# Psychological Consultation and Collaboration in School and Community Settings

## FIFTH EDITION

**A. MICHAEL DOUGHERTY**
Western Carolina University

BROOKS/COLE
CENGAGE Learning™

Australia • Brazil • Japan • Korea • Mexico • Singapore • Spain
United Kingdom • United States

# BROOKS/COLE
## CENGAGE Learning

**Psychological Consultation and Collaboration in School and Community Settings, Fifth Edition**

**A. Michael Dougherty**

Senior Acquisitions Editor: Marquita Flemming

Assistant Editor: Christina Ganim

Editorial Assistant: Ashley Cronin

Technology Project Manager: Andrew Keay

Senior Marketing Manager: Karin Sandberg

Marketing Assistant: Ting Jian Yap

Marketing Communications Manager: Shemika Britt

Content Project Manager, Editorial Production: David Woodbury

Creative Director: Rob Hugel

Art Director: Caryl Gorska

Print Buyer: Rebecca Cross

Permissions Editor: Margaret Chamberlain-Gaston

Production Service: Newgen–Austin

Copy Editor: Allen Michie

Cover Designer: Gia Giasullo

Compositor: Newgen

For product information and technology assistance, contact us at **Cengage Learning Customer & Sales Support, 1-800-354-9706**

For permission to use material from this text or product, submit all requests online at **www.cengage.com/permissions**. Further permissions questions can be e-mailed to **permissionrequest@cengage.com**.

Library of Congress Control Number: 2007939363

ISBN-13: 978-0-495-50780-2
ISBN-10: 0-495-50780-6

**Brooks/Cole**
10 Davis Drive
Belmont, CA 94002-3098
USA

Cengage Learning is a learning provider of customized learning solutions with office locations around the globe, including Singapore, the United Kingdom, Australia, Mexico, Brazil, and Japan. Locate your local office at **international.cengage.com/region**.

Cengage Learning products are represented in Canada by Nelson Education, Ltd.

For your course and learning solutions, visit **academic.cengage.com**.

Purchase any of our products at your local college store or at our preferred online store **www.ichapters.com**.

Printed in the United States of America
1 2 3 4 5 6 7 11 10 09 08

*Dedicated with love to my parents, Arthur and Cecilia;
and to my family, Leslie, Matt, and Ashley*

# Contents

v

# Preface

*Psychological Consultation and Collaboration in School and Community Settings* is written for graduate and undergraduate students in the helping professions. Students in counseling, psychology, social work, human resource development, and other helping-profession training programs will find this book helpful as they seek to acquire the knowledge and skill bases that lead to the effective practice of consultation and collaboration. This book can be used either as the primary text in consultation and collaboration courses or as a supplemental text in courses in the helping professions. Many instructors have found the text useful in introductory and "roles and settings" courses in counseling psychology, school counseling, school psychology, student development, mental health and community counseling, social work, and human resource development. Moreover, practicing consultants and collaborators can find in this book a wealth of practical and theoretical information to help guide their practice.

In this text, I use *human service professional* as a general term that encompasses counselors, psychologists, social workers, human resource development specialists, and members of other helping professions. At the same time, I have tried to respect the terminology used by the professions covered in this text.

## PURPOSE

This book provides a thorough overview of what students and practicing mental health/human service professionals must know and be able to do to effectively practice consultation and collaboration. It provides a balance of theory and practice and illustrates their interrelationship. The book presents a generic model for application, surveys the various models to consultation and collaboration, discusses their organizational context, and reviews the many ethical and professional issues faced in delivering these services.

I have found that students learning about consultation and collaboration appreciate a practical model for delivering these services before they study specific approaches. As a result, I have provided a generic model of consultation and collaboration at the beginning of the text before discussing specific models. Students will also find a large number of case studies that illustrate how to deliver consultation and collaboration services in real life. Furthermore, many professors note that the greatest challenge in teaching consultation and collaboration is to make them practical; therefore, I have included the numerous case studies to bring their concepts to life.

Finally, students say they benefit more from learning about consultation and collaboration when they are involved personally. As a result, I have structured the book so students can develop a personal model of consultation and collaboration. Each chapter begins and ends with questions that stimulate and encourage the reader to reflect on the material in that chapter. In the case studies, students are asked to make decisions about a particular consultant's or collaborator's behavior. Each chapter ends with some recommendations for effective practice. I have attempted to write a text that is interesting, current, informative, and oriented toward practice with a solid grounding in theory and research.

## ABOUT THE FIFTH EDITION

In this edition, I have updated the material and refined the discussion of the topics. I have also included many new topics and more extensive coverage than in the fourth edition. Throughout the text, I have provided significant additional coverage of cultural diversity as it affects consultation and collaboration. I have included material on prevention as there is a trend to increasingly view consultation and collaboration in this way. The most broad-based change is an increased focus on school-based consultation. I have again revised Chapter 12, which focuses on school-based consultation and collaboration with administrators, teachers, and parents. Chapters 3–10 each still contain a detailed case study on school consultation and community consultation; I have changed some of the case studies to reflect issues such as positive behavioral support and school violence. These revisions create a balance that will appeal to instructors preparing students for practice in school settings.

Each chapter has been carefully examined and reviewed. I have updated the introductory chapter and have added coverage of promoting consultation and collaboration in your work setting, the multicultural limitations of consultation and collaboration, and the levels of prevention. Chapter 2 has been significantly updated as well, particularly the section on research. Additions to Chapters 3–6 include discussions of the implications of cultural diversity on a particular stages of consultation and collaboration. Chapter 3 provides updated coverage of the social influence process, as well as a case study that illustrates each phase of the entry stage. Chapter 4 contains new coverage of qualitative data gathering and material on functional behavioral assessment. Chapter 5 contains additional coverage on treatment integrity and treatment acceptability. Chapter 6 includes additional material on qualitative evaluation. Chapter 7 contains new material on cultural diversity and crisis consultation, and updated codes of ethics of various professional organizations.

I have also revised Chapter 8. For this edition, I have added material on culturally responsive organizations. I have retained a section entitled "Implications for Consultants and Collaborators" for each theory of organization. Chapter 9 retains an in-depth discussion of Caplan's model of mental health consultation while including new material on the increasingly eclectic nature of mental health consultation. In particular, new material on consultee-centered consultation is included. Chapter 10 updates and expands coverage of Bergan and Kratochwill's model of behavior consultation. I have expanded coverage of the behavioral consultation process. Chapter 11 has additional material on Schein's models for organizational consultation as well as education/training consultation. Chapter 12 has been significantly revised and updated in general. I have included new material on working with nonmainstream families and the topic of prevention. In Chapter 13, I have retained a shortened version of the case study of Acme Human Services Center because it illustrates how the approaches covered in the text are applied to a non-educational setting. In addition, I have retained a transcript of a school consultation case and a school collaboration case, along with a reflective analysis of each. I hope that these additions will help the text become even more valuable and practical for the reader.

## OVERVIEW

What will you discover as you read this book? *Psychological Consultation and Collaboration in School and Community Settings* is divided into three parts. Part I sets the stage for understanding consultation and collaboration and how they are practiced. Chapter 1 is an orientation to the practice of consultation and collaboration: It contains an introduction, a definition of consultation and collaboration, a brief historical overview, and information on how you can promote consultation and collaboration within your work setting. Chapter 2 includes a discussion of the characteristics of effective consultants and collaborators and of the roles in which they engage; it also reviews the current status of research in consultation and collaboration.

Part II describes in detail the ins and outs of the consultation and collaboration processes using a model that involves four stages: entry, diagnosis, implementation, and disengagement. Chapter 3 is about the entry stage—that is, how the consultation or collaboration process starts. Chapter 4 discusses diagnosis—how the consultant or collaborator can help determine the problem to be solved. Chapter 5 describes the implementation stage—how the parties involved attempt to solve the problem. Chapter 6 examines the ending of the consultation or collaboration process, including the difficulty consultants and collaborators face in assessing success and how they can say goodbye in a personal yet professional manner. Chapter 7 focuses on the ethical, legal, and professional issues consultants and collaborators encounter in their practices, such as those related to confidentiality, diversity, and crisis situations. Chapter 8 deals with the pragmatic issues of working within an organization. This chapter emphasizes that all consultation or collaboration takes place within some type of organization and that the forces in that organization impact, for better or worse, your efforts.

Part III surveys mental health, behavioral, organizational, and school-based consultation and their implications for collaboration. Chapter 9 reviews mental health consultation; because of the traditional popularity of Caplan's model, I have made it the central focus of the chapter, while recognizing the increasing eclecticism in this model. Chapter 10 explores behavioral consultation, which uses behavioral technology both to benefit clients and organizations and also as an aid in training human service professionals and others. Chapter 11 discusses organizational consultation, including four specialized applications: education/training, program, doctor–patient, and process. Chapter 12 covers school-based consultation and collaboration, including how these services can be provided to administrators, teachers, and parents. Chapter 13 presents case study applications to give a better sense of the nuts and bolts of consultation and collaboration.

## HOW TO USE THIS TEXT

This text can be used in several ways. Some instructors might want students who are preparing for work in schools to read Chapter 12 first and students who are training for work in community settings to read Chapter 13 first. This would give each student a sense of how consultation and collaboration are practiced in his or her field. Other instructors might want to begin with Chapter 7 to instill an understanding of the complexity and seriousness of the ethical and professional issues faced in the process of providing consultation or collaboration. Still others might want to start with the generic model and cover the specific approaches later, or vice versa. I have designed this book so that the material can be covered in the most logical order regardless of how a particular course is taught.

In addition, this text can be used in conjunction with *Casebook of Psychological Consultation and Collaboration in School and Community Settings,* Fifth Edition, also published by Cengage–Brooks/Cole. The casebook contains several cases that describe real-life examples of consultation and collaboration and illustrate various approaches.

An instructor's manual and PowerPoint slides are also available at this text's website: academic.cengage.com/counseling/dougherty. It contains a variety of materials, including test questions, suggested class activities, and recommendations for teaching. I have taught courses in consultation and collaboration for over 20 years, and I believe this instructor's manual and the related slides will be very helpful to you in teaching the concepts and skills of consultation and collaboration.

# ACKNOWLEDGMENTS

I would like to thank the many graduate students in counseling and psychology—as well as student personnel and human resources staff at Western Carolina University — who contributed indirectly yet significantly to the development of this text. Their feedback on the consultation and collaboration course I teach was an invaluable asset in determining the final form this text would take. I also wish to thank my graduate assistant, Sara Stephens, who assisted me in various ways.

I would also like to acknowledge my reviewers, including:

Michael Cox, Webster University
Suzanne Faykus, Francis Marion University
John W. Fick, Siena Heights University
William Lawrence, North Carolina Central University
Sang Min Lee, University of Arkansas
Amelia Lopez, Millersville University
Michael B. Madson, University of Southern Mississippi
Cheryl A. Notari, Montclair University
Glenda P. Reynolds, Auburn University Montgomery
Charles Richards, Spring Arbor University
William Ross, Prairie View A&M University
Kumea Shorter-Gooden, Alliant International University
Jeff Thomas, Arizona State University
Karen S. Weston, Gannon University
Wendy Neifeld Wheeler, College of Saint Rose
Jesse B. DeEsch, Rider University
Richard K. James, University of Memphis
Arthur M. Horne, University of Georgia
James Bergin, Georgia Southern University
Scott Young, Mississippi State University

These individuals furnished me with a wealth of helpful ideas and many valuable comments.

Special thanks go to Dixie McGinty of Western Carolina University, who reviewed the material on evaluation in Chapters 5 and 6, and Candace Boan of Western Carolina University for her review of the entire text. I continue to thank Gerald Corey, professor emeritus of California State University at Fullerton, and Mary Deck of Western Carolina University for their suggestions over the years concerning the organization of the text and the instructor's manual.

To my wife and life partner, Leslie, my deepest appreciation for her love, support, and understanding during the preparation of this text and for helping me remember that work is always there and love is not always as accessible. To my children, Ashley and Matt, thanks for helping me remember how to play.

Finally, to the talented people at Cengage–Brooks/Cole, I extend my gratitude for being able to work with a first-class group of professionals. It was a true pleasure to work with them and others who helped make this book a reality.

# To the Student

Consultation and collaboration are "head, heart, and hands" processes. You come to understand them, then you become a strong advocate for them, then you do them with a passion. The often-used metaphor of the bicycle rider sheds light on what it takes to be an effective consultant and collaborator. The front wheel provides direction, the back wheel provides the force, and the rider guides the bike to its destination. The rear wheel represents your technical skills (what you do when you consult or collaborate), the front wheel represents your skill with people (how you consult or collaborate), and the rider represents your personhood (who you are). When all three elements are in sync, it becomes more probable that you will succeed in your consulting and collaborating endeavors. This book will help you become an even better "bicycle rider." You might want to take special note of the questions at the beginning of each chapter. They are designed to stimulate thought about each chapter's main points as you read. In addition, the questions at the end of each chapter will assist you in applying what you have learned through your reading. I hope you will take the time to reflect on these questions after you have completed each chapter. Each chapter concludes with a few suggestions for effective practice, which will help you determine how to use the chapter's material in your practice of consultation and collaboration.

In addition, supplementary readings are suggested at the end of each chapter. I have chosen these readings carefully and encourage you to read those that interest you. You will note that there are a variety of case studies throughout the text. The focus of some cases will not be in your professional training area. Nonetheless, the analysis of these cases can be quite beneficial to you, because it is the process of the analysis and not the cases themselves that is critical.

I also suggest that you look over Chapters 7 and 8, and 13 after you read Chapters 1 and 2. Chapter 7 discusses ethical, professional, and legal issues. Even a cursory glance at this chapter will show you the many important issues you will face in your practice of consultation and collaboration.

Chapter 8 covers a variety of issues related to working in an organizational context. By skimming through this chapter, you can appreciate the complexity of organizations and, consequently, of consultation and collaboration within them.

Chapter 13 presents the case of Acme Human Services Center and illustrates how various consultation approaches can be applied to that case. This chapter also includes a case study transcript of both a consultation session and a collaboration session. By looking through this chapter, you can get a feel for the nuts and bolts of real-life consultation and collaboration. Once you have obtained a perspective on how consultants actually consult and how collaborators actually collaborate, you can more readily see the critical importance of such procedures as creating relationships with the people with whom you are going to work and determining the interventions that emerge for use with the client system.

This is a book about consultation and collaboration: what these services are, how they are effectively practiced, and the forms they can take. I sincerely hope that after reading this book you will be motivated and empowered to perform consultation and collaboration confidently and effectively.

# Psychological Consultation and Collaboration in School and Community Settings

✳

# Consultation and Consultants, Collaboration, and Collaborators

Consultation and collaboration are forms of service delivery that are expected from today's mental health professionals. What is consultation? What is collaboration? What do psychologists, counselors, social workers, college student personnel and human resource specialists do when they consult and collaborate? What special knowledge and skills do consultants and collaborators need to practice effectively? What roles do consultants and collaborators take on in their work? Students can begin to develop a personal style of providing consultation and collaboration by familiarizing themselves with the answers to the aforementioned questions. To that end, Part I explores these and related questions.

Consultation and collaboration are specialized professional services. They are performed by mental health/human service professionals in a variety of settings. When these professionals consult, they work with individuals and groups for the purpose of helping them to work more effectively on the individual, group, organizational, or community level. Consultation is a helping relationship in which human service/mental health professionals work with individuals and/or groups in a variety of settings (such as agencies, schools, and businesses) to help them work more effectively.

This apparently simple process is actually quite complex. You'll learn that consultants not only try to help the people with whom they are working (called *consultees*) with their immediate problems at work; they also try to improve their consultees' future professional functioning. Part of this assistance is in helping consultees become more aware of new choices or alternatives for working with their client systems. Consultants engage consultees in joint problem solving, typically of a collaborative nature, and consultees are free to accept or reject any consultant suggestions. You'll discover that the client system can consist of an individual, a group, an entire organization, or the community at large.

Consultation is based on several assumptions (Noell & Witt, 1996; Zins & Erchul, 2002).

- Consultation is a cost-effective use of resources relative to direct services such as counseling.
- A collaborative approach frequently leads to a successful outcome.
- Discussing cases and programs with consultees, in a problem solving format, is sufficient for consultees to change their behavior.
- Consultees will generalize the problem-solving skills they learned in consultation to future situations.
- Direct contact between the consultant and client system is often unnecessary.

As you will note as you read this text, collaboration is quite similar to consultation. Those parties with whom the human service professional collaborates are termed *fellow collaborators*. The majority of what holds for consultation also holds for collaboration. For example, both are problem-solving activities. However, the last assumption in the list above reflects one area in which consultation and collaboration differ. In collaboration, it is assumed that *direct* service between the professional and the client system is integral to successful outcomes.

We will discuss later in this text the importance of multicultural variables as they relate to the effective practice of consultation and collaboration. As noted many times over in this text, the ever-changing makeup of our society dictates the necessity of including a multicultural context to the work

of consultants and collaborators. In your professional practice, you'll spend a great deal of your professional time performing consultation and collaboration, perhaps in situations similar to the following examples.

## The Case of Billie: Consultation

Billie is a therapist working with a client who reveals during a session that he has AIDS. As therapy continues, Billie is increasingly aware that there are several AIDS-related issues that may need to be dealt with in subsequent therapy sessions. Billie notes her anxiety about working with an AIDS client and her lack of knowledge about AIDS-related issues. By taking advantage of the consultation opportunities that her employer provides, Billie meets for three consultation sessions with a psychologist, who helps her examine her views concerning AIDS patients and recommends a variety of resources that provide pertinent information on AIDS. In addition, the psychologist helps Billie develop both short- and long-term plans to become more effective in dealing with clients with AIDS.

## The Case of Chris: Collaboration

Chris Gonzalez is the head counselor at a large urban secondary school that has a severe substance-abuse problem among its student body. The counseling department of the school has a well-defined procedure for referring substance-abuse cases to community resources. Chris has been studying several drug-prevention programs but is uncertain about which one would be best for the school. Chris contacts Leslie, who is a substance-abuse counselor at the community mental health center, and invites her to collaborate with him.

Leslie is quite familiar with a number of substance-abuse programs for schools. Chris and

Leslie agree to collaborate and meet for three two-hour sessions over a three-week period. During the first meeting they explore the school's substance-abuse problem in detail, and Leslie observes the overall operation of the school. In the second meeting, Leslie provides Chris information on possible substance-abuse programs with which Chris was not familiar. Chris helps Leslie understand the unique characteristics of the school and how they would affect any program. In the final meeting, Leslie and Chris problem solve and decide which program would be best for the school.

These examples are typical of the many opportunities for consulting and collaborating available to human service professionals. Indeed, consultation has become an increasingly powerful force in the helping professions (see ASCA, 2003; Kratochwill, Elliott, & Callan-Stoiber, 2002), and collaboration is increasing in its importance. A tremendous social demand for this kind of professional service has developed, in part due to the effects of the realignment of the world's economy and the increasing demographic changes in our society (Lewis, Lewis, Daniels, & D'Andrea, 2003). Whereas three decades ago consultation was considered an "emerging role" (Kurpius, 1978, p. 335), today it is an accepted and valued service of human service professionals. Consultation has become one of the services routinely provided in the work settings of human service professionals. As one example of this trend, a special workgroup on consultation and interprofessional collaboration across the specialty areas of psychology (see Arredondo, Shealy, Neale, & Winfrey, 2004) validated consultation and interprofessional collaboration as important activities for psychologists. What Gutkin and Curtis (1999) have said for the school psychology profession and consultation likely holds for other human service professions: "With each passing year, consultation seems to

grow in importance as a foundational role for the professions" (p. 599). There has been an increase over the past decade in the number of research studies conducted on consultation and collaboration. In essence, consultation has emerged as a primary service provided by helping professionals to assist a variety of other professionals (such as teachers) and caregivers (such as parents). Collaboration, as a direct service, has emerged as an alternative to consultation, particularly in settings where both the would-be consultant and consultee are employed in the same setting.

Consultation continues to be a cornerstone activity for mental health professionals. Mental health professionals frequently seek consultation primarily for the purpose of assisting their clients, with a secondary goal of avoiding possible lawsuits based on malpractice. The onset of managed care and limited counseling sessions has led to the increased need for consultation among mental health counselors, psychologists, and social workers (Sperry, 2005). For example, mental health consultants may assist with organizational downsizing, issues related to mergers, mental health policy, violence prevention, and conflict resolution. Managed care has also given impetus to interagency collaboration. Community consultants are called upon to assist in a variety of programs (Staton et al., 2007), such as programs designed to prevent elder abuse (Wolf & Pillemer, 1994). Community psychologists and community counselors have been expanding their application of consultation (Zins, 1998) by engaging in areas such as trial consultation (Myers & Arena, 2001), systems consultation (Lewis et al., 2003), and mental health consultation with juvenile correction facilities (Cowles & Washburn, 2005). They are also acting as cultural mediators to close the gap between mainstream schools and nonmainstream families (Nastasi, 2005). Whereas social workers used to be only the recipients of consultation, they now have provided consultation services to a variety of constituencies for over three decades. The 1980s saw a significant rise in the number of counselors providing services to organizations and their personnel (Maher, 1993). Serious social issues like the AIDS epidemic have led many psychologists to take on community involvement through education/training consultation (Douce, 1993; House & Walker, 1993) as well as by providing mental health consultation services to primary care physicians (Gongora, 2004). Music therapists spend a significant amount of their time consulting and collaborating (Register, 2002). School counselors spend at least 12 percent of their time performing consultation (Partin, 1993) and an undetermined amount taking part in collaboration activities. In some studies, elementary school counselors report spending more time consulting than in any other activity (Hardesty & Dillard, 1994). School psychologists, though consulting more than ever before, indicate a desire to do even more (Anton-LaHart & Rosenfield, 2004) and most likely will in the future (Cole & Siegel, 2003; Cummings et al., 2004a; Merrell, Ervin, & Gimpel, 2006). Recent reviews of the role of school psychologists indicate increased attention to collaboration as a service (Zins & Erchul, 2002). Human resource development specialists, as well as members of other helping professions, are frequently being called on to consult with organizational programs such as those related to employee assistance programs (French & Bell, 1999). Student affairs specialists are increasingly being asked to provide consultation in postsecondary educational settings (Conyne, Rapin, & Rand, 1997; Knotek, 2006; Kressel, Bailey, & Forman, 1999). Clearly, consultation and collaboration have increased in popularity as a role for human service professionals.

What kinds of things might you do as a consultant or collaborator? Consider the following list, which notes some broad examples:

- provide requested information and/or training
- assist other human service professionals with difficult clients
- provide solutions to a given problem
- conduct a diagnosis of a problem
- provide recommendations about actions to be taken
- build consensus among selected members of an organization
- improve organizational effectiveness
- improve the effectiveness of individuals in their work

Part I introduces you to the worlds of consultation and collaboration, provides a frame of reference for their practice, and focuses on the knowledge, skills and attitudes needed.

# 1

✳

# Introduction and Overview

This chapter introduces the concepts of consultation and collaboration, defines them, and shows how they differ from one other and from other services performed by human service professionals.

Here are five questions to consider as you read this chapter:

- How would you define consultation and collaboration?
- What are the differences between consultation and collaboration?
- What do consultants and collaborators actually do when they provide services?
- In what ways are the prototypical roles of healer and technological advisor compatible?
- What are the implications of the phrase "There is no one best way to consult or collaborate"?

Consultation is practiced by most human service professionals in a variety of settings for a variety of reasons. Consider the following examples:

- A psychologist helps a therapist deal with problems she is having with one or more clients in her caseload.
- A counselor works with a schoolteacher to improve classroom management techniques.
- A counseling psychologist consults with a nursing home director about recreation programs for patients suffering from Alzheimer's disease.
- A family therapist trains school counselors in family systems theory.
- A professor of human services assists a job corps center staff in becoming culturally skilled professionals.
- A team of school-based consultants assist teachers in finding ways to help students cope with school violence.

- A psychologist diagnoses the reasons for high turnover in a social services agency.

- A counselor assists the staff of a counseling center in identifying its major work concerns and in making plans to solve them.

- A mental health worker assists a Head Start program in evaluating its parent training program.

- A social worker assists a group of rural human service agencies to build a network for responding to common issues.

- A community mental health worker trains a group of other mental health professionals in developing outreach and client advocacy strategies for assisting ethnic minorities.

- A group of mental health consultants assist a university in examining the mental health aspects of its crisis communication plan.

These examples illustrate how human service professionals engage in *consultation*.

Human service professionals also collaborate. In its most generic form, collaboration involves a process in which two or more parties work together to assist another party or program toward some desired outcome (Allen, 1994).

Consider these examples:

- A community counselor serves on an interagency team designed to help a family at risk.

- A school psychologist serves as part of a site-based management team in an urban school.

- A human resource management specialist serves as a member of a self-directed work team that is a permanent structure in a health care setting.

- A psychologist works with a large industry to examine the turnover of women in leadership positions.

- A school counselor and teacher collaborate to assist a student, with the counselor providing counseling services to the student and the teacher changing the way she instructs the student in the classroom.

- Two mental health professionals in the same agency team up to help a client suffering from AIDS, each working with a different aspect of the case.

- A school psychologist and teacher work together on a prereferral intervention for a disruptive student in the teacher's classroom.

These examples illustrate how human service professionals can provide assistance to others (as well as receive assistance) through collaboration.

Consultation and collaboration have become important roles for many professionals (Cowan, 2007); practicing these roles has become increasingly scientifically based (Cowan, 2007; Zins, 2002). Human service professionals provide consultation to, or collaborate with, individuals, groups, and organizations, usually in one of three organizational settings. One setting is within some type of human service agency, whose mission in part is to provide consultation/collaboration services to the community—for example, a community mental health center. A second setting is a private firm or independent practitioner offering consultation/ collaboration services to the community—for instance, a psychologist in private practice offering stress management training to the employees of a job corps center. In the third setting consultants work "in house" and consult and collaborate within the organization that employs them—for example, a school psychologist or school counselor consulting with a teacher about a student's behavior.

When human service professionals consult, their primary purpose is to help others work more effectively to fulfill their professional responsibilities to an individual, group, organization, or community. The typical focus in human service consultation is changing behavior in some way, whether it is the behavior of a client or the behavior of program participants. The consultant's role varies with the needs of the consultee (Williams, 2000).

Whereas the consultee maintains responsibility for managing the problem and carrying out any intervention procedures, the consultant maintains the ethical responsibility of making appropriate recommendations and overseeing the professional well-being of the consultee. Consultation is a helping relationship that is interpersonal and has a problem-solving focus in which consultant and consultee have meetings to assist a third party called the client system. Collaboration differs from this process in that all parties involved have responsibility for some part of the outcome and reciprocally consult with one another.

Human service professionals generally consult or collaborate with other human service professionals, other professionals (such as teachers or managers in organizations), and parents. There is a preventative aspect to all consultation and collaboration, in that one of the goals is to prevent the problem at hand from becoming more severe and another is to prevent additional problems from arising (Zins & Erchul, 2002). As we will find out, this latter goal is often pursued by attempting to assist change at the systems level (e.g., an entire school or organization). By focusing on systems, human services professionals can often determine the conditions inherent within the organization that contribute to the development and maintenance of problems within individuals (Zins & Erchul, 2002).

To consult and collaborate effectively you need to develop an understanding of how these services are practiced. A general framework for understanding and practicing consultation and collaboration will help you develop a cognitive map and a sense of direction for performing these services. A familiarity with the types of consultation—usually categorized as mental heath, behavioral, and organizational—will provide you with models that have some applicability in particular situations. Collaboration has evolved as a derivative of these models. We will see that there are different types of consultation and collaboration within each of these models.

Achieving these steps provides you with the basic rudiments from which you can develop a personal model of consultation and collaboration. You will consult and collaborate most effectively when you have integrated your knowledge and skills with your unique personality. For example, I am a very social person; I prefer people around me. One way I use this trait in my own personal model of consulting and collaborating is by appreciating the importance of relationships in these contexts.

I make five very basic assumptions in this book. First, I assume that consultation and collaboration are very similar in terms of the skills needed and the processes engaged in. Throughout this text, what I write about consultation basically holds for collaboration. The main point to remember is that in collaboration, as opposed to consultation, the mental health professional assists in the intervention and also receives and gives consultation to other collaborators. In order to enhance the readability of the text, I will frequently use the term *consultation* instead of phrases like *consultation and collaboration*. When it is necessary to differentiate consultation from collaboration, I do this explicitly in the text.

The second assumption is that *how* a consultant or collaborator performs is as important as *what* he or she does. This is very important because the perceptions of these processes by the parties involved are critical in determining their success. For example, as a consultant I might know what I need to do to help a particular consultee, but if I don't know how to do it in a way that he or she sees as helpful, then the consultation is less likely to be successful. Of importance is how the working relationship is established. By consulting and collaborating under the supervision of well-trained professionals, you will understand *how* you consult and collaborate and the impact your behavior has on the effectiveness of these processes.

The third assumption is that consultation and collaboration are human relationships. Consultants and collaborators work *with* people. The personal sides of these services become as important as their professional sides. Human service professionals need to identify and clarify their values about both life and the professional services they offer so that they do not fall into the trap of inadvertently imposing those values when providing these services. Such an imposition, in addition to being unethical, can restrict the professional growth of the persons with whom they are working. In addition, a lack of self-knowledge about values can place blinders on a professional and lead to mistakes during the course of consultation and collaboration. However, when consultation and collaboration are viewed as human relationships, the respect, dignity, and welfare of the parties involved become paramount. Effective professionals excel by behaving in ways that demonstrate respect for their consultees and fellow collaborators and protect their welfare.

The fourth assumption is that human services professionals need training in these services. In the past many people consulted and collaborated without ever having any proper training; they learned to provide these services through a series of consulting and collaborating experiences alone. Only by chance do they develop a frame of reference for approaching consultation and collaboration opportunities. Flying by the seat of one's pants is dangerous in the delivery of any professional service; the professional (and sometimes the personal) aspects of other people's lives are involved. Consultants should not view their counseling/psychotherapy skills as sufficient to get them by when consulting (Welfel, 2002). Consequently, human service pro-

fessionals need to be well-grounded in models and interventions related to consultation and collaboration (Alpert & Taufique, 2002a; ASCA, 2003). This knowledge creates an objective frame of reference for delivering professional services. Further, only such knowledgeable and skillful professionals lend credibility to consultation and collaboration as legitimate services for human service professionals to provide.

The fifth assumption is that how one goes about the process effectively depends on the large number of factors that make up the situation that led to the request for service. Cultural competence is a must for practicing consultants and collaborators, and consultation models and practice need to be adapted to the cultural context of the consultee and client system. Maintaining an open mind about the various approaches to consultation and collaboration is also important. Some readers are turned off by the term *behavioral* because it reminds them of horror stories about the misuses of behavior modification. Others are prejudiced against the term "mental health" because they automatically identify it with "having a permanent disability" or using psychotherapy. Some readers may not like the term *organization* because it leads them to think of a bureaucratic structure in which rules and regulations are more highly valued than the people within it. However, since effectiveness in consultation and collaboration depends upon the context in which the services occur, an effective human services professional develops a broad repertoire of skills and a large knowledge base from which to provide service. Then, depending on the situation, the professional can use the most pertinent knowledge and appropriate skills available. Finally, I encourage a systems view of events. A systems view of events allows you not only to see the big picture, but also to see the interconnectedness of events, their multi-causal nature, and the great realm of possible ways of intervening.

## HISTORICAL OVERVIEW

Like most other human service/mental health functions, the roots of consultation go back to ancient times. Decades ago, Gallessich (1982) pointed out that two prototypical roles of consultation emerged: the healer and the technological advisor. The healer had the power to improve well-being, and the technological advisor could tell someone how to fix something or how to proceed to the next step in solving a problem. As human knowledge expanded, so too did the need for people who could help solve problems and provide technical expertise.

As consultation developed into a tool of human service professionals, the familiar medical consultation provided a model. If a physician noticed something about a patient that might require the attention of a specialist, he or she consulted with the specialist. Frequently, that meant turning the patient over to the specialist (in other words, the consultant). The physician who originally handled the case frequently did not treat the patient again. Hence, in the original form of consultation, the consultant saw and treated the patient.

Such was the state of consultation around the turn of the 20th century. Then it became increasingly apparent to medical professionals that the referring personnel could benefit from participating in treating the patient further. This change in perspective fostered the emergence in the human service professions of consultation as we now know it. Additional forces that contributed to the emergence of human service consultation were the growth of the organization development movement and the community mental health movement (Brown, Kurpius, & Morris, 1988). These forces viewed the consultee as an active participant in the consultation process and viewed consultation as a developmental, preventative force that would continue to balance direct and indirect service activities. This

shift led to the idea of consultant as trainer, that is, a professional party who would give away the skills of helping. The basic essence of consultation, as it emerged as a service delivery, was to enhance the methodological repertoires of consultees (Johnson & Pugach, 1996). The consultant was the expert who accomplished this task in a series of transactions with the consultee. Gerald Caplan's 1970 landmark book *The Theory and Practice of Mental Health Consultation* promoted mental health consultation as a primary prevention service to mental health providers. This book was, in part, based on Caplan's professional experiences in the late 1940s and early 1950s. Consultation became a primary activity for workers in the schools such as counselors and psychologists. The community counselor's role as a consultant has been less well-established (Keys, Bemak, Carpenter, & King-Sear, 1998). Along with these developments, there has been a great expansion of the empirical literature on consultation (Alpert & Taufique, 2002a).

Consultation today, common in such human service professions as psychology, counseling, social work, and human resource development, has developed into three broad types: organizational, mental health, and behavioral. I will cover the historical development of each of these types in later chapters.

More recently, the changing nature of organizations such as schools has changed the amount of emphasis placed on the expert role (e.g., a counselor helping a teacher improve classroom management skills) to a more collaborative approach (e.g., a counselor and teacher working simultaneously on goals related to improved classroom behavior) (Bradley, 1994). Collaboration as a distinct service emerged in education as a response to legislation involving the education of students identified as eligible for special education services. There has been a parallel increase in interest in collaboration as a mode of service delivery in profit and nonprofit organizations (Sherwood, 1993). For example, in the mental health arena, collaboration emerged as an alternative to traditional consultation, primarily for internal consultants. In fact, the increase in having providers and recipients of consultation employed in the same organization made it increasingly difficult for some of the assumptions of consultation to be met and thereby gave impetus to the popularity of collaboration.

Finally, the increased complexity of organizations has demanded a more system-level approach to problem solving. The literature concerning consultation and collaboration has reflected increased interest in providing these services at the systems level. It is now common for consultants and collaborators to work on organization-wide issues and deal with problems that affect the entire organization (Merrell et al., 2006). For example, counselors and psychologists are involved as consultants and collaborators in dealing with system-level issues such as those related to school reform. Consequently, today's human service professional needs to have the skills to consult and collaborate, not only at the individual level, but also at the systems level.

## CONSULTATION DEFINED

What is consultation? This simple question does not have a simple answer. For example, later in this book you will be exposed to definitions of mental health, behavioral, and organization consultation. With that said, there are some common elements. Basically, consultation is a type of service performed by counselors, psychologists, and human resource workers in which they assist another person who has responsibility for a case or program. However, defining the term "consultation" is as difficult as defining such terms as "counseling" and "psychotherapy," and there is no widespread agreement (Gutkin & Curtis, 1999; Kurpius & Fuqua, 1993a). In fact, the continued ambiguous use of this term makes quality research on the subject difficult (Zins, 2002).

Consultation tends to be defined in terms of the role and function of the consultant. However, this method de-emphasizes the *process* of consultation. A variety of generic definitions of consultation have been suggested over the years (see Parsons, 1996). These definitions generally agree about the role of consultation, but they differ on such issues as whether

the consultee must be a human service professional or whether the consultant must be from outside the system in which consultation occurs.

General agreement does exist on several aspects of consultation that can be used in formulating an acceptable definition. Most authors consider that the goal of all consultation is to solve problems. What constitutes a "problem" can, of course, vary significantly. An organization could seek a consultant to assist in such problems as alleviating poor staff morale or determining how best to evaluate the effects of a substance-abuse program. The term "problem" does not necessarily imply that something is *wrong*. It may simply refer to a situation that needs attention or enhancement. That is, consultants not only assist consultees in developing solutions to defined problems (such as assisting an administrator in working out the glitches in a program), but they also empower consultees by assisting them in recognizing their needs and tapping the unused potential and resources necessary to meet those needs (such as through strategic planning) (Egan, 2007; Knoff, 2002). The positive psychology framework (Gerstein, 2006) has influenced consultation with the increased focus on strengths and optimal human functioning. The consultee's problem with the client system can be dealt with in either a remedial or developmental manner, depending on what the situation dictates.

Consultants help consultees view the problem as part of a larger system to understand how it has developed, is maintained, and may be solved (Kurpius & Fuqua, 1993b). Hence, consultation can occur in a very broad range of problem-solving situations. In this sense, consultation is a unique activity (Auster, Feeney-Kettler, & Kratochwill, 2006; Kratochwill, Elliott, & Stoiber, 2002).

A second commonly accepted aspect of consultation is its tripartite nature (Williams, 2000); that is, it involves three parties: a *consultant*, a *consultee*, and a *client system*. The consultant delivers direct service to a consultee, who delivers direct service to a client system.

The client system receives indirect service from the consultant through an intermediary (the consultee). Thus, the consultant provides assistance

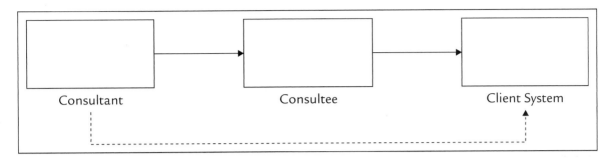

**F I G U R E  1.1**   Relationships of the parties in consultation

to the consultee that can positively affect the consultee's work with the client system.

Figure 1.1 shows the relationships among the parties involved in consultation. The solid lines represent direct service; the broken line represents indirect service.

The reader should not assume from Figure 1.1 that the relationship among the consultant, consultee, and client system is a linear one. There are times when the consultant may want access to the client system (e.g., for assessment, testing, or observation). Further, the consultant has an ethical and moral obligation to ensure that interventions designed to assist the client system are appropriately carried out (Kurpius & Fuqua, 1993b). Having contact with the client system when necessary meets this obligation. Figure 1.2 shows one way of viewing the relationships among the parties in consultation with these ideas in mind.

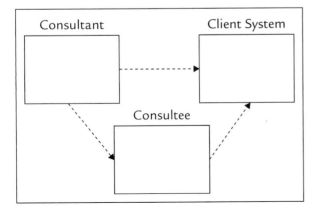

**F I G U R E  1.2**   The triadic relationships in consultation

In human service consultation, the consultant is often a human service professional, such as a counselor, psychologist, social worker, or human resource development specialist. The consultee is often a parent, another human service professional, or another professional with some caretaking role (e.g., a work supervisor, administrator, or teacher). There can be one or more consultees involved in consultation, and the client system can consist of one person, a group, an organization, or an entire community.

A third aspect of consultation on which there is substantial agreement is its goal of improving both the client system and the consultee (Zins & Erchul, 2002). The term *improve* can, of course, mean many things, and hence a large number of approaches to consultation and a great many interventions become available to consultants. For example, a consultant might help a consultee, not only to work more effectively with a given moderately depressed client, but also to improve the consultee's ability to work with similar clients in the future.

Agreement on these aspects of consultation leads to a general and widely accepted definition: *Consultation is a process in which a human service professional assists a consultee with a work-related (or caretaking-related) problem with a client system, with the goal of helping both the consultee and the client system in some specified way.* The *content* of consultation deals with what is discussed, and the process refers to the problem-solving process and the nature of the interaction between consultant and consultee (Kurpius & Fuqua, 1993a). The consultant and consultee pool their expertise to assist the client system.

## COMMON CHARACTERISTICS OF CONSULTATION

Can consultation be identified by certain common characteristics? A survey of the literature on the nature of consultation (e.g., Gutkin & Curtis, 1999) suggests it can. In addition to the three aspects just discussed, some general agreement exists on the following characteristics of consultation:

- Either the consultee or the client system may be given priority over the other at a given time, depending on the consultation approach that is taken.

- The consultant provides indirect service to the client system by providing direct service to the consultee.

- Consultation can be remedial or preventative. In remedial consultation, the consultant helps the consultee develop an effective intervention. In preventative consultation, a main focus is to assist consultees to increase knowledge and skills for future use.

- Consultants can be either separate from or part of the system in which consultation is to occur; that is, external consultants or internal consultants.

- Participation in consultation is voluntary for all parties involved.

- Consultees are free to do whatever they wish with the consultant's suggestions and recommendations. They are under no obligation to follow the consultant's recommendations. The need for monitoring or being on call when the consultee implements the consultant's recommendations is necessary to ensure treatment integrity, which is the appropriate implementation of the recommendation by the consultee.

- The relationship between the consultee and consultant is one of two equal peers. Although the consultation relationship is equal in terms of the power and decision making, it is unequal in terms of need; that is, the consultee needs help with a problem and the consultant does not (at least as far as the consultation relationship is concerned). The primary reason for consultation occurring is that the consultee expects the expertise of the consultant to be of some value with the situation at hand. Hence, a consultant can be both directive and collaborative (Gutkin & Curtis, 1999; Kratochwill and Pittman, 2002).

- The consultation relationship is temporary. Depending on the type, consultation may range from a single session to weekly sessions for more than a year. Whatever its length, however, the relationship is always temporary (the consultant does not replace the consultee).

- Consultation deals exclusively with the consultee's work-related or caretaking related problems. By definition, it never deals with the personal concerns of the consultee. The consultant can take on a variety of roles in consultation, depending on the nature of the problem, the skills of the consultee, the purpose and desired outcomes of consultation, and the skills of the consultant.

- Consultation tends to be collaborative in nature; that is, consultants and consultees work together to complement each other in solving the problems defined in consultation. The consultant brings expertise to bear on the problem and engages the expertise of the consultee to solve the problem (Gutkin & Curtis, 1999). One cardinal exception is in carrying out the agreed-upon consultation plan. The consultee carries out the plan with the consultant remaining on call for further assistance. Another exception is when consultees have the skills but not the time to do a given task. For example, a consultee might ask a consultant to lead a workshop on substance abuse counseling for the consultee's organization, even though the consultee is skilled in that task.

- Consultation usually occurs in an organizational context. Three key variables within an organization can influence the success of consultation: the people involved in consultation, how the process of consultation unfolds, and how change procedures are implemented. It is quite important that consultants understand the dynamics of the consultee's workplace.

## COLLABORATION DEFINED

Collaboration is very similar to consultation in that, as a stand-alone service, it follows the same problem-solving process. It involves the interactive exchange of resources, interdependence, and a focus on decision making (Rubin, 2002; Welch, 2000). Collaboration refers to "two or more people working together, using systematic planning and problem-solving procedures, to achieve desired outcomes" (Curtis & Stollar, 2002, p. 226). Collaboration requires the development of shared goals, bidirectional communication, and joint problem solving (Minke, 2006). There is an inherent respect of the views and skills of fellow collaborators (Arredondo et al., 2004). Collaboration is a role in which the helper accepts responsibility for the mental health aspects of a case, including carrying out planned interventions and assuming joint responsi-

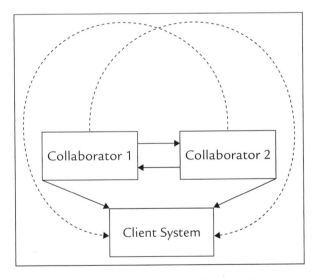

**FIGURE 1.3** The relationships of the parties in collaboration

bility for the case (Schulte & Osborne, 2003). For example, a school counselor might work with a student on decreasing verbal aggression while consulting with the teacher about decreasing the student's disruptive behavior in the classroom. Figure 1.3 illustrates the relationships of the parties involved in consultation.

Collaboration permits people with diverse expertise to combine efforts to accomplish the goal of helping a client, program, or organization. In collaboration each participant "alternately plays the consultant/expert and the consultee/recipient role in a forum where solution finding is jointly and equally shared among people with different knowledge and experience" (Thousand, Villa, Paolucci-Whitcomb, & Nevin, 1996). Collaboration improves upon the solutions the parties may have come up with independently. It involves shared ownership of problem definition and solutions, shared knowledge and expertise, and increased willingness to work together again. A key element in collaboration is focus on the end result and the connection between the purpose of collaboration and its goals (Gibbons & Shinn, 2002). Further, collaboration may be useful in situations where a consultee does not have the skill or time to effectively take total responsibility for implementation of the intervention (Kratochwill & Pittman, 2002). Recent research on collaboration as a service has socially validated collaboration as a valued service by practitioners (Welch & Tulbert, 2000).

It is important to remember that a distinguishing difference between consultation and collaboration is that, in consultation, the consultee retains responsibility for the outcome, is considered to be the determiner of the suitability of possible interventions, and is responsible for ensuring treatment integrity through adequate implementation of the intervention (Zins & Erchul, 2002). The basic trick of consultation is for the consultant to exert interpersonal influence while maintaining a cooperative relationship (Zins & Erchul, 2002).

In collaboration, the parties involved share the power in the decision-making process (Macmann et al., 1996). Decisions are made by the people involved, which allows for multiple views to be put forward. For example, in a school setting, a teacher's perspective is involved as well as that of the school counselor and school psychologist. Further, the teacher influences their behavior through his or her input. All collaborators are considered to have unique expertise and are accountable for applying it in helping the client system (Welch, 2000).

Collaboration as an option for service delivery has been around since the early 1970s and has been steadily growing in popularity ever since (see ASCA, 2003). It emerged as a way to help consultees take on a greater sense of ownership in the problem-solving process, most particularly in the carrying out of interventions (Johnson & Pugach, 1996). In this way, both parties reciprocally influence one another in all aspects of the case, engage in joint problem solving, and have responsibility for some aspects of the case related to its outcome. Collaboration sometimes remains a one-on-one experience, but most frequently it is a small group process that emphasizes teams (Paisley & Milsom, 2007; Rosenfield & Gravois, 1999). For example, many schools have an Instructional Consultation (IC) Team (Rosenfield & Gravois, 1999). It has recently evolved another aspect in which all members of the organization work "together and support each other on a set of multidimensional collegial interactions" to enhance the organization's effectiveness (Johnson & Pugach, 1996, p. 197).

Collaboration can occur in a variety of settings. For example, in schools, collaboration can occur during screening for special education services, development of individualized education plans (IEP), periodic review of students, and also with problem-solving intervention teams and site based management teams (Shaw & Swerdlik, 1995).

Collaboration often occurs in groups called teams, which are established whenever there is a collective effort to accomplish a goal such as helping the client system. Teams in which collaboration is the primary activity include task forces, work groups, and multidisciplinary teams. To be effective, teams have to manage their problem-solving business activities and maintenance (giving and receiving feedback) activities well (Rosenfield & Gravois,

1999). In school-based consultation and collaboration, family–school teams can be developed to assist in enhancing student achievement (Nastasi, 2005; Paisley & Milsom, 2007).

Like consultation, the context or setting of collaboration can shape its nature. There are typically two contexts in which collaboration can occur: intraagency and interagency. For example, in intraagency collaboration, people from the same school setting work together to help some children and their families in increasing the children's academic achievement.

In interagency collaboration, a group from two or more agencies attempts to help a child make a successful transition from a juvenile evaluation center to a public school setting.

Interagency collaboration is particularly common in early childhood settings (Harris & Klein, 2004). Collaboration in both these contexts presents its own unique challenges. In intraagency collaboration, the major challenge is for the parties-at-interest to find the time to actually meet and implement the nuts and bolts of the collaborative process (see Chapter 12). In interagency collaboration, the major challenge is one of coordination of the efforts of two or more organizations to a common end.

Defining the parameters of collaboration can sometimes be difficult. When the consultant and prospective consultees are employed in the same setting, it is difficult to meet some of the fundamental assumptions underlying consultation. For example, maintaining confidentiality at necessary levels can be challenging, the voluntary nature of consultation becomes questionable, and it is often difficult to relieve the consultant of *any* responsibility for the outcome of consultation (Zins & Erchul, 2002). Considering some of the challenges a school counselor or school psychologist might face in attempting to provide consultation services in a school, some authors (e.g., Caplan & Caplan, 1993) have suggested that collaboration is the intervention of choice when the mental health professional is internal to the organization.

In collaboration, the school-based professional has equal responsibility for the overall outcome and primary responsibility for the mental health outcome of the case. In addition, the collaborating partners do not have the freedom to reject any aspect of the assistance to be provided to the client system. They must go along with the consensus about how to proceed. Perhaps the best way to conceptualize collaboration is as consultation with a direct service component added. School-based mental health professionals need to be aware that they should be open to reciprocal consultation; that is, they too may take on the consultee role as necessary.

The following three brief and simple examples illustrate the scope of consultation and collaboration.

## Case Example 1: Consulting with Juvenile Court Counselors

A juvenile court counselor group asks you to conduct a two-day, interactive workshop on approaches for counseling adjudicated maladjusted and non-maladjusted youth. First you conduct a needs assessment. What do the consultees know, and what can they do? What do they need to know and do when it comes to working with adjudicated youth? You then design a workshop based on your findings, conduct the workshop, evaluate it, and follow up.

## Case Example 2: Collaborating with a Teacher

Mary Smith, a teacher, and you agree to try to assist a student whom Mary says is "incorrigible" and whom you view as lacking proper social skills with adults. You and Mary meet and establish a relationship. Mary describes what the student does that makes her label him as "incorrigible" and how often these negative behaviors occur. You give your opinions about the student's behavior. With that data in hand, you and Mary determine the acceptable level of the negative behaviors to be sought as well as the level of new desirable behaviors. Together, you then develop a program that has Mary implementing some token economy procedures with the student in the classroom while you provide counseling services to the student. You help her with the token economy procedures and she assists with information that is helpful in counseling the student. At a later date, you both evaluate the effectiveness of the collaborative experience.

## Case Example 3: Consulting with Another Human Service Professional

George is a community counselor seeking help for a situation that is new to him: providing therapy to a family who has a dying child. George asks you for some suggestions in helping the family deal directly with the impending death of the child since this is causing severe problems within the family. You interview the family without performing any therapy and provide George with specific written recommendations for him to assist the family in dealing with this issue. You then follow up and help George assess the progress he has made with the family.

# CONSULTATION AND COLLABORATION COMPARED WITH OTHER HUMAN SERVICE ACTIVITIES

Consultation and collaboration can be compared with the four other common human service functions—counseling and psychotherapy, supervision, teaching, and mediation—as a way of making the concepts underlying consultation and collaboration clearer. Such comparisons were popularized by Caplan in the 1970s.

*Consultation* and *collaboration* are different from counseling and psychotherapy in two fairly obvious ways. First, counseling and psychotherapy are dyadic in nature (they involve two parties, the therapist and the client) whereas consultation and collaboration are triadic. Second, counseling and psychotherapy deal with the personal problems of the client, whereas consultation and collaboration deal with work-related or caretaking-related concerns only. This is not to say that the effects of resolving a work-related problem cannot be therapeutic to the consultee or fellow collaborators. Still, consultants and collaborators, even if they are trained therapists, never provide counseling or psychotherapy to consultees or fellow collaborators, even if the work- or caretaking-related problem being solved is determined to be due to a personal problem of the other professional or caregiver. In such cases, the human service professional brings up his or her concerns and then refers the other party for assistance. In another difference, there is evidence that consultants tend to be more controlling of the consultation relationship than counselors are of the counseling relationship (see Henning-Stout & Conoley, 1987). A final point to remember is that when the consultant or collaborator is trained in counseling and psychotherapy, it is quite easy to inadvertently turn the consultation or collaboration session into a therapy session.

Another human service function that is different from consultation and collaboration is *supervision*. Supervision can be either clinical or administrative. Clinical supervision involves "consistent observation and evaluation of the counseling process . . . provided by a trained and experienced professional," while administrative supervision focuses "on the issues surrounding the supervisee's role and the responsibilities in the organization as an employee" (Haynes, Corey & Moulton, 2003, p. 3). Supervision tends to be performed in dyads and implies an ongoing relationship, whereas consultation and collaboration are usually temporary, tripartite relationships. More significantly, supervision implies the power of one person over another. If I am your supervisor, I have the power to perform ongoing evaluations of your effectiveness on the job. These evaluations will be used in personnel decisions that affect you in many ways at work and thus create inequity in the relationship. Therefore, consultants or collaborators do not become supervisors of the people to whom they provide these services.

*Teaching* is also different from consultation and collaboration. Traditional teaching involves a predetermined, detailed lesson plan, whereas events in consultation and collaboration often dictate more spontaneous behavior by the parties involved.

Further, teaching is an unequal relationship in which teachers have power over students and evaluate them, traditionally by some grading process. Human service professionals may assess consultee or fellow collaborator learning, but in a manner different from that used by teachers. A consultant or collaborator may, however, take on a teaching role on occasion. For example, a mental health collaborator might teach a fellow collaborator how to perform a behavioral counseling technique with a client, or an organizational consultant might teach a consultee the basics of survey design. Later in this text you will read about one of the most commonly requested approaches to consultation, education/training.

*Mediation* is different from consultation and collaboration, although many consultants and collaborators use mediation techniques in group or organizational work. Mediation is a form of conflict resolution (Fisher, Ury, & Patton, 1991) in which the mediator takes on the role of a third-party, neutral observer. Mediation is similar to consultation and collaboration in that it has a problem-solving orientation, is tripartite in nature, uses collaboration extensively, and involves a peer relationship among the parties. Mediation is different from consultation and collaboration in that it necessarily deals with conflict, never uses a teaching role, and does not allow room for suggestions or recommendations by the third-party neutral.

## CONSULTATION, COLLABORATION, AND LEVELS OF PREVENTION

Throughout this text, you will note examples that illustrate consultation and collaboration as either remedial or preventative. As you know, a remedial approach fixes a problem after it occurs with the idea of preventing occurrences in the future, while preventive approaches attempt to stop problems from occurring in the first place and attempts to decrease the need for services and resources (Love, 2007). The remedial perspective is reactive, and the preventative model is proactive (Blom-Hoffman & Rose, 2007). One of the founders of consultation, Gerald Caplan, used the public health model to develop his model of mental health consultation. His impact is felt today in consultation and collaboration. The public health model includes three levels of prevention: primary, secondary and tertiary (remedial). As Lewis et al. note: "Primary prevention focuses lowering the incidence of emotional problems and on promoting positive mental health among people not identified as having any special difficulty. It can be distinguished from secondary prevention, which aims at early identification and treatment of problems, and from tertiary prevention, which attempts to decrease the long-term effects of disabilities" (2003, p. 25). Primary prevention tries to prevent problems from occurring in the first place, secondary prevention tries to prevent problems from occurring in at-risk populations, and tertiary prevention (remedial) tries to prevent problems from reoccurring once they have been effectively resolved with a given client system. For example, a school-based consultant might engage in primary prevention by working to effect a system-level change in a school that creates a safe and caring school climate conducive to all students learning at optimal levels; secondary prevention by working with an administrator to develop at special program for students at risk for dropping out of school; and tertiary prevention by working with a teacher to assist a student with a history of acting out in the classroom. In another example, a community-based consultant might engage in primary prevention by consulting with neighborhood organizations to promote human development; secondary prevention by working with a community-based alternative mental health program to prevent teenage pregnancies; and tertiary prevention by consulting with the counselors of pregnant teens and their partners.

As you will note throughout this text, there is increasing consensus among mental health specialists in our society that we need to focus more on the psychological health and well-being of our society during the twenty-first century (Lewis et al., 2003). As a result, consultation for primary prevention is receiving increased attention in the literature [see, e.g., Zins (1995)]. The idea is consultation enhances consultee's abilities to successfully deal with similar issues in the future and serves as a method of delivering prevention services through the intermediary of the consultee (Zins, 1995).

In conclusion, consultation and collaboration, because they can focus on both remediation and prevention, are ideal services for mental health providers as they attempt to better meet the needs of people in a rapidly changing, culturally diverse, and technological society. All models of consultation and collaboration have both remedial and preventative aspects, but do vary in the degree to which one or the other is emphasized (Zins, 1995).

## MULTICULTURAL LIMITATIONS OF CONSULTATION AND COLLABORATION

It is very likely that you will practice consultation and collaboration in multicultural and cross-cultural settings. The 2000 U.S. Census showed that our society is very diverse. This diversity is reflected in all of the institutions in our society and thus requires culturally competent practice on the part of consultants and collaborators. In and of themselves, cultural differences are complex and subjective (Hall, 2005; LaRoche & Maxie, 2003). Further, there is a complex connection between culture and consultation. Culture is viewed as a context that permeates all aspects of consultation rather than simply a related variable (Hoffman et al., 2006; Tarver Behring & Ingraham, 1998). In other words, the culture of the client system is an aspect of the ecology dealt with in consultation (Ortiz, 2006; Ramirez & Smith, 2007). Further, most models of consultation are ethnocentric and are therefore limited (Nastasi, 2006).

Ingraham (2000, 2004) has built a framework that conceptualizes consultation from multicultural and cross-cultural perspectives. Multicultural competence is brought to the forefront and traditional consultation models are adapted accordingly

(Ingraham, 2004). This framework considers the influence of culture on the consultation process and the individuals involved in it. This framework can be applied to all models of consultation. In *multicultural consultation,* the consultant, in a culturally sensitive manner, adjusts services to accommodate and value cultural differences (Ingraham, 2003). In *cross-cultural consultation,* consultation occurs across cultures. Ingraham's comprehensive framework focuses on structures and processes of consultation, thus allowing consultants to identify and reflect upon multicultural issues and increase the chances of a successful consultation experience. This framework has five components:

- consultant knowledge, skills and dispositions related to cultural competence in consultation;
- understanding consultee needs for development in knowledge, skill, confidence and objectivity;
- cultural variations in the parties involved in consultation (e.g., consultant–consultee similarity);
- contextual influence (e.g., organizational culture) and power influences (difference in power among parties in the consultation relationship); and
- methods for supporting consultee success in multicultural situations.

Nastasi (2006) points out the necessity of cultural specificity in delivering services such as consultation and collaboration. Cultural specificity refers to the idea that all aspects of services such as consultation and collaboration are relevant to the targeted culture (Nastasi, 2006).

Huffman et al. (2006, p. 127), although not developing a framework for consultation as such, have presented major ideas that could lead to the development of a feminist and multicultural framework. The major themes include:

- a nonhierarchical approach provides greater benefits than a hierarchical one;
- a hierarchy in the consultation relationship is not inevitable;
- an open triad structure examines the complex interplay of interpersonal and extrapersonal forces within the context of the system;
- the consultation experience is used an opportunity to transform the system;
- patriarchal structures in organizations are based on greater privilege for some rather than others;
- the consultant's expertise and skills should be used to empower;
- the role of the consultant is that of an active agent for change;
- the consultation process can prevent similar systemic problems in the future; and
- informed advocacy on the part of the consultant for the consultee and client system is appropriate.

Through employing the framework and/or concepts like those described above, consultants are in a better position to provide services with multicultural competence. Without such a framework, the chances for successful consultation and collaboration are diminished (Ramirez & Smith, 2007). As Salzman (2005) notes, "no symptom or observation can be accurately interpreted without due consideration to social, historical, political and cultural considerations" (p. 235). Consultants will want to ensure that they are culturally sensitive at each phase of the consultation process. As an example, the concept of "happiness" for the client system may vary by culture (Gerstein, 2007).

In addition to striving to be multiculturally competent, consultants will want to bear in mind that the traditional models of consultation, which are typically derived from models of counseling and psychotherapy, may be based on worldviews that are irrelevant to some cultural groups (Corey, 2005; Hoffman et al., 2006). As Corey notes: "With respect to many of the traditional theories, assumptions made about mental health, optimum human development, the nature of psychopathology, and the nature of effective treatment may have little relevance for some clients" (2005, p. 42). For example, many cultural groups do not embrace the emphasis on individualism that many counseling theories value. As a result, consultants need to take a "person-in-the-environment perspective" (Corey, 2005; Lum, 2007). By focusing on both individual and environmental factors, consultants can modify and adjust the model they are using (Diller, 2007; Ramirez & Smith, 2007) to accommodate consultees and their client systems. For example, a consultant might reconceptualize treatment goals for a consultee of a culturally different group by taking the consultee's cultural beliefs into consideration (Diller, 2007). In other examples, a consultant may suggest that a consultee spend more time in relationship building with the client system, making recommendations regarding how the consultee may approach a culturally different client from a cultural style perspective (Ramirez & Smith, 2007). According to Diller (2007), another possibility is adding culture-specific helping strategies, as appropriate, to existing models. By behaving in this manner, consultants ensure that they take into account the subtle variables influencing the consultation process. The use of a multicultural framework will help consultees with a variety of issues that block consultee objectivity. One of these issues is *intervention paralysis,* in which consultees are multiculturally aware yet afraid of acting due to concern over making a multicultural blunder and coming across as culturally insensitive (Ingraham, 2004). This can result from the common predicament of a consultee knowing that each case is individual and also that common cultural variables may be at play (Ramirez & Smith, 2007).

## WHETHER TO CHOOSE CONSULTATION OR COLLABORATION

You will frequently be faced with the decision to choose between consultation and collaboration as the service of choice in particular situations. Below I describe some guidelines to assist you in this choice process.

First, ask and answer the question, "How does the organizational culture view each of these services in terms of preference?" In some instances, it might well be that collaboration is regarded as the "new kid on the block" and therefore is not perceived to be as legitimate as consultation. On the other hand, for professionals who are internal to the organization in which services are to be provided, collaboration may be preferred because it presents many stakeholders with a piece of the action of implementation.

Second, ask yourself, "How do I really feel about consultation and collaboration? Do I think consultation puts me too much in the expert role? Do I think collaboration forces me to give up too much power in the case?" It is important for you to know where you stand on issues like these as they will affect your choice of services. Before you proceed with consultation you need to determine if the assumptions underlying consultation (e.g., confidentiality, the voluntary nature of the relationship, nonhierarchical status within the relationship) are met. If they are not met, collaboration may well be the method of choice.

Your own skill level will also influence your decision to use consultation or collaboration.

On the one hand, consultation demands the ability to guide and control the problem-solving process while empowering the consultee. On the other hand, collaboration demands the ability to balance the reciprocal influence that the parties exert on each other in collaboration. As you gain experience in both consultation and collaboration you will become equally comfortable with both processes.

The level of skill of the prospective consultee or collaborator will also influence your choice of services. If the other party is not skilled in what is most likely to be implemented and time for training is not feasible, then collaboration is in order. If time is not a factor or the other party is relatively highly skilled in terms of possible interventions, then consultation may well be in order.

The bottom line is that the choice between using consultation or collaboration is frequently a judgment call with either choice being an adequate one. As in determining whether to provide any other service, the nature of the problem, the context in which it occurs, and the skills of the parties involved interact together to influence your choice.

## PROMOTING CONSULTATION AND COLLABORATION IN YOUR WORK SETTING

There are a variety of strategies available to you to promote consultation and collaboration services in your work setting. McLean (2006) has identified several successful approaches to finding the "points of focus" (p. 45). You can make a point to learn the ins and outs of your organization including its people. This task allows you to be able to identify the needs for consultation and collaboration at both the individual and organizational levels. You can proactively publicize and promote awareness of your services within the organization. These processes assist the members of the organization to determine how your work can assist them and the organization. When you share examples of their work and related successes, others in the organization are more likely to trust your expertise as well as make connections about how they can benefit from consultation and collaboration. When you are frequently visible and engaging others at all levels of the organization, you are more likely to be invited to engage in activities related to organizational-level and individual-level initiatives that lead to consultation and/or collaboration. Engage your immediate supervisor as champion of your consultation and collaboration services, and invite those who have engaged in consultation or collaboration with you to share their experiences with others in the organization.

## SUGGESTIONS FOR EFFECTIVE PRACTICE

- Know the focal points in your work environment that can be improved through your services.

- Develop a working definition of consultation and collaboration with which you feel comfortable.

- Become very familiar with the characteristics of both consultation and collaboration so that you can do both well and differentiate between the two when necessary.

- Make a point to differentiate consultation and collaboration from the other professional services you will be providing.

- Strive to take into account the social and cultural factors affecting your consultees and their client systems.

## QUESTIONS FOR REFLECTION

1. How do the roles of consultant, consultee, and client differ from one another?

2. What is the basic difference between indirect and direct service that consultants and collaborators provide?

3. In what ways can consultation and collaboration be called problem-solving processes?

4. Why is it important for consultants and collaborators to have a personal theory of these two services?

5. In what ways are consultation and collaboration similar? Different?

6. How can you promote consultation and collaboration services in your work setting and also emphasize both the preventative and remedial aspects of these services?

7. How can consultation and collaboration have the goal of improving the consultee (or fellow collaborator) and the client system at the same time?

8. Because consultants by definition work with consultees who have work-related problems, how can the consultation relationship be that of equals?

9. How would you as a collaborator determine which roles to take on during collaboration?

10. How can you practice consultation and collaboration in a culturally competent manner?

## SUGGESTED SUPPLEMENTARY READINGS

Started in 1990, the *Journal of Educational and Psychological Consultation* is put out by the Association for Educational and Psychological Consultants and published quarterly by Lawrence Erlbaum Associates. This journal serves as a forum for the exchange of ideas, theories, and research among professionals in the human services and education.

*Consulting Psychology Journal: Practice and Research.* This quarterly is the official journal of Division 13, Consulting Psychology, of the American Psychological Association. It presents various ideas related to the practice of consultation. In recent years, the journal has tended to emphasize organizational consultation.

"Consultation I: Conceptual, Structural, and Operational Definitions" (Special issue). (1993a). *Journal of Counseling and Development,* 71, 596–708. This special issue is an update of the special issue of the *Personnel and Guidance Journal* entitled "Consultation I: Definitions, Models, Programs," which was published in 1978. This update, edited by Kurpius and

Fuqua, is divided into five sections: Section 1 addresses conceptual and operational foundations of consultation; Section 2, assessment and organizational diagnosis: Section 3, organizational culture; Section 4, consultation in different settings; Section 5, research in consultation. This journal issue and the one described next still represent much of the current thinking in consultation.

"Consultation II: Prevention, Preparation, and Key Issues" (Special issue). (1993b). *Journal of Counseling and Development,* 72, 115–223. This special issue is an update of the special issue of the *Personnel and Guidance Journal* entitled "Consultation II: Dimensions, Training, Bibliography," which was published in 1978. The new update, edited by Kurpius and Fuqua, is divided into three sections: Section 1 addresses primary prevention consultation; Section 2, professional preparation of consultants; Section 3, trends and topical issues such as ethical, legal, and multicultural issues. This issue is a fine complement to "Consultation I."

## SUGGESTED WEBSITES

**http://www.counseling.org/Publications/ CounselingToday.aspx** This site presents *Counseling Today* online. You can explore this site for references to consultation.

**http://www.counseling.org/Publications/ Newsletters.aspx** This site is by subscription only, and the newsletter is available to be read on the website.

**http://members.apa.org** If you join the American Psychological Association (APA),

you can enjoy the convenience of searching APA journals, a database of abstracts, and general information. The search engine allows easy retrieval of information related to consultation and collaboration.

**http://www.nasponline.org** This is the website of the National Association of School Psychologists. It contains a wealth of invaluable information, including information on consultation and collaboration.

# 2

✳

# Consultants, Consultees, and Collaborators

I f you were looking for a consultant or collaborator to work with people in your human service organization, what type of person would you hire? If you were going to permanently hire a mental health professional in your organization and part of his/her job was to consult and collaborate, what you be looking for in candidates? What kinds of professional knowledge and skills would be needed in such a person, and how would you be able to tell if the consultant/ collaborator truly possessed them? What roles would you want this person to take during his or her activities? What would be the most critical factor for you in determining whether or not to hire this prospective helper?

This chapter provides some answers to these questions—it discusses the characteristics that effective consultants and collaborators possess, the skills critical to successful consultation and collaboration, and the various roles that professionals take on when providing these services. In addition, we will examine two other important areas: the position (internal or external) of the consultant/collaborator to the organization in which service is to occur, and the current status of research on consultation and collaboration.

As you read this chapter, consider the following questions:

1. How are the personal characteristics of consultants and collaborators likely to influence the delivery of their services?
2. What skills seem necessary for consultants and collaborators, regardless of the role they assume in delivering their services?
3. Do any of the roles of consultants and collaborators tend to contradict one another?
4. In what ways should consultants and collaborators be multiculturally skilled?

5.  To what degree can the research related to these services guide your practice?

As I have noted in Chapter 1, you can assume in this and in the following chapters that the discussion of a given topic applies equally to consultation and collaboration unless I make a distinction otherwise. I avoid using the terms "consultation" and "collaboration" together in order to enhance the readability of this text.

## INTRODUCTION

Consider the following two cases:

### Case Example 1:
### An Ineffective Consultant

Dale Jones, a counselor, and Jackie Cheng, a social worker, work together in a community mental health center. Jackie approaches Dale for consultation regarding a migrant family that is part of Jackie's caseload. It seems that the family has had difficulty adjusting to the community, which consists primarily of retirees who have their summer homes there. When Jackie asks Dale for help in facilitating the family's adjustment, Dale makes light of the request by noting that by late fall, both the retirees and the migrant family will be long gone.

### Case Example 2:
### An Effective Consultant

Terri Brodski, a psychologist, and Jamie Stewart, a social worker, work together in a community mental health center. Jamie approaches Terri for consultation regarding a migrant family that is part of Jamie's caseload. It seems that the family has had difficulty adjusting to the community, which consists primarily of retirees who have their summer homes there. When Jamie approaches Terri about the family's problems, Terri asks her to present her concerns about the family in detail, and she listens

to and clarifies Jamie's concerns. When Jamie expresses pessimism about the possibilities of helping the family, Terri offers encouragement and support, and she asks how Jamie's work with the family ties into their agency's role and mission. Finally, they establish a verbal contract between them and agree to meet twice more about how Jamie can work more effectively with the family.

First, Terri observes Jamie working with the family. During the next consultation session, they exchange their impressions about the family; divide the family's adjustment problem into three smaller, more specific problems; and set goals to solve them. Terri then leads Jamie through a brainstorming session during which possible interventions are generated. Once they agree on an intervention for each problem, Terri assists Jamie in formulating their ideas into a feasible plan, which Jamie agrees to carry out.

During their final consultation session one month later, Terri and Jamie formally evaluate the degree to which each problem was solved and the effectiveness of the consultation process itself (that is, how well they worked together). They plan additional follow-up strategies for Jamie to use in later contacts with the family and agree that, within 30 days, Terri will make a follow-up call to Jamie concerning the family's progress. Then they say their goodbyes.

Terri clearly spent much more time and used more finesse with Jamie than Dale did with Jackie. Terri displayed many of the characteristics of effective consultants. She used interpersonal skills when offering support and encouragement to Jamie. When Terri listened to and clarified Jamie's concerns, she used communicated effectively. She used several problem-solving approaches with Jamie to identify ways to help the migrant family. Terri showed the sensitivity of a multiculturally aware consultant when she asked Jamie to share in detail her views of the family's problems. Terri also showed skill in working with organizations when she asked how Jamie's work with the family tied into the agency's role and mission, and she displayed ethical and professional behavior by spending the time and effort needed to help Jamie. As you can see from these two cases, there are characteristics and skills that differentiate effective consultants from ineffective ones. Let's examine these characteristics next.

## CHARACTERISTICS OF EFFECTIVE CONSULTANTS AND COLLABORATORS

Because consultation and collaboration are demanding, the requirements to perform them successfully are a challenge. Some research suggests that the best consultants seem to be guided by the need to make a difference in the lives of others (Bianco-Mathis & Veazey, 1996). Beyond an internal motivation, however, effective consultants must possess the following:

- a personal and professional growth orientation
- knowledge of the content and process of consultation and collaboration as well as human behavior
- consultation and collaboration skills

What Arredondo et al. (2004) pointed out for psychologists applies to all consultants and collaborators in that they "need to acquire and demonstrate the knowledge, skills, attitudes and values necessary to work in a collegial, integrative, and informed manner across specialty and practice areas" (p. 791).

A *personal growth orientation* involves the willingness of a consultant to grow and change as a person. Because consultation involves problem solving, which requires change on the part of the consultee, consultants need to be willing to model that change. A personal growth orientation does not necessarily mean that consultants must experience personal growth counseling or therapy, although such experiences can be quite beneficial. Rather, the concept of personal growth orientation entails any aspect of a consultant's life in which he or she endeavors to "stretch." For example, one consultant might decide to accomplish the feat of hiking to every waterfall in a national park within a certain time frame, another consultant might volunteer 10 hours a week of free

consultation services to a church group, whereas another consultant might participate in a personal growth group to improve his or her interpersonal effectiveness. In short, personal growth orientation is an attitude toward life that helps consultants become more effective human beings by periodically "stretching" themselves in some way.

A *professional growth orientation* refers to consultants' participation in activities that enhance the effectiveness of their consultation practices (Cooper, Monarch, Serviss, Gordick, & Leonard, 2007). Consultants often participate in workshops, training programs, academic courses, and supervised practice so as to remain current in their fields. In addition, many consultants seek additional training and knowledge to expand the parameters of their consultation practices. For example, one consultant, a university professor by training, might take a series of management and organizational behavior courses and so expand her consultation services to include human service agencies. Thus, a personal and professional growth orientation helps consultants to practice what they preach more effectively. By experiencing growth in their own lives, consultants are better able to empathize with consultees about the barriers to growth that consultees normally experience, and to be more authentic role models for those with whom they work.

Effective consultants, of course, also possess *knowledge of consultation* and a basic *knowledge of human behavior* (Arredondo et al., 2004). Effective consultants know the ins and outs of consultation; that is, they possess a generic model of consultation and are knowledgeable about the various types of consultation and related multicultural and ethical issues. Such knowledge provides them with a sense of meaningfulness and adds direction to their practices.

Effective consultants must also possess knowledge about human behavior—including both individual and group behavior—for consultation involves having, first and foremost, a human relationship. Because consultants spend much of their time working with individual consultees, they need to know the basics of personality theory, normal and abnormal behavior, interpersonal relationships, and human communication. Knowledge of these topics is essential for maximizing the effectiveness with which each stage of consultation is accomplished. Furthermore, a basic knowledge of group dynamics and organizational theory and behavior is a necessity for almost all consultants because most consultation occurs in, and is affected by, an organizational setting. Therefore, consultants need a working knowledge of organizations to maximize the effectiveness of their activities.

Even when consultants have a growth orientation and are knowledgeable, if they are to be effective, they need to possess *skills in consulting*. Consultants must be able to *do* as well as *know*. Effective consultants have a broad repertoire of consultation skills that range from basic communication skills to sophisticated problem-solving intervention skills.

# SKILLS NECESSARY FOR CONSULTATION AND COLLABORATION

Many skills are required of effective consultants and collaborators. You will want to remember that the skills described below are not the consultation process itself. Rather they are the tools with which you will implement the process. Many authors point out the importance of competent interpersonal and communication skills (see, e.g., Dougherty, Henderson, & Lindsey, 1997; Egan, 2007). Skills in working with culturally diverse populations are increasingly important (Ingraham, 2004, 2004; Lum, 2007; Miranda, 2002), as are problem-solving skills (Welch, 2000) and skills in working with organizations (Knoff, 2002). Because consultants, and even more so collaborators, are increasingly being called on to work with groups of consultees, skills in group work are a must (Paisley & Milsom, 2007). Finally, well-developed ethical and professional behavior skills are essential to competency (Corey, Corey, & Callanan, 2007). The limited empirical research on the importance of the skill areas also supports the hypothesis that they are related to

consultation success (see Knoff, McKenna, & Riser, 1991; Knoff, Sullivan, & Liu, 1995; Randolph & D'Ilio, 1990). For example, Knoff and coauthors (1995) found that there were two primary skill areas when prospective consultees were queried regarding consultant effectiveness: consultant knowledge, process, and application skills and consultant interpersonal and problem-solving skills. It is very likely that the same holds for collaboration as its skill sets represent the same competencies (Arredondo et al., 2004).

## Interpersonal and Communication Attitudes

Consultation is a human relationship that involves extensive communication. Interpersonal and communication skills, which are related to creating and maintaining effective human relationships, are essential for a consultant. Furthermore, the attitudes from which these skills flow are as important as the skills themselves (Kurpius & Rozecki, 1993).

In the early 1960s, Carl Rogers demonstrated that the desirable underpinnings for these skills are unconditional regard, empathy, and genuineness. These attitudes form the core conditions on which an effective consultation relationship can be built. Without these attitudes in the consultant, the development of rapport with the consultee may take longer to achieve or may not occur at all. These attitudes exist on a continuum; their presence in a person is not an all-or-nothing proposition (Egan, 2007). However, to the degree that consultants possess these attitudes, the conditions for successful consultation will be established (Kurpius & Rozecki, 1993).

*Unconditional regard* (often referred to as "acceptance" or "respect") refers to the willingness of the consultant to respect and accept the consultee as a human being who is worthwhile, has dignity, and can be liked or cared for by the consultant, in spite of the consultee's imperfections. The consultant often manifests regard as nonjudgmental and nonpossessive behavior toward the consultee (e.g., assuming the consultee's and client system's good will).

*Empathy* refers to the consultant's ability to understand—to tune in to and accurately perceive the consultee's experience without losing his or her objectivity. It is a posture of putting oneself in another person's shoes. Empathy helps in establishing rapport, trust, open communication, and a common ground from which consultation can proceed (French & Bell, 1999). Empathy is both a value and a communication skill (Egan, 2007).

*Genuineness* is demonstrated when consultants feel free to be themselves in the consultation relationship—when they need not hide behind roles, become defensive, or lose spontaneity with the consultee (Egan, 2007). Perhaps one of the greatest contributions of genuineness to successful consultation is the modeling effect it can have for the consultee (Bellman, 1990). When consultees view consultants as genuine, they too can become more genuine (Block, 2000).

In summary, although your skills are critical to your success as a consultant, your perspective may be just as important (Bellman, 1990). For decades, these attitudes and the behavioral characteristics that reflect them are linked to professional skills and knowledge in such a way that they affect how a consultee perceives a consultant's helpfulness (e.g., see Bardon, 1986).

## Interpersonal Skills

The interpersonal skills of creating, maintaining, and terminating relationships refer to our ability to get along with other human beings. Because consultation is a helping relationship, consultants need relatively high levels of these skills (Arredondo et al., 2004; Zins & Erchul, 2002).

The creation and maintenance of consultation relationships require the following major interpersonal skills:

- putting the consultee at ease (e.g., making small talk)

- setting expectations about the relationship (e.g., contracting behaviors)

- creating an environment conducive to collaboration (e.g., determining early on what the consultee can and cannot do)

- creating an environment conducive to change (e.g., talking implicitly and explicitly about how consultation is related to change)

- creating an appropriate consultant's image in the eyes of the consultee (e.g., explaining early on who the consultant is and what he or she can do for the consultee)

- developing a social influence base built on prestige, trustworthiness, and similarity (e.g., making explicit use of expertise, benign intent, and similarities to the consultee)

- being comfortable with oneself as consultant (e.g., exuding confidence)

- noting and responding not only to consultee verbalizations, but also to emotions and non-verbal behaviors (e.g., reflecting a therapist's anxiety about working with a client who has AIDS)

- using appropriate humor (e.g., being willing to laugh at oneself)

Interpersonal skills assist consultants in developing and sustaining strong relationships with their consultees. The strength and outcome of the consultation relationship are often directly related to consultee motivation, a commitment to change, and a positive attitude toward consultation (see Curtis & Stollar, 2002). Gibbs (1980) was one of the first authors to note that consultant interpersonal skills are integral to working effectively in cross-cultural consultation. Kurpius and Rozecki note that "if the consultant does not have a mastery of the art of communication and an understanding of the intricacies of interpersonal interaction, the consultation process will most often appear lifeless and unlikely to be of long-lasting help" (1993, p. 143).

## Communication Skills

The communication process between consultant and consultee can be considered central to the process of consultation (Rosenfield, 2002b). As Rosenfield notes, "The consultant functions as the architect of the dialogue, creating space for and facilitating the consultation conversation" (2002a, p. 611).

Everything consultants do when they consult involves a system of language constructs (Daniels & DeWine, 1990); that is, a system of symbols used to make sense of life events and experiences. Communication skills refer to people's ability to send and receive meaningful messages. Such skills tend to be more specific than relationship skills. As we know from our experiences with others, communicating is sometimes quite difficult.

Consultants need to use a broad repertoire of communication skills to increase the probability of a successful outcome to consultation. There is some research that highlights the importance of communication in consultation (Dougherty et al., 1997; Erchul, 1993b).

There are many "basic" communication skills. Among the more important ones for consultants are:

- nonverbal attending (e.g., keeping an open body posture)

- listening (e.g., actively discerning a consultee's intended meaning)

- expressing empathy (e.g., understanding the consultee's experience and accurately communicating that understanding back to the consultee)

- questioning (e.g., asking consultees to expand on a subject or be more specific)

- clarifying or paraphrasing (e.g., putting consultees' expressions into the consultant's own words to demonstrate understanding or to help consultees understand themselves better)

- summarizing (e.g., putting together the main points of discussion in order to determine the next step in the consultation process)

- providing feedback (e.g., providing consultees with information about themselves for the purposes of examination and change)

- giving information (e.g., informing the consultee of the possible ways a given client might be effectively helped)

- "speaking the same language" (e.g., choosing plain language that avoids jargon)

Communication skills such as these are related to a successful consultation outcome in that they allow the consultant and consultee to exchange meaningful and accurate information, which facilitates more effective problem solving and aids relationship maintenance throughout the consultation process. Jargon should be used with caution (Knotek, 2003). Through the use of effective communication skills, the consultant is able to view the situation and the consultee from a variety of perspectives and enhance the possibilities of a successful outcome to consultation (Kurpius & Rozecki, 1993). In fact, communication and interpersonal skills build the foundation for the success all of the stages of consultation.

## Skills Related to Cultural Diversity

Cultural considerations can affect consultation practice (Nastasi, 2006). Although consultation models tend to be deficient in the areas related to cultural diversity (Ingraham, 2000, 2003, 2004) and gender issues (Henning-Stout, 1994), the literature related to multicultural issues in consultation has expanded greatly since the turn of the millennium. Several organizations such as the American Psychological Association, the American Counseling Association, the Council on Social Work Education, and the National Organization of Human Service Education have developed materials on multicultural preparation and practice. The increasing diversity within our society demands skills on the part of consultants in dealing with that diversity: "Consultants almost inevitably provide services to individuals who are different from themselves in their culture of origin" (Ramirez et al., 1998, p. 479). One of the major challenges human service professionals encounter is discerning the complex role cultural diversity takes on in their work (Hays, 2001). As early as 1970, Caplan pointed out how cultural variables could adversely affect communication in consultation.

Indeed, the culture of the parties involved in consultation may well affect the efficacy of the mode of consultation being used (see Brown, 1997; Rosenfield & Gravois, 1999). There is no doubt that consultants need to be culturally competent and take cultural differences into account (Frisby, 2006; Hoffman et al., 2006; Holcomb-McCoy, 2004; Miranda, 2002; Ortiz, 2006; Rogers, 2000). For example, by the year 2025, the Hispanic and Asian combined population will approximate one-quarter of the population in the United States (Ortiz & Flanagan, 2002). Consultants will increasingly be asked to consult with and about culturally diverse people and with organizations owned, managed, or populated by culturally diverse people (Jackson & Hayes, 1993). Competencies in becoming multiculturally skilled as a consultant include those related to beliefs, attitudes, knowledge, and skills (Arredondo et al., 2004; Nastasi, 2005), as well as assessment and intervention (Quintana et al., 2000; Rogers, 2000).

Multicultural competence is basic to effective consultation (Ortiz & Flanagan, 2002). Corey et al. (2007) note that one of the major issues facing human service professionals is understanding the complex role that cultural diversity plays in their work. Sue (1998) suggests that cultural competency involves making hypotheses rather than premature judgments about culturally different people, knowing when to generalize and when to individualize regarding culturally different people, and having culture specific expertise. When consultants work from a multicultural perspective, they attempt to understand and deal with the socio-cultural forces affecting the helping relationship (Gibbs, 1980). There are a significant number of multicultural competencies that have been established for human service professionals by Arredondo and her colleagues (1996, 2004). Ingraham (2000) has developed eight domains for consultant competency in multicultural consultation. Consultants should bear in mind that all consultation is multicultural if the concept of culture is broadened to include diversity indicators such as gender and age (Das, 1995).

Understanding your own cultural framework provides a context for understanding different cultural contexts (ACA, 2005; APA, 2002, 2003). Being multiculturally competent is essential for consultants and involves interpersonal, communication, problem-solving, ethical, and professional behavior skills such as the following (Ramirez et al., 1998):

- understanding the impact of one's own culture on practice

- valuing and understanding the impact of other cultures

- adapting a culturally responsive consultation style

- integrating a knowledge of cultural diversity into effective practice

- not making value judgments about consultees (or client systems) who are culturally different

- challenging any stereotypic beliefs about culturally diverse groups

- viewing cultural differences as issues to meet, not as impediments

- using methods consistent with the life experiences and values of different minority groups

- possessing specific knowledge about the particular minority group served in consultation

- ensuring that definition of problems and development of goals take place within a cultural context

By increasing the level of our skills in working with those from different cultures, and addressing the complexities of culture and gender as they relate to consultation, we can move toward effective consultation practice. For an example of a culturally congruent consultation, see Salzman (2002). Flanagan (2002) provides an excellent resource on competencies related to cultural diversity. For excellent resources for working with people from different cultures, see, Atkinson (2004), Diller (2007), Hall (2005), Lum (2007), and Ortiz and Flanagan (2002).

The bottom line in dealing with diversity is pointed out by Ortiz (2006, p. 159): "the development and application of interventions in a diverse setting or with a multiethnic population does not automatically make it an example of multicultural practice."

## Problem-Solving Skills

Because consultation is by nature a problem-solving activity, consultants need to be highly skilled in that area (Arredondo et al., 2004; Meyers, 2002). There is some empirical evidence that problem-solving skills are essential even in the presence of effective interpersonal and communication skills (Curtis & Stollar, 2002). Some of the many problem-solving skills available to consultants are:

- setting the stage for problem solving (e.g., defining consultation as a problem-solving activity)

- defining the problem (that is, isolating "what is to be fixed" during consultation)

- examining the conditions surrounding the problem (e.g., noting antecedents and consequences)

- gathering, analyzing, and interpreting data pertinent to the problem (e.g., surveying organizational personnel and providing feedback on the results)

- identifying any facilitating and restraining forces (that is, determining which forces are working for and against a given plan)

- designing interventions for a particular situation (e.g., identifying consultee strengths that increase the likelihood of successful plan implementation)

- evaluating problem-solving attempts (that is, determining the degree to which a selected intervention worked)

- determining who will do what, how, and when during the problem-solving process (that is, arranging the responsibilities involved in carrying out the plan)

- predicting the ramifications and implications of solving the problem (that is, examining how change can affect other parts of the system)

Consultants use problem-solving skills such as these to assist their consultees in solving work-related problems. Many consultants attempt to facilitate the development of more sophisticated problem-solving skills in their consultees. The critical implications of these skills for successful consultation will become apparent in later chapters (Chapters 4 and 5) that discuss specific problem-solving skills.

## Skills in Working with Organizations

As the cases presented at the beginning of this chapter indicate, almost all consultation occurs within some organizational context. Because of this, consultants need to have some basic skills—specific behaviors—in working with an organization as a whole. When successfully demonstrated, these skills increase the likelihood of a successful outcome of consultation.

Some of the more important skills consultants need when they work with organizations are:

- becoming accepted by the members of the organization in which consultation is to occur (e.g., creating working relationships with prospective consultees)

- using organizational analysis (e.g., determining who talks to whom under what conditions)

- providing feedback (e.g., giving the consultee objective information about some aspect of the organization's functioning)

- using systems theory (e.g., dealing with complex organizational issues)

- gathering information (e.g., using surveys to determine the attitudes of the organization's members)

- using a repertoire of organization-wide interventions (e.g., providing a stress management program)

- determining the cultural competence of an organization (that is, its working atmosphere related to cultural differences)

- determining the culture of the organization (that is, its norms, standards, and values)

- using program planning (e.g., assisting consultees in executing effective programs)

- determining how to utilize human resources within the organization (e.g., assisting consultees in improving managerial styles)

As the list suggests, human service consultants need not have all the skills required to give the organization with which they consult everything it needs.

However, such consultants do need selected skills that allow them to operate at an optimal level within the organization and assist with selected organization-wide changes. Without these skills, consultants and the consultation process itself can become victims of those organizational forces that have negative effects. The importance of a repertoire of skills for working with organizations will become even more apparent in Chapter 8, which provides an orientation to organizations and how they function.

### Group Skills

Because they are increasingly being called on to work with groups of consultees, effective consultants need to be skilled in working with a variety of groups (Conyne & Mazza, 2007; Gutkin 2002; Webster, Knotek, Babinski, Rogers, & Barnett, 2003). Several of the types of consultation you will be reading about later—such as education/training consultation, program consultation, process consultation, and behavioral system consultation—frequently demand the use of group work on the part of consultants. Furthermore, group skills are particularly critical for collaborators because most collaboration occurs in teams (Iverson, 2002; Meyers et al., 2004; Paisley & Milsom, 2007). Some of the many group skills needed include:

- focusing and maintaining attention on task and work issues (e.g., gently reminding the group when it gets off task)

- managing conflict within a group of consultees (e.g., using mediation skills in assisting two conflicting group members)

- managing agendas of meetings (e.g., helping group members determine what items should be on an agenda and how those items are to be dealt with)

- providing feedback to group members (e.g., confronting members, avoidance of important issues)

- facilitating concrete and specific communication among group members (e.g., reflecting the true meaning of vague generalities)

- linking the comments of one group member to pertinent comments from others (e.g., tying in a consultee's statement about one of her clients to another consultee's remark about one of his clients)

- facilitating the development of the group process (e.g., knowing when to move from the getting-acquainted stage to the working stage)

- using group management skills (e.g., knowing how to terminate a group session)

- sensing and using group dynamics to help consultee groups meet their goals (e.g., calling attention to the emotional current running through the group).

Increasingly consultants and collaborators are interacting in group modalities, such as teams, thus amplifying the importance of group-related skills.

### Ethical and Professional Behavior Skills

To be successful, consultants need to behave ethically and professionally. The necessary skills are often associated with internal feelings or beliefs that are explicitly demonstrated in consultants' behavior. Throughout their careers, all consultants encounter professional situations that require a set of skills based on sound ethical judgment (Corey et al., 2007). For example, what would you do if, as a consultant, you were "over your head" in trying to help a consultee work with a difficult client?

Some of the myriad important skills that can help consultants act in an ethical and professional manner are:

- acting with integrity (e.g., maintaining confidentiality)

- adhering to an ethical code (that is, adhering to accepted guidelines for professional behavior)

- engaging in consultation only within one's professional limits (that is, declining consultations for which one is not qualified)

- maintaining personal and professional growth (e.g., engaging in professional development activities)

- having the intent to help (e.g., being as thorough as possible)

- effectively coping with the stress of consulting (e.g., using stress management skills)

- ensuring cultural competence (e.g., adapting procedures to cultural context)

- using effective writing skills (e.g., writing high-quality reports)

- using power for legitimate purposes only (that is, using one's skills to influence others appropriately)

Acting in an ethical, professional manner creates positive perceptions among the consultant's coworkers and contacts. Such perceptions contribute to the successful outcome of consultation because consultees are able to attribute to the consultant the social influence necessary for maximum effectiveness during consultation. Chapter 7 deals extensively with the ethical and professional behavior of consultants.

Possessing all these skills seems a tall order. The extent of a consultant's skills is best understood if they are seen as part of a continuum; no consultant either completely lacks or completely possesses each skill. And although it is important to note that effective consultants are not necessarily expert in all of these skills, they possess most of these skills to a moderate or high degree. Developing the skills to be even more effective is a process that continues for the entire career of every consultant.

## ROLES CONSULTANTS AND COLLABORATORS ASSUME

### The Nature of Consultant Roles

Consultants can wear many hats. They use the skills described in the preceding sections in a variety of consultation roles or functions performed at any given time during the consultation relationship. Just as consultation is not easily defined, neither are the roles in which consultants function.

Consultants can take on any number of roles during a particular consultation relationship. The nature of the roles is usually defined in the consultation contract. Effective consultants are able to determine which roles are necessary, define them to the satisfaction of all parties involved, and then perform those roles.

The primary role a consultant takes on depends on several factors, including his or her abilities and frames of reference, the consultee's expectations and skill levels, the nature of the problem that consultation is attempting to solve, the model of consultation used, and the environmental context in which consultation occurs. Based on this assessment, the consultant will be directive or nondirective as appropriate (Kratochwill, Elliott, & Callan-Stoiber, 2002).

### The Categorization of Roles

Most categorization schemes put consultation roles on some sort of continuum. The most popular categorization approach still used was developed in the 1980s by Lippitt and Lippitt (1986), in which consultants' roles lie on a continuum ranging from directive to nondirective roles. In directive roles the consultant is something of a technical expert, whereas in nondirective roles consultants tend to facilitate the consultee's expertise. Another popular approach to consultants' roles, developed by Margulies and Raia (1972) in the 1970s, includes task roles (those related to expertise) at one end of a continuum and process roles (those related to facilitation) at the other.

Regardless of how consulting roles are categorized, the bottom line is that categorization schemes tend to reflect the consultant's degree of involvement in the consultation process relative to that of the consultee. They guide the consultant in determining who is responsible for what tasks and how the consultant should proceed in consultation. For most human service professionals, the directive–nondirective categorization scheme of Lippitt and Lippitt (1986) seems most appropriate; the terms are familiar to most human service professionals, and they provide a very helpful rule of thumb because they imply the amount of control the consultant should have over the consultation process. The following discussion of common consultation roles is grounded in the categorization scheme of Lippitt and Lippitt (1986).

## Common Consultation Roles

Consultants can engage in the consultation process in a broad range of roles that vary in terms of how much the consultant directs the activity occurring in consultation (Lippitt & Lippitt, 1986); that is, some roles are more directive than others. Next we'll consider six consultation roles: advocate, expert, trainer/educator, collaborator, fact finder, and process specialist.

**Advocate.**    The most directive consulting role is that of advocate. At first glance you would think that advocacy would not be a typical role the consultant takes on. As an advocate the consultant attempts to persuade the consultee to do something the consultant deems highly desirable. For example, a consultant relying on her superior knowledge about data collection in organizations might advocate the use of several methods in addition to what the consultee thinks is necessary. However, in the last two decades the advocacy role has been defined more in terms of advocating for the rights of those who are unable to help themselves (see, e.g., Hoffman et al., 2006; Lewis et al., 2003; Lott & Rogers, 2005). In this sense, advocacy is often combined with outreach: the promotion of available services to selected populations. For example, a mental health professional may advocate at a variety of levels to get barriers related to client access or growth examined (ACA, 2005).

Consultants can act as advocates in a variety of ways (Kurpius & Lewis, 1988): as process consultants assisting groups in working effectively or becoming self-advocates; as identifiers of target groups needing advocacy, finding necessary resources and facilitating the advocacy attempts; and as agents who attempt to prevent target groups from needing advocacy at a later time.

On the one hand, consultants have a professional obligation not to engage in inappropriate advocacy roles (Remley, 1988). Yet they should not avoid situations that dictate that they become advocates. Some authors (e.g., Conoley & Conoley, 1992) promote a very positive view of advocacy, even to the point of calling it a type of consultation in and of itself.

However, to get a feel for the possible turmoil in which an advocacy role might place a consultant, consider the following: A school counselor is an advocate for a student (client system) identified as a possible dropout. Some school personnel (consultees) feel strongly that because the student cannot be adequately educated in the system as it stands, the student is better off in some setting other than the school. The counselor agrees that the system cannot meet the student's needs but maintains that it should obtain the resources to do so. This advocacy position places the counselor in a lose–lose situation. By attempting to change the system to benefit the client, the consultant risks losing consultee support. If the consultant does not attempt to change the system, the client may drop out.

There are times, situations, and issues for which advocacy is the most appropriate role for a consultant. One common example of an appropriate advocacy role is when the consultant detects within an organization a discrepancy between the way an organization is supposed to treat its clients and the way it actually treats them (Lott & Rogers, 2005). Consultants can avoid misusing the advocacy role by maintaining a high level of self-awareness and skills about such matters as poverty, racism, and value-related issues and by maintaining a collaborative relationship with the consultee.

**Expert.**    The most common role that consultants take on is that of expert or technical advisor. In this circumstance, the consultee needs some knowledge, advice, or service that the consultant can provide on request (Stroh & Johnson, 2006). When consultants are retained as experts over a long period of time, it seems apparent that the consultees (or organizations) retaining the consultants know what they need from the consultants. However, this is often not the case (Schein, 1988).

Consultants who consult with agencies about their programs—perhaps they are asked to make a diagnosis of what is wrong with an agency's client system—typically act in the role of expert. Consultants also function as experts when they are asked to recommend solutions to previously defined problems. For example, a consultant might recommend a training program in stress management for the members of the counseling department at a large secondary school. As in most other consulting roles, the consultant does not treat the client system directly.

Consultants who engage in the role of expert need to be aware of the possibility that they can create dependence on the part of their consultees (Lippitt & Lippitt, 1986). The consultee can get used to having the consultant do the work and can effectively give the problem away to the consultant.

Consultants engaging in the expert role need to be aware that under such circumstances their consultees may not improve their own problem-solving abilities, especially if the consultant does not take the time and energy to help them to do so.

**Trainer/Educator.** Very closely related to the role of expert is that of trainer/educator. Whereas the role of "technological advisor" does not imply change in the professional functioning of consultees, the role of a trainer/educator does. Consultants can engage in both formal and informal training and/or educating. Some authors (e.g., Conoley & Conoley, 1992) contend that formal education/training activities such as workshops are not truly consultation because of the amount of preplanning involved. Others (e.g., Lippitt & Lippitt, 1986) see the trainer/educator role as a legitimate and distinct approach to consultation itself. Perhaps these differences in viewpoint result because education is compared with consultation as if it were a different human service. One way to reconcile these different perspectives is to take the view that whereas consultants frequently train and educate, both formally and informally, this role is only one of several in which they engage.

Consultants are often asked to act in the capacity of trainer/educator. The role of trainer implies that

the consultant has both the expertise in certain skills and the ability to create the conditions under which consultees can acquire those skills. The role of educator implies that the consultant possesses a body of knowledge that consultees desire and has the ability to teach them that knowledge. Formal training and education sessions usually take the form of workshops and seminars. For example, a consultant might train a group of program leaders in a human service agency in methods of motivating subordinates. Informal training/educating usually occurs between the consultant and the consultee during some other aspect of the consultation relationship. Thus, a consultant might teach a consultee how to gather baseline data on certain client behaviors.

One advantage of the trainer/educator role is that the consultee receives skills and/or knowledge that can perhaps be used repeatedly in the future, and thus the consultee's professional development is enhanced in some specific way. However, it is possible to erroneously assume that the consultee will actually use the newly acquired skills and knowledge in some way. Unless the consultant incorporates into the training the context in which the skills and knowledge are most useful, there is a strong likelihood that they will not be adequately put into practice in the future.

Consider this example, which uses the trainer/educator role: You are a practicing school consultant in a middle school. Your principal asks you to conduct some in-service training for the school staff on "Motivating the Underachieving Middle School Child." You agree to conduct the workshop and follow through.

**Collaborator.** Nowhere in the consultation literature is there more confusion than that over the term of "collaborator" (Schulte & Osborne, 2003). That said, consultants generally take a collaborative approach to consultation in that the consultant and consultee pool their resources and work together on the task of creating a successful consultation experience. Whereas the expert role in consultation acknowledges the consultee's need for assistance, the collaborator role acknowledges the consultant's need for the consultee's assistance. The consultee is encouraged to express his or her own ideas and modify the consultant's contributions. When used to describe consultants, *collaborator* refers to that role in which the consultant engages the consultee in a joint endeavor to accomplish a particular task at a particular time. The concept of complementarity is important in the collaborator role. Consultants do not perform for consultees tasks that the consultees could perform for themselves; they contribute expertise that consultees need to accomplish those tasks. Collaboration is frequently needed in identifying alternative solutions to a problem, in determining the positive and negative forces operating on various alternatives, and in making decisions about how to approach a given problem. You should note that collaboration, as a *role* for a consultant, is distinct from the *service* of collaboration. As I have noted earlier, in the service of collaboration, each collaborator takes responsibility for some aspect of the case.

In one example of a collaborative role, a consultant and a consultee might compare their observations of a client and come to a mutually agreed-upon diagnosis of the client's problem. In another case they might mutually agree on how much and what kinds of data need to be gathered about the consultee's organization.

Among the relatively few risks involved in engaging in the collaborator role is that consultants may not realize that they are affected by consultees' behavior. Perhaps the most common mistake human service professionals make as collaborators is to overestimate their consultees' abilities and consult in such a way that consultees' knowledge and skill inputs hinder effective consultation. To avoid this pitfall, consultants need some assessment of consultees' problem-solving abilities before assuming the collaborator role.

Conditions to enhance consultees' professional development are built into the role of collaborator. When the consultant takes on a collaborative role, consultees' problem-solving skills are enriched for the future. In addition, their confidence is likely to increase because they feel a sense of contribution to the consultation process. Some limited empirical evidence suggests that consultees prefer a collaborative approach by consultants (Gutkin, 1999a). At

the same time there is an ongoing debate about whether collaboration is an integral element in consultation (Erchul, 1999; Gutkin, 1999a, 1999b). Further, there is little agreement in the field as to the definitions of the terms "collaborator" and "collaborative" (see Schulte & Osborne, 2003). This lack of agreement has stifled research on the collaborator role and its effective implementation.

The following example uses the collaborator role: You are a consultant working in a community mental health center with a colleague who has difficulty with a client. Together, you and the colleague pool your resources and contribute your respective strengths and abilities to resolve the difficulty.

**Fact Finder.**    The role of fact finder is one every consultant takes on frequently. In its simplest form it merely involves obtaining information. In the typical fact-finding role, the consultant gathers information, analyzes it, and feeds it back to the consultee (Lippitt & Lippitt, 1986). The consultant often takes on the fact-finding role to collect information necessary in clarifying or diagnosing a problem. Methods for gathering information include reading records, interviewing, observing, and surveying. (We will discuss several ways to gather information in Chapter 4.) Consultants can gather information on a consultee's client or on an entire organization. Fact finding can range from a simple, quickly accomplished task to a very complex, time-consuming one. A school psychologist (consultant) might administer an individual intelligence test to a student (client system) who is being seen by a school counselor (consultee) and report the findings back to the counselor. In another example, a consultant might design and send out a survey to an organization's members to determine the level of morale within the organization.

One question the consultant should ask before beginning fact-finding activities is "Why am I (and not the consultee) gathering this information?" If the answers relate to lack of consultee expertise, political sensitivities, time constraints, or the consultant's need to learn more about the environment in which the problem is occurring, then the role of fact finder is a legitimate one. If the answer is because it's the consultant's job—not that of the consultee—to gather the facts, then the consultant should reexamine whether or not that role is appropriate.

Consider this example of a fact-finding role: You are consulting to determine why the personnel at a human service agency are exhibiting poor morale. You spend a great deal of time in the agency observing and interviewing personnel concerning the quality of work life. You put the data together and interpret it for the head of the agency.

**Process Specialist.** The least directive role of the consultant is that of process specialist. When consultants take on the role of process expert, they focus more on the *how* than the *what*. Instead of asking, "What's going on?", the process specialist asks, "How are things going?" When a problem is being solved, the consultant as process specialist does not examine the content but rather the problem-solving process itself. The focus is not so much on the nature of the problem-solving steps but on how those steps are accomplished. One approach to consultation with organizations, called process consultation, was developed in the 1980s by Edgar Schein. Process consultation has as its major goal the enhancement of the consultee's understanding of the process events that affect everyday behavior. Two process roles seem to be emerging: the *process observer* role and the *process facilitator* role (Kormanski & Eschbach, 1997). In the process observer role, the consultant provides periodic feedback concerning the group's process, models problem-solving processes, assists the group in dealing with communication issues, and facilitates the group process. There has been some discussion that process consultation, although primarily a group consultation model, can be used with individual consultees and focus on the consultant–consultee interaction as a source of data. The point is that the process specialist works in such a manner that the consultee becomes a better and more independent problem solver in the future. We will discuss process consultation again in Chapter 11.

In one example of a process specialist role, a consultant might sit in on a school's faculty meeting and, at the end, ask the faculty questions to assist them in analyzing their interpersonal behavior relative to what was accomplished in the meeting. In this example the consultant merely puts into exploratory questions what he or she observed. In another case, a consultant might help an administrator learn how to have more effective meetings by using agendas. In this instance the consultant assists the consultee in making an intervention designed to give people more time to participate in meetings.

Because consultants typically focus on structure and content, they are often uncomfortable in the process specialist role. And because the role of process specialist frequently requires the consultant to work with more than one consultee, group process skills are necessary. One common mistake consultants make in the process specialist role is to assume they have permission to bring up interpersonal issues (Schein, 1988). Consultees should first ask if feedback is wanted or raise questions concerning interpersonal issues.

The following example illustrates the process specialist role: You are a consultant called on to help a team of middle-school teachers work "more effectively." You sit in on the group's meetings several times, get a sense for the group's "process," that is, how they do what they do, and then invite the group to examine their own functioning in a non-defensivemanner.

Clearly, consultants need to be able to move easily among the various roles described in this section, or at least know their limitations to the degree that they can make referrals when appropriate (Schein, 1990c).

## INTERNAL AND EXTERNAL CONSULTANTS

Consultants may or may not belong to the system in which consultation is to occur. An *internal consultant* is part of the organization in which consultation occurs. An *external consultant* consults within an organization to which she or he is not permanently employed on a temporary basis. The entire consultation process remains the same regardless of the locus of the consultant.

Some authors (e.g., Brown, Pryzwansky, & Schulte, 2001) recommend that the concepts of internal and external consulting be viewed as ends of a continuum rather than as discrete entities. For example, an itinerant elementary school counselor may serve three different schools. Depending on one's viewpoint, the consultant can be seen as internal or external. A staff member at the school system's central office may note that, because the school counselor is employed by the system that runs the three schools and because everyone involved in the consultation also belongs to the school system, the counselor functions as an internal consultant. But consider another point of view: Because the counselor is at a given school only infrequently, he or she is not really a part of that school. Thus, to most of the school's staff—those at the school every workday—the counselor is seen as an outsider, an external consultant. Therefore, whether the consultant is internal or external is determined to some degree by the perceptions of the members of the organization served by the consultation. Historically speaking, other authors (e.g., Bell & Nadler, 1985) suggest that the internal–external distinction receives too much attention; a consultant is always external to the problem to be resolved whether or not he or she is external or internal to the organization itself.

Case, Vandenberg, and Meredith (1990), in investigating managerial consultants, found that the value orientations of internal consultants are less likely than those of external consultants to reflect humanistic and democratic concerns, that external consultants were more likely to suggest structural changes in organizations than their internal counterparts, and that internal consultants were more likely to conduct more rigorous program evaluations than were external consultants. In extrapolating from this limited finding, there is one possible message for internal human service consultants: Don't get so caught up in the system that you lose your objectivity about the necessity for change.

It seems reasonable to suggest that effective consultants are effective whether or not they are permanently attached to the system receiving consultation (Stroh & Johnson, 2006). This contention is further supported by the fact that internal con-

sultants are taking on many of the functions historically reserved for external consultants (Caplan, Caplan, & Erchul, 1994). There are, however, advantages and related disadvantages to being either an internal or an external consultant (McLean, 2006). External consultants seem to be characterized by marginality; that is, they are only marginally admitted into the organization. They are likely to be objective, neutral, and comfortable with conflict, ambiguity, and stress (Stroh & Johnson, 2006; Tobias, 1990). On the other hand, internal consultants are affected by the hierarchy (Caplan & Caplan-Moskovich, 2004) and the politics of the organization; that is, they "operate more by mandate than by choice" (Block, 2000, p. 131).

Many organizations with internal consultants hire external consultants with the expectation that the two will work as a team (Kelley, 1981). Such a team approach can blend the objectivity, expertise, and "newness" of the external consultant with the knowledge of the organization, expertise, and continuity provided by the internal consultant.

There has been an interesting twist in the literature on internal consultants. In the past decade, there has been a movement to suggest that collaboration is preferred to consultation when delivered by professionals who are internal to the system. Because mental health or human resource specialists are considered experts in their area, they can provide and receive assistance from their fellow collaborators while also directly serving the client system. A driving force for this shift in thinking is that in organizations such as schools there is a very limited amount of time to assist clients, and multiple treatment options can help compensate for this potential barrier to success.

## CONSULTATION RESEARCH

As a practicing consultant, you will want to verify that your practice is legitimate. One way to verify this is through examining the empirical foundations of consultation (Henning-Stout, 1993). Research in consultation is only about four decades old and is therefore not yet very sophisticated. But there is a growing body of research supporting the efficacy of consultation. Research on consultation usually involves one or more of the following areas: what consultants do (i.e., consultant practice), the interaction between consultant and consultee (i.e., consultation process), and the effectiveness of interventions (Froehle & Rominger, 1993).

Armenakis and Burdg (1988) note four types of consultation research, numbered in terms of increasing sophistication. First, there are experience-based writings (e.g., case studies), typically written by the consultant, that describe a given consultation experience. Second, there is quasi-scientific research in which there is not adequate control over the variable being assessed, as distinguished from the third type, scientific research, which requires adequate control over the experimental conditions. The fourth type of research is meta-analysis that attempts to tie together the results of several studies (Kratochwill & Stoiber, 2000a).

What do the results of the various types of research suggest about consultation? Meade, Hamilton, and Yuen (1982) pointed out long ago the difficulties surrounding research in consultation. In summarizing the research to date, these authors suggested that outcome studies found consultation to be effective (although they questioned the methodological soundness of most studies), that process studies were so limited that very few conclusions could be made, and that research on consultant characteristics was methodologically so poor that the whole area of research should be reconceptualized. They recommended that future research use time-series designs in outcome studies, and that consultation process studies use the case study method and take multiple measures.

After reviewing later research in organizational consultation, Armenakis and Burdg (1988) concluded that: (1) the very limited scientific research on consultation creates a condition in which meta-analysis is not possible at this time, (2) organizational politics should be included as a research topic in consultation, (3) there is a need for more research on consultation success criteria, and (4) more research is needed on how consultation strategies are selected.

In reviewing the research on school consultation, which appears to be more or less representative of research in other areas of human service consultation, Gresham and Kendall (1987) noted that a lack of precision in defining consultation has led to a lack of precise research. Pryzwansky (2003) echoed this criticism. Gresham and Kendall also noted that most research is descriptive and has not considered environmental variables. The authors summarized the research in consultation in the following manner: "Most consultation research can be described as limited in scope, univariate in nature, non-experimental, devoid of a strong theoretical base, and unsophisticated in terms of research design and statistical treatment of data" (Gresham & Kendall, 1987, pp. 313–314). Some of the more important things these authors described that we know about consultation include the following:

- Most outcome research is conducted on behavioral consultation (see Bergan & Kratochwill, 1990; Hughes, 2000).

- The empirical research support base is strongest for behavioral consultation.

- Dependent variables tend to include the frequency of consultation use by consultees and changes in clients, consultees, or both as a result of consultation.

- Long-term follow-up is typically a part of outcomes research.

- In process research, problem identification is the best predictor of problem solutions.

- Perceived communication skills of consultants by consultees is related to perceptions of consultant effectiveness.

- Consultees dislike jargon.

In a later review, Gibson and Chard (1994) evaluated 1,643 consultation outcomes using meta-analysis. These authors concluded that consultation is at least moderately effective. Sheridan, Welch, and Orme (1996) reviewed consultation outcome research in educational settings from 1985 to 1995. They found that three-fourths of studies reported positive outcomes and that behavioral consultation research studies were most prevalent. The authors point out advances in methodological aspects of research such as design and multiple measures.

Sheridan, Kratochwill, and Bergan (1996) found empirical support for change in both client system and consultee behaviors. These same authors investigated the research on consultation processes and determined that successful behavioral consultation was characterized by variables that included a cooperative attitude, clearly defined roles, and active involvement by all parties.

How can research in consultation continue to evolve? According to Froehle and Rominger (1993), five topics need attention: (1) agreeing on a definition of consultation, (2) encouraging methodological diversity in consultation research, (3) addressing multi- and cross-cultural issues in consultation research, (4) enhancing the connection between research and practice, and (5) training consultants in research (pp. 694–695). Others (see, e.g., Alpert & Taufique, 2002a; Gutkin & Curtis, 1999; Love, 2007; Meyers, 2002; Zins, 1995) point out the need for research in the areas such as consultant training, consulting with groups and in teams, consultation's effectiveness in providing preventative-oriented services, and consultee resistance. Pryzwansky and Noblit (1990) suggest that case study approaches can be valuable assets in developing a knowledge base for consultation.

Dixon and Dixon (1993) add that consultation research can be improved through expanding the measures used to evaluate it and by defining its "boundary" conditions. They suggest that consultation outcome research should measure changes in the consultant and the consultee; in the interactions between the consultant, consultee, and client system; and in the system in which consultation occurs. Gutkin (1993) notes that consultation research needs to move from defining the broad boundaries of consultation services to "qualitatively more refined and sophisticated levels of research ... that will move us closer to answering questions such as what forms of consultation are most effective with which types of consultees having what kind of clients with which sort of problems under what sets of circumstances" (p. 241).

Gresham and Noell (1993) recommend that future consultation research should address "socially significant goals ... using socially acceptable intervention methods that produce socially important, reliable, and cost-beneficial changes in behavior" (p. 269). Watson, Sterling, & McDade (1997) add that areas such as the effect of adherence to the integrity of the consultation objectives need attention.

Kratochwill, Elliott, & Busse (1995) and Kratochwill, Elliott, & Callan-Stoiber (2002) have suggested that future research in consultation needs to ensure stricter data presentation, collection procedures, and more sophisticated designs. These authors have also recommended that future research expand the use of effect sizes to allow for single-case and within-study meta-analyses, thus allowing for an examination of connections between training and treatment outcomes. Zins (2002) recommends more consistency across studies in terms of outcomes assessed, measurements used, and quality of implementation criteria. Gutkin (2002) suggests that research that takes into account the multivariate contexts of conducting consultation is critical. Hughes (2000) adds that outcome studies need to include follow-up evaluation.

There is very little research related to cross-cultural consultation (Henning-Stout & Brown-Cheatham, 1999; Ingraham, 2000, 2003), and what research exists on cross-cultural consultation is in its infancy (Ramirez, Lepage, Kratochwill, & Duffy, 1998). Empirical research addressing cultural factors, however difficult it is to conduct, must be performed (Ramirez et al., 1998). There is very little research in this area, especially that related to Hispanics (Ramirez & Smith, 2007). To date, most of the research in this area is analogue research and qualitative case studies. Results suggest that the sensitivity of the consultant to racial issues is more important than the race of the consultant, and that consultants may want to specifically address racial issues in the consultation session. More sophisticated research that identifies consultation methods that are effective in multicultural contexts is sorely needed (Ingraham, 2000; Ingraham & Meyers, 2000b). As Ingraham (2000) notes: "Empirical research with real consultation sessions is needed to investigate fully the influence of race, consultant style, and consultee perceptions of consultant effectiveness" (p. 322). This need holds for cultural variables in addition to race. Researchers should also consider investigating traditional consultation approaches and modifications with culturally diverse consultees and client systems (Tarver Behring, Cabello, Kushida, & Murguia, 2000) such as parents (Cox, 2005; Guli, 2005; Hoard & Shepard, 2005). For example, does it take more time for the consultant to build rapport with consultees from certain cultural groups? Ingraham and Meyers (2000b) add that research is needed in the area of culturally different communication styles in the consultation relationship. Meyers (2002), Ingraham (2003), and Ingraham and Meyers (2000b) have suggested that qualitative research methodology may be particularly appropriate for research on multicultural consultation in terms of clarifying relationships among variables. The limited qualitative research to date is promising (see, e.g., Goldstein & Harris, 2000; Ingraham, 2003).

Gresham and Lopez (1996), Meyers (2002), and others have pointed out the necessity for consultation research to have practical applicability. For example, Henning-Stout (1994) and Sandoval (2004) suggest research on the communication of expert consultants as they relate to their impact on consultees. On the other hand, Jones and Lungaro (2000) point out that school-based behavioral consultation has been successful in part due to detailed attention to social validity. Zins (2002) points out that consultation research needs to be more useful to practitioners and that the adoption of a consistent terminology is important for generalization and drawing conclusions. As Watson and colleagues note: "[I]t behooves those who do research . . . to determine, experimentally, what should be accomplished during the consultation interaction to make it maximally effective for both the consultee and client" (1997, p. 472). Kratochwill and Stoiber (2000b) recommend that

consultation research examine which interventions provide evidenced-based outcomes and encourage the use of multiple measures.

There has been very limited research on collaboration as a service. One study (Welch & Tulbert, 2000) socially validates some of the aspects of collaboration that have been espoused by practitioners. Other research (see Meyers, Meyers, & Gelzheiser, 2001) stresses the importance of clarity of the roles of team members, shared decision making, and the necessity of a school vision for collaboration to be optimally effective. But there are major definitional issues surrounding terms like "collaborative," "collaboration," and "collaborator," all of which great create major difficulties in conducting pertinent research. Schulte and Osborne (2003) raise issues that need to be addressed in research on collaboration such as: a) how should collaboration be defined; b) which definitions of collaboration are linked to specific outcomes in consultation; and c) how, if at all, direct service ties into definitions of consultation. Cox (2005) points out that the research on parent collaboration is promising but that additional research needs to be conducted.

A summative view of the research, however limited, suggests that consultation has efficacy even if consultation practice has far outpaced the body of research on consultation (Dunson, Hughes, & Jackson, 1994; Erchul & Martens, 2002; Gutkin & Curtis, 1999). Qualitative research efforts in consultation are just beginning (Athanasiou, Geil, Hazel, & Copeland, 2002) and may increase along with the use of these methods in counseling research (Berrios & Lucca, 2006), and they may particularly useful when combined with quantitative approaches into a hybrid model (Kratochwill & Stoiber, 2000b). On a disconcerting note, Hylander (2003) notes that there has actually been a decline in research on consultation practice except in the area of behavioral consultation.

## SUMMARY

The characteristics of effective consultants result from their desire to grow personally and professionally, to acquire knowledge in consultation and human behavior, and to enhance their consulting skills. Consultants need interpersonal and communication skills that flow from a genuine attitude based on respect, as well as skills in problem-solving, working with groups and organizations, dealing with cultural diversity, and maintaining ethical and professional behavior.

Consultants take on a variety of roles during any given consultation, ranging from nondirective ones, such as process specialist, to directive ones, such as advocate. The role a consultant takes is a result of his or her abilities, the consultee's needs, and the nature of the problem.

The research on consultation is limited. Although there is general support for the fact that consultation is an effective human service function, there is relatively little specific guidance for practitioners.

## SUGGESTIONS FOR EFFECTIVE PRACTICE

- Make a commitment to try to consistently grow personally and professionally, increasingly learn about the knowledge of human behavior and consultation, and develop the skills of consultation.

- Practice the various roles that consultants and collaborators take on so that you can become comfortable with them.

- Develop each of the skills areas identified for effective consultants and collaborators.

- Become familiar with the empirical and qualitative research on consultation and collaboration as means to guide your practice.

## QUESTIONS FOR REFLECTION

1. Which criteria indicate that you have an adequate personal and professional growth orientation as a consultant?

2. The basic attitudes from which a consultant's interpersonal and communication skills flow are critical to effective consulting practice. Why?

3. Why are interpersonal skills as important for the consultant as communication skills?

4. What are the most essential problem-solving skills for a consultant to possess? Why?

5. With which of the consultant roles discussed in this chapter do you feel most comfortable? Why?

6. Why are the skills in working with cultural diversity so critical?

7. What are the basic differences in consultant and consultee behavior when a consultant changes from a directive to a nondirective role?

8. What are the factors that determine the role a consultant will take on?

9. If you were a consultant starting a relationship with a consultee, what consultee characteristics would you consider especially crucial for successful consultation?

10. If the research results on consultation are so sketchy, how can consultants use them to enhance their effectiveness?

## SUGGESTED SUPPLEMENTARY READINGS

Lippitt, G., and Lippitt, R. (1986). *The consulting process in action* (2nd ed.). La Jolla, CA: University Associates. This book is a classic in the consultation literature. Chapter 3, "Multiple Roles of the Consultant," presents a comprehensive approach to categorizing the many roles that consultants can take. This article is a classic about consultation roles. The authors discuss each role and then speculate on the factors that influence when a given role will be taken on. Chapter 7, "The Consultant's Skills, Competencies, and Development," contains a survey performed by the authors on the necessary components of an effective consultant. These two chapters present a concise overview of the roles consultants can take on and the skills and attitudes necessary to fulfill them effectively.

Ingraham, C. L., & Meyers, J. (2000a). Annotated bibliography for the miniseries on multicultural and cross-cultural consultation in schools. *School Psychology Review, 29,* 426–428. This bibliography presents some of the cutting-edge thinking in multicultural consultation. It puts in one place a list of important articles that will help you better understand the nature of multicultural consultation.

Erchul, W. P., & Sheridan, S. M. (Eds.). (2008). *Handbook of research in school consultation: Empirical foundations for the field.* New York: Lawrence Erlbaum Associates/Taylor & Francis Group. This book provides an up-to-date analysis of the current state of research in school consultation. The book discusses related research perspectives and methodologies, findings and future research directions. This is an excellent resource if you are interested in research in consultation.

✳

# PART II

# The Stages of Consultation and Collaboration

Now that you have an idea of what consultation and collaboration are, what professionals do when they provide these services, and the skills they need, let's examine a generic model of consultation/collaboration. This straightforward model provides a framework for performing these services and also allows for the inclusion of the intricacies and the complexities of consultation and collaboration. It represents what counselors, psychologists, college student personnel professionals, social workers, human resource specialists and other human service professionals need to know to effectively consult and collaborate. As you can see in Figure II.1, consultation and collaboration follow a problem-solving format consisting of four stages: a relationship building process, the definition of the problem, an implementation and evaluation of some plan, and a termination stage. Due to the relatively few empirical studies performed on the processes of consultation and collaboration, there are few evidence-based guidelines for effective practice. However, there is a significant amount of evidence in the literature that indicated that a formal problem-solving approach to consultation and collaboration is effective (Meyers, 2002). Furthermore, please note that in every aspect of the problem-solving endeavor, the way consultees and fellow collaborators perceive your communication is every bit as important as what you actually say. Let me remind you that I will not use the phrase "consultation and collaboration" continuously throughout this and subsequent chapters; if there are differences between the two services at any of the stages, I will use the individual terms to differentiate.

Stage One of the generic model represents the starting up of the consultation process. It is called *entry* because the consultant enters the organization and/or

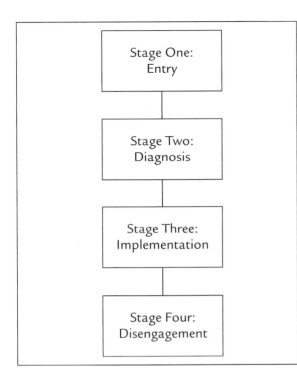

Stage One:
Entry

Stage Two:
Diagnosis

Stage Three:
Implementation

Stage Four:
Disengagement

**FIGURE II.1**   The stages of consultation and collaboration

flect its primary focus on action and its secondary emphasis on planning.

Stage Four winds down the process; it is the period of disengagement. Consultation is evaluated and consultant involvement is reduced. Goodbyes are said and leave is taken. The term "disengagement" implies that the process of consultation goes through a gradual reduction in activity and is used instead of "termination," which implies a more abrupt ending to the process.

Each of the four stages in the consultation process consists of four phases. I have chosen the term "phase" because it implies process, whereas terms like "step" imply more static events and fail to acknowledge that consultation is a very human endeavor that goes through its own life cycle.

There is nothing magical in having four phases for each stage; they merely result from the way I choose to view the consultation process. The important thing to remember at this point is that consultation can be divided into certain stages and phases. The stages (and the phases within them) can frequently overlap and interact with one another, depending on what happens during consultation. Consultation is a flexible and dynamic process; it rarely proceeds in textbook fashion. For example, while a consultant and consultee are in the process of implementing a plan, a different aspect of the problem might emerge that would require returning to the diagnosis stage. Furthermore, some experts consider the implementation stage to occur continuously; that is, each of the consultant's actions during the entire consultation process is viewed as an implementation. You should note that it is normal, in real-life consultation and collaboration, for there to be movement back and forth between the various phases and stages (Allen & Graden, 2002; Curtis & Stollar, 2002). In addition, consideration of cultural issues should take place throughout the stages and

enters into relationships with consultees. In this stage, relationships are built, the parameters of the problem are examined, and a contract is agreed upon with the organization or individual consultees. This stage lays the foundation on which the remainder of the consultation rests.

Stage Two of this model is concerned with shedding light on the problem that was broadly examined during entry. In this stage, the problem is understood more clearly and deeply. The consultant and consultee set goals based on this understanding and begin to think of ways to meet those goals. The term "diagnosis" is used (as opposed to "problem definition") because it implies an ongoing process.

Stage Three involves taking action to solve the problem: a plan is formulated, implemented, and evaluated. This stage is called *implementation* to re-phases (Ingraham, 2000, 2003, 2004; Miranda, 2002). Consultants require a perspective that facilitates their familiarity with the cultural frame of reference of the consultee and client system's culture (Ramirez et al., 1998) while also attending to the "personal culture" of the parties involved (Egan, 2007). This generic model describes the consultation process in a general enough manner to include the models we will be examining later on in this text and provides a set of guidelines and behaviors to follow irrespective of the particular model you implement. It is designed to take consultees where they are and can be adapted to their style of problem management and cultural context. The model provides direction and focus while allowing for the flexibility necessary for effective consultation. A final point: Remember that the skills and attitudes noted in Chapter 2 are essential for adequately implementing the generic model.

## THE PHASES OF THE ENTRY STAGE

Stage One, entry, consists of the following phases:

- exploring organizational needs
- contracting
- physically entering the system
- psychologically entering the system

*Exploring organizational needs* refers to the process in which the consultant, consultee, and perhaps other parties-at-interest discuss the concerns that brought them together and then determine whether consultation should proceed. *Contracting* refers to the process of formalizing the agreement that consultation should take place. Expectations for all parties involved are stated in the contract, as are fees for services to be rendered and deadlines to be met. When a consultant *physically enters the*

*system,* relationships are built, a work site is obtained, the organization is studied, and contact with the consultee begins. *Psychologically entering the system* entails the ongoing process in which the consultant gains acceptance as a temporary member of the organization. This phase actually lasts the duration of the consultation process, and it is a task that requires continual attention if consultation is to be fully successful.

## THE PHASES OF THE DIAGNOSIS STAGE

Once the entry is accomplished, the consultation process proceeds to the diagnosis stage, which consists of the following phases:

- gathering information
- defining the problem
- setting goals
- generating possible interventions

When *gathering information,* the consultant and consultee also attempt to increase the chances of understanding the problem by isolating factors that precipitate it. Data can be gathered through a variety of means, including surveys, interviews, observations, and examination of records. When *defining the problem,* the consultant and consultee analyze and interpret the data that have been gathered. It is especially important for the consultant and consultee to remain objective during this phase. A biased interpretation of the data can lead to an erroneous definition of the problem. Once the problem has been defined to the satisfaction of the parties involved, they *set goals* to overcome the problem. The consultant has the responsibility to make sure that any goal meets the criteria of effectiveness. Once goals have been set, the consultant and consultee move on to *generating possible interventions* that could resolve the problem.

## THE PHASES OF THE IMPLEMENTATION STAGE

Once a list of possible strategies has been generated, the consultation process moves to Stage Three, implementation, which includes:

- choosing an intervention
- formulating a plan
- implementing the plan
- evaluating the plan

This stage begins with *choosing an intervention* or group of interventions—activities the consultant and consultee think have the best chance of effectively solving the problem. Using these interventions, the consultant and consultee embark on *formulating a plan* that incorporates these interventions. The pros and cons of a variety of possible plans are carefully scrutinized until a plan that is likely to succeed is chosen and tailored to the unique requirements of the client and/or the organization. In collaboration, each party involved is assigned to, and responsible for, carrying out a part of the plan. The third phase is *implementing the plan,* and the consultant usually monitors the plan's progress once it has been implemented. In collaboration, unlike consultation, the human service/mental health professional takes responsibility for the mental health aspects of the case and is hence part of the implementation process. In collaboration, the parties involved carry out their pieces of the plan and provide ongoing assistance to one another as necessary. The final phase is *evaluating the plan*. Based on the results of the evaluation, the consultation process moves either back to a previous phase of some

stage (e.g., defining the problem) or on to the stage of disengagement.

## THE PHASES OF THE DISENGAGEMENT STAGE

Stage Four, disengagement, consists of the following phases:

- evaluating the consultation process
- planning postconsultation matters
- reducing involvement and following up
- terminating

*Evaluating the consultation process* can range from assessing consultee satisfaction with consultation to measuring the impact of a system-wide intervention on the behavior of the members of an organization. Evaluation must be a planned event so that consultant and consultee alike will know what will be evaluated, by whom, how, and when. We will see that there is a trend toward the increased use of qualitative measures of consultation effectiveness. *Planning postconsultation matters* involves deciding how the effects of consultation are going to be maintained by the consultee and/or the organization. This phase is essential in increasing the probability that follow-through occurs after the consultant's involvement ends. *Reducing involvement* is the phase in which the consultant creates conditions of decreasing contact with the consultee. This is also the time when more and more responsibility for the results of consultation is taken on by the consultee. *Follow-up* is the process in which the consultant monitors this transfer of responsibility so as to iron out any unforeseen problems. *Terminating* is the formal ending of the consultation process. It has professional aspects (e.g., collecting final fees) and a personal side (e.g., saying goodbye). Effective consultants successfully accomplish both the professional and personal sides of termination (Dougherty, Tack, Fullam, & Hammer, 1996).

## PUTTING THE GENERIC MODEL INTO PRACTICE

There are three important points to make about putting the generic model of consultation into practice. First, consultation is a dynamic, interactive process that uses the various stages as needed (Meyers & Yelich, 1989). Things rarely, if ever, go in a textbook fashion. Equal attention should be paid both to *what* you are doing and to *how* you are doing those things.

Second, it is very important to get supervised practice in consultation. By "trying on" the model and putting it into practice, you can get a sense of yourself as a consultant. The more experience you get, the higher the probability that you will increase your effectiveness as a consultant.

Third, the collective wisdom concerning consultation suggests that the generic model be implemented in a collaborative manner whenever possible. You should be aware, however, that there is very little empirical evidence to support this point of view. Therefore, your own experience in each consultation will assist you in determining what roles to take on. Some limited empirical evidence suggests that consultants should be at least minimally in charge of the consultation process (Witt, 1990a; Gutkin, 1996). Consultees tend to view some degree of consultant dominance in which they follow the consultant's leads as being positive (Erchul & Chewning, 1990). Erchul and Chewning (1990) intimate that consultants may be more in control of their consultation relationships than they realize and that this control is positively perceived by consultees as indi-

cating consultant competency. You may want to examine with your consultees the degree of your directiveness and their reaction to it during your supervised practice. For example, you may want to gain feedback from consultees regarding your questioning style (Hughes & DeForest, 1993). In collaboration, you will often be viewed as the expert in a certain area relative to the goals of helping the client system. For example, a school counselor might be viewed as the most knowledgeable about a child's capacity for learning.

## EXAMPLES

The following two case studies are designed to show how the consultation and collaboration processes generally work. Although oversimplified, they will provide concrete examples to which you can continue to refer as you read and study the next five chapters. They represent idealized cases—for consultation and collaboration, like other human service activities, rarely proceed so smoothly—but, nonetheless, they provide a rough outline of how the processes work.

## RESISTANCE TO CONSULTATION

No matter how many precautions consultants take to ease their physical and psychological entry into the system, some resistance to consultation is typical throughout the entire consultation process. Although such resistance is normal, this lack of cooperation with the process can present significant challenges to your consultation activities. *Resistance* is the failure of a consultee or organization to participate constructively in the consultation process

---

**CASE II.1      Consultation**

---

Assume that you are a school counselor who is going to act as a consultant. Your consultee is a schoolteacher and the client is his student. You meet with the teacher, who discusses the student's behavior, particularly his rarely turning in homework. You help the teacher explore the problem and at the same time build rapport with him. You both agree that working on the homework problem is mutually agreeable, so you contract to meet three or four times to work on that problem. You agree to observe the student in the teacher's classroom and continue to use effective communication skills and gain the teacher's acceptance of you as a person he can trust. At this point you have completed the entry stage.

You and the teacher now start to gather information on the student; together you examine the student's cumulative folder. The teacher keeps track of when homework is not turned in and the conditions surrounding that behavior. Based on the data, you note that the student does not turn in homework on Tuesdays and Fridays but does on the other school days. An interview with the student's parents reveals that they both attend school on Monday and Thursday nights and that the child is left with a babysitter. Based on this information you and the teacher redefine the problem as lack of parental supervision on Monday and Thursday nights. You and the consultee set the goal of having the student turn in all homework every other Tuesday and Friday for the first month, and every Tuesday and Friday thereafter. When generating possible strategies you come up with several ideas, which

include the loss of recess time when homework is not turned in and the use of a parent-child contract for getting the homework done. You have now completed the diagnosis stage; you are ready to begin the implementation stage.

Weighing the pros and cons of each intervention, you and the teacher determine that the parent-child contract is the best alternative. You then formulate a plan that consists of obtaining parental cooperation and assisting in the formulation of a parent-child contract for getting homework completed on the nights the parents are not home. When the parents agree to the plan, you and the teacher assist them in carrying it out. Strategies for appropriately reinforcing both the child and parents are included. The parents carry out the plan effectively; based on your evaluation, the goal has been met. The third stage, implementation, has just been accomplished. Now you go on to the disengagement stage.

In this final stage, you have the teacher rate his satisfaction with your efforts to assist him during each of the previous three stages. You then lay the groundwork concerning the way he will carry on with the student after you cease consulting. You check in with the teacher every two weeks or so to see how things are going. A month or so after your last contact you follow up to make sure that the homework is still being turned in. Toward the end of the next grading period you again check in about the student's performance. Because everything is proceeding well, you and the teacher agree to terminate consultation.

---

(Wickstrom & Witt, 1993). A related term, "reluctance," refers to the hesitancy of the consultee to engage in consultation.

Overcoming resistance involves accurately diagnosing its source. A common mistake made by consultants is to assume that resistance is due to a negative attitude on the part of the consultee (Kratochwill et al., 1995; O'Keefe & Medway, 1997; Watson & Robinson, 1996). Consultants will need to differentiate resistance from lack of skill on the part of consultees to carry out interventions.

## Organizational Resistance

When consultants enter organizations ready to initiate change, they frequently encounter a healthy resistance (Fuqua et al., 1999; Block, 2000). This is an important survival mechanism that protects the organization from outside threats. However, all organizations must adapt to change, and resistance can impede the progress of this adaptation. Although resistance to consultation received a significant amount of attention in the literature during the 1990s, relatively little has been written recently.

---

**CASE II.2     Collaboration**

---

Now consider the same case, only this time from the perspective of collaboration. Pay particular attention to the italicized aspects of the case. Assume that you are a school counselor who is going to act as a collaborator. Your fellow collaborator is a schoolteacher and the client is a student. You meet with the teacher, who discusses the student's behavior, particularly his rarely turning in homework. You help the teacher explore the problem and at the same time build rapport with him. You both agree that working on the homework problem is mutually agreeable, so you contract to meet three or four times to work on that problem. You agree to observe the student in the teacher's classroom and continue to use effective communication skills and gain the teacher's acceptance of you as a person he can trust. At this point you have completed the entry stage.

You and the teacher now start to gather information on the student; together you examine the student's cumulative folder. The teacher keeps track of when homework is not turned in and the conditions surrounding that behavior. Based on the data, you both note that the student does not turn in homework on Tuesdays and Fridays but does on the other school days. An interview with the student's parents reveals that they both attend school on Monday and Thursday nights and that the child is left with a babysitter. Based on this information you and the teacher redefine the problem as lack of parental supervision on Monday and Thursday nights. You and the teacher set the goal of having the student turn in all homework every other Tuesday and Friday for the first month, and every Tuesday and Friday thereafter. When generating possible strategies you come up with several ideas, which include the loss of recess time when homework is not

turned in and the use of a parent-child contract for getting the homework done. You have now completed the diagnosis stage; you are ready to begin the implementation stage.

Weighing the pros and cons of each intervention, you and the teacher determine that the parent-child contract is the best alternative. You then formulate a plan that consists of obtaining parental cooperation and assisting in the formulation of a parent-child contract for getting homework completed on the nights the parents are not home. When the parents agree to the plan, you and the teacher assist them in carrying it out. Strategies for appropriately reinforcing both the child and parents are included. *You agree to counsel the child concerning the issues related to the child's lack of academic performance when the child is not under parental supervision.* The parents carry out the plan effectively; based on your evaluation, the goal has been met. *In evaluating your work with the student, you determine that the goals have been met.* The third stage, implementation, has just been accomplished. Now you go on to the disengagement stage.

In this final stage, you and the teacher rate your satisfaction with your respective efforts to assist one another. *You then lay the groundwork concerning the way each of you will carry on with the student after you cease the collaboration process.* You check in with each other every two weeks or so to see how things are going. A month or so after your last contact you follow up to make sure that the homework is still being turned in. Toward the end of the next grading period, you again check in about the student's performance. Because everything is proceeding well, you and the teacher agree to terminate.

---

There are four sources of organizational resistance to consultation (Parsons & Meyers, 1984): the desire to keep things the way they are, the view of the consultant as an outsider, the rejection of anything new as non-normative (a "we-just-don't-do-things-that-way-around-here" attitude), and the desire to protect one's own turf or vested interest (the "silo mentality"). Resistance is common even in those organizations that want to change and that support consultation with appropriate degrees of money,

time, and effort. In fact, the very title "consultant" can be threatening because it implies change. Because the organization's perception of the consultant's role early on in the consultation process is often unclear, resistance can be preempted by providing a clear picture at the outset of what the consultant is to accomplish (McLean, 2006). Obtaining support from the leadership of the organization for consultation also diminishes resistance (Kratochwill, Elliott, & Callan-Stoiber, 2002). French and Bell (1999) add that extensive and ongoing communication about the expected changes from consultation, and engaging organizational members in planning how consultation will be implemented, help to reduce resistance.

Nontraditional views of organizational resistance assume that resistance is present only to the degree that organizations are conceptualized in terms of power and conflict (Kress et al., 1998; Merron, 1993). In these cases, what is labeled "resistance" is regarded as simply the expression of alternative views of organizational events and a consultant's focusing on what is *wrong* in the organization.

### Consultee Resistance

Whereas relatively little has been written about organizational resistance to consultation, a great deal has been written over the past few decades about consultee resistance (Dougherty et al., 1991; Erchul & Conoley, 1991; Hughes, 1983; Meyers & Yelich, 1989; Randolph & Graun, 1988; Tingstrom et al., 1990). In any helping relationship, resistance is both unavoidable and potentially helpful (Blom-Hoffman & Rose, 2007; Otani, 1989). Consultants must manage resistance to maximize a positive consultation outcome (Blom-Hoffman & Rose, 2007). From a behavioral viewpoint, resistance can arise from the consultee's aversion to the consultation outcome. Consultees may believe that the benefits of consultation are not worth the costs (e.g., it will take too much of their time) or that consultation will result in some form of punishment (e.g., criticism by one's supervisor) (Piersel & Gutkin, 1983). Therefore, to minimize resistance, the consultant should ensure that the cost of participating in consultation is at least matched by the benefits.

Cognitive dissonance theory can be used to analyze sources of consultee resistance (Hughes, 1983).

Dissonance occurs when a person has concepts that are either not in accord with each other or illogical. For example, being a consultee and not liking it are dissonant concepts, and there is a strong likelihood that consultee resistance will ensue. Dissonance is minimized when a consultee buys into the consultation process. Ways to involve a consultee include keeping consultation a voluntary and peer relationship, showing how consultation can help but making no "guarantees," and making sure that the consultee puts forth some effort in the consultation process (Hughes, 1983). By involving the consultee in these ways, the consultant creates a relationship in which the consultee is more likely to cooperate.

Hughes and Falk (1981) examined resistance to consultation from the perspective of reactance theory, which suggests that when a person perceives that a freedom is taken away, he or she will try to restore it (Brehm, 1966; Hughes & Falk, 1981). One implication for consultants is to avoid the overuse of persuasion and recommendations, and instead provide consultees with choices whenever possible during consultation. In this way, consultees are most likely not to experience any infringement on their freedom. Dougherty et al. (1991) suggest that resistance can be due to a consultee's misconception concerning the nature of consultation, some dysfunction in the consultation relationship, fear related to the discomfort of disclosing need, or cognitive distortions that cause misunderstandings and lead to increased resistance. Kratochwill and Pittman (2002) indicate that resistance may be related to the consultee's perception of the acceptability of the intervention. Jeltova & Fish (2005) note that consultants need to be knowledgeable about the content of the resistance and the resistors.

## Dealing Effectively with Resistance

There are several things consultants can do to minimize resistance:

- Create a strong relationship to build trust and alleviate fear.
- Demonstrate cultural competence and sensitivity.
- Collaborate whenever possible.
- Create conditions so that a consultation has a satisfying outcome and is worth the effort.
- Allow the consultee as many choices as possible.
- Throughout the process, point out how consultation might be helpful.
- Distribute the workload in consultation so that the consultee does his or her share.
- Give the consultee as much freedom as possible in all aspects of the process.
- Be clear about the nature of consultation from the outset.
- Challenge any cognitive distortions with specific disputing examples.
- Be as clear and specific as possible about what is expected of the consultee.
- Use examples to illustrate points.
- Try to minimize the new things a consultee has to learn.
- Link interventions to the consultee's explanation of the causes of the problem.
- Ensure that the consultee has the skills necessary to carry out the interventions.

Perhaps the best method of dealing with resistance is to prevent its occurrence in the first place through understanding and emphasizing referent power (Wickstrom & Witt, 1993), viewing some resistance as normal (Egan, 2007), and applying motivational interviewing (Blom-Hoffman & Rose, 2007). Understanding refers to the consultant's ability to comprehend and appreciate the consultee's views of events. Using referent power refers to consultant's attempt to use a collaborative and cooperative style in approaching the consultee. Motivation interviewing assists consultees in dealing with ambivalence-related resistance by allowing them to convince themselves that change is in order.

## A Brief Example of Resistance to Consultation

As you consult with a mental health practitioner about a client, you increasingly note that the consultee avoids direct eye contact with you as he discusses his client. As you reflect on the consultation relationship, you note that you and the consultee are locked into a "Yes, but . . ." kind of interaction in which you make suggestions regarding the case, and he explains how none of them could possibly work with this client. You acknowledge the issue by noting that you are getting frustrated with what is going on and that you imagine the consultee is, too. You suggest both starting anew by focusing on what the consultee wants to have happen in the case and how both of you can collaborate to achieve it.

## PERSONALIZING THE CONSULTATION AND COLLABORATION PROCESS

Discussing consultation and collaboration in terms of stages and phases leaves out the human side of the process. As a consultant or collaborator, you are your best intervention (Bellman, 1990). That is, who you are as a person can affect the outcome of consultation or collaboration as much as what you do when you engage in these services. I developed this idea after reading Gerard Egan's book *The*

*Skilled Helper* (2007). Egan describes his counseling model as a series of steps for "being with" clients. To include this human side, here is how you can be there for the people with whom you're working throughout the phases of the consultation process:

1. Listen well at the outset and take the time to build rapport.

2. Assist in formulating a contract that will make explicit the expectations you have for each other.

3. Start the consultation/collaboration process on the consultee's or collaborator's turf as soon as possible.

4. Proactively attempt to gain acceptance, not only by the consultee or fellow collaborator, but also by the organization in which the service is being provided.

5. Do your best to determine what information should be gathered on the problem and how best to do it.

6. Attempt to be unbiased as you assist in analyzing and interpreting the gathered data.

7. Ensure that the goals you and the consultee or collaborator set are effective goals that have a good probability of being successfully accomplished.

8. Be as creative and sharp as you can be when it comes to generating possible interventions.

9. Assist in examining the pros and cons of each possible intervention you and the consultee or collaborator consider.

10. Collaborate in putting together the best possible plan and considering the available resources.

11. As a consultant, be available to monitor the progress that is being made; as a collaborator, fulfill your part of the plan.

12. Provide assistance and encouragement in evaluating the plan.

13. Ask for evaluations of yourself and your services.

14. Assist in planning what needs to be done regarding the consultation or collaboration after you have left the scene.

15. Avoid dependence by the consultee or fellow collaborator through a gradual reduction in your involvement and foster their independence through intermittent follow-ups.

16. Say goodbye professionally and personally and let go of the relationship when that is in everyone's best interest.

My main goal in this part of the book is to provide you with an understanding for how to go about the general process of conducting consultation and collaboration. As you read the next several chapters, I also hope that you will gain an appreciation of the complexity of the ethical, professional, and legal issues that surround the consultation/collaboration process. A final goal is for you to become aware of some of the pragmatic issues involved in consulting, such as the influence of the organization in which consultation occurs.

# 3

# Entry Stage

Just like a good novel, the consultation process should have a beginning, middle, and an end. Frequently referred to as *start-up activities,* the entry stage can consist of one telephone call or several exploratory meetings. Entry is the initial contact the consultant has with the consultee. It involves examining the consultation request, building a strong working relationship, and determining whether consultation should occur (French & Bell, 1999). Throughout this stage, the consultant and the organization contact person try to determine how advantageous consultation can be. The consultant should bear in mind that the success of the consultation depends in part on how well these start-up activities are accomplished. It is important to note that consultants will also have to "enter" every relationship they form with consultees.

The purpose of this chapter is to explain this beginning, or entry, stage of the consultation process. Entry, as both a distinct stage of consultation and a process in which the consultant begins to create relationships within the consultee organization, is complex and consists of four phases: exploring organizational needs, contracting, physically entering the organization's system, and psychologically entering the system.

Here are five questions to consider as you read this chapter:

1.  In what ways is the entry stage a complex process?
2.  Why is the entry stage both a critical and delicate stage of consultation?
3.  How directive should a consultant be in guiding the course of consultation during the entry stage?
4.  "There is more to a contract than what is written on the paper." What are the implications of this for consultants?
5.  How can a consultant psychologically enter the consultation system effectively and efficiently?

## INTRODUCTION

To get a feel for the entry stage, consider the following situation:

### Case Example

You are a professor of human services at a state university. A former student, now director of advising at a nearby community college, telephones and wants to come and talk with you about enhancing the quality of his advising services. You set up an appointment, which will take place in your office.

During the appointment, you assist the advising director in exploring the advising office's specific needs in regard to enhancing the quality of advising. You ask the director to make up a wish list to stimulate preliminary exploration. You ask what is going well and what is not going so well. You ask about the organizational environment in which advising occurs, and you ask for the advisors' views on the process of advising, its rewards, the level of administrative support for advising, and the advising director.

Based on this information, you agree to conduct two sessions with all the advisors. The first session is a workshop on effective advising, and the second is a troubleshooting meeting with the advisors to help them feel more heard by those who coordinate advising services. You and the advising director sign a contract to that effect. The week before the workshop, you visit the community college and all of the workshop participants. You are supportive and ask them what things they would like to talk about. Next you arrange for the room at the community college in which the workshop is to occur. Then, when you open the first session, you ask the participants what they want and what they do not want out of the workshop.

*Entry* is the general process by which the consultant enters the system in which consultation is to occur. Glidewell (1959), in a now classic article, defines entry by an external consultant as the attachment of a consultant to an existing social system

through the creation of temporary membership in an organization for a person who is to help that system. This temporary membership is accomplished by creating relationships that assist in determining which functions a consultant should provide to best help the organization accomplish its ends. Internal consultants (those permanently employed by the organization in which they consult) also have to enter, because elements of each consultation situation will be new to them every time. Figure 3.1 shows the four phases of the entry stage of consultation.

## PHASE ONE: EXPLORING ORGANIZATIONAL NEEDS

Consultation typically begins when a representative of an organization contacts a consultant for the purpose of *exploring* the possibilities of initiating a consulting relationship. It is not unusual for an organization to contact a consultant without

**FIGURE 3.1** The phases of the entry stage

knowing the precise or even the appropriate reason why consultation is needed. In fact, the toughest aspect of entry is making a quick and accurate assessment of what is troubling the organization. Some authors (Conoley & Conoley, 1992) note that an organization rarely uses refined techniques to determine its need for a consultant, and frequently the organization has misidentified its problem. Therefore, consultants should be cautious about moving too quickly into planning implementation steps during the beginning of the entry process (Sperry, 2005).

Whether or not there is a firm grasp on what is needed in consultation, an organization usually contacts a consultant because it perceives it has a concern that cannot be solved within the organization or because there is an unfilled gap within the organization (Schein, 1988). In contrast, the process can also begin when a consultant contacts an organization and attempts to sell consultation services related to the typical concerns of organizations.

Before actual physical and psychological entry into the organization occurs, the consultant must deal with certain preentry issues (Cherniss, 1993; French & Bell, 1999), such as deciding whether the consultant appears to be the right person to help the organization and determining the things to focus on during consultation. Other issues include dealing with possible disagreements on the nature of the problem, as well as the ramifications of whose interests are being served by the consultation (Cherniss, 1993; Sperry, 2005). The process of considering these issues usually begins with an exploratory meeting referred to as the *first contact*.

First contact may be initiated by either party and usually involves the organization's contact person, perhaps some parties-at-interest (stakeholders), and the consultant. Ideally those involved should be knowledgeable about consultants and favorable toward their use (French & Bell, 1999).

The initial meeting for exploring organizational needs can occur either at the organization or in a neutral setting such as a restaurant. The advantage for meeting at the organization is that it allows the consultant on-site observations of the organization and the ways its personnel interact.

There, the serious nature of the consultation relationship is reinforced because the meeting is not in a social setting. The advantages of meeting in a neutral site are that it gives the organization's contact personnel more of a sense of control and provides an informal setting that minimizes pressures to commit to a contract for consultation services.

## Determining whether Consultation Should Take Place

The primary decision to be made during the preliminary exploration of organizational needs is whether or not consultation should be undertaken. Over the years, six issues that relate to this decision have emerged (see Cherniss, 1993; Holtz & Zahn, 2004; McLean, 2006; Stroh & Johnson, 2006):

- the degree of congruence between the consultant and the consultee system (e.g., as regards value systems)

- the amount of resources the organization is willing to commit toward change (e.g., the amount of administrative sanctioning for consultees' participation)

- the appropriateness of the consultee's or the organization's characteristics (e.g., the amount of flexibility within the organization with regard to the changes consultation may involve)

- the ways in which the organization perceives the need for change (e.g., the degree to which prospective consultees see consultation as important in meeting the organization's goals)

- mutual understanding of the expectations for consultation (e.g., the consultant and consultees being able to agree on how consultation should proceed and on desirable outcomes for all parties involved)

- agreement on who constitutes the consultee system, the client system, and parties-at-interest (e.g., the consultant agrees to consult only with the crisis intervention team in a mental health center regarding approaches in counseling their clients)

In the 1980s, Bell and Nadler (1985) developed four shared questions to determine whether or not consultation is necessary and worthwhile: Why am I here? Who are you? What is likely to happen? What will be the result? The degree to which the four questions are answered to the satisfaction of both the consultant and the contact person eventually determines the success of the preliminary exploration (Stroh & Johnson, 2006).

The answers to these questions constitute the *task of familiarization,* during which consultants learn the ins and outs of the organization —for example, its history, mission, philosophy, and procedures (Caplan & Caplan, 1993). Another part of this task is determining what the organization has done so far to solve its perceived problems, to what degree these activities were successful, and what factors prevented them from being more successful (Mann, 1983; Strohn & Johnson, 2006). To determine this, the consultant conducts a "mini-assessment" of the perceived problem (McLean, 2006).

## Why Am I Here?

The question "Why am I here?" is important to contact person and consultant alike. From the contact person's perspective, this question concerns perceived need. From the consultant's perspective, the question involves assisting the consultee in defining an appropriate problem or concern and assessing whether the consultant is the right person for the job.

## Who Are You?

The question "Who are you?" concerns defining the roles taken on by the consultant, contact person, and others involved in consultation. Answering this question entails identifying the roles and responsibilities of the consultant and the contact person. By discussing views, attitudes, and perceptions pertinent to organizational needs, values, and working styles, the consultant and contact person can determine the "goodness of fit" between the contact person's needs and the consultant's abilities. In determining their respective roles, both consultant and contact person need to remember that they represent their respective organizations as well as themselves (Caplan & Caplan, 1993; Caplan, Caplan, & Erchul, 1994; Stroh & Johnson, 2006).

## What Is Likely to Happen?

The third question, "What is likely to happen?", is really about means and ends. What is the goal of consultation? How will the goal be accomplished? What are the desired outcomes? (See Stroh & Johnson, 2006.)

## What Will Be the Result?

From the consultant's perspective, the question "What will be the result?" addresses how the impact of consultation will be assessed and evaluated. From the contact person's perspective, the answer depends on how much change the consultation requires.

## What Can Go Wrong?

The initial exploration of the organization's needs can go awry due to inadequacies in both the consultant's and the contact person's behavior. As Ford (1979) noted long ago, echoed by French and Bell (1999) and still holding today, a consultant can jeopardize the consultation relationship during the entry phase in several ways:

- fail to identify the real problem
- promise too much
- fail to specify consultant roles adequately
- fail to recognize a lack of competence about the problem
- fail to adapt to the organization's particular problems and concerns

By bearing these potential pitfalls in mind and by monitoring their own behavior accordingly, consultants can frequently save the consultation process from difficulties. Consultees can also prevent entry from proceeding smoothly. The following are some of the many things a consultee or contact person can do during the entry phase to jeopardize the consultation relationship:

- fail to screen a prospective consultant properly

- neglect to clarify how the consultant intends to operate within the system

- fail to clarify specific expectations of the consultant's role and behavior

- fail to identify the organization's problem accurately

- fail to explain to the consultant how the organization's resource limitations might affect the potential consultation experience

Consultants must be aware of these potential pitfalls as they assist the organization's contact person in exploring the organization's needs. Perhaps the best way to prevent such pitfalls is by allotting sufficient time to develop a mutual understanding, which leads to open communication and discussions that are as specific and detailed as possible. Effective questioning by the consultant is particularly important in avoiding these pitfalls.

**A Brief Example of Exploring Organizational Needs.**    A mental health consultant is approached by the members of a religious organization to help them develop a program for enhancing the self-esteem of its youth group members. The consultant meets with three members of the organization's governing board and the youth group leader. Together the group explores the possibilities of what such a program might look like, the history of the program's idea, and the consultant's comparable experience. The consultant is satisfied that she can assist, and the consultees believe that she can be of assistance. The resources necessary for program development are available, and everyone agrees on what is expected from the parties involved. The consultant agrees to draw up and submit a proposal and contract.

In summary, preliminary exploration of the organization's needs includes deciding who the consultees and client system will be, determining the

consultant's role in the consultation process, and defining the organization's responsibility with regard to expectations about the consultant. Once this has been adequately accomplished and it is determined that consultation should occur, the information gathered in this phase can be used in contracting.

## PHASE TWO: CONTRACTING

With a decision that consultation is to take place, the consultant and the consultee or contact person begin to discuss and negotiate the terms of consultation. This activity begins the phase of *contracting*. A good contract not only provides mutual understanding of the consultation process and clarifies roles and responsibilities, but it can also provide legal protection for consultants (Remley, 1993; Remley & Herlihy, 2007) and is one method of obtaining informed consent (Rosenfield, 2002a).

### The Nature of Contracts

Every relationship is based on expectations, which, in the context of the consultation relationship, are usually made explicit in formal contracts. Stroh and Johnson (2006) point out that the terms "proposal," "letter of agreement," and "contract" are often used interchangeably. For our purposes, the term "contract" has a variety of meanings when used in the delivery of human services. A contract in consultation is between the consultant and the organization and is typically an oral or written agreement that defines the parameters and character of the consultation relationship and provides a form of self-protection for both the consultant and the organization (Holtz & Zahn, 2004; McLean, 2006; Caplan et al., 1994; Sperry, 2005). In consultation relationships, the contract is an agreement "spelling out the expectations and obligations of each party, the frequency of meetings, the scheduling of appointments and access to personnel in the consultee system, the data to be collected, the provisions for review and modification of the program, and the amount and manner of payment of any fees involved" (Mann, 1983, p. 108). The contract reflects and clarifies the shared understanding between consultant and consultee in three critical areas: what each expects from the relationship, how much time each will invest, and the ground rules everyone will follow.

In collaboration, contracting is often informal, with the parties involved agreeing to take responsibility for the aspects of the case related to their area of expertise (Block, 2000). There is an increase in the use of contracts even by internal consultants (Stroh & Johnson, 2006). The consultant should bear in mind, however, that a detailed written contract has the advantages of framing participants' roles and providing a focus for evaluating consultation services. Whatever form a contract takes, its particulars must be clear. Some authors (e.g., Wilcoxon, 1990) recommend a formal, written contract at all times as a legal safeguard for the consultant.

The specificity of a contract depends upon how precisely the problem has been defined. To the degree that the contract is structured and specific, the consultant's role will be relatively constant. To the degree that the contract is general and unstructured, the consultant's role may vary and the more likely it is that the contract will be renegotiated during the consultation process (French & Bell, 1999). Since specificity can be an issue, it must be agreed upon when the contract is being drawn up. It is in the consultant's best interest to make the contract as specific as possible as it defines the ground rules for consultation (Rosenfield, 2002a).

The stage of change in which the consultee's problem exists can be an important factor in developing the contract. There are typically four stages of change during which the consultee may seek help: the *development* stage, as a problem begins; the *maintenance* stage, once a problem is established; the *declining* stage, when an existing problem begins to get worse; and the *crisis* stage, when the consultee is in dire need of immediate assistance. The consultant, through the use of judicious questioning, can determine the existing stage of change and create an appropriate contract (Kurpius, Fuqua, & Rozecki, 1993).

A contract has both formal and psychological aspects. The formal aspect of a contract covers such things as services to be rendered, type and amount of payment, and the length of consultation (French & Bell, 1999). The psychological aspect of a contract refers to what each party hopes to gain from the relationship. The "psychological contract" is based on interpersonal trust, which cannot be put in writing, and it reflects a collaborative effort between the consultant and the organization's contact person concerning what each expects from the consultation process (Boss, 1993).

## The Formal Aspects of a Contract

The formal aspects of contracting refer to the types of contracts used and their elements. There are several types of contracts that can be used in consultation. For example, a contract may be a simple working agreement or a written and detailed technical document. Contracts can vary to the agency in which consultation is to occur. A school district might well have a boilerplate contract with type of service, dates, fees, and legal/disclaimer information, while state and federal agency contracts will have significantly more detail. Internal consultants often use verbal agreements. Consultants should be willing to help the contact person choose the type of contract that the nature of the consultation dictates.

## Elements of a Contract

To develop and maintain a good working relationship between the consultant and the organization, certain key issues pertinent to the consultation should be covered in the contract. A well-defined contract will minimize the possibilities of role conflicts, dual role relationships, and resistance—all of which can contaminate the consultation relationship. Consultation contracts typically cover the following elements noted by Remley & Herlihy, 2007, p. 326):

- Clearly specify the work to be completed by the consultant.

- Describe in detail any work products expected from the consultant.

**Mountain City School System**

**Mountain City, USA**

**Contract**

This is a contract between the Mountain City School System, herein called the party of the first part, and L. G. Shandi, herein referred to as the party of the second part. This contract is entered into on the sixth day of February 2009 as follows:

The party of the second part agrees to serve as a consultant between March 1, 2009 and December 31, 2009, by providing group case consultation regarding the students with whom the counselors and psychologists in the school system are working. Specifically, the party of the second part agrees to provide group case consultation services at the school system's central office from 1:00 p.m. until 4:00 p.m. on the first and third Monday of each month. The party of the second part further agrees to provide individual case consultation at any of the system's schools upon request at a mutually agreeable time. The party of the second part agrees to use Bernie Thompson, Director of Psychological Services of the Mountain City School System, as the contact person for all matters pertaining to this consultation, including the possible use of additional consultants or the addition of other consultees.

The party of the first part agrees to pay the party of the second part a total of six thousand dollars ($6,000) plus expenses for travel and materials paid in nine equal monthly payments for the group case consultation sessions. In addition, the party of the first part will pay one hundred dollars plus travel and materials for each individual case consultation session for up to fifty individual sessions during the length of the contract with payment being on a monthly basis.

This contract is subject to renegotiation at any time and either party is free to terminate it with twenty-four hours notice if either determines the consultation progress to be unsatisfactory. Signatures of appropriate parties indicated agreement to the terms of the contract.

For the Mountain City School System

_____

Party of the Second Part ————————————————
Signature ————————————————
Address ————————————————
Date ————————————————

**FIGURE 3.2**    A sample contract

- Establish a time frame for the completion of the work.

- Establish lines of authority and the person to whom the consultant is responsible.

- Describe the compensation plan for the consultant and the method of payment.

- Specify any special agreements or contingency plans agreed upon by the parties.

Figure 3.2 is a sample contract between a school system and a mental health consultant who is going to provide case consultation to school counselors and school psychologists regarding students with whom they are providing services. This sample represents a relatively informal, simple contract that contains only those elements pertinent to the nature of the consultation.

## The Psychological Aspects of a Contract

Contracting has psychological as well as formal aspects. The psychological aspect reflects a partnership in which the consultee's investment in the consultant's abilities is balanced by the consultant's investment in the opportunity to consult provided by the consultee (Bellman, 1990). The psychological aspects of a contract refer to the set of expectations that govern the consultation relationship (Boss, 1993). These expectations are not always directly communicated, agreed upon, or written down; however, they are just as crucial to the consultation's success as a legal contract, and once broken they are difficult to repair. Therefore, early in the relationship it is imperative that the consultant assess and shape any expectations deliberately or unwittingly withheld by the organization's contact person (Schein, 1988). In effect, the consultant must determine what psychological and business needs are to be met through consultation. The psychological contract needs to be based on mutual honesty, realism, and interpersonal sensitivity (Boss, 1993; Block, 2000). Harrison (2004) points out that psychological contracts are likely to be rooted in fundamental worldviews (p. 86). For example, "The psychological contracts operating between different genders and racioethnic groups will almost always be significant factors in any interactions that occur during the consulting process" (Harrison, 2004, p. 96). Clearly, cultural competence includes ensuring that the psychological contract excludes dimensions of bias and prejudice. The psychological contract is also very important in collaboration because each of the parties involved has some responsibility for directly helping the client system. The following examples illustrate how psychological contracts can be broken:

**Case Example 1.** A consultant hired by a human service agency to assist in program development expected an office but was not provided one. The consultant's resulting resentment made it more difficult to focus objectively on the tasks to be accomplished.

**Case Example 2.** An organization's contact person wanted to be reached by the consultant each time he or she visited the organization. The contact person neither expressed this wish nor put it into the formal contract. When the consultant innocently restricted communication with the contact person, the contact person felt rejected and covertly began efforts to sabotage the consultant's activities.

The following is a summary of a case study reported by Reed, Greer, McKay, and Knight (1990) that further illustrates the importance of the psychological aspects of the contract. The authors report that they conducted a consultancy of nine meetings over a six-month period for the staff of a school for troubled students with the purpose of reducing staff stress levels. Prior attempts to reduce such stress were not successful, so the consultants were called in by the school administrators. However, the staff expected the consultants to provide consultation regarding difficulties they were having with individual students. The authors point out that although the administrators' expectations were covered, the nature of the consultation could have been better clarified for the staff. Consequently, a psychological contract was formed with the administration but not with the staff. The authors point out the need to ensure that all consultees are aware of and agree to the nature of the consultation process.

To avoid unfortunate occurrences like those just described, consultants should be clear about what is expected from both the organization and themselves. By explaining their roles to contact persons and consultees, consultants can build trust with key members of the organization (Rosenfield 2002a; Schein, 1988, 1999). Block (2000) suggests a contracting meeting to both formalize the consultation and to identify process issues that may occur during the consultation process. Consultants should explain what behaviors will occur and the rationale for them. Thus, a consultant who will observe the inner workings of an organization should clearly state that such observations will be made for the purpose of understanding organizational dynamics, not for gathering personal data about individuals.

In summary, if the consultant has effectively completed the preliminary exploration of an organization's needs, then the psychological aspects of contracting need less attention because mutual expectations have already been verbally expressed and agreed upon. The consultant's primary concern with regard to the psychological aspects of contracting is in involving the organization's contact person in mutual development of the formal contract. To the degree that this involvement happens, the ground rules for the consultation process and mutual cooperation on future issues and problems will be established (Boss, 1993). Such involvement of the contact person, of course, requires the investment of more time at the outset of the entry stage. Consultants will want to remember that as consultation proceeds, there may well be the need for renegotiating the contract (Caplan, 1993).

**A Brief Example of Contracting.**   The head of a group home for abused adolescents currently has five male and five female clients. The head has concerns about physical contact between clients and staff, and she contacts you to consult about this matter. After an initial exploration of the organization's needs, you and the head develop a contract that will guide your consultation. You first agree to interview each of the three staff members and the head independently and then observe them discussing this issue in the next two staff meetings. You both agree that all information you gather will be held confidential, you set a fee, and you put the contract in writing.

## PHASE THREE: PHYSICALLY ENTERING THE SYSTEM

Once a contract has been formalized, the consultant is ready to physically enter the system. *Physically entering the system* begins when the consultant first comes into contact with the members of the organization (Gallessich, 1982) and, where appropriate, creates consultant–consultee relationships. Physical entry is different from psychological entry, which is the ongoing process by which the consultant achieves increasing acceptance by the members of the organization. Internal consultants have usually already established the infrastructure for their work (McLean, 2006).

A very important feature of physically entering the system is the consultant's work site within the organization. Should the consultant be assigned a private office, meet in designated meeting rooms, or in the offices of other staff members? The reality of organizational life is that having one's own office is a sign of status and prestige. By providing the consultant with a temporary office, the organization makes a symbolic statement of strong support for the consultant, one that sanctions and demonstrates the administration's willingness to allocate the organizational resources needed to support the consultation process. Because site-based consultants and collaborators are frequently internal to the organization, they may have often already accomplished the task of physical entry.

Having an office and always being in it are two different things. When beginning the physical entry process, consultants should move about the work areas to begin building relationships with members of the organization. Consultees often feel most comfortable when the consultant is willing to meet them on their own turf. Thus, as soon as possible after entering the system, consultants should seek out everyone connected with the consultation. A specified time schedule that makes the consultant's comings and goings predictable is very useful in successfully accomplishing physical entry.

The consultant should proceed in a deliberate, cautious manner. Organizations are slow to change, and the consultant would do well to realize that appropriate physical entry will enhance the organizational members' acceptance so crucial to successful psychological entry. The consultant should adapt to the organization's schedules and thereby minimize any interruptions in the workday.

The consultant should remind the organization's contact person to inform the parties-at-interest of the consultant's upcoming entry into the organization. The members affected by consultation should be informed of the consultant's role and function, why that particular consultant was hired, what is to be accomplished within what time frame, and who is to be involved (Boss, 1993). McLean (2006) suggests accomplishing this communication by setting up a project management system by which the consultant's work can be tracked and a status-reporting process for communicating with all stakeholders. Further, the work setting in which consultation services are to be delivered should be common knowledge (Schein, 1988, 1999). Such advance notification prepares the people involved for the consultant's entry. Finally, an open discussion concerning confidentiality and its limits is important because it informs both administrators and consultees of what they can reveal to the consultant, and it can avoid problems later on (Conoley & Conoley, 1992).

**A Brief Example of Physically Entering the System.** Reread the preceding brief example of contracting and assume you are the consultant in that example. Since the length of your consultancy is brief (three weeks or so), you realize that you do not need an office at the site. Yet you will need a place to conduct interviews with the staff and suggest to the head that you use one of the staff offices so that you will not become overly identified with the administration of the home. You then ask the head to discuss your coming at least a week in advance. At your first visit, you mingle with the staff and clients and try to get a feel for the atmosphere that permeates the group home.

# PHASE FOUR: PSYCHOLOGICALLY ENTERING THE SYSTEM

In actual practice, physical and psychological entry cannot be separated. *Psychological entry* refers to the gradual acceptance of the consultant by members of the organization in which consultation is being performed. Effective accomplishment of the first three phases of entry can enhance the consultant's acceptance by the organization. Because collaborators are frequently internal to an organization, they frequently have attained psychological entry.

In gaining psychological acceptance in an organization, the consultant should consider the two levels of operation in any organization. The process level concerns how an organization does what it does (Schein, 1999); that is, how it makes major decisions. The second level involves the personal interactions among its members; for example, how peers are encouraged to support each other on the job to build the organization's morale. By quickly learning and adapting to the organization's norms, consultants can increase the probability of a successful outcome.

Consultants who achieve psychological entry relatively quickly can be said to be "working smart." Because they realize that organizations attempt to maintain a state of equilibrium and stability (Parsons, 1996), such consultants create the conditions in which only minimal stress is placed on the organizational personnel involved in the consultation. They follow existing rules, regulations, and communication channels, and they ask to be judged on their deeds rather than on what they say.

When consultants try too hard to be like their own stereotype of an organization's members, adverse effects can occur. For example, Deitz and Reese (1986) provided examples of how a mental health consultant tried to take on the jargon used by the members of a law enforcement agency. Rather than being seen as "family" by the officers, the consultant was seen as an oddball who would never be trustworthy or deserving of respect. Clearly, psychological entry can be made more difficult if the consultant falls into the trap of not being perceived as genuine by appearing to take on the behaviors of consultees that are not part of his or her everyday behavior.

The consultant's acceptance by the organization can be enhanced by keeping matters pertinent to consultation as simple as possible. The consultant should describe consultation interventions in concrete and specific terms (McCarroll & Ursano, 2006), and changes in the organization's structure that result from consultation should be minimized.

Furthermore, the consultant will want to ensure that consultees perceive that the consultant is able, at the outset of consultation, to translate assistance to meet the needs of the consultee. To effectively psychologically enter, the consultant must be perceived by the consultee as appreciating the consultee's role demands and stressors (Kelly, 1993).

## Interpersonal Influence in Consultation

**Social/Interpersonal Influence.** Psychological acceptance can be accomplished through the use of social influence or the popular and broader term "social/interpersonal influence" (Strong, 1968). There has been increased attention paid to this area in recent years, due in part to the fact that consultants in any setting spend most of their time working with other adults even when the clients targeted for assistance are children (Gutkin, 1997). The trick is for consultants to impact the consultee while maintaining a relationship among equals. Social influence theory states that the people affected by consultation are more open to influence to the degree that they view the consultant as being attractive, trustworthy, and competent. Increasingly, consultation in the human service professions has been recognized as an interpersonal influence process (Erchul, Raven, & Ray, 2001; Erchul, Raven, & Whichard, 2001; Noell et al., 2005). Blom–Hoffman and Rose (2007) note the importance of "knowingly weaving social influence into consultation" (p. 152). For example, a consultant uses interpersonal influence such as persuasion when directing the focus of the consultation process onto the problem-solving process and away from mere chitchat. In another example, a consultant attempts to influence a consultee's perception of a given client. Interpersonal influence should not be mistaken for controlling or manipulation, but rather is a tool to assist in problem solving and dealing with the relational aspects of consultation (Erchul et al., 2007; O'Keefe & Medway, 1997). For example, interpersonal influence may help minimize resistance and may, in fact, help consultees believe they have the self-efficacy to implement the plan they are

discussing with the consultant and subsequently enhance their commitment to follow through (Noell et al., 2005). Social influence does not diminish consultee responsibility for dealing effectively with the client system (Egan, 2007), but rather can enhance it ( Blom-Hoffman & Rose, 2007).

Consultants are seen as attractive when the people with whom they work perceive similarities between themselves and the consultant. They can increase their attractiveness by identifying with and manifesting as many of the organization's values as are congruent with their own. To this end, consultants can accept and abide by the organization's routines, use the terminology common within it, and abide by its dress codes.

Consultants are perceived as trustworthy when they demonstrate understanding, appropriate use of power, respect for confidentiality, and credibility. Consultants can create trustworthiness (Egan, 2007) by avoiding behaviors that imply ulterior motives, using the power of social influence carefully, promoting the best interest of the consultee or the organization, and being realistic but optimistic about the ability of the consultee or organization to handle the demands of consultation.

Expertness is the perceived possession of specialized knowledge or skills to solve a problem (Short, Moore, & Williams, 1991). One method of enhancing perceived expertness is to cite one's experiences relative to the situation at hand.

One of the most valuable tools consultants have for obtaining acceptance is the effective use of questioning. During entry, it is better if consultants ask good questions about the system (to obtain some understanding of how organization's members perceive consultation) than if they rattle off what they already know about the consultee or the organization (Caplan & Caplan, 1993).

Consultants will not want to gain social influence at the expense of the consultee's need for self-responsibility (Egan, 2007). Consultants can become too accepted within the system. Those who become too accepted risk losing their objectivity and having members of the system blindly accept what they say (Egan, 2007). On the other hand, if consultees feel pushed to accept the consultant's point of view, they might well become resistant. Thus, consultants should strive to obtain enough social influence to make the necessary impact while facilitating the consultee's reflectivity on the consultant's input. Ultimately, consultants' social influence may be as critical as their having skills and knowledge in determining the effectiveness of consultation (Erchul & Raven, 1997; Erchul et al., 2001; Martens, Kelly, & Diskin, 1996).

**Models of Interpersonal Influence.** Consultation involves either direct or indirect attempts to influence change in consultees. Hence, I next explore two models related to attitude change, the Elaboration Likelihood Model (ELM) and French and Raven's bases of social power model, and discuss their significance with regard to working with consultees. You should note that an underlying assumption of this discussion is that any attempt to influence or change a consultee will be accomplished in an ethical and professional manner.

The ELM offers a method to make sense of the antecedents and consequences of attitude change. Central to ELM is the idea that "attitude change can result from relatively thoughtful (central route) or non-thoughtful (peripheral route) processes" (Petty, Heesacker, & Hughes, 1997, p. 107). Thoughtful processes include examining the underlying assumptions of the consultant's information. Non-thoughtful processes rely on the idea that the information makes the consultee pleased or that the consultee simply acquiesces to consultant expertise (i.e., consultant-knows-best type of thinking). Non-thoughtful processes do not challenge the consultee to put any kind of rigor into thinking about what the consultant is saying. As you might guess, thoughtful attitude change is more likely to be permanent than that which is non-thoughtful.

The essence of this model is that consultants have a better chance of interpersonally influencing consultees when consultees have the motivation and the ability to think about the benefits of the data provided by the consultant and its underlying assumptions. On the other hand, if consultees are less involved, it is highly unlikely that they will change their attitudes and behavior in a way

deemed desirable by the consultant. In other words, change is more likely when the consultee has internalized and accepted the consultant's message and is not simply being compliant at the time of the recommendation.

Ways to motivate consultees to consider information reflectively include making the information personally relevant to the consultee, restricting the focus to areas for which the consultee is accountable, ensuring that the consultee has an adequate amount of information, avoiding being forceful in delivering information, taking measures to be viewed as a credible source of information, and keeping a positive emotional atmosphere in the relationship. Ways to make sure that the consultee has the ability to think about the merits of the information include minimizing distractions when information is being considered, providing adequate time for processing the information, avoiding technical language, using written follow-ups to consultation sessions, and avoiding trying to consult during chance encounters.

In addition to motivating and facilitating consultee thought, it is important to create the conditions that will help the consultee think and feel favorably about the consultant's recommendations. Two ways to accomplish this are to make the recommendations from the consultee's perspective (i.e., self-schemas) and to recommend an intervention that is congruent with the consultee's thinking about the problem. For example, a consultee with a humanistic bent has the client's problem explained from a humanistic perspective by the consultant.

As noted in Erchul and Raven (1997), French and Raven (1959) developed a typology that contains six bases of power that can be used for social influence. These bases, accompanied by examples, include:

- coercion—a consultee is fearful of confrontation by the consultant ("If I don't follow through with the plan, I will get in trouble.")
- reward—a consultee views praise from the consultant as rewarding ("It feels good to be validated by the consultant.")

- legitimate—a consultee views the consultant's attempt to help as appropriate to the consultant's role ("It's right for the consultant to try to help me with this; it's part of the job.")

- expert—the consultant is viewed as being more expert in the consultee's opinion ("I should follow this recommendation. After all, the consultant knows more than I do.")

- referent—the consultant is viewed by the consultee as being similar ("Since we are all in this together, the least I can do is my part.")

- informational—the methods of persuasion by the consultant are viewed by the consultee as relevant ("I think I can really use these ideas to help my client.")

As you can note, each of the bases of power can be of use to consultants in their attempts to help their consultees. In addition, these bases of power can be used by all parties involved in collaboration, where the influence is more reciprocal than in consultation. Whatever the basis of power that is used in social influence, the method by which the power is exerted is critical to the success of the influence (Erchul & Raven, 1997). Consultants and collaborators will want to reflect upon available power bases and their mode of implementing in order to have maximum influence on their consultees. Recent research (Erchul, Raven, & Whichard, 2001) suggests that consultants prefer using informational, expert, and referent power bases, which are considered "soft." Riley-Tillman and Chafouleas (2003) discuss the process consultants go through to implement social influence on consultees.

**A Brief Example of Psychologically Entering the System.** As a consultant you are preparing to conduct a workshop for teachers in an elementary school on indicators of child abuse. Before you conduct the workshop, you visit several of the teachers' rooms, introduce yourself, start to learn names, and begin building relationships. In your conversations you note that you were once a schoolteacher and a school counselor. You mention how serious the topic is and that hopefully a child or two can be saved from being victimized as a result of the workshop. You are friendly, professional, and genuine.

## MULTICULTURAL ASPECTS RELATED TO ENTRY

Consultants and collaborators will want to initiate the relationships by using "dynamic sizing," which is the ability to take into account cultural characteristics without stereotyping; and "culture-specific expertise," which is specific knowledge of the cultural groups with whom they work (Castillo et al., 2000; Sue, 1998). The point is consultants interact with consultees and their clients systems as individuals while maintaining cultural sensitivity (Egan, 2007). Culturally different consultees may perceive consultants in terms of interpersonal orientation (the ability to positively socially influence others) and instrumental orientation (the ability to be perceived as competent) (Gibbs, 1980). For example, an African American consultee may be primarily concerned about the interpersonal orientation of a white consultant, whereas a white consultee may be more interested in determining whether or not the consultant can be of assistance (i.e., instrumentally competent) (Gibbs, 1980). Clearly, consultants and collaborators will want to be knowledgeable about culturally different groups (Castillo et al., 2000) and take that knowledge into consideration as they accomplish the entry stage. For example, consultants will want to bear in mind that the amount of information communicated by words versus by context varies among cultures, and it is likely that minority consultees will make a commitment to the consultation process based upon their perception of the consultant's ability to relate and the consultant's familiarity with the meanings of specific nonverbal behaviors across cultures (Ortiz & Flanagan, 2002).

Some consultees or collaborators from differing cultural backgrounds may view the consultant as the expert. Consequently, consultants will have to determine whether they wish to enter the relationship in this context or aim for a more non-hierarchical, collaborative relationship.

Clearly, communication and relationship building are essential to culturally skilled consultants, and how they use these skills will to a large extent determine the success of consultation (Jackson & Hayes, 1993; Ramirez et al., 1998). One method consultants and collaborators can use to determine their suitability to work with consultees or fellow collaborators is to determine their level of comfort in dealing with any cultural or ethnic issues related to the problem being dealt with (Ingraham, 2003, 2004). Awareness of cultural differences and how they might impact the consultative relationship should be considered before contracting. Cultural awareness is particularly influential on outcomes during the entry phase (Duncan, 1995).

## A FINAL NOTE ON ENTRY

Part of your work as a consultant may involve the work-related concerns of individual consultees. For example, you might consult with counselors in a community human service agency about their clients, with teachers concerning students about whom they have concerns, or with parents about issues regarding raising children. If you are going to be working with individual consultees within an

---

**C A S E  3.1    Entry for School Consultants**

Maurice is a school-based consultant in a large, urban elementary school and frequently consults with many staff members, including the school's four administrators. The administrators ask Maurice to assist them in developing a dropout prevention program. Although Maurice is internal to the school, he realizes that he is external to the problem and must go through the entry stage very carefully.

In a first meeting with the administrators, Maurice and the group explore the possibilities of his being a consultant for the program. Maurice wants to make sure that he can be of assistance as well as ensure that the administrators see him as someone who can help. Together the group explores the underlying values concerning counseling that will guide the development of the program, how the program will be staffed, the kinds of resources that will be provided, and the flexibility available for fine-tuning the program. Maurice asks the administrators why they are interested in the program in the first place and what they think it will do for the school. He then interacts with the group concerning what they view his role to be in helping develop the program and, correspondingly, their own roles. Finally, the group discusses the limits of Maurice's involvement given his other duties in the school.

Based on this exploration, all agree that Maurice should be a consultant for the program's development. Maurice suggests that a formal, written contract, although internal to the school, will help the parties involved stay on track with the project. He agrees to develop a contract for approval and submits one that describes the general goals related to the program's development, what roles he and the administrators will take on, a time frame, and a brief evaluation design for assessing the quality of the work accomplished through consultation.

In a brief meeting Maurice and the administrators review and agree to the contract, as well as make sure everyone involved has the same set of expectations. To enhance physical and psychological entry, Maurice suggests a location for program development meetings, makes sure that he follows protocol in gaining access to the administrators, and acknowledges the fact that just because he is a consultant to the group does not make him an administrator or more important than any other staff member at the school.

**Commentary**

This case illustrates the importance of the maxim: You always have to enter. Even though Maurice was an internal consultant, he recognized that he was external to the problem and the consequent importance of appropriately entering. Notice that Maurice clarified his role very carefully and put things in writing. Even though he was functioning as an internal consultant, Maurice did not fall into the trap of making the consultation process so casual that it would be difficult to keep it on task and remain in a problem-solving mode.

organization, you will have to "enter" with each one, that is, explore their perceived needs that led to their requests for consultation.

You will have to develop a suitable contract with your consultees or fellow collaborators, be willing to meet them on their own turf, and psychologically enter through building a good working relationship with them. Evidence suggests that how well you can establish relationships with consultees is related to consultation success (Hughes & DeForest, 1993). There is also strong support for the importance of a strong relationship from writers in the area of consultation theory such as Caplan

and Caplan (1993). On the other hand, you have the potential to strongly affect consultees in their thinking (Granda, 1992)—you must successfully complete the entry stage not only with the organization, but with each consultee as well. You may have to orient the consultee to the consultation/collaboration process, engage them in a professional relationship, and understand the nature of the organization in which consultation occurs (Gutkin & Curtis, 1999; Larney, 2003).

The limited research on entry with individual consultees suggests that the consultant's knowledge is not as important to consultees as are the

---

**C A S E   3.2    Entry for Community Consultants**

Marie, a mental health consultant operating out of a mental health satellite center, is contacted by Kristine, the director of a human resource development department of a local municipal government, to engage in some "train-the-trainer" consultation. She is interested in having her human resource development staff trained in consultation skills. During their first contact, Marie thoroughly explores what Kristine would like to accomplish in the training, shares her own related professional experiences as well as her values regarding consultation in general and training in particular, and asks Kristine about her views of training and consultants.

They discuss the human resource development department, its staff and mission, and how it is perceived by the rest of the organization. They also discuss the practical use of the consultation training to the department's staff and the resources that the department is willing to put into training. At the end of their discussion, both Marie and Kristine are positive about the prospect of working together. Before she agrees to become a consultant, Marie asks if she could have a brief meeting with the human resource development department's five staff members to inform them about the proposed consultation.

Marie meets with the staff for an hour, during which she gets to know the members in a leisurely fashion, briefly describes the proposed training and her own related professional experiences, and allows time for questions and discussion. At the end of the meeting, there is a consensus among group members that they are favorable about the training.

Marie contacts Kristine soon thereafter and clarifies the few issues that were raised in the meeting with the staff. Kristine mentions that the local municipal government has a form contract that is to be used by all departments when they hire consultants and that there was some flexibility in it for writing in items specific to a given consultation. Marie and Kristine agree to add a statement about the consultant's roles and the responsibilities of the director of the department.

Stopping by the human resource development office the day before the training sessions are to start, Marie makes a point of interacting with each of the participants and, with a couple of the participants, looks over the room in which the training is to be conducted. She provides a schedule for the training to the staff members as well as a couple of handouts on consulting ideas for human resource development specialists.

**Commentary**

It is of particular importance, as this case illustrates, for consultants to enter with each consultee as they enter the system. Marie wisely held a brief meeting with the consultees prior to beginning her training sessions with them. Notice how she also made personal contact with each of them on the day before the training. By taking the time to create relationships with consultees, consultants not only build trust and minimize resistance, but they also quickly move the consultation relationship to a partnership that allows for effective collaboration.

relationship-building activities of the consultant (Martens, Lewandowski, & Houk, 1989). There is additional attention being paid to the consultees' cognitive responses to the help they are receiving (Uhlemann, Lee, & Martin, 1994). In other words, consultees' perceptions about what is happening in the consultation relationship can be as important as what is actually happening. Therefore, as a practic-ing consultant you may well put a high priority on establishing solid working relationships with your consultees. In doing so, consultants will want to be aware that consultees may want a balance of direction and collaboration (Buysse, Schulte, Pierce, & Terry, 1994) and prefer some leadership from the consultant in determining the content of consultation (Gutkin, 1996).

## SUMMARY

The entry process in consultation is a critical stage. When successfully completed, it increases the prob-ability that the entire consultation process will turn out successfully. The success of the entry process relies heavily on the consultant's skills and how well these skills are used to accomplish the tasks of the entry stage. The most critical skills in the entry stage relate to exploring problems, contract-ing, relating, and communicating. By effectively ac-complishing the stage of entry, consultants not only set the stage for successful consultation, but they also minimize possible resistance from organizations and individual consultees.

Consultants should avoid the temptation to go quickly through the entry stage to get on with problem-solving activities. By effectively exploring the organization's needs, the consultant can help it determine its priorities for consultation. A well-designed contract makes the expectations of every-one involved explicit and prevents misunderstand-ings regarding consultation later in the process. Effective physical entry makes consultants less in-trusive as they join in the organization's activities. By taking the time necessary for building relation-ships and gaining acceptance, consultants can be-come insiders and accomplish the difficult phase of psychological entry.

The research on the entry stage is quite limited. There is some evidence that consultees prefer a blend of facility and expertise in consultants and that the readiness for change (and a consultee's abil-ity to bring it about) are more likely to lead to a successful consultation experience than will factors like consultee interest in the subject of the consul-tation (Armenakis & Burdg, 1988).

## SUGGESTIONS FOR EFFECTIVE PRACTICE

- Remember the maxim: "You always have to enter."

- A contract is one of the best ways of docu-menting expectations.

- Consider resistance to be a normal part of the consultation and collaboration process.

- Make a deliberate effort to psychologically enter the system and create a relationship with *each* consultee, even if you are internal to the setting in which consultation and collaboration occur.

## QUESTIONS FOR REFLECTION

1. What do you think is meant by the phrase "You always have to enter?"

2. Why is it important for the consultant to obtain sanctions for performing consultation from the organization's upper echelon?

3. Recall a situation in which an outsider entered your classroom. What were your immediate reactions? Relate your feelings to how members of an organization must feel when they encounter a consultant for the first time.

4. What characteristics would you look for in an organization or a consultee before you would agree to consultation?

5. Under what circumstances can resistance in consultation be seen as normal?

6. How can the power attributed to the consultant due to expertise or trustworthiness be useful in ameliorating resistance?

7. What are the key points consultants should consider in assessing their performance during the entry phase?

8. How would you as a consultant go about accomplishing psychological entry? That is, how would you go about the task of building accepting relationships with staff with whom you had no previous contact?

9. How would you go about the task of physically entering into consultation with an organization?

10. Under what circumstances do you think consultants should use formal contracts?

## SUGGESTED SUPPLEMENTARY READINGS

If you are interested in reading in more depth and detail about the entry stage of consultation, here are some useful selected readings:

Marks, E. S. (1995). *Entry strategies for school consultation.* New York: Guilford. This text is dedicated to the nuts and bolts of helping consultants open the doors to effective consultation. The author emphasizes entry in school consultation, but consultants and collaborators in any setting will find useful information.

Glidewell, J. C. (1959). The entry problem in consultation. *Journal of Social Issues, 15*(2), 51–59. Don't let the date on this article fool you. This article is a

classic and well worth reading. Glidewell was one of the first authors to promote the idea of the consultant as a person who temporarily attaches to a social system; he does an excellent job of pointing out that the process of entry can be accelerated or retarded by the perceptions of the members of the organization in which consultation is to occur.

Cherniss, C. (1993). Preentry issues revisited. In R.T. Golembiewski (Ed.), *Handbook of organizational consultation* (pp. 113–118). New York: Marcel Dekker. This is an excellent review of preentry issues. Two particular aspects of this article are dealing with conflict during preentry and choosing a primary focus.

# 4

✳

# Diagnosis Stage

The nature of the diagnosis stage depends on the type of consultation being performed. But just as some kind of diagnosis, either formal or informal, is made in counseling and psychotherapy, so too is one made in consultation or collaboration. A mental health consultant working with a therapist may assist in diagnosing a client's problem and in prescribing a treatment plan. A behavioral consultant may examine the antecedents and consequences of students' selected classroom conduct and assist a teacher in implementing behavioral strategies to change that conduct. An organizational consultant may help an organization improve its efficiency by focusing on an individual, a group, a subsystem, or the organization as a whole. The process of diagnosis remains the same for all consultation, although the types of data gathered will depend on the type of consultation being performed. The bottom line is that diagnosis develops the foundation for, and is interdependent with, intervention (Gutkin & Curtis, 1999), and it is a prerequisite for goal setting (French & Bell, 1999).

The preceding chapter discussed the entry process, in which the consultant engages in a preliminary exploration of organizational needs, formulates a contract, and physically and psychologically enters the system. The stage following entry is called the diagnosis stage and has four phases: gathering information (which answers the question "What information do we need to find out where we are?"), defining the problem (which answers the question "Where are we?"), setting goals (which answers the question "Where do we want to be?"), and generating possible interventions (which answers the question "What are some things to do that might help us get there?").

Figure 4.1 shows how diagnosis, data gathering, and intervention relate to one another. The consultant's relationship with the consultee is critical to the successful completion of this stage. Unless the consultant is able to obtain accurate, pertinent

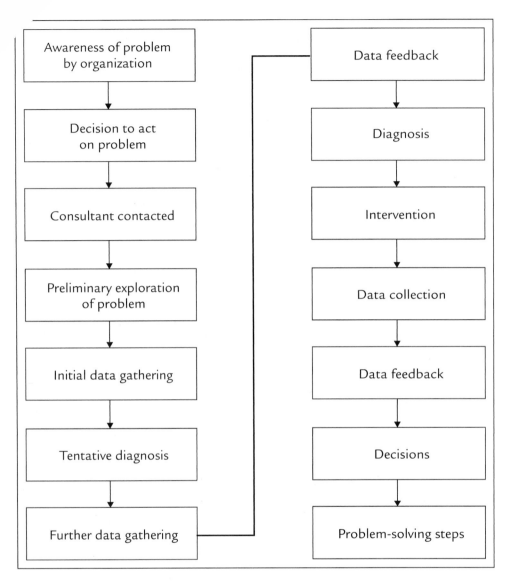

**FIGURE 4.1**   The interrelationships among diagnosis, data gathering, and intervention (French, 1972)

information and assist consultees in translating this data into a list of functional and viable interventions, then it is likely that the wrong problem will be solved. As you read this chapter, consider these questions:

1.  How does a consultant determine where to collect information within the organization?

2.  How does a consultant determine who should gather the data needed to define the problem?

3.  What factors should be considered in setting goals?

4.  How can a consultant assist a consultee in developing a set of possible interventions?

5.  In what ways is diagnosis an ongoing event?

## INTRODUCTION

Assume for the moment that you are the consultant described in the following example:

### A Case of Diagnosis

You are a human service professional in private practice with a caseload of clients, and you perform consultation with other therapists and human service organizations. The director of a county social service agency requests that you assist in resolving some of the agency's problems. You have successfully completed the entry stage and therefore have a rough idea of what the agency's problems are. You have a contract, have gotten to know the staff, and are set up in the office of a part-time staff member. The director is concerned about the morale within the agency: people work behind closed doors, put-downs of clients are frequently heard, backlogs of paperwork are large, and little camaraderie is apparent.

When consulting with the director, you agree to design and conduct a survey about what it is like to work in the agency. You agree to interview a random number of the staff about their personal views of their professional work site, and, based on the results of this information, you assist the director in determining what's the matter. You divide the problem into three smaller problems: morale, high caseloads, and little administrative support and encouragement. You then assist the director in setting some goals to ameliorate these problems. You break these down further into more specific subgoals (e.g., more oral and written praise and support from the director for jobs well done). Once goals have been set, you and the director come up with a variety of intervention alternatives for meeting the set goals. As this example illustrates, consultants are sometimes asked to assist in determining the nature of a problem prior to making some form of intervention. Thus, this stage of consultation—in which the consultant performs this assessment in the roles of information seeker and detective—is called the *diagnosis stage*.

*Diagnosis* is the identification of the forces underlying or precipitating the current way things are in a given situation. From another perspective,

diagnosis is the "meaning or interpretation that is derived from assessment information when it is interpreted through the use of a diagnostic classification system" (Hohenshil, 1996, p. 65). It identifies "strengths, opportunities, and problem areas" (French & Bell, 1999, p. 105). Diagnosis may pertain broadly to the present state of a system, including the many positive forces giving rise to desirable outcomes, or may be narrower in the sense of focusing on the dysfunctional forces that are producing undesirable outcomes, or may focus on changes in the state of the system over time (Harrison & Shirom, 1999).

A critical part of diagnosis is determining that part of the organization in which the problem is located. How the consultant approaches the diagnostic stage depends on the purpose of consultation, the complexity of the problem, and the time available (Harrison & Shirom, 1999). For example, Tichy (1983) listed three types of organizational diagnoses based on complexity that are still valuable today:

- radar-scan diagnosis (which involves a quick examination of the organization to locate problem areas)

- symptom-focused diagnosis (in which information is examined relative to known problem areas)

- in-depth diagnosis (which involves a systematic, detailed organizational analysis)

Another important aspect of the diagnosis stage involves determining who constitutes the client system—an individual, a group, a subsystem, or the entire organization—for the nature of the client system affects diagnosis. As the client system increases in size, the complexity of the diagnostic stage usually increases as well: The more complex the diagnostic stage, the greater the need to use several methods to collect data from a larger group of people.

What French, Bell, and Zawacki (1978) noted long ago still holds true today: Every consultant brings at least three theories to the diagnostic process. The first, descriptive and analytical in nature, is the theory by which the consultant attempts to understand the client system in terms of the behavior and events surrounding them. In this view, for example, behaviors might be considered rather more critical than attitudes in understanding events. A second theory, one of change, consists of the consultant's views of how events change and influence one another. For example, one view of this theory might state that structure, not people, determines change. Finally, consultants have diagnostic theories, which consist of a set of notions to determine what is dysfunctional or wrong (Sandoval, 2003). One example is the viewpoint that a problem must be a long-standing one in order to be severe. Another is a view based on the positive psychology movement that focused on what is going right and related solutions (Gerstein, 2007).

Assessment refers to the kind of information used in diagnosis (Hohenshil, 1996; Kamphaus, Reynolds, & Imperato-McCammon, 1999). The kind of information used for diagnosis depends on a given consultation model's view of what must be examined. Three major areas or domains that consultants may examine in their diagnoses are consultee characteristics, client system characteristics, and environmental characteristics. Consultants' theories of description-analysis, change, and dysfunction significantly affect which domains are examined and how a diagnosis is made. By being aware of their own theories, consultants can use them to accomplish accurate, effective diagnoses and avoid being unwittingly victimized by them during the diagnostic stage. As an example, let's consider a behavioral approach to change called *functional behavioral assessment (FBA),* often referred to as the "ABCs" of behavior. In this process the consultant and/or consultee gather data regarding the conditions (also called contingencies) that control a specific behavior. The idea is that by determining how antecedents and consequences surrounding a behavior in a given context interact with the behavior, the consultant and consultee can manipulate those antecedents and consequences to develop interventions tailored to the client system's specific problem (Crone, Hawken & Bergstrom, 2007; Denton et al., 2003; Lee & Jamison, 2003). A little later in the chapter, Figure 4.3 illustrates a form used in functional behavioral assessment. For a detailed discussion of FBA consult Watson & Steege (2003).

The diagnosis stage, like the entry stage, is very complex. It involves the four interrelated phases depicted in Figure 4.2: gathering information, defining the problem, setting goals, and generating possible interventions.

## PHASE ONE: GATHERING INFORMATION

### The Nature of Information Acquisition

Consultants will want to remember that even though the information gathered is critical, the method of gathering information and how that information is used is also important (French & Bell, 1999). An accurate diagnosis requires accurate information (Gregory, Armenakis, Moates, Albritton & Harris, 2007). The terms "data" and "information" are used interchangeably in this discussion. Although data gathering does not cease during the consultation process, there is a formal time for the process of gathering information.

The first step is to conceptualize the problem. Some idea of the problem is obtained during the

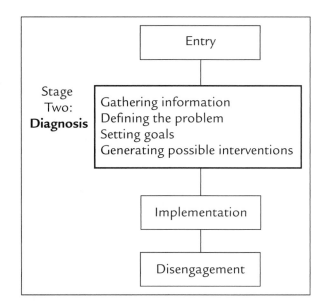

**FIGURE 4.2** The phases of the diagnosis stage

preliminary exploration of organizational needs. The results of the preliminary exploration are, in part, determined by the model of consultation to be used, for each model has its own view of human behavior, of what is necessary for change, and of what constitutes the client system. These factors in turn will determine the types of methods used to gather data.

Still, the consultant must assign some parameters to the task of consultation before diagnosis (Gregory et al., 2007; Kratochwill, Sheridan, Carlson, & Lasecki, 1999). These parameters help to determine the scope of data gathering and assessment. To determine which intervention may have the best opportunity to be successful, relevant data should be gathered and analyzed (Gutkin & Curtis, 1999). For example, in school-based consultation, client system behavior is often examined in terms of child's daily routine at school and home. Depending on the model of consultation in use, the consultant can draw from several data sources: genetic data, current descriptive data, process data, interpretive data, consultee–client system relationship data, and client system behavior data (Bergan & Kratochwill, 1990; Caplan & Caplan, 1993).

- Genetic data: This type of data includes easily accessible, common information (e.g., an organization's role and mission statement) and historical information (e.g., reports and memos). (Example: A consultant might read the role and mission statement of a human service agency and decide to determine the degree to which the agency's members are aware of it.)

- Current descriptive data: As its name implies, this type of information describes an organization as it currently exists. The organization's physical layout, and its command and salary structures, are all descriptive information. (Example: A human service agency asks for a consultant's help with its internal communication problems. The consultant examines the agency's organizational structure as a prelude to determining how superiors and subordinates

within the agency communicate with one another.)

- Process data: Process data involve the organization's methods, including how decisions are made and how meetings are conducted. (Example: A consultant acts as an observer at a crisis intervention team's staff meeting to determine who talks to whom about what.)

- Interpretive data: This kind of information tends to be subjective and have emotional aspects to it. Interpretive data include members' attitudes, beliefs, and perceptions about the organization, its means of functioning, and the ways members relate to one another. (Example: A consultant gathers information about how school counselors perceive the support given them by the teachers in their school.)

- Consultee–client system relationship data: The dynamics between the consultee and the client system constitute this type of data, including the nature of interpersonal relationships, their direction, and how communication takes place. (Example: A consultant watches a videotape of a consultee providing therapy to a client to help the consultee work more effectively with the client.)

- Client system behavior data: This type of information includes characteristics of the client system, such as level of intelligence, nature of the problem, levels of coping, the frequency of adaptive and maladaptive behaviors, and related environmental conditions. (Example: A school psychologist consulting with a school counselor administers an individual intelligence test to the counselor's client in order to suggest some effective helping strategies.)

A great number of data sources are available to consultants, depending on the nature of consultation. For example, consultants working with consultees whose client system is an organization may want to examine genetic data (e.g., forms for writing up client reports from past years), current descriptive data (e.g., current forms for writing up client reports), process data (e.g., how the decision to use a given form for writing client reports was made), or interpretive data (e.g., the results of a survey, that reveal how staff feel about the current form used to write up client reports). Consultants working with consultees who have individual clients tend to rely on data from consultee–client system relationships and behavior for purposes of classification (Kamphaus, Reynolds, & Imperato McCammon, 1999). Whatever the type of data being gathered, it must be precise and meaningful. Imprecise data can intensify existing problems due to misdirected interventions (Stroh & Johnson, 2006). Data should also be selective, relevant, understandable (Golembiewski, 1993a), and adequately defined (Kratochwill et al., 1999). Further, consultants will want to assure that their consultees engage in culturally sensitive diagnostic practices in order not to misdiagnosis or use unnecessary diagnoses with their client systems (see Hays, 2001 and White Kress et al., 2005). For example, in culturally sensitive assessment, the consultant focuses on the strengths of the client's system as well as its social supports. In addition, culturally sensitive assessment gathers data from multiple sources and encourages the assessor to be knowledgeable and experienced with the cultures of the consultee and the client system (Hays, 2001). If information gathering is well done at this stage, the method chosen may well be helpful in the evaluation process (McLean, 2006).

## Scanning

Using the presenting problem as a starting point, it is a good idea for the consultant to scan the context in which the problem is thought to occur. *Scanning* is the process of looking at the big picture, including information about events and relationships within the organization's internal and external environment (Gallessich, 1982; McLean, 2006). Scanning prevents a premature focus on the problem's more obvious major elements to the exclusion of other pertinent factors. Scanning procedures can provide data for determining the validity of the problem, for identifying forces supporting or inhibiting effective change, and for detecting problems that are deeper

than the ones identified in the preliminary exploration. In addition, scanning can prevent an a priori determination of the problem's nature and can counteract the consultant's professional and personal biases.

Hypothetically, a consultant could scan the entire domain: consultee, client system, and environment; in practice, however, scanning must be cost effective. Therefore, consultants typically use their theories of description analysis, change, and dysfunction to scan these systems. To avoid biases, the consultant describes these theories and the results of scanning to the consultee, who can then add additional perspectives to the analysis of the diagnosis stage. Once the entire context of the problem has been scanned and the results of the scanning interpreted, the consultant and consultee are ready to focus on more specific data.

## Methods for Gathering Information

Data gathering can be done by the consultant, the consultee, or both. Some authors (e.g., Noell & Witt, 1998) recommend a hybrid data collection strategy that involves both the consultant and the consultee. The information used in consultation is obtained by either unobtrusive or obtrusive data-gathering devices. Unobtrusive devices would disclose historical data (e.g., memos), external data (e.g., interviews with former clients of the organization), and observational data (e.g., observing a meeting in action) (Bell & Nadler, 1985). Unobtrusive measures are not likely to interrupt the organization's normal flow of everyday activities or be seen as threatening by the organization's members. Obtrusive data-gathering activities include those that in some way ask for a reaction.

Examples of this type of data gathering include questionnaires, surveys, and interviews. Because these activities directly assess the organization through its members and may imply impending changes within the organization, they can be threatening and elicit resistance. Regardless of the method of data gathering used, the consultant can minimize resistance by ensuring that all appropriate personnel are informed of the data's anticipated uses.

Data can be soft, such as subordinates' impressions of the organization's leadership, or hard, such as statistical data on the number of clients who perceive that the organization has helped them in some way. A general rule for data gathering is to move from less to more structured methods (Parsons & Meyers, 1984). For example, concerning the morale of an entire organization, it is best to gather general information first (such as a survey of a selected sample about the level of morale) and more specific information later (such as views concerning specific causes of the quality of morale). Instruments and procedures used to gather data should, whenever possible, be designed to take into consideration the uniqueness of the consultation situation.

The methods used for gathering information in consultation depend on the nature of the client system and the perceived problem (Stroh & Johnson, 2006). A consultant working with a therapist experiencing difficulty with a case requires different information than would a consultant working with an organization suffering from poor morale. Nonetheless, the most common information-gathering methods used in consultation include examining documents and records; giving questionnaires, surveys, and interviews; and observation. There are some very specific models used. For example, there is a functional behavior assessment model used in school consultation which can be used to gather information about antecedents, behaviors, and consequences in order to design interventions (Gresham, Watson, & Skinner, 2001).

**Documents and Records.**  Consultants and consultees sometimes erroneously assume that they have to collect all of the data needed to make a diagnosis. All organizations generate a wealth of information and keep some form of records, including numerical data and written communications (Harrison & Shirom, 1999). This information is often referred to as *secondary data* (McLean, 2006). Use of records is often considered unobtrusive because their examination does not interrupt the organization's normal flow of work. Records are frequently referred to as

secondary data because the information in them has already been collected.

The consultation party who is responsible for data collection searches these documents without the aid of any structure or procedure. Gallessich (1982) was among the first to note that a variety of documents supply the consultant with data for use in making a diagnosis: job descriptions, agency policies and manuals of operating procedures, historical records, annual reports, budgets, audits, personnel statistics, orientation procedures, promotion policies, program descriptions, grant proposals, client demographic profiles, surveys of client use of services, public information brochures, logs and appointment calendars, and case records.

By comparing an organization's current and past records and documents, the consultant may be able to identify trends and forces influencing the organization and can determine who corresponds in writing with whom, how critical information is disseminated throughout the agency, and so forth. Reviewing relevant documents is a data-gathering technique that is frequently underused by consultants.

Examining records as an information-gathering technique has several strengths, including the use of existing information, cost efficiency, the wealth of relevant material, the provision of a historical context, and the data's credibility with members of the organization (McLean, 2006). In addition, records are typically free from response bias and are nonreactive. Furthermore, the development of discourse analysis has created a methodology for interpreting records (MacNealy, 1999).

The use of documents as an information-gathering device also has weaknesses, among which are potential inaccuracy and incompleteness, limited availability, difficulties in data analysis, long times for review, and the possibility of increasing resistance among consultees and the organization as a whole (Fuqua & Newman, 1983; McLean, 2006). Records frequently can have little relation to reality. In addition, the consultant must frequently rely on the consultee's assistance in determining the validity of existing data and in identifying which data might be diagnostically useful.

**Questionnaires and Surveys.**   Questionnaires and surveys are actually self-administered interviews that allow for simultaneous collection of information from several sources. They can be extremely useful (Stroh & Johnson, 2006) and contribute to understanding the behavior of individuals and organizations and reveal possible targets for change (Westaby, 2006).

*Standardized* questionnaires are available either commercially or in research journals. Their validity and reliability have been demonstrated in the research literature. *Modified* questionnaires are usually standardized questionnaires that have been adapted in some way to meet specific needs of the data-gathering process. For example, a school counselor might adapt a questionnaire used in a mental health center for use in a school setting. When a questionnaire is *custom made*, it is developed by the consultant, perhaps with the assistance of the consultee, for a specific purpose. Custom-made questionnaires require a substantial amount of time to construct and often lack high levels of validity and reliability. The type of questionnaire or survey a consultant chooses depends on the precise nature of the information needed to make an adequate diagnosis.

Most questionnaires and surveys use fixed responses for respondents' information about their attitudes, perceptions, or points of view. There are several advantages of using surveys and questionnaires as data-gathering techniques. They allow sampling of large numbers of people simultaneously, are cost effective, can be administered in a variety of formats including the Web, and can be used for a variety of purposes. Responses can be quickly and easily collated and statistically analyzed. Questionnaires and surveys are probably the most powerful data-gathering tools for yielding maximum information in the most efficient manner (French & Bell, 1999; McLean, 2006). They can be used to gather data for defining a problem, to provide clues about which data gathering techniques (e.g., interviews) should next be used, or to work in conjunction with interviews of a sample of the respondents.

Questionnaires and surveys also have disadvantages. They are non-empathic—the instrument does not interact with the respondent in a personal way—which can cause indifference toward the questionnaire on the part of the respondent. They lack adaptability; that is, they are prestructured. If some questions are inappropriate for some respondents, nothing can be done about it. They can also be difficult to interpret; different respondents may interpret the same question differently. The items on a given survey make not be tapping the most pertinent information (Westaby, 2006). Further, surveys and questionnaires can suffer from response bias, in which the respondent answers all items in a set way rather than each item on its own merit. Questionnaires can produce canned results and consultants frequently use them when direct human communication, such as interviews, is more appropriate.

**Interviews.**   One of the best ways to understand a client system or an organization is to ask the people in them what they think and feel (Stroh & Johnson, 2006). Such a technique, the interview, is another commonly used form of data gathering (Busse & Beaver, 2000; Kratochwill et al., 1999). Interviews allow increasing understanding of the client system and facilitate selection of an intervention (Beaver & Busse, 2000). Even though interviews are used in all phases of the diagnostic stage, the nature of the interviewing process will depend on the type of model from which the consultant operates, the issues the interviews are to explore, and the consultant's earlier observations (Beaver & Busse, 2000). Effective interviewing demands that the consultant be sufficiently skilled to note the interviewee's nonverbal and verbal behavior during the interview. Depending on how the interview is conducted, the consultant can uncover both positive and negative opinions and attitudes as well as information on a large number of relevant topics.

The interviewing process can be formal or informal, as can its setting, which can affect the type of information shared by the interviewee. Both groups and individuals can be interviewed, though interviewees are less likely to distort data in a group interview and are also less likely to share their true views and feelings (Greiner & Metzger, 1983). The process by which interviews take place is usually determined by such factors as cost and the data-gathering potential of the interviewing style.

Different types of interviews produce different types of responses from different people (Egan, 1985). There are three common types of interviews: unstructured, structured and open ended, and structured and fixed response. *Unstructured* interviews are typically characterized by a minimal direction of their content by the interviewer (consultant). *Structured and open-ended* interviews consist of a set of preselected questions that the consultant asks the interviewee. This type of interview is considered more flexible than procedures such as surveys and checklists. The behavioral interview discussed in Chapter 10 is of this type. *Structured and fixed-response* interviews provide both predetermined questions and responses from which to choose. They allow for standardization and tend to have a high level of reliability (Beaver & Busse, 2000).

Interviews have several advantages (Busse & Beaver, 2000; Kratochwill et al., 1999). They are adaptive—the interviewing process can be modified depending on the course of the interview. For example, if an interviewee provides an ambiguous response, the consultant can ask for clarification or an example of what the interviewee means. Interviews can be a source of detailed information on several topics and can provide rich sources of data about problems and their causes (Kratochwill et al., 1999). Furthermore, interviews allow the consultant to express empathy and understanding to the interviewee, and as a result, the interview process can be used to build rapport with some members of the organization.

Interviews also have their disadvantages. They are one of the most costly forms of data gathering in terms of both time and expense (McLean, 2006). The interviewee's responses can be affected by the consultant's biases to the degree that these biases dictate the types of questions asked. Interviewee bias can also affect the data obtained because the consultant can record not only the interviewee's perceptions, but also the observations of the consultee's behavior (Beaver & Busse, 2000). Consequently, the results of interviews should be carefully vali-

dated. Two additional potential disadvantages of interviews are the inaccessibility of interviewees and the perceived threat that what interviewees say could somehow later be used against them. The reasons for interviewing and the uses made of the interview data should be made known to all parties-at-interest prior to the onset of the interviewing process.

**Observation.** Data can be collected through observation—the deliberate viewing of events. It is used to gather objective features of behavior (Gresham et al., 2001; Skinner, Dittmer, & Howell, 2000). There are two types of observation: naturalistic and systematic direct (Hintze, Volpe, & Shapiro, 2002). *Naturalistic observation* refers to observation within a particular environment, such as a classroom, without any specific behaviors being targeted for observation. *Systematic direct observation* refers to using a standardized method to measure specific behaviors that have been operationally defined. This most obvious way to collect information puts the consultant in direct contact with the people, activities, and/or environment about which information is being collected (Rosenfield & Gravois, 1996). Observation is widely used to gather data, particularly in schools (Hintze, Volpe, & Shapiro, 2002). Consultants must make choices about what, when, and how much to observe; such choices lend observations structure that can range from a strictly defined to a general framework. The consultant's basic question regarding observation is, "How can the observation be structured so that meaningful and useful data can be collected?" The point is that direct observation "allows an outside observer to record data on the behavior of interest within the environment where the behavior is of concern" (Skinner et al., 2000, p. 22). The three types of observation—structured, semistructured, and unstructured—differ in the degree to which observers watch and record the observations.

*Structured* observations typically use procedures or instruments that specify what type of behavior is to be observed and how it is to be recorded. For example, functional behavioral analysis (FBA) uses several types of structured observations, such as observing specific behaviors between the times they start and stop, or their occurrence during specified time interval (Watson & Steege, 2003). *Semistructured* observations have relatively unstructured observations but highly structured recording. *Unstructured* observations have no strict guidelines for what is to be observed, what is to be recorded, or how recording should take place. Figure 4.3 illustrates a form used in a structured observation.

Observation has several advantages. It provides data on behavior rather than on reports of behavior and can note behaviors unrecognized by organization members or the client system. It can also be one of the more objective data-gathering methods; technology can allow for electronic data entry during the observation process. Observational data have strong face validity; that is, such data have concrete referents to back them up, whereas interviews and questionnaire data can be accused of being overly subjective. Further, this type of data is also current, whereas questionnaires generally sample respondents' past perceptions. Finally, observation, like interviewing, is adaptive: The consultant can adjust what is to be observed as the situation demands. For example, consultants can use observation to identify and prioritize target behaviors and indicate effective interventions (Skinner et al., 2000).

Observation is not without its liabilities as a data-collection method (Gresham et al., 2001; McLean, 2006). Observation only gives information at one point in time. Like interviewing, observation is expensive. The coding and interpretation that must be applied to observational data is subject to observer bias, and the less structured the observation, the more likely observer bias will enter into the process. As is the case with questionnaires, sampling is also an issue in observation. Observations require sampling with regard to people, time, space, and activities, and such intensive sampling can be costly in time and money. Finally, observation has the potential liability of observer effect. *Observer effect* is the impact observers have on the behavior of those being observed. For example, counselors being observed by a consultant may be more empathic than usual with clients simply because they are under observation. Therefore, training in observation is important (Kratochwill et al., 1999).

In summary, each data-collection method has its advantages and disadvantages. Consultants should consider using multiple and valid data-gathering methods as a way of both overcoming the liabilities of a given method and eliminating inaccurate or distorted data. Consultants should ensure that the information gathered is as valid and accurate as possible and have an agreement with the consultee as to how to integrate the data from multiple sources (Macmann et al., 1996).

**A Brief Example of Gathering Information.** A counseling psychologist has contracted to assist a preschool program in determining how parents view its strengths and weaknesses. As the psychologist meets with the program director to develop a plan, they decide to gather survey and interview data from a random sample of half the parents (one-fourth of the selected group will be interviewed, the other three-quarters will be surveyed). The consultant agrees to develop a structured interview and develop a survey that is compatible with the interview. The consultee suggests that the consultant be responsible for conducting the interviews while the consultee takes care of getting the surveys sent out and the results collated.

# PHASE TWO: DEFINING THE PROBLEM

After the data has been collected, it must be analyzed. The importance of defining the problem cannot be overemphasized (Gutkin & Curtis, 1999; Upah & Tilly, 2002). This phase is quite critical because the task to be accomplished is defined and thus affects the rest of the consultation process (Gregory et al., 2007; Kratochwill, Elliott, & Callan-Stoiber, 2002) and has long been linked to eventual success in consultation (Bergan & Tombari, 1976). Furthermore, an accurate definition of the problem determines what behaviors are associated with the problem (Upah & Tilly, 2002).

To define a problem the consultant and the consultee should have a systematic, deliberate, and

## Form to Report Functional Relations over Several Days and Time Periods

Day, Date, & Time (Class Period): _____

Location (Classroom): _____

### TEASING
Defined as negative comments to others about something they have done, how they look, or a threat.

### Setting Events/Antecedents
Activity when teasing occurred: _____

Others nearby: _____

Activity before present activity: _____

Any other events before that seemed relevant: _____

### Consequences
Actions of teacher: _____

Actions of peers: _____

Any other consequences: _____

### NONTEASING
Peer-directed comments that are positive or neutral. Comments about eternal activities or events (e.g., sports, class), compliments, statements of fact (e.g., about the assignment) not about the peer.

### Setting Events/Antecedents
Activity when nonteasing occurred: _____

Others nearby: _____

Activity before present activity: _____

Any other events before that seemed relevant: _____

### Consequences
Actions of teacher: _____

Actions of peers: _____

Other: _____

**FIGURE 4.3** Observations for functional assessment

SOURCE: From Kazdin, A. E. (2002). *Behavior modification in applied settings* (6th ed.). Pacific Grove, CA: Brooks/Cole. By permission of publisher.

predetermined plan for analyzing the data. This avoids "slippery slopes" and the possibility of unintended consequences. For example, from a behavioral perspective, the difference or "gap" between what the client system is expected to do and its actual performance is determined (Tilly, 2002). The consultant and consultee may engage in functional behavioral analysis (Watson & Steege, 2003) (see Chapter 10) and examine the relationships among antecedents, behavior and consequences. As another example, consultants can use "discrepancy analysis" (French & Bell, 1999) to determine differences between the current and desired situations. In addition, cultural sensitivity needs to be shown and technician-like diagnostic procedures avoided (Diller, 2007; Smart & Smart, 1997). When involved in the details of gathering information, it is easy to forget that the purpose of the collecting is to shed light on the problem (Heppner, Kivlighan, & Wampold, 1999). Thus, the consultant and consultee should consider working together as a team to analyze a situation and choose the proper strategies that are likely to lead to the accomplishment of desired goals (Armstrong & Wheatley, 1990). In addition, there is some evidence to suggest that consultants who openly model the problem-solving process as they go through it create a road map that enhances consultee understanding and use of the process (Zins, 1993).

Data analysis is made up of a conceptual model and a technical component (Nadler, 1977). The conceptual component—the diagnostic perspective described earlier—should have been agreed upon by the consultant and the consultee before data are gathered, as should the techniques for analysis. Analysis of the data may suggest new hypotheses concerning the problem that require collection of additional data and subsequent analysis.

As the consultant and consultee examine the data, a more complex conceptualization of the problem often occurs. There is some evidence that defining the problem is not as easy as the literature suggests (Conoley, Conoley, & Gumm, 1992). Thus, consultants will want to take into account the problem-solving approach used by their consultee in examining the data. The analysis of the data may suggest more than one problem, in which case the consultant

and the consultee should prioritize them in terms of importance (Zins & Erchul, 2002). Furthermore, how the consultee conceptualizes the problem might well influence the consultant's conceptualization.

During the significant amount of time spent on analyzing and interpreting data, the consultant and consultee determine how a broad range of factors affects the problem: how it develops over time, how past events are causing the present problem, or how future expectations are related (Allen & Graden, 2002). A clear, specific problem statement with corresponding objectives is crucial in assuring that the correct problem is attacked. Consultants have long been encouraged to frame their problem statements in language that is acceptable to the consultee (Dustin & Ehly, 1984). To this end, Osterweil (1987) suggests generating several alternative definitions of the problem from which the consultant and consultee can choose using three criteria:

- reasonability—the degree to which the definition seems logical to both consultant and consultee

- workability—the degree to which the definition seems practical and leads to new directions of action

- motivation—the degree to which the consultee will be willing to take action on the defined problem

In addition, ignoring cultural variables in the problem identification stage could lead to misidentification of the problem (Miranda, 2002). Rushing straight to problem solving prior to adequately defining the problem is a common pitfall (Allen & Graden, 2002).

**A Brief Example of Defining the Problem.**    A school administrator asks a school counselor for assistance in determining which programs the school's counseling department should implement. The counselor interviews a select group of administrators, teachers, parents, and students about the types of programs suitable for counseling department sponsorship. Based on these interviews, the department uses four surveys designed for a random sample of each group: administrators, parents, teachers, and students.

The counselor and administrator agree to conceptualize the data analysis based on the common themes that emerge from each of the four surveys. In addition, they agree to look for any program suggestions that are unique to any given set of responders. They ask themselves the following questions: Is there a consensus among the groups concerning the programs the counseling department should sponsor? What program suggestions are unique to each group? What are the implications of this information for planning programs? Survey items are tallied and their relative ranks determined for each of the four groups. A given program would be seriously considered if it is ranked in the top four in importance by two or more groups. The remainder of the data, though not given priority for the development of a particular program, is to be taken into account as the counseling department reviews its entire set of activities.

In general, defining the problem requires the consultant and consultee to interpret the analyzed data according to some mutually accepted conceptual scheme and then determine the data's meanings and limitations. These efforts ideally result in both an appropriately defined problem and a cognitive map for the consultee's future use. Once the problem has been defined to the mutual satisfaction of consultant and consultee, the consultant facilitates a commitment from the consultee to act on it.

# PHASE THREE:
# SETTING GOALS

Setting goals is an important phase in the diagnostic stage because consultation includes solutions and outcomes. Consultants need to be experts in goal setting because it is likely that their consultees will not be (Egan, 1985). Goal setting focuses on which actions will effectively solve or ameliorate the identified problem or problems (Curtis & Stollar, 2002). From a behavioral perspective, a goal is the intended result from an intervention designed to change behavior (Upah & Tilly, 2002). From another perspective, a goal sets the stage for closing the gap between "where we are" and "where we want to be" (French & Bell, 1999).

## The Process of Setting Goals

Goal setting is the central point of the diagnostic process (Egan, 2006, 2007). Because choosing goals establishes what specific ends are to be accomplished, goal setting should not be rushed (Allen & Graden, 2002). If it is, inappropriate or poorly refined goals may be chosen.

Goal setting, then, is a process of shaping, a movement toward concreteness and specificity from a broader, more general perspective. If the problem is complex, the goal of resolving the problem will likely be complex, too (Egan, 1985).

The first step in goal setting is to determine the possible goals related to the problem. Once goal possibilities have been determined, the consultant and consultee engage in the following goal-setting steps (Locke & Latham, 1984, 2002):

1. Specify the task or objective.
2. Specify how the task or objective will be measured.
3. Specify the target or standard to be reached.
4. Specify the time span involved.
5. Prioritize possible goals.
6. Rate goals with respect to difficulty and importance.
7. Determine coordination requirements.

Based on these goal-setting steps, the consultant and consultee choose the most appropriate goal, which is then evaluated and adjusted in light of the characteristics of effective goals.

## Characteristics of Effective Goals

A *goal* is a specific outcome that is sought to solve or improve a problem; a *complex goal* is one that can be divided into subgoals (Egan, 1985). In the context of consultation, success is a complex goal that can be broken down into subgoals: success in each phase of each stage of consultation.

For the goal-setting process to be successful, goals should be written in clear, specific, behavioral terms (Upah & Tilly, 2002). Such specificity facilitates selecting appropriate interventions to solve the problem and evaluating those interventions. Specific goals allow the consultant and consultee to regulate and evaluate the effectiveness of interventions designed to meet those goals. If, for example, a consultant and a consultee determine that the goal is improved morale, it would be insufficient until they specified what they meant by *morale* and *improved*.

Effective goals are verifiable in some way, preferably by measurement. They should be stated in terms of outcomes. Consultants and consultees must determine what should be measured, how it should be measured, and when measurement should take place. Accomplishment of goals can be verified either quantitatively or qualitatively. Measures of quantity include volume and rate, whereas measures of quality include accuracy and novelty (Egan, 1985). Cost-effectiveness—whether the expense in meeting a goal was worth the benefits derived from accomplishing it—should also be taken into consideration. Worthwhile goals are those that are meaningful to the people involved in achieving them; they are considered to be worth the effort required to accomplish them.

Three factors determine whether a goal is realistic: resources, control, and obstacles (Egan, 1985). The consultant and the consultee must determine the adequacy of available resources for accomplishing the goal. Thus, a mental health consultant whose consultee is a teacher may have to determine whether the school has the resources needed to help the teacher's student who suffers from an emotional disturbance. The consultant should ensure that the consultee has some control over whether or not the goal is met, and the consultant and consultee must determine if the goal is adequate.

Obstacles to the accomplishment of any goal must be expected. For example, even though a consultant and consultee may have chosen as a goal the accomplishment of a treatment plan for the consultee's client, the client may not be willing to attend the number of counseling sessions required for effective implementation of the plan. The consultant and consultee should try to anticipate and eliminate any obstacles to the successful accomplishment of a goal.

Goals reflect the values of the people attempting to accomplish them, and they should conform to the values of the consultant, consultee, client system, and the organization. Consultants may occasionally need to help consultees clarify their values so as to set effective goals. Furthermore, consultants may also need to reflect on their own values so that they do not inadvertently impose them on their consultees during this phase of the diagnostic process.

The consultant and consultee should determine who else needs to be informed about goals. Clear communication about goals to parties-at-interest is essential to receiving the cooperation crucial to the accomplishment of the goals, especially when the accomplished goals will affect many of the organization's members. In summary, goals are useful in that they:

- help to focus attention and action

- assist in mobilizing energy and effort

- provide an incentive to determine strategies to achieve them

- promote persistence when they are clear and specific (Egan, 2007, p. 250)

**A Brief Example of Setting Goals.** A social worker is consulting with the principal of a rural school on how to increase involvement with community agencies. In setting goals to accomplish this, the consultant engages the administrator in both brainstorming and scenario writing. They brainstorm on the types of organizations that could become more involved with the school and write scenarios depicting the nature of the involvement for each agency. Based on examining goal possibilities, the consultant and consultee determine that they will contact seven agencies within the next two months and sell them on the idea of becoming more involved with the school. Together they assess the feasibility of the goal, and the social worker agrees to coordinate attempts to accomplish it.

## PHASE FOUR: GENERATING POSSIBLE INTERVENTIONS

Once the consultant and consultee have chosen an acceptable goal, they are ready to enter the last phase of the diagnosis stage—generating possible interventions, sometimes referred to as "strategies," to accomplish the goal. Effective interventions are essential to consultation and collaboration (Upah & Tilly, 2002).

Like goal setting, generating possible interventions is a critical step in the diagnostic stage. Whereas the goal suggests what the consultant and consultee want to accomplish, interventions are things they can do to accomplish that goal. An *intervention* is a force that attempts to modify some outcome. Evidence-based practice refers to the use of interventions that have scientific evidence related to their effectiveness. In consultation, interventions are the actions or activities that, when put together in a systematic manner, make up a plan to achieve a goal.

It would be a mistake for the consultant to assume that because consultees know what goals they want to accomplish, they also know all of the ways to go about accomplishing them. By discussing alternative interventions, consultants can ascertain both the consultee's knowledge of various types of interventions and what the consultee has tried so far to solve the problem. Developing a broad array of interventions to choose from is related to consultee willingness to implement the selected intervention (Gresham & Lopez, 1996). At the same time, only interventions with demonstrated effectiveness should be seriously considered (Allen & Graden, 2002). Evidence-based interventions refer to those that are supported by research evidence (Auster et al., 2006). For example, some consultees may be used to employing interventions with which they are familiar even though there is no empirical evidence or observed consistency that suggest that the interventions are effective. Consultants can encourage effective practices by monitoring the implementation process and providing assistance to consultees as needed to ensure treatment integrity.

Consultants can assist their consultees in generating possible interventions by using prompts (stimuli or reminders) that stimulate the consultee's creativity. These prompts include (Egan, 2006, 2007):

- *people* who might assist the consultee in achieving goals, such as resource people or role models (e.g., a program evaluator for a newly implemented program)

- *places* that might be more appropriate for implementing a plan (e.g., an off-campus location for a faculty retreat)

- *things* that may lead to an easier way of accomplishing a goal (e.g., computer technology for a proposed corporate reorganization)

- *organizations* that could sponsor or assist the consultee in some way (e.g., a private charitable foundation to provide funding for a pilot program)

- *prepackaged programs* whose goals are similar to the consultee's (e.g., a stress management program for teachers at a school)

- *consultee resources* that can be used to a large degree to generate possible interventions, particularly when the consultee will carry out the intervention that is ultimately selected (e.g., the consultee being the counselor for a client about whom a goal has been set)

Brainstorming is a powerful strategy that consultants can use to help consultees generate a list of possible interventions (Curtis & Stollar, 2002; Zins & Erchul, 2002). Such a technique assists the consultant and consultee in going beyond the usual consideration of only one or two intervention alternatives. Whenever a consultee's work-related problem has some unknown factors and some uncertainty about the best way to solve it, it is appropriate to take the time necessary to generate and analyze a list of alternative interventions (Curtis & Stollar, 2002). By following the rules of brainstorming, consultants can increase the probability that consultees will generate an adequate list of possible interventions. The rules of brainstorming include the following (Egan, 2006, 2007):

- Suspend judgments on strategies as they are being generated.

- Generate as many interventions as possible.

- Use piggybacking: use one idea to stimulate others.

- Creativity and novelty are at a premium when generating a list of possible interventions.

Once the consultee understands the ground rules, the consultant and consultee brainstorm for an agreed-upon period (e.g., five minutes). The consultant and consultee should write down or record interventions as they come to mind. After the brainstorming period, the consultant and consultee reconsider and clarify each item to complete this list of possible interventions.

If the consultee is unfamiliar with the brainstorming process, the consultant should provide some practice sessions first. For example, the consultant and consultee could brainstorm ways people could stay dry after being caught out in the rain. Brainstorming does not replace the sound professional judgment of either the consultant or the consultee. Rather, it is simply a technique to enhance the quantity and quality of inputs into the decision-making process. Consultants should be aware that brainstorming is very demanding intellectually, because one must consider the future, examine complex situations, recall previous experiences, and use creativity.

**A Brief Example of Generating Possible Interventions.** A consulting school psychologist and a high school counselor agree that their goal is to alleviate the test anxiety of an international student. To bring to mind possible interventions, the school psychologist asks the school counselor questions, including the following:

- "Who do you think can assist you in your work with this student?"

- "What do you think is the best setting for working with the student?"

- "What things such as CD-ROMs and booklets might be available for you to use?"

- "Are any organizations that work with international students available to be of help?"

- "Do you know of any companies who have prepackaged programs for test anxiety or for helping international students get acclimatized to American schools?"

- "What professional abilities do you have that you can use directly with the student?"

## MULTICULTURAL ASPECTS RELATED TO DIAGNOSIS

Multicultural influences can impact the diagnosis stage (Jackson & Hayes, 1993; Quintana et al., 2000). Consultants will need to adapt accordingly to maximize the conditions for success (Ramirez et al., 1998). For example, a consultee's or fellow collaborator's view of the methods used for data gathering may be influenced by cultural variables such as context (Ortiz & Flanagan, 2002; Sheridan, 2000). Consultees or fellow collaborators from high-context cultures may prefer interviewing or observational methods, whereas those from low-context cultures may prefer methods such as reading documents or conducting surveys.

Consultees of different cultural backgrounds may prefer a fluid definition of the problem, while others prefer a concrete and detailed process of defining the problem so that the major cause is clearly defined (Ramirez et al., 1998; Sheridan, 2000). There can be cultural differences related to perceptions of what goals need to be set. For example, whereas one collaborator may view a whole family as the focal point of the goals, another collaborator may believe a particular member of the family should be the focus. Therefore, consultants need to ensure that goals and problems are defined with cultural context and sensitivity. Cultural differences can play a part in determining what kinds of data are gathered and what interventions are generated. Consultees or fellow collaborators influenced by high cultural context may want to avoid interventions that that they see as time bound, perceive to be overly structured, or view as exclusively dealing with authority figures. Furthermore, the cultural aspects of the client system are a variable in determining the types of interventions that might be successful (Ortiz, 2006; Ortiz & Miranda, 2002; Sheridan, 2000). In addition, collecting information about a culturally different client may necessitate multiple sources and contexts (Castillo et al., 2000; Ortiz, 2006).

## SUMMARY

Diagnosis is a critical stage in consultation. Indeed, if the wrong problem is defined, then the wrong problem is solved. During this stage, the consultant and consultee collaborate in gathering information by various means, in defining a problem from that information, in setting a goal to resolve the problem, and then in generating some possible interventions to accomplish the goal. Diagnosis should not be rushed; consultants should encourage their consultees to remain patient and avoid the tendency to define the problem hastily.

This stage of consultation requires that the consultant and consultee gather the appropriate information necessary for defining the problem. To do this effectively, the consultant and consultee need to know both what information they seek and the

---

**CASE 4.1    Diagnosis for School Consultants**

Geri is a school-based consultant who is working with a teacher concerning a child who has difficulty remaining in his classroom seat. During the diagnosis stage, Geri and the teacher decide that Geri should observe the child in the classroom on at least three different occasions and conduct an informal interview with him. During the observation, Geri is to observe the social conditions that surround the child's getting out of his seat as well as the antecedents and consequences of this behavior. In the interview, Geri is to inform the child that the teacher is concerned about his behavior. The teacher has asked Geri to talk to him about it and about his feelings toward the class, the teacher, his studies, and his own behavior.

Geri conducts the observations, interviews the child, and then meets again with the teacher. Together they determine that the child's behavior is most likely due to the attention he receives from his buddies for disturbing the class. Geri and the teacher discuss what is reasonable behavior for the child, and on the basis of that discussion, they set a reasonable goal for the child to decrease his inappropriate out-of-seat behavior by 50 percent the first month and 75 percent the second month. They decide on a second goal—for the child to increase the frequency of socially acceptable classroom behaviors by 25 percent over a 3-month period. Geri and the teacher begin to brainstorm possible interventions, but they don't evaluate any of the items at this time. They come up with interventions such as a change in the child's seat, a teacher contract with the child, a teacher face-to-face talk with the child, a parent conference that includes the child, a student assistant program, and a realignment of the entire structure of the classroom.

**Commentary**

Diagnosing the problem is a very important element in the consultation process. It is very easy for consultants and consultees to pay lip service to diagnostic procedures in organizations such as schools when there are numerous time constraints. Look at it this way: Would you prefer physicians to perform cursory examinations (that is, data-gathering procedures) on you? Certainly, you wouldn't because they might well be missing significant information related to your well-being. So too in consultation, it is better to ensure that you and the consultee have adequate data so that you have a higher probability of accurately defining the problem.

methods by which they are going to gather it. Because each method of data gathering has its advantages and disadvantages, the consultant and consultee must carefully weigh the pros and cons of each. Furthermore, they need to analyze the data using some valid method that is consistent with the goal of consultation. Both quantitative and qualitative methods can be used in defining the problem.

Once the problem has been defined to the satisfaction of the parties involved, goal setting is initiated. Goal setting, like all phases of diagnosis, should be collaborative to enhance the likelihood that the consultee will obtain an effective set of diagnostic skills for future use.

After setting goals, the consultant and consultee generate a list of possible interventions. This is one

---

### CASE 4.2    Diagnosis for Community Consultants[1]

Martin, a community consultant, was asked by a local hospital to assist in the development of a community AIDS prevention program. Martin's consultees are a community health practitioner, a hospital-community relations coordinator, and a physician with a strong interest in the prospective program.

At one of their first meetings, Martin brought up the idea that a lot of information needed to be gathered to get a focus on how the program might look. He noted that it would be valuable to determine the success of several existing AIDS and HIV education programs. The group reached a consensus that it would be foolish to try developing a program without proper study.

Their first task was to find out about as many of the existing programs as possible. Through Martin's facilitation, the group would review the literature, make calls to existing programs, and visit a few programs that were close to the community. The physician agreed to call several programs, Martin and the hospital/community relations coordinator agreed to review the literature at a local university library, and the entire group agreed to make site visits to three existing programs.

As they reviewed all of the gathered information, one theme became quite evident: Many AIDS and HIV education programs were unsuccessful due to poor planning and lack of community involvement. Martin then helped the group define the problem in terms of the question, "What is the best type of AIDS prevention program for this community?" Once the problem was defined, Martin and the group developed and prioritized a set of goals. In developing the goals by writing a scenario of what a quality program might look like, they realized that a quality program might be beyond the scope of the hospital's resources.

The prioritized goals were to start a publicity campaign to promote the need for an AIDS/HIV education program, develop a task force to promote and plan the program, develop targets for the programs within the community, and develop short- and long-term plans that demonstrate sensitivity to the social and cultural contexts of AIDS/HIV.

The following are some of the series of possible interventions they felt would help in meeting their goals: involve possible target group members in the development of the program; ask target group members to be part of the task force; include culturally relevant content and media in publicizing the need for the program; use community recognition to reward members who assist in the development of the program; and maintain the use of Martin as a consultant for developing short- and long-term plans.

#### Commentary

External scanning can be one of the most effective diagnostic procedures consultants, consultees, and collaborators employ. In your work as a consultant or collaborator, scanning will prevent you from working in a vacuum and from reinventing the wheel. The use of goal setting by writing desired scenarios can be an interesting process for the consultant and consultee to engage in. Such scenarios provide a rich narrative that is often lacking from traditional goal setting statements. Putting goals in priority order enables the consultant and consultee to remain aware of the most important tasks at hand while providing them with a map to guide their efforts. Clearly, diagnosis involves more than figuring out what's the matter.

---

1. The idea for this case study came from the articles in the section entitled, "Special Feature: AIDS and HIV," *Journal of Counseling and Development,* 71(3): 1993, pp. 259–309.

of the more creative phases of diagnosis, and it is also one of the most difficult because consultees may experience conflict and uncertainty about having so many possible courses of action, especially if the majority of them appear to be equally effective in reaching a desired goal (Ashford & Cummings, 1983). Therefore, the consultant may need to assist the consultee in selecting some of the better alternatives. There is some evidence that such direction by the consultant is not a detriment to the consultation process (Houk & Lewandowski, 1996). Ultimately, the major goal of the consultant during this phase is to assist the consultee in developing an adequate number of possible interventions.

The research on diagnosis is sparse. There is some evidence about the frequency with which diagnostic models are used, but none on the relative effectiveness of different approaches to diagnosis. The research on providing consultees with feedback regarding the result of the data-gathering stage indicates that feedback is necessary and desired by consultees, and the response to such feedback is affected by how it is presented (Armenakis & Burdg, 1988).

There is some evidence that enhancing the problem-solving techniques of consultees improves consultee performance during consultation (Zins, 1993). To this end, Zins (1993) suggests that consultees be trained directly in problem-solving and intervention techniques, that consultants provide overt modeling of the problem-solving process for consultees, and that potential consultees receive direct training in problem solving prior to receiving consultation services as part of preservice training.

## SUGGESTIONS FOR EFFECTIVE PRACTICE

- Remember that diagnosis can be an ongoing process and that numerous aspects of the problem may change as time goes on.
- Define the problem and related goals as specifically as you can.

- Use scanning as a tool to give direction to your choice of interventions.
- Involve consultees and fellow collaborators as much as possible in the data-gathering process. Avoid the temptation to bypass the phase of generating possible interventions.

## QUESTIONS FOR REFLECTION

1. What do you envision as the most difficult phase of diagnosis for you to function in? Why?
2. Which 10 skills are most needed by consultants to increase the chances that the diagnosis stage will be successful?
3. Consider your answer to the previous question: in which of these skills do you think most of your consultees will be deficient? Why?
4. What is the most practical way to scan a presenting problem? How would you determine what to scan?
5. How can you best teach consultees to enhance their skills in diagnosis?
6. Which methods of gathering information would you be most likely to use? Why?
7. Once the data have been collected, how does a consultant go about assisting a consultee in defining a problem?
8. Of the characteristics of effective goals mentioned in this chapter, which do you think are the most difficult to meet?
9. How would you assist a consultee in generating a list of several possible interventions?

10. You have now read about the entry and diagnosis stages of consultation. In what ways does the diagnosis stage build on a successfully completed entry stage?

## SUGGESTED SUPPLEMENTARY READINGS

Hohenshil, H. (1996). Editorial: Role of assessment and diagnosis in counseling. *Journal of Counseling and Development, 75,* 64–67. Although published over a decade ago, this article presents a concise and valuable perspective on the role of assessment and diagnosis. Although it focuses on a counseling context, you will find a wealth of information to employ in consultation and collaboration.

# 5

✳

# Implementation Stage

The "action stage" of consultation is implementation. The consultant often functions as a resource person and trainer during this stage. The various models of consultation (Chapters 9–11) conceptualize the implementation process differently and use different types of interventions. A mental health consultant might carefully determine whether the problem in consultation is due to the consultee or to the client before identifying possible interventions. A behavioral consultant might determine which types of reinforcement are most effective with a given client and then choose an intervention that includes those types of reinforcements. An organizational consultant might spend a lot of time determining the level of the organization at which to intervene and then selecting an intervention appropriate to that level. Regardless of the model of consultation in use, however, the process of implementation remains the same.

This chapter covers the implementation stage of consultation, which is composed of four phases: choosing an intervention, formulating a plan, implementing the plan, and evaluating the plan.

As you read through this chapter, here are some questions to consider:

1. How does a consultant assist a consultee in choosing the most appropriate interventions from among those generated at the end of the diagnosis stage?

2. What are the pros and cons of the various types of interventions?

3. How do the consultant and consultee tailor the chosen plan to the organization in which it is to be implemented?

4. What is the consultant's role in implementing the plan?

5. How can the consultant and consultee determine the degree to which the plan was successful?

## INTRODUCTION

Consider for a moment the following:

### A Case of Implementation

A staff development coordinator in a human service organization has been working with a consultant on some of the organization's concerns about improving the quality of its work environment. The co-ordinator's immediate superior calls the coordinator in and asks what progress has been made with the consultant. The coordinator indicates that the problem has been identified, explored, and analyzed. Furthermore, several prospective interventions have been identified. The supervisor then asks what the next steps will be. The staff development coordinator replies that a plan will be formulated and the logistics of implementing it worked out. The plan will then be put into action and evaluated. The supervisor then asks for a time frame within which all of this will occur.

This sequence of events is quite common in consultation. Often, people within the organization in which consultation is occurring have relatively little idea about how complex and time consuming effective consultation is. The staff development coordinator was in essence telling the supervisor that consultation had progressed to the implementation stage. She and the consultant were ready to choose among the several possible interventions they had devised, formulate a plan, tailor it to the organization's needs, put it into action, and then evaluate the degree to which it works. Clearly, good planning is essential to successful consultation, yet it is very easy to neglect. Because every plan has its advantages, disadvantages, and possible glitches, there is no one best plan, but rather one that has the highest probability of succeeding.

Figure 5.1 illustrates the phases of the implementation stage. In choosing an intervention, the consultant and consultee answer the question, "What are we going to do?" In formulating a plan, they answer the question, "How are we going to do it?" They actively try to solve the problem in the phase of implementing the plan, and in evaluating the plan they

ask "How did we do?" As was the case in the entry and diagnosis stages, the implementation stage is critical in the consultation process: Imagine the difficulties that would be encountered if an inappropriate plan were chosen for a given problem. The consultant and consultee would come up with the wrong solution for the right problem. Or if a proper plan was chosen but the wrong interventions were used, the consultant and consultee might have the right solution put together in the wrong way.

In the implementation stage, the client or client system is now ready for some form of direct assistance from the consultee or indirect service from the consultant. The consultant must make sure that the consultee formulates an appropriate plan and correctly implements it; evaluating the plan is one of the consultant's highest priorities. Consider a situation in which the right plan, the right strategies, and correct implementation are combined, but the consultant and consultee have failed to design an appropriate evaluation of the plan. In this situation, the consultant and consultee have no way of accurately determining the degree to which the plan actually worked.

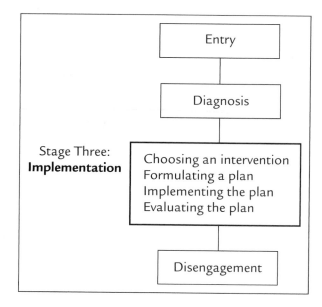

**FIGURE 5.1**    The phases of the implementation stage

The consultant may need to train the consultee in the interventions implemented during this stage; for example, a mental health consultant might need to train the consultee, a school counselor, in a specific procedure for assisting a child with school phobia. As in other stages in the consultation process, consultants take a collaborative approach whenever possible and avoid doing anything for consultees that they can do for themselves. In addition, the consultant typically relies on the consultee for information about the culture of the consultee's organization and the exact role of the consultee relative to the client system (Erchul & Schulte, 1993).

The implementation stage is important to the consultee because it represents some action on the problem that prompted the request for assistance in the first place. In this stage, the consultee either makes some intervention with a client system or benefits directly from some intervention by the consultant, who assumes that the experience will give the consultee useful skills for handling similar work-related concerns in the future.

# PHASE ONE: CHOOSING AN INTERVENTION

One of the most formidable challenges is to identify effective interventions prior to their implementation (Kratochwill & Shernoff, 2004; Noell et al., 2000). Since consultees may have a large number of interventions available to them, they may experience conflict because all of the interventions look good. The selection of interventions needs to be linked to assessing those interventions (Levinson, 2002). Furthermore, consultees may prefer interventions that they are familiar with, they think are easy to implement, are the most practical (Martens & Ardoin, 2002), and for which they perceive that they have the necessary knowledge and skills (Egan, 2007). Therefore, the first phase of the implementation stage involves selecting one or more interventions that have a high probability of success.

One way to accomplish this is to make sure that all of the interventions under consideration have research to back their efficacy, that is, they are evidence-based (Barnett, Vander Heyden, & Witt, 2007; Gibbs, 2003; Hoard & Shepard, 2005). Other ways involve addressing the social factors that bear upon the problem (Farmer, 2000), considering the costs and benefits of the intervention (Topping & Ehly, 2001), and developing an intervention that readily fits into the consultee's other responsibilities (Allen & Graden, 2002; Noell & Witt, 1998). In addition, consultants should remember that knowing about a wide range of potential interventions is not enough. As Elliott and Busse (1993) note, consultants must also be "sensitive to the skills and perceptions of their consultees and be able to clearly communicate treatment procedures so that they are implemented with integrity" (p. 194).

Although proposed over three decades ago by Janis and Mann (1977), one effective procedure the consultant can still use in helping a consultee choose among possible interventions is based upon their decision counseling. Although developed for use in counseling and psychotherapy, this procedure is useful for ensuring that the consultee goes through the process of choosing an intervention in an appropriate manner. The process of *decision consultation,* which is based on effective decision making, consists of eight questions consultants can ask consultees. The following questions are adaptations of those developed by Janis and Mann (1977, p. 371):

- To what degree has the consultee developed a wide range of alternative interventions?

- To what degree has the consultee considered the objectives and related values of the possible interventions?

- To what degree has the consultee weighed the potential negative consequences, risks, and potential payoffs of each intervention?

- To what degree has the consultee searched for new information relative to each intervention?

- To what degree has the consultee processed the consultant's comments about potential positive and negative factors related to the interventions?

- To what degree has the consultee made a final determination of the interventions' potential positive and negative consequences, as well as the driving and inhibiting forces that affect their implementation?

- To what degree does the consultee have the capacity to successfully execute the chosen intervention?

- Which interventions have been set aside for use in contingency plans?

By engaging the consultee in the pursuit of answers to these questions, the consultant can help the consultee make a reasonably effective choice of interventions and can ascertain not only the degree to which the implementation appears satisfactory to the consultee, but also whether any adaptation of the intervention by the consultee will negatively affect its impact. The use of this process helps to ensure that the intervention selected is logically related to the information gathered and is congruent with the reasons the problem is believed to exist (Allen & Graden, 2002). In addition, the process involved in this kind of assistance can rub off on the consultee, who can then be more effective in choosing interventions for similar problems in the future.

By engaging in decision consultation, the consultant can increase the probability that the consultee will follow through with the agreed-upon intervention. Research suggests that consultees do not always follow through on the intervention they are supposed to implement. Later in this chapter, you will read about the concept of treatment integrity and the way to enhance consultee commitment to interventions. Whether consultees will accept an intervention appears to be a function of their perception of the fit between the problem and the intervention, their beliefs about the intervention (e.g., humaneness), the level of difficulty in implementing it (Erchul & Chewning, 1990), the quality of the consultant-consultee relationship (Conoley, Conoley, Ivey, & Scheel, 1991), the consultee's values (Egan, 2007), and its compatibil-

ities with behavioral routines in the consultee's work setting (Noell & Witt, 1998). Therefore, the consultant should address these considerations when developing a rationale for an intervention. In addition, in selecting an intervention, the consultant and consultee should examine the following questions (Gutkin & Curtis, 1999):

- Do we believe that the intervention will really work?

- Can the consultee implement with high levels of treatment integrity?

- Does the consultee see it as part of his or her duties to carry out the intervention?

- Is the intervention in line with the consultee's perception of what needs to be done?

- Does the intervention fit relatively easily with the consultee's routine?

Being able to explain a wide variety of interventions from several different perspectives is a very desirable skill for consultants (Conoley et al., 1991), and it helps to avoid considering a limited number of interventions due to bias or favored interventions. Decision consultation also helps facilitate the use of more idiosyncratic, innovative, research-oriented interventions (Barnett & Lentz, 1993). Consultants should be aware of potential obstacles to the successful completion of this phase. First, the consultee and consultant must process a tremendous amount of information in selecting the intervention (Wheeler & Janis, 1980). Second, it is difficult to predict realistically the specific outcomes of various interventions due to the possibility of unforeseen events and potential human error (Lentz, Allen, & Erhardt, 1996). In order to facilitate discussion about the possible impacts of given interventions, the consultant should therefore consider having the consultee keep a consistent, detailed set of notes concerning alternative interventions. One possible method of maintaining such a record is to use a balance-sheet method that deals with the acceptability and unacceptability of benefits and costs of various interventions (Egan, 2007). The process of supporting the intervention should also be taken into consideration. In other words, the technical components need to be blended together with an ecological understanding of the problem setting (Lentz et al., 1996). There are some additional guidelines that can assist consultants and consultees in choosing an adequate intervention (Gutkin & Curtis, 1999; Zins & Erchul, 2002):

- Try to use positive interventions first.

- Avoid complex and intrusive interventions.

- If the consultee is to learn a new skill, incorporate it into daily routines as much as possible.

- Promote interventions that require the least amount of time.

- In addition to empirical research on the intervention, rely on the consultee variables discussed previously.

The issue of *empirically supported interventions* (ESI), also often referred to as *evidence-based interventions* (EBI) (Cox, 2005; Gibbs, 2003; Guli, 2005), has come to the forefront in the consultation/ collaboration literature, particularly in school-based consultation (Graden, 2004; Stoiber & Kratochwill, 2000; Wilkinson, 2005). School reforms—such as those dictated by the No Child Left Behind Act, developments in the field of special education, and gap between research and practice—have all stressed the importance of evidenced-based activities (Kratochwill & Shernoff, 2004; Merrell et al., 2006). These developments have risen, not without implementation issues (Kratochwill & Shernoff, 2004), from the idea that scientific inquiry should guide practice. For community consultants, our nation's health care delivery system and its focus on accountability has led to an emphasis on evidenced-based interventions. Depending on the consultee's skill level related to implementing the intervention, the consultant should be prepared to provide indirect training (e.g., didactic instruction) or direct training (e.g., modeling) (Sterling-Turner et al., 2002). The main idea is that by having a catalog of evidence-based interventions, consultants can be linked to research in their practice. This practice, of course, puts the consultant in the expert mode. The major strategies for introducing EBI include developing a practice-research network, promoting research on the efficacy of EBIs, and establishing guidelines for the implementation and evaluation of EBIs by practitioners (Kratochwill & Shernoff, 2004). EBI is not without controversy. For a pertinent discussion, see Egan (2007).

## Types of Interventions

You are hungry, so you decide to go to a restaurant that offers a smorgasbord. As you walk through the smorgasbord, you have a difficult time selecting from among the offerings because they all look so good. You decide to choose one item that is representative of each of the four food groups. So you choose one meat, one dairy product, one cereal product, and one green vegetable—and then you proceed to enjoy your meal. You have, in effect, just classified all of your possible food choices into four categories and then chosen from each of them. By categorizing your options, you made your decision about what to eat much easier.

Indeed, consultants and consultees have a smorgasbord of interventions available to them. Therefore, consultants typically categorize all the possible interventions that might be put together in order to expedite the decision-making process. In dealing with a problem situation, an intervention can be a single task, a series of related tasks, or a series of unrelated tasks organized around a common theme. One or more unique interventions can be put together systematically into a plan that is tailored to the identified problem.

Effective consultants have a large number of interventions in their repertoire to most effectively assist their consultees. Such expertise allows the consultant flexibility in combining programs to meet the goals of consultation. Do you know about the carpenter who could only use a hammer? He saw every problem as a nail to be hit. Consultants who do not have knowledge of and skill in many types of interventions tend to conceptualize solutions in terms of what they know how to do instead of what is really needed.

A useful device for obtaining a broad perspective on interventions is a classification system. A categorization of interventions based on primary target groups is a convenient one and is used in the following discussion. The target group is usually the client system. A classification scheme developed by French and Bell (1999) includes the following targets: individuals, dyads/triads, teams and groups, intergroup relations, and the total organization. Though developed for interventions in organizational consultation, this scheme can easily make up a generic classification system useful to all consultants.

## Individual Interventions

Because individual interventions can also be designed to assist the organization as a whole by improving the functioning of selected individual members, individual interventions can apply in a variety of consultation settings. The previous chapter discussed ways to determine when individual interventions are appropriate. Fuqua and Newman (1985) suggest that consultants commonly use two general types of individual interventions: consultee-focused intervention and educational/training intervention. In effect, all individual consultation interventions attempt to assist the consultee by alleviating a lack of knowledge, skill, confidence, or objectivity.

Consultee-focused interventions are used when the consultee is experiencing a work-related problem due to a lack of objectivity or confidence or a lack of skill in problem solving and decision making (Caplan & Caplan, 1993). Educational/training methods are used when the consultee has a knowledge or skills deficit in a given area or desires self-improvement in a given area. In school-based consultation, individual interventions are typically either academic or behavioral. These interventions are often used in prereferral intervention programs before considering eligibility for special programs (McDougal, Clonan, & Martens, 2000).

**Academic Interventions.**  For many school-based consultants, student academic problems are the most common source for consultation (Bramlett et al., 2002; Jitendra et al., 2007). Academic difficul-

ties can be caused by a variety of variables, including student behavior (Noell, 2002; Noell & Witt, 1998). In some cases, students don't have the academic skills to learn. In others, students have the appropriate academic skills but still don't learn adequately, thus suggesting a disability or an inadequate learning environment. Academic interventions typically include those related to students' learning behaviors, teachers' instructional behaviors, and instructional materials and practices (Elliott, Busse, & Shapiro 1999; Kampwirth, 2006). Among the academic interventions with strong empirical support are school-home notes (e.g., daily report cards); providing students with constructive feedback on their performance, training students in self-management techniques, peer tutoring, and cooperative learning (Elliott et al., 1999); as well as other instructional principles such as pacing (Kratochwill, Elliott, & Callan-Stoiber, 2002).

**Behavioral Interventions.**  Consultants have a broad array of interventions available to assist consultees in changing the behavior of the client system. However, detailed discussion of behavioral interventions is beyond the scope of this text. From a school-based perspective, problem behavior can result from lack of knowledge or skills, the fact that the problem behavior is more rewarding than non-problem behavior, and that problem behavior is a way to avoid the demands of things like school work (Martens & Ardoin, 2002). Interventions should then be designed using positive behavioral support in such a way that appropriate behavior is rewarded. For example, a student can be reinforced with praise from a teacher for engaging in a new behavior (Martens & Ardoin, 2002). Kampwirth (2006) lists commonly used behavior-related interventions in schools:

- general preventative techniques (e.g., classroom rules)
- contingency management and contracting
- non-contingency interventions (e.g., modeling appropriate behavior)

- social skills training
- conferencing

## Consultee-Centered Case Consultation

This intervention is one approach to the mental health consultation model and is given in-depth coverage in Chapter 9. This approach suggests that the problem in consultation resides in the consultee (e.g., lack of skill). Consultee-centered consultation is given renewed attention in the consultation literature (Caplan & Caplan-Moskovich, 2004; Knotek & Sandoval, 2003).

## Dyadic and Triadic Interventions

Sometimes consultants are called on to make interventions that are most effective with groups of two (dyads) or groups of three (triads). Interventions aimed at these small groups are limited but popular due to frequent use of dyadic and triadic work groups in human service organizations. Some of the types of interventions that are useful with individuals can be used to increase effectiveness of dyads and triads. Furthermore, many of the interventions typically aimed at large groups, such as team building, are appropriate for use with these small groups.

**Third-Party Peacemaking.**   Conflict, common in most organizations, usually stems from parties' different perspectives on the same events. Consultants will frequently be called upon to deal with conflict management (French & Bell, 1999; McLean, 2006). Differences between two consultees can be effectively dealt with in a variety of ways, including third-party peacemaking (Golembiewski & Rauschenberg, 1993), an intervention unique to dyads and triads, which is used to resolve interpersonal conflict.

The consultant guides a process in which two parties directly confront one another and use conflict resolution techniques, such as those developed by Fisher, Ury, and Patton (1991) or Walton (1987). The term "third party" refers to the consultant, who presumably is skilled and objective in

terms of the conflict's resolution or management. The consultant is interested in improving the conditions and the manner in which the conflicting parties manage the conflict.

## Interventions for Groups and Teams

Organizations make extensive use of teams and groups (French & Bell, 1999), and consultants are frequently called on to make interventions to enhance the effectiveness of an intact group or team. Interventions with groups or teams can be one of the most powerful of consultant interventions. The most common group or team intervention is the education/training approach, which is covered extensively in Chapter 11. Other interventions are described here.

**Team Building.**   A team is a group of individuals working together in a coordinated effort. There is increasing attention being paid to developing leadership teams through team building (Rawlings, 2000), particularly in the area of cross-cultural team building which includes cross-cultural training (McLean, 2006). Team building is the process by which a team's individuals attempt to improve the group's functioning through analyzing and evaluating their interactions (French & Bell, 1999). The term "team building" came about because selected interventions lead to increases in team cohesiveness and effectiveness. Note that the consultant is not a member of the team with which he or she is working.

During team building the consultant acts as a facilitator and a collaborator. The consultant typically interviews each team member individually, examining the strengths and weaknesses of the team. The strengths and weaknesses are grouped and presented to the team for prioritization. The team then analyzes the selected issues and sets an action plan to effectively deal with them. The consultant follows up periodically to determine if the expected results have been achieved. Special attention is paid to how the team's various members use power.

**Nominal Group Technique.**   The nominal group technique (NGT) was originally developed by Delbecq, Van de Ven, and Gustafson (1975) in the mid-1970s. The NGT is a group problem-solving process designed specifically for engendering the members' involvement and creativity. Its purpose is to involve groups in determining solutions to issues and problems.

The NGT is based on two assumptions: that all group members need only the proper encouragement to induce them to express their ideas, and that the exchange of ideas and group decision making contribute to greater acceptance of decisions by the individuals involved. The NGT is a structured problem-solving meeting with a "one-person-one-vote" orientation; superiors and subordinates all have equal status in the NGT. The technique yields a large quantity of high-quality, specific ideas and encourages independent thinking by participants.

The process is highly motivating, and participants experience the satisfaction of task accomplishment, as well as the social reinforcement of having worked effectively together. The consultant acts as a facilitator of the problem solving process, as well as a taskmaster who ensures that the steps of the NGT process are completed (Sandland & Dougherty, 1985).

**Quality Circles.** Quality circles are small problem-solving groups (French & Bell, 1999) whose members are typically from the same work area. The groups meet for one to two hours per week to discuss concerns, investigate the sources of those concerns, make recommendations, and take authorized corrective action. A primary purpose of these circles is to enhance product quality. The sharing of information is essential in quality circles (Kovach, 1998). According to one of the early writers in this area (Dewar, 1980), the objective of quality circles is to improve work quality, productivity, and motivation.

The consultant's primary role with regard to quality circles is educating and training potential members and administrators in the ways quality circles work. Consultants may want to recommend that quality circle participants are highly rewarded because of the stress of participation (Jennings, 1988). The quality circle concept has expanded to include quality improvement teams. The primary difference is that quality circles tend to focus on one task or

issue, whereas quality improvement teams tend to be more permanent and focus on issues related to emerging issues of quality.

**Work Teams.** Work teams are "small groups of interdependent individuals who share responsibility for outcomes for their organizations" (Sundstrom, DeMeuse, & Futrell, 1990, p. 120). Consultants can make use of work teams in meeting the goals of consultation, usually by taking on the role of facilitating an environment in which the team can function effectively (Conyne et al., 1997; Kovach, 1998). There are four basic applications of work groups: advice and involvement, production and service, projects and development, and action and negotiation.

Teams whose purpose is advice and involvement typically have a short group life, are not extensively linked to other units in the organization, and provide proposals and recommendations (Sundstrom et al., 1990). For example, a consultant facilitates a group of therapists in determining ways to provide more timely services to clients while at the same time cutting down the length of time allocated to staffing.

Production and service groups are teams that may have a brief or extended group life, relate their work to what other units in the organization are doing, typically repeat their processes, and provide coordinated services (Sundstrom et al., 1990). Consultants assist groups such as these by using group dynamics principles and processes to enhance communication and productivity (Conyne et al., 1997), as well as explaining the advantages of team versus individual work (French & Bell, 1999). For example, a school counselor works with an individualized education program (IEP) team to provide the best service to a student with behavior disorders.

Teams that handle projects and development usually have a brief group life, are made up of individuals from a variety of specialties, and generally produce a report as their output. For example, a consultant assists a community task force charged with developing an AIDS awareness program.

Action and negotiation teams often engage in the same brief event many times, have specialists as members of the team, and coordinate their actions with other parties-at-interest (Sundstrom et al., 1990). For example, a group of consultants provides training in mediation skills for a group of school counselors and psychologists.

## Interventions for Use between Groups

Human service organizations are made up of several groups that interact with and affect one another. One group frequently experiences tension or conflict with one or more other groups within the same organization. Consultants can assist groups to relate more effectively by using strategies designed to alleviate group conflict. Two or more interdependent groups are put together as a single unit and engage in joint activities (French & Bell, 1999).

The two major types of intergroup interventions—team building and organizational mirroring—work because the group interactions are structured to maintain control (French & Bell, 1999). All information is shared between groups: there are no secrets, and the consultant engenders a spirit of constructive problem solving (French & Bell, 1999).

**Intergroup Team Building.** Intergroup team-building activities attempt to improve the communication and cooperation between two groups, reduce inappropriate group competition, and develop recognition of group interdependence (French & Bell, 1999). The accomplishment of these tasks can lead to more harmonious functioning within and between the groups.

**Organizational Mirroring.** When the increased effectiveness of three or more groups is desired, including reducing conflict (McLean, 2006), organizational mirroring is frequently used (French & Bell, 1999). In this technique, one group, called the host group, receives feedback from other groups about the ways it is perceived; the technique's goal is to change the host group. To keep the number of participants manageable, representatives of each of the groups (rather than the entire membership of each group) are involved. As in intergroup team building, the consultant acts as the process's facilitator, enforcer of norms, and coordinator. As an example, a consultant might lead while a group of school counselors (host team) receives feedback from select groups of administrators and staff on their perceptions of the counseling department's programs.

## Interventions for the Entire Organization

Interventions that attempt to enhance an entire organization's effectiveness are called organizational interventions. Many interventions used primarily at the organizational level can also be used as intergroup and team interventions. Consultants who intervene at the organizational level must be experts in organizational theory and dynamics, in addition to having the basic skills required of all consultants. The most common organizational interventions include total quality management, survey feedback/action research, parallel learning structures, and strategic planning.

**Total Quality Management.** Total quality management (TQM) is a combination of many of the interventions discussed in this chapter. Also called "total quality improvement," this model, along with its offshoot, Six Sigma, emphasizes teams, a focus on service, measurement of objectives, and a major emphasis on continuous training (David & Strang, 2006; McLean, 2006). Major concepts include "customer focus, reduction of variability, continuous improvement and employee participation" (David & Strang, 2006, p. 216). The role of the consultant is to assist with the training in any of the methods or in providing instruction in total quality philosophy. For example, a school-based consultant might work with a group of teachers on implementing total quality concepts into their classroom instruction.

**Survey Feedback/Action Research.** Survey feedback/action research owes much of its development to the social psychologist Kurt Lewin (1945, 1951). It is a problem-solving intervention designed to systematically collect data about some system (through surveys and/or interviews), analyze the data, and feed results back to appropriate personnel in workshop settings (French & Bell, 1999). The problem is diagnosed and action steps are planned during the workshop meetings. One underlying assumption of this approach is that whatever discrepancies are noted from interpreting the data will create the motivation to change things (French & Bell, 1999). Another underlying assumption is that ongoing feedback is necessary to keep the organization on course in terms of its role and mission. Survey feedback/action research takes on a cyclical approach: research, data collection, feedback, planning, action, and evaluation (McLean, 2006). Depending on the outcome of evaluation, the process may be repeated.

**Parallel Learning Structures.**   One common organizational intervention consultants can recommend is the parallel learning structure (also called a collateral organization)—a small unit within the existing organization. It is very much like a task force except that it is permitted to work outside the existing norms of the larger organization. This license to create its own norms allows the collateral organization the freedom necessary to attack problems that are difficult for the larger organization to solve. This intervention is used with high-priority, systemwide problems that involve people from more than one section of the organization. Parallel structures allow for the determination of the type of change needed, and this determination then becomes the vehicle for leading the change initiative (French & Bell, 1999). The consultant acts as a resource person to administrators and to the members of the collateral organization itself. However, the consultant does not meet formally with the collateral group except on an as-needed basis.

**Strategic Planning.**   Strategic planning is a forward-looking visionary intervention process that helps organizations deal better with the future (Fuqua & Kurpius, 1993; Kormanski & Eschbach, 1997). It emphasizes process over product, separates vision from the steps to accomplish that vision, sees change as a positive force, involves as many people in the

organization as possible, is long term by nature, and takes into consideration the needs and security of the people involved in the planning (Fuqua & Kurpius, 1993). The process typically involves goal development, environmental analysis, strategy development, strategy evaluation, strategy implementation, and strategic control (French & Bell, 1999). It often employs SWOT (strengths, weaknesses, opportunities, threats) (McLean, 2006). The main roles of the consultant are to make sure everyone involved understands the process (such as how to engage in internal and external scanning), guide the consultees in determining where they want the organization to go and how they are going to get there, as well as develop specific action and monitoring plans. Strategic planning has been increasingly used in educational settings (Knoff, 2002).

Because choosing an intervention varies somewhat in consultation and collaboration, I use the same scenario to provide examples below of choosing an intervention in each.

**A Brief Example of Choosing an Intervention in Consultation.**   Ellen, the head of a community agency serving developmentally disabled adults, has been consulting with Lisa, a mental health worker specializing in consulting to management. Ellen is feeling all of the pressures associated with being placed in charge of an important program. The diagnosis has pointed to Ellen's deficiency in management training. Lisa and Ellen discuss the large array of interventions that could be made in this situation and select several interventions that seem likely to be successful. Lisa leads Ellen through the decision consultation by asking her eight questions related to her concern about the lack of management skills. Based on outcomes to these questions and a determination of Ellen's beliefs about the possible interventions, Lisa and Ellen choose a general intervention, shadow consultation, in which Lisa will follow Ellen at work for three days. Lisa will then provide feedback on possible management skills Ellen may want to pursue as part of her professional development plan.

**A Brief Example of Choosing an Intervention in Collaboration.**   Ellen, the head of a community agency serving developmentally disabled adults, has been collaborating with Lisa, a mental health worker in the agency specializing in consulting to management. Ellen is feeling all of the pressures associated with being placed in charge of an important program. Lisa is concerned that she needs to be more effective in her work of providing more effective services to the management of the agency. The diagnosis has pointed to Ellen's deficiency in management training and Lisa's lack of a systematic plan for assisting management. Lisa and Ellen discuss the large array of interventions that could be made in this situation and select several interventions that seem likely to be successful. Together, Lisa and Ellen engage in decision consultation by asking and answering the eight questions related to their concerns. Based on outcomes to these questions and a determination of their beliefs about the possible interventions, Lisa and Ellen choose a general intervention, shadow consultation, in which Lisa will follow Ellen at work for three days. Lisa will then provide feedback on possible management skills Ellen may want to pursue as part of her professional development plan. They also choose a focus-group approach through which Lisa will determine more effective approaches for her providing her services. Ellen, who has expertise in conducting focus groups, agrees to help monitor Lisa's progress.

## PHASE TWO: FORMULATING A PLAN

Once the consultant and consultee have been able to decide on one or more interventions that have a high probability of helping meet their goal, they begin formulating a plan. For our purposes, formulating a plan refers to joining the pieces of the interventions into a sequence and generating appropriate time lines (Egan, 2007). It is critical in this planning phase that the consultant emphasize the collaborative nature of consultation to ensure that the consultee has a ready-made commitment to the plan (Erchul & Chewning, 1990). It is usually best for the consultant and consultee to formulate a few possible

plans and then choose the plan that appears to have the highest probability of succeeding.

Good plans shape successful consultation outcomes. When formulating a plan, the consultant and consultee should consider the *what* (objectives), the *where* (locale of the implementation), the *when* (time frame), the *how* (methods, procedures, sequence), and the *who* (who is responsible for which elements) (Upah & Tilly, 2002). In doing so, the consultant and consultee can plan more effectively.

Plan formulation is a complex activity that requires time to accomplish adequately. The consultant and consultee first determine the plan's objectives, choose its procedures, and establish the time frame in which it is to be carried out. Next, they assign responsibility for carrying out each part of the plan. Each step is scrutinized again and adjusted as necessary. Finally, they assess the plan in terms of its feasibility, cost effectiveness, and capability to succeed.

Consultants and consultees should adhere to several principles of formulating plans (Egan, 1985). Plans should be clearly linked to the established goals; a connection must exist between what the consultant and consultee want to accomplish and how they are going to accomplish it. A variety of plans to accomplish set goals should be constructed and examined. Brainstorming is a helpful procedure for generating a variety of plans. Plans should be evaluated in terms of the criteria of effectiveness, efficiency, and ability to meet human needs. Steps in plans should be viewed as subgoals, and measures should be taken to see that the subgoals meet the criteria of effective goals. Plans should have reasonable time frames for completion and be sufficiently detailed. Finally, plans should be examined in terms of their feasibility as contingency plans. It is a good practice to have a "Plan B."

Once plans have been formulated, the consultant and consultee choose a plan. One common way of choosing the best plan is *force-field analysis,* a method of determining the driving and restraining forces affecting the accomplishment of a goal (Egan, 2007; Lewin, 1951). Restraining forces inhibit movement toward a plan's successful implementation, and driving forces support the plan's successful outcome. Force-field analysis helps consultees gain perspective on possible plans' pitfalls and strong points, and such awareness allows consultees to adapt plans to the specific settings in which clients are being served.

In using force-field analysis, the consultant has the consultee review each plan that has been generated. For each plan, the major restraining and driving forces, identified by brainstorming, are listed and examined in detail. Depending on the plan, one or more restraining and driving forces over which the consultee has some control are identified for modification. The consultee and consultant then brainstorm ways to minimize the selected restraining forces and maximize the selected driving forces for each of the plans. They look at the relative weights of the restraining and driving forces, and those plans whose restraining forces outweigh their driving forces are discarded. From the remaining plans, one plan and a backup contingency plan are chosen. Specific adaptations of the plan to the unique needs of the client or client system are worked out.

In addition to using techniques such as force-field analysis, the consultant and consultee can work together to create a checklist to avoid the following pitfalls, which frequently contribute to the failure of plans (Egan, 2007):

- trying to accomplish too much
- formulating too large a plan
- overanalyzing the plan, which causes disinterest and resistance
- under-analyzing the plan and failing to anticipate pertinent problems
- failing to consider the plan's system-wide impact
- inadequately defining the plan's desired outcomes
- failing to consider the human-side factors

As a final safeguard, the consultant and consultee may want to "walk through" the process one time to see who is affected in what ways by the plan.

In summary, to choose a plan, the consultant helps the consultee consider each plan's compre-

hensiveness, positive and negative consequences, and the adequacy of the consultee's information about each plan. The consultant checks out the acceptability of the treatment by helping the consultee make a judgment of the appropriateness and likely effectiveness of the selected intervention (Dunson et al., 1994). High treatment acceptability indicates a high level of willingness to proceed with the intervention in the situation at hand, making it more likely that the consultee will both stick with the intervention and implement it appropriately (Kratochwill & Stoiber, 2000a). Furthermore, the consultant helps the consultee integrate the consultant's input regarding the plans and makes a final check of each plan's potential positive and negative consequences. The plan builds upon the natural interaction between the consultee and the client system and the realities of the environment in which the plan is to be carried out (Lentz et al., 1996). Plans can keep the consultee from being overwhelmed and uncover unanticipated obstacles. Finally, the consultant assesses the consultee's capacity to carry out plans and develop contingencies successfully.

**A Brief Example of Plan Formulation in Consultation.** A school counselor is consulting with a school principal about the most appropriate type of in-school suspension program. They develop three possible plans for operating the program: a punitive approach, a "time-out" approach, and a counseling approach. The pros and cons of each approach are weighed, and the consultant makes sure that the administrator possesses adequate knowledge of the basis for each plan. The consultant's input into the various plans is clarified and a force-field analysis is applied to each. Together they decide that the in-school suspension plan with a counseling focus is the best plan; the "time-out" approach is chosen as a contingency.

**A Brief Example of Plan Formulation in Collaboration.** A school counselor and a school principal are collaborating about the most appropriate type of in-school suspension program. They develop three possible plans for operating the program:

a punitive approach, a "timeout" approach, and a counseling approach. The pros and cons of each approach are weighed, and the school counselor makes sure that the administrator possesses adequate knowledge of the basis for each plan. The administrator ensures that the school counselor is aware of how to deal with the organizational dynamics of program implementation. A force-field analysis is applied to each possibility. Together they decide that the in-school suspension plan with a counseling focus is the best plan; the "time-out" approach is chosen as a contingency. They agree to implement the program by each taking on a variety of the responsibilities.

## PHASE THREE: IMPLEMENTING THE PLAN

Now that the consultee and consultant or collaborators have narrowed the possibilities and formulated a plan, they are ready for action. The plan designed in the previous phase is now put into operation, and the focus of consultation turns to making sure that the plan is followed in such a way that it achieves the desired results.

Although putting a plan into action seems quite straightforward on the surface, it is actually a very complex process; planning needs to involve strategies for effective implementation (Ervin & Erhardt, 2000; Riley-Tillman & Chafouleas, 2003). This phase dictates that consensus needs to be reached on items such as the roles taken and the timing of any monitoring by the consultant (Kratochwill, Elliott, & Callan-Stoiber, 2002). For example, the consultant and consultee should engage in role analysis (Golembiewski, 1993b) to ascertain who is responsible for the tasks involved while recognizing that each brings unique skills to the problem-solving process (Lentz et al., 1996). Furthermore, the consultant should reassure the consultee that events sometimes get in the way of the plan's implementation and that most often this is due to factors in the complex real-life environment in which all interventions must eventually be made.

The consultant can increase the probability of successful plan implementation by providing logistical and tactical assistance. *Logistics* refers to the provision of resources in a timely manner. *Tactics* is the art of adapting a plan (program) to the immediate situation (Egan, 2007), possibly on short notice. Therefore, consultants should consider maintaining contact with consultees during the implementation phase.

Consultant availability can be a critical factor in the success of an intervention because of the reliance on the consultee (who may not be as well trained as the consultant) to carry out the intervention. By monitoring the consultee's implementation of the intervention, the consultant is, in effect, providing a quality control mechanism to the process (Tilly, 2002). Careful monitoring by the consultant will help to ensure that the consultee has or acquires the skills necessary for reflective implementation. It will also provide the contact necessary to prohibit consultees who think they have the necessary skills from implementing a procedure which, in reality, they lack the ability to implement (Caplan et al., 1994).

Because the consultant and consultee made plans jointly, it is reasonable to assume that the consultee may welcome contact with the consultant during implementation (Conoley & Conoley, 1992). Such contact can be in the form of technical assistance (for example, plan revision) or emotional and cognitive support (for example, encouraging the consultee to take risks). For example, the consultant may engage in the functional outcome analysis (FOA) in order to evaluate or monitor interventions (Noell & Gresham, 1993) or assist with a response to intervention initiative (Barnett et al., 2007). In collaboration, of course, both parties are responsible for some aspect of the implementation of the plan. As a result, they will provide the necessary support to one another during the implementation.

Some consultants monitor the consultee's intervention efforts through a series of brief interviews and/or observations of the consultee during the implementation process (Bergan & Kratochwill, 1990). Such contact allows consultants to gather data from the consultee concerning the effectiveness of the intervention; this data can range from a description of the consultee's and client's behavior during the intervention to measurements of changes in the client. A note of caution: during the implementation phase the consultant must exercise care to prevent excessive dependency in some consultees who may inadvertently rely too heavily on the consultant's expertise (French & Bell, 1999). For example, a school counselor consulting with a teacher might judiciously use questions to stimulate the teacher to take more responsibility for implementing the plan. In collaboration, the monitoring is typically accomplished through team meeting in which team members report on their progress and receive input from the others.

There are some principles of effective implementation that I have extracted from the work of Egan (2007) with counseling clients, and I have applied them to consultation and collaboration:

- develop a strong commitment to specific interventions to accomplish goals

- ensure that consultees don't jump on the first implementation they brainstorm

- assist consultees who are subject to inertia

- engage in force-field analysis

- identify benefits for persisting with the intervention

### Treatment Integrity

Choosing a proper intervention and formulating an effective plan do not guarantee successful implementation. Consultees may not carry out a carefully designed plan effectively (Ervin & Erhardt, 2000; Kratochwill & Stoiber, 2000a; Noell et al., 2005; Wilkinson, 2006) and, in fact, many don't. An improperly implemented intervention, even though it has empirical support, can damage the consultation process. Treatment integrity refers to the degree to which the intervention is implemented as intended (Lentz et al., 1996; Wilkinson, 2006). For example, effectively implemented interventions are used with the proper frequency, consistently, and with suffi-

cient intensity (Riley-Tillman & Chafouleas, 2003). If the intervention is a program, for example, then many issues can arise in the implementation (Larsen & Sandal, 2007). In recent years, there has been a significant amount of research conducted on treatment integrity (see Sterling-Turner et al., 2001). One reason for the lack of implementing interventions as designed is the cost incurred by the consultees during the phase of implementation (Noell & Gresham, 1993). There are two types of costs in implementing interventions: objective (e.g., time) and subjective (e.g., inconvenience). So too, there are two types of benefits: objective (e.g., a change in the client system's behavior) and subjective (e.g., a sense of accomplishment).

Interventions that are complex and time consuming are particularly at risk. To help reduce this cost, consultants can train and coach consultees to use interventions (Noell & Witt, 1998; Watson & Robinson, 1996) and follow up with performance-based feedback on intervention implementation (Noell et al., 2005; Riley-Tillman & Chafouleas, 2003). Assessing intervention costs allows consultants to help consultees determine the conditions under which interventions are implemented and maintained with minimal adverse by-products so that the benefits outweigh the costs (Gresham & Noell, 1993).

One method of assessing the cost-benefit ratio for interventions is *functional outcome analysis* (Gresham & Noell, 1993). In short, FOA determines the amount of effort required to accomplish a desired outcome and answers the question: "How much does it cost to get the desired change in the client system?"

Methods for assessing treatment integrity have received recent attention. Interviews, observation of implementation, training in the intervention, and use of scripted intervention plans can assess treatment integrity (Upah & Tilly, 2002). Treatment integrity is likely enhanced by choosing high probability interventions and promoting correct implementation (Telzrow & Beebe, 2002). High probability interventions are those that focus on key behaviors, are empirically supported, and are acceptable to the consultee. Interventions should be easy to implement, positive, perceived to be effective, and fit easily into the consultee's routine (Riley-Tillman & Chapfouleas, 2003). Promotion of correct implementation of interventions involves things such as treatment manuals and guided practice in monitoring of the implementation (Martens & Ardoin, 2002), as well performance feedback during follow-up (Noell et al., 2005) and the addition of a treatment-monitoring interview to the consultation process (Wilkinson, 2006).

*Social validity,* an aspect of treatment integrity, refers to the notion that the parties involved agree to the value of the intervention (Lentz et al., 1996). It involves the social significance of goals, the social acceptability of the procedures, and the social importance of effects (Gresham & Lopez, 1996). Consultees are more likely to follow through on an intervention if they see the goals of consultation as socially significant and worth the cost of meeting them.

*Treatment acceptability* refers to the concept that the parties involved believe that the intervention is in line with their value systems and their perceptions of what it takes to help the client system. If consultees view the intervention and the plan to implement it as acceptable, then they are more likely to be willing to self-monitor or be monitored by the consultant (Erhardt, Barnett, Lentz, Stollar, & Reifin, 1996). They are also more likely to proceed with the implementation as planned and increase the likelihood of accomplishing treatment integrity (Kratochwill & Stoiber, 2000a; Noell et al., 2005; Truscott, Cosgrove, Meyers, & Eidle-Barkman, 2000). When dealing with large numbers of people in organizational consultation, consultants will want to assure "group treatment acceptability" by ensuring that organization members see the intervention as: (1) existing within the parameters of their roles, and (2) tailored to the specific needs of the organization (Truscott et al., 2000). Not all interventions developed by the consultant and consultee are viewed as equally acceptable. Acceptable interventions are usually simple, time effective, and free of jargon; they also tend to deal with a severe situation and involve something that the consultee is knowledgeable about (Gresham & Lopez, 1996).

There is some evidence that consultees find interventions based on functional assessment as more acceptable than those that are not (Jones & Lungaro, 2000). On the other hand, some authors suggest there is little empirical support for the idea that treatment acceptability is related to the effectiveness of the intervention (Watson et al., 1997). Questionnaires are typically used to assess treatment acceptability. More recently, focus groups and other qualitative measures have been used (Finn & Sladeczek, 2001). For an interesting study regarding treatment acceptability, consult Cowan and Sheridan (2003).

*Social importance* refers to the consultees' view that the intended changes are important to long-term functioning of the client system. Consultees are more likely to follow through with plans when they view the intervention as making significant differences in the life of the client system.

**A Brief Example of Implementing the Plan in Consultation.**   Mary, a school counselor, is consulting Louise, a third-grade teacher, in helping a student diagnosed as having test-taking anxiety. The plan they have devised together involves a cognitive behavioral approach that focuses on the child's "self-talk." The teacher instructs the child in a variation of stress inoculation training. As the child is applying this strategy during an exam, he starts saying aloud the coping phrases that were to be said silently to himself. Mary, who had been monitoring Louise's implementation of the plan, assists Louise in revising the procedures for instructing the child in stress inoculation training procedures. At the same time, Mary is quite cautious in avoiding the creation of any dependency on her by Louise.

**A Brief Example of Implementing the Plan in Collaboration.**   Mary, a school counselor, and Louise, a third-grade teacher, are collaborating together to help a student diagnosed as having test-taking anxiety. The plan they have devised together involves a cognitive behavioral approach that focuses on the child's "self-talk." The teacher instructs the child in a variation of stress inoculation training. As the child is applying this strategy during an exam, he starts saying aloud the coping phrases that were to be said silently to himself. Mary provides individual counseling to the child in terms of stress management procedures the child can use. Mary, who had been monitoring Louise's implementation of the plan, assists Louise in revising the procedures for instructing the child in stress inoculation training procedures. At the same time, Louise assists Mary in understanding the various strategies that might help Mary's work with this particular child.

## PHASE FOUR: EVALUATING THE PLAN

After the plan has been implemented, it must be evaluated. In this phase, the question is: "To what degree were our goals met?" Evaluating the plan is a part of a larger evaluation effort that assesses the effectiveness of the entire consultation process. As it relates to the plan implementation, *evaluation* refers to the collection of data/information about the implementation to determine its effectiveness in meeting the specified goals (Upah & Tilly, 2002). Both the plan itself and how it was carried out need to be evaluated (MacMann et al., 1996). If the evaluation suggests that the plan has been successfully implemented to an appropriate degree, the consultation proceeds to the disengagement phase. If the analysis finds that the plan was not successfully implemented to the degree sought, then the consultation relationship will revert back to a previous phase (such as defining the problem) and proceed from there.

Evaluation of the plan within consultation frequently involves two processes: implementation evaluation and outcome evaluation. First, implementation evaluation determines whether the implementation occurred as originally planned, what problems were encountered in the implementation, and how these problems affected the outcomes (Upah & Tilly, 2002). You will remember in the discussion of the third phase of this stage—the actual implementation of the plan—that we discussed such items as tactics, unforeseen glitches that might occur, and treatment integrity. Implementation evaluation reviews these items in case the consultant and the

consultee choose to develop alternative plans and strategies.

Second, outcome evaluation determines whether, and the degree to which, the goals of the plan have been achieved. Questions to answer include: "To what degree was the plan successfully implemented?", "What are the next steps that need to be taken?", and "How can the glitches that occurred be eliminated?" If the plan did not meet its goals, the evaluation may shed some light on reasons why. In this case, the consultant and consultee can revisit the problem and determine the subsequent phases that need to be repeated in the problem-solving process.

Evaluation of the plan is frequently considered to be out of the realm of expertise of the typical consultant and consultee. However, consultants are increasingly being held accountable for the quality of their services. They must at least be able to evaluate their own interventions, and they should also assist in evaluating their consultees' plans. Unfortunately, there are an inadequate number of well-researched methods to measure the costs and benefits, either objective or subjective, of interventions (Barnett & Lentz, 1993; Barnett et al., 2007).

Outcomes can be measured in terms of what happened to the client or client system as a result of some plan. The consultant and consultee have a variety of instruments and techniques available for this purpose, but basically there are three ways to evaluate a plan's outcome: individualized goal attainment measures, standardized outcome assessment devices, and consumer satisfaction surveys.

*Individualized goal attainment measures* are "techniques whereby the efficacy of services is measured according to criteria that have been specifically tailored to the needs, capacities, and aspirations of the person(s) receiving services" (Anderson, Frieden, & Murphy, 1977, p. 293).

One example is concrete goal setting used with goal-oriented progress notes. Ideally the consultant and consultee have already performed concrete goal setting during the diagnosis stage of consultation. Plan evaluation then becomes a simple procedure of determining the degree to which each goal was accomplished. For example, if the plan called for the client to reduce the number of cigarettes smoked from 20 to 6 a day, then it is relatively easy to monitor the degree to which this goal is being met.

Measurement of individualized goal attainment is often accomplished through goal attainment scaling (GAS) (Illback et al., 1999; Sladeczek et al., 2001). In this technique the dimensions representing desired changes in client behavior are scaled (e.g., from 1 = minimally attained to 5 = totally attained), expected levels of attainment are set, and scores are determined at the end of the plan's implementation. As Sladeczek and others note: GAS involves "the selection of the target behavior . . . an objective description of the desired intervention outcome, and the development of three to five descriptions of the target behavior . . . that increasingly approximate the desired outcome" (2001, p. 46). These authors note that GAS is individualized, personalized, inexpensive, and non-intrusive.

*Standardized outcome assessment devices* measure the accomplishment of goals through some norm- or criterion-referenced device. Checklists and ratings scales are typically used in consultation. For example, if a consultee assessed a client's career maturity on a standardized instrument and later retested the client on the same measure, the client's progress toward the goal of increased career maturity could be ascertained by the differences between the scores.

*Consumer satisfaction surveys* attempt to assess the opinions and attitudes of the client or client system regarding the services and effects of the plan provided to them. These data, typically gathered through an interview or questionnaire, are quite subjective and of questionable validity if used as the only indicator of the plan's success.

For a more in-depth and step-by-step discussion of evaluation methods in consultation, see the section entitled "Evaluating the Consultation Process" in Chapter 6.

**A Brief Example of Evaluating the Plan.** Yvonne, a community projects consultant, is working with Ashley, the head of an Upward Bound program, concerning the implementation of per-

sonal counseling to the program's teenage participants. Their efforts over several sessions have given birth to a personal counseling program. They are now at the stage of evaluating its implementation. Because they conducted ongoing evaluations of the program, Yvonne and Ashley have a sense of its success. The goal attainment measures they developed for each of the program's 20 participants show that the average participant benefited from the program to a level of 4.1 on a 5-point scale. On a standardized problem checklist, the students also reported fewer concerns after counseling. Student opinion surveys showed that they preferred group counseling over individual counseling, although the latter was also beneficial.

## MULTICULTURAL ASPECTS RELATED TO IMPLEMENTATION

Cultural differences can influence the perception of how interventions are selected and implemented. For example, interventions focusing on the use of groups may be preferred, and the time required for implementing an intervention may not be highly valued by some cultural groups. There is some evidence that cultural variables may not play an important part in the level of intervention acceptability (Naumann, Gutkin, & Sandoval, 1996). Nonetheless, the cultural views and expectations of the parties involved should be considered when selecting and planning for an intervention (Jackson & Hayes, 1993) as well as modifying one (Ingraham, 2000, 2003), as these might well affect how the intervention is perceived and implemented. In cases such as these, even collaborators will want to make sure that the team doesn't attempt to divvy out the responsibility for various aspects to individuals, but rather they will want to keep more of a team approach to implementation.

---

**C A S E   5.1     Implementation for School Consultants**

---

Barbara, a human service professional working in a large urban secondary school, is consulting with Shirley, who is the school's chief administrator. Both have spent time in the business world prior to entering education and are familiar with "total quality management" programs. Shirley is very interested in implementing quality management concepts throughout the school. At this point in the consultation, they are ready to choose from several goals and a long list of possible interventions to get the program into place.

To obtain the support of the entire staff, Barbara and Shirley have thought of numerous ways to help them freely buy into learning and utilizing total quality management concepts. Ideas ranged from having the district superintendent make an announcement that the school would implement the program to having a series of departmental meetings led by heads in which teachers and staff could freely discuss the proposal.

To develop school-wide ownership of the program, Barbara and Shirley tested each intervention using decision consultation questions to assess how the intervention would fit the environment of the school, the kinds of resources and personnel necessary to do an adequate implementation, and the glitches that might occur if the intervention was put into place.

They decided that a grassroots approach to getting the program accepted is probably the best plan since the school district had a history of imposing new programs on schools without their input. How they attempted to get the program accepted, therefore, was the most important step. First they decided that Shirley would hold a schoolwide faculty meeting to present the program as a possibility along with her personal recommendation as chief administrator. However, she would also make it clear that she was not going to force the program on the school. She would discuss her rationale for wanting the program, what it would do for the school, and also what it would cost in terms of staff behavior.

Department heads would then be taken on a one-day retreat during which the program would be discussed and debated. The heads would then use regularly scheduled departmental meetings to discuss and debate the program with staff. Shirley would hold an-other regular faculty meeting dedicated to the total quality management idea and have open discussions about it.

Shirley put the plan into action and frequently used Barbara as a resource. She bounced ideas off Barbara concerning ways to approach certain resistant department heads. After the plan was implemented, Shirley conducted an anonymous survey of the staff's views of the program and how they had been approached about it. The survey's results were very positive, and Barbara and Shirley took the next step toward implementing the program.

**Commentary**

Decision consultation is an excellent method for selecting an intervention given the context in which it is to be implemented. This case shows how, through decision consultation, the history of prior programs in the school affected what intervention was selected and how that intervention was implemented. Note also the importance of consultants "staying online" while the consultee implements the intervention.

When a plan is being formulated, differences in opinion about the importance or necessity of a time frame for the plan's implementation can exist. In addition, people with some cultural backgrounds will prefer collaboration to consultation based on their views of interdependence.

In terms of evaluation of the plan, input from consultees or fellow collaborators is critical so that the perspectives of different cultures are considered. People from high-context cultures, for example, may approach evaluation of the plan in a quite different manner, relying more on a constructivist model. For example, efficiency—a must in a plan in a traditional low-context culture—may not be of particular interest to a person from a high-context culture. Similarly, whether the plan was executed in a timely fashion may not be nearly as relevant as the social impact the plan will have. Even the preferred model of evaluation itself may be framed in a social-consensus, constructivist model rather than the traditional positivist, empirical model so frequently employed in consultation and collaboration.

---

**C A S E  5.2    Implementation for Community Consultants**

---

Roy is a mental health consultant who has been working with Robbie, a counselor for a residential summer program for academically gifted students at a small state university. Robbie is working on his master's degree in counseling at the university. During their second session, Roy and Robbie have gotten to the point of generating several possible interventions for helping Zachary, one of the program's students.

Zachary has been having a series of interpersonal conflicts with many of the other academically gifted students in the program. It appears that he offends his peers by playing the game "Who's most gifted?" During their third session, Roy helps Robbie select an intervention to help Zachary. Through use of decision consultation, they choose individual counseling with Zachary as the best approach. Robbie has the counseling skills, and he and Zachary have a good working relationship already established. Robbie's beliefs about individual counseling seem congruent with making it the method used, and Zachary's needs for some skills in dealing with his peers would be accomplished by this method. Robbie realizes that Zachary would probably benefit most from being in a counseling group with his peers but strongly believes that Zachary is not ready to be in such a group. Robbie designates the group as a possible contingency plan in case the individual counseling relationship falls through.

In formulating a plan, Roy and Robbie decide that both supportive and behavioral approaches are needed to help Zachary. A supportive approach would help him to not feel singled out or considered sick in some way, while the behavioral approach could help him quickly learn some interpersonal skills to enjoy and benefit from the summer program. Roy and Robbie determine that the best things to use for evaluating the success of counseling will be the self-report of Zachary as well as Robbie's observations of Zachary and his peers during the next three weeks of the program.

In deciding to be tactful yet honest with Zachary, Robbie invites him to become involved in counseling. Robbie hopes to get Zachary excited about their project in which Zachary can design his own methods for relating more effectively to his peers.

As they conduct a brief force-field analysis on the plan, the only loose end that emerges is the possible rejection of Zachary by his peers in spite of any constructive changes he might make. Roy helps Robbie choose an initial target group of Zachary's peers for him to try his new skills with first. The target group will be students with whom Zachary has had no known conflicts. After success with these students, Robbie could help Zachary target those students with whom he has had some difficulties. Robbie then implements the plan with Zachary. Robbie consults with Roy over the next two weeks about behavioral rehearsal procedures and methods of giving specific feedback. As the summer program ended, Robbie notices Zachary being more positive about his peers and less in need of being the best at everything. Zachary's peers seem to make less of a big deal about Zachary to the degree that Zachary made less of a big deal about himself. They accept him as one of them.

**Commentary**

The development of a contingency plan is an important part of the planning process. Without a contingency plan, consultees are left in a "sink-or-swim" predicament if the primary plan falls through. Force-field analysis teases out possible glitches in a plan and enables the consultant and consultee to better align the plan with its goals. Force-field analysis procedures enabled Robbie and Roy to refine their plan to accommodate Zachary's situation. Notice also the importance of Robbie's staying in touch with Roy during Roy's work with Zachary in terms of behavioral rehearsal.

## SUMMARY

The implementation stage of consultation consists of choosing an intervention, formulating a plan, implementing the plan, and evaluating it. In this stage, the consultant provides the consultee with practical assistance to meet the goals set to help the client or client system.

A vast number of interventions are available for use in plans. Interventions can be categorized in a variety of ways, but classification by target level is the most common. Although interventions usually focus on improving the efficiency of the consultees' workplace by increasing the effectiveness of the targeted level, they may be effective at more than one level.

As a consultant, your role in interventions can range from that of facilitator to that of trainer/educator. Make sure that you have the expertise in a variety of interventions and keep abreast of the burgeoning number of interventions available to you.

Once the appropriate intervention or interventions are chosen, consultants help consultees formulate and choose an appropriate plan. During plan implementation, the consultant provides the consultee with tactical assistance and also monitors his or her procedures. After the plan has been implemented, evaluation is performed to assess the degree to which it was effective in realizing its goals. Then the consultant and consultee determine whether consultation should continue. If the plan is considered to have worked satisfactorily, consultation moves to its next stage—disengagement. As in entry and diagnosis, the research on the implementation stage is quite limited. Research on developing a plan suggests that consultees who feel that they can have a positive impact regarding plan imple-

mentation are more willing to take responsibility for the planning process, as opposed to those who feel their efforts may have no impact (Armenakis & Burdg, 1988). Research on the implementation stage in organizational consultation suggests that getting a change institutionalized as a result of implementation is related to several factors, including commitment of the individuals involved and continued sanctioning by high-level administrators (Armenakis & Burdg, 1988).

A final note on the implementation stage: Many consultants report that they do not engage in evaluation of the plan; when they do, consultee verbal reports about the client system are more about the source of the evaluation rather than observations of actual client system behavior (Bramlett et al., 2002). Evaluation of the plan also creates a mechanism for feedback to researchers on the application of empirically supported interventions (Stoiber & Kratochwill, 2000a). It is important to remember that evaluation is essential to determine the effects of consultation and that it should be integral to your practice.

## SUGGESTIONS FOR EFFECTIVE PRACTICE

- Ensure that consultees and fellow collaborators have the skills and an accepting attitude toward the interventions being considered.
- Have a plan that is the result of the input of all stakeholders.

- Have a monitoring mechanism in place that will examine the progress the plan is making.
- Avoid the temptation to disregard evaluation of the plan.

## QUESTIONS FOR REFLECTION

1. What is unique about the consultant's behavior during the implementation stage?
2. How would you as a consultant help a consultee choose an appropriate intervention?
3. Look over the interventions discussed in this chapter. How many of them could be used at more than one level?

4. Which of the interventions for individuals have the most danger of turning from consultation into counseling or psychotherapy? Why?
5. Which of the interventions described in this chapter could be most effectively implemented by a group of consultants rather than by one alone? Why?

6. What are some ways in which consultants can learn new interventions?

7. Under what circumstances would you monitor a consultee's implementation of a plan?

8. What kinds of tactical assistance might most consultees require during plan implementation?

9. What are the basic differences between plan evaluation and evaluation of the process of consultation?

10. What should the consultant and consultee do if the evaluation of the plan indicates that little success in meeting the plan's goal was achieved?

## SUGGESTED SUPPLEMENTARY READINGS

French, W. L., and Bell, C. H., Jr. (1999). *Organization development: Behavior science interventions for organization improvement* (6th ed.). Englewood Cliffs, NJ: Prentice-Hall. This book provides an interesting and practical overview of various interventions available to consultants. Of particular interest is the authors' discussion of the various ways in which interventions can be categorized. This book has become a classic for many who work as organizational consultants. This book has a tremendous amount of information that consultants in any setting will find invaluable.

Elliott, S. N., Busse, R. T., & Shapiro, E. S. (1999). Intervention techniques for academic performance problems. In C. R. Reynolds and T. B. Gutkin (Eds.), *The handbook of school psychology* (3rd ed., pp. 664–685). New York: Wiley. This chapter contains a wealth of information for school-based consultants on academic interventions. It provides a performance-based model for understanding academic intervention. The chapter also surveys various academic interventions aimed at remediating academic performance problems.

Telzrow, C. F., & Beebe, J. J. (2002). Best practices in facilitating intervention adherence and integrity. In A. Thomas and J. Grimes (Eds.), *Best practices in school psychology* (4th ed., pp. 503–515). Bethesda, MD: National Association of School Psychologists. This chapter presents a comprehensive view of treatment integrity with a focus on practical ways to ensure the appropriate implementation of interventions. Consultants will find a substantial number of practical ideas.

# 6

✳

# Disengagement Stage

If the entry stage is characterized by the question "Hello, what would you like to change?", then the disengagement stage is characterized by the question "What do we need to take care of before we say goodbye?" In effect, the disengagement stage winds down what was started up in the entry stage. Disengagement refers to the ending of the consultation or collaboration relationship.

The purpose of this chapter is to discuss and explore the disengagement stage, during which the consultant and consultee evaluate the consultation process, make plans for integrating the effects of consultation into the system after the consultant leaves, go through a period of reduced contact, make provisions for follow-up, and terminate the consultation process itself. Figure 6.1 illustrates the phases of disengagement.

Once the consultant and consultee have evaluated the plan, they must decide whether to continue or discontinue consultation. The length and complexity of the consultation or collaboration process can complicate this decision (Dougherty et al., 1996). The decision to continue most often results from an evaluation that indicates the goal was not met satisfactorily (Brack, Jones, Smith, White, & Brack, 1993). The consultant and consultee usually return to the end of the diagnostic stage and generate other possible interventions; occasionally, they may need to re-define the problem. In some other cases, continued consultation may be needed because the consultee or organization has an additional work-related concern about which consultation is desired. In these cases, the consultation process typically reverts to the entry phase of exploring organizational needs.

Consider the following situation: You are a consultant who for two years has been working with a human service organization for an average of four hours a week. You have worked with several individual consultees, have done a lot of team building and organizational-level interventions, and have had your own

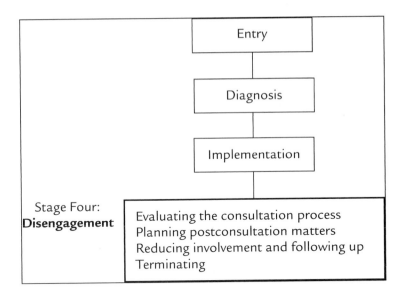

**FIGURE 6.1**  The phases of the disengagement stage

office space and clerical assistance. Leaving would not be as simple as packing your briefcase and walking out the door. What would you need to accomplish before you left? To whom would you say goodbye? How would you help the system plan to maintain the benefits of consultation after you have gone? How would you evaluate the process of consultation? What arrangements for follow-up would you make?

## INTRODUCTION

As you are reading the chapter, here are some questions to consider:

1. When does the process of disengagement really begin?

2. What issues need to be taken into consideration during postconsultation planning?

3. What are the basic differences between evaluating the process of consultation and evaluating the plan in the implementation stage?

4. How would you arrange for follow-up with a consultee organization?

5. What effect does the length of time the consultant has spent with the consultee or organi-

zation have on what the consultant should do during the disengagement stage?

### A Case of a Botched Disengagement

Consider the following scenario in which disengagement is poorly done:

You have worked very closely with a certain consultee who has assisted as your co-leader in many of the interventions you have made. Without any warning, you announce to him that after two years of working together, today is your last day on the job and you wish him the best of luck in the future. He leaves the room upset and slams the door. As you track him down and discuss the situation, you find out that he has grown close to you over the two years and now resents being treated so impersonally; your decision to tell him that you were leaving for good at the end of the day caused the resentment. He feels that you should have said earlier that you were going to terminate the relationship.

Consultants and collaborators can minimize problems during disengagement by accurately timing its initiation, properly developing postconsultation/collaboration planning, gradually reducing involvement, and by planning a formal time to terminate (Dougherty et al., 1996).

# PHASE ONE: EVALUATING THE CONSULTATION PROCESS

## The Role of Evaluation

As it relates to consultation, evaluation might be defined as the systematic collection of information about the activities and outcomes of consultation for the purpose of making judgments and decisions about how consultation is proceeding and the effect it is having (Patton, 1986). Evaluation is helpful to understand if the goals of consultation have been met and if the consultee is more likely to be effective with similar cases in the future (Knotek, 2004). Lack of agreement in the field on definitions of consultation and collaboration make accurate evaluation difficult (Pryzwansky, 2003). Consultants may well need expertise in qualitative assessments methods in order to adequately take cultural variables into account (Rogers, 2000). In addition, human service consultants often do not do a good job of evaluating their services (Gibbons & Shinn, 2002; McLean, 2006). Conducting an effective evaluation can be difficult and time consuming. With that said, a properly performed evaluation can provide the consultant with a quality control device, a learning device, legal protection, and a marketing tool (Kelley, 1981).

When evaluating consultation or collaboration, the parties involved will want to evaluate both instrumental and expressive elements (Chowanec, 1993; O'Driscoll & Eubanks, 1992). *Instrumental performance* refers to how well the party providing assistance did in helping to solve the situation presented. *Expressive performance* refers to the human side of the relationship and deals with the level of comfort for the parties involved. The bottom line is this: to enhance their performance, consultants should consider evaluating not only what they did, but the way the consultees perceived their behavior.

Because the evaluation process is not always easy to perform, it is not unusual for consultants to consult others about how to evaluate both their services and the consultation process itself. Still, consultants and consultees should realize that they do not need to be experts in evaluation or research to adequately per-

form the practical evaluations required in consultation. Whereas merely going through the motions of evaluation is professionally inexcusable, a simple yet credible evaluation can be very informative (Caplan & Caplan, 1993). Consultants need to be aware that at the opposite extreme, they can spend so much of their time evaluating the consultation process that its human side can get lost in the volume of information collected and interpreted. Basically, they need to identify what to measure and find a way to collect appropriate data in an evaluation (Gibbons & Shinn, 2002).

Pertinent evaluation information should be provided to the consultant, the consultee, administrators of the organization in which consultation has occurred, and (in some cases) the client. The consultant should take measures to see that the results of evaluation are not used in the following covert and inappropriate ways: for protection of an ineffective consultee or program, to avoid decision making, as a public relations tool, or for getting rid of an effective but unpopular consultee or program.

Consultants and consultees need two primary skills to perform evaluation effectively: the ability to identify the consequences of their actions, and the ability to compare results to some standard. Although these skills were identified in the context of counseling clients on skills they need to change their behavior effectively (Egan, 2007), they are certainly needed by the consultant and consultee as well.

Deciding who should conduct the consultation evaluation is difficult, and perhaps the best rule of thumb is "It depends." The consultant and consultee will usually make this decision during the contracting stage. In some cases the consultant helps the consultee gather and make sense of the data; in other cases the consultee gathers the data, and the consultant assists in its interpretation; in still other instances someone other than the consultee (e.g., the organization's contact person) conducts some aspects of the evaluation. Some organizations even have special departments to evaluate services like consultation. So long as the people who perform the evaluation are qualified to do so and have no conflict of interest, it probably does not matter who conducts given aspects of it. Regardless of who performs it, consultants are responsible for arranging an evaluation of their services, and they should also conduct a separate self-evaluation. Evaluation is an *ongoing* process that should be performed throughout the consultation, not just at the end.

Three steps are common to all evaluation processes: formation of criteria, assessment of attainment of the criteria, and utilization of results. *Formation of criteria* refers to the creation or designation of the criteria (frequently goals) that will be used to assess those aspects of consultation under evaluation (Anderson et al., 1977). Decades ago, Lippitt (1969) noted that developing evaluation criteria is one of the most difficult problems facing consultants. *Assessment of attainment of the criteria* means systematically determining what, how, and by whom information is to be gathered, as well as how it is to be analyzed. *Utilization of results* involves disseminating the results to appropriate parties, often for some form of decision making. For example, an organization might use the results of consultee satisfaction surveys to decide whether or not to retain a particular consultant.

Consultation is typically evaluated by examining pertinent data gathered from observations, questionnaires, surveys, interviews, and the organization's documents. The use of a multi-method approach to evaluation, which provides more than one perspective on the results obtained, may add information valuable in interpreting the data and can reduce response bias. The use of devices for gathering data is discussed in .

When evaluating consultation, it is appropriate to gather data from the client system, the consultee, the consultant, and other parties-at-interest. To make evaluation manageable, the consultant and consultee should determine during the formation of the contract which kinds of evaluative information should be gathered from which parties. Consultants may want to evaluate three general consultation topics: the plan that was carried out in the implementation stage, the overall effects of consultation and the consultant's behaviors, and the efficacy of certain stages and phases along the way. The decision concerning which topics to evaluate depends on the type of evaluation, the nature of the problem, and the level at which consultation oc-

curs. For example, an organizational consultant might be interested in evaluating the impact of consultation on total organizational effectiveness, participants' attitudes toward the change process itself, or the efficacy of a specific intervention. It is very important that the consultant, consultee, and (if necessary) other parties-at-interest plan what is to be evaluated, how evaluation is to occur, and who is going to perform it and when. Such planning prevents evaluation procedures from becoming overwhelming.

The following questions provide a starting point for identifying the many things that can be evaluated at the end of consultation:

- To what degree has behavior in the client or client system changed in the desired direction?
- To what degree was the consultant able to enter the system psychologically?
- In what ways has the organization changed as a result of consultation?
- To what degree have the goals established in the contract been met?
- To what degree have established timetables been met?
- How successfully has a given intervention been carried out?
- How effectively has the consultant established an effective working relationship with the consultee?
- To what degree has consultation been worth the cost in time, effort, and money?

Specific items that can in some way be evaluated:

- consultee preference for given models of consultation
- initial planning of the consultation process
- quantity and quality of consultee reports about the work-related problem
- progress made relative to each consultation stage

- organizational variables that affect the consultant process
- consultant behaviors at each consultation stage
- consultee behaviors throughout the consultation process
- client behaviors throughout the consultation process
- consultee satisfaction with consultation
- the degree to which goals are being attained
- adequacy of each consultation contact
- interpersonal behaviors of the consultant and consultee
- institutionalization of change

Changes in behavior are looked for in the client or client system, but consultees can also be examined for such changes. For example, an evaluator could look for a reduction in the number of physically aggressive behaviors by a student (client) or an increase in the number of open-ended questions a consultee asks a client.

Cost effectiveness is a judgment call: Were the costs in the terms of time and resources needed for consultation worth the returns? Thus, the administrator of a human service agency might weigh the time and resources it took to have a consultant help reorganize the agency against the perceived benefits of the consultation. Attitudes and opinions about benefits of the consultation can range from indexes of consultee satisfaction with the consultant to views about the overall success of the consultation.

Consultation evaluation can be viewed throughout the consultation process, or it can be considered once it has run its course. Just as the consultant is continually entering the system, continually diagnosing, and continually intervening, so too should he or she be continually evaluating. The evaluation performed along the way by the consultant and consultee is referred to as *formative evaluation*. The question answered by formative evaluation is "Is consultation working?" (Upah & Tilly, 2002). The process of consultation is evaluated without respect to the ultimate product. For example, a consultant and a consultee

might use formative evaluation to investigate the degree of success of the diagnosis stage.

When the consultant and consultee evaluate the effects of the consultation process at its conclusion, such an evaluation is referred to as a *summative evaluation*. Its role is to determine the effects of consultation outcomes; it sums things up at the end of the process and evaluates the product. For example, the consultant and consultee might decide to assess a training program's effect on the participants' morale.

### Formative Evaluation

One of the best ways to conduct formative evaluation in consultation is to perform evaluations at the end of each phase (Curtis & Stollar, 2002). Such evaluations will assist the consultant and consultee in determining whether to stick to the current course of consultation or modify the process (Gibbons & Shinn, 2002). Frequent formative evaluation has been linked to consultation success (Noell & Witt, 1998). Formative evaluation allows for feedback along the way on processes and outcomes (Egan, 2007). Evaluation can be formal (such as using written surveys or performing observations and monitoring on some combination of consultant, consultee, and client behaviors) or informal (such as a discussion between the consultant and consultee or other parties-at-interest concerning how a given phase has progressed).

Human service professionals are traditionally positive toward the use of surveys. Thus, consultants may want to develop questionnaires and surveys related to each of the phases of the consultation process. Sample evaluation questions for the phases of each stage of the consultation process are provided later in this chapter. These questions can be helpful in developing a frame of reference, whether evaluation is conducted by surveys, observations, interviews, or the examination of records.

**Formative Evaluation across the Consultation Process.**   Certain useful questions can be asked in the various stages of consultation, and their answers are helpful in evaluating the progress and subsequent direction of consultation. The following questions are adapted from an evaluation form developed by Parsons and Meyers (1984):

- How many contacts have been made with the consultee?

- What is the average length of the contacts?

- What is the average length of time between contacts?

- What progress has been made so far?

- What issues have come up that still need to be handled?

- Who needs to be apprised of what has been done so far?

- What does the consultee think about what has happened to date?

- To what degree is the consultee satisfied about what has happened?

- What does the consultee think about the consultant's style?

- What details need to be worked out?

- What does the consultant think about what has happened so far?

- To what degree is the consultant satisfied with what has happened?

- What are the consultant's impressions of the consultee?

- Are there any changes needed in the way the consultation is being conducted?

As noted earlier, it is useful for consultants to evaluate their effectiveness at the end of each phase of the consultation process. In the following section, I provide questions that may be asked during each phase of the entry stage. Consultants can convert these questions into surveys or checklists, use them for directing observations, or develop them as a basis for interviewing: Figure 6.2 is an example of a survey for use in the formative evaluation of the exploration of organizational needs, whereas Figure 6.3 is a sample checklist for evaluating the contracting phase of the entry stage. The following example of formative evaluation of the entry process can easily be

extended to each of the other stages; the consultant simply evaluates each phase of the current stage before moving on to the next stage.

**Formative Evaluation of the Entry Stage.**   In the entry stage, the consultation process progressed through the phases of exploring organizational needs, contracting, physically entering the system, and psychologically entering the system. The consultant and consultee can evaluate each of these phases as a guide for conducting subsequent consultation phases.

*Exploring Organizational Needs.*   Some questions used in formative evaluation during this phase include:

- To what degree was the level of congruence between the consultant's abilities and consultee system's needs determined?

- Was the amount of resources the organization was willing to commit to consultation adequately defined?

- To what extent was the identification and clarification of the need for change accomplished?

- How well was the organization's readiness for change explored and defined?

- How well was the potential for working together explored by the parties involved?

- To what degree were role expectations made clear?

- How well were the roles of consultee and client defined?

*Contracting.*   The questions that can be asked about contracting are more specific than those for the previous phase:

- How effectively were the professional expectations of the involved parties spelled out in the contract?

- To what degree were the personal expectations of the involved parties made explicit?

**Directions:** Please rate each item according to the five-point scale listed by circling the number that most accurately expresses your opinion on the following statements:

> 5 = strongly agree        2 = disagree
> 4 = agree                 1 = strongly disagree
> 3 = undecided

1. The level of congruency between the consultant's abilities and the consultee system's needs was adequately determined.

   5            4            3            2            1

2. The amount of resources the organization was willing to commit to consultation was adequately defined.

   5            4            3            2            1

3. The identification and clarification of the need for change was adequately accomplished.

   5            4            3            2            1

4. The organization's readiness for change was adequately explored and defined.

   5            4            3            2            1

5. The potential of the parties involved for working together was adequately explored.

   5            4            3            2            1

6. Role expectations for those involved were made clear.

   5            4            3            2            1

7. The roles of the consultee and client system were adequately defined.

   5            4            3            2            1

**F I G U R E  6.2**   Sample survey for evaluating the exploration of organizational needs

- Were the amount of time and other resources each party would invest, the times they would invest them, and the costs of those investments adequately defined?

- How precisely specified were the ground rules under which the parties involved would operate?

- How well were the boundaries of consultation defined?

- To what degree was the nature of the contract reviewed with the appropriate parties?

- Were arrangements made for the periodic review and evaluation of consultation?

*Physically Entering the System.*   Evaluation of the physical entry into consultation is relatively straight-forward. Some questions useful in evaluating this phase include:

- Is the selected work site conducive to effective consultation? Is the selected work site strategically located?

**Directions:** Please place a check mark on the line under the appropriate response.

Yes  No

1. Were the professional expectations of the parties involved spelled out in the contract? ___ ___
2. Were the personal expectations of the parties involved made explicit? ___ ___
3. Were the conditions under which each party involved would invest time and other resources adequately defined? ___ ___
4. Were the ground rules under which the parties involved would operate specified clearly? ___ ___
5. Were the boundaries of consultation defined? ___ ___
6. Was the nature of the contract reviewed with all appropriate parties? ___ ___
7. Were arrangements made for the periodic review and evaluation of consultation? ___ ___

**FIGURE 6.3**   Sample checklist for evaluating the contracting phase

- Is the consultant appropriately balancing the amount of time spent at the work site with the time spent moving throughout the organization?
- To what degree does the consultant adapt the schedule for consultation activities to the regular schedule of the organization?
- To what degree have the parties affected by consultation been informed about the nature of consultation, its purpose, and its time frame?

*Psychologically Entering the System.*   Even though psychological entry cannot be divorced from physical entry, its aspects can be evaluated by the judicious selection of questions. Some questions that can be used in evaluating this phase include:

- To what degree has consultation placed minimal stress on the parties involved?
- To what degree has consultation placed minimal stress on the organization's structure and processes?

- To what degree has the consultant developed social influence within the organization?
- How effectively has the consultant obtained some sanction for consultation from the organization's top-level administrators?
- How effectively has the consultant built strong professional relationships with all parties affected by consultation?

In summary, evaluation of the entry stage—as with any of the other stages—is best applied to each of its phases. The consultant and consultee must agree on the most appropriate methods of evaluation and must limit the number of events that will be evaluated.

**A Brief Example of Formative Evaluation in the Consultation Process.**   Monica, a mental health consultant, has been consulting with Wendell, the director of a community council on aging program, on a "Reminiscences on Life" program series the council has been holding once a month in the community services center in a small rural town. The program was designed to bring seniors of the community together to recall wholesome reminiscences of their life experiences and share them with youth volunteers who were being trained by the council on aging to work with the elderly. Monica and Wendell came up with an evaluation scheme for the program prior to its inception. After five program sessions, they evaluated the program by means of a survey with the 12 seniors participating in the program, the program's two other staff members besides the director, and the 24 youth to whom the seniors had been sharing their reminiscences. After they conducted the evaluation, Monica and Wendell decide to "evaluate the evaluation." They determined that perhaps they should have spent more time on interviewing the participants and less time on surveying. Although the program's staff members had no complaints about the evaluation, some of the seniors had trouble seeing and said they couldn't read the survey very well. Several of the youth said it was hard to take the survey seriously and that they found it to be an unwanted demand on their time. As Monica and Wendell examined the results, they determined that a structured interview approach to evaluating the program would lend the most valid data. The seniors would appreciate the time given to them by a program member one-on-one, and the youth would be offered not only time to speak about how they felt, but also some coupons for free pizza. Monica and Wendell concluded that although the evaluation plan was appropriately linked to the goals of the program, the data-gathering methods were not adequately chosen or implemented. In addition, more methods of data collection like a combination of interviews, observation, and surveys were in order.

## Summative Evaluation

Summative evaluation refers to the evaluation of outcomes or products; indeed, it is often referred to as *product evaluation*. It assesses how well consultation worked (Upah & Tilly, 2002). Consultants and consultees use summative evaluation to determine if the objectives of consultation were met (Gibbons & Shinn, 2002). In some circumstances

consultants can benefit from consulting with experts in evaluation concerning the design of summative evaluation procedures. Evaluation methods in consultation and collaboration are typically based on research design. Evaluation methods can be quantitative, qualitative, or a mixture of both. These methods are not opposed to each other; they are merely different (Polkinghorne & Gribbons, 1999). Both methods can provide valid information (Berrios & Lucca, 2006; Padgett, 2004; Tashakkori & Teddlie, 2003).

An exhaustive treatment of the many possible designs used in summative evaluation is beyond the scope of this book. Excellent resources already available to consultants and consultees can provide guidance in designing evaluations of the consultation process; they include *Research Design in Counseling* (Heppner et al., 1999), *Single Case Experimental Designs* (Barlow & Hersen, 1984), *The Scientist Practitioner* (Barlow, Hayes, & Nelson-Gray, 1999), *Experimental and Quasi-Experimental Designs for Generalized Causal Inference* (Shadish, Cook, & Campbell, 2002), *The Qualitative Research Experience* (Padgett, 2004), and *Handbook of Mixed Methods in Social and Behavioral Research* (Tashakkori & Teddlie, 2003). There is also a trend in using a mix of quantitative and qualitative methods (Waszak & Sines, 2003) and some support for the single-case methodology for which some of the quantitative methods below are appropriate (Bangert & Baumberger, 2005).

## Quantitative Methods

**The Pre-Post Method.** The pre-post method attempts to assess changes that result from consultation by measuring variables related to desired changes before and after the consultation process. For example, a consultant might measure an organization's morale before and after an intervention designed to improve it. The advantages of this method are that it is relatively simple and requires a minimum of time to perform. The pre-post method is particularly valuable when the variables being measured are specific and observable. Because there is no control group, however, this method is of limited value.

Changes that were sought and achieved may not be directly attributable to consultation because other factors—such as changes in the organization and life experiences—may just as well explain the results. Still, this method is a step above nonstandardized observation and anecdotal accounts in that it provides more useful information and more conclusive evidence.

**The Group Comparison Method.**  The group comparison method strengthens the evaluation's validity by including a comparison or control group. This method is recommended to empirically validate interventions (Stoiber & Kratochwill, 2000). This method allows the consultant and consultee to be more confident that any changes found in the measurement are specifically attributable to consultation itself and not to extraneous variables. For example, a consultant might train half of an agency's crisis intervention team in cognitive therapy strategies for crisis situations. The other half of the team, which would receive no training, would be used as a control group. The performance of both groups is assessed and compared on selected criteria.

Sometimes consultants use a no-contact control group or an attention-only control group. In using a *no-contact control group*, the only contact with the group occurs during the assessment of the dependent variables (measures of the factors to be changed by consultation). In an *attention-only control group*, the assessment of the dependent variables is made and the group is informed of the nature of consultation services without receiving these services directly. Attention-only control groups are useful in that they eliminate the possibility that the attention paid to the consultees and clients, not consultation itself, led to differences in the dependent variables. Several potential problems can be associated with the group comparison method of evaluation: management of the control groups, developmental complexity of the experimental design, and required statistical knowledge beyond the expertise of consultant and consultee.

The group comparison method is particularly useful in a follow-up assessment using the same measurements taken in posttesting. Because of the complexity of the group comparison method, it is a desirable, but relatively infrequently used, method of consultation evaluation (McLean, 2006).

**Time-Series Method.**  The time-series method involves establishing a series of measures on one or more given variables over time (Barlow et al., 1999). The primary difference between the time-series method and the group comparison or pre-post methods is that it uses more frequent assessments of designated variables. The effects of intervention are then assessed in terms of the variability of their level of occurrence and possible trends (Barlow et al., 1999). Pertinent information can therefore be gathered on a measurement's changes over time (Barlow & Hersen, 1984). This method may or may not use a control group. Single-case experimental designs in which the client system is assessed before, during, and after the intervention are increasingly popular (Steege et al., 2002). As an example, a consultant and consultee might make a series of observations on how an imagery program affects a client's eating behavior at breakfast, lunch, and dinner.

*Multiple baseline designs* are one example of the time-series method. Multiple baselining reduces the effects of random influences on behavior change by replicating the change obtained in one period with that in subsequent periods; each subsequent period serves as a control for the earlier period (Barlow et al., 1999; Steege et al., 2002). Time-series methods are most effective when it is likely that a large number of variables are affecting the outcome of consultation.

### Qualitative Methods

Qualitative evaluation is an umbrella for the many methods in which data can be interpreted from a qualitative perspective (Hanson et al., 2005). There is increasing acceptance of qualitative methods (Berrios & Lucca, 2006; Haverkamp, Morrow, & Ponterotto, 2005) and they are increasingly being used alongside quantitative methods (Ponterotto,

2005). Qualitative evaluation methods can extend consultants' abilities to effectively evaluate their efforts (Denton et al., 2003; Polkinghorne & Gribbons, 1999). Qualitative evaluation is really more of an attitude of inquiry that uses particular types of procedures (Athanasiou et al., 2002). Qualitative evaluation methods include methods such as the case study and the self-evaluation. Data for these methods include transcripts of interviews, notes from observations, descriptions from appropriate stakeholders, and scores from assessment instruments. Qualitative evaluation deals with specific situations and is directly related to decision making.

**Case Study Method.**   A case study is an example of a qualitative evaluation method in which the focus is on an individual or a group of individuals, and a broad range of data sources are obtained from the natural setting. Case studies have "a unique strength in providing a format to understand the dynamics of a situation, linking context, processes, and outcomes" (Pryzwansky & Noblit, 1990, p. 297).

Narrative in nature, case studies are often conducted under naturalistic conditions (Bergan & Kratochwill, 1990; Denton, Hasbrouck, & Sekaquaptewa, 2003). The case study method can be used to monitor or analyze the effects of consultation on the consultee or client system (Pryzwansky & Noblit, 1990); for example, a consultant might conduct a case study on the effects of quality circles on job satisfaction in a community service agency. Although it is descriptive in nature, the case study method does not excuse the consultant and consultee from identifying specific and behaviorally defined goals at the outset of consultation (Bergan & Kratochwill, 1990; MacNealy, 1999). It does, however, permit application of consultation evaluation to an individual consultee or client with a minimum of statistical work even though it requires detailed data collection (Pryzwansky & Noblit, 1990).

The case study can provide insight into previously unsuspected relationships affecting consultation. The case study is, however, very susceptible to bias, and use of this method requires careful

judgments about the efficacy of consultation. Because of its uncontrolled nature, consultants and consultees can have only limited confidence about the cause of any observed effects (Barlow et al., 1999) and generalizability (MacNealy, 1999). On the other hand, Lincoln and Guba (1985) point out mechanisms of dealing with bias. To the degree that a case study is comprehensive, it can be quite time consuming. Case studies are often viewed as lower-level evaluation tools, but they can also be used to evaluate consultation adequately (Barlow et al., 1999).

**Self-Report Assessment Method.**   The self-report assessment method is frequently used at the end of the consultation process to evaluate the effects of consultation. This method makes use of such instruments as rating scales, surveys, checklists, and questionnaires, which can all be developed by the consultant and consultee or are available in some standardized form. When using assessment and evaluation instruments for any purpose, the consultant will want to bear several important points in mind (Cooper & O'Conner, 1993): first, develop a specific connection between the goals of consultation and the instruments chosen; second, consider using a combination of assessment instruments that reflect hard, soft, and qualitative methods; third, use repeated measures; and fourth, inform consultees of the limitations of any instruments used, which is an ethical obligation.

In summative evaluation, self-assessment can be used in all of the previously mentioned methods, including a postconsultation assessment measure. The method tends to lack rigor in terms of experimental design and can easily provide inaccurate results if the precision of the instruments used is inadequate. However, this is a very common method of evaluating consultation, and its use has been enhanced by significant improvements in the development of questionnaires and surveys (e.g., see Oher, 1993). The self-report method is particularly appropriate for evaluating consultation in terms of consultee satisfaction, consultant satisfaction, and perceived consultant effectiveness.

**Focus Groups.** Focus groups are both an intervention and a qualitative research technique (Kormanski & Eschbach, 1997; Tashakkori & Teddlie, 2003). They usually consist of 7–10 members who are chosen due to their relationship to the topic under consideration, led by a moderator. Although the consultant selects the topics that will be focused on, the objective is to determine the consultees' perspectives on these topics. The reactions of the consultees guide the direction the focus group takes. Focus groups allow consultants to observe group process.

They also act as source of rich data about selected topics and provide a detailed data bank from which to draw conclusions. Focus groups have the advantage of having high face validity but the disadvantage of producing data that are difficult to analyze (Marshall & Rossman, 1995). Focus groups can be used for a variety of purposes, such as determining workers' beliefs about diversity management in their work settings (Russell-Chapin & Stoner, 1995) and evaluating programs for children and families (Nabors, Ramos, & Weist, 2001).

**Grounded Theory.** Grounded theory is a method in which a theory is derived inductively out of the data gathered (Padgett, 2004). It emphasizes constant comparison (see below). Grounded theory also employs theoretical sampling, in which the characteristics of the sample are determined as the evaluation progresses (Oktay, 2004). This is purposive sampling which increases the diversity of your sample, searching for different properties of the subjects.

**Triangulation.** Triangulation is an approach in which multiple methods and/or sources of data are put together to validate a given explanation of a situation (Lincoln & Guba, 1985; Tashakkori & Teddlie, 2003). Data are examined across sources to look for consistencies in patterns (Goldstein & Harris, 2000).

**Ethnographic Interviews.** This method assumes that the evaluator is familiar with and understands the unit such as an organization so that the reports of members of the unit are meaningful. The main premise is that the evaluator adequately understands the frame of reference of the persons providing data (Truscott et al., 2000). There are two types of ethnographic interviews: causal and systematic (Macnealy, 1999). Casual interviews are very similar to the unstructured interviews discussed in  of this text. Systematic interviews are very similar as the structured interviews described in the same chapter.

**Constant Comparative Method.** This evaluative method is much like the formative evaluation discussed above. As data are collected, they are interpreted and additional information is gathered based upon the questions raised by the previous data collected from multiple sources and methods (Strauss & Corbin, 1990; Truscott et al., 2000). This method allows for the identification of critical themes or incidents through grouping and regrouping of selected data (Goldstein & Harris, 2000; Oktay, 2004). Consensus is then determined regarding thematic patterns.

**Member Checks.** Member checks involve a process by which the original data and evaluation scheme are fed back to the participants for their evaluation (Lincoln & Guba, 1985; Truscott et al., 2000). This method is used to increase the credibility of collected data (Goldstein & Harris, 2000). You might view this method as a specialized focus group.

**Recursive Data Collection.** This is the method in which multiple data sets are collected over time and analyzed to try to verify previous findings (Truscott et al., 2000). An example would be following a student's behavioral adjustment over several years of schooling.

In summary, the evaluation of consultation effects moves the consultant into the realm of experimental design, either quantitative or qualitative, which may require more sophistication in this area and/or statistics than the consultant and consultee possess. Under such circumstances, they must either seek outside assistance or develop a suitable evaluation method that is within their levels of expertise. Because of the time, effort, and expense that outcome evaluation can require, the evaluation plan used must be cost effective. The consultant must ensure that evaluation results are described completely and accurately and are disseminated to the appropriate parties, such as the consultee, organization contact person, administrators, and other appropriate parties-at-interest.

**A Brief Example of Summative Evaluation in the Consultation Process.** Bonnie has been consulting with Dorothy concerning a "Back on Your Feet and on Your Own" program at a local shelter for battered women. Half of the women in the shelter have agreed to be trained in a program designed to help them reestablish themselves as independently functioning members of the community. The other half were promised the same training provided that the evaluation of the training was positive. After three months, the group comparison method was used in the evaluation. Differences were found between the experimental group and the control group on several measures ranging from personality inventories and interviews to survey results and the impressions of the experimental group's counselors. Results of the evaluation suggested that the training might well benefit the women. The control group was immediately provided with the training.

The consultant and consultee can effectively plan the postconsultation by following many of the procedures used in the formulating-a-plan phase of the implementation stage. You may want to review the planning process in , including determining objectives; establishing procedures; defining steps; assigning responsibilities; and testing for feasibility, cost effectiveness, and capabilities. A classic technique called force-field analysis (Lewin, 1951) is a useful technique in assessing the forces that may aid or impede the accomplishment of plans. With the proper planning, then, the consultant can help the consultee and organization effectively follow through on the results of consultation.

**A Brief Example of Planning Postconsultation Matters.** A marriage and family therapist has been consulting with a counseling psychologist who is working with a couple on enhancing their relationship. The family therapist has assisted the consultee in using therapeutic metaphors with the couple. Consultation has proceeded effectively. Together the consultant and consultee formulate a plan for how the consultee will proceed with the couple after consultation has ended. Part of the plan to enhance their emotional intimacy involves helping them write their own metaphors.

# PHASE TWO: PLANNING POSTCONSULTATION/ POSTCOLLABORATION MATTERS

The consultant can increase the chances that the results of consultation will be maintained after his or her departure by using effective postconsultation planning. Plans for this purpose rely heavily on the resources available to the consultee and the organization. In collaboration, this phase involves all of the collaborators "getting on the same page" with regard to what activities, if any, they will be engaging in after the collaborators stop formally meeting about the client system.

# PHASE THREE: REDUCING INVOLVEMENT AND FOLLOWING UP

Once postconsultation plans have been formulated to the satisfaction of the parties involved, the consultant initiates a period of reduced involvement and enacts follow-up procedures.

## Reducing Involvement

Reduced involvement refers to the gradual reduction in the consultant's contact with the consultee and the organization, which effectively prevents abrupt termination. The consultee and other appropriate parties begin to pick up the slack left by the consultant's declining involvement. In collaboration, reducing involvement refers to the gradual reduction of contact of the collaborators with one another.

One method proved effective in reducing involvement is called *fading,* a lessening of contact and involvement with the consultee and the organization. For example, if a consultant has been meeting with a consultee on a weekly basis, contact might be faded to once every two weeks, then to once every three weeks, and so on. Similarly, the consultant's visits to the organization are reduced over time. As the consultant is fading contact, his or her roles are gradually taken over by the consultee. The reduced involvement reinforces independence in the consultee and the organization.

Some authors (e.g., Bell & Nadler, 1985) advocate that the consultant be available on an as-needed basis while the consultee and the organization try to manage the changes brought about by consultation. Others, such as Noell et al. (2005), suggest specific feedback on consultee implementation as a way to ensure treatment integrity. However reduced involvement is accomplished, it should be negotiated, for then it is clear to everyone involved that reduced involvement does not mean no involvement (Schein, 1999). For example, consultees may still need emotional, practical, or technical support (Atanasiou et al., 2002).

**A Brief Example of Reducing Involvement.** A school counselor has been meeting weekly with a teacher regarding some classroom management problems the teacher has been having. As a result of consultation the teacher has made great strides in eliciting appropriate behavior from the students. The consultant has helped the teacher plan how the class will be managed for the entire term and how data on the students' behavior will be collected. To reduce the consultant's involvement, the consultant and consultee set two final meetings at three-week intervals before terminating the consultation.

### Following Up

Although follow-up is a critical phase, it is often not conducted (Myrick, 2003; Zins & Erchul, 2002).

Planning follow-up procedures can reduce the stress that comes with winding down consultation. Follow-up helps to develop a sense of how the gains made are being maintained. It helps to deal with things like "quirks" in the implementation, unanticipated resources that are needed to be successful, unanticipated issues such as the nature of consultee communication with the client system, the need to check the "goodness of fit" between the intervention and the environment in which it is being implemented, needed consultee support, and the professional development of the parties involved (Gutkin & Curtis, 1999) as well as treatment integrity (Riley-Tillman & Chafouleas, 2003).

Follow-up refers to the process of periodically determining how well the results of consultation are being maintained over time and how well the consultee and organization are performing postconsultation efforts. In the language of behavioral consultation, the term *monitoring* is often used (Noell & Witt, 1998). Follow-up provides the consultee and organization with a regular "check up" (Kelley, 1981). For example, follow-up can help to determine if certain target behaviors have been generalized or if a certain behavior has been maintained by the client system (Kratochwill et al., 1999). Follow-up is important because it provides some indication of consultant availability, an opportunity to salvage plans that have not been effectively carried out, some assistance while promoting independence on the part of the consultee and the organization, and some prevention of future problems (Kelley, 1981) as well as an opportunity to celebrate successes. There has been some criticism that follow-up is generally not well done (Zins & Erchul, 2002) and that the conduct of follow-up can make a difference in the integrity with which interventions are applied (Noell et al., 2005).

According to recent research, when done properly and effectively, follow-up often includes performance feedback to the consultee (Noell et al., 2005). Performance feedback involves monitoring the implementation and then sharing with the consultee, in a structured manner, specific information of the level of treatment integrity and client performance (Noell et al., 2005). There is evidence that performance feedback leads to superior treatment implementation and child behavioral outcomes whereas simply talking about the implementation does not (Noell et al., 2005). When properly accomplished, reduced involvement and follow-up fill a gap between postconsultation planning and termination.

**A Brief Example of Follow-Up.** A human resource development specialist has been training volunteers who work with incarcerates in a rehabilitation program. Three months after the training has concluded, the specialist calls the program director to check on how the volunteers are doing according to a format agreed upon during postconsultation planning.

## PHASE FOUR: TERMINATING

Like human relationships, consultation requires closure; termination provides that closure in a formal, ritualistic manner. Termination formally ends a process and ideally leads to a sense of satisfaction with whatever has been accomplished. It also provides an appropriate time for celebrating whatever successes have been achieved. However, the termination process has received relatively little attention in the consultation literature (Dougherty et al., 1996; Gilmore, 1993; Stroh & Johnson, 2006).

Termination is a critical element in the consultation process. If performed properly, it can lead to subsequent requests for consultation (Dougherty et al., 1996). If performed inappropriately, it can result in the dissatisfaction of the consultee and the organization. Inappropriate termination can affect the manner in which postconsultation planning and subsequent consultation experiences are perceived. Inappropriate termination procedures include a unilateral decision (by either the consultant or consultee) to terminate, abrupt termination, indefinite retention of consultation (with no formal end point), and the attempt to unnecessarily extend the consultation process by any of the parties involved.

Abrupt termination is a shock and can be a distraction (French & Bell, 1999). Conversely, unnecessary extension of consultation is a particular danger to consultants in private practice and to consultants internal to the organization who feel they must always have something to do. As the termination process is begun, consultants should maintain awareness of their need to be needed and avoid engendering dependence (French & Bell, 1999; Huckabay, 2002). A lingering consultation prevents the human side of termination from receiving adequate consideration.

A meeting that concludes postconsultation planning is an excellent time to deal with any unresolved issues before the consultant or collaborator's formal departure, and such a ritual can set the termination process in motion. A formal review of the consultant's final report is one proven method of effectively accomplishing termination (Gilmore, 1993); a debriefing conversation on lessons learned is another (McLean, 2006). Here participants can discuss the progress made in consultation relative to the contract and stated goals of the consultation, and a clearly defined point of termination can be set. This definite ending point can prevent unnecessary dependence on the part of the consultee or the organization (French & Bell, 1999). Finally, discussing future possibilities for consulting is another way of easing the stress of termination.

**A Brief Example of Terminating.** Sherill, a school-based consultant, has worked with several teachers for a period of four semesters on managing work-related stress. The stress management program was now being phased out, and it was time for Sherill to terminate the consultation relationships she formed. At the last meeting of the group, Sherill gave her work phone number to each participant and conducted a brief discussion in which each member responded to the question, "What have I learned from this experience?" Sherill then provided a light snack over which each group member sent every other member a "telegram."

---

### CASE 6.1    Disengagement for School Consultants

Rosie, a school-based human service consultant, has been working with Wilma, a fourth-grade teacher, about a boy in Wilma's class named Leo. Leo had become increasingly withdrawn over the first grading period of the academic year, and Wilma had contacted Rosie for consultation. The two professionals evaluated the plan they had put into motion and determined that Leo's level of participation in class activities had increased dramatically thanks to an increase in group activities and special attention from Wilma.

As they wound down the consultation process, Rosie and Wilma reviewed their work together and shared their perceptions of the experience. Rosie engaged Wilma in a reflective discussion of each stage of consultation they went through. By use of selected questions, Rosie and Wilma concluded that although the majority of the process went quite smoothly, they had some difficulties in actually defining how Leo's withdrawing behavior manifested itself. They determined that Wilma saw Leo as more withdrawn than Rosie did and that these different perceptions led to some difficulties in defining the problem. Wilma agreed that the quick manner with which Leo responded to her interventions suggested that perhaps she had misconstrued his behavior.

Rosie and Wilma reviewed the results of pre- and postconsultation measures, which included a behavior checklist and observational data they had both periodically filled out on Leo. Rosie discussed how she had statistically analyzed the data and cautioned Wilma about the limitations of the data. The two then focused their discussion on whether the results obtained with Leo were worth the cost of having Wilma work with him in the classroom rather than having him sent for individual

and group counseling. Wilma admitted that at first she wanted Rosie to take Leo and "fix" him so that she wouldn't have to continually prod him to get involved in classroom life. She had to admit that she was pleasantly surprised with the quick progress that Leo had made.

Rosie and Wilma then changed the focus of their meeting to discuss the kinds of behaviors that Wilma would engage in after consultation was completed to keep the gains Leo had made. They agreed that informal contacts with Leo as well as verbal reinforcement for social interactions should be continued on an intermittent level. Rosie agreed to check in with Wilma at two-week intervals for a month after which they would terminate their relationship. During the next academic year, Wilma contacted Rosie again for assistance with two other problematic students.

**Commentary**

Evaluation of the plan is essential to having the parties involved believe in the process. Notice the effort Rosie made to ensure that Wilma had a thorough understanding of the nature of Leo's behavior change. Notice further how this might well be linked to Wilma's seeking additional consultation with Rosie about different students the next school year. Part of disengagement is planning postconsultation procedures with the consultee.

In this case Rosie and Wilma made plans to assist Leo in maintaining the progress he had made. The first part of the telegram read, "I encourage you to keep on . . ." The second part of the telegram read, "I encourage you to work on . . ." Members then shared what others had written to them. Sherill then thanked the group and the meeting was adjourned.

---

## MULTICULTURAL ASPECTS RELATED TO DISENGAGEMENT

Multicultural influences can have a strong effect on the disengagement stage, particularly the evaluation of the consultation process. For example, the cultural experiences of some consultees or collaborators may suggest that the evaluation be informed by general questions rather than checklists or questionnaires.

Just as in evaluating the consultation plan, consultants and collaborators should be cautious about assuming what kind of evaluation process is acceptable to consultees of differing cultural backgrounds (Sheridan, 2000). Cultural differences can relate to perceptions of what needs to be accomplished during postconsultation and postcollaboration planning. For example, whereas the consultant may judge the progress to date as time to begin withdrawing from the relationship, the consultee may have a perception that there needs to be increased

---

**C A S E   6.2       Disengagement for Community Consultants**

---

Hernando, a hospital social worker, has been an internal consultant to a long-term care team at a community hospital. The team consists of an activity therapist, a patient advocate, the charge nurse, the director of physical therapy, and a part-time social worker. The two-fold problem of staff and patient morale led to the consultation.

With its 55 beds typically filled, the long-term care program was continually experiencing severe stress, and the problem was considered to be significant. Hernando's reputation throughout the hospital led to his being asked to consult. For the past three months he had worked intensely with the team members, who in turn took the resulting ideas to their units for review and decision making.

Consultation had resulted in a complex plan of interventions that was evaluated and determined to be fairly successful. The primary changes for staff included flexible work scheduling and a stress management group. Improved caregiving to patients including getting them fed and taken to bathroom facilities within proper time frames. In addition, significant changes to the activities program made it more appealing to the patients.

To begin winding down the consultation process, Hernando requested a special two-hour meeting with the team, during which he and the group evaluated the consultation process. Hernando asked the group for face-to-face as well as written feedback in the form of a consultee satisfaction survey he had developed for his work at the hospital. Hernando provided his observations of what had transpired and how effective he thought the process had been. The group discussed what had happened as a result of the consultation and

how much these changes had cost—the group agreed that the changes had been somewhat painful. They noted that, at first, there was a tendency for the different work groups assigned to the program to feel severely understaffed and to believe that this was causing the problems.

Only after discussions with the different shifts—led by Hernando and the appropriate team member—did any kind of group ownership of the problems begin to emerge. Only then were goals set and implemented. The group of consultees and Hernando decided that he should follow up with them during the next two months to work out any glitches. The team would continue to take responsibility for monitoring the impact of the recent changes. Six months after the beginning of the consultation, Hernando followed up with the team one last time. Since things were continuing to go smoothly and the morale of the staff and patients alike was improved, Hernando and the team officially terminated their intense yet successful relationship.

**Commentary**

Evaluating the consultation process is good business on the part of consultants. In this case Hernando, through a face-to-face evaluation process, allowed the consultees to express their deeper feelings about the consultation process and most likely created the conditions for the consultees to communicate more genuinely among themselves in the future. Follow-up procedures, such as those implemented by Hernando, demonstrate the consultant's commitment to the consultee as well as provide opportunities for refining any postconsultation planning.

---

collaborative activity, including additional monitoring (Ramirez et al., 1998).

The cultural experiences of the parties involved can influence follow-up. For example, some fellow collaborators may desire frequent follow-up contacts, not due to dependency, but to their view of social professional relationships. The critical nature of termination becomes even more apparent when consultants and collaborators take cultural experi-

ences into consideration. Depending on one's cultural experiences, the termination process may be considered as rather drawn out. For example, the rituals of some cultures suggest that consultants terminate with an approach that involves a series of brief meetings. To ignore cultural differences in disengagement is to risk jeopardizing the current relationship as well future consultations.

# SUMMARY

Disengagement in the consultation process involves a sense of letting go on both professional and personal levels. Its four phases include evaluating the consultation process, planning postconsultation matters, reducing involvement and following up, and terminating. Disengagement, which should be differentiated from termination, should not be rushed; it should be a well-planned and well-executed procedure.

Evaluation of consultation is frequently done poorly, and as a result, it often does not provide consultation participants a chance to examine how well they have done or how they have grown. Therefore consultants should be ready to assist their consultees in evaluating consultation and should ensure that their own services are included in the overall evaluation procedure.

In postconsultation planning, the consultant asks the consultee, "How are you going to follow through after I am gone?" This planning process places increased responsibility on the consultee and the organization to make effective use of the products of consultation. Postconsultation planning is an appropriate time for consultees to express their concerns about the consultant's leaving and for the consultant to encourage them to realize that they have the abilities to follow through.

The egos and self-esteem of everyone involved in consultation are affected during reduced involvement. Being needed as ing, and thus it is sometimes follow through on what the instrumental in accomplishi can more effectively reduce involvement by remembering that one goal of consultation is to help the consultee and the organization continue to function without the consultant. Consultants can take pride in being instrumental in enabling consultees to use the new skills they have learned.

During follow-up the consultant takes on a troubleshooting role in which help is provided to the consultee or organization on an as-needed basis. It is important to define what is meant by "as-needed" so that dependence is not fostered.

Termination is the formal ending of the consultation process. Saying goodbye is not always easy. Consequently, formal termination does not always occur or may be done in a stiff, artificial manner. By being perceived as fair, competent, human, and effective, consultants can take leave with an enhanced reputation, which can be intrinsically satisfying and earn them subsequent consultation opportunities. You should bear in mind that very little of the consultation/collaboration literature related to stages has focused on the disengagement stage (Dougherty et al., 1996).

# SUGGESTIONS FOR EFFECTIVE PRACTICE

- Design all evaluation procedures prior to carrying out the plan.

- Remember that formative evaluation can be as valuable as summative evaluation.

- Use fading procedures for reducing involvement.

- Bear in mind that follow-up procedures, although frequently neglected, help to sustain gains made by the consultee or fellow collaborators.

- Avoid abrupt terminations.

## QUESTIONS FOR REFLECTION

1. How does the term "disengagement" differ from the term "termination"?

2. In what ways is disengagement a winding down of the consultation process?

3. For what purposes can evaluation of the effects of consultation be used?

4. As a consultant, when in the consultation process would you start to plan evaluation procedures?

5. How does a consultant proceed in determining what events to evaluate?

6. How would you handle evaluation of consultation if both you and your consultee lacked the expertise to perform sophisticated evaluation procedures?

7. What kinds of things should be accomplished in postconsultation planning?

8. What is the major difference between reduced involvement and follow-up?

9. How would you go about the process of psychologically terminating the consultation process?

10. What does the following statement mean: "The consultant begins termination upon entry into the consultation process"?

## SUGGESTED SUPPLEMENTARY READINGS

Heppner, P. P., Kivlighan, D. M., Jr., and Wampold, B. E. (1999). *Research design in counseling* (2nd ed.). Pacific Grove, CA: Brooks/Cole. This book provides invaluable evaluation information for consultants, whether or not they are trained as professional counselors. I recommend this as a handbook to help consultants determine how to evaluate the effects of consultation. Even though the book's focus is on research, its concepts are easily translatable into evaluation procedures. Chapter 14, "Process Research," should be of high interest to consultants. I strongly recommend this book to consultants who believe their evaluation skills need a boost.

Dougherty, A. M., Tack, F. E., Fullam, C. B., & Hammer, L. A. (1996). Disengagement: A neglected aspect of the consultation process. *Journal of Educational and Psychological Consultation, 7,* 259–274. This article, one of the few on the topic, examines and summarizes the existing literature on disengagement in consultation. The authors describe the stage of disengagement, identify important stage-specific consultant skills and roles, examine relevant psychological dynamics, and suggest how to avoid pitfalls during this stage. The authors conclude with recommendations for further study.

# 7

✳

# Ethical, Professional, and Legal Issues

Throughout their careers, all consultants and collaborators encounter ethical, professional, and legal dilemmas about which they must make decisions. Decisions of this type require sound judgment. Frequently, the problems do not suggest clear and specific courses of action for resolution. This should not be surprising, for most consultation issues are complex and ethical dilemmas will be frequent (ACA, 2005).

In this chapter, we will examine how ethical, professional, and legal issues may affect your consultation practice. We will also examine how consultants can make ethical decisions regarding them. There are few cut-and-dried answers when it comes to the ethics of consultation. Consultants frequently have to depend on their sound professional judgment when they make ethical decisions. For example, you could face issues related to the ambiguity about how to proceed in providing consultation in extreme situations such as those involving disasters (Halpern & Tramontin, 2007) or you could have to determine the impact of consultee actions on client welfare. However, studying the issues that consultants encounter will provide you with a better understanding of the importance of ethics and the complexity of consultation. Furthermore, exposure to these ideas can help you develop the competencies and professional perspective necessary for effectively delivering your consultation services.

Here are some questions to consider as you read this chapter:

1. What professional and ethical obligations do consultants have beyond those to their consultees?

2. What are the basic legal issues that consultants encounter?

3. Why are codes of ethics important to guiding the practice of consultants and collaborators?

4. What are some professional and ethical issues related to consultant effectiveness?

5. How do multicultural issues affect the ethical practice of consultation?

## INTRODUCTION

Consider the following scenario of an ethical dilemma:

### Case Example

You are a consultant working with a group of consultees in a human service organization. The consultees are all section heads within the organization, and you are training them in becoming more effective decision makers. It was clear from the outset that you were in no way to report to the organization's administration your opinions about any of the section heads' decision-making abilities. It was further understood by all the parties involved that you were to maintain total confidentiality about all aspects of the consultation.

After two months of training, the chief administrator asks you to evaluate the decision-making skills of a particular section head so that a personnel decision can be made about her. The administrator assures you that the information will not go beyond your conversation with her and that no one will know that you ever said anything about the section head's decision-making skills. When you reiterate that confidentiality was guaranteed at the outset of the training, the administrator becomes angry, demands that you share the requested information, and threatens to terminate consultation immediately if you do not cooperate.

What would you do if you were the consultant in this case study? Would you be tempted to share the information secretly? What are your ethical obligations to the section head? What are your ethical obligations to the organization in which consultation is occurring? What is your ethical obligation to your profession?

Although ethics has been a neglected topic in consultation in the past, it has been receiving more attention in recent years. For example, for a period of time, the *Journal of Educational and Psychological Consultation* had a column entitled "Legal and Ethical Issues in Consultation." While very little has been written about specific ethical issues related to consultation and collaboration, these services are receiving increasing attention in the codes of ethics of many professional organizations. Several ethical, legal, and professional issues have arisen as consultation has become more widely practiced and as the number of people directly and indirectly affected by consultants' behavior has grown. Therefore, consultants need to become increasingly aware of the ethical and professional dilemmas they may encounter. For example, when consulting with organizations, human service consultants may have to make decisions about issues related to deception, coercion, risk to people, invasion of privacy, and the probability of the success of selected interventions (Tannenbaum, Greene, & Glickman, 1989).

As human service professionals, consultants have an obligation to behave in such a way that they bring no harm to themselves, their consultees, the client system, the organizations involved, or society at large. Because consultation is by nature complex, the consultant is frequently caught in ethical dilemmas. In addition, consulting is a powerful activity that involves changing the parties involved. Finally, our society is demanding a higher level of accountability for human service professionals.

Just as ethical issues are receiving more attention in consultation, so too are legal issues. Since consultants can be sued for malpractice, breach of contract, and a variety of other actions or inactions, they need to learn about the laws affecting their practices and perform in a manner that reflects that knowledge.

## ETHICS AND PROFESSIONAL ISSUES

As it pertains to consultation, *ethics* refers to standards of moral and professional conduct. *Morality,* on the other hand, deals with perceptions of right and wrong behavior and is based on judgments of behavior from a broad view such as religion or culture (Corey et al., 2007). You may want to note that there has been some discussion about morality and its relationship to consulting with organizations (Fuqua & Newman, 2006).

Ethical conduct comes from putting together an awareness of an ethical code and its underlying principles (Bersoff, 1996). Ethical issues in the mental health professions are regulated by both laws and professional codes (Remley & Herlihy, 2007). Ethics are aspirational goals that reflect the ideal standards of the profession and are enforced by the appropriate organization (Remley, 2007). Corey et al. (2007) distinguish between mandatory ethics and aspirational ethics. *Mandatory ethics* refers to complying with minimal standards, a kind of "dos-and-don'ts" way of behaving. From this perspective, professionals basically look to things outside of themselves, such as rules of an organization, for guidance in dealing with ethical dilemmas (Newman, Gray, & Fuqua, 1996). Although the concept of mandatory ethics is useful, the complexity of the consulting relationship does not easily lend itself to using mandatory ethics (Newman et al., 1996). Consider, for example, the complexity of issues related to confidentiality due to the triadic nature of consultation.

*Aspirational ethics* refers to "the attempt to accomplish the maximum in moral and ethical outcomes" (Newman et al., 1996, p. 231). The concept of aspirational ethics can help the professional aim for the highest standards of professional behavior and go beyond the "letter of the law" (Corey et al., 2007). Compared to mandatory ethics, aspirational ethics are more general. Examples of aspirational goals include integrity and social responsibility (Newman et al., 1996).

When a human service professional functions in the capacity of a consultant and follows broad, written ethical guidelines, such guidelines are typically referred to as an *ethics code*. An ethics code serves to discourage inappropriate practice and protects the recipients of the services being rendered. In a positive sense, ethics codes stress adherence to rigorous professional standards, clarify expectations,

and promote exemplary behavior. Most human services professions have codes of ethics to guide practice (Jacob, 2002). Recent ethics codes, such as those of the American Counseling Association (ACA) and the American Psychological Association (APA) have both a mandatory and an aspirational component.

Because codes of ethics tend to be general, they do not dictate specific courses of action. Further, the ethical codes of most human service professional groups contain very few, if any, guidelines specific to the practice of consultation. As a result, in your practice, you will often face ethical dilemmas with no specific guidance for action. Each consultant can only apply the code of ethics of his or her profession and make the best possible professional decisions when applying the code to a particular situation. Many consultants belong to various professional organizations. Most of these organizations—for example, the ACA, the APA, the National Board for Certified Counselors (NBCC), the National Association of Social Workers (NASW), the National Association of School Psychologists (NASP), the American Mental Health Counselors Association (AMHCA), and the National Organization for Human Services Education (NOHSE)—have developed a code of ethics. Thus, many consultants enjoy the privilege of having (and have the responsibility of following) some general guidelines that apply to the professional behavior of any human service professional.

By belonging to one of these organizations, the human service professional agrees to adhere to that organization's code. Some organizations, such as the ACA, have specific statements about the ethical conduct of consulting behavior. The result is that there are some guidelines for acting as a professional in the general areas of competence (e.g., not providing services for which one is not competent) and responsibility (e.g., maintaining confidentiality) (Robinson & Gross, 1985). But there are few guidelines specific to consulting behavior, such as applying principles of confidentiality in an organizational setting.

In conclusion, consultants can use the ethics codes of their organizations only as general guidelines. These guidelines cannot identify appropriate actions for all situations, and the final decision for what constitutes a correct course of action in a given situation rests with the professional. Further, there is an emerging issue that the ethics codes of many mental health organizations may be subject to cultural bias (Pedersen, 1997). As Pedersen (1997) notes, "not only do ethical guidelines need to be interpreted in each situation, but they must also be interpreted for and within each cultural context" (p. 230). Thus, developing personal methods for making ethical decisions is crucial for the consultant. The bottom line is that consultants, within the broad guidelines, need to make informed, sound, responsible, and culturally competent judgments (Corey et al., 2007).

In consultation and collaboration, ethical issues are often multidimensional and very complex. As a result, these issues can be a challenge to resolve effectively. There are many gray areas that require decision-making skills. The process entails not only learning information about ethical standards, but also learning how to define and work through a variety of difficult situations. To assist human service professionals in making such judgments, I recommend the following steps:

1. Identify the problem or dilemma.
2. Identify the potential issues involved.
3. Review the relevant ethics codes.
4. Know the applicable laws and regulations.
5. Obtain consultation from trusted colleagues.
6. Consider possible and probable courses of action.
7. Enumerate the consequences of various decisions.
8. Decide on what seems to be the best course of action. (Corey et al., 2007, pp. 20–22)

For an alternative decision-making strategy based upon constructivism, consult Cottone (2001).

In addition to mastering and using an ethical decision-making process, consultants themselves can engage in peer consultation activities (Gottlieb, 2006). Peer consultation is a process in which professional development activities and support are mutually provided by one or more professionals. For example, if I am experiencing difficulty with some of my consultation activities, I might seek some consultation for the consultant. Peer consultation can occur in support groups and by telephone or the Internet. Peer consultation activities can be valuable assisting consultants in coping with ethical dilemmas, preventing legal entanglements, and enhancing their professional competence.

What kinds of professional and ethical issues do consultants face in their practices? The following issues are all involved, and I will address them throughout this chapter: values, multicultural issues, competence, training, the consultant-consultee-client relationship, the rights of the consultees, group work, and interventions. I have also included a discussion of ethical issues related to crisis/disaster consultation, organizational consultation, and web-consulting because human service professionals are increasingly being called upon to deal with these types of issues.

## Values and the Consultant

As in any helping relationship, values play an integral role in the consultation process. The consultant, consultee, members of the client system, and parties-at-interest to consultation all have values formed by their life experiences, and each party involved in or affected by consultation is in turn influenced by each other's values. Consequently, the sheer number of people involved (usually three or more) suggests that conflict of values should be expected (Parsons, 1996). The trick is for the consultant to use values to enhance the consultation process without abusing power (French & Bell, 1999).

It would be naive for consultants to think that their own values do not influence the consultation process while thinking that those of the other parties do (or vice versa). Clearly, it is important for consultants to possess a reflective understanding of their values and how they influence the practice of consultation. In fact, the ethics codes of the ACA (2005), the APA (2002), and the NBCC (2005) note that self-awareness, including awareness of one's values, is important when consulting. Consequently, consultants will want to understand the role their own values play in the creation and resolution of the ethical dilemmas they face in their practice.

A significant professional issue for consultants is the degree to which they let their values dictate their behavior in consultation. Consultants who impose their values on consultees or other parties-at-interest are on very shaky ethical ground because they are depriving others of their due freedom. There are, however, some sets of values that inform consultants' work. Community psychologists, for example, tend to value self-determination, and that value will affect the consultation process (Prilleltensky, Peirson, & Nelson, 1998). At the other extreme, when consultants are overly cautious about imposing their values on others involved in consultation, they risk rendering the consultation impotent. A middle ground appears to be one in which consultants are aware of their values, make a commitment not to impose them on others, and go about the consultation process as effectively as they can.

**Value Conflicts.** In our culturally diverse society, the potential for value conflicts is high. When consultants' and consultees' values do conflict, effective progress in consultation can be blocked. The bottom-line for consultants is whether or not to refer the consultee to another consultant. Just as when value conflicts arise in other helping relationships such as counseling (Corey et al., 2007), there are no easy conflict resolution solutions in consultation. Consultants experiencing value conflicts should be honest with themselves in determining whether they can remain objective enough to work with those with whom they disagree.

When value conflicts do occur, they are typically best met head-on. The consultant can model effective conflict resolution skills for the consultee as they work through the conflict, and together they can determine whether and how consultation is still feasible. There are three areas in which value conflict issues are likely to arise in consultation: worldviews (including cultural perspectives), views of organizations, and views of the client or client system. Consider the following examples of values conflicts:

*Example 1: Differences in Worldviews.* Gene and Phil, both mental health professionals, are consulting regarding several clients in Phil's caseload. Gene's cultural background is different from Phil's. As consultation ensues, Gene is increasingly disturbed by Phil's apparent lack of concern about being prompt for their sessions. When Gene questions him on this, Phil notes that from his perspective, time is a convenience for humans to use and not an indicator of politeness. Phil relates that in his culture time just "happens" and is viewed more as a convenient way to track events rather than something that drives events. Gene's view is that time is very critical and important and that every act on the job must be completed in an efficient and timely fashion. To act otherwise is certainly unprofessional and possibly unethical. If you were Gene, how would you attempt to manage these different views so that effective consultation might take place? Should Gene refer Phil to another consultant? Do you think Gene is open to examining his view of life and accommodating differing views?

*Example 2: Differences in Views of Organizations.* Bobbie is a mental health consultant assigned to work with the law enforcement professionals in a large urban police department. Bobbie has to negotiate constantly between the often-conflicting values associated with mental health and law enforcement. When a high-ranking police officer used a consultation session to deal with ways to prevent bypassing the chain of command, Bobbie inadvertently made light of the situation and was puzzled when the police officer did not return for a second consultation session. Why do you think that one minor slip-up caused the officer not to return? In what ways do you think Bobbie could have prevented such a slip-up? What Bobbie didn't recognize was the taboo in law enforcement circles against bypassing the chain of command, whereas in a mental health setting, such behavior might be viewed as inappropriate and worthy of reprimand but is certainly not such a big deal. A perceived value difference concerning views of behavior probably caused the officer's absence. Because the officer did not perceive the consultant to be knowledgeable about or respectful of law enforcement values, he prematurely terminated consultation.

*Example 3: Differences in Views of the Client System.* A consultant working with the administrator of a substance-abuse program in a human service agency finds that the administrator thinks of the program's clients as "welfare bums" who are "sponging off" society and the agency. The consultant, in contrast, views the clients as sick and in need of rehabilitation. How would you proceed if you were the consultant? How would you specifically deal with the value conflict in which you find yourself? Clearly, this situation has no easy answer.   In summary, because values are connected to every important decision made during the consultation process, consultants must be aware of their own values (Corey et al., 2003) and make a commitment not to impose them on consultees. The consultant's values can, however, be used to make appropriate decisions. The issue concerns how much consultants should allow their values to influence their behavior in consultation and when they should reveal their values (Snow & Gersick, 1986). When value conflicts emerge, the consultant should deal with them in a non-defensive, professional manner.

## Multicultural Issues

Multicultural issues are important elements in ethical and professional decision making (see, for example, the APA, 2003). Ethical practice dictates that consultants take the cultural context of consultees and client systems into account. In fact, some authors (e.g., Ingraham, 2000, 2003; Tarver Behring & Ingraham, 1998) have called for making culture a central component in the field of consultation. Increasingly, our society is becoming culturally diverse (Kanel, 2007). This diversity is reflected in the workplace (Steward, 1996; Plummer, 1998). As a result, as a consultant or collaborator, you will most likely have contact with people with varying cultural backgrounds. When working with consultees or fellow collaborators who are culturally different or with consultees or fellow collaborators whose clients are culturally different, you may

well encounter many ethical dilemmas and issues (Corey et al., 2007). Fortunately, most ethics codes underscore the helper's responsibility to take cultural contexts into consideration when delivering services. For example, the ethics codes of the ACA (2005), the APA (2002), and the NASW (1999) all cite respect for cultural diversity as essential to the best practices, and diversity perspectives are increasingly being incorporated into these codes. In their practice, consultants can place themselves in ethical jeopardy by ignoring diversity factors because such neglect can infringe upon rights of consultees with different worldviews and values.

The experiences of growing up in a different culture can create language patterns, learning styles, and ways of acting that differ from those of the majority culture. For example, speech in high-context cultures, such as Native American cultures, relies heavily on nonverbal aspects of communication, whereas low-context cultures like that of the majority culture rely more heavily on the use of words (Miranda, 1993). It is easy to imagine a person from a low-context cultural background wanting a person from a high-context cultural background to think, act, and speak more concretely and quickly. The implications for the development of ethical dilemmas in consultation and collaboration are obvious.

People from differing cultural, ethnic, or racial backgrounds can vary in a variety of ways including values, language patterns, and child rearing patterns (Thomas, Correa, & Morsink, 1995). Obviously, there can be differences within cultural groups regarding these same constructs which make generalization difficult (Tobias, 1993). As a result, specific cultural characteristics may assist professionals with information in dealing with consultees, fellow collaborators, and their clients to the degree those people possess those characteristics (Correa & Tulbert, 1993; Wubbolding, 1991b). Nonetheless, working effectively with people from differing cultural backgrounds requires knowledge of, and respect for, their cultural heritage and worldviews (Henning-Stout, 1994; Ingraham, 2000; Ramirez & Smith, 2007).

To practice ethically with cultural differences, consultants need to demonstrate sensitivity and respect when they provide their services to families, schools, or any other organization (Hogan, 2007; Remley & Herlihy, 2007). If consultants or collaborators do not take such differences into account, they can inadvertently cause difficulties in the helping relationship or exploit others. When consultants or collaborators do not act with multicultural sensitivity, they often become frustrated in attempts to be of service, get locked into their "expert" role, and become more content oriented (as opposed to process oriented) (Dougherty, 1996, 1997). There is some likelihood that the effectiveness of their communication will suffer.

Consultants and collaborators have a professional and ethical obligation to be aware of the influence of their culture and gender on their work with people of different cultural identities (Lum, 2007; Ramirez & Smith, 2007). Consultants and collaborators should recognize that their models of service delivery, and perhaps even their ethics codes, are deficient in the areas related to ethnic, racial, and cultural diversity (Jackson & Hayes, 1993; Soo-Hoo, 1998; Weinrach & Thomas, 1998).

Clearly, multicultural influences need to be taken into account when providing consultative and collaborative services. Consultants and collaborators should possess an awareness and comprehension of their own cultural group as well as the cultural group of their consultees and fellow collaborators. Consultants need perceptual sensitivity toward their own personal values and beliefs as well as those of consultees and fellow collaborators, and they should have a comprehension of the impact of the experiences of the mainstream culture on the parties involved in the helping process.

*The Case of Sidney.* Sidney is a Caucasian consultant who has a private consulting practice in a large urban area. Sidney is contacted by a minority neighborhood group because of his reputation for advocacy work. The neighborhood group is interested in forming a network that provides neighborhood members access to resources related to their personal and social welfare as well as enhancing their own sense of empowerment. Sidney agrees to provide consultation free of charge. As he begins work with the consultees from the neighborhood organization, he starts out by sharing the importance of advocacy. As he continues, many members of the group believe him to be condescending. He even occasionally uses terms like "you people" and "you need to get on with it!" When one of the members approaches Sidney about his behavior, Sidney explodes and says: "I am helping you people and not even charging you! You're lucky I just don't stop the whole deal right now. Remember, I am an expert on advocacy for disenfranchised groups." How could Sidney's worldview have gotten him in this unfortunate predicament? What values was Sidney using that seemed to make the consultation go awry? Assuming that Sidney had good intentions, what might you suggest to him about the way he went about trying to help?

*The Case of Maria.* Maria, a Hispanic counselor, is consulting with Michael, an African American psychologist, about one of Michael's cases. As Michael describes the case of an abused child, Maria immediately focuses in on the family unit for discussion and directs Michael to talk in more of a "family therapy" mode. Maria is aware of her own strong views about how families influence their individual members and how treatment should focus on the entire family (and perhaps the extended family). When Michael refocuses the discussion on the child, Maria confronts what she believes to be Michael's resistance. Maria ends up persuading Michael to look at the problem from her perspective. Do you see any possible ethical conflicts for Maria in this case? Can you identify any ways in which Maria could have acted differently when consulting with Michael? Could cultural variables have played a part in the way both Maria and Michael conceptualized the case?

## Consultant Competence

The issue of consultant competence has received much attention: the ethics codes of the major organizations in which many consultants have membership (e.g., the ACA [2005], the APA [2002]) all make statements to the effect that members should deliver only those services and accept only those positions for which they are qualified. The ethics code of the NBCC (2005) explicitly makes this statement for consulting. These qualifications are usually determined by the consultant's training and experience.

The parameters of competence are maintaining high levels of professionalism, knowing one's professional limitations, knowing when to decline and refer, and avoiding consultation activities when personal concerns could affect professional performance (Corey et al., 2007; French & Bell, 1999).

**Maintaining High Levels of Professionalism.** Consultants can do several things to maintain high levels of professional competence:

- Belong to and participate in professional organizations.

- Obtain the appropriate national and state credentials, certificates, and licenses for the profession in which they are trained.

- Participate in continuing education activities in general.

- Participate in continuing education activities (both didactic and experiential) that pertain to the consultation services they deliver or would like to deliver.

- Co-consult with more experienced colleagues.

- Consult under the supervision of a trusted colleague or a designated supervisor.

Underlying the maintenance of professionalism is consultants' desire to grow in their work. Consultants with such a growth orientation attempt to stretch themselves so that the depth and breadth of their knowledge and skills increase. This willingness to grow professionally also provides consultees with a positive role model that stimulates their growth and desire to participate more fully in consultation.

*The Case of Roger.* After Roger earned his doctorate in a human service profession, he proudly thought that he had "done it all." He became an active consultant and worked with many community groups on what he liked to call "family dynamics." Mary was one of Roger's consultees several years

before. When she again became one of his consultees, Mary got the eerie feeling that she was hearing the very same thing she had heard from Roger almost 10 years earlier. New terms like "empowerment" were thrown in for some of the same old ideas. When Mary challenged Roger and asked him his views on family systems and codependency as they related to the topic being discussed in the consultation, Roger became flustered, noted quickly that there was probably no connection, and promptly changed the subject. Has Roger kept updated in his field? Do you feel he has behaved ethically or demonstrated a high level of professionalism?

**Knowing One's Professional Limitations.**    Prior to entering a consultation relationship, consultants must assess whether their personal and professional competence is adequate for the task. Although it is easy to suggest ways of maintaining high levels of professionalism as a consultant, it is more difficult to suggest methods of knowing one's limitations. Most ethical codes such as those of the ACA (2005) and the APA (2002) state that a knowledge of one's limitations and abilities is essential. The ACA *Code of Ethics* (2005) makes direct reference to consultant competency.

Probably the most important thing that consultants can do in recognizing their limitations is to make a commitment to maintain high levels of objectivity and integrity while placing the needs of the consultee and the organization above their own. By asking themselves the following four questions in order, consultants can stay focused on their limitations:

1.  What can I do, given this situation?

2.  What is the right thing to do in this situation?

3.  Do I have the ability to do the right thing?

4.  What is the right thing to do that is in the best interests of the consultee and the organization?

By carefully pondering these questions, consultants are less likely to make errors in judgment with respect to their limitations. There is no substitute for the combination of personal and professional self-awareness and the commitment to put forth one's best effort when consulting.

*The Case of Shirley.*   Shirley recently received her master's degree in one of the helping professions, which included taking a course in consultation. She received a phone call from a church group offering her a fee for providing a workshop on eating disorders. Although Shirley was not knowledgeable about eating disorders, she took the consultation. She studied the topic for a week and then presented a two-day workshop. How well do you think Shirley knows her professional limitations? Did she have the right to conduct a workshop just because the group asked her to? If you were Shirley's work supervisor, how would you handle the situation if you became aware of it?

**Knowing When to Decline and Refer.**   When consultants realize they are "in over their heads" in terms of what is expected of them, they need to decline and make an appropriate referral. The story of the consultee walking up to a consultant and asking, "Are you an expert in X?," to which the consultant responds, "Sure, just give me an hour," should never occur. Several professional organizations' ethical codes state that services should be delivered only if it is anticipated that the provider can effectively manage the existing problem as well as any others that may arise.

A related issue involves the representation of oneself as a consultant. Consultants must state explicitly what they stand for, who they represent, and what they can and cannot do as consultants. This obligation to represent oneself honestly and accurately includes advertising. The ACA (2005) and the APA (2002) all make explicit statements with regard to honest disclosure about oneself both in person and through advertising. In fact, the ethical code of the APA (2002) devotes more coverage to public statements than to any other ethical principle.

Closely tied to the issue of representing oneself honestly is the issue of remuneration. Consultants typically charge the "going fee" for a given type of consultation service with a given type of organization in a given geographic area. The ACA (1995) specifically states that its members must refuse any type of remuneration when consultation recipients are due those services through the member's orga-

nization. Consultants must consider for each potential consultation whether they are in a position to charge fees in the first place and, if so, how much.

How do consultants respond when they are asked to provide services for which they are not qualified? The answer lies in referral procedures. Consultants have the responsibility to determine at the outset of consultation (in exploring organizational needs) whether or not they can be of assistance. When consultants determine that they cannot be of assistance, they should consider making a referral to a qualified consultant; even if a referral is not possible, the provision of services should be declined anyway.

*The Case of Jackie.*   Jackie holds a doctorate in a helping profession and has been working with a mental health center for 10 years. She is actively seeking another professional position in another part of the country and is approached by a community group to consult with them in developing a two-year self-advocacy project for the homeless in the area. Although Jackie has a great deal of expertise and interest in this area, she refers the community group to another consultant because of the possibility that she might be relocating. This scenario reflects a common concern in our mobile society: The consultant may not be around to finish what he or she agreed to complete. In this case, Jackie clearly knew when to decline and refer.

**When Personal Concerns Affect Professional Performance.**   Consultants, of course, have the same kinds of personal concerns and problems as anyone else, and these can negatively affect their professional performance to the degree that consultation services are not adequate. In this case the consultant should consider stopping the services and making an appropriate referral. In fact, the APA code of ethics (2002) states that when members suffer from personal concerns that affect professional functioning, they should "take appropriate measures, such as obtaining professional consultation or assistance and determine whether they should limit, suspend, or terminate their work-related duties" (APA, 2002, p. 9). Therefore, consultants who are experiencing high levels of stress should be particularly aware of their ability to provide adequate professional services.

Consultants need to be aware of their personal needs throughout each phase of the consultation process and should take measures so that those needs do not replace the needs of the consultee (Corey et al., 2007); such an awareness decreases the probability that the consultant will behave unethically. If an exception must be made with regard to consulting despite a lack of competence, Wallace and Hall (1996) suggest that this should be done only when certain conditions are present:

- if it can be clearly established that there is no other consultant in the area who is better qualified

- if the consultant possesses parallel training and experience for the consulting task

- if the consultant has adequate time to prepare for the consulting task

- if the consultant makes all these limitations clear to the employing agency

- if it is a crisis situation that requires immediate intervention

### Training as an Ethical Issue

Training is actually an aspect of consultant competence. Consultants must make sure they have the adequate training to perform the services for which they contract (Welfel, 2002). Consultation is not "watered-down" counseling/psychotherapy and its skills do not come naturally from being trained in these methods (Caplan, Caplan, & Erchul, 1994).

Although there are some guidelines for training, it is ultimately up to individual consultants to decide whether they have received sufficient training to deliver competent services in a given consultation situation. The development of ethical behavior in consultants has most likely been enhanced by the focus in recent literature on consultation training (see Gutkin, 2002; Meyers, 2002). There has been a paucity of empirical research conducted on training in consultation, but recent literature in the field has critically examined the training needs

of prospective consultants (see, e.g., Alpert & Taufique, 2002b).

With regard to school-based consultants, it is safe to assume that most have adequate training in consultation and collaboration. The training of community-based consultants, however, is apparently not as well articulated. Regardless of how they receive training, consultants are still ethically bound to determine whether they are adequately trained to provide services in each consultation situation as it arises.

### The Consultant–Consultee–Client Relationship

The consultant–consultee–client relationship is very complex. What obligation, for example, does the consultant have to the consultee's client? What parameters of this relationship relate to the consultant and consultee? Can the consultant–consultee–client relationship be examined only in the context of the organization in which consultation is occurring? In general, the consultant–consultee–client relationship can be examined in isolation or within an organizational context; both views shed light on ethical issues. When considered in isolation, ethical issues revolve around each party's obligations and how well these are fulfilled.

In an organizational context, ethical issues go beyond the isolated relationship. For example, when confidentiality is to be maintained, where within the organization do we set its limits? Next we'll consider the ethical issues surrounding the complex consultant–consultee–client relationship in terms of work-related focus, dual relationships, and freedom of choice.

**Work-Related Focus.**  The code of ethics of the ACA (2005) states that the focus of the consultation relationship, from the outset and throughout, should be on work-related problems and not on the parties involved. It can be inferred from this code that personal relationships with consultees and their clients is questionable ethical behavior. Further, this same code of ethics also implies that the consultation relationship should be contractual and based on well-defined, mutually agreed-upon expectations (e.g., the nature of the problem, goals of consultation, and desired results). This straightforward assumption must also be considered in light of the consultant and consultee representing their respective organizations (Snow & Gersick, 1986); either party may have obligations to others not directly involved in but directly affected by consultation. Attempting to sort out these obligations can be very difficult.

*The Case of Sheila.*    Sheila is a talented school counselor with a knack for relating effectively to students and teachers alike. As part of her consultation role, Sheila's principal asked her to conduct a teacher support group to focus on work issues. Sheila agreed, and as the support group developed, some members increasingly asked for help on personal domestic issues such as relationships with spouses and children and eating disorders. Sheila expressed her concerns that the group was getting too far away from its original intent and tried to refocus the group.

Was Sheila right in refocusing the group? Might she have taken any other measures under referral to help the members meet their perceived needs? If you were Sheila, would you find it somewhat difficult not to let the group go where it wanted to go?

*Dual Relationships.*    Increasing attention has been paid to dual relationships in consultation (Dougherty, 1992b, 2006a, 2006b; Herlihy & Corey, 2006; Moleski & Kiselica, 2005). The APA code of ethics (2002) suggests a thorough assessment of the potential for harm before engaging in such relationships. *Dual relationships* are those in which a professional has more than one role with another person. As an extreme example, a consultant experiencing sexual intimacy with a consultee has dual relationships—one professional, the other personal. Dual relationships can occur due to a shift in roles (Pearson & Piazza, 1997). For example, a consultant may be appointed to an administrative position in which a current consultee now also becomes a subordinate. Dual relationships frequently cause conflicts of interest as well as role conflicts. Maintaining two professional roles in the consultation relationship can be particularly hazardous to consultants and their consultees.

The two potentially most common second roles in consultation relationships are counselor/psychotherapist and supervisor. There is often a fine line between where consultation ends and counseling begins. Therefore, it is relatively easy for a consultant who is a trained counselor or therapist to move the consultation relationship into one that also provides counseling or therapy. When this occurs, the act of counseling contaminates the consultation relationship by focusing on personal problems and by deemphasizing the work-related problems on which consultation was contracted.

The use of counseling or psychotherapy in the consultation relationship, when it occurs, usually results once the consultant has determined that the basis for the work-related problem resides more in the personal issues of the consultee than in the client. Rather than providing direct counseling services to the consultee, consultants should refer the consultee for assistance. Dual relationships also occur when supervision is somehow incorporated into the consultation relationship. It is relatively easy for the consultant who has had supervisory training and administrative experience to include supervisory activities in what should be an exclusively consultative relationship. Because supervision implies the use of evaluation, control, and power over someone, supervision violates the peer nature of the consultation relationship.

Use of supervision in consultation allows the consultant to build an illegitimate power base, creates the potential for conflicts of interest, and violates the original consultation contract. What are some of the potential problems that result from a dual role relationship? There are several reasons for caution when determining whether to engage in dual relationships (after Dougherty, 2006b):

- The complexity of the consultation process has led to difficulties in determining the boundaries of the consultant's role and consequent difficulties in discriminating between appropriate and inappropriate practice.

- The difficulties in defining consultation lead to difficulties in defining the roles of consultants.

- Multiple roles in relationships can cause conflicts of interest that can reduce the efficacy of consultation.

- Multiple roles can cause the consultee to have contradictory expectations.

- Trained counselors can zero in on affective concerns and personal problems. Therefore, there is a possible danger for turning consultation into counseling.

- Consultees may have an obligation to their organizations not to use consultation for personal purposes (such as counseling).

- Publicity about a consultant engaging in dual role relationships could dissuade potential consultees from seeking consultation.

The bottom-line question consultants must ask themselves concerning dual relationships is, "Do the potential conflicts outweigh the potential benefits of serving in both capacities?" (Herlihy & Corey, 2006). As I have noted elsewhere (Dougherty, 2006b), human service consultants should be very cautious about engaging in dual professional relationships. Extreme caution should be used before engaging in supervision or counseling relationships with consultees (Knoff, 1988). I agree with the position of Kitchener and Harding (1990) that human service professionals "should never enter such relationships when the potential for harm is high unless there are strong offsetting, ethical benefits for the consumer and the risks are clearly discussed" (p. 153).

*The Case of Freddie.*    Freddie, a social worker, is consulting with Norma, the director of a religious counseling center, about some problems she is having with some of the staff at the center. As Norma is discussing the problems, she brings up some very significant aspects of her private life that are affecting her relationships with the staff. Out of the blue, Norma asks Freddie for personal counseling as well as consultation. If Freddie agrees, is he involved in an inappropriate dual relationship? If he agrees to the dual role, how can Freddie assess whether the benefits outweigh the possible dangers? If you were Freddie, what would you do?

**Freedom of Choice.**    Providing consultees and their clients with freedom of choice is one of the major ethical obligations of consultants. Because freedom of choice is about the consultee acting in the client's best interests, it therefore involves issues of dependence, the misuse of power, and inappropriate manipulation of consultees by consultants.

Consultees should always perceive that they have the freedom to do whatever they wish with consultants' recommendations (Kratochwill & Pittman, 2002). This relieves the consultant from being responsible for the consultee's behavior, assuming that the consultee acts in a professionally responsible manner. However, this also requires consultants to take certain steps when they consider consultees' actions to be negative (Snow & Gersick, 1986). The first step is to point out the inappropriate behavior to the consultee. Beyond this, there is little consensus as to how the consultant should proceed. The consultant may have the option of pointing out the consultee's behavior to the consultee's employer or may terminate the consultation relationship, thereby placing the behavior beyond the consultation relationship.

Consultees cannot have complete freedom of choice if they are dependent on their consultant. This issue is addressed by the ACA (2005), whose code of ethics specifically states that the consultation relationship should be such that the consultee does not become dependent on the consultant and learns increased self-direction. It is the consultant's responsibility to make sure that dependence does not occur. Because the very purpose of consultation is to assist consultees and their organizations to function more effectively and autonomously, it is unethical for consultants to create and maintain dependence on the part of consultees (NBCC, 2005).

Closely related to the issue of dependence is that of power. The potential for an imbalanced power relationship is a common ethical issue for consultants (Corey et al., 2007). One of the most common abuses of power in the consultation relationship occurs when the consultant violates the peer nature of the relationship and pressures the consultee to get something accomplished. For example, a consultant might push a certain plan of action on the consultee. Consultants need to remember that, although the consultation relationship is equal in terms of status, it is unequal in terms of need. This inequality due to need raises issues about maintaining the peer nature of the consultation relationship. The consultant is helping the consultee meet a need. If the consultant gets anything out of this process, it is simply as a by-product. Taking a collaborative stance toward consultation, whenever possible, helps to ensure that the misuse of power is minimized.

A second abuse of power involves misusing the relationship with the consulting organization's administrators to achieve something that should be accomplished through other channels (French & Bell, 1999). For example, a consultant might ask an administrator to send a memo concerning preferred action plans through regular administrative channels when it was agreed at the outset that consultees would develop action plans independent of the administration.

A third misuse of power occurs when a consultee is forced to participate in consultation. Because such coercion violates the voluntary nature of consultation, it is unethical behavior. In addition, consultants must ensure that their consultees are not receiving undue pressure to participate from their administrators.

A fourth misuse of power relates to the advocacy role a consultant might take on for personal reasons (Brown, 1988). For example, a mental health consultant might exploit the director of a program for the homeless who prefers to go through proper channels by demanding immediate change in the program. In this case, the consultant's hidden agenda might be to gain a power position with the program's board of directors.

Consultees cannot have freedom of choice if they are being manipulated by consultants (Newman, 1993). From the outset, therefore, consultants should discuss with their consultees the ways in which consultants will attempt to influence them. Consultants can maintain their consultees' freedom of choice by discussing their own values and by helping consultees to critically consider consultants' suggestions on their own merits (Hughes, 1986). This can also be accomplished by ensuring that there is agreement and understanding in terms of the goals of consultation (ACA, 2005). In summary, clear expectations concerning the relationship, avoidance of dual relationships, and freedom of choice for all parties involved contribute to maintaining ethical behavior on the part of consultants.

*The Case of Teresa.* Teresa is an internal consultant in the human resource development department of a large psychiatric hospital. Part of her role is to consult with heads of other departments on topics such as "total quality management." Marcie, one of the hospital's department heads, was told by her supervisor that she had to get help in running her department from Teresa. Teresa is keenly aware that Marcie needs some assistance and at the same time has a negative attitude about consultation. If Teresa proceeds with consultation with Marcie, is Marcie's freedom of choice being violated? If you were Teresa, how would you handle this situation in an ethical manner?

### Rights of Consultees

Closely related to the issues concerning the consultant–consultee–client relationship are those surrounding the rights of consultees, which include two major issues: confidentiality and informed consent. As it applies to consultation, confidentiality is an ethical responsibility of the consultant to protect the consultee and the consultee's clients from inappropriate disclosure of information shared within the consultation relationship. The ethics codes of the ACA (2005) implicitly deals with confidentiality as it relates to consultation, while that of the APA (2002) mentions it explicitly. Informed consent refers to sharing with the consultee information pertinent to consultation so that the consultee will know what is involved and will participate fully and effectively in the process. The codes of ethics of the ACA (2005) and the APA (2002) mention informed consent, although not specifically regarding the practice of consultation.

**Confidentiality.**    Confidentiality in consultation and collaboration is both important and complex (Jacob & Hartshorne, 2003). Confidentiality is meant to protect privacy and promote trust (Taylor & Adelman, 1998). Consultees should feel safe in stating their concerns (Gutkin & Curtis, 1999). Even unintended breaches of confidentiality can severely damage the consultation relationship (French & Bell, 1999). The consultant is obligated to develop guidelines that safeguard the confidentiality of parties involved in consultation and collaboration as well as educate consultees about the nature and limits of confidentiality (Corey et al., 2007). These guidelines should be developed during the entry stage and put into the consultation contract (Rosenfield, 2002a). In fact, it is a good idea for the contract to state clearly how information gathered during consultation will be used, by whom, and when (Jacob, 2002). Guidelines should be structured to protect the consultee's oral and written communications and records (Robinson & Gross, 1985). It is a good idea to follow the practice noted in the APA (2002) ethics code of protecting the identity of parties involved in consultation and sharing only that information necessary to achieve the purposes of consultation. In other words, it is important to use the "need-to-know principle" (Jacob & Hartshorne, 2003). Two aspects of confidentiality that should be considered are the tripartite nature of consultation and the limits on confidentiality (Snow & Gersick, 1986).

Consultation is by definition tripartite, which implies that three parties (and possibly more) can have knowledge of information that is disclosed during consultation. The simplest example is a consultee sharing information about a client to a consultant. In a more complex example, an external agency might require a report from a consultant about some aspect of consultation. The potential for several parties to acquire information may create trust issues in consultation and makes confidentiality a primary ethical concern for consultants. The consultant must create procedures for determining what information is to be shared with whom, when, how, for what reasons, and what the likely impact of sharing will be.

Consultants can increase their awareness of the complexity of confidentiality by asking themselves the following questions:

- What can I tell my own organization about what is said both in consultation and in the consultee organization?

- With whom can I share information in the consultee organization?

- What steps do I need to take to ensure the safety of computer-accessible information?

Posing and answering such complex questions at the outset of consultation, getting consensus on the answers, and publicizing this consensus can prevent problems from occurring later on in the consultation process. There is no such thing as total confidentiality. Confidentiality has limits, and it is up to the consultant to forge some agreement concerning those limits (Gutkin & Curtis, 1999). This is particularly true with the advent of interagency collaboration and interdisciplinary teamwork (ACA, 2005; Taylor & Adelman, 1998). The limits of confidentiality refer to those instances that would dictate that confidentiality be set aside. It is usually assumed that consultants must get permission from their consultees or from members of the organization affected by the consultation before sharing information. But in cases where permission is not granted, what do consultants do when they have what they feel are good reasons for revealing the information? Specifically, what should consultants do when they determine that a consultee is mistreating a client or that a program is counterproductive for the client system? There are no clear-cut answers in determining when confidentiality should be set aside in consultation. I am of the opinion that confidentiality should be set aside when consultants determine to the best of their ability that the client system is being violated in some way, or the best interests of society are not being met. When setting aside confidentiality, the consultant determines and takes responsibility for who is to be told, what they are to be told, and in what manner.

The second way in which the limits of confidentiality are discussed involves the concept of anonymity (Snow & Gersick, 1986). Such a strategy is in line with the APA ethical principles which state: "psychologists do not disclose confidential information that reasonably could lead to the identification of a . . . person or organization with whom they have a confidential relationship unless they have obtained prior consent of the person or organization or the disclosure cannot be avoided . . ." (APA, 2002, p. 8). When maintaining confidentiality, the consultant can share information only with the permission of the consultee or an appropriate member of the organization. When maintaining anonymity, the consultant can share the information but must protect its source. The use of anonymity has the advantage of facilitating a flow of information, which can be critical to the success of consultation that focuses on an organization as a whole. Using anonymity can be a very useful strategy for consultants: It prevents them from having "one helping hand tied behind their backs" when they have confidential information that could be helpful if they only had permission to share it.

*The Case of Gus.* Gus, a mental health consultant with a large number of community service agencies, is asked to consult for six months with several of the staff in an area nursing home concerning the use of reminiscences as a tool for improving the quality of life of the elderly. Midway through the consultation period, Gus is approached by the administrator of the nursing home. She relates that she is going to have to cut several of the staff in a downsizing move and would like Gus's opinion on whom to lay off. As a consultant, what ethical issue is facing Gus? Does the fact that the administrator hired Gus give her any rights with regard to her request?

**Informed Consent.** Informed consent is very important in delineating the rights of consultees (Clayton & Bongar, 1994; Herlihy & Corey, 2006; Remley & Herlihy, 2007). To determine whether they want to be involved in consultation in the first place, consultees need to be as fully informed as possible about the nature and goals of consultation, issues of confidentiality, their right to privacy, the voluntary nature of participation, and complete freedom in

following or not following through on the consultant's recommendations. Consultees have the right to know about how any information obtained from the consultation process will be used (Newman, 1993). The guidelines suggested by Corey et al. (2007) for counselors and therapists who work with clients seem quite appropriate for consultants and their consultees. ACA (2005) makes direct reference to informed consent in consultation.

Informed consent should be considered an ongoing process and not a one-time event (Remley & Herlihy, 2007). This view of informed consent prevents the consultant from making the mistake of overloading the consultee with too much information at the outset of consultation, and it permits candid discussion of the most critical information about which the consultee needs to be apprised.

Even though consultants should view informed consent as an ongoing process, they must still ask themselves what consultees need to know at the outset. Providing the consultee with a copy of the ethics code of the consultant's discipline can be a good starting point. A good practice for answering this question is for consultants to place themselves in their consultees' shoes and ascertain what they would like to know at the outset of consultation. By empathizing with their consultees, consultants are in a better position to answer questions patiently and provide information. Instead of merely being a routine exercise, the sharing of information to obtain informed consent can be a rapport-building event for consultant and consultee.

*The Case of Sid.* As part of his job as a staff development specialist in a community mental health center, Sid provides a group of consultees an instrument designed to assess their ability to work effectively on a team. Based on their performance on the instrument and other measures, the consultees will be assigned to autonomous work teams. As the training is coming to a close, several of the consultees' supervisors contact Sid regarding what he found out about the consultees' suitability as team members. If Sid shares what he knows, is he violating the consultees' right to informed consent? What is Sid's obligation to the center in this situation?

Does the employing organization have any rights in this situation? How could this problem have been avoided in the first place?

## The Consultant and the Group

For a variety of reasons, an increasing amount of a consultant's practice is with a group of consultees or part or all of an organization (see Conyne & Mazza, 2007 and Paisley & Milsom, 2007). Because consultation with groups raises unique ethical and professional issues, it is given separate consideration here. If you are interested in consulting with groups, I strongly recommend that you refer to the *Professional Standards for the Training of Group Workers* (2000) published by the ASGW.

**Consulting with Groups with Caseloads.**   When a consultant considers working with the same group of consultees for an extended length of time, a basic issue that is raised is one of competence. To what degree is the consultant experienced and trained in group consultation? How aware is the consultant of group process and group dynamics? Because consulting with a group is much different from and more complex than working with an individual consultee, it is critical that consultants have some form of training in group consultation before embarking on such a venture.

A second issue that reemerges when consulting with a group is informed consent. To what degree have the consultees been made aware of the differences between individual and group consultation? Has participation been made voluntary? Have the consultees been made aware of what is expected of them within the group? As in individual consultation, informed consent should be an ongoing process.

A third issue that resurfaces in group consultation is confidentiality. Clearly, the consultant cannot guarantee confidentiality for anyone in the group except him- or herself. In fact, many consultees will subscribe to professional standards such as those of the ASGW (2000), which specifically mention that group cases be discussed only for professional consultation and educational purposes. Even in these cases, group members should be informed

of any limits to confidentiality regarding their cases. Because most consultees are also professionals, it is not unreasonable to expect them to live up to their obligations with respect to confidentiality. Many authors (e.g., Corey et al., 2007) suggest that group leaders encourage confidentiality by providing a written policy statement at the outset and casually but seriously mentioning confidentiality throughout the life of the group.

A final issue that reemerges is that of cultural sensitivity. ASGW (2000) points out the importance of collaborative consultation with targeted populations to enhance the ecological validity of planned group interventions. This is an important factor whether one is consulting with groups about caseloads or with training groups (as discussed later in this chapter).

*The Case of Lucy.*   Lucy, a mental health practitioner who is consulting with a group of school counselors about their cases, is very concerned about confidentiality because the consultation is occurring at a variety of school sites. She prepares a statement about confidentiality, distributes it during the first meeting with the consultees, and mentions confidentiality intermittently throughout the course of the consultation relationship. In your opinion, has Lucy acted in an ethical manner? Is there anything else she could do to encourage confidentiality? What are the consultees' obligations regarding confidentiality in this situation?

**Consulting with Training Groups.**   Consultants are increasingly being retained to educate or train consultees. In their extensive treatment of the ethics of training groups decades ago, Pfeiffer and Jones (1977) listed five basic issues of concern to consultants engaged in education or training: deception, co-optation, inappropriate techniques, inattention to application, and rehashing.

In this context, *deception* refers to the willful misleading of consultees as a part of an educational or training strategy. Consultants are obligated to correct any misconceptions that may result from such deception and duly inform consultees of the goals and objectives of training activities by some form of debriefing.

*Co-optation* involves forcing a consultee to do something he or she does not want to do by such means as excessive persuasion or group pressure. Such a practice of course violates informed consent and the right to privacy. Co-optation in any form is unethical and can be minimized by making the learning/training environment a safe one for all involved.

The use of *inappropriate techniques* frequently stems from the consultant's need to use some "pet" methodology, either due to a lack of understanding between consultant and consultees concerning what is to be accomplished or possibly due to poor planning by the consultant. A way to avoid this predicament in educational and training experiences is to take the norms of the consultee group into consideration during planning.

*Inattention to the application of training* occurs when measures to apply the lessons of the educational experience are not taken. The consultant is ethically bound to assist consultees in applying what they have learned. Consultants have an ethical obligation not to repeat or rehash the same educational/training experience with the same consultees. In addition, consultants should keep their education and training offerings current and full of vitality. Consultants involved in education and training should take their own professional growth as seriously as that of their consultees.

*The Case of Selli.* Selli is known as a hotshot consultant who can entertain the most subdued groups of trainees. She has a well-polished "dog and pony show." Some of her consultees comment, "See Selli once and you know everything she knows!" Selli suggests to her organization contact person that she offer a series of 10 training sessions. When asked for a proposal with a list of objectives, Selli comments that she views such things as unnecessary. "After all," says Selli, "the show's the thing." What are your views about Selli's behavior? Could she possibly be guilty of rehashing the same thing in her session time and time again? Does she seem to allow for application of her training by her consultees?

## Ethical Issues in Intervention

The ethical as well as the technical adequacy of interventions must be determined (Newman et al., 2002). Three important intervention areas that involve ethical issues are individual-versus systems-level interventions, use of assessment data, and the empirical validity of interventions (Newman, 1993).

When considering individual-level interventions, the consultant needs to determine that the intervention is in the best interest of the client system and not merely accommodating the organization's needs (Jacob, 2002). Consultants will need to avoid cultural bias in their assessment activities (Diller, 2007). For example, it would be unethical for a consultant to recommend a certain developmental guidance program for use by teachers merely as a way to cut the number of school counselors in a school. If the consultant determines that the system is "sick," interventions at the individual level may also be ethically questionable because of their marginal effect on the problem.

The use of assessment data can present many ethical issues (Fuqua et al., 1999). Primary among these is the improper use of assessment devices so that freedom of choice and the principle of informed consent are violated (Newman, 1993; Newman et al., 2002). The potential for unethical behavior occurs often in personnel decisions. Consultants need to make sure that all parties-at-interest are properly informed about the use of any assessment instruments.

Consultants should also bear in mind the impact of culture on assessment procedures and consider using multiple assessment and "indigenous consultants" (an appropriate representative of the client system's cultural group) in both assessment and intervention in cross-cultural consultation (Diller, 2007; Moseley-Howard, 1995; Quintana et al., 2000). For example, research-based interventions should be made available as culturally appropriate. On the other hand, culturally sensitive decisions need to be made in selecting interventions, such as those using concrete reinforcers (Sheridan, 2000). Consultants must make every effort to see that their interventions have some desired effect. There has been very little attention paid to this in the consultation literature. The scale and scope of available interventions makes their selection, implementation, and evaluation very difficult. Consultants should be familiar with the empirical research as it relates to the efficacy of interventions and should attempt to make sound judgments when selecting interventions.

*The Case of Ozzie.*   Ozzie is hired as a consultant by a human service agency to help determine if the child and adolescent services sections could be combined as a cost-cutting measure. As Ozzie is gathering data, the director of the agency pushes the reorganization as the only recommendation she wants to hear. Ozzie determines that the reorganization is not an appropriate strategy because it would put an excessive burden on the personnel who serve the agency's clients. In his report, Ozzie suggests that reorganization is not a feasible alternative and makes other cost-cutting recommendations. Did Ozzie act in an ethical manner? What types of pressure do you believe he experienced when the director attempted to influence him? Did Ozzie attempt to recommend the best possible solution?

## Issues Related to Crisis/Disaster Consultation

Consultants are increasingly being called upon to provide service in crisis and disaster situations (McCarroll & Ursano, 2006; Stock, 2007). Tragedies like those of September 11 and at Virginia Tech University have called attention to the need for organizations to implement or create crisis management plans. They have also shown the need for training organizational personnel in how to react to various crises, including events such as workplace violence. Areas of ethics important in crisis situations include self-awareness, dual relationships, confidentiality, elder/child abuse, informed consent, and supervision/training (Kanel, 2007; McCarroll & Ursano, 2006; Stock, 2007). Consultants will want to bear in mind the acute vulnerability of the client system in crisis and disaster situations as well as the heightened ethical

considerations from the resulting chaotic environment (Halpern & Tramontin, 2007). In addition, consultants will need to assure that cultural competence is exhibited when engaging in crisis consultation, since responses to a crisis vary according to given cultures (Remley & Herlihy, 2007).

## Ethical Issues in Organizational Consultation

Mental health/human service professionals are increasingly being called upon to provide services at the organizational level. A school psychologist might, for example, assist a site-based management team in developing methods to prevent staff burnout. In another example, a community counselor might work with the board of directors of a church group in examining and revising the administrative structure of the church's operation in order to facilitate effective communication. Organizational consultation is one of the most complex types of consultation. Consequently, the ethical issues can also be highly complex (Block, 2000). Confidentiality may be an important issue due to the fact that the organization is the client system (Kratochwill & Pittman, 2002; Newman, Robinson-Kurpius, & Fuqua, 2002). As you will read in later chapters, the goal of organizational consultation is to help the organization function more effectively in some specified way. Ethical issues can easily arise when this overarching goal is being pursued. If you review the case example at the beginning of this chapter, you will note how easily ethical dilemmas can arise during organizational consultation.

The nature of organizations can lead to a variety of ethical issues for consultants (Newman et al., 1996; Newman et al., 2002):

- Consultants have significant ethical responsibility to ensure the proper effects of interventions, and those effects can be difficult to determine at the organizational level.

- Consultants frequently rely exclusively on the subjective reports of consultees, although consultees can have biased and distorted views of the organization and its functioning.

- Conflicts of interest within the organization itself can complicate the goals of consultation.

- Differing views of the organization can make setting goals difficult.

- Voluntary participation on the parts of consultees can be difficult to ascertain.

Because of the complexity of organizational consultation, consultants may want to consider adopting *aspirational ethics* (Newman et al., 1996; Newman et al., 2002). Aspirational ethics is also called "virtue ethics" (Jordan & Meara, 1990). Virtue ethics attempts to integrate the character of the professional with his or her practice. Aspirational ethics is not based on the question "What shall I do?" but on the question "Who shall I be?" (Newman et al., 1996). The use of virtue ethics by consultants lays the foundation for moral considerations as part of the organizational consultation process. By taking this orientation, consultants will continually be examining their own behavior in terms of whether it is the right course of action to take (French & Bell, 1999; Fuqua & Newman, 2006). This orientation considers consultation to have powerful moral influences. These influences can be used to promote moral discourse in the organization, impact the organization's leadership structure, and impact the moral elements of the organization's structure (Fuqua & Newman, 2006).

*The Case of Bryan.*   Bryan is a human resource development specialist in a community college. A trained counselor, Bryan has been asked to assist the academic affairs committee of the college to make recommendations for new programs to the college's president. As Bryan attempts to assist the group in making its decision, it becomes obvious that a lot of the committee members are allowing politics rather than the best interests of the college to guide their decision making. Bryan asks the group for some time to share his thoughts on the committee's processes to date. At a meeting he directly yet professionally shares his views that the committee may be having their own special interests in mind when determining the academic future of the college. Was Bryan, in

your opinion, using aspirational ethics in this situation? Was he taking a big risk with the group? What would you have done in this situation?

## Issues Related to Consulting over the Internet/Telephone

As telecommunications and technology continue to impact our society, so too do they have the potential to affect how consultation is delivered. With the onset of e-mail, listservs, chat rooms, and file transfer protocols, consultants are able to develop a variety of methods for providing consultation, often to consultees in rural areas. For example, a group of counselors can engage in peer consultation via a web-camera, e-mail or a chat group (Kruger & Struzziero, 1998; Miller, 2006). In another example, a mental health consultant may deal with a consultee about a case exclusively through e-mail. There is some evidence that consultees perceive the use of e-mail as effective in helping them accomplish the goals of consultation (Kruger, Struzziero, Kaplan, Macklem, Watts, & Weksel, 2001) and that consultants can help facilitate an online support community for beginning teachers (Babinski, Jones, & DeWert, 2001). Although there is no data that demonstrates the amount of consultation that occurs over the Internet, there were at least 88 online counseling websites located (Shaw & Shaw, 2006).

Extrapolating from the ideas of various authors (ACA, 2005; AMHCA, 2002; Corey et al., 2007; ISMHO, 2000; Meyers et al., 2004; Sampson et al., 1997) on web counseling and applying them to consultation suggests the following consultation applications on the information highway: computer-based networking with consultees regarding cases, marketing of services via web pages, delivery of consultation services over the Internet and through videoconferencing, data collection and assessment through the use of computer-assisted instruction, videoconferencing with more than one consultee at various remote sites, and the delivery of self-help materials and resources with the consultant being "on call" to assist as needed. As a side note, advances in technology have the potential to impact the way consultants use face-to-face meetings in unique ways. For example, face-to-face meetings may be used more for relationship building and less for the transmittal of information (Corey et al., 2007; Sampson et al., 1997). However, the impact of technology on consultation raises a variety of ethical issues (Miller, 2006; Shaw & Shaw, 2006). The APA (2002) has included a section in its code of ethics regarding the use of technology in service delivery; ACA (2005) has a separate set of standards. Other organizations such as the NBCC (2005) have adopted standards for Web-Counseling. Consultants can adapt and use standards such as these and APA (2002) and ACA (2005) to assist them in dealing with related ethical issues that arise in their practice. Issues raised by the use of what I refer to as "web consulting" can be categorized as technology-related aspects of the basic issues already discussed in this chapter. These include confidentiality and obtaining permission to consult with members of an organization without physically entering the system. Examples of issues related to confidentiality include the privacy of material sent over the web, the use of encryption methods, how long transmission will be preserved, difficulties in verifying the identity of the parties involved, crisis situations being dealt with from remote locations, and appropriate procedures for releasing information with other electronic sources (NBCC, 2005; Shaw & Shaw, 2006). In a related issue, consultants will want to remember that lack of attention to information security can violate consultee confidentiality (APA, 2002; Shaw & Shaw, 2006). Consultants need to ensure that the messages they receive and send electronically are protected as needed, and that the consultee has access to privacy when sending information to the consultant.

Another issue revolves around location-specific factors. Consultants need to make sure they assess the impact of local variables as they attempt to assist consultees. For example, a mental health counselor should be aware of the limitations imposed on the counseling activities of school personnel prior to making recommendations regarding interventions.

Consultants should also be aware of how relationship development can be affected by technology.

Trusting relationships tend to develop rich and more valid discourse than do those based on superficial acquaintance. Consultants will want to keep this in mind as they determine the depth of relationship necessary to accomplish the goals of consultation. A minimal consideration is contact with consultees over the phone or through video-conferencing.

Little has been written in the area of web-consulting. The bottom line is that potential benefits need to outweigh the potential risks.

## THE CONSULTANT AND THE LAW

Due to the training of most human service consultants, there can be a dynamic tension between their mental health orientation and how the law impacts that orientation (Rowley & MacDonald, 2001). Relatively little has been written on the legal issues that concern consultants, but more is being written on legal issues for mental professionals (Egan, 2007; Sales, Miller, & Hall, 2005). Most professional organizations note the importance of knowing and respecting the law (Jacob, 2002). Relatively few guidelines on professional behavior exist to guide the courts when consultants encounter legal entanglements. Still, as human service professionals, consultants deliver their services in a socio-legal environment and should be aware of legal matters that affect them (Swenson, 1997). For example, school-based consultants need to be aware of the legal considerations of offering advice to school personnel about students (McCarthy & Sorenson, 1993). Some authors such as Remley and Herlihy (2007) caution that lawsuits brought against human service professionals, although few, are on the rise.

Consultants will want to remember that mandatory law, if it applies to a given consultation situation, almost always takes precedence over ethical or other concerns, and consultants who violate the law are subject to legal consequences (McCarthy & Sorenson, 1993). The importance of attention to legal issues in the helping professions is emphasized by the fact that the ACA and the APA have set up legal defense funds for members involved in certain types of litigation (Anderson, 1996). The bottom line is this: When dealing with issues that may have legal ramifications, consultants may well want to consider seeking legal advice (Remley, 1996; Remley & Herlihy, 2007).

## Malpractice

We'll now consider a legal issue of paramount importance to consultants: malpractice. Human service professionals are accountable for the quality of their services. In malpractice, the service recipient is in some way damaged by improper services offered without good faith or through neglect or ignorance. Malpractice cases allege that the professional in some way induced psychological, financial or physical damage on someone in the course of providing services (Sales et al., 2005) Corey et al. (2007) note that malpractice is the failure to render professional services or to exercise the appropriate degree of skill that is ordinarily expected of professionals in a given situation. Consultants can be sued for performing the wrong services or for failing to provide the correct services. How can the right or wrong type of service be determined? The court would attempt to determine whether a typical professional consultant would act in a way similar to the way the consultant in question acted. An answer in the affirmative would likely lead to no liability, whereas a negative answer could lead to liability (Anderson, 1996).

Tort lawsuits are the most common type involving malpractice (Swenson, 1997). To determine whether a consultant was guilty of malpractice, a court would seek answers to the following questions:

- Did the defendant (consultant) have a professional obligation to the plaintiff?

- Was that duty breached by the consultant?

- Is there a causal link between the breach and the damage to the plaintiff?

To answer these questions, the court would probably attempt to determine whether or not the consultant showed *requisite skill and care* (Anderson, 1996). However, because these terms are not yet adequately defined for consultants, courts tend to rely on already-established standards for appropriate professional consulting behavior (Anderson, 1996). Courts often use the *ordinary reasonable person* concept which refers to the evaluation of a legal issue from "the standpoint of what would be the most reasonable course of action to most reasonable nonprofessional people," namely people who are always reasonable, prudent, careful, informed, and up to standard (Harrison, 2004, pp. 139–140).

Malpractice suits can occur in just about any area of consultation practice. A recent literature review of the causes of malpractice (Corey et al., 2007; Sales et al., 2005) cites the following behaviors that could cause legal entanglements for consultants:

- misrepresenting one's training and skills

- failing to respect integrity and privacy

- using improper diagnosis and assessment techniques

- using improper methods to collect fees

- making inappropriate public statements (libel and slander)

- failing to honor agreements (breach of contract)

- failing to keep adequate records

- failing to provide for informed consent

- providing poor advice

Of these torts, those based on lack of skill are the most prevalent (Swenson, 1997). In summary, consultants can be sued for malpractice whenever there is the likelihood that they have provided services either without the proper skill or without the proper care.

## Avoiding Legal Entanglements

It is safe to assume that the vast majority of consultants want to avoid legal entanglements. How

**C A S E  7.1**     **Ethics for School Consultants**

Terry is a consultant based in a junior high school, and she is consulting with a newly hired and inexperienced in-school human service professional, Burt. Burt is conducting a group for students who received more than three Fs on their latest report card and has asked Terry to consult with him regarding "helping these kids out." As Burt describes the group's progress, Terry notices that he has not informed the group of its purpose or made any attempt to promote confidentiality. She also notes that Burt talks to teachers readily about the members' behavior and puts several of the members down by calling them "airheads." At the same time, he exhibits a commitment to the members and to the success of the group.

It is apparent to Terry that Burt does not want feedback on his behavior but rather desires techniques for more effectively helping the students in the group. Terry feels very frustrated during two of her consultation sessions with Burt and perceives him as having a low level of self-awareness and being impervious to how others might perceive him. She has come to resent what she sees as a basic contradiction in Burt—namely, his enthusiasm to help students and the disrespectful way in which he talks about them outside of the group.

During a third session, as Burt keeps asking for techniques to achieve this or that, Terry becomes angry not only at Burt, but also at herself for being angry with Burt. In the middle of the session, she excuses herself for a couple of minutes to check on an appointment. While out of the room, she uses some stress management techniques on herself. Her internal dialogue is saying things like, "It's awful that he talks about kids that way and still thinks he's committed to help them." As she continues to process her feelings, Terry begins to manage her anger effectively and realizes what she wants to do.

Upon returning to the room and before Burt can start talking again, Terry tells him that she has something to discuss. She briefly shares her perception that the reason Burt is having trouble with his group may not be due only to the kids, but perhaps also to his own actions in and out of the group. Terry assures Burt that she believes in his commitment to the students,

mentions the behavior that she is concerned with, and asks him if that is the image he wants to project to students, parents, and staff members. In a gentle yet straightforward way, Terry refers to the ACA code of ethics and some of the questions she has about Burt's conduct.

As Terry is talking, Burt shows surprise and becomes genuinely interested in what she is saying. He notes that his attitude may be because of his father's flippant attitude about life. He praises Terry for her sensitivity and perceptiveness and asks her to help him work on his attitudes and behavior, saying, "After all, if my personal life is messing up my professional life, I guess I'd better start there." Terry shares with Burt her appreciation for his willingness to look closely at himself and his interest in counseling. Because she is a school consultant, Terry points out that she feels very uncomfortable doing this and details how being both his counselor and his consultant might destroy their ability to work effectively together. She mentions to Burt the positive results of counseling she received from a local therapist and refers Burt to that counselor.

When Burt comes back for two more consultation sessions, the mood of the relationship is relaxed and yet very work oriented, with Burt speaking compassionately of one of the group member's difficulties.

**Commentary**

This case illustrates the importance of self-awareness on the part of consultants. If Terry had not possessed a strong sense of self-awareness and insight into herself, her anger might well have jeopardized her relationship with Burt. This case further demonstrates how easy it is for consultants to slip into possibly damaging dual relationships with their consultees. Given Terry's feelings of anger toward Burt combined with her strong willingness to help him, she might easily have trapped herself in a relationship that involved both consultation and counseling. By taking such steps, consultants can dramatically reduce the likelihood of legal entanglement. Consultants who know what they are doing and why they are doing it have relatively little to fear, even though the boundaries of their professional behavior remain relatively indistinct in the eyes of the law.

---

**C A S E   7.2**      **Ethics for Community Consultants**

---

Cindy is the director of a prerelease center for incarcerates. Cindy and her five staff members all have master's degrees in one of the helping professions. The center runs a coeducational, seven-week program for incarcerates who are eligible for parole no more than six months after the program's conclusion. Part of the center's role is to assess the suitability of the program participants for early parole.

The center staff have been experiencing difficulties in communicating with incarcerates who are known to suffer from substance abuse. At a needs assessment meeting, the staff concluded that they would like to hold a communication skills workshop that focused on working with substance abusers. As a result, Cindy contacts Sharon, a social worker in the community. Sharon has several years' experience in corrections and an excellent reputation for conducting workshops and making presentations. Cindy contracts with Sharon for a four-day workshop on "Communicating Effectively with the Substance-Abusing Incarcerate."

Sharon does an outstanding job in conducting the workshop. The staff are very open about their views and feelings about communication and how the center responds to known substance abusers. An evaluation of the workshop indicates that the staff felt very positive about the knowledge and skills they had gained from the workshop.

Two weeks later, Cindy calls Sharon to tell her that she is being promoted to a new position and that her immediate supervisor has asked her to choose an interim director from the staff of the center. Cindy also states that she values Sharon's opinion highly and that she realized how close Sharon got to each staff member dur-

ing the workshop. Cindy asks Sharon to analyze each staff member, rank them, and name her top three choices for the interim director position. Sharon feels uneasy as she talks with Cindy. She puts off agreeing or rejecting Cindy's proposal by telling her she will respond before the week is over. As Sharon considers the reasons for her uneasiness, she realizes that Cindy's request is inappropriate. After all, Sharon was not hired to evaluate anyone but to conduct a workshop. Further, if she were to comply with Cindy's request, she would be depriving the staff members of their right to know about and consent to Sharon's imparting her impressions of them to their director. As Sharon reviews her professional organization's code of ethics, she realizes that her uneasiness was well founded. She calls Cindy and politely yet assertively denies her request.

**Commentary**

As you see from this case, Cindy put Sharon, perhaps inadvertently, in an ethical dilemma revolving around both informed consent of consultees and knowing one's limitations as a consultant. For Sharon to comply with Cindy's request for information about the workshop participants would clearly violate the consultees' right to informed consent. Further, when Cindy asked Sharon to analyze and rank the workshop members, Cindy was assuming that Sharon has expertise in staff evaluation procedures. Sharon did not, in fact, possess those skills and was put in the position of having to decline Cindy's request for an additional reason; namely, she did not possess the expertise to do what Cindy was asking regardless of whether the consultees had consented to being evaluated.

---

should they go about doing this? It is most important that consultants learn about any state laws that may have implications for their practices (Remley & Herlihy, 2007). Ignorance of the law is not an excuse if a consultant is called into court. Consultants are not held legally accountable for negligence of the consultee (Remley & Herlihy, 2007).

However, consultants should provide proper services—only those services in which they are skilled—with care. The old adage "An ounce of prevention is worth a pound of cure" could not be truer when it comes to avoiding legal entanglements.

Consultants should consider joining a professional organization that has an ethics code and should adhere to that code's principles and standards. Such adherence facilitates delivering consultation services with the proper skill and care and assists the consultant in determining standards of professional conduct.

Consultants need a personal and professional growth orientation based on a healthy and honest self-awareness. Knowledge of one's limitations and abilities as a person and as a professional enhances a consultant's ability to make the correct decision concerning whether a given consultation service should be undertaken in the first place. Consultants can participate in professional development activities that review the law as it relates to their profession (Rowley & MacDonald, 2001).

Consultants should do well each of the things their profession demands of them:

- Use a written contract.
- Keep accurate records.
- Discuss fees at the outset of consultation.

- Discuss confidentiality and its limits as a matter of course at the outset of every consultation relationship.
- Make sure that any advertising or promotional activities provide current and accurate information.
- Seek consultation from a trusted colleague or a supervisor when in doubt about proper procedure.
- Foster open communication at all times.

## SUMMARY

This chapter has presented an introduction to the closely related ethical, professional, and legal issues that pertain to consultation in the human service professions. The complexity of consultation increases the complexity of the ethical issues consultants face in their work. Consultants can maintain professional standards by being aware of issues involving values, competence, training, the consultation relationship, the rights of consultees and their clients, and consultation in groups. Most legal issues that consultants encounter concern malpractice. Consultants can maintain a sense of ethical and professional responsibility and avoid legal entanglements by being committed to their own personal and professional growth. Finally, for consultants to be more confident in their ethical behavior, more specific ethics codes and more deliberate training of consultants in ethical decision making are needed.

## SUGGESTIONS FOR EFFECTIVE PRACTICE

- Strictly adhere to the ethical code of your profession.
- Seek out consultation from trusted colleagues when you are in doubt about how to proceed in consultation or collaboration.

- Avoid legal entanglements by documenting all procedures you employ and by rigorously adhering to your profession's ethical code.
- Only consult in areas in which you have expertise.

## QUESTIONS FOR REFLECTION

1. If ethical guidelines are by definition general in nature, how can consultants apply them in specific situations?

2. To what degree do you agree that ethics codes of most human service organizations are culturally biased? Explain your position.

3. As a consultant-in-training, how would you want to be trained in ethical decision making?

4. To what degree do consultants require specific training to consult in a given area?

5. What are the consultant's professional and ethical obligations to the consultee?

6. What are the consultant's professional and ethical obligations to the consultee's client?

7. In what ways are consultants most likely to violate the rights of their consultees during consultation?

8. How does a consultant go about developing a personal and professional growth orientation?

9. If you were a judge in a court of law and a consultant was being sued for malpractice, what information would you want to know to determine whether malpractice had occurred?

10. How can there ever be a code of ethics for consultants when there are so many different professional groups whose members perform consultation as one of their primary functions?

## SUGGESTED SUPPLEMENTARY READINGS

I hope you are interested in learning more about the ethical, professional, and legal issues that affect consultants. I strongly recommend the following readings for study and reflection:

APA. (1990). *APA Guidelines for providers of psychological services to ethnic, linguistic, and culturally diverse populations.* Although close to two decades old, these guidelines provide excellent information consultants can use to ensure culturally competent practice. The guidelines are available at http://www.apa.org/pi/oema/guide.html.

Corey, G., Corey, M.S., and Callanan, P. (2007). *Issues and ethics in the helping professions* (7th ed.). Pacific Grove, CA: Brooks/Cole. This book provides a wealth of information for professionals and students in any of the human service professions. Ethics and issues specifically related to consultation are given adequate coverage, and the authors' ideas on several issues have relevance for consultants. Chapter 3,

"Values and the Helping Relationship," provides excellent information that consultants can extrapolate and apply to their practices. Chapter 4, "Multicultural Perspectives and Diversity Issues"; Chapter 6, "Confidentiality: Ethical and Legal Issues"; and Chapter 7, "Managing Boundaries and Multiple Relationships" all present important information that consultants can use in developing their own standards of conduct.

Swenson, L. C. (1997). *Psychology and law* (2nd ed.). Pacific Grove, CA: Brooks/Cole. This thorough text provides a broad coverage of a variety of legal issues practicing human service professionals encounter. Part 2 of the text, "Practice and Malpractice," provides four chapters from which practicing consultants can extrapolate and apply material to consultation situations. This text puts consultants into the world of legal realities, a world far different than that in which most of us practice. Swenson's point that satisfied consumers rarely sue is well taken.

# 8

---

✳

# The Pragmatic Issues
# of Working within
# an Organization

There are a variety of issues and forces that you will encounter in your practice of consultation and collaboration. All consultation occurs in some organizational context which contains complex forces that affect, for better or worse,
the consultation process (Lewis et al., 2003; Truscott et al., 2000). This chapter
provides the working knowledge of the pragmatic issues related to providing
consultation in an organization. Because consultation is one way to help organizations change so that they can function more effectively, consultants need to
know what organizations are; how they develop, grow stagnant, and change;
and what the connection is between an organization's individuals and its ability
to meet its goals and objectives. Knowledge of organizations also helps consultants better understand their consultees' position in an organizational context.

As you read this chapter, keep the following questions in mind:

1. How can you cope with the time constraints imposed upon you by the
   structure and culture of the organization for which you are consulting?

2. If organizations are so complex, how can a consultant or group of consultants accomplish real changes in them?

3. How are organizations like live organisms?

4. What factors are involved in organizational change?

5. How does organizational culture affect the behavior of individuals within
   the organization?

An organization is a complex social system that interacts with its environment and is, therefore, subject to influences from without and within. It is important for consultants to be familiar with the technical and social forces and structures that will impinge on the consultation environment (Knoff, 2002) so that they can help to ensure consultation success. These forces and structures include organization climate, the administration's view of consultation and collaboration, and the organization's authority, decision-making structure, and communication structures (Forman, 1995). This awareness is essential as consultants "must be able to conceptualize problems and interventions from an organizational perspective and utilize information about organizational processes in their consultation activities with agencies and organizations" (Illback & Zins, 1993, p. 87).

Both school-based and community-based consultants are increasingly being called on to engage in organizational consultation and need to take into account the organizational context of consultation, as well as consultation theory and practice, so as to maximize the probability of being successful (Illback & Zins, 1993; Knoff, 1995). This is particularly true with school-based consultants. As a result, school-based consultants will want to be familiar with organizational change processes so that the programs they assist can be fully integrated into the school (McDougal, Clonan, & Martens, 2000). Further, human service consultants must be versed in the nature of organizations and must be skilled in working with them. For example, Kelly (1993) noted long ago that mental health consultants are subject to the forces of the environment in which they consult, but their training is basically in individual therapy. Organizational factors about which consultants may want to be knowledgeable include recent changes in organizations and our society, the theory of organizations

that consultants themselves hold, the nature of organizational change, dealing with organizational culture, issues in assessment, cultural sensitivity in the organization, and time constraints.

## INTRODUCTION

Consider this situation:

### Case Example

In your job as chief administrator of a large human service agency, you notice an excessive turnover rate in two of your organization's six departments. You have made several unsuccessful attempts to rectify the problem; you know what is wrong, but you don't know how to fix it. As a last resort, you decide to call in a consultant. In preparing for the first meeting with the consultant, what exactly would you tell him or her about your organization, the people in it, the problem, and the solutions you've tried? Where would you suggest the consultant begin to try to help? If you were the consultant in this situation, what information would you want to know? What values and biases about "how to fix things" would you bring into the consultation setting? Which personnel would you want to interview? How would you go about solving the problem? How would you know whether consultation had been successful? The answers to these and many other important questions depend on how well you (the consultant) and the human service agency's administrator understand the nature of organizations.

Organizations of all kinds abound in our society: schools, businesses, human service agencies, and industries. People organize because they think it is the best way to reach their goals. To be effective in organizational consultation, consultants need to understand organizations themselves, as well as what prompts people to think and behave as they do within organizations.

An organization has the following: cooperation among many individuals, certain common goals, a division of labor, and a hierarchy of authority (Jerrell & Jerrell, 1981). Organizations can be defined in terms of what they do, how they are set up, and what their goals are. Management is a specialty task in organizations that helps them meet those goals. How organizations are managed raises many values issues, and organizations are often criticized for their values and the ways they are run. For example, some human service organizations are criticized for valuing rules and regulations more than the clients they serve. An organization's values and behaviors become quite evident when it must face several constantly changing issues. Regardless of the specific issues an organization faces at a given time, the basic issues remain constant: complexity, organizational size, and technology.

Organization development consultation attempts to explain the whats, hows, and whys of organizations and to help them increase their effectiveness. When a consultant goes into an organization, the first step is to develop a basic definition of the organization. The theoretical frame of reference with which the consultant enters the organization determines what the consultant sees. The consultant defines the organization by performing an assessment to clarify its basic nature. Consultants usually have training in one of the four components of organizations—environment, people, structure, and process—but consultants also need a general perspective on organizations to be able to compare one with another.

## RECENT CHANGES IN SOCIETY AND ORGANIZATIONS

Some understanding of recent changes in society and organizations provides consultants a framework for being more effective in assisting the organizations with which they consult. In the new millennium, basic societal change has affected new workers: There has been a diminishing percentage of young people entering the work force, new

workers are less skilled than those of previous generations, and women and minorities continue to make up a very large proportion of the workforce. Issues in the workplace in the 1990s (Luke, 1993) that are continuing include those related to dependent care, substance abuse, AIDS, women at work, stress (e.g., violence in the workplace), advances in technology, the creation of a "flat world," a realignment of the world's economy, and cultural diversity. The effects of catastrophic events such as September 11 and Hurricane Katrina have tested the way our society goes about its business by making the incomprehensible comprehensible.

In addition to societal changes, organizations themselves are changing. Organizations, including human service organizations, have been going through several changes (Burke, 1993). Organizations have been experiencing change at an increasingly rapid pace. Implications for consultants include how to best gather and process information in order to react to ever-changing conditions. A further implication of rapid change is that consultants themselves must be willing to deal effectively with ambiguity and uncertainty.

Organizations have become more complex; the number of specialized people performing different tasks has increased. This increased complexity and diversification makes it much more difficult for an organization to have a common purpose and makes coordination difficult for management. The managers of organizations and agencies have moved from being unaware of organizational change concepts to being quite familiar with them. The challenge to consultants is to make sure that managers and others are capable of acting on their awareness of the meaning of terms such as "vision," "organizational culture," and so forth.

There is a greater competition among all types of organizations (Beer & Walton, 1990), including human service organizations. Organizations, therefore, will be looking for longer term consultation rather than touch-and-go advice, gearing consultation to long-term effects through help with immediate problems and providing specific (not general) help. The atrocity of September 11 and the tragedy at Virginia Tech have changed the nature of the workplace in terms of dealing with terrorist threats or attacks and tragic events (Knotek, 2006; McCarroll & Ursano, 2006; Stock, 2007).

**Implications for Consultants.**   Human service/mental health consultants will be increasingly called upon to assist organizations and their members manage and cope with such changes. Organizations are likely to want help in the following areas that impact organizational culture and climate: focusing more on the human side of management, resolving the human resource problems caused by mergers and acquisitions, and providing training in effective communication regarding the impact of change (Offermann & Gowing, 1990). Organizations are also likely to need consultants in the following areas related to maintaining organizational productivity: optimizing organizational structure, restructuring the nature of work toward increased use of team approaches, maximizing the use of technology, creating effective work environments, improving services and products (Offermann & Gowing, 1990). The increase in technological developments in the workplace will add to problems of stress among management and staff, leading to increased use of consultants in stress management training capacities (Turnage, 1990). The increased competitiveness among organizations will require that consultants help managers become more effective in the following areas: taking the leadership in accomplishing needed changes through better use of the skills of empowering others, envisioning desired outcomes, providing resources, and modeling desired practices (Beer & Walton, 1990). Increases in workplace violence as well as the increased possibility of terrorist attacks and natural disasters have created a need for consultants who can assess the risk of workplace violence, review and update crisis management plans, work with members of the organization's crisis management team and others to prepare for violence when it occurs (Stock, 2007), as well as provide consultative services during crises and disasters (Halpern & Tramontin, 2007; McCarroll & Ursano, 2006). As examples, consultants can work with organizations to develop or improve crisis management plans, increase social

cohesiveness to minimize the psychological impact related to a trauma in the workplace (McCarroll & Uranus, 2006), and conduct post-crisis audits (Simola, 2005).

Because many of these organizational needs are related to the human factor, human service consultants will find themselves increasingly involved in work with business and industry as well as the traditional areas of public and nonprofit organizations. Education/training consultation will be in demand because so many organizational needs relate to maximizing the talents of personnel (Goldstein & Gilliam, 1990). Regardless of how they will be employed, consultants will need to be competent in using power, blending structural changes with people changes, and learning quickly yet thoroughly the nature of the organizations that they are consulting (Beer & Walton, 1990; Illback & Zins, 1993). Consultees are increasingly open to collaborative, qualitative organizational consultation methods (Truscott et al., 2000).

# THE INFLUENCE OF ORGANIZATIONAL THEORY

Consultants develop a broad perspective on the nature of organizational forces by considering each organization with which they work relative to some organizational theory. The consultant's organizational theory is the glue that holds together events into a meaningful form. Organizations' day-to-day functioning are guided by the particular theories of organization they adhere to. By being aware of such theories, human service consultants will understand the ways things are done in a particular organization and, just as importantly, the ways the forces that impact that organization are interpreted (Harrison & Shirom, 1999). Further, the theory on which an organization is based affects the way processes such as consultation and collaboration are performed.

Historically speaking, *organizational theory* is the study of the structures and processes of organizations and the behavior of groups and individuals within them. Because they attempt to explain these complex entities and how they are best designed, most theories must simplify organizations; how this is accomplished depends on which factors are considered relevant. (A comprehensive coverage of different organizational theories is beyond the scope of this text; interested readers can gain in-depth information from such classic books as *The Social Psychology of Organizations* [Katz & Kahn, 1990].) The following overview of two organizational theories highlights the different perspectives from which organizations can be studied. I particularly believe that a view of the bureaucratic model and the systems model provide a contrast for consultants to consider as they analyze organizations.

Before the turn of the century, organizations were considered individual entities such as church, government, and so forth. With the rise of capitalism in the late 19th century, organizations came to be viewed as a "class of collectivities" (French & Bell, 1999). The classical model of organizations came into vogue near the beginning of the 20th century and was epitomized by Max Weber's model of bureaucracy (Katz & Kahn, 1990). This model is considered a "machine" theory. *Machine theory* is a generic term that implies that each organization is built according to the blueprint derived from its purpose, just as each machine is built according to a set of specifications (Katz & Kahn, 1990).

## The Bureaucratic Model

Weber designed the bureaucratic model as the ideal of organizational effectiveness. Its principles, which are "means to ends" in nature, emphasize the structure of the organization over the human element (Harrison & Shirom, 1999). Rules and regulations are important and provide order and continuity. Jobs are analyzed in terms of what is required to do them effectively, and the most highly qualified people are placed in them. Communication patterns are vertical rather than horizontal, with each unit under the direct control of a higher unit. Emphasis is placed on the written record, with all decisions, acts, and regulations written down (Katz & Kahn, 1990).

According to this bureaucratic theory, organizations were meant to be efficient, effective, and equitable. However, the potentially counterproductive elements in this model can lead to red tape, rigidity, apathy, and resistance to change.

**Implications for Consultants.**  Consultants encountering an organization emphasizing bureaucratic values will want to be sensitive to the lines of authority, the dedication to the written word, and the importance of rules and regulations. They should be on the lookout for apathy/morale issues, views of leadership among the organization members, concern over confidentiality, and the nature of the informal power structure.

The classical models of organizational theory, such as the bureaucratic model, emphasize specialization of tasks, standardized role performance, uniformity of function, and avoidance of duplication (Katz & Kahn, 1990). These models are inadequate in that they do not provide for interaction between the organization and its environment and thus deny the organization a means to change (Katz & Kahn, 1990).

## Open Systems Organizational Theory

One of the most popular models of organizational theory is systems theory, which provides a broadly based perspective on organizations developed from attempts to understand biological events (Adelman & Taylor, 2007; Curtis & Stollar, 2002; Kurpius et al., 1993). Systems theory is integral to the consultation-related activities of community psychologists and is becoming increasingly popular with other human service professionals (Harrison & Shirom, 1999; Juras, Mackin, Curtis, & Foster-Fishman, 1998; Lewis et al., 2003).

A "system" can be defined as "the orderly combination of two or more individuals whose interaction is intended to produce a desired outcome" (Curtis & Stollar, 2002, p. 224). The idea is to understand interdependencies, multiple causes, and multiple effects (French & Bell, 1999). In systems theory, "organizations" can be defined as "dynamic entities continually interacting with their environment, changing and adapting to develop congruence between people, process, structure, and external environment" (Beer, 1980, p. 15). According to systems theory, everything is interrelated and interdependent. When applied to organizations' and consultants' behavior in organizations, system theory suggests that events impact and are impacted by whatever transpires. There are two types of systems: closed and open. Closed systems are not affected by their environments: They have a finite amount of energy, and when that energy is used up the system runs down. Open systems, in contrast, have permeable boundaries and can obtain energy from and send energy back to the environment. Organizations can be viewed as open systems (French & Bell, 1999). Open systems have an input-throughput-output mechanism. These three systems must work well together for an organization to work effectively.

The systems view of organizations identifies four components: a framework (pattern of activities), goals, methods and operations, and people (Kurpius et al., 1993). The systems theory of organizations assumes that organizations are open systems; they are not isolated, closed entities, but instead are subject to internal and external influences (Curtis & Stollar, 2002). Systems theory considers the organization to be a totality, and it directly examines the interrelationships among an organization's subsystems and between the organization and its environment.

The most fundamental property of a system is the interdependence among its parts (Curtis & Stollar, 2002). The systems approach is helpful in conceptualizing the multidimensional parts of a system as an integrated whole and it assumes that an organization is more than the sum of its parts. Organizations (and the people within them) are seen as adaptive and as social systems operating within larger environments (French & Bell, 1999).

**Characteristics of Systems.** When viewed as open systems, organizations have nine characteristics (Henning-Stout, 1993):

1. *Importation of energy.* No social structure is self-sufficient: the organization must draw new energy from other organizations, the material environment, and people such as consultants.

2. *The throughput.* Energy is transformed as it goes through the organization. In a human service organization, throughput can be service to clients, training of existing personnel, addition of new staff, and so forth.

3. *The output.* The organization exports some product into the environment, such as some new service to the client system.

4. *Systems are cycles of events.* Organizations have an input-throughput-output cycle; the output product supplied to the environment provides energy for repetition of the cycle.

5. *Negative entropy.* Entropy is the degradation process of all organisms toward death or disorganization. Organizations can arrest this entropy by importing more energy than they expend. This process of energy storage is called negative entropy.

6. *Information input, negative feedback, and the coding process.* Information input can give the organization signals about the environment and the organization's relationship to it. One type of information input is negative feedback, which allows the organization to stay on its chosen course or, if necessary, change course. The reception of inputs into the organization is selective; that is, the organization can attend to only so many inputs, and those inputs are the only ones among many that the organization tunes in. This selective mechanism is called coding, and the coding procedures of an organization are determined by its functions. (For example, if a mental health center learns that the community would fund a dropout prevention program, it might make plans to develop and implement such a program.)

7. *The steady state and dynamic homeostasis.* The importation of energy can maintain constancy in the flow of energy such that an organization is characterized by a steady state. Dynamic homeostasis refers to the basic preservation of the system's character. In preserving its

character, the organization must import more energy than it exports. In adapting to its environment, an organization moves toward assimilating the external resources considered necessary for survival. Hence, organizations attempt to grow both quantitatively and qualitatively over time.

8. *Differentiation.* Organizations move in the direction of differentiation and elaboration: roles within the organization become specialized and the number of such roles tends to increase. (For example, a mental health center might differentiate from a single team to a crisis-intervention team, a substance-abuse team, and any number of other specialized teams.)

9. *Equifinality.* The principle of equifinality proposes that organizations can reach the same end by different means: this is the "there's-more-than-one-way-to-skin-a-cat" principle. (For example, a single human service organization might use any of several methods to improve its public relations image.)

**Subsystems within the Organization.** The subsystems of an organization are integrated by means of the norms, roles, and values present within the system. Role behavior is sanctioned by norms that are justified by values. Five subsystems within organizations are built around the organization's norms, roles, and values (Katz & Kahn, 1990):

- the technological or production subsystem
- the support subsystem
- the maintenance subsystem
- the adaptive subsystem
- the managerial subsystem

The *technological subsystem* is concerned with the quantity and quality of the work accomplished within the organization. For example, in a counseling center, the direct delivery of services to the client system—the throughput—constitutes the technological subsystem. Organizations are often classified according to the type of product they provide, and the products of human service organizations are the clients they serve. (More precisely stated, the product of human service agencies is "better" people.) The technological subsystem is responsible for the input-throughput-output cycle.

The *support subsystem* is concerned with the procurement of inputs, the disposal of outputs, and the maintenance of an environment favorable to the organization. For example, a university might seek funding (procurement of inputs) for a counseling program for learning-disabled college students. Upon termination of the program, a written report is submitted to the funding agency (disposal of outputs), and the program is widely publicized to attract students and strengthen its public image (maintenance of a favorable environment).

The *maintenance subsystem* is concerned with connecting people within the organization to their roles. It is not concerned with the material being worked on (typically the client system in human service organizations), but rather with the equipment used to get the work done. In human service organizations, this concern relates to getting people who work for the organization into their proper roles: patterned human behavior. This subsystem integrates people into the system through recruitment, socialization, training, rewarding, and sanctioning, and it is concerned with input with respect to maintenance (for example, recruitment of personnel).

The *adaptive subsystem* helps an organization exist in a changing environment. It is specifically concerned with sensing and interpreting important changes in the external environment. Functions such as long-range planning, research and development, and market research are part of the adaptive subsystem.

The *managerial subsystem* controls, coordinates, and directs the other subsystems of the organization and adjusts the total system to its environment. There are two major types of managerial subsystems: regulatory mechanisms and the authority structure.

*Regulatory mechanisms* gather and interpret data about the organization's input-throughput-output cycle and give feedback to the system about its output in relation to its input. In a human service organization, a follow-up study of clients' perceived benefits from the organization would be an example of a regulatory mechanism.

Organizations must have a defined and established decision-making framework called the *authority structure*. This structure describes the organization of the managerial system in terms of the decisions it makes and the routes through which they are implemented.

**Implications for Consultants.** Because of the current popularity of the systems view, I have provided extensive coverage of the implications of this perspective. O'Neill and Trickett (1982, pp. 4–5) have pointed out six implications that still hold today for consultants taking on a systems view of organizations:

- Consultation is an activity designed to intervene in the social context.

- An important source of knowledge is understanding the social context where consultation is occurring.

- Cultural and institutional diversity is a positively valued fact of life for the consultant.

- Consultation interventions should be matched to the organization within which consultation occurs.

- Priority should be given to predicting the side effects of consultation.

- Interventions should be designed in such a way that the organization's resources are managed and preserved.

In addition, just as each person is unique and special, so too is every system (Curtis & Stollar, 2002). Consultants need to take a fresh perspective each time they enter a new consultation setting. They need to view behavior from a systems perspective, remembering that everything is connected to everything else, and use collaborative procedures (McLean, 2006). Furthermore, because the effects of consultation can go far beyond those intended, consultants should ensure that communication flows smoothly and accurately throughout the subsystems of an organization. You no doubt have heard horror stories about organizations such as schools or mental health centers in which the staff in one area was

totally unaware of what the staff in other areas was doing and planning, even though they would be affected by those decisions.

Other implications of systems theory for consultants include helping an organization maintain focus on its core mission, promoting the use of feedback as a self-regulating mechanism to expedite change, and assisting with the maintenance of internal and external boundaries so that work flow goes smoothly (French & Bell, 1999; Lee, 1993). The field of community psychology has added the additional element of the community as a part of the system in which organizations exist (Kloos et al., 1998). The community is viewed as both a possible target for consultation and collaboration as well as a force impacting the organization (Lewis et al., 2003).

The goal of consultation using systems theory can be a change in the *microsystem* (i.e., the closest social elements of the defined client system), the *mesosystem* (i.e., the near but not immediate influences, such as the general influence of family and friends), and the *exosystem* (i.e., the most remote factors, such as ethical and legal procedures; see Kurpius et al., 1993, pp. 416–417). Conceptualizing at these levels permits the consultant to design interventions at multiple levels. Effective consultants using systems theory will take into account the relationships between the problem at hand and systems variables. The interaction between the client system and the environmental context (i.e., the various systems levels) will be assessed in consultation.

The bottom line is that consultation based on systems theory has as its goal an increase in the level of problem-solving expertise of the system. While the immediate goal is to assist the system with a specified problem, the ultimate goal is to assist the system to be a more effective problem solver on its own. As a result of this perspective, the use of training in problem-solving activities for consultees is strongly encouraged.

Now that we have examined the bureaucratic and systems theories of organizations, it should be clear that when consultants enter an organization, they regard it and analyze it based on some theory of organizations. Whether you realize it or not, you have your own theory of organizations. The more you are aware of it, the more you will know what you are looking for and also what you are likely to overlook; you will also be in a better position to understand how your consultees view their organizations and the concomitant implications this has for your consultation.

Will you see the organization relative to the bureaucratic theory and assume that the members of the organization need to be controlled by certain highly regulated structures? Will you adopt the position of the systems theorists and look at the interdependencies and interrelationships among the organization's subsystems to understand the organization? Whatever questions you ask, the variety of organizational theories available to consultants suggests that consultants should take a flexible view in analyzing organizations.

## ORGANIZATIONAL CHANGE

Consultants, both internal and external, frequently help organizations change. The following discussions incorporate current thinking about effective organizations and the principles of organizational change.

### Approaches to Change

All organizations change in response to pressure from internal or external forces; this change can be deliberate or accidental (French & Bell, 1999). Most organizations, including schools, are not adept at making changes (Lee, 1993). Depending on how well an organization monitors its internal and external environments, change may be either well planned or forced on the organization through a crisis situation.

When an organization senses the need for change, it looks for new directions to proceed. From a philosophical perspective, there are three views of planned change: the empirical-rational approach, the normative-reeducative approach, and the power-coercive approach (Chin & Benne, 1985). Although conceptualized decades ago, these views of change remain current and influential in planned change initiatives (French & Bell, 1999).

The *empirical-rational approach* assumes that people are rational by nature and will follow their rational self-interests once these are made known. Thus, any proposed changes are presumed to be congruent with the self-interests of the organization and its members. Because the organization and its members are presumably rational and motivated by self-interest, changes will be adopted only if they can be rationally justified and gains are evident. In other words, according to this approach, changes in cognitions produce changes in behavior. This approach's credibility is based on scientific research and the process of educating people for change.

The *normative-reeducative approach* does not deny the role of rationality in change but points out that change is supported by sociocultural norms based on attitudes and values. Change involves a shift in those attitudes and values away from old patterns and a commitment to new patterns. This approach views people as social by nature; their shifts in emotion about something will bring about change. This position holds that change is not only intellectual; it also involves feelings and attitudes.

The *power-coercive approach* to change focuses on the ingredients of power and the ways it is used in bringing about change. This approach relies on the use of political, economic, and moral sanctions in the exercise of power; it assumes that externally based sanctions are necessary for change to occur. Most consultant activities related to organizational change involve the normative-reeducative category, although some activities may be a combination of normative-reeducative and empirical-rational approaches (French & Bell, 1999).

Change can also be examined in terms of the source from which the impetus to change comes. These "power structures" are top-down, bottom-up, and shared (Beer, 1980). In the *top-down approach,* change is implemented on authority of the organization's leadership, which also defines the problem and determines the solution. The change that is to occur can be communicated in the following ways:

- decree (e.g., memorandum)
- introduction of technology (e.g., personal computers)

- replacement (e.g., changing key personnel)

- changes in structure (e.g., reorganization of a subsystem)

Top-down changes are usually unilateral, are usually introduced rapidly, and involve only a few key, top-level administrators in the decision-making process.

The *bottom-up approach* to change is the opposite of the top-down approach. Because responsibility for change is delegated to members lower in the organization, administrators typically are not involved but are typically kept apprised about the changes. Bottom-up change can occur in the following contexts:

- training sessions (e.g., team building)

- staff groups (e.g., peer teaching and training in different managerial approaches)

- experimental units (e.g., groups designed to take services to locations near the residences of the client systems' members).

In the bottom-up approach, leadership in the organization relinquishes significant amounts of power and authority.

Bottom-up changes are usually slow and subject to the influences of special-interest groups. The *shared approach* involves a continuous interaction among members of the organization's different levels, and a process of mutual influence ensues (Beer, 1980). The shared approach to change can involve the following (Beer, 1980):

- iterative communication (e.g., a top-level administrator defines the problem and assigns staff to gather data and develop solutions; the process is reviewed frequently by members throughout the organization)

- decision-making task forces (e.g., top leadership defines the problem and the parameters of the solution but has the task force generate solutions; top leadership then makes the final selection of the most appropriate solution)

- diagnostic and problem-solving task forces (e.g., a group composed of individuals from all

levels of the organization defines the problem and implements a solution)

Because they typically involve personnel from throughout the entire organization, shared approaches to change are usually slow; and because so many people are involved, ownership of changes is usually strong (Lippitt, 1993).

## The Nature of Organizational Change

Change is a part of the daily routine of any organization; it can be precipitated by internal or external forces and can be planned or unplanned. If these forces are adequately monitored, then change can occur in a planned and systematic way. If these forces are not adequately monitored, crises ensue and the organization is forced to cope in a less orderly, less effective manner. Pressure to change can be strong and can demand great adaptability from an organization. Nonprofit organizations frequently have a more difficult time coping with and planning for change because they are not necessarily subject to the same marketplace forces that act on for-profit organizations.

Organizations are subject to the following changes occurring in our society (Backer & Porterfield, 1998): the pace of change has increased; an increasing amount of change involves diminishing resources, thus necessitating reactions such as downsizing; and the nature of change itself is changing all of the time. Efforts to achieve change must be responsive to organization–environmental interfaces; it is no longer practical to improve internal effectiveness without explicit attention to the relationship between an organization and its environment.

Real organizational change will not take place and be maintained unless the following three conditions exist:

- There must be a sufficiently high level of dissatisfaction with the status quo to mobilize energy toward some change.

- Leaders must have some vision of the desired result of change.

■  Leaders must envision and communicate some practical first steps to mobilize the energy to begin change.

Burke (1993) points out that attempts to change organizations should aim for change in the following areas in the presented order: behavior, attitudes, and values. Behavior change leads to change in attitudes which can, in turn, change culture.

**Implications for Consultants.**  Human service consultants in any setting generally consult with the purpose of achieving change in an organization (or in an individual or group within that organization). Clearly, to be most effective, consultants must be familiar with many models for conceptualizing organizational change and understand how change is viewed in the organization in which they are consulting (Fuqua & Kurpius, 1993). Consultants are well-advised to buy into the method of change typically used by the organization prior to recommending or implementing their own views. Because change is such a sensitive issue for people, consultants should minimize the stress of change whether for an individual or an entire organization. They will also want to ensure that ideas for change are integrated into the organization, that changes are conducted by members of the organization with top-level sanctioning and involvement, and that change strategies are well planned and implemented. For example, consultants can use *learning diagnosis,* which involves organizational members in the diagnostic process and assists them in acquiring the "willingness, skills, and ability to discuss the undiscussable" (Beer & Spector, 1993, p. 644) while tailoring the diagnosis to the strategic tasks of the organization.

Finally, consultants will need to develop an operational view of organizational effectiveness (Ridley & Mendoza, 1993) which can help the consultant and consultee develop a framework for effective change. By using such activities, consultants will better understand the change process within an organization and can thereby minimize resistance and enhance the probability that their efforts will be successful.

# DEALING WITH
# ORGANIZATIONAL CULTURE

Organizational culture has a large impact on individual and group behavior (Schein, 2004). Although the term "organizational culture" is not well-defined, the concept is important for consultants to be aware of in terms of designing and implementing successful strategies (Schein, 1990b; 2004). The forces in an organization that are derived from its culture are powerful. Members of the organization need to understand them so that can adequately deal with them (Schein, 2004). I have dedicated extensive coverage to organizational culture because of its potential to significantly impact the behavior and effectiveness of an organization.

"Culture" can be defined as "a pattern of shared basic assumptions that was learned by a group as it solved its problems of external adaptation and internal regulation, that has worked well enough to be considered valid and therefore, to be taught to new members as the correct way to perceive, think, and feel in relation to those problems" (Schein, 2004, p. 17). Manifestations of the organization's culture include climate, group norms, roles, systems, politics, and values.

The culture is maintained by the socialization of members new to the organization. Successful organizations have the following cultural attributes: uniqueness in their philosophy, a focus by management on maintaining the philosophy, deliberate attempts to integrate the philosophy throughout the organization, and involvement by all staff in communicating and reinforcing an organization-wide view of events and decisions (Lundberg, 1993).

Consultants need to be aware of an organization's culture because it has a very strong impact on whether or not a given plan of action will be successful (Harrison & Shirom, 1999). For example, if school-based human service professionals are expected to have large caseloads, then there will be limited time available for consultation and collaboration (Bramlett & Murphy, 1998). Clearly, consultants need to have a sense of how an organization defines itself in terms of its culture. In addition, different segments of an organization may define themselves in terms of culture differently than does the entire organization (Jenster & Bigler, 1989). For example, school teachers may have a different organizational culture than school administrators. Consider the situation in which you are a consultant asked to conduct a professional development experience for junior high school teachers on the characteristics of the middle school child. Although the administrative unit sees this as an important step in moving the school toward a middle school concept, the teachers might see the training as another unnecessary imposition on valuable time and another set of expectations without any subsequent reward. You can readily see that the intervention would not likely be successful without the consultant's understanding of how the two units within the school tend to view the use of the consultant's training.

What does a consultant look for when attempting to understand an organization's culture? According to Schein (1990b; 2004), culture manifests itself in terms of the interaction of artifacts, values, and basic underlying assumptions. *Artifacts* refer to relatively superficial things such as dress codes, annual reports, role and mission statements, and the various interpersonal rituals people engage in. Consultants may intervene at this level by helping the organization reorganize the way people problem solve (e.g., by setting up quality circles). *Values* refer to the espoused ways people think and feel in the organization. Consultants can intervene at this level by conducting team building exercises among various subgroups within an organization (e.g., between teachers and support personnel). *Basic underlying assumptions* refer to those views of the organization that are taken for granted and are unconscious. A basic implication for consultants is that interaction with members of the organization is essential to get to these assumptions. Another implication is that getting to the underlying assumptions of the organization can assist the consultant in suggesting the right type of interventions. Consultants can intervene at this level through leading exploratory groups in which consultants raise focused questions and consultees volunteer to analyze their deep-seated views of the organization. Table 8.1 summarizes Schein's (1990b) ideas regarding the underlying dimensions of organizational culture and their underlying assumptions.

**Implications for Consultants.** By having the skills to understand an organization's culture, consultants are better able to get a feel for an organization's history, current behavior, and future aspirations (Schein, 1990b, 1999; 2004), which will help them determine how to select the best interventions. By understanding an organization's culture, consultants will be better able to help the organization deal with the sets of problems with which organizations most often need assistance: dealing with its environment and internally integrating daily functions and the ability to adapt (Schein, 2004). By understanding an organization's culture, consultants are better able to manage the cultural forces that impact their consultation and to help an organization change in constructive ways. For example, they can promote their consultation and collaboration services in the framework of "how things are done" and fitting these services into the routines of the organization (Welch, 2000). In addition, they and their consultees might well attain a better understanding of the behavior of the organization, which can be linked to effective change within the organization. Knowledge of culture is essential when consultants are asked to help clarify individual roles within the organization, restructure for accommodating change, develop the management function within the organization (Lewis, Lewis, & Souflee, 1991), and understand how contextual variables shape behavior within the organization (Kuh, 1993; Schein, 2004).

## ISSUES IN ORGANIZATION ASSESSMENT

Organizations offer challenging issues to consultants regarding assessment. Due to the complexity inherent in most organizations, determining what to assess can be difficult. Further, there are limited instruments for assessing organizations. When looking at assessment of organizations, consultants need to

**T A B L E  8.1**    **Some Underlying Dimensions of Organization Culture**

| DIMENSION | QUESTIONS TO BE ANSWERED |
| --- | --- |
| The organization's relationship to its environment | Does the organization perceive itself to be dominant, submissive, harmonizing, searching out a niche? |
| The nature of human activity | Is the correct way for humans to behave to be dominant/proactive, harmonizing, or passive/fatalistic? |
| The nature of reality and truth | How do we define what is true and false, and how is truth ultimately determined in both the physical and the social world—by pragmatic test, reliance on wisdom, or social consensus? |
| The nature of time | What is our basic orientation in terms of past, present, and future, and what kinds of time units are most relevant for the conduct of daily affairs? |
| The nature of human nature | Are humans basically good, neutral, or evil, and is human nature perfectible or fixed? |
| The nature of human relationships | What is the "correct" way for people to relate to each other, to distribute power and affection? Is life competitive or cooperative? Is it best to organize society on the basis of individualism or group mind? Is the best authority system autocratic/paternalistic or collegial/participative? |
| Homogeneity versus diversity | Is the group best off if it is highly diverse or highly homogeneous, and should individuals in a group be encouraged to innovate or conform? |

Source: From Schein, E. H., *Organizational Culture and Leadership: A Dynamic View,* Table 3, p. 86. Copyright 1985 by Jossey-Bass, Inc., Publishers. This material was used with permission of John Wiley & Sons.

avoid the usual perspective used to assess an individual because organizational factors are more complex. Two particular challenges faced by consultants in assessment of organizations include the necessity of taking a systems perspective and developing a wariness of defining organizational concerns in terms of behavioral constructs (Fuqua, Newman, & Dickman, 1999). What is needed for effective assessment by organizational consultants is an integrated, theory-based model with well-defined and evidenced-based constructs (Fuqua et al., 1999).

A systems view of organization assessment assumes that the "whole is greater than the sum of its parts." Assessment must try to capture the dynamic interactive factors of an organization to be most accurate. For example, it may be more effective to analyze the interaction between the model of discipline used in a school and the school's administrative unit, instead of focusing only on one or the other.

**Implications for Consultants.**    Consultants will need to be well-grounded in organizational theory and approaches to organizational consultation. Assessment should focus on the interactions of the parts of the organization rather than separate parts (Beer & Spector, 1993). Consultants will want to avoid interpreting individual data in group terms and vice versa (Fuqua et al., 1999). Consultants can effectively use both objective measures (e.g., the number of in-school suspensions) and subjective measures (e.g., teachers' perceptions of the efficacy of in-school suspensions) as well as qualitative and quantitative measures (Fuqua et al., 1999).

## THE CULTURALLY SENSITIVE ORGANIZATION

As the changing demographics of our society have reached the workplace, the need for diversity awareness and skill has grown. We are beyond looking at diversity in organizations in terms of legal compliance and human rights protection and seeing it as a value-added opportunity to maximize the potential of the organization (Cox, 2001; Hoffman, 2006). As Hogan (2007) notes: "Cultural awareness, coupled with the skills needed to interact successfully with people of diverse cultural backgrounds living and working in the same place, is called *diversity competence, cultural competence,* or *cultural diversity competence*" (p. 1). Hogan goes on to note that "Culturally competent organizations have congruent structures, policies, programs, protocols, and processes that enable the entire system to work with culturally diverse people" (p. 1). Culturally competent organizations are proactive in responding to the constant diversity-related, economic, political and social conditions. These organizations have a sense of open-mindedness and a commitment to continuous learning (Arredondo, 1996). Culturally competent organizations have the ability to identify the organization's needs; increase awareness, understanding and skills of all employees; implement a strategic plan; effectively monitor progress in becoming a strategic organization (Hogan, 2007); and allow for how diversity can impact services such as coaching (Thomas, 2006). From a human service organization's perspective, the bottom line is that a culturally competent organization can effectively provide services cross-culturally (Diller, 2007).

Diversity competence is promoted in organizations by maintaining awareness of cultural awareness throughout the organization, recruiting culturally diverse employees, providing career development op-

portunities for all employees, creating working conditions conducive to the needs of all employees, and monitoring the change process related to cultural issues (Hogan, 2007; Washburn, Manley, & Holiwski, 2003). As Lum (2007) notes about cultural competence in organizations, "workers are trained in the skills necessary for diversity sensitive practice, and multicultural awareness and functioning are promoted in organizational structure and program delivery" (p. 9). Lum notes further that culturally competent organizations "value diversity, have the capacity for cultural self-assessment, be conscious of the dynamics of cultural interaction, institutionalize cultural knowledge, and develop programs and services that promote diversity between and within cultures" (p. 11). Management, of course, plays a major part in developing and maintaining a culturally responsive organization. There are models of diversity management (e.g., Arredondo, 1996) that attempt to develop the organization in a diversity-sensitive manner while encouraging organizational-level change and employee empowerment. The goal for consultants is to help to develop and maintain an organization that is culturally competent in its functioning through a variety of interventions at different levels within the organization. There is some empirical evidence that organizations with multiculturally competent mission statements and multicultural training tend to have employees who perceive themselves to be multiculturally competent (Darnell & Kupermine, 2006).

## TIME CONSTRAINTS

One of the biggest issues you will face in work as a consultant or collaborator is finding the time to perform it adequately (Bramlett & Murphy, 1998; Gottlieb, 2006; Noell & Witt, 1998). Whether you work in a school, a clinic or agency, or a business and industry setting, you will be challenged to cope with time constraints. Part of the time constraint issue involves the mindset by many consultees that consultants are professionals to whom a problem is given to be fixed. In this mindset, consultees

---

**C A S E   8.1     Organizational Concepts for School Consultants**

---

Sharon is a school-based consultant who has transferred to an elementary school after 15 years of working in a middle school. The central office of the school system has recently mandated that each school must develop a wellness program for its staff and students within the first 9 weeks of school. Sharon's principal has assigned her the task of designing the program. Because Sharon is new to the school, she decides that she must carefully do her "homework" to design an effective program. It's an opportunity for her to learn about her new work environment and get a project done at the same time. Yet Sharon is disconcerted by the nagging question of why the principal would give a new staff person a project like this.

As Sharon began to familiarize herself with students, staff, and the physical plant of the school, she found out many interesting things. The school was run in a very businesslike manner. Sharon was expected to develop her proposal and send it directly to the principal without discussing it with anyone. She was to schedule a weekly 15-minute appointment with the principal in his office to update him on her progress. She found out that rules and regulations were of paramount importance to the principal. Staff had to sign in and out of school, and a high priority was put on keeping detailed records. Teachers appeared to be very friendly with one another, and the "informal power structure" of the school kept up the morale of teachers and staff alike. It was obvious to Sharon that there was a rather large communication gap between the faculty and administration. The principal was highly respected yet seen as overly concerned with the mechanics of running the school at the expense of its "human side." The students dreaded going to his office but typically liked their teachers.

Sharon felt the principal gave her the job because of her qualifications and because he didn't want to take time away from any teacher's instructional obligations. To the principal, the teachers' job was to teach. Similarly, ancillary personnel like Sharon were to do ancillary tasks.

Sharon was very used to the middle school concept. What she found out as she began developing her project shocked her; she would have to be careful not to let her own values about how the school should be run interfere with her project and her attitude toward the principal. Sharon sensed that the values of the teaching staff were basically those related to a humanistic view of education, whereas the administration valued "getting the job done." A deeper underlying assumption appeared to be "the administrators are the bosses, let them do their thing, but don't let them get in the way of our doing our thing." "Like two ships passing in the night and not noticing each other," thought Sharon.

The wellness program would mean some changes, which in this school meant in a somewhat autocratic "top-down" manner. She also noted that the informal power structure of the school supplemented the principal's authority and got things done in a less legalistic and more personal manner. In reflecting on how to proceed with developing her proposal, Sharon made a list of as many of the school's organizational characteristics as she could come up with and then looked at them in terms of force-field analysis.

**Commentary**

As experienced consultants will tell you, there is more to organizational change than appears on the surface. Wisely, Sharon took the time to analyze the organizational context in which her project was to take shape. She further had the insight to look at the development of her project in terms of both the formal and informal power structures in the school, thus increasing the chances of having a "politically correct" yet "user friendly" program. Notice her attempt to creatively use a force-field analysis of her school's characteristics to guide her planning. This case clearly illustrates the importance of consultants being aware of the organizational forces that impact their practice and the importance of taking these forces into consideration in their attempts to be of service.

---

frequently see themselves functioning mainly as referral sources for the consultant. Some managers, for example, do not see their role as collaborating with the consultant and then implementing the recommendation, but rather view the consultant as one who can come up with a traditional training intervention that should fix the problem. Managers often think, "If employees are not motivated, then come up with a training application that will get them motivated and then implement it." Rarely will the consultant hear: "Help me figure out what *I* can do to help motivate my employees."

---

**C A S E   8.2    Organizational Concepts for Community Consultants**

---

Ward is a counseling psychologist asked by a hospital-based hospice program to provide consultation services to its staff. Because the program had been in existence only a few years and Ward had limited experiences with the hospice staff, he decided to proceed cautiously in developing his consultation for the staff. Part of his approach was to ensure that he first studied the organization in which he was going to consult before proceeding further.

He had been introduced at a staff meeting, and the director of the program had taken Ward around the unit for a day introducing him to the staff members on an individual basis. Ward then spent three days orienting himself to the hospice program. He observed and interacted, paid attention to a variety of aspects of the program's culture, and noted that the staff dress code was less rigid than that of the rest of the hospital. He found that families were encouraged to visit their loved ones at any time and were warmly seen by the staff as participants in the care of their loved ones. There was a sense of camaraderie among the staff as being special people serving a higher need of society.

As Ward tried to determine the theoretical nature of the problems, he constantly kept in mind the influence of his lengthy experience as a psychologist in the military. With this perspective in mind, he noted that the hospice program was designed with a human relations approach. The people in the program held frequent team meetings, program decisions were made through consensus-seeking meetings, and the program

director acted as a buffer against the strong bureaucratic element of the hospital at large. Both staff and patients concurred that teamwork was important and that interdependence was more valued than independence.

Although they were not espoused as values, the program seemed to work on the underlying principles that satisfied staff contribute more compassionately to patient welfare, and that people and love were more important than rules and regulations. In interviewing staff, patients, and the patients' families, Ward determined that changes in the program were based often on a normative-reeducative basis and on a shared approach involving everyone. Based on what he had learned about the hospice program, Ward set about to develop a proposal that would outline a consultation program suitable for the type of "mini-organization" the hospice program seemed to be.

**Commentary**

Ward, as any perceptive external consultant would, took the time to analyze the organization in which he was going to work. Notice that Ward investigated the manifestations of the organization's culture by noting indicators such as employee dress and attitudes. Ward also attempted to grasp the "philosophy" of change in the hospice unit in order to make sure that he could minimize resistance to his consultative efforts. Finally, notice how Ward attempted to design a program with the unique characteristics of the organization in mind.

---

Involving consultees in more collaborative approaches frequently entails educating them about the nature of consultation and training them in problem-solving procedures. Administrators and supervisors who sanction consultation as a desired activity in the organization also legitimatize the use of time for consultation purposes. In some organizations, the use of consultants is considered a professional growth activity that is rewarded during the annual review process.

An even more critical issue is the severe time constraints faced in most organizations. Increasingly organization members are being asked to do more with less. This makes time an even more precious commodity in organizations. As a result, school-

based, as well as external, consultants will need to take the risk of consulting on the run (for example, discreetly in the hallway of a school) and keep initial attempts to establish consultation simple and time efficient (Bramlett & Murphy, 1998).

Methods to create time for effective consultation include scheduling meetings in advance as much as possible, doing as much data gathering as possible early on in the consultation process, and training prospective consultees in the problem-solving process prior to consultation. In schools, teachers can be given more time to be consultees by being given release time, having teacher aides assigned to them, and by using some team meeting times for consultation. Another possible method of dealing with time constraints is to have an "entry presentation" at a faculty meeting that orients teachers to consultation and allows the consultant to begin entry on a group basis (Zins & Curtis, 1984). Training consultees directly in selected interventions is another effective method of dealing with time constraints (Watson & Robinson, 1996).

Indirect ways for finding time to consult and collaborate include publicly articulating the rationale for consultation/collaboration, having leadership participate in these activities, defining staff roles to include consultation/collaboration, creating a schedule that allows time for these activities, providing occasional additional time for these activities during the work day, and providing incentives for engaging in these activities (Thousand et al., 1996). Ferguson (2006) adds the Adlerian concept of encouragement and mutual respect as time-tested strategies for expediting motivation (and consequently effective use of time) on the part of consultees.

Perhaps the best solution to dealing with time constraints is to have the consultation process unfold in a series of short meetings that meet the schedules of the parties involved. Rather than leaving important elements of the process out and using a bare-bones approach, distributing the process out allows for a quality experience and increases the probability of a successful outcome.

## SUMMARY

Whether they are internal or external to organizations or in an educational or community setting, consultants will need a basic understanding of organizations to maximize their effectiveness.

How consultants view the broad range of organizational theories—from those that emphasize organizational structure to those that emphasize the human side of organizations—determines how they think organizational change should occur. Because the process of change within organizations is very complex, consultants can use a variety of approaches and many methods to assist organizations in the process. Consultants will want to study an organization's culture to understand it well enough to implement change effectively.

## SUGGESTIONS FOR EFFECTIVE PRACTICE

- When deciding how to proceed in a consultation or collaboration, consider the culture of the organization.

- Be able to clearly articulate your view of organizations as part of your professional development as a consultant.

- Have a sense of organizational change procedures in the organization in which you are delivering services.

## QUESTIONS FOR REFLECTION

1. Do you think that most members of a typical human service organization could explain how their organization really operates? Why or why not?

2.  What is organizational theory?

3.  Why is a firm understanding of organizational theory important for a consultant?

4.  Why should a consultant have a "personal" theory of organizations that is carried into the consultation process?

5.  How could a consultant teach members of an organization about their own organization?

6.  What are the advantages for consultants of the systems model of organizational theory?

7.  You are hired as a consultant to a human services organization. As you enter the organiza-tion for the first time, what types of things and activities would you look for? How would you find out more about these things and activities?

8.  What are some of the ways that the adaptive subsystem of an organization can monitor its internal and external environments?

9.  Which approach to change do you hold to most firmly: the rational-empirical, the normative-educative, or the power-coercive? Why?

10. Why is promoting understanding of cultural competency in an organization essential?

## SUGGESTED SUPPLEMENTARY READINGS

Schein, E. H. (1990b). Organizational culture. *American Psychologist,* 45(2), 109–119. Schein is one of the leaders in organizational consultation. Although many of the examples in this article relate to business and industry, human service consultants will find a wealth of information related to organiza-tional culture. Schein does an excellent job of pro-viding both the theoretical and practical aspects of organizational culture as they relate to consultation. Don't let the date on this article deter you from reading it.

# PART III

---

❋

# Models of Consultation

Now that you have studied the process of consultation in general, we will consider some popular models. (Because there are no detailed models of collaboration, I will limit discussion of this service to its applications for consultation models.) Each model of consultation provides a conceptual definition for practice (Kratochwill & Bergan, 1990). The models of consultation we will cover have the common characteristics and assumptions of all consultation (Gutkin & Curtis, 1999). These were covered in Chapter 1. All models of consultation can help consultees deal with a work-related concern through a problem-solving process (Kratochwill et al., 2002). The ways problem solving is accomplished varies according to the model under consideration. In addition, these models can help consultees be more effective with similar or related problems in the future.

Some models of consultation are more structured than others, and the consultant may act in the role of technical expert, expert diagnostician, or expert facilitator. Although all models have a well-defined approach to solving problems, no model has developed a theoretical basis from research to prescribe how the consultant and consultee should interact with each other. Three factors impede the development of adequate theories of consultation: the very attitude among consultants that consultation is an atheoretical process, the rapidity of change in consultation practices, and problems in performing research on consultation and its effects (Gallessich, 1985). To overcome these obstacles, Gallessich (1985) suggests that consultation models be categorized by value structure, which results in three models:

- a scientific-technological model (based primarily on the values of the scientific method)
- a human development model (based primarily on the values of human growth and development)

- a social/political model (based primarily on the values from the social/political aspect of the consultee's work)

In spite of such suggestions as these, most authors still rely on the more traditional way of characterizing consultation models—in terms of their derivatives. These models, which will be covered in this part of the book, include mental health, behavioral, and organizational consultation. Traditionally, models of consultation differ with respect to five dimensions: conceptualization of the problem, goals, methods and assumptions, consultant roles, and professional values (Gallessich, 1982).

*Mental health consultation* focuses on the implications of human service professionals' mental health-related programs and their work with clients. Mental health consultation focuses both on helping consultees help their clients and on helping consultees become more effective professionals. In the past, mental health consultation was strongly influenced by psychodynamic theory, but today is practiced from a variety of theoretical points of view.

*Behavioral consultation* focuses on specific changes in clients, client systems, and consultees. Behavioral consultation conceptualizes the problem in terms of reducing the difference between the current frequency of some problem behavior and the desired frequency of that behavior. This behavioral goal is accomplished through the use of interventions based on the principles of learning. The consultant acts as both expert and guide and advocates that behavior be changed in a precise, scientific manner. Behavioral consultation is based on social learning theory. The range of behavior change can be from the individual level to that of an entire organization.

*Organizational consultation* tends to consider the entire organization to be the client. Organizational consultation conceptualizes the problem in terms of an organization's structure and processes, and the goal is to ameliorate some problem through carefully designed interventions that affect the organization's system. The consultant takes on one or more roles to assist consultees. Values are advocated that enhance the organization's overall effectiveness by helping its members become more satisfied and productive. An increasing number of organizations outside of business and industry settings use organizational consultation to enhance their effectiveness.

There is no one "organizational consultation," but rather a series of approaches. Program consultation and education/training consultation are included in the discussion of organizational consultation because of their similarities to other organizational approaches: Both can improve the effectiveness of the organization in which consultation occurs, even though their roots are not specific to organizational consultation.

As the field of consultation has developed, the differences among these three major models have become increasingly less distinct. All consultation is organizational in that it occurs within an organization of some kind. All consultation concerns mental health by either directly or indirectly affecting the psychological well-being of the consultee and the client system. All consultation is behavioral because by its very nature it implies change: when consultees, clients, and client systems such as organizations respond positively to consultation, they change their behavior.

Indeed, there are probably more similarities than differences among these models. At the same time they differ in regard to elements such as the roles consultants typically take on, the types of interventions employed, and the organizational level which is the target of consultation (Zins & Erchul, 2002). Organizational consultation, for example, has become increasingly aware of mental health issues. Empirical research on organizations suggests that satisfied personnel work more productively than do dissatisfied personnel.

Behavioral consultation increasingly focuses on how behavioral technology can be used to help organizations more effectively meet their missions. Unfortunately, there is one other similarity among these three models—a lack of an adequate body of literature on how they apply to multicultural consultation situations (Ingraham & Meyers, 2000b).

The context in which consultation occurs is important (Zins & Erchul, 2002). I have therefore provided a chapter on school-based consultation. The models that are commonly used in schools—Adlerian consultation and instructional consultation—are covered in Chapter 12. Adlerian case consultation is a form of mental health consultation. The Adlerian C-group consultation is a unique approach to education/training consultation that is often used with teachers and parents.

Four emerging theories of consultation include Gestalt (Nevis, 1987; Melnick, 2003), psychoanalytic (Kets de Vries & Associates, 1991), rational emotive therapy consultation (Criddle, 2007; Greiger 2007a, 2007b; Lange & Greiger, 1993; Bernard & DiGiuseppe, 2000; see also Brack et al., 1993), and

feminist consultation (Huffman et al., 2006). Because the development of these approaches to consultation is still in its infancy, they are not covered in detail in this text.

Most writers still categorize the models of consultation according to the primary focus of each. Hence, in the next few chapters we'll discuss the mental health, behavioral, and organizational models of consultation separately, all the while noting the rapidly disappearing differences among them. One caution: consultants should not become too reliant on models. Although models can help consultants guide their practice (Brack et al., 1993), models can also overly focus their attention on aspects of the model instead of the features of the consultation setting. Further, practicing consultants, irrespective of what model they employ, will want to be aware that "consultation represents an ongoing process that is often mediated by factors such as interpersonal skills, relationship dynamics, problem severity, willingness of participants, competencies of consultees and clients, and many other issues" (Sheridan et al., 1996, p. viii).

# 9

---

✳

# Mental Health Consultation and Collaboration

It is difficult to promote the mental health of society in a preventative way, but mental health consultation attempts to do just that. Consider the difficulty: how would you promote the unique mental health needs of each of the numerous subgroups in our culture? In this chapter we'll consider the historical development of the mental health consultation model and examine Gerald Caplan's model (Caplan, 1970; Caplan & Caplan, 1993) of mental health consultation. This model is included both because of its historical and practical utility and because Caplan is considered to be the one person who put consultation on the human services landscape. Included are the approaches the model can take, their respective goals, the consultant's role, the consultee's experience in consultation, and the techniques and procedures used. We will examine a relatively new professional role called *mental health collaboration*.

We will also consider the ecological perspective to mental health consultation. Finally, we will cover some contributions and criticisms of the model and cite some trends in mental health consultation that have led to modifications of Caplan's model.

As you read this chapter, consider the following questions:

1. What are some of the differences and similarities between mental health consultation and the generic model we've already examined?

2. What difference would it make if a mental health consultant's primary goal in working with a human service worker was to make him or her a better worker in general, rather than to help the client under discussion?

3. What are the basic differences between mental health collaboration and mental health consultation?

4. How would a consultant best determine the reasons that a human service worker or administrator is having difficulties with a work-related problem?

5. Are there really differences between work-related and personal problems? If so, what are they?

Mental health consultation has provided the foundation for the development of consultation as service delivery approach (Henning-Stout, 1993). Mental health consultation is based on the idea that society's mental health can be promoted through the efforts of consultants who work with human service personnel (such as counselors) or with administrators of human service programs (such as the director of a factory's employee assistance program). The recipients of the consultant's efforts are the "primary agents in preventing mental disorders in a population" (Caplan, 1993, p. 41). If the consultant can enhance the effectiveness of the consultee, some emotional problems will be reduced, making referral to an expert unnecessary (Meyers, Brent, Flaherty, & Modafferi, 1993). More precisely, mental health consultants assist their consultees with specific work-related problems, such as a difficult case or glitches in a mental health-related program. An important goal of mental health consultation is not only to help consultees cope with their specific work-related problems, but also to improve their general level of functioning so that they can be even more effective in the future. As Caplan et al. note, writers in the field need to "underscore the importance of mental health consultation *in the service of primary prevention*" (1994, p. 6).

Mental health consultation has been used in schools, nursing homes (Meeks, 1996), hospices (Lindberg, 1996), religious settings (Maloney, 1991), medical settings (Quirk, Strosahl, Kreilkamp, & Erdberg, 1995), police hostage negotiation teams (Butler, Leitenberg, & Fuselier, 1993), community residences for people with developmental disabilities (Hyman, 1993), employee assistance programs (Shosh, 1996), postsecondary education settings (Amada, 1993), youth shelters (Grigsby, 1992), the postwar theater (Garland, 1993), and a variety of other settings. It has been used for many purposes including assistance with cases, organizational change, and diversity training (Russell-Chapin & Stoner, 1995; Shosh, 1996).

## HISTORICAL BACKGROUND

Mental health consultation is a part of the community mental health concept that asserts that services should be available as needed within the community and should be integrated with other human services.

Mental health consultation began in the late 1940s with the passage of the federal Mental Health Act of 1946, which created the National Institute of Mental Health (NIMH) and provided states federal moneys for the purpose of supporting mental health services. Public acceptance for community-based mental health services increased in the 1950s; the idea that mental health services were limited to treating severely disturbed individuals in residential treatment centers waned. In 1963, Congress passed the Community Mental Health Centers Act, which provided federal funds for the construction of mental health facilities in local communities and called for consultation and education services to the community.

The concept of the prevention of mental illness became very important both because there was a large discrepancy between the need for services and the ability to meet those needs (Caplan & Caplan, 1993) and also because the efficacy of psychotherapy in treating mental illness was under criticism. The ability of local mental health centers to provide preventative services thus became one of the criteria for being considered for these federal funds. Consultation services were seen as one type of preventative service to public and private human service professionals, who would become more effective as they attempted to meet the mental health needs of their clientele. Consultation was to be a method for helping non-mental health professionals to learn the mental health skills necessary to assist those people for whom they had professional responsibility (Watson & Robinson, 1996).

A trend that paralleled public and federal interest in preventative services was a shift in the conceptualization of consultation. Before 1950, consultation in agencies was considered to be an extension of clinical psychiatric consultation. In other words, consultation was viewed in terms of the medical consultation model: the psychiatrist examines the patient, makes a diagnosis, and prescribes treatment to the professional in charge. Two trends emerged around 1950 to change this view: Professionals other than psychiatrists came to be viewed as legitimate consultants, and it became clear that problems in treating cases could be due, not only to a lack of knowledge or skills on the part of those in charge of treatment, but also to the consultee's personal concerns or to organizational factors present in the consultee's work site. A few articles incorporating these trends began to appear in the early 1950s, and evidence increased substantially in the mid-1950s.

Around this time, Gerald Caplan arrived on the scene. A psychiatrist by training, Caplan's name has become synonymous with mental health consultation. In fact, mental health consultation is frequently referred to as the *Caplanian model*. He is often credited with "discovering" the usefulness of mental health consultation and describing its various forms.

Caplan attempted to incorporate and apply the ideas of public health in his consultation model. By improving a community's ability to create resources for the promotion of mental health, the prevalence of mental illness would be diminished. By having consultants work with consultees to serve their clients better, mental health would be promoted more widely than possible by a mental health practitioner working individually (Kelly, 1987). For example, if a mental health consultant helped a group of three teachers raise the self-esteem of the students in their classrooms, the consultant, by working directly

with three people, would indirectly affect the lives of over 90 students in a relatively short time. Contrast this with the idea of having the practitioner work individually with all 90 students, or even working in each of the three different classrooms one at a time. Clearly, consultation could be a time-saving and efficient mode for promoting mental health.

Caplan's 1970 book, *The Theory and Practice of Mental Health Consultation,* reflects his experiences as a consultant and his research in consultation. Caplan relates that his interest in mental health consultation began around 1949 when he was a member of a team of psychiatrists, social workers, and psychologists at a child guidance center in Israel. Part of the team's duties was to attend to the mental health needs of over 16,000 immigrant children who were cared for in about 100 residential centers. Referrals to the team far outweighed its ability to provide direct services to the children.

The operation of the team under these circumstances led to five discoveries by Caplan. First, the caretakers seemed to have a very restrictive perception of possible management strategies. Second, many of them had very stereotypic perceptions of the children and their difficulties. Third, they were frequently quite upset, and their personal concerns affected their ability to be objective about the children with whom they were working. Fourth, their narrow perceptions, stereotypic attitudes, and personal issues could be ameliorated by particular consultant attitudes and interventions. Finally, the team could learn a substantial amount of relevant information about the children and caretakers by visiting the institution, rather than by bringing the caretakers and children to the team's central office.

Out of Caplan's experiences in Israel, the basic rudiments of his model began to take shape. Consultation could be viewed as working with another person to help a client. Consultation typically would take place on the consultee's turf, and the consultee's perceptions of the client would be the basis for consultation. The consultant would need to be especially observant of the consultee's perceptions and would look for possible distortions, stereotypes, and personal issues that might adversely affect working with the client. The consultant would be objective yet sympathetic and would focus on the client as a person with problems, not as a problem who happens to be a person. When the team members working with the children were treated in this way, they seemed to be able to return to their duties with renewed enthusiasm and a broader perspective on working with clients (Caplan et al., 1994).

After his experiences in Israel, Caplan continued to develop his model of consultation at Harvard's Schools of Public Health and Medicine, where he began to use the term "mental health consultation." He formally developed the concept of the consultation as a collaborative relationship among equals. Techniques of group consultation emerged, along with the idea that consultation need not occur only in a crisis situation, but could also be used for preventative measures. Through Caplan's efforts, mental health consultation became conceptualized as a "method whereby a small group of mental health specialists would guide and support ...non-mental-health-specialist caregivers, such as doctors, nurses, teachers, clergymen, and welfare workers, in mastering the cognitive and emotional challenges of ... their traditional duties" (Caplan, 1993, p. 45). Professionals in the human service professions were now able, through consultation, to work at a systems level. Caplan continued updating his views over the years (Caplan, 1974, 1977), including a revision of his first text entitled *Mental Health Consultation and Collaboration* (Caplan & Caplan, 1993, 1999).

Mental health consultation has expanded over the years in spite of federal spending cutbacks. Most models remain adaptations of Caplan's although the theoretical bases underlying these adaptations vary. There has been a move away from the psychodynamic orientation toward other approaches; that is, mental health consultants are free to conceptualize their consultees, clients, and the dynamics of the organizations in which they work from any number of perspectives and approaches. One of the more common perspectives is the ecological perspective covered later on in this chapter. In addition, mental health consultants now regularly consult with other

mental health professionals and parents as well as non-mental health professionals such as teachers. Learning to conduct mental health consultation can be a challenge (Pinkerton & Temple, 2000). Some experts consider it more difficult to master than psychotherapy (Iscoe, 1993).

## MENTAL HEALTH CONSULTATION DEFINED

### Case Example

Consider this relatively simple form of mental health consultation:

You are a social worker who consults with psychiatric nurses on dealing with relatives of Alzheimer's disease victims. One of your consultees is having difficulty with a family of a certain patient. As you listen to the consultee describe the case, you get the impression that the patient's "Jekyll-and-Hyde" personality is keeping the family off balance. You suggest that the nurse teach the family some self-talk strategies they can use when the patient is acting out. You refer the nurse to several sources of information on self-talk strategies and agree to provide the consultee with a training session.

This example erroneously suggests a relatively simple definition of mental health consultation. Various attempts have been made to define mental health consultation. The most consistently recognized definition of mental health consultation is from Caplan and Caplan, who describe it as

> a process of interaction between two professional persons—the consultant, who is a specialist, and the consultee, who invokes the consultant's help in regard to a current work problem with which he is having some difficulty and which he has decided is within the other's area of specialized competence. The work problem involves the management or treatment of one or more clients of the consultee, or the

planning or implementation of a program to cater to such clients. (1993, p. 1)

Subsequent attempts at defining mental health consultation (for example, Hodges & Cooper, 1983; Mannino, MacLennan, & Shore, 1975) elaborated on the type of help the consultant provides while holding to the basic ideas in Caplan's definition. Notice this emphasis in the following definition by MacLennan, Quinn, and Schroeder:

Mental health consultation is the provision of technical assistance by an expert to individual and agency caregivers related to the mental health dimension of their work. Such assistance is directed to specific work-related problems, is advisory in nature, and the consultant has no direct responsibility for its acceptance or implementation. (Bloom, 1984, p. 155)

This definition suggests that the consultant will function as a technical expert in an advisory capacity.

Hodges and Cooper expanded on Caplan's definition by adding some of the specific role behaviors the consultant uses in helping consultees:

Community mental health consultation can be defined as the process by which a mental health professional interacts with community-based professionals and other service providers (the consultees) to supply information, skill training, and individual process change or system change in order to help the consultee or the system better serve the mental health needs of the people in the community. (1983, pp. 19–20).

The bottom line is that the consultant serves to assist the consultee with the psychological elements of a current work-related or care-giving problem related to a specific client or program (Erchul & Schulte, 1993). The consultant uses knowledge and skills to assist the consultee with the specific concern and, in addition, attempts to improve the consultee's ability to function in the future. The consultee has the freedom to choose whether or not to apply the assistance provided in consultation and remains responsible for the client or the program.

# KEY CONCEPTS OF MENTAL HEALTH CONSULTATION

## Basic Characteristics

From Caplan's point of view, mental health consultation has several basic characteristics, awareness of which is essential for understanding his view: (The following list is adapted with permission of Waveland Press, Inc. from Caplan & Caplan, *Mental Health Consultation and Collaboration,* pp. 21–23. Long Grove, IL; Waveland Press, Inc. [reissued 1999]. All rights reserved. Reprinted by permission of the publisher.)

1.  Mental health consultation is a method used by two professionals in respect to a lay client or a program for such clients.

2.  The consultee's work problem must be defined by him or her as being mental health related, such as a mental disorder or personality idiosyncrasy of the client, the need to promote mental health in the client, or interpersonal aspects of the work situation. The consultant must have expert knowledge in these areas.

3.  The consultant has neither administrative responsibility for the consultee's work nor professional responsibility for the outcome of the client's case. She or he is under no compulsion to modify the consultee's conduct of the case.

4.  The consultee is under no compulsion to accept the consultant's ideas or suggestions.

5.  The basic relationship between the two is coordinate; there is no built-in hierarchy or authority-subordinate tension, which in our culture potentiates the influence of ideas. The consultees' freedom to accept or reject what the consultant says enables them to take

quickly as their own any ideas that appeal to them in their current situation.

6.   The coordinate relationship is fostered by the consultant's membership (typically) in another profession and his or her arrival into the consultee's institution from the outside.

7.   The coordinate relationship is further supported by the fact that consultation is usually given as a short series of interviews—two or three on average, which take place intermittently in response to consultees' awareness of their current need for help with a work problem. The relationship in individual consultation is not maintained and dependence is not fostered by continuing contact. In group consultation there may be regular meetings, but dependence is reduced by peer support.

8.   Consultation is expected to continue indefinitely, for consultees can be expected to encounter unusual work problems throughout their careers. Increasing competence and sophistication of consultees in their own profession improves the likelihood of their recognizing mental health complications and asking for consultation.

9.   Consultants have no predetermined body of information that they intend to impart to a particular consultee. They respond only to the segment of the consultee's problems that the consultee exposes in the current work difficulty. The consultant does not seek to remedy other areas of inadequacy in the consultee but instead expects other issues to be raised in future consultation.

10.   The twin goals of consultation are to help consultees improve their handling or understanding of the current work difficulty and through this to increase their capacity to master future problems of a similar type.

11.   The aim of consultation is to improve consultees' job performance, not their sense of well-being. It is envisaged, however, that, because the two are linked, consultees' feelings of personal worth will probably be increased by

successful consultation, as will their capacity to deal in a reality-based socially acceptable way with certain life difficulties. In other words, successful consultation may have the secondary effect of being therapeutic to consultees.

12.   Consultation does not focus overtly on personal problems and feelings of consultees.

13.   It respects their privacy. The consultant does not allow discussion of personal and private material in the consultation interview. This does not mean that consultants disregard the feelings of the consultee. They are particularly sensitive to the feelings and to the disturbance of task functioning produced by personal problems. They deal with personal problems, however, in a special way, such as by discussing problems in the context in which they relate to the client's case and the work setting.

14.   Consultation is usually one of the professional functions of a specialist—even if he is titled "consultant." He should use the consultation method only when it is appropriate. At other times he should use different methods. Sometimes the demands of the situation will cause him to put aside his consultation. For instance, if he gets information during a consultation interview that leads him to judge that the consultee's actions are seriously endangering the client (such as failing to prevent a suicide or to pursue treatment for a dangerous psychosis), he should set aside his consultant role and revert to the basic role of a psychiatrist, psychologist, or social worker. He will then give advice or take action that the consultee is not free to reject. This destroys the coordinate relationship and interrupts the consultation contact in favor of a higher goal. Such dramatic occasions are rare, but the possibility demonstrates the realistic limits of this method.

15.   Finally, it is worth emphasizing that mental health consultation is a method of communication between a mental health specialist and other professionals. It does not denote a new profession, merely a special way in which existing professionals may operate.

These fourteen characteristics represent the basis for the practice of mental health consultation from Caplan's perspective. Although the consultant is the expert, the relationship is an equal one. The nature of the consultant–consultee relationship is crucial: the consultant assists with work-related problems only and does not deal directly with the consultee's personal concerns. The consultee's work problems may be viewed from a psychodynamic perspective, and the goal of consultation is to enhance the consultee's current and future ability to function professionally. The consultant does not take any supervisory authority over the consultee's actions and has no responsibility for the client/program (Caplan, 1993). Further, it is essential that the consultant take organizational influences into account when conducting consultation (Conoley & Wright, 1993).

## Psychodynamic Orientation

The Caplan model uses a *psychodynamic approach* to consultation, for, as a trained psychiatrist, Caplan was heavily influenced by the work of Sigmund Freud. The Caplan model relies on an intrapsychic view of behavior change, and this psychodynamic orientation makes the Caplan model one of the most complex consultation models (Conoley & Conoley, 1992). (A detailed discussion of the psychodynamic approach is beyond the scope of this book. Those interested in reviewing Freud and his modifiers should consult a good text on theories of counseling and psychotherapy, such as Corey's *Theory and Practice of Counseling and Psychotherapy* [2005]). The psychodynamic approach fosters the concept that our behavior is a product of unconscious motivation and that most of our personal issues result from early childhood experiences. These issues often lead to inner conflicts that affect our behavior and cause us problems. Because these inner conflicts are usually unconscious, we are often unaware of the causes of our behavior. True behavioral change must deal with these unresolved conflicts from the past; merely dealing with the behavioral manifestations of a person's problems only results in the emergence of another problem because the core problem has not been adequately addressed. This phenomenon is often referred to as symptom substitution.

Not every difficulty a consultee has with a case or program is due to inner conflict. A difficulty might stem from a lack of appropriate professional knowledge about some aspect of the case. But from Caplan's perspective, when the consultee's inner conflicts are causing problems with a case or program, they must in some way be addressed to ensure the consultee's adequate functioning with the current case and with similar cases in the future. Changing overt behaviors will only provide temporary change. Because the consultant does not provide psychotherapy to the consultee, the consultee's inner conflicts must be dealt with indirectly.

In his recent writings (e.g., Caplan et al., 1994), Caplan has stressed the importance of taking into consideration not just the psychodynamics of the individuals involved but also those forces operating in the organizations represented by the consultant and consultee in addition to those in the community itself. Hence Caplan's thought has evolved into one that takes into consideration the larger systems context of consultation.

## Transfer of Effect

Transfer of effect refers to the concept that what is learned in one situation should be usable in similar, future situations, which is central to the Caplanian model. Consultee-centered consultation improves the consultee's capacity to function effectively and to benefit current clients as well as similar ones in the future. By listening to the consultee's perceptions of the client or program and extrapolating the pertinent information concerning the consultee's difficulty, the consultant by indirect means can help the consultee be more objective. In addition, by retaining responsibility for the case or program, the consultee is set up for optimal learning and generalization to future cases (Erchul & Schulte, 1993).

**T A B L E  9.1**    **Caplan and Caplan's Consultation Classification in Terms of Level, Target, and Goal**

|  | CLIENT-CENTERED CASE | CONSULTEE-CENTERED CASE | PROGRAM-CENTERED ADMINISTRATIVE | CONSULTEE-CENTERED ADMINISTRATIVE |
|---|---|---|---|---|
| **Level** | Case | Case | Administrative | Administrative |
| **Target** | Client | Consultee | Program | Consultee |
| **Goal** | Behavioral change in client | Enhanced consultee performance in delivering services to clients | More effective delivery of program | Enhanced consultee performance in programming |

## Types of Consultation

The manner in which mental health consultation is conceptualized is a critical factor in terms of how it is practiced. The consultant should have a system to anticipate what is likely to happen in each consultation situation and to identify effective strategies with which to approach the consultation. To accomplish this end, Caplan (1970) devised a classification system with two major divisions. The first concerns whether the consultant *focuses on a case* (e.g., a client at a halfway house) or *focuses on an administrative problem* dealing with a mental-health-related program (e.g., helping a health science teacher implement a unit on substance abuse).

The second division concerns whether the consultant's primary goal is "giving a specialized opinion and recommendation for a solution" (Caplan, 1970, p. 32) (e.g., observing a client and recommending a specific therapeutic technique) or "attempting to improve the problem-solving capacity of the consultees and leaving them to work out their own way of solving it" (Caplan, 1970, p. 32) (e.g., helping a parole officer be more objective about a case with a parolee). The goal is thus to change either the *client* (or program) or the *consultee*.

These two divisions make up four types of consultation: *client-centered case consultation, consultee-centered case consultation, program-centered administrative consultation*, and *consultee-centered administrative consultation* (Caplan & Caplan, 1993). This classification formed the early organization of consultation types, and most reconceptualizations of types are summaries of Caplan's work.

Each of the four types of consultation has a different level of intervention, an identifiable target, and an identifiable goal (Bloom, 1984). Table 9.1 presents Caplan and Caplan's (1993) classification as defined by these three factors.

# THE CONSULTATION PROCESS

Next we'll examine these four types of mental health consultation in terms of their goals, the consultant's function and role, the consultee's experience in consultation, and the use of consultation techniques and procedures. Because of its unique nature and its impact on the development of mental health consultation, consultee-centered case consultation is covered in more depth than are the other three types.

## The Client-Centered Case Consultation Process

**Consultation Goals.**   Client-centered case consultation is the most commonly used form of mental health consultation. It typifies what most human service professionals think of when they hear the word *consultation*. The consultant is viewed as an expert or specialist who can diagnose and recommend an intervention. The consultee presents a case in which a client has mental health problems that are causing the consultee some difficulty. The primary goal of this type of consultation is to develop a plan to help the client. Secondarily, the consultee is better able to handle similar cases alone in the future as a result of contact with the consultant. However, only limited educational benefit to the consultee is expected from this type of consultation because the consultant spends very little time with the consultee.

**Consultant Function and Roles.** The consultant functions primarily as an expert in assessing the situation, diagnosing the client, and making recommendations for the consultee's use in the case. Specifically, the consultant builds a relationship with the consultee (in ways previously discussed); assesses the client's difficulty by gathering information from the client and other sources; assesses the consultee's strengths, weaknesses, and work setting by visiting the consultee at work; and files a written report, usually a letter or a case record, which should (if possible) be reviewed in a meeting with the consultee. In this way, the consultant can improve the consultee's functioning in similar cases in the future. It is the consultee's responsibility to use the written report and the conference with the consultant in dealing with the case. In other words, the consultee takes the consultant's report and develops and implements a plan of action. Finally, the consultant plans for a follow-up session with the consultee.

**Consultee Experience in Consultation.** Consultees in client-centered case consultation focus on providing the consultant with as much pertinent information and professional opinion as possible regarding the case, such as the consultee's role relative to the client system and any constraints that have been laid upon the consultee.

Even though the consultant is likely to observe, interview, or test the client, the consultant wants to know how the consultee views the case. The consultee, then, is not only a link between the consultant and client, but is also a professional collaborator who knows the client better than the consultant and knows how to best deal with the client within the consultee institution.

The consultee's primary responsibility is to adapt and carry out the consultant's recommendations, but the consultee is free to accept or reject any or all of them. The consultee may require the assistance of the consultant in implementing a given recommendation but must ask for such assistance. Finally, the consultee participates in a scheduled follow-up session with the consultant.

**Application: Consultant Techniques and Procedures.** It is not unusual for a written note to accompany a consultee's request for consultation, and it is best for the consultant to respond to the consultee with some form of personal contact so as to build a relationship, clarify what the consultee desires from the consultant, and obtain more information on the client.

In assessing the client, the consultant has two basic questions: Should the client be referred for specialized treatment? What can the consultee do to help the client in the consultee's work setting? These are answered by listening to the consultee (and perhaps the client and his or her significant others when applicable; see Karg & Wiens [2005] for interviewing hints).

It is quite risky to provide client-centered case consultation in the consultant's office. Otherwise the consultant can rely only on the client's report about the consultee and the work setting. Because the consultant needs to know about the strengths and weaknesses of the consultee and the consultee institution to make effective and realistic recommendations, the consultant should visit and perform consultation in the consultee institution.

One of the consultant's major tasks in client-centered case consultation is writing a report for the consultee. This report, typically supplemented by a face-to-face meeting with the consultee to clarify the report and answer questions related to it, should be written in language appropriate to the consultee's institution, should be practical, and should avoid condescending terminology.

The main body of the report should focus on how the client is or is not coping in major areas of life and include some recommendations as to how the consultee can facilitate improved client functioning in appropriate areas.

*A Sample of a Consultant's Written Report.*   The following is a portion of a consultant's report prepared by a counselor working with a teacher having difficulty with Dana, a third-grade student who steals from other children in the classroom:

> The stealing behavior is most likely caused by Dana's need for security. The objects taken are usually food (for example, snacks) or school supplies (for example, pencils). The fact that Dana makes little attempt not to get caught perhaps suggests that there is the perception on her part of too little attention. Stealing objects thus helps Dana feel more secure and get attention.
>
> I recommend that the teacher make a deliberate attempt to praise Dana throughout the school day for appropriate classroom behaviors. In addition, she could be assigned some classroom responsibilities (for example, erasing the board) and then be reinforced for acting responsibly. Dana's security might be increased if the teacher frequently communicated to her that she belongs in the classroom taking care of all the children. Such verbalizations can reduce insecurity.

Implementation of the consultant's recommendations is the consultee's prerogative because he or she has responsibility for the case. However, the consultant can help determine whether the consultee has the knowledge and skills required to perform the suggested interventions. Such a judgment is best achieved by having a history of sustained contact with the consultee so that an assessment of consultee strengths and weaknesses is possible before the formulation of recommendations.

Follow-up by the consultant is crucial: it provides the consultant a rough evaluation of the effects of consultation; it pro-

vides feedback on how the consultant's interventions affected the consultee in the case under discussion, which could be useful to the consultant in improving future interventions; and it conveys consultant interest to the consultee and improves their relationship so that the consultee may actively seek additional consultation about the current (or some other) case.

**Case Example of Client-Centered Case Consultation.**   Tracy is a resident psychologist consulting with Kim, an activity therapist, concerning a patient in a residential psychiatric hospital. The therapist reports that the patient, a 15-year-old, refuses to engage in any activity therapy. The client shows up on time but just sits and watches as the other patients engage in the therapy.

Tracy observes the patient in several hospital settings, including activity therapy, and interviews the patient's primary therapist concerning the case. She determines that the patient appears to have few friends at the hospital but is friendly and approachable. She also concludes that Kim has the ability and motivation to assist the patient to begin participation in activity therapy.

Tracy writes a brief report suggesting a "buddy system" for the patient. Kim would implement the program, in which one or two higher-functioning patients could become friends with and accompany the patient to the activity therapy group, where they could perform the activities together. Tracy shares this recommendation in a final consultation session with Kim, who agrees to the recommendation, and takes steps to implement the program. Tracy follows up after two weeks to monitor the intervention.

## The Consultee-Centered Case Consultation Process

**Consultation Goals.**   The primary goal of consultee-centered case consultation is improvement of the consultee's ability to work effectively with a particular case as well as with similar cases in the future. "In consultee-centered case consultation the consultant's primary focus is upon elucidating and remedying the shortcomings in the consultee's professional functioning that are responsible for his difficulties with the case with which he is seeking help" (Caplan & Caplan, 1993, p. 101). Improvement of the client is the secondary goal. As in client-centered case consultation, the case is the focus of discussion, although usually the consultant does not see the client because the goal is to help the consultee. The consultant helps the consultee by focusing on his or her subjective view of the case.

**Consultant Function and Roles.**  In consultee-centered case consultation, the consultant plays the roles of detective, expert, and educator. In the role of detective, the consultant seeks out the consultee's cognitive and emotional problems through active listening and judicious questioning. The consultant discusses the case with the consultee in the role of an expert mental health professional. As an educator, the consultant provides the consultee the information and/or training needed to solve problems with this and similar cases in the future. Thus, the consultant builds a relationship with the consultee, assesses his or her problem with the case, and intervenes to alleviate the problem.

The consultant asks the consultee to discuss the case, and the remainder of the consultation relationship involves such discussions. The consultant, however, is more directive than in client-centered case consultation in that the consultee is asked to discuss selected aspects of the case, which provides the consultant information about the consultee's work difficulty. As the consultee discusses the case, the consultant categorizes the consultee's work difficulty as a lack of knowledge, skill, confidence, or professional objectivity. The consultant intervenes to resolve the consultee's particular work problem. The so-called "grist for the mill" in consultation comes from the consultee's "subjectively determined story" (Caplan & Caplan, 1993, p. 101), not from the real facts about the case.

**Consultee Experience in Consultation.**  In consultee-centered case consultation, the consultee's

task is to enter into the consultation relationship and discuss a case that is causing difficulty. Under the consultant's guidance, the consultee elaborates on the particulars of the case. When the consultant makes interventions to assist the consultee, it is up to the consultee to implement those recommendations, which often include ways the consultee can improve professional functioning. The consultee maintains full responsibility for the case under discussion.

During the initial stages of consultation, the consultee may have a very narrow view of the case. Indeed, consultees often do not know why they are having difficulty with cases. In responding to the consultant's judicious questioning, the consultee's perceptions of the case are enriched and broadened so that the "cognitive grasp and emotional mastery" (Caplan & Caplan, 1993, p. 101) of the particulars of the case are increased.

**Application: Consultation Techniques and Procedures.**  There are four approaches to consultee-centered case consultation, one for each of the four reasons that consultees may have difficulty with cases: lack of knowledge, skill, self-confidence, and professional objectivity. Now we'll consider each of these four approaches, which can be performed individually or in groups.

*Lack of Knowledge.*  When the difficulty with a case is due to lack of knowledge, the consultee might not have sufficient understanding of the client's problem, some important client characteristics, or both. According to Caplan, the consultee may lack either factual or theoretical knowledge needed to deal effectively with the case. The consultant imparts the missing knowledge to the consultee in a manner conducive to the consultee's success in the case under discussion as well as for possible similar cases in the future. It is very important that the consultant provide this information without violating the coordinating nature of the relationship, a task best accomplished by capitalizing on the consultee's motivation to learn information relevant to the case at hand. The consultee's education results from applying the needed knowledge to the current case, which also maintains the desired consultant-consultee relationship.

*Lack of Skill.* The consultee may well have the knowledge required to understand a case but lacks only the skill to intervene effectively. In this situation, the consultant should avoid the temptation to supervise the consultee's conduct of the case.

Procedurally, the consultant and the consultee conduct a joint appraisal of the case: they explore the problems, what the consultee has tried so far to help the client, and what the consultee could yet do to resolve the issue. Such a procedure broadens the consultee's perspective on the case, provides a broader context for perceiving subsequent similar cases, maintains the coordinate nature of the relationship, and preserves the consultee's self-esteem. The consultant determines the degree of the consultee's skill deficit, describes what skills are needed to deal effectively with the case, and explores with the consultee the means to get the appropriate skills training within the consultee institution. If such training is not available within the consultee institution, the consultant can provide the training.

*Lack of Self-Confidence.* Lack of self-confidence can cause confusion and uncertainty about how to handle a case. It can result from consultee inexperience (for example, being assigned a particular client problem for the first time or being a beginner on the job) or be a generalized trait within the consultee that manifests itself in reduced on-the-job functioning.

The goal of the consultant is to provide support and encouragement by fostering hope, confidence, and courage by affirming the consultee's strengths and capabilities. Reassurance, which damages the nonhierarchical nature of the relationship, should be avoided. The consultant's second goal is to help the consultee find a peer support group within the consultee institution.

*Lack of Professional Objectivity.* The consultant considers lack of objectivity only after lack of knowledge and lack of skill are eliminated (Erchul, 1993a). Lack of objectivity is the most common problem

among consultees who work in institutions that have a knowledgeable, skilled staff and a supervisory system; hence, most consultee-centered case consultations are of this type. The consultee's lack of professional objectivity is a defective judgment—an inability to maintain an appropriate professional distance. The consultee's role functioning, perceptions, and judgments are impaired by subjective factors that make him or her unable to apply existing knowledge and skills to the case effectively.

By the time the consultee seeks out consultation, confusion, frustration, incompetence, and declining self-esteem are often evident and can cause a lack of professional poise. The coordinate nature of the consultant-consultee relationship is in greatest jeopardy in consultee-centered case consultation because the consultant appears to be in control of personal issues in the professional setting, whereas the consultee is not. Therefore, the consultant should *indirectly* help the consultee recapture professional objectivity by discussing the client, the consultant, or some fictitious client in a story or parable. The consultee's problem should not be dealt with directly. The consultee's confidence and poise must be maintained (Caplan, 1993).

Lack of objectivity in even the most knowledgeable and skilled consultees can result from five somewhat connected reasons: direct personal involvement, simple identification, transference, characterological distortions, and theme interference (Caplan & Caplan, 1993).

When a consultee loses professional objectivity due to *direct personal involvement,* the relationship changes from a professional to a personal one. An obvious example is when a consultee falls in love with a client. Because of the emotional nature of personal relationships, objectivity is lost. Professionals should keep a certain distance from their clients to maintain objectivity, and personal involvement alters the balance of that relationship by causing the consultee to be either too close or too distant from the client. Consultees are frequently unaware of their personal involvement with their clients and do not realize they are fulfilling their own personal needs at the expense of those of the client.

*Simple identification* occurs when the consultee does not merely empathize with but instead identifies with the client (or some person in the client's life) and loses the sense of neutrality so essential to maintaining objectivity. The consultee identifies with some real characteristic of the client (or person in the client's life) such as race, gender, or some behavior pattern the consultee considers idiosyncratic. For example, a consultee who is a minister might over-identify with a client who is also a minister. The client is then described in a positive, sympathetic manner, while others in the case are viewed in derogatory terms. The consultant can relatively easily identify simple identification because of the obvious similarities between the consultee and some person in the case.

A *transference* distortion occurs when the consultee transfers onto the client feelings and attitudes from key relationships in the past. Once the consultee's predetermined attitudes and feelings are imposed on the client and objectivity is lost, the consultee is unable to assess the client's real situation. For example, a consultee who has difficulty with authority figures due to her childhood relationship with her mother might have difficulty dealing with a female client who is the head of a large company. The transference relationship tends to be repeated over time in similar cases.

Minor disturbances in consultees, often referred to as *characterological distortions* of perceptions and behavior, can cause consultees to lose their professional objectivity. Caplan defines these distortions as personality problems that interfere with the effective delivery of human services to the client. To illustrate this point, Caplan (1970) tells of a teacher, with a tendency toward sexually acting out, who anxiously attributed harmful sexual behaviors to several of her students that a consultant later described as quite normal.

Caplan's concept of *theme interference* is a special type of transference reaction that causes consultees to lose their professional objectivity. Theme interference becomes apparent to a consultant when the consultee is "blocked" from progressing with a case for no explicable reason. For example, a consultee who has difficulty dealing with anger might impose this trait on the client, in effect saying, "Unless this client deals with his anger during our sessions

together, no progress can be made in this case." For whatever reason, the consultee has identified with some aspect of the client's case.

According to Caplan and Caplan (1993), theme interference develops in the following manner: "A conflict related to actual life experiences or to fantasies in the consultee that have not been satisfactorily resolved is apt to persist in his preconscious or unconscious as an emotionally toned cognitive constellation which we call a 'theme'" (p. 122). The theme is a recurring symbol of an unresolved problem and has a preemptory quality. When suffering from theme interference, the consultee sees the case as being hopeless and makes several inappropriate problem-solving efforts (Erchul & Schulte, 1993). Themes generally repeat themselves, carry a negative emotional valence, and take the form of a syllogism. This syllogism has two statements that constitute a prejudicial stereotyped notion and are perceived by the consultee to be linked in such a way that they are inseparable: an "initial category" followed by an "inevitable outcome."

The initial category is a statement that signifies the condition that was characteristic of the original unresolved problem in the consultee's life. In reality, the client may or may not fit the stereotype, but still the consultee applies the stereotype to the client. The stereotype is imposed when consultees form their impressions of the client; certain pieces of information are put together and the initial category is formed. Placing the client in the initial category leads to expectations that are typified in the inevitable outcome, which is a rigid assumption that the worst case scenario will occur. When put together, the initial category and inevitable outcome take the following form: if A (initial category) happens to anyone, then B (inevitable outcome) must occur. One example might be, "If my client doesn't deal with his anger, we will never make any progress in therapy." In such cases the consultant must assume that the consultee has a problem in dealing with anger and that the client may or may not have the same problem.

The problem with theme interference is that, by losing objectivity, the consultee is unable to see that there are many possible outcomes to any problem and that several possible interventions are available. This lack of objectivity causes inconsistent, sometimes panicky behavior in the consultee, and the subsequent lack of progress in the case reaffirms the belief in the inevitable outcome. Thus, a vicious cycle develops. There is, however, one source of consolation for the consultee: the inevitable outcome happens to the client, not the consultee. Theme interference tends to recur as long as the theme is manifest.

There are two basic methods the mental health consultant can use to relieve theme interference in consultees. These methods are subtle and designed to "alter the emotional theme underlying the lack of objectivity" (Henning-Stout, 1993, p. 21). First, the consultant helps the consultee reassess the cues in the client's case that led to placement in the incorrect category in the first place. Such a reevaluation helps the consultee see that the original perceptions were erroneous and return to professional objectivity because the inevitable outcome is no longer pertinent. Caplan and Caplan (1993) label this technique *unlinking* (p. 125) because it unlinks the client from the consultee's theme.

Whereas unlinking attempts to invalidate the initial category, the second approach, called *theme interference reduction,* attempts to invalidate the inevitable outcome. The consultant invalidates the "If A, then B" syllogism by helping the consultee reexamine the evidence on which the inevitability of the outcome is based. The consultee is then able to view the previously inevitable outcome as merely one of an array of possible outcomes (and not necessarily a very likely one at that). The influence of the consultee's theme then begins to wane.

Theme interference reduction affects the consultee on both cognitive and affective levels. Theme interference reduction techniques neither exacerbate resistance nor cause a loss of face because the consultant accepts the consultee's view of the initial category: the consultant does not try to deal with the consultee's inner conflicts directly but rather through their discussion of the case. When properly carried out, theme interference reduction helps consultees by lowering their level of tension, raising their level of objectivity, weakening the theme, and reducing the likelihood that the theme will be displaced onto subsequent cases.

Several techniques are effective in theme interference reduction, and all of them have the following steps occurring over a three- or four-week period: assessment of the theme, the consultant's intervention, and ending and follow-up (Caplan & Caplan, 1993). The expression of intense feelings by the consultee is permitted as long as the consultee expresses feelings about the case and does not believe that the feelings are about him- or herself (Caplan, 1993). Part of the consultant's job is to help the consultee feel safe while expressing emotionally sensitive material.

In assessing the theme, the consultant examines the consultee institution, the affective and cognitive reactions of the consultee to the case, indications of an initial category and inevitable outcome, and the possibility that there is more than one theme. Once the existence of theme interference has been established, the consultant can make one or more of the following interventions (Caplan & Caplan, 1993):

- verbal focus on the client
- verbal focus on an alternative object—the parable
- nonverbal focus on the case
- nonverbal focus on the consultation relationship

A *verbal focus on the client* is the most commonly used technique in theme interference reduction. The consultant discusses with the consultee the evidence for the inevitable outcome by examining in significant detail the facts concerning the case, by which the so-called inevitable outcome is seen instead as one possible outcome among many others. The likelihood of the inevitable outcome's occurrence is explored specifically and in depth to ensure that the consultee does not consider the consultant to be prejudiced against that outcome. By such a thorough examination, the consultee realizes that the inevitable outcome is not even among the most likely outcomes. For example, when a consultee thinks a client must deal with the issue of avoidance of competition, a consultant might help the consultee consider several other therapeutic approaches to pursue with the client.

*Parables* are used when the consultant thinks it important to create greater distance between the consultee's growing awareness of the theme and its connection to the personal issues in his or her life. It must be remembered that consultation is not psychotherapy; the consultee's personal issues are not to be discussed, even though they may be affecting the case. Once the consultant identifies the initial category and the inevitable outcome and decides that the case under consideration is not a good vehicle to break the connection between the two, they can discuss alternatives.

In using a parable, the consultant artistically creates a believable story concerning the identified theme but uses a fictitious client in a fictitious case (Caplan & Caplan-Moskovich, 2004; Mang, 2004). The details of the current case are used as a springboard for creating the anecdote, but details are changed significantly so that only basic similarities to the client and consultee remain. Discussion of the fictitious case then results in the realization that the so-called inevitable outcome was only one of many possible outcomes and that the fictitious case did indeed have a different outcome. Thus, for example, when a consultee suggests that a client must agree to assertive training to overcome shyness, the consultant might relate a story about a fictitious client who overcame shyness by going through a cognitive behavioral form of counseling.

Because the consultee is likely to consider the consultant a role model, the ways the consultant responds nonverbally to the consultee's anxieties about the case can be a very powerful tool in theme interference reduction. When the consultant uses a *nonverbal focus on the case,* the consultant's nonverbal behavior demonstrates to the consultee, in a relaxed state free of anxiety, that the consultant is not really worried that the inevitable outcome must occur. This technique works only if the consultee perceives that the consultant has dealt with the case seriously and thoroughly and has appreciated both the consultee's concern for urgent action and the client's situation. In a simple example, when a consultee nervously relates the specifics of a case, the consultant would maintain a calm demeanor.

A *nonverbal focus on the consultation relationship* is needed when the consultee transfers themes not onto a case but onto the consultant, particularly when the consultation relationship is well developed and contains emotional connections between the two parties. If the consultee transfers a theme by ascribing a certain role to the consultant and then plays the complementary role, the consultant needs to show the usual acceptance of the initial category and then invalidate the inevitable outcome through discussion of the case. However, the expectation of the inevitable outcome should be dealt with in a nonverbal manner, that is, by remaining calm, objective, and free from anxiety. By staying "cool, calm, and collected" both about the case and the transference occurring in the consultation relationship itself, the consultant is working on both planes simultaneously. For example, when a consultee suggests that the consultant should be as upset about the case as the consultee is, the consultant shows appreciation for his or her view but remains calm about what is happening in the consultation session.

## Innovations in Consultee-Centered Consultation

Consultee-centered consultation has received a great deal of attention in the first decade of the new millennium. Consultee-centered consultation has evolved over time beyond Caplan's original conceptualization, creating the need for a new definition. This new definition has two important components. First, the consultant assists the consultee to "pinpoint critical information and then consider multiple views about well-being, development, intrapersonal, interpersonal, and organizational effectiveness appropriate to the consultee's work setting. Ultimately, the consultee may reframe his or her prior conceptualization of the work problem" (Knotek & Sandoval, 2003, p. 245). The second point deals with the goal of consultee-centered consultation which is "the joint development of a new way of conceptualizing the work problem so that the repertoire of the consultee is expanded … As the problem is jointly reconsidered, new ways of approaching the problem may lead to acquiring new means to address the work dilemma" (Knotek & Sandoval, 2003, p. 245). As a result, the working relationship between the consultee and the client system is improved (Sandoval, 2003). Knotek and Sandoval (2003) point out the significance of these changes to the definition of consultee-centered consultation. First, rather than a psychodynamic orientation, the process employs a constructivist approach that emphasizes constructing *conceptual change,* that is, how the consultee (and often the consultant) understands and views the problem (Sandoval, 1996, 2004). Second, the consultee-centered consultation now encompasses more than metal health consultation (e.g., instructional consultation) and can occur in a variety of settings beyond mental health clinics (Caplan & Caplan-Moskovich, 2004).

In the new consultee-centered consultation, consultants build strong relationships with consultees and help them tell their stories about their experiences with their clients. Through judicious questioning, the consultants determine their consultees' conceptualization of the problem and their efforts to date in resolving the problem (Sandoval, 2003). Consultants then share their view of the problem with consultees and make their thinking transparent and explicit. By explaining their views and their rationale for reconceptualizing the problem, consultants help consultees to begin to think differently about the client system. At this point consultants often point out anomalous (e.g., atypical) data that may cause dissonance for the consultee that can lead to richer and deeper thinking on the part of the consultee. This leads to a mutual reconstruction of the focus of consultation and answering why the client system is behaving in a particular manner.

Caplan and Caplan-Moskovich (2004) have modified consultee-centered consultation to include a range of techniques that consultants can use given the specific consultation situation. They have also made the point that theoretical conceptualizations beyond psychodynamic theory are legitimate for the consultant to use.

**Case Example of Consultee-Centered Case Consultation.** A mental health consultant is working with a social worker whose caseload consists primarily of indigent families. The consultee brings up a case about the members of a particular family the consultee thinks are "just plain lazy" and are becoming more so because of the welfare they are receiving. The consultee notes that the middle class is the ultimate loser. The consultant listens carefully to the consultee's subjective view of the case, notes the consultee's defective judgment, and determines that the consultee's difficulty in working effectively with the family is due to theme interference.

The consultee views hard work and effort as vehicles for achievement. The theme interference takes the form of the syllogism: unless the family overcomes its laziness (initial category), family members will never amount to much (inevitable outcome). The consultant notes that the consultee appears to be fixated on the "laziness" of the family.

In attempts to reduce the theme interference, the consultant calls this case a tough one and suggests that three consultation sessions over a three-week period might help alleviate the problem. During the consultation sessions, the consultant listens and reacts calmly to the consultee's frustrations concerning the case. The consultant then describes two cases involving "lazy" families in which therapeutic benefits were attained, even though the families remained "lazy." As a result of these fictitious case examples, the consultee feels more comfortable about working on the case and begins to consider alternative approaches to it, such as training in child-rearing practices. The consultant agrees to follow up at a later date concerning the consultee's progress with the case.

## The Program-Centered Administrative Consultation Process

**Consultation Goals.** In program-centered administrative consultation, the consultant comes into an organization and consults with an administrator with regard to the mental health aspects of some program or the internal functioning of the organization. The consultant enters the organization, assesses and defines the problem, and makes a written report that includes a series of recommendations. It is up to the consultee to adapt the consultant's report and implement it within the organizational setting. Consider this example based on an article by Petti, Cornely, and McIntyre (1993): The mental health unit of a university medical center was asked to conduct an assessment of a mental health program for at-risk children and adolescents in a rural county. The scope of the consultation was to evaluate the services of the local mental health center to the county, examine independent service providers as supplements to the programs of the local mental health agency, and recommend a scope of services for at-risk children and adolescents. The consultation resulted in a five-year plan developed by the mental health center in conjunction with representatives from the county. A follow-up study after the implementation of the five-year plan indicated separate service units for children and adolescents and a successful mechanism for coordinating services by all mental health providers in the county. In another example, Cowles and Washburn (2005) describe a consultation on program design of intensive management units in juvenile correctional facilities.

The specific goals of this type of consultation depend on the nature of the consultation request and could include recommendations to deal with problems in program development, organizational planning, or program functioning. A secondary goal is that the consultee will learn to deal more effectively with similar program problems and issues in the future. Just as client-centered case consultation makes recommendations for working with a given client, administrative-centered program consultation makes recommendations for an administrative plan of action. As with client-centered consultation, a minimum of time is spent in direct contact with the consultee. The goals of program-centered administrative consultation are met in a relatively brief time, generally ranging from several hours to a few days. The consultant is seen as an expert who comes in, assesses the situation accurately, and writes knowledgeable recommendations.

**Consultant Function and Roles.**   The consultant needs sufficient data-collecting, action planning, and communication skills to be able to make findings and present recommendations in a form understandable to the principal consultee and other members of the consultee institution. The consultant should be a content expert, that is, have a thorough knowledge of the problem area in which the program administrator (principal consultee) requests assistance. The consultant also should be knowledgeable and experienced in organizational theory and practice, program development, fiscal policy, administrative procedure, and personnel management.

The consultant must be particularly careful to create effective relationships with staff members of the consultee institution because their help might be needed in gathering data. For example, the consultant may obtain significant amounts of information from individual and group interviews with staff including information about the internal and external forces working on the organization.

The consultant must consider two issues when performing program-centered administrative consultation. The first concerns being responsible for collecting and analyzing the data required to solve the problem and make recommendations. Therefore, the consultant must do more than merely help the organization's staff determine what data they want to collect since they may lack the knowledge, skill, and confidence necessary to make that determination. Because the consultant bears responsibility for the content of the assessment and the recommendations, the amount, type, and timing of data collection should ultimately be based on his or her expert knowledge and objectivity.

The second issue relates to the consultant's authority among the organization's staff members affected by the consultation. In program-centered administrative consultation, the consultee is the administrator who requested the consultant. This administrator, like any consultee, needs a coordinate relationship with the consultant and is free to accept or reject any or all of the consultant's report and recommendations. The consultant's relationship to the administrator's subordinates, however, is not coordinate. Therefore, in this type of consultation, the sanctioning process should guarantee that the consultant's requests for information and cooperation will be honored by all involved.

**Consultee Experience in Consultation.** The consultee in program-centered administrative consultation is the program administrator who expedites the hiring of the consultant in the first place. (This may or may not be the person who initially contacts the consultant.) The administrator should be the principal consultee because of the power of that position to both sanction the consultation and ensure that the consultant's recommendations are carried out at the end of consultation.

The consultee's task is to meet with the consultant to discuss the main reasons the consultant is being hired, any strategies for clarifying the problem that involve some of the organization's staff, the time frame for consultation, as well as the selection of methods to approve the consultant's activities throughout the organization.

Because the consultant needs considerable knowledge about the organization to determine which data to collect and make realistic recommendations, the administrator should make available as much information as possible concerning the organization's nature and methods of operation. The administrator also produces a rank-ordered list of administrative problems about which the consultant's assistance is being requested.

During the consultation the consultee should have as much contact with the consultant as the consultant deems necessary and should complete two primary tasks: provide the consultant an ongoing broad view of the organization and the interactive nature of its subsystems, and react to the consultant's tentative findings so that he or she can modify the recommendations at key times during the consultation process.

After the consultant's report has been filed, the consultee is responsible for the degree to which the recommendations are accepted and implemented. Finally, during follow-up the consultee is expected to assist the consultant in assessing the impact of consultation.

**Application: Consultant Techniques and Procedures.** How does the consultant proceed in program-centered administrative consultation? In the beginning of consultation, needs are explored, the contract is negotiated, the administrator is identified as the principal consultee, and the approximate amount of time the consultant and the consultee will spend together is established.

In obtaining an overview of the problems and their ramifications, the consultant makes a rapid initial assessment of the consultee institution's structure and culture and the nature of its problems. At this stage, the consultant is interested in forming general impressions and hunches that will provide a procedural blueprint for the remainder of the consultation.

Once the principal problems are identified, the consultant must gather additional information to shed light on them and to formulate potential solutions. Data are gathered by conducting formal and informal interviews with both individuals and groups, by observing the behavior of the organization's members in their routine work patterns, and by occasionally using questionnaires.

Based on the information gathered, the consultant begins to develop interim recommendations which are then provided to the principal consultee and other authorized parties-at-interest. The consultant incorporates the received reactions into progressively more detailed, complex, and sophisticated recommendations.

During assessment and the reformulation of interim recommendations, the consultant should maintain as much contact with the primary consultee as is feasible. Such contact provides the consultant with reactions from the organization's administration, maintains the consultee's interest in the consultation, and increases the likelihood that some of the consultant's skills will "rub off" on the consultee. By progressively modifying the recommendations made to solve the problem, the consultant has used a collaborative approach.

The final recommendations should have both a short-term and a long-term focus and should detail procedures required to implement the recommendations.

Because the consultant's report is typically distributed widely and throughout several levels in the consultee institution, it should be written in a formal style and should cover the issues and problems investigated well enough to be understandable to parties-at-interest who had no direct contact with the consultant.

Finally, the consultant should set up a follow-up schedule before terminating the consultation and should arrange to receive the results of the implementation of the recommendations.

**Case Example of Program-Centered Administrative Consultation.** Marilyn, a mental health consultant, is working with an administrator, the head counselor, and the dropout prevention coordinator of a large urban secondary school. The focus of consultation is the school's dropout prevention program. The dropout rate for the school is one of the highest in the state and is still increasing in spite of the dropout prevention program, which has been in existence for three years. Marilyn has been asked to make recommendations to improve the program. Before the onset of consultation, Marilyn made a thorough study of other dropout prevention programs in the state.

She spent one day in the school to get a feel for a typical school day and during the next week conducted in-depth interviews with the administrator, the head counselor, and the dropout prevention coordinator about their perceptions of the program. A few "high-rise" public housing students and some teachers were also interviewed. The results of these interviews led Marilyn to conclude that the program was viewed as a stigma or as "Mickey Mouse" by virtually everyone except the school's principal and the program coordinator. The program coordinator was viewed as being inadequately trained, as having a "cake" job, and as not being sensitive enough to the needs of the students in the program.

Based on these findings, the consultant made some interim recommendations for changing the program's image and for getting the coordinator additional training. These recommendations were shared with the appropriate staff members and were modified according to their input. The following is part of the consultant's final written report:

> Problem 1.1. The image of the dropout prevention program is poor among students and many staff members. The interviews conducted by the consultant suggest that most students view the dropout prevention program as "not a cool place to be." Students in general perceive students associated with the program as "rejects." The school counselors see the program as a "dumping ground" for students who are having a difficult time adjusting to school. The teachers tend to think of the program as one more "non-academic" activity at school. The administration and dropout prevention coordinator see the program as being adequate.

The following suggestion is made: The administration of the school should appoint a Dropout Prevention Program Advisory Committee with representatives from the administration, the program, students, the counseling department, and teachers. The dropout prevention coordinator would present the committee an annual plan for working with potential dropouts as well as methods of promoting the program's image throughout the school. Special attention needs to be paid to student views of the program.

The consultant followed up three months later and found that the school was actively engaged in carrying out these recommendations. The dropout prevention coordinator was enrolled on a part-time basis in a master's degree program in counseling.

## The Consultee-Centered Administrative Consultation Process

**Consultation Goals.** Consultee-centered administrative consultation is the most complicated, interesting, and demanding type of consultation. The consultant is hired to work with an organization's administrative-level personnel to help solve problems in personnel management or the implementation of organizational policy. The goal is to enhance the professional competency of an administrative staff (Erchul & Schulte, 1993). The consultant gathers information from within the organization to identify its problems and help consultees overcome them. The consultant can work with an individual, although most often there is more than one consultee.

The primary goal of consultee-centered administrative consultation is an increased level of consultees' professional functioning with regard to program development and organization so they help the institution accomplish its mission in the future—this form of consultation is educative in nature (Mendoza, 1993). A secondary goal is producing positive program change.

**Consultant Function and Roles.**  In consultee-centered administrative consultation, the consultant may work with one or more administrators referred to as *principal consultees*. The consultation is expected to be long-term, ranging from a few months to more than a year. Depending on the size of the consultee institution and the nature of the requested consultation, more than one consultant may be used. The consultant needs the same skills required for program-centered administrative consultation, including expertise in group consultation and specialized knowledge of social systems, administrative procedures, and organizational theory. In particular, the consultant must be able to understand how these skills relate to individuals and subgroups within the consultee institution, as well as to how the institution relates to the broader community. A final skill needed is the ability to scan the entire organization and make quick judgments about portions of the organization to examine in more depth.

Upon determining who the consultees are, the consultant enters the organization, performs relationship-building activities, studies the social system of the institution, plans an intervention, intervenes at the individual, group, or organizational level, and then evaluates and follows up.

The consultant is more or less "free to roam" through the organization and assists in defining problems and gathering data. Consultants present ideas to consultees and encourage them to discuss and act on them.

Recent trends in consultee-centered administrative consultation suggest that consultants should focus on trying to achieve lasting organizational change (Caplan et al., 1994). This can be accomplished by attempting to reduce stressors in the organization, by assisting in developing programs that deal with crises that may arise, and by creating mechanisms such as EAPs that permit individuals to seek psychological assistance on an easily accessible basis.

**Consultee Experience in Consultation.**  The principal consultee in this type of consultation is the administrator who hired the consultant. This administrator has the job of helping the consultant decide whether additional forms of consultation are required, whether there are to be other consultees, and how they are to be involved in the consultation process. As in consultation of any kind, the principal consultee negotiates the contract, assists in getting sanctions from the top administrator, and provides the consultant logistical support for studying the organization's social structure.

The consultee must determine the extent of contact with the consultant and arrange meetings at which the consultant can present findings to all consultees involved. It is important that consultees know from the start that the consultant will discuss the findings with them for their consideration and input. Although the primary focus of consultation is on organizational problems, an important goal is for consultees to use the consultant's input to further develop their own skills.

**Application: Consultant Techniques and Procedures.**  The beginnings of consultation are the same as in the other types of mental health consultation and more or less follow the entry procedures discussed in Chapter 3. The consultant in consultee-centered administrative consultation, however, has two unique problems at the onset of consultation. The first is determining who, in addition to the administrator, will be consultees. The administrators may want the consultant to have contact with subordinates so that they can inform the consultant about the organization. The consultant would then use this information while consulting with the administrator. However, the administrator may want the consultant to consult with the subordinates concerning issues and problems within the organization. Whichever is the case, it is very important for the consultant to be sure that everyone involved is aware of the nature of the consultant's role.

The second problem is to ensure that members of the consultee's institution understand that the consultant is an independent agent of change who can move freely within the organization. Members of the organization may suspect that the consultant is a spy for the administrator, an agent who will use psychological influence to get them to do what the administrator wants, or an outsider who wants to mold the institution into some preconceived form. This perceived threat can be minimized by building proper relationships, including maintaining coordinate relationships, communicating openly, and proceeding cautiously when introducing interventions.

As the consultant studies the organization's social system, problems and issues are identified and then presented to the consultees concerned. The consultant's intervention is a neutral one that is restricted to "increasing the range and depth of their [consultees'] understanding of the issues and to augmenting their emotional capacity to use such knowledge productively. It is then up to them to work out solutions in the light of their own personal and role-related choices" (Caplan & Caplan, 1993, p. 272). The most effective way for the consultant to remain neutral is to keep in mind the consultation processes of collecting information, making a consultation plan, and intervening to implement the plan.

Data collection has more constraints in consultee-centered administrative consultation than it does in program-centered consultation. First, staff participation in data collection is voluntary, even though it is administratively authorized. Second, because the people from whom the consultant is collecting data are potential consultees, relationship building must be accomplished as well. Third, although consultants have

the freedom to collect data about any aspect of the organization, they would do well to focus on issues that are both important to the staff and related to changes the staff would like to make.

In planning the intervention, the consultant should avoid the temptation to intervene too quickly and should review the findings, set some goals, and determine how these goals are to be met. Each intervention has a time limit, should be related to a problem the consultee thinks is important, and targets an individual, a group, or an organization.

As in all types of consultation, the consultant schedules a follow-up session in which to evaluate. If the consultation is ongoing, the consultant is then free to move on to another problem.

**Case Example of Consultee–Centered Administrative Consultation.**   A community counselor was consulting with the staff of a community mental health center that was working with an increasing number of clients with special problems, including AIDS. A former staff member had, in fact, recently contracted the disease. The staff members seemed familiar with the controversies surrounding AIDS, but were ill at ease about such problems because of denial of the disease by some patients. The consultant decided to use a consultee-centered approach but did not focus directly on the AIDS issue until some consultees brought it up. Once the subject was broached, the consultant attempted to extend the consultees' knowledge of denial in some AIDS patients.

The consultant met with the group of consultees for four sessions to discuss coping with client denial and shared information on the feelings helpers often have when working with chronically ill patients. After the four sessions, the consultant evaluated the consultation process with the principal consultee and arranged for a follow-up in six months.

### Modifications of the Caplanian Model

Caplan and Caplan have recently updated the ideas expressed in *The Theory and Practice of Mental Health Consultation* in a text entitled *Mental Health Consultation and Collaboration* (1993, 1999). The vast majority of Caplan's original ideas remain the same, though several have been expanded.

In addition to developing the concept of collaboration as an alternative to consultation, Caplan and Caplan have modified the earlier model in some relatively minor ways. For example, they more strongly support consultation with groups of consultees so that members can assist one another. The support that group members can provide one another allows the consultant to maintain a peer relationship with the consultees.

The consultant roles—mediator and conciliator—have been advocated by Caplan and Caplan for use in specific situations, such as helping divorcing parents form a collaborative relationship in order to safeguard their children's rights.

Some of Caplan and Caplan's techniques, such as theme interference reduction, have received criticism for being manipulative in nature. For example, Henning-Stout (1993) recommends referral to other mental health professionals in the case of loss of professional objectivity. However, Caplan and Caplan (1993) argue that the intention of the consultant is what determines whether or not the manipulation is unethical and that the consultant and the manipulator both try to note the other person's weaknesses—the manipulator to undermine the person, the consultant to help the consultee overcome those weaknesses. Thus, they conclude that if the consultee knew about the benign nature of the consultant's manipulations, he or she would judge the manipulation as positive. Furthermore, Caplan and Caplan suggest that when consultees seek consultation, they are giving tacit or explicit consent for any interventions, including benign manipulation. These authors also conclude that not every consultee is suitable for consultee-centered consultation and that, in such cases, consultants should move to a client-centered method that excludes any manipulation. They also note that many of the principles and basic techniques of mental health consultation are quite appropriate for use by consultants outside of the mental health field.

## The Ecological Perspective

New models of mental health consultation are increasingly examining the human-environment interface, which has led to greater emphasis on systems,

behavior modification, and human ecology (Gutkin & Curtis, 1999; Smith et al., 1997). Termed the *ecological approach,* this view emphasizes that behavior is a function of the interaction of the characteristics of the environment and those of the individual (Conoley & Haynes, 1992; Kloos et al., 1998). This trend implies less emphasis on case-oriented models and more on those concerned with ecology and events (Jason et al., 2005; Thomas, Gatz, & Luczak, 1997). As Jason et al., (2005) note, "The ecological perspective helps school and community consultants consider and work with the broader social systems and institutions within the community that reflect community norms and ultimately people's lives" (p. 207). Hence, mental health consultants are increasingly moving into the area of organizational consultation.

The ecosystem, the interacting systems related to individuals and their environments, provides the context for understanding human behavior. The ecological perspective provides consultants with ways of making changes within a given system, helps individuals contribute significantly, and helps people adapt to the setting in which something is expected of them.

The ecological perspective suggests that a strong consultation relationship and shifts in consultee attitudes are insufficient to effect change (Kelly, 1983). Rather, the resources in the organization must be taken into account. In such models, the consultant becomes part of the community's system and changes the ecological interactions to produce a milieu that promotes mental health. Prevention is a key goal of the ecological perspective. The setting constitutes the client system in this perspective and is usually either an organization or the community at large. Interventions are "aimed at developing long-term adaptive processes for the betterment of the setting and its members" (Trickett, 1986, p. 189). Interventions and strategies for any model of consultation can be used when appropriate. Consultation is successful when the organization or community is able to locate and develop its own resources, which are then linked to external resources (Kelly, 1987). Each setting is viewed as having its own unique physical and social characteristics. In its own way, the ecological perspective has several of the characteristics of the doctor–patient model discussed in Chapter 11, namely, an emphasis on diagnosis and the attempt to tailor intervention to the setting. The ecological perspective is radically different from the doctor-patient model in that it has a preventative orientation, a strong emphasis on the consultant–consultee relationship, a strong focus on ecological variables, a consideration of the way an organization is conceptualized, and a focus on collaboration throughout the consultation. Two guiding principles for the consultant are that the client system is a part of a functioning social system, and disturbances are not things inside the individual but rather discordances in the system. The term "discordance" refers to the differences between the individual's abilities and the demands of the environment (Conoley & Haynes, 1992).

Proponents of the ecological perspective (Tindal et al., 1990) suggest that a great deal of mental health consultation fails to consider the environmental context within which it takes place. For example, whereas consultants typically realize that consulting in a school is vastly different from consulting in a hospital's human resource development program, they rarely consider that one school differs vastly from another (Kelly, 1987). Consider a second example in which a consultant helps a therapist effectively assist a client, but the client returns because he or she is unable to fit into the community.

In contrast, to think ecologically is to consider how people, settings, and events can become resources for positive developments in individuals and total organizations, as well as how these resources can be managed and conserved (Trickett, Kelly, & Vincent, 1984). This model assumes that consultee power is needed to effect true change—for example, in reducing the constraints due to social structure and processes within an organization. The ecological model is based on principles that emphasize the interactions between individuals and their environments.

There are three premises of the ecological perspective that guide the consultant:

- Each social setting has a finite number of resources to maintain and develop itself.

- An adaptive environment has members who have a variety of competencies.

- The purpose of a preventative intervention is to activate and develop resources (Kelly, 1987, p. 3).

The role of the consultant is to identify the social resources of the setting and help members help one another. This is accomplished in part by the consultant being as aware of the setting and its external environment as the individuals in that setting. Such mutual assistance helps the organization or community adapt, cope, and become empowered. In short, the ecological perspective provides consultation that nurtures the opportunity to acquire competencies for self-development in the presence of social support.

There are several principles that guide the behavior of the parties involved in consultation from an ecological perspective (Kelly, 1987). I have selected five of these to provide an overview of this approach:

- People, settings, and events are resources for the development of the consultation, which takes into account the fact that these features are present in all social settings and make up the raw material from which change occurs. Thus, consultants scan the entire social organization for resources to develop preventative actions within the everyday life of the organization (Kelly, 1987). For example, a consultant notes that the teachers' lounge in a school may be an excellent setting for teachers to discuss innovative ideas.

- The ecological paradigm advocates the conservation and management of resources, which taps the vast social energy within the individuals in a given setting so that they become resources for each other. Thus, the consultant assesses the resources within an organization with an eye toward developing those that are used extensively while saving those that are overused. For example, a consultant determines how sensitive topics can be discussed with impunity in a human service agency.

- The positive qualities of people, settings, and events in every organization can be activated to empower the membership. Activating qualities such as enthusiasm, informal settings such as the coffee room, and events such as birthday celebrations should be encouraged. Thus, consultants identify and employ such qualities as personal initiative, social settings, and informal events as growth opportunities for the organization. For example, a consultant organizes a series of "brown bag" luncheon meetings whose topics emerge from the informal interactions of the participants.

- The dominant means of growth and change are coping (how members of the organization deal with stress) and adaptation (how they undergo changes in "fitting into" the organization). Thus, consultants maximize the qualities of coping and adapting, for example, by sponsoring a series of wellness activities such as stress management or exercise programs.

- Consultation is a flexible improvisational process with no set way of proceeding. Thus, consultants may want to maximize networking within the setting to identify resources and strategies.

- In conclusion, the ecological perspective involves all members of the setting in preventative measures by identifying its strengths and weaknesses. With a systems view, the resources are then developed so that the setting is self-enhancing. The goal is the creation of an effective social setting in which all members contribute to its maintenance and growth by serving as resources for each other. As you might have surmised, this approach to consultation is very demanding and can be quite time consuming. The ecological perspective is just that—a perspective. It does not attempt to be a model of consultation. Therefore, it is up to consultants to interpret the principles of this perspective as guidelines for effective practice. The ecological approach, although valuable, has yet to reach its promise as a way to aid communities and community groups (Trickett, 1993).

**Case Example of the Ecological Approach to Consultation.** A community psychologist was consulting with a family service center concerned about its work environment. By coming from an ecological perspective, the consultant had a lot of leeway in how she might proceed. Realizing that each family service center is a unique setting, the consultant investigated how the people at the center interacted within their work setting.

She reviewed the history of the center, observed the people in their work environment, and conducted interviews to determine how newly hired people were oriented and how employees were acknowledged during the everyday course of events. The consultant provided a survey that assessed the workers' views of their real and ideal work settings. In noting discrepancies between the real and the ideal, she found that employees had issues with the degree of autonomy they felt, the amount of work-related stress they experienced, and the quality of communication with supervisors. Areas of strength included reward for productivity, acknowledgment for effort, and opportunities for professional development.

Based on her findings, the consultant and staff engaged in a variety of interventions to enhance the center's quality of life. First, they capitalized on informal elements of the center. People were encouraged to take breaks together, flexible work scheduling was introduced, and a staff volleyball team was formed. Quality circle problem-solving groups with participation at all levels of the center were created. Finally, a community advisory group for the center was created and an internal network was formed to smooth the flow of communication. These empowering interventions were designed to prevent the center from experiencing major problems.

The consultant's final report noted that assisting the center from an ecological perspective would have been much more difficult if the director had not been supportive of change. Further, it appeared that the center staff were now involved in daily operation of the center to a degree that they could be self-supporting.

## COLLABORATION FROM A MENTAL HEALTH PERSPECTIVE

As you may recall, Caplan developed his model of consultation in the context of an external consultant who becomes a temporary member of the consultee organization. As increasing numbers of mental health professionals such as school psychologists and school counselors were hired in the schools and started providing consultation services, there were some strong effects on Caplan's original consultation model. These effects included the idea that it would be more difficult for the consultee to reject the consultant's recommendations; that the level of expertise of the consultant would make a nonhierarchical relationship impossible; and that an in-house mental health expert would, under normal circumstances, be expected to participate in the intervention and thereby would be responsible to some degree for the outcomes of the case (Caplan et al., 1994). As a result, Caplan and Caplan (1993) have expanded the concept of *collaboration* into a process complementary to, but different from, *consultation.*

Collaboration does not take away from consultation but adds to it (Erchul, 1993a). The difference is this: In collaboration, the mental health practitioner determines which cases to discuss, takes responsibility for the mental health outcomes of the cases, and typically joins in the treatment of the client and seeks changes in the host organization that will benefit the clients. In consultation, the consultee chooses which cases to discuss, remains responsible for the interventions and outcomes of the cases, and does not seek changes in the host institution unless asked to do so. Caplan and Caplan (1993) make the distinction between collaboration and consultation in this way:

> The essential difference between *collaboration* and *consultation,* as I use the terms, is this: In *collaboration,* the mental health specialist joins the care-giving team inside the community institution, such as a school system or a general hospital, and accepts responsibility for the mental health outcome of its cases. The specialist may fulfill his or her mission by ensuring that the other team members deal effectively with the clients, in line with his or her assessment of their needs, or else he or she may undertake to implement part or all of the diagnostic and remedial plan him- or herself. (p. 46)

As you can see, in collaboration, the collaborating specialist takes primary responsibility for the mental health outcome of the case or program and equal responsibility for the overall outcome of the case or program (Caplan et al., 1994).

The major implication of Caplan and Caplan's recent ideas for practicing consultants seems to be the necessity for the human service professional to determine at the outset of the helping relationship whether consultation or collaboration is in order. This determination can be made by assessing the skill level of the consultee: if high, then perhaps consultation is in order; if low, then the consultee can either be trained to manage the case and then consulted with, or the human service professional can suggest a collaborative relationship and take part in the treatment. In any case, the counselor or psychologist may want to consider collaborating in all cases and programs by the very fact of being an in-house professional.

Mental health collaboration can be particularly suitable for school-based human service professionals (Caplan et al., 1994). Caplan and Caplan (1993) use the terms "collaborating professional" and "collaborating specialist" to describe the counselor or psychologist in a school providing collaboration. For example, a school-based mental health professional might consult with a teacher about classroom management procedures for an acting-out student while collaborating with the teacher by providing counseling services to the student to help reduce the behavior. As this example demonstrates, there is no inherent conflict between collaboration and consultation. In addition, as this example suggests, the mental health professional is responsible for certain aspects of the case (helping the student adjust to the situation behaviorally), as is the teacher (making sure appropriate academic learning occurs). Caplan's recent writings strongly suggest that mental health collaboration should replace consultation as the method of choice by mental health workers who are staff members of an organization. At the same time, Caplan cautions against ignoring the differences between human service and for-profit organizations when considering mental health collaboration (1993). Table 9.2 summarizes the differences

**T A B L E   9.2**    **Mental Health Consultation and Mental Health Collaboration Contrasted on Key Dimensions**

| DIMENSION | MENTAL HEALTH CONSULTATION | MENTAL HEALTH COLLABORATION |
|---|---|---|
| Location of consultant's home base | External to the organization | Internal to the organization |
| Type of psychological service | Generally indirect with little or no client contact | Combines indirect and direct services, and includes client contact |
| Consultant–consultee relationship | Assumes a coordinate and non-hierarchical relationship | Acknowledges status and role differences within the organization and thus the likelihood of a hierarchical relationship |
| Consultee participation | Assumes voluntary participation | Assumes voluntary participation, but acknowledges the possibility of forced participation |
| Interpersonal working arrangement | Often dyadic, involving consultant and consultee | Generally team based, involving several collaborators |
| Confidentiality of communications within relationship | Assumes confidentiality to exist, with limits of confidentiality (if any) specified during initial contracting | Does not automatically assume confidentiality, given organization realities and pragmatic need to share relevant information among team members |
| Consultee freedom to accept or reject consultant advice | Yes | Not assumed to be true, as a collaborator's expertise in his or her specialty area is generally deferred to by team |
| Consultant responsibility for case/program outcome | No | Shares equal responsibility for overall outcome, and primary responsibility for mental health aspects of case or program |

SOURCE: From Caplan, G. R., Caplan, R. B., and Erchul, W. P. (1994). Caplanian mental health consultation: Historical background and current status. *Consulting Psychology Journal*, 46, p. 7. © 1994 by the Educational Publishing Foundation and Division of Consulting Psychology. Reprinted with permission.

between mental health consultation and mental health collaboration.

## MULTICULTURAL ASPECTS RELATED TO MENTAL HEALTH CONSULTATION

Just as organizational consultation offers more than one type of consultation, so too does mental heath consultation. Caplan's client-centered case model allows for minimal disclosure on the part of the con-

sultee. Consultee-catered case consultation is suitable for consultees wanting assistance from a knowledgeable authority figure. Ingraham (2003, 2004) points out that consultee-centered consultation can be effectively used in multicultural consultation to help consultees construct culturally sensitive understandings of problems. The focus of both of these types of consultation on the case (and not the consultee) makes them safe for consultees from cultural groups that do not value self-disclosure. Caplan's model is flexible enough to account for other worldviews due to the coordinate, nonhierarchical relationship between consultant and consultee (Harrison, 2004). As a result, mental health consul-

---

**CASE 9.1     Mental Health Consultation for School Consultants**

---

Micheline is a school counselor assigned to a large urban junior high school. The school has been experiencing an increase in gang behavior along with an alarming increase in the number of students bringing weapons onto campus. Micheline was asked by representatives from a group of language arts teachers to consult with them on stress management.

In a meeting with the teachers, it was apparent to Micheline that they were experiencing a great deal of stress over possible violence in the classroom. Teachers noted that the increase in stress had begun to affect the quality of the group's communication adversely, had increased the number of teacher leave days, and had led many of the teachers to leave school at the earliest possible moment after student dismissal. The teachers related their concerns that the school administration had neither taken a strong enough stand with the gangs nor implemented adequate security procedures to prevent weapons on campus. Having discussed the matter with the principal and been told that the procedures for making the school secure were appropriate, adequate, and approved by the local superintendent's office, the teachers concluded that their only recourse was to create a self-help group to cope with the ongoing stress.

Micheline agreed to meet with the group for one hour after school once every two weeks to form a peer support group and train teachers in stress management strategies. The first two meetings dealt with the nature of peer support groups among teachers, and subsequent meetings were divided between stress management training and dealing with issues individual teachers raised.

Micheline began to feel that the teachers tended to look at her as the ultimate authority in the group instead of focusing on how to help one another, perhaps because she was training the group. In bringing up her concern, she was very surprised at the reaction: several of the teachers felt that although they were in a support group, Micheline would be the one who would be the leader and the expert, while others wondered why Micheline kept the group focused on work even when some members brought up very personal issues.

On hearing this feedback, Micheline suggested that she and the group renegotiate her role and had each member write down and then read what he or she expected from the group and from Micheline. As it turned out, most members wanted Micheline to be more active and directive. There was also a trend among the members to discuss how to make their classrooms more secure from gang activity and weapons.

Micheline agreed to the group's request, moving away from stress management training and toward teachers' concerns about particular students with regard to gang behavior or potential violence. She acted as a resource on gang behavior and ways of minimizing violence in the classroom. The group's evaluation of the consultation experience reflected a very positive attitude toward Micheline's role as a resource person. The evaluation also indicated that the teachers felt very supportive of one another even though the concept of a direct support group had been abandoned.

**Commentary**

Regardless of the initial contract and expectations of the parties involved in consultation, things change. Micheline showed both flexibility and resiliency in her work with the group as indicated by her willingness to renegotiate the nature of role with the group members. This case also brings out another very important point about mental health consultation: even though the consultant can make group-focused interventions such as stress management training, it is typical for individual consultees to want assistance with their own agendas, in this case, strategies for dealing with particular students.

---

tation may be seen as desirable by disenfranchised groups. The move toward eclecticism on the part of mental health consultation allows for a broad conceptualization of the problem and a wealth of interventions for assisting the client system. The increased breadth and flexibility that has emerged in mental health consultation has created the conditions that allow for sensitivity toward cultural variables and modifications of the process to meet the needs of culturally diverse groups. Harrison (2004) noted one criticism: The concept of theme interference and its related issues of control over one's psychodynamic issues may be discrepant from the worldview of groups such as Native Americans, Inuits, women, and racioethnic minorities.

---

**C A S E   9.2       Mental Health Consultation for Community Consultants**

The consultee, Clover, is a family resource coordinator for a New Start program for low-income single mothers. The program provides support in such areas as finding work; raising children; developing budgets; personal, career, and family counseling; and advocacy. The program helps women set and meet goals that lead to self-sufficiency. Clover is a support person for the women and maintains contact with them over a two-year period. She was having some difficulties in helping one client meet her program goals and had asked Della, a community counselor with a local mental health center, to consult. Clover had made several home visits with the client, who avoided any significant discussion of her problems and had difficulty being assertive. The woman also had difficulty with minor bouts of depression and exhibited self-esteem issues. Clover had asked Della for assistance in building stronger rapport and for methods to promote assertiveness and motivation with the client..

Della took time during the first session to build rapport with Clover, and then asked how she had proceeded with the case so far—in particular what interventions had already been implemented to resolve the problems. In looking for any lack of skill, confidence, or objectivity in Clover, Della determined that client-centered case consultation was appropriate. Clover admitted that she had resorted to persuasion and a few gentle confrontations. In looking over the client's written goals and history, Della wanted more data so she could further determine Clover's strengths and limitations in managing the case and better assess the client's difficulties. She asked Clover to contact the client for a home visit and for permission to go along.

During the home visit Della took a low profile, observing Clover and the client as Clover again went over the client's goals and the lack of progress being made toward them. As Della drove back with Clover to her office, they discussed what happened during the

home visit. Della questioned Clover about alternative approaches to focusing directly on the client's goals. Della mentioned that she saw the client as reluctant rather than resistant. Perhaps taking the first step toward accomplishing her goals was just too much for the client.

Della then wrote a detailed report that contained recommendations on how Clover might manage the case, a brief analysis of the client including her lack of any type of social support system, and the conclusion that such a support system should be the primary goal for Clover to help the client develop. Della listed several interventions that she knew Clover was familiar with or could obtain resources for, among which were peer counseling, a singles support group, strength bombardment, and goal attainment scaling.

Della met with Clover one more time to go over the report and encouraged her to follow through. They agreed to meet in a month to discuss Clover's progress with her client, and Della encouraged her to call if any glitches showed up in the plan.

**Commentary**

This case illustrates the skill of determining which type of mental health consultation to employ. Notice that this decision, although not irrevocable, did guide Della in her work with Clover. If Della had determined that consultee-centered case consultation was in order, she would have proceeded in a very different manner. Notice that Della was not reluctant to share her expertise with Clover and that she based her recommendations on direct observation of the client. Such observations are time consuming and raise the issue of whether alternative ways of observing through audio or videotapes are as legitimate as direct observation. This case also highlights the importance of assessing the consultee's skills to ensure that the consultant's recommendations are possible.

## SUMMARY

In mental health consultation, a mental health expert (consultant) helps a human service worker or administrator (consultee) with a work–related problem. The approach is historically identified with Gerald Caplan (1970, 1974, 1977; see also Caplan & Caplan, 1993, 1999; Caplan & Caplan-Moskovich,

2004) and has its origins in the psychodynamic school of psychotherapy. This model stresses the importance of the consultant-consultee relationship and emphasizes enabling consultees to apply what they learned in consultation to similar situations in the future.

The combination of two levels of mental health consultation (case and administrative) with two possible targets (the client or program and the consultee) produces the four types of mental health consultation: client-centered case, consultee-centered case, program-centered administrative, and consultee-centered administrative. Consultees can have work-related concerns due to a lack of knowledge, skill, confidence, or objectivity. Depending on the type of consultation and the nature of the consultee's difficulty, consultants have at their disposal a broad array of techniques, including the most innovative and controversial of these techniques—theme interference reduction. All of these approaches to mental health consultation share the common goals of helping the consultee be more effective in the present and future.

## RECENT TRENDS

Several trends have occurred in mental health consultation since Caplan published his inaugural work in 1970. It is to his credit that many of these trends involve adaptations of his model, such as reconsideration of who may qualify as a consultee and innovations in methods of working with them.

One trend, described earlier in this chapter, is the move toward using collaboration when internal consultants need to take some direct responsibility for part of the plan to help the client system. This is a rather dramatic move away from traditional consultation, in which the consultee maintains responsibility for the outcome of the plan. The concept of reciprocal consultation, which is implicit in collaboration, is not well developed in Caplan's writings. Rather than focusing on how professionals working with the same client system can consult with one another about the client system, Caplan's writings emphasize each professional implementing a part of a mutually agreed-upon plan.

Another trend in mental health consultation is the continued inclusion of nonprofessionals as consultees. Parents, volunteers (such as hospice workers), and paraprofessionals (such as mental health technicians) all work with people in ways that can loosely be described as providing human services. Consultants can help these workers deal more effectively with the people they serve by using essentially the same methods used with professionals. However, Caplan's consultee-centered model does not apply to parents because it is unlikely that they can be objective about their children. Over the years, experts in the field of mental health consultation (Altrocchi, 1972; Heller & Monahan, 1983; Hodges & Cooper, 1983; Knotek 2003, 2004; Kuehnel & Kuehnel, 1983b; Osterweil, 1988; Parsons & Meyers, 1984; Schmuck, 1983) have modified Caplan's original formulations.

The issue of whether the consultant should directly confront consultee defenses has received some attention. Some authors (Dougherty et al., 1996; Parsons, 1996) take a positive view of such confrontation. These authors disagree with Caplan's contention that direct confrontation takes away a consultee's defenses and that the time available in consultation for providing defensive coping strategies is too short. Proponents of direct confrontation argue that it is time effective, much less dangerous than Caplan implies, and does not diminish self-esteem.

Theme interference reduction has also been modified. Heller and Monahan (1983) reconceived theme interference as being due to stereotypes and produced a method for alleviating these stereotypes without having to focus on manipulating the consultee or on the psychodynamic influence that originated the theme interference reduction methods. Theme interference can be reconceptualized in terms of irrational beliefs and corrected using the principles of Rational Emotive Therapy (RET) developed by Albert Ellis (Harrison, 2004).

Group consultation has received positive attention because of its cost-effectiveness and the realization that it may be as effective as individual consultation, particularly in promoting innovation (Caplan, 1974, 1977; Caplan & Caplan, 1993, 1999; Counselman & Weber, 1994; Davis & Hartsough, 1992). For example, school-based and external consultants are involved in teacher retention through the use of support groups using a consultee-centered model to group consultation (Babinski & Rogers,

1998). Drum and Valdese (1988) developed a system for determining levels of client system needs and the degree to which advocacy is appropriate for each level. Advocacy consultation can also be linked to network-building consultation in which human service consultants work with community groups and/or agencies for the purposes of sharing information, promoting linkages, and developing a unified response to mental health issues that arise. For example, a mental health professional might proactively assist a small rural community in developing a network for assisting the community's AIDS patients. Advocacy can also be involved in grassroots consultation, in which mental health consultants assist groups and/or agencies in dealing with issues that have mental health implications for them or their community. For example, a mental health worker might help neighborhood groups develop strategies for keeping drug pushers out of their neighborhoods.

Mental health consultants are getting more involved in staff development. Mental health consultants are also increasingly working with different types of support groups for, parents, teachers, families with special needs, and others. For example, consultants assist support groups for families of the mentally ill, families being served by hospice, teachers under stress, and workers considering career changes. This trend capitalizes on the increasing popularity of the mutual help movement. In addition, there is a demand for mental health consultants to increase their skills in helping groups organize, recruit members, and make themselves known to the larger community (Werner & Tyler, 1993).

Another trend is the increasing amount of mental health consultation performed in medical settings (Sears et al., 2006). For example, a mental health consultant may be asked to assist a physician concerning a patient's unwillingness to take medication. In another example, administrators of nursing homes often rely on mental health consultants to assist with issues residents present such as depression, combative behavior, and confusion (Crose & Kixmiller, 1994). Mental health consultants are increasingly being asked to conduct organizational consultations in medical settings, such as the areas of program development or communication between hospital departments.

Also on the increase is the technical assistance mental health consultants provide agencies (Lewis et al., 2003; Sears et al., 2006). Such assistance frequently takes the form of outreach consultation and involves the direct dissemination of knowledge and skills to human service agencies (Sullivan & Rapp, 1991). For example, mental health consultants are increasingly being called on to assist in programs that lead to independent living, are designed to decrease psychiatric hospitalization, and whose objectives are to increase the number of clients served by human service agencies. In another example, consultants engage in psychoeducational group intervention that addresses the needs of adults caring for aging parents (Schwiebert & Myers, 1994, 1997). Finally, in yet another example, mental health consultants may serve as key members of the multidisciplinary team with hospice organizations (Lindberg, 1996).

The onset of managed care has also impacted mental health consultation. Having to "do more with less" has created opportunities, particularly for psychologists, in providing consultation (such as that based on personality assessment) to other therapists and clients' families (Quirk et al., 1995; Sears et al., 2006). Increasingly, psychologists are marketing themselves and the clinical utility of their assessment skills with organizations such as HMOs. Even mental health centers themselves are increasingly seeking organizational consultation from mental health providers (Backer, 1993). Caplan's administrative consultation models can be particularly appropriate for mental health centers because the models are user-friendly for practitioners and can be adapted to deal with the impact of managed care yet still remain innovative. "The adaptation of organization development concepts in mental health organizations has made those organizations amenable to consultation in their attempts to manage the change that is happening anyway" (Backer, 1993, p. 157). Increasingly, organizational constructs such as culture are being used to assist consultants in helping human services agencies cope with change.

There has been an increase in the involvement of personnel from counseling and psychological services centers in post-secondary education settings to participate in consultation with other units in the educational institution (Knotek, 2006; Silverman, 1993).

Consultants provide guidance on retention efforts, students in academic difficulty, relationships between culturally different groups, and issues surrounding fraternities and sororities. Particular attention is being paid to working with faculty and administrators concerning disruptive students (Amada, 1993) and student-athletes (Gabbard & Halischak, 1993).

There has been a move toward increased use of mental health consultants in business and industry settings, particularly through Employee Assistance Plans (EAPs) (Shosh, 1996) and organization development initiatives (Sears et al., 2006). One of the most common tasks for consultants is in helping employees adjust to major changes in companies, such as changes from line production to team production, and in outplacement activities (see Chapter 8).

There is a trend for mental health consultant to work with schools and school systems using a public health model which focuses on prevention (Nastasi, 2004). These mental health services will be based in the school and focus on health and competence at the class or school level, thus moving away from a "deficit" model (Cummings et al., 2004b)

Finally, there is a trend for consultants to look beyond the problem-solving paradigm, as well as increasing support for the concept of empowering consultees, with the consultant taking on the role of resource person (Lewis et al., 2003). For example, a consultant may act as a resource person for assisting the administrators of a domestic violence program and the administrators of a substance-abuse program communicate more effectively. In reality, this is what consultants who take on a collaborative mode do when they are with a very skillful consultee. There is a corresponding move away from the problem-solving approach, which places the consultant in the expert mode.

## CONCLUSIONS

Mental health consultation has contributed significantly to the psychological well-being of our society. First, it has made possible increased and better delivery of human services to client systems through the use of a pyramid structure in which consultants assist consultees working with clients or programs. Thus, a relatively large segment of the population can be served by a relatively small number of professionals. Second, it has promoted mental health and has helped to create positive public attitudes concerning the delivery of human services. A significant portion of our society now views mental health as everyone's business. Third, it has allowed untold thousands of human service professionals to improve and refine their skills, which has benefited the clients with whom they work. Fourth, mental health consultation has taught us a hard lesson in regard to our fast-paced society: namely, unhurried and systematic reflection increases the consultee's awareness of the range of options available, counteracts premature and emotionally based closure,

and reestablishes a state of equilibrium (Caplan et al., 1994). This position has tempered the tendency on the part of consultants to give in to the time constraints placed on them and their consultees' efforts in organizations such as schools where a quick fix is often considered better than nothing. Finally, it has reemphasized the notion that personal issues can affect our work lives for better or worse. Indeed, human service professionals may bear the following dictum in mind throughout their careers: "Physician, heal thyself."

Even though there is no doubt that mental health consultation has had a broad and positive impact, it is not without criticism. One basic criticism is that even though "mental health consultation" has been defined, it has been done so more in terms of what consultants *do* than in terms of what the concept itself *means*. This has led to some controversy over the boundaries of consultation. Long ago, Mazade (1983) contended that the boundaries of mental health consultation are too broad: until there is a better definition of mental health consultation and a more consistent set of expectations concerning what mental health consultants do, research and attempts to define relevant delivery of services to consultees will suffer.

Bloom (1984) related several criticisms of mental health consultation that are, unfortunately, still all too true today. First, because mental health consultation focuses on clients and their issues, consultees seek new cases rather than perform preventative measures. Hence, mental health case consultation may work at cross-purposes with primary prevention. Second, the value of consultation is limited when the individual consultee (instead of the consultee institution) is the target for change. Third, mental health consultation can erroneously assume that consultees are not functioning effectively with their cases and programs when in fact they are (Caplan & Caplan, 1993).

Most of the criticisms of mental health consultation have been directed at Caplan's model. For example, some authors criticize Caplan for creating a model that only works in an ideal situation that is rarely, if ever, obtained. Caplan's model has also been described as elitist, a vestige of a time when consultees had limited training in their field and few well-trained consultants were available to assist them. A more preventative perspective would characterize consultee-centered case consultation, for example, as the development of knowledge, skill, confidence, or objectivity in the consultee (Knotek, 2003, 2004; Meyers et al., 1993). As it stands, the model has a deficit perspective in that it assumes there is something wrong with the consultee. Hence, the model focuses on problem solving rather than prevention and has thus not developed a larger plan to assist communities in creating structures that prevent mental illness (Trickett, 1993). Although Caplan views his model as preventative, there is little about prevention in his writing regarding consultation.

Caplan also underestimates the amount of time needed to build relationships with individual consultees, particularly in consultee-centered approaches to consultation. Even the psychodynamic assumptions underlying theme interference reduction have been questioned, and theme reduction techniques have been criticized as being manipulative and unsupported by research. Henning-Stout (1993) and even Caplan (1993) himself have suggested that Caplan was perhaps too preoccupied with theme interference reduction when he developed his model.

Furthermore, consultants who are also therapists may have much more difficulty than Caplan suggests in avoiding direct therapeutic interventions to consultees who are too emotionally involved in their cases. The transfer of effect, discussed earlier as a key concept, has been increasingly questioned; only minimal research supports this concept's existence. Finally, Caplan's view of a coordinate, nonhierarchical relationship is criticized because consultants, particularly in consultee-centered case consultation, do not always act as if the relationship were equal.

## SUGGESTIONS FOR EFFECTIVE PRACTICE

- Listen to how the consultees describe the situation for which they requested assistance as a guide to determine whether to use client-centered or consultee-centered consultation.

- Avoid using techniques like theme interference reduction unless you have been trained and directly supervised in their use.

- Consider the importance of administrative consultation, even though the primary work you will do will be case consultation.

- Don't do for consultees and fellow collaborators what they can do for themselves.

## QUESTIONS FOR REFLECTION

1.  How did the psychodynamic perspective influence Caplan?

2.  Do you believe that the transfer of effect really takes place in mental health consultation? On what do you base your belief?

3.  What does Caplan mean when he describes the consultation relationship as coordinate and nonhierarchical?

4.  What are three basic differences between program-centered administrative consultation and consultee-centered administrative consultation?

5.  To what extent do you agree that mental health collaboration is the service of choice for in-house mental health practitioners?

6.  What ethical issues are raised by the use of techniques for reducing theme interference?

7.  Is manipulation ever a legitimate consultant intervention? Why or why not?

8.  Which of Caplan's four types of consultation would you feel most comfortable using? Why?

9.  Do you feel that the consultee-centered case type demands too much skill on the part of the consultant to be used effectively by the majority of mental health consultants? Justify your position.

10. What does the ecological perspective add to mental health consultation?

## SUGGESTED SUPPLEMENTARY READINGS

If you are interested in more detail and depth about mental health consultation, the following selected readings are recommended:

Caplan, G. (1970). *The theory and practice of mental health consultation*. New York: Basic Books. This classic on mental health consultation was the primary source for this chapter and presents a nice blend of theoretical and practical aspects. Of particular interest is Caplan's discussion of consultee-centered case consultation. Many of today's mental health professionals have used Caplan's ideas as a basis for developing their own particular style and approach to consultation.

Caplan, G., & Caplan, R. B. (1999). *Mental health consultation and collaboration*. Prospect Heights, IL: Waveland. (Original work published in 1993). The first part of this text is a reprint of the majority of Caplan's 1970 text. The latter part is filled with Caplan and Caplan's ideas on mental health collaboration and methodological and technical issues. New material includes discussion of the significance of manipulation, when to use consultation, and key modifications in Caplan's theory since 1970. The ideas and case studies on collaboration are quite informative.

# 10

✴

# Behavioral Consultation
# and Collaboration

In 1977, John Bergan introduced behavioral consultation as a way to provide more service to larger numbers of clients (Watson et al., 1997). Behavioral consultation evolved from the behavioral paradigm based on positivism (Henning-Stout, 1993). Behavioral consultation is a popular approach to consultation that applies behavioral technology to the consultation process (Elliott & Busse, 1993) and is most likely the most frequently used model of consultation (Anton-LaHart & Rosenfield, 2004). The expanding application of behavioral technology to mental health and educational concerns has led to behavioral consultation's immense popularity (Noell, 1996). While behavioral consultants specialize in this approach, all consultants make at least occasional use of behavioral approaches to consultation. In essence, the consultant in this model assists the consultee to be specific about behaviors to be changed. This allows for the determination of the contingencies controlling the behavior, thus permitting the development of specific interventions to accomplish behavior change.

A consultant functioning within this framework needs to be skilled in behavioral theory and practice (Kratochwill & Bergan, 1990) and should become familiar with the work of such leaders in behavioral psychology as B. F. Skinner and Albert Bandura. Because behavioral consultation places heavy emphasis on assessment and evaluation, you may want to review the various methodologies for data collection described in Chapter 4, the discussion of treatment integrity covered in Chapter 5, and the various evaluation methods described in Chapter 6.

This chapter presents three models of behavioral consultation suggested by Vernberg and Reppucci (1986) and, most recently, Kratochwill, Elliott, &

Stoiber (2002). In *behavioral case consultation,* the consultant helps as consultees apply behavioral principles to a case. *Behavioral technology training* teaches specific behavioral technology skills to consultees. *Behavioral system consultation* analyzes and modifies an organization's processes and structures using behavioral technology principles. Because of its popularity, I provide the majority of the coverage to case consultation.

As you read this chapter, consider the following questions:

1. What makes behavioral consultation "behavioral"?

2. What unique ethical issues, if any, might arise from the use of behavioral consultation?

3. Is this model's emphasis on measurement an asset or a liability?

4. What are the basic differences among the three approaches to behavioral consultation described in this chapter?

5. What special skills does a behavioral consultant need?

## INTRODUCTION

The following is an example of behavioral consultation:

### Case Example

You are a schoolteacher who asks a school counselor to consult with you concerning one of your students who causes disturbances by talking at inappropriate times throughout the school day. The counselor asks you to describe exactly those behaviors you consider to be "inappropriate" as well as your and the child's behaviors immediately before and after the undesirable behavior occurs. Based on your description and direct observations of the child, the school counselor leads you through a problem-solving process to eliminate the child's inappropriate behavior. You discuss strategies that you can implement and appropriate positive behavioral supports. You agree to implement the program, and the school counselor agrees to help you measure the subsequent frequency of the child's inappropriate behavior.

Chances are excellent that the school counselor in this example was using a model of behavioral consultation. Behavioral consultation is based on behavioral psychology, which has had a tremendous influence on all areas of human services. Behavioral psychology applies theory and research findings to behavior change techniques in systematic, problem-solving procedures (Gmeinder & Kratochwill, 1998; Martens, 1993). It stresses the principles of learning in understanding how behavior is acquired and changed. Behavioral models of consultation are based on the idea that because most behavior is learned, it can be unlearned and new behavior can take its place. The result of consultation is some change in the consultee and/or the client system's behavior. Therefore, the principles of behavior change are combined with indirect service by the consultant to form the basis for consultation.

When the behavioral consultant uses principles of learning to help consultees bring about desired changes in themselves or their clients, these principles are translated into empirically validated behavioral techniques. Two key aspects of this type of consultation are a focus on *behavior change* and an extensive use of the *scientific method.*

Behavioral consultation can be used in a variety of settings, including mental health centers, schools, and other human service organizations. In addition to its wide applicability, behavioral consultation is one of the most frequently practiced forms of consultation (Kratochwill et al., 2002). It is, for example, the most frequently reported method for working with other professionals in school classroom management (Schottle & Peltier, 1996).

## HISTORICAL BACKGROUND

Behavioral consultation has its roots in behavior therapy: it developed out of experimental psychology, which encompasses not only operant and classical conditioning but also social, developmental, and cognitive psychology.

In the early 1900s, John Watson founded the behavioral school of psychology, which shunned covert events such as cognitions and restricted the parameters of psychology to observable behaviors only. As behaviorism became a strong force in experimental psychology, it was applied to the study of people's personal problems (Lutzker & Martin, 1981). Behaviorism strongly influenced operant conditioning, classical conditioning, modeling, behavioral ecology, and cognitive-behavior modification.

In the 1940s behaviorism became the dominant force in psychology under the guidance of Harvard psychologist B. F. Skinner. In developing the concept of operant conditioning, Skinner researched such principles of behavior change as reinforcement, punishment, and shaping, as well as their applications to humans (Skinner, 1953). From the 1950s through today, many behaviorists have applied learning theory in developing treatment techniques for a variety of personal problems.

Psychotherapists such as Wolpe, Lazarus, and Eysenck were pioneers in applying the Pavlovian model of classical conditioning to the treatment of human psychological disorders. Until the 1960s, behavior therapy was based primarily on the learning principles known as operant and classical conditioning. In the late 1960s Albert Bandura popularized modeling, a powerful social learning theory based on observation and imitation of certain behaviors (modeling) under conditions of reinforcement (Bandura, 1977). His views related to cognitive events as influencing human behavior set the stage for cognitive behavioral interventions.

In the 1970s and early 1980s, behavioral ecology (Willems, 1974) and systems theory (Morasky, 1982) began to receive attention. In behavioral ecology, people are considered a part of a multilayered ecological environment. The settings in which people behave are interactive, and a change in behavior for one setting could affect behavior in another setting. For example, the assertiveness behaviors a client learns in the workplace may produce different results when used in the home.

In the mid-1970s, the cognitive-behavioral therapy movement became popular. This movement asserts that what we think or say to ourselves can affect our behavior for better or worse, and there is a connection between what someone thinks and whether or not a personal problem is likely to develop.

Donald Meichenbaum (1977, 1985), a leader in this field, has shown that changing self-statements in an appropriate way can lead to desirable behavior change. For example, people who instruct themselves to cope with perceived stress are more likely to be able to manage it effectively than are people who engage in self-talk that expresses doubt in their ability to deal with stress.

The behavior therapy movement has grown to include nationwide societies such as the Association for the Advancement of Behavior Therapy. At the same time, this growth and expansion have produced such diversity that it is more accurate to speak of multiple behavior therapies rather than one, and consequently behavior therapy has become a difficult concept to define. The unifying factor underlying behavioral therapies is their derivation from experimentally established principles and procedures and the focus on the importance of learning and the careful assessment of behavior (Kazdin, 2001).

As the effectiveness of behavioral therapy became increasingly apparent, there occurred a parallel increase in requests from human service providers for assistance in the design and implementation of behavior change programs. The role of the behavioral therapist or counselor was therefore expanded to include that of behavioral consultant. Behavioral consultation was first practiced in organizations that require high levels of client control, such as state mental hospitals (Gallessich, 1985). As behavior therapy came to be used in a variety of settings, behavioral consultation was increasingly used in mental health centers, schools, and other human service organizations. Most of the consultation provided by behavioral consultants consists of casework; that is, the consultant helps a consultee apply behavioral principles to a specific problem so as to help a client or group of clients. Recently, there has been a movement to call behavioral consultation "problem-solving consultation" to reflect the increasing diversity of approaches that extend behavioral consultation (Kratochwill et al., 2002). Bergan's (1977) text was the first definitive expression of behavioral case consultation. Although this model tended to focus on interventions that relied on behavior modification, it has expanded to include interventions from diverse theoretical origins (Kratochwill, Elliott, & Callan-Stoiber, 2002). The influence of behavioral ecology and behavioral training models in the 1970s broadened the role of today's behavioral consultant to include behavioral system consultation and training in behavioral technology. Proponents of behavioral consultation tend to lead the way in designing and conducting research related to consultation with most of the focus being on school-based consultation. In fact, behavioral consultation has done much to establish consultation itself as a legitimate service for human service professionals. For an interesting description of the development of behavioral consultation as it relates to its use in the schools, consult Bergan (1995).

## BEHAVIORAL CONSULTATION DEFINED

Behavioral consultation "encompasses a wide variety of activities conducted in a broad range of settings with diverse populations" (Vernberg & Reppucci, 1986, p. 65). Because the conceptual framework that underlies behavioral consultation (behavior therapy) has become diffuse, behavioral consultation does not possess a central theory of consultation. According to Keller (1981), "behavioral consultation is based upon a theory of change that is derived from a broad-based social learning model encompassing diverse streams of psychological and social science research and theory" (p. 64). When all these factors are taken into consideration, defining behavioral consultation clearly becomes a difficult task.

In its broadest sense, behavioral consultation is a problem-solving process that has its foundation in behavioral theory (Kratochwill et al., 2002). According to Keller (1981), behavioral consultation involves a "relationship whereby services consistent with a behavioral orientation are provided to a client through the mediation of important others in that client's environment, that is, indirect service" (p. 65). Note that this actually defines behavioral case consultation because its major emphasis is on helping a consultee help a client. Keller's (1981) definition reflects a traditional classification scheme: mental health consultation focuses on the consultee so that the client will be helped; behavioral consultation focuses on the client so that the client can be helped; and organizational consultation focuses on helping the system so that the client system can function better.

Four characteristics typify behavioral consultation of any form (Kratochwill et al., 2002; Vernberg & Reppucci, 1986):

- the use of indirect service delivery models

- a reliance on behavioral technology principles to design, implement, and assess consultative interventions

- a diversity of intervention goals ranging from solving problematic situations to enhancing competence to empowering

- changes aimed at various targets (e.g., individuals, groups, organizations, and communities) in different settings (from single to multiple)

In effect, these characteristics broaden behavioral consultation from a case-oriented concept to one that includes the training and system forms of consultation.

Combining Keller's (1981) definition with ideas suggested by Vernberg and Reppucci (1986) produces the following definition of behavioral consultation that is still used today: a relationship whereby services consistent with a behavioral orientation are provided either indirectly to a client or a system (through the mediation of important others in the client's environment or of those charged with the system's well-being), or directly by training consultees to enhance their skills with clients or systems.

Such a definition is consistent with nine characteristics or assumptions that typify behavioral consultation and account for its uniqueness (Henning-Stout, 1993, pp. 25–26):

- All behaviors are learned.

- The establishment, maintenance, and change of social behavior can be explained through observation of functional interactions of the individual, his or her behavior, and the environment.

- Assessment, intervention, and evaluation of the intervention's effectiveness are directly linked.

- Behaviors of focus must be observable, measurable, and quantifiable.

- Environmental antecedents provide powerful points for initiating change.

- Because learning histories vary, intervention is necessarily idiosyncratic.

- Understanding and intervening with any behavior are guided and modified according to systematically collected data reflecting the frequency, intensity, or duration of that behavior.

- For one person's behavior to be changed, behaviors in other individuals interacting within the environment of focus must also be modified.

Recent additional characteristics include a problem-solving orientation, emphasis on a collegial relationship, and a focus on a structured interview process (Bergan & Kratochwill, 1990; Sheridan, Kratochwill, & Bergan, 1996). For example, emphasis on the collegial relationship focuses on the idea that the behavioral consultant is a content expert and the consultee is an expert on the situation at hand. These characteristics and assumptions reflect behavioral consultation's emphasis on quantification and measurement, as well as its perspective regarding how behavior is learned and changed.

All three forms of behavioral consultation tend to follow a set problem-solving sequence (Kratochwill, Elliott, & Callan-Stoiber, 2002):

1. description of the problem in behavioral terms
2. a functional analysis of the problem's antecedents and consequences
3. selection of a target behavior(s)
4. generation of behavioral objectives
5. design and implementation of a behavior change plan
6. evaluation of the process.

It might occur to some that the behavioral technology training form of consultation does not fit this sequence perfectly. In this form of consultation, the implementation step of the sequence consists of the training sessions. (Steps 1 through 4 will already have been accomplished prior to the training.)

## KEY CONCEPTS OF BEHAVIORAL CONSULTATION

Next we'll discuss the following key concepts of behavioral consultation: its scientific view of behavior, its emphasis on current influences on behavior, and the principles of behavior change. An understanding of these key concepts will help clarify why behavioral consultation proceeds as it does.

### Scientific View of Behavior

Behavioral consultation, like the behavior therapy that spawned it, is grounded in a scientific view of human behavior which implies the use of a systematic and structured approach to the delivery of human services such as consultation. Because knowledge obtained from empirical research is valued so highly by behavioral consultants, such research is subjected to scientific validation, or in other words is put to the scientific test. Such evaluation and subsequent validation are essential to the advancement of behavioral consultation beyond its current state of practice (Vernberg & Reppucci, 1986). The emphasis on scientific investigation also leads behavioral consultants to use empirically validated consultation interventions because they believe that such methods increase the likelihood that consultation will be successful (Bergan & Kratochwill, 1990).

## Emphasis on Current Influences on Behavior

Behavioral consultation focuses on current behavior as well (Kazdin, 2001). For the most part, behavioral consultation takes the position that because certain current behaviors constitute the problem in a particular situation, behavioral consultation should focus on those behaviors. Behavioral consultation, as Bergan notes, "defines problems presented in consultation as being outside the skin of the client" (1977, p. 26). It is the description of behavior, not the description of a person, which is essential (Gresham et al., 2001). Thus, by the standards of behavioral consultation it is better to describe a client's hitting behavior in terms of its environmental antecedents and consequences than to describe the client as aggressive.

By focusing on current behaviors, behavioral consultation is better able to discriminate between existing and desired behavior (Bergan & Kratochwill, 1990). Such discrimination allows for defining the goals of consultation in behavioral terms. The consultant and consultee can mutually determine what behaviors currently exist and what alternative behaviors are desired; they then set behavioral goals, which create the conditions for more rigorous evaluation of the effects of consultation. Past behavior is viewed as important only to the degree that it assists in present interventions. As a result, behavioral consultants do little to help consultees or the consultees' clients gain insight into their problems or concerns. Rather, they concentrate on directive and active treatment of current behavior (Kazdin, 2001).

## Principles of Behavior Change

Behavioral consultation assumes that behavior is lawful (that is, orderly, following a set of rules)

and that changing the consequences of behavior by using the principles of learning produces a change in behavior (Kazdin, 2001). The consultant helps the consultee select these principles for use in the problem-solving process (Bergan & Kratochwill, 1990).

Behavior consultants use such principles as reinforcement, punishment, extinction, shaping, and modeling in the behavior change process. The consultant uses these principles to examine and understand the client's behavior, to examine the consultee's behavior, and to determine how to proceed with the course of consultation (Bergan & Kratochwill, 1990). These principles can also be used by consultees in their own work with clients.

There has been a trend to use *social learning theory* to integrate different learning paradigms. Social learning theory uses various learning models to explain behavior while emphasizing the context of events, human social development, and internal perceptions of events. Social learning theory's major contribution is its recognition of multiple influences (such as cognitions and the environment) on behavior while at the same time offering a framework for explaining behavior (Kazdin, 2001). For an excellent, detailed introduction to the principles of behavior, consult Kanfer and Goldstein's *Helping People Change* (1991) or Kazdin's *Behavior Modification in Applied Settings* (2001). Table 10.1 illustrates common techniques based on the principles of behavior change.

## THE CONSULTATION PROCESS

Behavioral consultation can take three forms: behavioral case consultation, behavioral technology training, and behavioral system consultation. All three forms have the following characteristics: indirect service to the client system, use of behavioral technology principles throughout the consultation process, a problem-solving orientation, and empirical validation of interventions (Vernberg & Reppucci, 1986).

**T A B L E  10.1     Common Behavioral Methods**

| METHOD | PROCESS |
|---|---|
| Positive reinforcement | To increase the occurrence of desirable behavior, the application of positive conditions (praise, attention, privilege, tokens) if the subject's performance warrants it |
| Negative reinforcement | The removal of an aversive condition if the subject engages in desirable behavior |
| Punishment | To decrease the occurrence of undesirable behavior, the application of aversive conditions depending on the subject's performance |
| Extinction | Eliminating an undesirable behavior by terminating the conditions that reinforce the subject's performance |
| Ignoring | Eliminating the subject's undesirable behavior through inattention to it |
| Shaping | Changing the subject's undesirable behavior through the positive reinforcement of successive approximations of the desirable behavior |
| Differential reinforcement | Increasing the subject's performance of desirable behaviors through the selective reinforcement of desirable behaviors and ignoring the undesirable behaviors |
| Environmental cues | Environmental stimuli that prompt the subject's behavior |
| Inadvertent reinforcement | Inadvertently or unintentionally reinforcing the subject's behavior by creating conditions that have an effect opposite of that anticipated |
| Contingency contracting | The process of formalizing an agreement that specifies the behavioral conditions or plans associated with behavioral change |
| Behavioral rehearsal | An educational learning process in which subjects practice new, adaptive behavior in a controlled setting |

Next we'll examine each of the three forms of behavioral consultation in terms of goals, the consultant's function and role, the consultee's experience in consultation, and the use of consultation techniques and procedures.

## Behavioral Case Consultation

In *behavioral case consultation* a consultant provides direct, behavior-based service to a consultee concerning the management of a client or group of clients. Behavioral consultation requires an effective analysis of the problem and related intervention and an effective implementation of the intervention (Noell & Witt, 1998). Most case approaches to behavioral consultation (e.g., Bergan & Kratochwill, 1990) still rely heavily on operant conditioning. However, more recent models use a variety of

models such as the social learning theory developed by Bandura (1977). By far the most comprehensive approach to behavioral case consultation is that of Bergan and Kratochwill (1990); indeed, most other models are basic variations of Bergan's original model (1977).

Behavioral case consultation consists of a series of four stages that provide form and focus to the problem solving engaged in by the consultant and consultee (Kratochwill, Elliott, & Callan-Stoiber, 2002). These four stages deal with identifying the problem, analyzing it, implementing a treatment, and evaluating the treatment. According to Elliott and Busse, the challenge of behavioral consultation is to "select treatment strategies from a pool of potentially effective strategies that can be . . . managed by people who have not had specific training in behavioral change methods" (1993, p. 180).

As Sheridan notes: "Compared to other forms of consultation, behavioral consultation is characterized by (a) the use of a standard four-stage problem-solving process, (b) adherence to behavioral assessment, (c) reliance on behavioral intervention strategies, and (d) evaluation of outcomes based upon behavioral analysis and related methodologies" (200, p. 344). In a nutshell, this model consists of identifying the problem, analyzing it, intervening to treat the problem and evaluating the treatment—all from a behavioral context.

**Consultation Goals.** In behavioral case consultation, the consultee presents a work-related concern with a client to the consultant, who uses his or her expertise in the principles of learning to *manage the consultee's management of the case;* that is, to help the consultee make positive changes in the client's environment (Feld et al., 1987) and therefore in the client's behavior. Recently, some authorities on behavioral consultation (e.g., Bergan & Kratochwill, 1990) have suggested that a second, complementary goal is to effect change in the consultee.

**Consultant Function and Roles.** Behavioral consultants use a systematic problem-solving process to assist consultees with their clients (Bergan & Kratochwill, 1990). Behavioral consultants frequently act as experts to ensure that the stages of problem identification, problem analysis, plan implementation, and problem evaluation occur and are adequately accomplished.

Although the consultant is called on to provide expertise, most behavioral consultants take a collaborative approach to the consultation relationship. Even though the content and process of consultation are under the consultant's control, the consultee is encouraged to become involved in content- and process-related decision making to the degree his or her knowledge and skill in the behavioral approach permit. That said, the behavioral consultant is typically more in control of the relationship than a consultant coming from a mental health perspective. The consultant helps the consultee determine the best course of action in the case and suggests an array of choices from which he or she can choose. Because

the consultee is the primary instrument of change in the client, the consultant avoids dictating the consultee's behavior.

The consultant provides knowledge concerning those principles of learning pertinent to the case and whatever knowledge is needed to help the consultee accomplish each of the consultation stages. In some cases, the consultant must train the consultee in the use of strategies based on principles of learning. However, Bergan's model does not emphasize consultee training to a great degree. To ensure that the stages of consultation occur and are successfully accomplished, the consultant guides the consultee's behavior through the use of selected types of verbalizations.

Thus, the consultant makes sure that problem identification occurs, but the consultee controls its process. The consultant must inform the consultee about the use of this form of management at the outset of consultation and be satisfied that he or she is seeking services voluntarily. Management of the consultation process by using verbal skills in structuring the consultant–consultee interaction is therefore the major task of the consultant.

*Verbal Interaction Techniques.* Because consultation can be reduced to a series of verbal interactions between the consultant and the consultee, these interactions must not be left to chance (Bergan & Kratochwill, 1990). The consultant controls not only his or her own verbalizations, but also those of the consultee. There is some evidence that consultant verbalizations are related to successful consultation outcomes (Busse, Kratochwill, & Elliott, 1999). There is some empirical support that the content of the consultee's responses tends to match that of the consultant's questions, thus providing the consultant with a tremendous amount of influence in controlling all aspects of the consultation process (Turco & Skinner, 1991).

There is also some evidence to suggest that consultants with high dominance scores on personality inventories are perceived as more effective by consultees (Erchul et al., 1999). The consultant does not attempt to control the specific content of the consultee's verbalizations during consultation, but rather attempts to encourage him or her to produce the various type of verbalizations needed to achieve the task at hand in the consultation process.

Bergan produced a classification system to assist consultants in controlling the verbalizations in consultation (see Table 10.2). Verbal interchanges can be classified in terms of message source, content, process, and control. Judicious use of this classification system can enable the consultant to successfully guide the consultee through the consultation process.

*Message Source.*   The message source simply indicates whether the verbalization comes from the consultant or the consultee.

*Message Content.*   Message content refers to what the consultant and the consultee discuss. The consultant usually controls the content of verbalizations in consultation, which includes seven subcategories: background/environment, behavior setting, behavior, individual characteristics, observation, plan, and other. The verbalizations that occur in behavioral case consultation are to be controlled by the consultant because what is talked about in consultation directly relates to the course and degree of success of the consultation. By determining what to discuss and when, the consultant can help the consultee work with the client more efficiently and effectively.

*The background/environment* content consists of verbalizations that concern historical factors or current environmental factors related to the behavior under discussion and might affect the client's behavior. For example, if the major focus of consultation is the client's adjustment at work, a consultant might ask for information on a client's home life or for a developmental history of the client's problem. *Behavior-setting* verbalizations, which are among the most frequently used by behavioral consultants, are used to analyze the client's behavior so that appropriate plans to change that behavior can be made. These verbalizations concern the antecedent, consequent, and sequential conditions in the immediate environment that affect the client's behavior. Antecedent conditions occur just before the behaviors under discussion, so the consultant might ask the consultee to describe exactly what happens just before the client's behavior occurs. Consequent conditions occur just after and may reinforce the behavior in question; they reflect the patterns of antecedents and consequences or the timing of the client's behavior. For example, sequential conditions can become clear when the consultant asks about the events leading up to the client's behavior, when and how frequently the behavior tends to occur, and any special conditions that may be pertinent.

*Behavior* verbalizations allow precise specification of client behaviors so that they can be measured and discussed. Such verbalizations can also help identify which environmental factors affecting the client's behavior should be investigated. Verbalizations of

**T A B L E  10.2     Classification of Verbal Interchanges**

| MESSAGE SOURCE | MESSAGE CONTENT | MESSAGE PROCESS | MESSAGE CONTROL |
| --- | --- | --- | --- |
| Consultant | Background/Environment | Specification | Elicitor |
| Consultee | Behavior-setting | Evaluation | Emitter |
| | Behavior | Inference | |
| | Individual characteristics | Summarization | |
| | Observation | Validation | |
| | Plan | | |
| | Other | | |

this type include descriptions of the client's thoughts, feelings, overt behaviors, and their intensity, as well as discussions of written records concerning the client's behavior (for example, baseline behavior graphs). As an example, the consultant and consultee might discuss a client's written autobiographical statement, or the consultant might ask the consultee to describe as specifically as possible what happens when the client engages in a problem behavior.

The *individual characteristics* of verbalizations describe the unique features or traits of the client. They can help determine what is unique about the client and how that uniqueness is related to the client's problem. Consultant–consultee discussion of clients' attributes and traits can range from basic matters like age and weight to more complex personality characteristics and handicaps. For example, the consultant and the consultee might discuss the age, weight, and shyness of a teenage boy as it relates to his being the "class clown."

Often the consultant–consultee interaction produces a decision to obtain more information or data about the client's behavior. Verbalizations in this *observation* subcategory are related to documenting client behaviors. For example, a consultee might determine that data should be collected to compare the number of negative self-references a client makes in group therapy with those made during individual therapy. In another example, a consultant might help a consultee determine the best way to record observations of a client's behavior.

The *plan* subcategory is broad and consists of those verbalizations related to attempts to solve the consultee's problems. Planning in this context typically refers either to general strategies for the consultee to consider or the tactics for intervening with some specific strategy. However, any verbalization about a plan—how it should be implemented, how it should be evaluated, or how well it worked—falls under this category. For example, the consultant and consultee might plan a strategy called a "token economy system" to help a child stay on task when doing schoolwork, or discuss how well such a plan worked.

No classification can be fully comprehensive and concise, and in fact consultants and consultees make many other kinds of verbalizations during consultation. Therefore, a catchall subcategory, *other* verbalizations, is used for those not appropriate to the other six subcategories. For example, the consultant and consultee might "talk about the weather" or make statements only indirectly related to client behavior or to the consultation process.

*Message Process.*   Consultants control not only the things that are talked about, but also the way in which they are discussed—the message process, in other words. Consultant–consultee verbal exchanges can be categorized by type of verbal process. As noted by Bergan (1977), "the message-process category classifies verbal messages in accordance with the kinds of speaker actions they describe vis-à-vis the content of conversation" (p. 38). Process, then, refers to the type of verbal action conveyed in a message. The five message-process subcategories are specification, evaluation, inference, summarization, and validation.

*Specification verbalizations* ask for some detail or description concerning one of the content subcategories. Information about some behavior's background, setting, nature, or occurrence could be specified. This subcategory is used when more precision or detail is needed to assist the consultee. For example, a consultant might ask a consultee to specify exactly how an intervention will be implemented or to describe the consequences of a given client behavior.

*Evaluation verbalizations* involve some sort of value judgment or reveal emotions and attitudes about a topic. For example, a consultee might judge a plan to be ineffective, or a consultant might praise the consultee's behavior in implementing a selected strategy.

*Inference verbalizations* concern making and playing "hunches" as compared with acting on known fact. Such verbalizations are frequently used to predict the effects of certain interventions on the client's behavior or to demonstrate the set of assumptions under which the consultant and consultee are acting. For example, a consultant might think or feel a certain plan will be effective and might tell this to a consultee, or a consultee might surmise that a client is acting out because of some kind of inappropriate child-rearing practice.

*Summarization verbalizations* are reviews or summaries of previously discussed information that can help the consultant and consultee remember what has been discussed previously, keep them focused on the task at hand, and provide a review of what has been agreed on. For example, a consultant might review what has been accomplished during a given consultation interview or ask a consultee to review his or her perceptions of the client's problems.

*Validation verbalizations* give or ask for a yes-or-no response concerning the facts at hand and are used primarily to develop and maintain consensus between the consultant and consultee concerning each stage in the consultation process. They can be used at any time to make sure that the consultant and consultee are on the same "wavelength." For example, a consultee might review some implementation strategy and ask the consultant if he or she agrees on it, or a consultant might ask if there is agreement on the kind of observation that needs to be performed on a client's behavior. There is some evidence that the use of validating statements by the consultant early on in the consultation relationship may encourage consultees to move prematurely through the consultation process (Martens et al., 1989).

Thus, there are five message processes that can describe what is occurring in each of the content subcategories. Consider the content subcategory "plan." By using each of the processes, the plan could be specified, evaluated, inferred about, summarized, or validated. The consultant, then, should know not only what to talk about, but the way in which it should be talked about.

*Message Control.* The consultant is charged with guiding the consultee through a successful consultation experience and must control the consultee's verbal behavior to do so. To this end, the consultant must determine not only what (content) and how things are to be discussed (process), but also who is going to talk about them (control). In effect, the consultant uses message control to either give input or to get input from the consultee. (The consultee can also use message control for the same purpose.) In message control behavior, the speaker's verbiage is classified in terms of whether or not it will have a direct effect on the receiver's response.

If a direct verbal response is intended (and is thus considered controlling), the message is called an *elicitor*. If the message is not intended to obtain a direct response (and thus does not control the receiver's response), it is termed an *emitter*. Elicitors usually take the form of either direct or indirect questions that ask the consultee to engage in specification, evaluation, inference, summarization, or validation in one of the message content subcategories. The consultant could ask the consultee to use a verbal process about the conditions affecting the client's behavior, the behavior itself, related observations, or pertinent plans. There is some evidence that specificity when questioning consultees is related to the effectiveness of consultation (Bergan & Kratochwill, 1990). Four examples of elicitors and their classifications in terms of content and process follow:

- A consultant asks a consultee to describe the most problematic situation about the client's behavior (behavior-specification).

- A consultant asks a consultee to validate a plan that is to be implemented (plan-validation).

- A consultant asks a consultee how he or she feels about making a series of observations of a client's behavior (observation-evaluation).

- A consultant asks a consultee for some hunches on why the client is acting in a certain way (background/environment-inference).

An emitter does not call for a reaction from the listener. When consultants use emitters, they provide both content and process information to consultees without attempting to control the consultee's response. Emitters usually take the form of declarative statements. Consider the following examples of emitters and their classifications according to content and process:

- A consultant summarizes the individual characteristics of a client for the consultee (individual characteristics-summarization).

- A consultant summarizes for the consultee some plan they have agreed to use to help the client (plan-summarization).

- A consultant makes a statement agreeing with the consultee regarding the consequences of a given client behavior (behavior setting-validation).

- A consultant shares hunches with the consultee about suspected traits and habits that the client might have (individual characteristics-inference).

In summary, the behavioral consultant controls the verbal communication in consultation so as to help the consultee use the consultation process with maximum effectiveness and efficiency by controlling who should talk, what should be discussed, and how the discussion should proceed.

**Consultee Experience in Consultation.** The consultee is expected to work with the consultant toward the successful completion of the consultation process and be actively involved in the problem-solving process (Martens, 1993). As in other forms of case consultation, such as Caplan's (1970) client-centered case consultation, the consultee is a link between the consultant and the client and functions as a professional collaborator. The consultee's four primary duties in the consultation process are to specify or describe, evaluate or decide, provide direct services to the client, and supervise the client's actions. The consultee should describe as specifically as possible the details of the case and the nature of the work-related problem. The consultee should respond to the consultant's prompts and probes as accurately as possible and provide him or her with the most comprehensive, detailed picture of the work-related concern possible. The consultee's role as evaluator or decision maker reflects the peer nature of all consultation: the consultant may make a recommendation concerning a case, but it is the consultee's task to determine what to do with that recommendation. Bergan (1977) relates an example of this consultee role in noting that the consultant might help the consultee select a method for measuring client behavior, but the consultee would have to evaluate that measurement's effectiveness in achieving desired outcomes. Of course, a primary role of the

consultee is to continue to work with the client. Such work can include performing a particular care-giving role relative to the client (e.g., teacher to student or counselor to client) and collecting data regarding the client's behavior. Frequently, the consultee's work with the client will be adaptations of the consultant's recommendations. A critical part of the consultee's work with the client involves the client in the selection of the goals and processes of consultation; this is frequently accomplished by having the consultee discuss with the client what the consultant and consultee are considering in regards to the client.

A final (and relatively rare) consultee role is that of supervisor, such as when a consultee is a teacher and the client is a student under that teacher's responsibility. However, the consultee may also supervise the involvement of other people working on the client's treatment. For example, a teacher who is a consultee may supervise a teacher's aide who is collecting baseline data on a student's (the client's) behavior.

**Application: Consultant Techniques and Procedures.** Both types of behavioral case consultation—developmental and problem centered—concern changes in client behavior (Bergan, 1977). Developmental consultation deals with more-or-less long-term behavior change, whereas problem-centered consultation deals with problems that call for immediate attention (for example, crises). Most of the literature on behavioral case consultation refers to developmental consultation because it is by far the more extensively used, and thus our discussion of behavioral case consultation will be limited to developmental consultation.

According to Bergan and Kratochwill (1990), there are four stages to the behavioral consultation process. The first stage consists of the *Problem Identification Interview* (PII) during which the consultant focuses on "the specification of a problem by emphasizing the selection and definition of a target behavior and by the determination of baseline data collection procedures" (Kratochwill, Elliott, & Busse, 1995, p. 87). Problem analysis and plan implementation are dealt with through the *Problem*

*Analysis Interview* (PAI). The objectives of this interview are to "validate the problem through examination of baseline data, analyze the problem and related variable . . . and develop an intervention plan" (Kratochwill, Elliott, & Busse, 1995, p. 88).

The third stage, plan implementation, involves selecting and implementing an intervention (Kratochwill, Elliott, & Callan-Stoiber, 2002). The consultant is "on call" as the consultee implements the plan. The fourth stage of consultation, plan evaluation, is accomplished through the *Treatment Evaluation Interview* (TEI) during which the consultant and consultee assess the degree of success in meeting the plan's goals. There are typically three to four sessions between the consultant and the consultee in this model.

*Problem Identification Stage.*   This stage provides the momentum for the entire consultation process (Kratochwill et al., 1995). The term *problem identification* sounds quite simple, but from a behavioral perspective, defining the problem can be a complex and difficult matter. This stage is crucial; what occurs here will determine the direction that consultation takes and affects whether or not consultation will be successful (Kratochwill et al., 2002). In fact, this stage is considered the most critical because its outcome is the formulation and implementation of a plan (Kratochwill et al., 1995). Bergan and Tombari (1976) found years ago that if the problem identification stage was not successfully completed, the entire consultation process might be irreversibly damaged.

During the problem identification process, the consultant helps the consultee accomplish the following steps:

- Designate the general and specific client performance goals to be achieved in consultation.

- Determine how to measure the designated goals.

- Assess current client performance in terms of the designated goals.

- Examine the results of the assessment.

- Discern the discrepancies between current and desired client performance.

These steps are accomplished by two consultant-led interviews, the first being a problem identification interview in which Steps 1 and 2 are accomplished. Step 3 is accomplished by the consultee. The second is a follow-up interview in which Steps 4 and 5 are accomplished. The problem identification stage ends once the discrepancy between current and desired client behavior has been specified (Bergan & Kratochwill, 1990).

In the problem identification stage, the consultant uses more elicitors than emitters—more specifications, validations, and summarizations than inferences and evaluations—and more verbalizations in the behavior, behavior setting, and observation categories than in other content categories.

When successfully accomplished, the problem identification stage results in a well-specified problem defined by the discrepancy between current performance (as measured by collected data, including baseline data) and desired performance (as indicated by stated goals) (Kratochwill et al., 2002). Successful problem identification sets the stage for problem analysis.

*Problem Analysis Stage.*   In this stage, the consultant determines the conditions that maintain the client's problem behavior and formulates a plan to alleviate that behavior. The consultant jointly pursues these two tasks with the consultee.

This stage can thus be divided into two phases that contain a total of five steps:

*Phase One: Problem Analysis*

1.   Choose a procedure for analyzing the problem.

2.   Conduct a conditions and/or skills analysis.

*Phase Two: Plan Formulation*

3.   Develop plan strategies.

4.   Develop plan tactics.

5.   Establish procedures for assessing the plan's effectiveness.

These steps are accomplished by means of one or more interviews, during which the client's problem behavior is examined from one of two perspectives: internal and external conditions related to the behavior, or a skills deficit in the client. The consultant and consultee must first decide whether to conduct an analysis of the conditions surrounding the behavior, the skills of the client, or both.

Bergan and Kratochwill (1990) suggest that a conditions analysis be performed if the problem behavior tends to be variable over conditions; if the problem behavior remains constant over conditions, then a skills analysis is recommended, as in the case when increased self-direction on the part of the client is desired. Once the consultant and consultee decide on which type of analysis to perform, Step 1 is accomplished.

In Step 2, conducting an analysis of the problem, the consultant and consultee work together to determine what conditions and/or skills need to be changed to resolve the client's problem successfully.

Consultation next enters Step 3, developing plan strategies, during which a systematic course of action to use with the client is developed. The consultant usually starts out by suggesting a broad strategy that seems promising based on the conditions or skills analysis performed earlier. In general, the consultant and consultee determine which principles of learning should be used and convert them into strategies to help the client. For example, a consultant might suggest using positive reinforcement as a strategy to change the client's behavior, but allow the consultee flexibility in its use.

In Step 4, the consultant and consultee consider the tactics involved in implementing the strategy, and in Step 5 they establish procedures for determining the plan's effectiveness. If a conditions analysis was performed, then those same techniques are used for assessment purposes. If a skills analysis was performed, then methods for measuring skill acquisition need to be used. Bergan and Kratochwill (1990) suggest that items used in the skills analysis should be adapted to measure skill acquisition. Once assessment procedures have been established, consultation moves to the plan implementation stage. The bottom line is that the consultant and

consultee develop a plan that is acceptable both objectively (i.e., empirically sound) and subjectively (i.e., mutually acceptable) (Sheridan, Kratochwill, & Bergan, 1996).

In the problem analysis stage, as in the earlier problem identification stage, the consultant uses more elicitors than emitters and more specifications, validations, and summarizations than inferences and evaluations. Whereas the problem identification stage has a balance of verbalizations in the behavior, behavior-setting, and observation subcategories, the problem analysis stage has a balance of verbalizations in the behavior, behavior-setting, and plan subcategories. The problem analysis stage builds naturally on the problem identification stage (Kratochwill, Elliott & Carrington Rotto, 1995; Kratochwill, Elliott, & Callan-Stoiber, 2002).

*Plan Implementation Stage.* The result of successful problem analysis is a plan designed to assist the client system. In this stage, what was planned during the problem analysis stage is put into effect. Good planning does not necessarily lead to good implementation, and thus the consultant's task is to ensure adequate implementation. To this end, the consultant guides the consultee in accomplishing two steps of this stage: preparing for and carrying out the implementation. This stage is different from the previous two stages in that there is no formal interview between the consultant and the consultee.

In preparing for plan implementation, roles related to the implementation are assigned, required materials are gathered, and skills necessary for implementation are affirmed. The consultee generally takes the roles of the plan implementation director, plan executor, and observer of client behavior. The consultant is responsible for determining the need for training and providing it to the consultee (or a designee of the consultee) so they can adequately perform these roles. Training can be very time consuming, so any plans should take the strengths of consultees into consideration (Kratochwill, Elliott, & Callan-Stoiber, 2002). Often, the consultant trains the consultee in techniques like those in Table 10.1. Once the appropriate roles have been assigned and arrangements for use of materials made, the consultant and consultee implement the plan, during which the consultee attempts to help the client with the consultant's guidance. Plans should be time efficient, have few restrictions, and carry a low level of risk to the client system (Kratochwill, Elliott, & Busse, 1995). The consultant is available to assist with any revisions to the plan that become necessary as the implementation proceeds.

*Treatment Evaluation Stage.*   Behavioral case consultation stresses evaluation of consultation more than any other model of consultation. Considerable time is spent evaluating the goals of consultation and the effectiveness of the plan, which determines what happens next in the consultation process.

The problem evaluation stage has three steps: evaluating goal attainment, evaluating plan effectiveness, and postimplementation planning (Bergan & Kratochwill, 1990). In reality, plan evaluation is often not as rigorous as that used in research, but nonetheless there needs to be adequate support to verify outcomes. For example, outcome criteria should involve measures of the degree to which desired behaviors were demonstrated over time, such as with single case study designs (Kratochwill, Elliott, & Busse, 1995).

Goal attainment is assessed by determining whether the client's behavior change adequately meets previously set standards. Recall that the problem was defined in terms of a discrepancy between current and desired levels of behavior. In evaluation, the degree to which desired and observed behaviors coincide is judged in order to determine whether the goals of consultation have been met. There are three possibilities in terms of goal attainment: no progress, some progress, and accomplishment. If there has been no progress, the consultant typically suggests a return to the problem analysis stage, or perhaps to the goal identification step within the problem identification stage. In some situations, consultation may be terminated and replaced by another type of service. If there is some progress in goal attainment, the consultant usually suggests a return to the problem analysis stage. On occasion, the consultant might suggest a return to

the problem identification stage to reexamine goals; on rare occasions, he or she might recommend termination. If the goals have been accomplished, the consultant and consultee then proceed to evaluate the plan's effectiveness.

Behavioral consultants believe that even though the goals of consultation have been achieved, an appropriate design must be used in evaluating the plan so as to demonstrate that the plan was indeed responsible for the success of consultation. Plan evaluation has no direct bearing on the case, but it can be used in solving similar concerns in the future. Plan effectiveness is determined by applying an appropriate evaluation design that states when client behaviors are to be measured and when plan implementations are made relative to those measurements. (Interested readers should consult Bergan and Kratochwill (1990) for a discussion on evaluation design; a detailed discussion of this subject is beyond the scope of this book.)

Step 3 in problem evaluation is postimplementation planning. The consultant and consultee design a plan for use after consultation has formally been terminated. Such a plan prevents the problem from recurring and provides a way for the consultee to reestablish contact should the problem behavior return to undesirable levels. Sometimes this plan is left intact and maintained, especially when it is relatively easy to implement and when there is some likelihood that the client's behavior would return were the plan eliminated.

The implementation of a new plan often occurs when it is determined that it is equally effective as, but more convenient than, the first plan. Moving from tangible to non-tangible reinforcers is a common example of this type of strategy. Finally, a program can be removed once it has been determined that it is no longer needed to maintain the performance levels desired of the client. Whatever the postimplementation plan, behavioral consultants suggest that consultees continue to monitor client behavior for some period of time.

When the goals of consultation and the implementation plan have been evaluated and postimplementation plans made, consultation is terminated. During this stage, the consultant uses a balance of elicitors and emitters; more specifications, summarizations, validations, and inferences (instead of evaluations); and more verbalizations in the behavior, plan, and observation subcategories. On occasion, the consultant may want to formally communicate the results of an intervention program to a consultee. Figure 10.1 illustrates the format for such a report.

**An Example of Behavioral Case Consultation.**
A counselor working as a mental health consultant assists a family therapist with a family. The consultant has expertise concerning runaway youths. Two of the family's three teenagers have run away. The family therapist wants to consult with the counselor before using certain interventions with the family.

Together, the consultant and consultee define what is meant by "running away" behavior. They functionally analyze the behavior in terms of what occurs before and after its occurrence, and then devise a plan based on rewarding responsible behavior. The consultee then implements the strategy with the family and evaluates it at its conclusion.

## Behavioral Technology Training

This approach to behavioral consultation is used when consultees seek to increase general usage of behavioral technology principles when working with clients. Consultees tend to be professionals such as teachers or parents (Kratochwill and Pittman, 2002). Consultants train consultees in general behavioral principles or specific behavioral technology skills (Bergan & Kratochwill, 1990; Watson & Robinson, 1996) or both (Elliott & Busse, 1993; Vernberg & Reppucci, 1986). For example, Kratochwill and Pittman note: "One common format for technology training is teacher skill development that focuses on teaching specific information such as assessment techniques, discipline or child management tactics, the process of consultation, or a combination" (2002, p. 79). Technology training with parents can also cover a broad array of topics. Behavioral technology training can be formal or informal and be given to individuals (e.g., in training a therapist to perform

systematic desensitization) or groups (e.g., in training special education teachers in token economy procedures). The education/training model of consultation discussed in Chapter 11 is similar to the process involved in behavioral technology training.

Behavioral technology training has several justifications for its existence (Watson & Robinson, 1996). Consultees who use behavioral technology are frequently successful. An understanding of behavioral technology increases the likelihood that behavioral programs will be implemented appropriately. Consultees who understand behavioral technology are likely to generalize it to new situations and thus enhance other aspects of their lives. Behavioral technology is also cost effective and efficient.

The goal of behavioral technology training is increased consultee competence in the use of general and/or specific behavioral technology procedures. The consultant functions as a resource person and trainer. The consultee is a trainee expected to apply learned procedures with appropriate work-related concerns. As is the case in most types of education/training consultation, the steps involved are conducting a needs assessment, planning the training, performing it, and evaluating it. Behavioral technology training usually consists of behavior modification procedures and, more recently, a variety of other behaviorally derived methods. It has been provided to a variety of human service professions, especially schoolteachers. It has also been used with a variety of nonprofessional caretaking roles such as parenting and paraprofessional services in human service settings. There is strong empirical evidence that behavioral technology training of consultees leads to improved client behavior (Vernberg & Reppucci, 1986).

Problems encountered in evaluation of behavioral technology training revolve around whether it is generalized to settings beyond the training and whether consultees continue to use the results of training in intended environments (Elliott & Busse, 1993). Consultants who use behavioral technology training must decide what form of this training is best for which type of consultee and under what conditions. Behavioral technology training can be

I. Background Information
   A. Demographic Information on the Child
   B. Ecological Context of the Problem

II. Problem Definition
   A. Referral Problem
   B. Target Behavior
   C. Desired Outcome Behaviors
   D. Critical Setting/Situations for Change
   E. Preliminary Functional Analysis

III. Problem Analysis
   A. Description of Assessment or Data Recording Procedures
   B. Rationale for Use of Data Collection Procedures
   C. Presentation and Discussion of Data

IV. Intervention Plan
   A. Basic Design
   B. Contingencies
   C. Criterion for Contingencies
   D. Acceptability of Interventions to Teacher/Parent and Child
   E. Personnel Involved in Intervention Implementation
   F. Setting and Time
   G. Resources
   H. Procedures for Promoting New Behaviors
   I. Procedures for Increasing Existing Behaviors
   J. Procedures for Reducing Interfering Problem Behaviors
   K. Procedures for Facilitating Generalizations
   L. Treatment Integrity Checks

V. Plan Evaluation
   A. Change in Behavior via Direct Observation
   B. Change in Teacher/Parent Performance Ratings
   C. Mainstreamed Peer Comparison
   D. Outcome Interview with Significant Adults
   E. Intervention Side Effects

VI. Summary and Recommendations
   A. Summary and Results Obtained
   B. Discussion of Effectiveness
   C. Suggestions for Increasing Program Effectiveness
   D. Suggestions for Future Follow-Up

**FIGURE 10.1** Outline for writing a behavioral consultation case report

SOURCE: From Kratochwill, T. R., Elliott, S. N., and P. Carrington Rotto (1995). Best practices in school-based behavioral consultation. In A. Thomas and J. Grimes (Eds.), *Best practices in school psychology* (3rd ed., pp. 519–537). Washington, DC: National Association of School of Psychologists. Copyright 1995 by the National Association of School Psychologists. Reprinted with permission.

a particularly important intervention in the schools, though some authors (e.g., see Rosenfield, 2002a) suggest that teachers tend not to use its interventions in the classroom, or, if they do, they give up on them early before the desired outcomes have developed. This happens because (1) teachers using behavioral technology are responsible for solutions to the problem, though not for the child's problem, (2) teachers' working knowledge of behavioral technology is limited, and (3) the underlying assumptions of behavioral technology may be at odds with teachers' explanations of human conduct. Rosenfield (1985) cites an example in which an elementary school teacher gave up on a successful classroom management project agreed to in consultation because her aide didn't like it.

**Implications for Consultants.**  Rosenfield (1985) has made some suggestions for consultants regarding behavioral technology training. They should be seen as resources for classroom practice and need to encourage teachers to be resource persons among themselves. Teachers should be encouraged to use techniques that allow them to put some of themselves into the implementation. It is very important that they understand the underlying assumptions of behavioral technology since they frequently modify the consultant's suggestions and must do so constructively. Consultants need to be available to teachers since some research suggests that teachers turn to resources that are convenient. Other research suggests that teachers are not well trained in behavioral interventions as they relate to instruction (Crone et al., 2007).

Because the language of behavior modification can cause a clash of values, consultants need to choose meaningful and acceptable words in behavioral technology training. Time should be provided at the outset of training for discussion and experiential learning related to values regarding behavioral technology.

Teachers need to be in control of the use of behavioral technology and see interventions as congruent with their values. Consultants need to actively promote their suggestions rather than thinking teachers will use them only because they think they will

work. Behavioral consultants are advised to develop behavioral technology training with the consultee's frame of reference in mind. When working with teachers, the consultant should plan the training to accommodate their daily classroom routine incorporate behavioral technology training (via direct instructional methods) into traditional behavioral consultation (Watson & Robinson, 1996).

**An Example of Behavioral Technology Training.**  A school counselor acting as a consultant conducts a three-session workshop for teachers on "Catching Students Being Good." The workshop focuses on effectively using the principles of extinction and positive reinforcement and covers an overview of the concepts and what to expect in using them, situations from the classroom that illustrate how the principles can be used effectively, and general rules for using these kinds of reinforcement. The teachers then practice using the principles in comparable classroom situations and receive feedback on their performances as well as hints for remembering to use the principles in the classroom. Finally, the consultant agrees to observe each teacher applying the principles in the classroom and to provide feedback.

## Behavioral System Consultation

In behavioral system consultation, behavioral technology principles are applied to a social system (Lewis and Newcomer, 2002; Williams, 2000). Consultants use behavioral technology principles to analyze and change interactions among the various subsystems of a larger social system, such as a school or mental health center or between two or more interactive systems. For example, a behavioral consultant might interact with the staff at a substance-abuse clinic and the staff at a halfway house for substance abusers to assure proper coordination of treatment efforts. The goal of behavioral system consultation is to enhance the efficiency and effectiveness of a system in terms of its stated functions and to focus on the process and structure of the system itself (Curtis & Stollar, 1996), whereas behavioral case consultation focuses on an individual client within a system.

Behavioral system consultation is influenced by the research and theory of behavioral ecology and systems theory. Behavioral ecology, which states that humans are part of a multilevel system called an ecological environment (Willems, 1974), is a mix of individual approaches derived from traditional behavior modification and ecological approaches that study environments and social systems (Jeger & Slotnick, 1982).

Behavioral ecology assumes that the settings in which individuals operate are interdependent. For example, what happens to people in their work can affect their home life. The primary goal of behavioral system consultation is to help a social system function more effectively in terms of its stated mission. This goal is accomplished through a combination of individual, group, and system-wide interventions, the last of these being the most prevalent. The system itself is the client, and the people with whom the consultant works are the consultees. For example, in a school setting, the classroom is the client system, not an individual student.

Consultees' increased future functioning relative to their job duties within the system can be a secondary goal. As in the other types of behavioral consultation, the consultant acts as an expert, but in behavior system consultation the consultant must be an expert in the specifics of systems theory and behavioral ecology. The consultant guides the consultee through a systematic problem-solving process and ensures that the steps of system definition, assessment, intervention, and evaluation are accomplished. Even though the consultant is an expert in behavioral technology, systems, and behavioral ecology, the nature of the consultation relationship is collaborative; consultees participate to the degree their skills and knowledge permit.

The consultee's most important function is that of decision maker. Although the consultee and consultant are peers, in the end it is the consultee who decides how consultation is to proceed. The consultee is charged with providing the consultant with fully accurate information, which can include descriptions of the problem or of the system's parameters, suggestions for gathering data, or feedback on the feasibility of possible interventions.

In system definition, the consultant and consultee gather information about the behavior of members of the system relative to the system's goals and structures. There are the two steps of defining the system structure and defining the system process. In determining the *structure* of a system, the consultant and consultee or the collaborators define the system's parameters with regard to time and space, including such variables as physical setting and boundaries (e.g., where the system is located), environmental design (e.g., the system's physical plant), number of system members (that is, demographic data), and policies and procedures (e.g., rules and regulations).

In determining the *process* of a system, the consultant and consultee or the collaborators define the system's parameters in terms of the behavior of the system's members, including such variables as assessment functions (i.e., how behavior of various systems' groups will be measured), intervention functions (i.e., how the system tries to change on its own), evaluation functions (i.e., how the quality of the system's functions is determined), and communications functions (that is, who talks to whom, in what manner, and how often).

Once the system's structural and process factors are known, it is time to assess the system in terms of those factors. Assessment is a joint effort of the consultant and consultee or the collaborators to gather appropriate information concerning the interrelationships among identified structures and processes using direct observation, interviews, and appropriate standardized instruments. Based on the system's structural and process limitations, the parties involved can then decide which parts of the system are operating adequately and which are "dysfunctional" (Maher, 1981, p. 502). The consultant and consultee or collaborators then use three steps in system intervention to eliminate structural and process limitations: they prioritize system needs, specify behavioral outcomes goals, and design and implement an intervention program.

In system evaluation, the consultant and the consultee evaluate the intervention program operations and system change. In evaluating the operations of the intervention program, the parties involved determine whether the program was implemented in the way intended and with the results expected. This in turn helps to determine which activities were responsible for the outcome and how to modify the program for future use. In an example, Cooper and Newbold (1994) report an effective use of behavioral systems consultation in which a small and large group feedback was employed to help employees develop more safety with regard to lifting, equipment use, and hand/body positioning. For school-based examples see Sugai and Horner (1999) and Putnam, Luiselli, and Jefferson (2002).

**An Example of Behavioral System Consultation.**   A human service professor from a university is consulting with a human service agency about enhancing its effectiveness. The consultant and the designated consultee first define the system in terms of its structure and process. Although the first of these is easy, it takes them quite a bit longer to define the system's process. They examine each of the agency's subsystems (e.g., the technological subsystem, which consists of the case workers) in terms of how communication takes place, how the behavior of the subsystem is measured and evaluated, and how the subsystem attempts to solve its own problems.

After defining the system, the consultant guides the consultee in assessing the interaction between the identified structural and process factors. They determine that part of the system's limitations is due to poor "top-down" communication and lack of adequate autonomy for the agency's case workers. In intervening to rectify the matter, they identify poor "top-down" communication as the most important problem. They set the objective of having a regular weekly staff meeting in which all participants are allowed to submit agenda items and all important information is discussed. In addition, the final 10 minutes of each meeting is allocated for discussion of any topic that an individual wants to bring up. The consultant and consultee generate three possible programs, weigh their ad-

vantages and disadvantages, and decide that the consultant will be a participant/observer at the first meeting.

Based on feedback from the consultant, the group will decide how to modify procedures for conducting subsequent staff meetings. Following this intervention, the consultee agrees to monitor staff meetings on a regular basis to make sure the desired changes in "top-down" communication indeed occur. The changes in the system are evaluated six months later by surveying the staff.

# CONJOINT BEHAVIORAL CONSULTATION

There is a trend in behavioral consultation in schools to use parents and teachers as conjoint consultees (Auster et al., 2006; Sheridan, 2000; Sheridan & Kratochwill, 1992; Sheridan, Kratochwill, & Bergan, 1996). This method consists of involvement of teacher–parent pairs who together (simultaneously rather than individually) serve as consultees (Sheridan, 2000), considering both school and home settings (Grissom, Erchul & Sheridan, 2003; Sheridan, Clarke, Knoche, & Edwards, 2006). The process parallels that of behavioral case consultation (Guli, 2005). Designed to bridge the gap between the school and the home and maximize the spread of effects from one setting to another, conjoint behavioral consultation emphasizes continuous data collection and programming between the school, home, and community. This approach has been a logical step in attempting to link the significant settings in a student's life such as home, school, and primary community arenas and their reciprocal influence (Auster et al., 2006; Kratochwill, Elliott, & Carrington Rotto, 1995).

Conjoint behavioral consultation is defined as "a structured, indirect form of service-delivery, in which parents and others are joined to work together to address the academic, social, or behavioral needs of an individual for whom both parties bear some responsibility" (Sheridan & Kratochwill, 1992, p. 122). Although the addition of more consultees complicates this approach, the benefits can be more than worth the costs.

For example, this approach can expedite change across the home and school settings. This approach starts to build some empirical validity (Auster et al., 2006; Guli, 2005; Sheridan et al., 2001; Sheridan, Eagle, & Doll, 2006). For example, there is some evidence that parents and teachers prefer conjoint behavioral consultation over parallel, one-on-one consultation for each party (Freer & Watson, 1999), although some initial research suggests that parents may tend to dominate the sessions more than teachers (Grissom et al., 2003).In another example, there is growing evidence that this model accommodates multicultural variables that affect the consultation process (Guli, 2005; Sheridan, 2000; Sheridan et al., 2006). Research on this model is promising (Guli, 2005; Wilkinson, 2005). This consultation approach serves the two goals of bridging the gap between the home and the school, maximizing the potential of treatment effects in both places. Due to the increased attention this model is receiving, I include a summary of it here. Bear in mind that this model builds directly upon that of Bergan and Kratochwill (1990).

## COLLABORATION FROM A BEHAVIORAL PERSPECTIVE

Very little has been written about behavioral collaboration as distinct from behavioral consultation. This is most likely due to the fact that much of behavioral consultation is practiced in the schools, and many of the professionals in the typical school are not familiar with the intricacies of implementing behavioral interventions to the degree that treatment integrity can be ensured. As a result, the human service professional often has no choice but to take on an expert mode of consultation. The use of behavioral collaboration can be increased by individual organizations making effective use of behavioral technology training. To the degree that other professionals can become skilled in behavioral interventions and accept their use as methods of choice, behavioral collaboration can become a frequently used service. Another way to increase the use of behavioral collaboration is for the human service professionals to provide direct service to the client system while providing consultation to the consultee. In that way, the professional is taking some specific as well as general responsibility for the outcome of the case. As a caution, experts in behavioral interventions will want to ensure that they minimize their "expert" role as much as possible to allow for an equal relationship among the collaborators.

## MULTICULTURAL ASPECTS RELATED TO BEHAVIORAL CONSULTATION

The known effects of cultural issues on behavioral and conjoint behavioral consultation are very limited (Sheridan, 2000). However, behavioral consultation, with its focus on environmental events, may be appealing to cultural groups that do not freely express feelings, value linear thinking, or want concrete and predictable outcomes. Because some cultural groups value the nature of the relationship more than the expertise of the consultant, behavioral consultants may want to look at how to build effective relationships prior to consultation (Sheridan, 2000) and develop collaborative procedures within the consultation relationship (Sheridan et al., 2006). Groups that value independence and individual accomplishment may see value in this approach. Part of behavioral consultation's assessment procedures take into account social and cultural environments, thus setting the stage for modification of interventions due to the cultural context. Behavioral consultation's focus on monitoring and

---

**C A S E  10.1    Behavioral Collaboration for School Consultants**

---

Monica is a school-based consultant in an inner-city elementary school. She has received extensive training in behavioral case consultation and cognitive behavioral interventions. Her consultee is Jose, a fifth-grade math/science teacher. Jose has participated in some behavioral technology training sessions in the recent past.

In their first two meetings, Monica and Jose engaged in problem identification and analysis. Jose reported that he was having difficulties with four aggressive boys in one of his classes. Jose was concerned that the children in his class were not learning enough because of the time he had to spend "keeping his thumbs on" the boys, who exhibited verbal and physical forms of aggression to their classmates and each other. Jose was worried about the harm they were causing. He felt that they were well on their way to dropping out, and he wanted to do everything he could to keep them in school.

For one week Monica had Jose write down his descriptions of exactly what the boys did when they were "verbally and physically aggressive." In the meantime, she observed the boys in Jose's classroom on three different days and did the same thing. Based on a comparison of their notes, they came to a consensus on operationalizing the behaviors that were problematic. In their analysis they examined the boys' behavior, the classroom conditions, and Jose's behavior at the time of the undesirable behaviors. It was found that Jose used proximity control and appropriate verbal responses to the boys when they were acting out, as well as the "assertive discipline" techniques that were prescribed school wide. In analyzing the boys' behavior, they came to the conclusion that their verbal and physical aggression was due to poor anger coping techniques. The boys came to math class right after a physical education class whose focus was competitive sports. The boys seemed to be angry when they or their teammates didn't do particularly well in competition.

The physical education teacher wanted nothing to do with the attempt to help the boys and said, "If they can't cut it now, they never will." So Monica and Jose determined that the boys needed training in anger-coping skills but also, and most importantly, the ability to demonstrate the newly learned skills in Jose's classroom. So Monica agreed to counsel the boys using a cognitive behavioral and coping skills approach to anger control. As far as the consultation process with Jose went, he agreed to monitor the boys' behavior in the classroom and cue them when necessary to implement their newly learned skills. When they effectively used their coping skills, Jose would reward the boys with tokens that could be used to "buy" a variety of items Jose had for rewarding good conduct and academic achievement.

Jose implemented his monitoring program at the same time Monica began the coping skills training. Jose's charts showed slow but steady decreases in the boys' verbal and physical aggression. He contacted Monica on a couple of occasions to make sure that he was accurately identifying the boys' attempts to use their coping skills. After Monica had finished the training group, she met with Jose one more time to plan how he was going to fade out the cueing and reward system over the semester.

**Commentary**

Notice how this case nicely illustrates collaboration using a behavioral model. Both Monica and Jose own a piece of the helping "pie." At the same time Monica uses her expertise to assist Jose in developing a token economy program for the boys. She also follows up with him periodically to help him with the details of the program. This case shows how consultants, through collaboration, can serve the client system directly while assisting a fellow collaborator to work more effectively with that same client system.

---

follow-up may be welcomed by those from cultural groups that perceive themselves to be disenfranchised. Consultants are cautioned to be careful with the jargon-laden terminology that can be a turnoff to some cultural groups (Sheridan, 2000). Further, the consultant's control of the model can be an issue for some cultural groups (Harrison, 2004; Hoffman et al., 2006).

---

**C A S E 10.2**    **Behavioral Consultations for Community Consultants**

---

The consultee is a qualified mental retardation specialist with Washington County Citizens for the Handicapped, an organization that operates a six-resident intermediate care facility for the mentally retarded (ICF-MR). As a qualified professional, the consultee is responsible for ensuring that "active treatment" is provided for each resident in accordance with state and federal regulations governing ICF-MR group homes. The consultant was asked to help the consultee develop an appropriate program for each demonstrated need.

The 30-year-old client, Ms. Jones, has been demonstrating aggressive behaviors: striking other home members and some of the staff, particularly a female staff member. The consultee wanted assistance in developing a behavior program to increase Ms. Jones's positive social behavior and reduce her unacceptable behaviors in a nonrestrictive manner that would not violate her client rights.

The consultant built rapport with the consultee during the first session as they discussed Ms. Jones. They defined "striking" as hitting out at another and "socially appropriate behavior" as smiling at others, being next to others without striking, talking to others about routine matters, and engaging in social activities while following any rules.

The consultant then observed the client for five consecutive days at 15-minute intervals for one hour each in the morning and during social activities in the evening. A graph of the incidence of striking behavior showed that Ms. Jones tended to strike out at others in the evening during social activities. Her socially appropriate behavior index was fairly average during other times. The consultant and the consultee agreed that it would be important to create a reinforcement program for Ms. Jones so as to increase the number of socially appropriate behaviors during the evening hours.

During the next session they discussed Ms. Jones's strengths and skills as well as environmental conditions that might be influencing her striking-out behavior. By applying their mutual knowledge bases to the problem, they agreed that Ms. Jones tended to sit by Mr. Smith. Whenever she was not sitting by Mr. Smith in the evenings, she tended to strike at another group member, typically another female. She did not have a history of striking at Mr. Smith.

Based on this and other observations, the consultant and consultee developed a program that involved a type of "time out" procedure in which Ms. Jones would be escorted to her room any time she attempted to strike anyone. She would then be free to leave her room and join in social activities after a 10-minute period. Ms. Jones was also rewarded with additional activity therapy time when she fulfilled the token economy procedures indicated in her treatment plan. The program called for a 90 percent decrease in the striking behavior and a 30 percent increase in socially acceptable behaviors.

The program was approved by the Human Rights Committee and was signed by the client's guardian. The consultee implemented the program with the consultant being "on call" for any monitoring that was needed. It was obvious that within one month of implementing the plan, Ms. Jones had almost totally stopped her striking out behavior and had significantly increased the frequency of her socially acceptable behaviors.

Further data and information were gathered and analyzed. Every indication was that the plan was a success. In a final interview the consultant and consultee reviewed the case. Both were pleased with Ms. Jones's success, but they still wondered what part Mr. Smith had played in influencing her behavior.

**Commentary**

This case nicely illustrates the use of behavioral consultation in a somewhat delicate situation. The case also demonstrates one of the premises of behavioral consultation, namely, that the cause of a behavior does not necessarily have to be understood to effectively change that behavior. Notice how the consultant and consultee worked together in reinforcing the appropriate target behaviors exhibited by Ms. Jones while at the same time enforcing consequences for inappropriate behavior. Clearly, behavioral consultation focuses on assessing and operationalizing behavior prior to intervening. This strength of behavior consultation suggests to consultants the critical nature of knowing what it is that is to be changed through an intervention.

# SUMMARY

Behavioral consultation is a process in which a consultant uses the principles of learning to assist one or more consultees having a work-related problem with a client or client system. Behavioral consultation owes its heritage primarily to behavior therapy and behavioral psychology. The boundaries of behavioral consultation tend to expand in direct relationship to advances in these two areas.

The result of all behavioral consultation is a change in behavior in the client, the consultee, or both that is accomplished through a systematic problem-solving process. The consultant–consultee relationship is a collaborative one in which the consultant is an expert who guides the consultee through the consultation process using the principles of learning.

Behavioral consultation can be performed in case, training, or system approaches (Kratochwill & Pittman, 2002). In the case approach, by far the most common, the consultant helps the consultee manage a client's case. It has changed little since it was formulated by Bergan in 1977 (Noell & Witt, 1996). Behavioral technology training consultation involves preparing the consultee in the use of general or specific behavioral principles for future use with clients and client systems. In the system approach, a system or some part of it is modified through use of behavioral principles.

The basic assumptions of behavioral consultation are that behavior can be viewed scientifically, overt and current behavior is the focus of change, and behavior is lawful and subject to systematic change. Among the procedures advocated by behavioral consultants are use of direct assessment, operationalization of goals, objective measurement of target behaviors, and assessment of both the goals of consultation and the consultation plan. Behavior consultation has been successfully applied in a variety of settings but is most frequently used when there are high levels of client or system control. It is the best researched model of consultation (Kratochwill et al., 2002; Sheridan et al., 1996).

# RECENT TRENDS

The major trends in behavioral consultation are linked to developments in behavior therapy and behavioral psychology; findings in these areas are quickly incorporated into the practices of behavioral consultants.

A major trend in the field is the expansion of behavioral consultation to include behavioral system and behavioral technology training approaches, which has allowed the field to move beyond traditional case consultation (Williams, 2000). Kratochwill, Elliott, and Stoiber (2002) suggest substituting the term "problem-solving consultation" for "behavioral consultation" to allow for these expansions. Kratochwill and Pittman (2002) point out that in system-level consultation there is a trend away from school restructuring and toward building learning communities (see Senge et al., 2000).

Instead of relying solely on the current abilities of the consultee, consultants now are taking increasing responsibility for assessment and are teaching intervention procedures to consultees (Noell, 1996). Direct behavioral consultation (Ervin & Erhardt, 2000; Sterling-Turner et al., 2001) has been receiving increasing attention. This model differs from traditional behavioral case consultation in that the consultant does not use indirect instruction (e.g., didacticism) in teaching consultees the skills necessary to effectively implement interventions. Rather, the consultant uses direct instructional methods such as role playing, modeling, and coaching. There is a tendency to include more applied behavior analysis techniques in behavioral consultation (Noell & Witt, 1998). One implication of this trend is that there will be more emphasis on direct techniques for assessing behavior (such as observation) and less on indirect techniques (such as recollections gotten through interviews).

Behavioral consultants are increasingly engaging in positive behavior support (PBS) programs (Lewis & Newcomer, 2002; Luiselli, 2002;

Martens & Ardoin, 2002). Positive behavior support is an approach to intervention that uses positive, individualized support to promote positive and socially important behavior change using functional behavioral assessment. Positive behavior support is used at the school system, classroom, and individual levels. The idea is to create a system for optimizing the capacity of schools for addressing behavioral issues using evidence-based and culturally appropriate interventions (Sugai et al., 2000).

Another trend in behavioral consultation is an increased tendency to include other forms of behavioral technology in addition to those based on operant conditioning, classical conditioning, and observational learning in both behavioral and academic interventions (Kratochwill et al., 2002). The cognitive-behavioral and behavioral ecology movements have made strong headway and now have a place in all behavioral consultation approaches. Cognitive behavioral theory has greatly expanded the number of potential interventions available to consultants and permits more flexibility in developing plans (Lochman et al., 1989). Hughes et al. (2001) report the development of Responsive Systems Consultation (RSC) as an alternative to conjoint behavior consultation (CBC). RSC emphasizes a larger menu of interventions and a greater focus on improving client relationships with significant others than does conjoint behavioral consultation. Problems seen as being located in the client system are reframed as products of the interactions of the client system and the interpersonal contexts in which the client system behaves (Denton et al., 2003). All interventions can have a systemic effect even though they are responsive to the individual client. In school consultation, authors such as Gutkin & Curtis (1999) have suggested changing the name of behavioral consultation to "ecobehavioral consultation" in order to expand its parameters to include distal environmental events such as parental pressures affecting the consultation process. Behavioral consultants are becoming increasingly aware that the success of any approach to behavioral consultation is in part determined by the environment in which consultation occurs (Dickinson & Bradshaw, 1992; Kratochwill & Pittman, 2002).

In terms of the consultant–consultee relationship, behavioral consultants are devoting more attention to the development of relationships based on rapport with their consultees and the consultee variables that may affect the success of consultation (Kratochwill, Elliott, & Callan-Stoiber, 2002; Rosenfield, 1991, 2002b).

Behavioral consultation in general, and conjoint behavioral consultation in particular, places more attention on multicultural variables (Sheridan, 2000). Issues such as trust, acknowledgement of diversity, use of jargon, and even the effect of interpreters is under examination. More attention is being placed on the potential impact of multicultural variables during all stages of the consultation process (Sheridan, 2000).

## CONCLUSIONS

The major contribution of behavioral consultation has been its emphasis on approaching consultation in a systematic way. Consultants can be taught to perform behavioral consultation in a straightforward, step-by-step manner, which has reinforced the view that consultation is a sequential process made up of identifiable stages. There is considerable evidence that behavioral consultation is effective (Erchul & Schulte, 1996; Kratochwill & Pittman, 2002).

A second major contribution of behavioral consultation, its emphasis on specifics, has contributed to more effective methods in setting the goals of consultation, gathering data on the perceived problem, and most importantly, in evaluating the effects of consultation. Behavioral consultation's emphasis on specifics and measurement has encouraged consultants to be more accountable for their consultation efforts. Further, behavioral consultation's emphasis on specifics has allowed it to have the most research activity and empirical support among consultation models (Sheridan, Kratochwill, & Bergan, 1996).

Behavioral consultation has also emphasized treatment acceptability, treatment integrity, and treatment evaluation. More than any other model, behavioral consultation has focused on ensuring that consultees implement plans that they believe are satisfactory; that they are skilled to accomplish; and that they, along with the consultant, agree need to be rigorously evaluated. Another contribution of behavioral consultation is the training of consultants in techniques from behavioral and cognitive-behavioral approaches to counseling and psychotherapy. Hence, schoolteachers are frequently able to use behavior modification procedures, and many counselors can use stress inoculation training.

Behavioral consultation is not without its limitations and criticisms. Limitations include a lack of standardization of consultation procedures, little or no consultee training, and problems surrounding problem identification (Kratochwill & Van Someren, 1995). Additional limitations include lack of focus on treatment integrity (Sterling-Turner et al., 2002) and the fact that behavioral consultation has not really developed over the years (Watson et al., 1997). For example, in one study (Bramlett et al., 2002), less than one-half of the school psychologists surveyed reported using all of the stages of behavioral consultation.

One major criticism is that behavioral consultation does not adequately take into account consultees' thoughts and feelings regarding the use of behavioral principles with clients (Hughes, 2000). Many times consultees have reservations about using behavioral interventions with clients because of perceived technical problems or manipulative behavioral procedures and because of concerns about their ability to implement the required procedures. Researchers have begun to address this issue by exploring consultee reactions to consultant language (such as the use of jargon) and consultee involvement in selecting interventions as they relate to consultee acceptability of suggested interventions (Rhoades & Kratochwill, 1992; Sheridan, 1992). There have also been writings aimed specifically at the use of relational variables in the context of behavioral consultation (Kratochwill, Elliott & Callan-Stoiber, 2002).

Behavioral consultation is often criticized for the difficulties involved in applying behavioral procedures in real life or in natural environments (Kazdin, 2001; Witt, Gresham, & Noell, 1996a). For example, it is one thing to help a teacher make a plan to control the behavior of a seventh-grade boy, but quite another to implement the program in a classroom with 36 students.

Some consultants' neglect of a collaborative approach is frequently cited as a criticism of behavioral consultation. Because some work-related problems can be addressed simply by using behavioral interventions, some behavioral consultants adopt the role of expert and perform most of the consultation tasks except the intervention. The long-term positive effects on the consultee's future performance are likely to be negligible as a result. A closely related criticism is that some behavioral consultants rely too much on pet interventions (e.g., tangible reinforcers) when designing intervention programs with their consultees. Behavioral consultation is also criticized for not maintaining the *integrity of the treatment* (Elliott & Busse, 1993; Hughes, 2000). Frequently the agreed-upon treatment plan is not implemented as planned due to a lack of adequate financial and/or human resources. Therefore, behavioral consultation does not always practice what it preaches—adequate monitoring of program implementation.

Behavioral consultation has been criticized for creating a degree of orthodoxy that has led to a somewhat rigid model rather than an evolving model subject to change (Noell & Witt, 1996). Some authors challenge some of the fundamental assumptions of behavioral consultation, such as talking to consultees being an adequate method for getting them to change their behavior and generalize the problem-solving skills to similar situations in the future (Witt, Gresham, & Noell, 1996a, 1996b).

With one exception, each of these criticisms suggests that the shortcomings of behavioral consultation result from inadequacies of practicing behavioral consultants rather than from the failings of consultation approach. As with the other models of consultation covered in this text, the remedy to this situation may well be better training and a refinement of approaches to behavioral consultation.

## SUGGESTIONS FOR EFFECTIVE PRACTICE

- Avoid behavioral jargon at all times.

- Note the importance of relational issues.

- Consider training prospective consultees in behavioral interventions as part of their staff development training.

- Make the goals of consultation and collaboration as concrete and specific as possible.

- Recall the importance of evaluation of the plan and the consultation process.

## QUESTIONS FOR REFLECTION

1. Could any individual behavioral consultant incorporate the findings from operant conditioning, classical conditioning, observational learning, the cognitive-behavioral movement, and behavioral ecology into the practice of consultation? Justify your answer.

2. What are the essential characteristics of any approach to behavioral consultation?

3. To what degree are the underlying assumptions of each of the influences on behavioral consultation compatible with each other?

4. When would you, as a behavioral consultant, incorporate punishment into a treatment plan? Justify your answer.

5. How can a consultant using the behavioral case consultation approach avoid manipulating and excessively controlling the consultee's verbal behavior?

6. Which of the three subcategories of verbalizations would an organizational process consultant employ most frequently? How would this compare with a consultant employing behavioral case consultation?

7. Which of the three subcategories of verbalizations would a mental health consultant using consultee-centered case consultation employ most frequently? How would this compare with a consultant using behavioral case consultation?

8. What strengths does behavioral ecology add to behavioral system consultation?

9. Why does a consultant using behavioral technology training need to be a "good teacher"?

10. When you consider both the contributions and criticisms of behavioral consultation, what conclusions do you draw?

## SUGGESTED SUPPLEMENTARY READINGS

Those further interested in behavioral consultation should consult the following suggested readings:

Bergan, J. R., and Kratochwill, T. R. (1990). *Behavioral consultation and therapy*. New York: Plenum. This text is, in effect, a second edition of Bergan's classic text *Behavioral Consultation* (1977). This is "the book" on behavioral case consultation. Although the authors assume consultants will be working in a school setting, readers can easily apply the ideas in the text to any human service setting. The authors devote at least a full chapter to each of the four stages of behavioral consultation and provide extensive treatment of verbal interaction techniques. There is a case study section to demonstrate precisely how a behavioral consultant would proceed. The major difference in this text from Bergan's (1977) text is the addition of a chapter on methodological and conceptual issues in behavioral consultation outcome research. Be advised that this book is laborious reading but well worth the effort.

Kratochwill, T. R., and Bergan, J. R. (1990). *Behavioral consultation in applied settings: An individual guide.* New York: Plenum. This guide is a fine resource for those who want to better understand the basics of behavioral case consultation but who do not desire the in-depth discussion presented in the Bergan and Kratochwill text just described. It provides summaries of each of the stages of the behavioral case consultation model as developed by Kratochwill and Bergan, as well as exercises at the end of each chapter to help readers assess their understanding of the material.

Sheridan, S. M., Kratochwill, T. R., and Bergan, J. R. (1996). *Conjoint behavioral consultation: A procedural manual.* New York: Plenum. This model involves an expansion of traditional behavioral consultation to include conjoint consultation with parents and teachers. Of particular interest is Chapter 2, which discusses various approaches to working wit... ents such as parent education. Chapter 3 does a excellent job of discussing the conceptual bases of conjoint behavioral consultation and differentiates it from traditional behavioral consultation. This is an excellent resource for those interested in consulting with both parents and teachers from a behavioral perspective.

**http://www.pbis.org/english/** The Technical Assistance Center on Positive Behavioral Interventions and Supports (PBIS) has been established by the Office of Special Education Programs, a division of the U.S. Department of Education, to give schools capacity-building information and technical assistance for identifying, adapting, and sustaining effective school-wide disciplinary practices. This is an excellent site for information on PBS.

# 11

✳

# Organizational Consultation and Collaboration

G iven your basic familiarity with organizations and the ways they operate, we'll now examine how consultants operate within organizations. Why do consultants work in organizations? As Bellman notes, "in this imperfect world full of imperfect people, we try to get things done through large, imperfect organizations—organizations of our own creation" (1990, p. 69). Consequently, the main goal of organizational consultation is improvement in the organization's effectiveness, and this can take many forms and use a multitude of methods. It typically emphasizes data gathering, problem identification, and organizational well-being (Truscott et al., 2000; Zins & Erchul, 2002). Many types of organizational consultation originated in business and industry settings, whereas the mental health movement was influenced by others.

In this chapter we'll consider the historical development of organizational consultation and define some important terms. Then we'll examine a few of its key concepts, drawing from the discussion of the preceding chapter. We'll consider three specific models of organizational consultation: purchase of expertise, doctor-patient, and process consultation (Schein, 1969, 1987, 1999, 2006). In discussing the expertise model, we'll focus on education/training and program approaches. In the doctor–patient model, diagnosis is emphasized. In the section on process consultation, we'll explore Schein's model.

For each of these approaches we'll examine the goals, roles, and functions of the consultant and the consultee's experience in consultation. We'll explore some applications of organizational consultation by discussing its techniques and procedures, and we'll note some contributions and criticisms of this kind of consultation.

Here are some questions to consider as you read this chapter:

1. Why is consulting with organizations more complex than consulting with individuals?

2. Who or what makes up the client system in organizational consultation?

3. How can a consultant evaluate the effects of organizational consultation when the process is so complex?

4. How should a consultant select from the multitude of available interventions?

5. What are the basic differences among the various approaches to organizational consultation?

## INTRODUCTION

Consider the following example, which covers just one of several approaches to organizational consultation:

### Case Example

You are a human service professional who is asked to consult with a rehabilitation center staff. The center, which serves as a counseling facility for incarcerates nearing eligibility for parole, is having staff conflicts that are adversely affecting the success of its programs. The center's head administrator asks you to sit in on three of the regularly scheduled weekly staff meetings and provide the staff feedback concerning how they might resolve their conflicts. As you observe the meetings, you take notes on such things as what and how things are said, as well as who talks to whom. You provide feedback to the staff at a special meeting and then help the group process that feedback. As a result, three areas of conflict are identified: some staff members are perceived as being too hard on the clients, some staff members are perceived as being too soft on the clients, and the center has no evaluation system in place to determine whether it really helps its clients. You agree to spend an additional session with the staff to help them resolve their conflicts and to help a select group of staff develop procedures for evaluating the effectiveness of the center's services.

Increasingly, professionals who provide consultation (either internal or external) are being asked to assist with organization-wide concerns and issues. *Organizational consultation* is based on the concept that an organization can be made to function more effectively through the efforts of one or more consultants who work with some (or possibly all) members of the organization. Thus, the organization itself or one of its parts becomes the client and the members are the consultees. Consider a school counselor or school psychologist who assists a group consisting of seventh-grade teachers and parents to decrease the number of incidents of school violence. Or for another example, a school counselor might be asked to develop an intervention assistance program to assist teachers to meet the academic and behavioral needs of their students (Curtis & Stollar, 2002). Managed care, downsizing, and expanding ecology have created a variety of opportunities for human service professionals to consult with organizations to assist them in coping with these phenomena (Sears et al., 2006; Sperry, 1996).

Organizational consultants can fulfill the following functions (Schein, 1987, p. 20):

- provide information that is not otherwise available

- analyze information with sophisticated tools not available to clients or their subordinates

- diagnose complex organizational and business problems

- train clients or their subordinates to use diagnostic models that help them make better decisions

- listen and give support, comfort, and counsel during troubled times

- help implement difficult or unpopular decisions

- reward and punish certain kinds of behaviors (by using status as an "outsider" as a special source of authority)

- transmit information either up the normal chain of command or laterally as needed

- make decisions and give directives on how to proceed if for some reason line management cannot do so; and take responsibility for decisions, allay anxiety that may attend the uncertainties of consultation, and in other ways provide the emotional strength to help others through difficult situations

Human service professionals, through their specialized training, are particularly suited to provide organizational consultation (Lewis et al., 2003; Sears et al., 2006).

## HISTORICAL BACKGROUND

Organizational consultation first emerged in the 1890s in industrial settings. Consultants, experts who focused on manufacturing productivity, were called on to fix production problems. In open systems terminology, the early organizational consultants dealt with the technological subsystem of the organization. At the outset of organizational consultation, consultants combined industrial engineering with time and motion studies and were often referred to as management engineers.

During World War I, organizational consultants were frequently considered efficiency experts; they were concerned with functions such as input–output ratios and the relationships between humans and tools. During the 1920s, organizational consultation expanded into other subsystems of industrial organizations, particularly management and maintenance.

The Great Depression created a crisis in which many businesses, industrial and non-industrial alike, were forced to fight for survival. This financial crisis produced conditions conducive to a new consultant activity: helping "sick" organizations. Although "sick" referred to finances during the Great Depression, the term has since come to refer to any aspect of an organization considered to be problematic.

With the advent of group dynamics research and the call to improve work conditions during the 1940s and 1950s, psychology entered business settings, and motivation and leadership studies became quite

popular (French & Bell, 1999). Organizations, therefore, no longer needed to be sick to benefit from the assistance of a consultant; rather, healthy organizations could become more efficient and effective in meeting their goals by obtaining consultant services in motivation and leadership. Thus, consultants became increasingly involved in serving organizations in such matters as lines of authority, types of leadership, and the distribution of labor (Gallessich, 1982).

The national attention given to the concept of mental health and the emergence of mental health consultation (see Chapter 9) began to influence not only human service organizations, but business and industrial organizations as well. Greater emphasis was placed on the psychological well-being of the worker on the job. Organizational leaders began to realize that satisfied workers were crucial to effective and productive organizations. Coincident to the national emphasis on mental health was the emergence of organization development.

*Organization development* is the application of the behavioral sciences to an organization's internal workings to increase its efficiency, effectiveness, and its ability to change (French & Bell, 1999; McLean, 2006). The organization development effort focuses "on the characteristics of the workplace as a whole, with the consultant attempting to use a variety of interventions that can integrate organizational and individual needs" (Lewis & Lewis, 1986, p. 202).

Organizational consultation developed under the influences of applied behavioral science and managerial science (Shultz, 1984): From behavioral science came laboratory training methods, the use of the survey research and feedback method, and autonomous work groups; from managerial science came quantitative analysis of business activities, particularly managerial decision making (French & Bell, 1999).

The laboratory training methods are a series of experimental activities that focus on developing skills for more effective organizational functioning. Development occurs in a laboratory setting in which group members experiment with new behaviors and are given feedback. The new behaviors are then supposedly transferred to the work site.

In the survey research and feedback method, results of surveys about the organization are conveyed to the respondents to further pinpoint problem areas and to generate discussion. Such discussions are intended to improve relationships among the participants and help solve identified problems.

The Tavistock Institute of London developed a psychoanalytic theory of groups that influenced organization development (French & Bell, 1999). Much of this institute's work focused on study groups formed to examine how participants dealt with issues such as authority, leadership, and norms. Participants were to take their newly acquired knowledge and apply it in their own organizations. In 1969, Edgar Schein wrote a landmark text entitled *Process Consultation*. This text strongly influenced the human side of organizational consultation and gave great momentum to legitimizing organizational consultation in all types of organizations, including educational institutions.

Schein emphasized focusing on process elements such as leadership style, balancing individual needs, and organizational goals (Kormanski & Eschbach, 1997). Later, Blake & Mouton (1983) and others developed their famous "consulcube" which helped consultants determine the nature of the problem, the target of change, and the type of intervention.

Managerial science, which accompanied the development of management as a profession (Katz & Kahn, 1990), focuses on finances and quantitative analysis of all aspects of management. Unlike applied behavioral science, managerial science focuses almost exclusively on the tangible and the quantitative.

Organization development influenced another field called human resource development (HRD), which developed during World War II out of military and industrial organizations' needs for competent personnel (French & Bell, 1999). The philosophical framework of HRD is the development of human potential. Whereas organizational consultation focuses on the workplace as an entity, HRD focuses on the individuals within the organization. HRD consists of the learning experiences "that are organized, for a specified time, and designed to bring about the possibility of behavioral change" (Nadler, 1980, p. 5). HRD gained recognition when the ASTD emerged and promoted HRD

nationally. HRD can take place in educational as well as business and human service settings.

A current trend in organizations is to provide counseling for employees on the work site through, for example, employee assistance programs (Hopko & Hopko, 2003).

The emergence of organization development and HRD has given legitimacy to using either internal consultants (when present) or outside consultants (whenever internal ones are absent or unskilled in the area of service for which consultation is needed). This point of view exemplifies the philosophy that satisfied workers make productive employees and that democratically run organizations based on relationships lead to organizational success. Later, Deming's TQM (total quality management) concepts influenced organizational consultation in all settings. This movement gave legitimacy to the concept of *continuous improvement* in all organizations, irrespective of their mission.

## ORGANIZATIONAL CONSULTATION DEFINED

In spite of the many attempts to define it, there is no agreement on a single definition of "organizational consultation." What is clear is that there are many types of such consultation, and how they are performed depends on the theoretical orientation of the consultant, the nature of the organization, and the nature of the problem for which consultation is sought (Lewis & Lewis, 1986).

Organizational consultation can be defined in terms of what the consultant does. Three decades ago, Sinha provided the following definition:

> An organizational consultant is a professional, internal or external to the client system, who applies behavioral science knowledge in an ongoing organization with the explicit objectives of managing change and increasing its effectiveness. He [or she] engages in a wide variety of activities, often called interventions, such as

organizational diagnosis, team building, inter-group activities, survey feedback, training for managerial effectiveness, restructuring organization, role negotiation, socio-technical system design, planning and goal setting, counseling and career planning, etc. The type and choice of interventions and relationship a consultant establishes with the client system often define the approach and style of consultants (1979, p. 8).

A synthesis of many authors' views on organizational consultation might produce the following generic definition: organizational consultation is the process in which a professional, functioning either internally or externally to an organization, provides assistance of a technical, diagnostic/prescriptive, or facilitative nature to an individual or group from that organization to enhance the organization's ability to deal with change and maintain or enhance its effectiveness in some designated way.

Some confusion surrounds the terms "consultee" and "client system" in organizational consultation. Consultees are those people in the organization with whom the consultant works; frequently they are mid- to high-level managers or those who provide direct services to clients. In the organizational consultation literature, the term "client" often refers to the consultee, particularly when the discussion concerns those in the organization with whom the consultant is working. With respect to organizational consultation in this text, the term "consultees" refers to those with whom the consultant works directly; the "client system" is always the organization or some part of it.

## KEY CONCEPTS IN ORGANIZATIONAL CONSULTATION

Most of the key concepts concerning organizational consultation were discussed in Chapter 8. However, two are sufficiently important to highlight: the organization as client, and the fact that process is as important as content.

## The Organization as Client

The client system in organizational consultation is usually the organization or some part of it. In any case, the goal of organizational consultation is to enhance the overall effectiveness of the organization, making the organization the client system. This can be a hard concept to grasp because many consultants are used to viewing the client system as either an individual or a relatively small group.

The more complex the organization, the more complex the client system becomes. Organizations are systems made up of interactive and interdependent parts; consulting with one part of the organization can affect all of its parts. Organizations are made up of people, each of whom possesses a unique set of attitudes, values, beliefs, and behaviors. Individuals in an organization are affected not only by these attributes of their coworkers, but also by the social relationships that exist within the organization. When consultants provide services to one part of the organization, the potential impact on other parts must be considered.

Among the concepts important to understanding the complexity of the organization as client is the principle of *synergy,* which states that the whole of a set of products is greater than the sum of its parts. When buildings, offices, people, and machines are put together in a certain way, they become more than the sum of their parts (organizations). This concept makes understanding organizations even more complex. By viewing the entire organization as the client, consultants will understand the complexity of the potential ramifications of their interventions and avoid oversimplified consultation methods.

## Process Is as Important as Content

An important underlying assumption of organizational consultation is that process is as important as content; that is, *how* something is done can be as important as *what* is done. Thus, how people communicate with one another in an organization is as important as what they communicate, and how an organization goes about solving a problem is as important as the nature of that problem (Golembiewski, 1993e). If we think of the problem to be solved as the content, then the process can be thought of as the method by which the problem is defined and solved (Schein, 1978, 1999). There is even a specific kind of consultation, called process consultation, that focuses on the process of organizational behavior rather than on its content.

In organizations, process factors are distinguished from structural factors, such as departments and lines of authority. These structures coordinate and control tasks in an efficient and timely manner (Jerrell & Jerrell, 1981), but they are surrounded by process factors, such as informal relationships, traditions, and culture (Schein, 1987, 1999). Further, how people perceive a structure (e.g., their job's role) determines how they relate to others within the organization and how they act in that role (Schein, 1988). Only when its members are smoothly interacting with one another can the organization be functioning effectively. Consultants often help organizations become aware of the interactions between process factors and their members to assist them in functioning at optimal levels (Golembiewski, 1993e).

Process and content are often subtly related. There can be a connection between an organization's problem and how the problem is being worked on. Schein (1978) illustrates this connection by telling about a group that discussed leadership (content) while it was experiencing a leadership struggle (process) among several of its members. Consultants frequently have the difficult task of deciding whether or not to focus on the interaction between process and content.

## EDGAR SCHEIN'S MODELS OF CONSULTATION

Whereas Blake and Mouton (1983) developed a broad conceptual framework for organizational consultation, more specific conceptualizations such as those of Schein (1988, 1999; 2006) have been developed.

Schein conceived three models of consultation: the purchase of expertise model, the doctor–patient model, and the process model. Both the purchase of expertise and the doctor–patient models are versions of "expert" consultation (Schein, 1987, 1999). They focus on what needs to be done. In the *purchase of expertise model,* the consultee "purchases" a consultant who can provide expertise (knowledge or skill) to solve a previously determined problem. In the *doctor–patient model,* the consultee "purchases" the consultant's ability to both diagnose a problem and prescribe an appropriate set of solutions for it. The consultee retains control of defining the problem in the purchase of expertise model but not in the doctor–patient model. In the purchase of expertise model, the consultee has already identified the solution (what the consultant does), whereas in the doctor–patient model neither the problem nor the solution is defined prior to consultation.

The *process model* views consultation as a "set of activities on the part of the consultant which help the [consultee] to perceive, understand, and act upon process events which occur in the [consultee's] environment" (Schein, 1988, p. 11). It focuses on *how* problems are solved. In process consultation, the consultee "purchases" the consultant's ability to help the consultee focus on process (as opposed to content) events; this approach focuses on how problems are solved rather than on the content of problems.

There are two versions of the process model: the catalyst version and facilitator version. The *catalyst* version of process consultation occurs when the consultant does not know the solution to some problem but can help the consultee formulate his or her own solution. The *facilitator* version occurs when the consultant may have ideas (content) about solutions but withholds them to help the consultee clear up his or her own dilemma by going through the problem-solving process. Effective consultants use the version of process consultation that is most appropriate to the circumstances (Schein, 1987).

There is some evidence that consultee readiness and the amount of time available for consultation relate to the choice of Schein's models (Stayer & Dillard, 1986). Consultees with low readiness and little time may want, and be best suited for, the purchase of expertise model. Consultees with high readiness and sufficient time might be more suitable for process consultation. Schein's models of consultation are compared with one another in Table 11.1, which is adapted from O'Connell (1990).

Schein's models form the basis of the following discussion of organizational consultation. First, education/training consultation and program consultation are discussed as examples of the purchase of expertise model. Next, the process of diagnosis is given special attention in the discussion of the doctor–patient model, and then the process model of consultation is considered last.

**The Purchase of Expertise Model.**    When consultees request help from consultants, they are frequently seeking some form of expertise, which can take the form of the knowledge or skill to fix a predetermined problem. Some combination of information, methods, tools, and support is provided to the consultee (Lawson, 1998). The essence of this model is that the consultee knows what the problem is, what needs to be done to solve it, and who can be of help. The consultee is in effect saying to the consultant, "Here's the problem; fix it." This model is by nature very content oriented. The consultant functions as a content expert (Schein, 1990c). For example, a consultant leads a school system to assess and improve its crisis management plan.

For the purchase of expertise model to be effective, four basic assumptions must be met (Schein, 1987, 1988, 1999). The consultee must have made a correct diagnosis of the problem, chosen the right consultant, correctly communicated the problem, and thought through and accepted the consequences of consultation. If the consultee has not made the correct diagnosis, the entire consultation will be invalid: the right consultant may have been chosen, but the wrong problem will have been solved.

If it becomes apparent that consultation is solving the wrong problem, the consultant is under no obligation to assist the consultee in making a new diagnosis. It's the consultee's responsibility to ensure that the consultant has the skills and abilities to meet the consultee's needs and to correctly communicate the nature of the problem. By using effective communication skills such as clarifying responses, the consultant can assist the consultee in expressing the perceived problem in such a way that both parties agree about its exact nature. However, ultimately it is the consultee's responsibility to correctly communicate the problem. Inherent in the purchase of expertise model is the assumption that the consultee has thought through the consequences of consultation.

Things happen when consultation takes place; a change in one part of an organization often affects other parts. Sometimes consultees are not fully aware of the potential long- and short-term impact of consultation. For example, polishing the communication skills of mid-level managers might have the unwanted impact of making them too assertive in trying to improve the entire organization. From the outset,

**T A B L E  11.1    Schein's Models Compared**

|  | EXPERT | DOCTOR | PROCESS CONSULTANT |
|---|---|---|---|
| Defines problem | Consultee | Consultant | Consultee with consultant |
| Suggests an intervention | Consultee | Consultant | Consultee with consultant |
| Major responsibility for work in consultation | Consultant | Consultant | Consultee |
| Consultee learns more effective problem solving | No | No | Yes |

effective consultants help the consultee think through the consequences a consultant's activities could have.

In summary, the purchase of expertise model is often appropriate when a problem has been well defined, such as when a consultant can provide specific information or training or when a glitch arises in a human service program. It works best when the consultee has ascertained the consultant's suitability for the job and has thoroughly thought through the consequences of consultation. Two of the most common forms of purchase of expertise consultation provided by human service consultants are education/training consultation and program consultation.

**Education/Training Consultation.**    The education/training approach is the most frequently used kind of purchase of expertise consultation. However, it is but one method of assisting organizations to change and should not be viewed as a stand-alone experience distinct from other organizational change initiatives (Arredondo, 1996). The use of consultants in education/training is often referred to as "staff development" or "professional development activities." Recent changes in organizations (see Chapter 8) have dictated an increased need for education/training consultation (Arredondo, 1996). Consultants provide education/training services in any number of settings, and topics range from motivation techniques and classroom discipline to substance-abuse prevention and effective parenting. The reason for this type of consultation is the facilitation of change or improvement in an organization or one of its subsystems. Education/training consultation can occur in a group or on an individualized basis for a variety of purposes.

As its name suggests, this approach emphasizes the two most common roles of the consultant: educator and trainer. In this type of consultation, the consultant shares expert knowledge and skills by some education means (such as a lecture on motivation) or through some kind of on-the-job training (such as a workshop on techniques for motivating supervisors). Gallessich (1982) defines the education/training model as prearranged, organized services, in contrast to the impromptu educational and training activities that are incidental to most

forms of consultation. This cost-effective model, an exemplar of the technological approach to consultation, is information-centered and emphasizes the dissemination of concepts, information, and skills rather than the formulation of a diagnosis. One caveat: sometimes organizations erroneously view training with the "training-can-fix-everything" syndrome (McLean, 2006).

*Consultation Goals.*    The primary goal of the education/training consultation is the increased effectiveness of the organization that results from the consultee's improved professional functioning in the area on which education and/or training focuses. The idea is that consultees will learn something new related to their job or, in the case of parents and guardians, something related to their care-giving responsibilities. When consultation is educative in nature, some form of information is being provided; when the consultant acts as trainer, however, the learning is usually experiential and focuses on skill acquisition.

Whether a consultant uses an educational or a training approach depends on whether the goal of consultation is to affect cognitive learning or to change attitudes and behaviors (Arredondo, 1996). In an example affecting cognitive learning, a consultant might provide a junior high school faculty an in-service program on the differences between a junior high school and a middle school. In an experiential learning situation, a consultant might have mid-level managers practice different types of strategies to strengthen their leadership skills.

Education and training can also be combined in consultation. For example, a group of ministers might first be taught the characteristics of depression by a mental health consultant and then participate in supervised counseling sessions in which they attempt to detect these characteristics by role-playing. Whether the consultant emphasizes education, training, or both depends primarily on what the consultee perceives the problem and its solution to be.

*Consultant Function and Roles.*    The consultant in education/training consultation functions as an expert who possesses information or skills that the consultee needs and transmits that knowledge in one or more of the roles of advisor, educator, trainer or technical expert. The consultant's function is to provide the information and/or the training that best matches a consultee's interests and needs (Conoley & Conoley, 1992) and is designed in the context of the particular workplace with emphasis on workplace goals (Arredondo, 1996; Cox, 2001).

In addition to assisting in needs assessment and in planning and implementing education/training interventions, the consultant also assists in the evaluation of consultation. Although many organizations have standard evaluation forms to help in this task, many consultants prefer to use their own forms that can be specifically tailored to any particular evaluation.

The purpose of evaluation is to determine whether consultees have learned the appropriate knowledge and skills required for the intervention in use. Lippitt and Lippitt (1986) were the first to define the critical skills needed to function effectively as a consultant in education/training consultation:

- assessing the training needs related to the problem
- developing and stating measurable objectives for learning experiences
- understanding the learning and change process
- designing a learning experience
- planning and designing educational events
- going beyond traditional training and using heuristic laboratory methods
- using multiple learning stimuli, including multimedia presentations
- functioning as a group teacher or trainer
- helping others learn how to learn

Consultants should remember that they also have a commitment to the organization and should consider any organizational impact the education/training may have.

*The Consultee's Experience in Consultation.* The major role of the consultee is to be a good learner.

Consultees are expected to learn the knowledge or skills they are taught, adapt them if necessary, and use them on the job to contribute to the organization's overall effectiveness. Consultees accomplish these tasks by giving the consultant honest and accurate information during needs assessment, being cooperative and motivated learners during the education/training process, and attempting to implement their new knowledge on the job.

During the needs assessment, the consultee is interviewed (or fills out a survey form) to identify topics for education/training, to give opinions on the nature of the problems of concern during the consultation, and to provide some idea of his or her willingness to participate in the consultation.

Most consultants agree that if consultees must be coerced, however subtly, to participate, positive benefits will probably not accrue from consultation. If consultee participation is voluntary, cooperation and motivation can be enhanced during consultation by providing special incentives for participating. Consultees can also be taught to understand that consultation is a process, to know how to initiate consultation, to understand that the timing of a request for consultation can affect both the process and the outcome, and to determine when to choose consultation from among the available services. Consultees can be encouraged to implement what they have learned by education/training methodologies that help them to personalize the material. It is one thing to listen to a lecture on management styles; it is another to be asked to consider how the different management styles match or contrast with a consultee's own style. Responding to consultees' perceived needs during the entire consultation process is an effective way to maximize the likelihood that consultees will follow through on consultation activities. However, as in all forms of consultation, it is ultimately up to consultees to decide whether or not they'll use the information and/or training received.

*Application: Consultant Techniques and Procedure.* The education/training model consists of four steps: needs assessment, planning the education/training activities, performing them, and evaluation.

Either the consultant or the organization's contact person conducts the needs assessment, which identifies the content of education/training sessions and occasionally the problems that consultation can help ameliorate. Needs assessments help identify discrepancies between "what is" and "what is desired" (McLean, 2006). Through the use of interviews, needs assessment can obtain in-depth information and opinions. This method is comprehensive, but it is very expensive and time consuming. In other cases, needs are assessed through questionnaires, which are cost effective and provide information that is relatively easy to collate. However, questionnaires frequently lack depth, and the framing of questions can affect the kinds of responses obtained. An example of a needs assessment form is provided in Figure 11.1.

Consultants should consider the nature of adult learners when *planning* activities. Adults have learning behaviors that are influenced by past experience, current abilities and roles, and future aspirations (Knowles, Holton, & Swanson, 2000). For example, although adult learners tend to be conservative in their educational outlook, they still enjoy innovative teaching methodologies. Many corporations and other organizations have applied modern concepts of adult learning in their education/training consultation.

The term *andragogy* refers to the art and science of helping adults learn (Knowles et al., 2000). There are several important points about andragogy that consultants should consider in their planning: adult learners are internally motivated, task-oriented, and rich resources for one another. In addition, consultants should take the following interrelated points into consideration in their planning:

- generate activities that will work best in the existing organizational culture;

- determine how the education/training strategies will be linked to other strategies around the topic;

- ensure linkage of the education/training to organizations goals; and

- determine how the message about the education/training will be disseminated (Arredondo, 1996).

---

Our organization has set aside the week of April 10 for staff development training. Your frank and candid responses to the following items will assist the training division in arranging for training and development activities that coincide with your needs. In the next few weeks we will collate your responses and put them into a questionnaire that will help us to formulate specific training needs and activities. Please answer the following questions carefully and return them to the training division by the end of this week. All responses will be kept anonymous. Thank you for your participation.

1.  I would benefit from knowing more about the following recent trends in my field:
2.  I would benefit from discussing the following current issues in my field:
3.  I would like to know more about the following new skills areas that are currently receiving much attention in my field:
4.  List the needs within your part of the organization that you think staff development should address.
5.  List the needs within the entire organization that you think staff development should address.
6.  Add any suggestions you think are relevant to the week of staff development.

**FIGURE 11.1**  A sample needs assessment form

Such planning allows creates a roadmap for the delivery of the education/training experience.

In *performing* the education/training, the consultant should attempt to use methods that are appropriate to the consultees' characteristics and the objectives of the consultation. Many education/training consultants use designs that incorporate methodologies (Garmston & Wellman, 1992) such as lectures, media and materials, structured laboratory experiences, small group discussions, behavioral role modeling, movement, and feedback. Off-the-shelf programs should be used with caution (Arredondo, 1996).

How consultees respond to the consultant at the outset of education/training also affects the ultimate success of the consultation. Therefore, regardless of the methods used, the consultant should make an attempt to create a good working climate (Conoley & Conoley, 1992), including:

- using moderate levels of self-disclosure at the outset

- being open about any concerns that relate to how the education/training is proceeding

- treating consultees with respect

- being open to consultee feedback

- learning consultees' names as quickly as possible

- being able to laugh at oneself when things go wrong

In addition, consultants using this type of consultation should consider the culture of the organization and permit participation by the consultees in all aspects of the education/training.

During *evaluation* of the education/training, consultants often use questionnaires and pre- and post-intervention measures of pertinent material. Evaluation is typically made in terms of participant reactions, participant learning, behavior/skill acquisition, and organizational impact (Kirkpatrick, 1998). Evaluations of education/training interventions include feedback loops that allow continuous adaptation of procedures and methods for measuring the impact of education/training on the entire organization. In evaluation of education/training it is often effective to focus on *impact* rather than *change,* given the often short-term nature of the experience.

In summary, education/training is evaluated both formally and informally by participants who assess its usefulness, by consultants who assess "how it went," and by administrators who decide how the organization might be affected (Knowles et al., 2000). Chapter 5 and 6 of this text cover related points on evaluation in more detail and depth.

**Case Example of Education/Training Consultation.**  A human service professor at a university was asked by the director of personnel services of a large school district to conduct some workshops for the district's school counselors and psychologists. When the consultant asked the director what kinds of workshops were desired, the director responded: "You know, some of that new counseling stuff." The consultant advocated the use of a needs assessment instrument to give prospective participants input about the nature of the workshops, and the director agreed to gather the information by using a form developed by the consultant.

The needs assessment revealed that the participants desired information and training for dealing with AIDS, teenage pregnancy, and date rape. The consultant planned the activities by developing behavioral objectives to be accomplished through a variety of methods. A balance was struck between providing information and skills training. The consultant also took the needs of adult learners into consideration during the planning process.

One workshop was held on each topic. Additional input from the participants was obtained at the beginning of the first workshop. Several methods were used during the workshops, and a good working climate was developed and maintained throughout the workshops. At the conclusion of each workshop, the participants evaluated the consultant, the workshop content, and the usefulness of the session. The consultant's views concerning the workshop and its effects on the participants were sent to the personnel services director in a written report.

**Program Consultation.**   Most human service organizations have programs that frequently require programmatic consultative services. Community-based consultants frequently engage in this type of consultation (Staton et al., 2007). Program consultation is a form of purchase of expertise consultation in which the organization in some way uses the consultant to help plan a new program or revise or deal with factors that affect an existing program. Program consultation is unique in that it is restricted to a specific program and its goals (Gallessich, 1982).

In program consultation, the organization "purchases" some kind of technical assistance. The organization perceives a need with respect to the program and hires a consultant to help fulfill that need. For example, a consultant might be hired to help design an evaluation assessing whether a program has met its goals; indeed, evaluation is the primary reason consultants are hired to assist with programs. Even though program consultation does not require any new skills on the part of the consultant, it clearly demonstrates how consultants can work with organizations to meet their goals (Hosie, 1994).

Program consultation is becoming increasingly popular due to human services and for-profit organizations' increased emphasis on programs, the increasingly complex technology related to programs, and the trend toward cost effectiveness and accountability in organizations (Lewis et al., 2003; Sears et al., 2006). In addition, the professional standards of organizations in which consultants work demand that evaluation of programs be performed. Outside consultants frequently use program consultation as a way to "get their feet in the door" of an organization and eventually perform other types of consultation. Many internal consultants are also called on to assist in program evaluation (Lusky & Hayes, 2001; Staton et al., 2007).

Program evaluation is critical as it sheds light on program strengths and weaknesses, provides a sense of why things happened as they did, and provides feedback for improvement (Zins et al., 2000), yet it is often ignored (Meyers & Nastasi, 1999). Recently, there has been increased interest in the consultant's role in sustaining project/program in-novations (see Adelman & Taylor, 2003).

The primary goal of program consultation is to provide an organization technical assistance so that a given program is successful. Consultation services can be provided for any aspect of a program, including development and evaluation. Consultation is usually requested for some skill or knowledge that the organization neither possesses nor has time to use. Because program evaluation is the most frequently requested form of program consultation, we'll focus now on how program evaluation consultation is performed. Program evaluation is a systematic set of data collection and analysis activities. It involves "determining the worth or values of actions directed toward specific goals as a means of assessing credibility" (Staton et al., 2007, p. 389). The results of program improvement are typically used for program improvement, accountability, or assessment related to program continuation. You should keep in mind that the program planning evaluation steps listed in Chapter 6 are not applicable here since the program already exists.

*Consultation Goals.*   The goal of program evaluation is to improve current decision making in the program being evaluated and to help develop policy (Hosie, 1994). Thus, the effort, effectiveness, and adequacy of a program can be improved (Illback, Zins, & Maher, 1999). Organizations want to know if their programs are meeting their goals and objectives. When they are not sure how best to determine this, organizations frequently turn to program consultants who evaluate with a variety of methods and then transmit their findings to the organization so that program decisions can be made. For example, a consultant might assist in evaluating the effects of an employee assistance program in a large textile firm.

A secondary goal of evaluation in program consultation is increasing the consultee's ability to evaluate current and subsequent (similar) programs. If this goal is part of the consultation, the consultant might also function in the education/training consultation model described earlier in this chapter; in this case the consultant "gives away" the very skills that led to the need for a consultant in the first place. Such a process helps to build a "culture of evaluation" in the organization (Rosen, Young, & Norris, 2006).

The integration of consultation and evaluation skills creates an approach that can assess local issues and can be particularly useful in human service and educational settings (Illback et al., 1999). A newer approach to program evaluation is a constructivist approach that concentrates on evaluative instruments that are sensitive to the unique needs of the program and the menu of practices available (Lusky & Hayes, 2001).

*Consultant Function and Roles.*   In this model, consultants act as objective experts in program development and evaluation: they provide accurate, timely, and useful information to decision makers so that the program can be run more effectively. The consultant, as a technical expert, conducts exploratory meetings with consultees to determine the needs of program evaluation, develops a program evaluation design, obtains consultee feedback on the design, and redesigns the evaluation (Hosie, 1994; Rosen et al., 2006). Often, the consultant has been involved in the evaluation design from the onset of the program. The use of qualitative evaluation strategies has increased as has the inclusion of all stakeholders in the evaluation process (Arredondo, 1996). The consultant then carries out the evaluation by collecting and analyzing data and filing a report. The process of designing a program evaluation can be very time consuming; much of the consultant's time is spent in preparation and planning (Illback et al., 1999). In models such as that proposed by Lusky and Hayes (2001) that view program evaluation as a gradual process, the success of one phase depends upon the success of the prior phase. Qualitative methods of program evaluation are becoming popular (Illback et al., 1999; Polkinghorne & Gribbons, 1999).

*Consultee Experience in Consultation.*   The consultee's primary role in this model is to provide the consultant with as much accurate information as possible, which is critical in the initial stages of program evaluation, because the consultant needs as much information as possible to develop the appropriate design. Therefore the consultee must make a commitment to spend whatever time and effort are required to be interviewed or to react to the consultant's progress in formulating a suitable evaluation design. Ideally the organization's administrative structure will sanction the consultees' participation so that they feel free to cooperate.

Consultees should do everything possible to ensure that consultants can function independently, particularly when internal consultants are asked to do program consultation that focuses on evaluation. Consultees should inform consultants before the evaluation what they will do if the results are positive, neutral, or negative to the program. Furthermore, consultees can help consultants by determining the type of final report that will be submitted: Will the report be sent directly to a top administrator? Should the report be written in non-technical language? Finally, consultees should inform consultants of any recent events within the organization that might affect the results of the evaluation.

*Application: Consultant Techniques and Procedures.* Four steps in program consultation focus on evaluation: hold ongoing meetings with consultees to design the evaluation, collect data, evaluate it, and write a final report.

After program evaluation has been requested, the consultant completes the entry stage as in any other consultation situation. Once the consultant is given permission to consult, the parties to receive the consultant's findings should be determined. The consultant is then ready to develop the program evaluation design, which involves a series of meetings with the consultees, typically called the "program staff." The participants try to identify what decisions are to be made, determine who the organization's important decision makers are, and discuss how the program evaluation will tie into the decisions to be made (Rosen et al., 2006). Evaluative methods can involve retrospective monitoring or naturalistic monitoring (Illback et al., 1999) and can include qualitative methods. In retrospective monitoring, "self report information is obtained from program managers and staff about the extent to which the program has been operationalized" (Illback et al., 1999, p. 917). In naturalistic monitoring, the evaluator examines the program processes directly. Outcome methods include goal attainment scaling Chapter 6. The success of the evaluation will depend upon the degree of congruence among the program, the evaluation scheme, and the setting of the program (Unger et al., 2000).

The consultant meets with the consultees for as many meetings as necessary until both consultant and consultees are confident that all parties have an appropriate understanding of what is to occur and why. From all of this information, the consultant begins to put together an evaluation design that dictates the who, what, where, and when of the evaluation procedure.

Regardless of the model of evaluation the consultant uses, there are four evaluation standards to bear in mind: accuracy, utility, feasibility, and propriety (Matuszek, 1981). Accuracy standards relate to the methodological soundness of the evaluation. Utility standards relate to the concept that evaluation should have some practical application. Feasibility standards deal with whether the evaluation design is appropriate for the program in the first place. Propriety standards relate to any ethical or legal issues that are connected to the evaluation. Consultants will also want to include qualitative methods of evaluation (such as periodic discussions with program developers as a source of data about program implementation) and not rely exclusively on quantitative indicators (Domitrovich & Greenberg, 2002). Once the consultant has put together the program evaluation design, a final review is held with the consultees and parties-at-interest. Any needed modifications in the design are made at this time.

The consultant is now ready to carry out the design. Data are collected and analyzed according to the design plan. Program consultants anticipate problem areas in carrying out the evaluation and stay in contact with all parties involved during data collection and analysis (Hosie, 1994). After the data have been analyzed, the consultant writes and presents a formal report so that appropriate action can be taken. The consultant will frequently involve program staff in making use of the evaluation results (Illback et al., 1999). For an interesting description of program evaluation in school and community settings, consult Unger et al. (2000).

**Case Example of Program Consultation.** Pat, a psychologist in private practice, is selected by a human service agency to help evaluate its Big Brother Big Sister program, which has been in operation for three years. Although the agency thinks that the program is "doing okay," there appears to be a high turnover rate among its volunteers. Pat has had considerable experience with program evaluation and has worked with volunteer programs in the past.

He starts out by holding a meeting with the program's staff to design an evaluation. Four other meetings are held to make sure that the parties involved are in agreement about what is going on and that the evaluation is proceeding smoothly. Pat and the program staff then collect information on the volunteers and the children in the program, including how long volunteers tend to stay with the program. Methods are determined for assessing the program's impact on the children. Pat then analyzes the collected data and presents a report to the program staff. Among other things, the data show that volunteers last an average of nine months, receive little recognition or encouragement from the agency, and are not sure what is expected from them.

Pat recommends a training program for the volunteers, more personal contact with the volunteers by the program's staff, and some form of recognition for service as a volunteer. The program's impact on the children was deemed to be positive. Parents reported that volunteers gave their children additional, desirable adult role models and helped "keep the kids off the streets." The children liked the program because they "got to do a lot of extra things that were fun."

**The Doctor–Patient Model.** Sometimes consultees know something is wrong but don't know what it is. When consultation is requested, the consultant is given the power to make a diagnosis and prescribe a solution. It is as if the consultee says, "I don't know what's wrong. Find out and tell me how I can fix it."

In the doctor–patient model, another type of expert consultation, the consultee is "purchasing" the consultant's expertise in diagnosing and prescribing. Schein (1990c) points out that the consultant's role in the doctor–patient model differs from that in the purchase of expertise model because "it empowers the consultant to dig into the workings of the organization and to combine information gathering expertise with knowledge of organizations such that a deeper and consultee-relevant diagnosis can be reached" (p. 264).

For the doctor–patient model to be effective, the following assumptions must be met (Schein, 1987, 1988):

- The diagnostic process itself is seen as helpful and not disruptive.

- The consultee has correctly interpreted the organization's symptoms and has located the "sick" area.

- The person or group defined as "sick" will provide the information needed to make a valid diagnosis; that is, they will neither hide data nor exaggerate symptoms.

- The consultee understands and will correctly interpret the diagnosis provided by the consultant and will implement whatever prescription is offered.

- The consultee can remain effective after the consultant leaves.

The very act of calling a consultant to perform a diagnosis is an intervention, and the consultant should make sure that the consultee is aware of this. If the consultee is unaware that diagnosis is an intervention or does not explain the consultant's presence adequately, then the consultant's efforts can meet considerable resistance that can adversely affect the results of consultation.

Because organizations are very complex entities, faith that the consultee has correctly interpreted the symptoms and knows where the organization is "sick" is a very large assumption. Consultees can easily misconstrue and misjudge events on the job. In addition, consultees and consultants can easily get caught in a cycle of incorrect diagnoses due to the consultee's desire for help and the consultant's desire to give it.

The doctor–patient model assumes that consultees and other members of the organization are straightforward and honest with the consultant about their perceptions of the organization's problems. The nature of this honesty is a function of the organizational climate: If the climate is one of mistrust, then the consultant is not likely to get the real story; if the climate is one of trust, the consultees and other organization members are likely to tell the consultant everything and may even exaggerate the problem. The consultant also needs to be cautious about creating dependence among consultees.

What will happen if the consultee doesn't like the consultant's diagnosis? Even if the diagnosis is accepted, what guarantees are there that the prescription is going to be implemented? It may not be accurate to assume that the consultee will accept diagnosis and prescription and remain effective after the consultant leaves—especially if the consultee did not learn any problem-solving skills during the consultation. If a similar problem arises for the consultee in the future, the consultant will have to be called in again.

Clearly, the relationship between the consultant and consultee is critical in the doctor–patient model of consultation. The consultant must be able to gain the trust of the consultee so that open communication can occur. If the consultee trusts the consultant, then real issues helpful to the diagnosis are more likely to emerge. In addition, if the consultant is able to create an effective relationship with the consultee and develop professional credibility, the prescription provided to the consultee also has more credibility.

In summary, the doctor–patient model works best when the consultee is willing to use a consultant, has observed and described the symptoms accurately, does not have the ability to perform the diagnosis and prescription, and is willing to follow through on the consultant's recommendations. A possible drawback of this model is that consultees might not enhance their problem-solving skills and may become dependent on the consultant. Because many ideas in the doctor–patient model, including diagnosis, are covered in Chapter 4, only a brief overview of this model is given now.

*Consultation Goals.*    The consultant's primary goal in the doctor–patient model is to define the organization's problem and to recommend realistic interventions to ameliorate that problem. Enhancing the consultee's diagnostic skills is not a goal in this model.

*Consultant Functions and Roles.*    The consultant functions as an expert who enters the system, interviews consultees and parties-at-interest, collects data, makes a diagnosis, and recommends a solution. The consultant may well be hired to implement the solution, in which case he or she would change to the purchase of expertise model. Whereas the latter model demands content expertise on the part of the consultant, the doctor–patient model demands expertise in diagnostic and prescriptive skills.

Consulting skills that are critical to the doctor–patient model include:

- diagnostic skills
- a broad repertoire of prescriptive skills
- an in-depth knowledge of organizational theory
- the ability to "read" organizations
- data collection skills
- data interpretation skills
- human relations skills

*Consultee Experience in Consultation.*    The main task of the consultee is to be a good "patient"—that is, to tell the consultant in as honest, objective, and accurate a way as possible the areas in which the organization has problems. The consultee should realize that the very act of using a consultant will affect the organization in some way. The consultee's tasks also include assisting the consultant in gathering additional data, ensuring that the consultant's diagnosis is

fully and accurately understood, and advocating that the consultant's prescription be implemented.

*Application: Consultant Techniques and Procedures.*
In the doctor–patient model consultants enter the system as they would in any other consultation model. The major step in this model is to determine how best to go about making a diagnosis which is based on the situation. The method used to diagnose the organization's problems should obtain information about how its people see the organization's internal processes (Beer, 1980). It is crucial for the consultant to ensure that people involved in the diagnosis feel free to express their true thoughts, opinions, and feelings.

After the data have been gathered, the consultant analyzes it and formulates a diagnosis. The diagnosis defines problems in the organization in terms that the consultee can both understand and utilize.

The consultant typically follows one of three paths after making the diagnosis (Schein, 1990c): The consultant shares the diagnosis with the consultee as the basis for collaborating on finding a solution, shares the diagnosis and ends the consultation relationship, or makes recommendations and then helps implement them. In the latter case, the consultant then moves from the doctor–patient model to the purchase of expertise model.

Usually the consultant determines what is best for the consultee to do about the problem. However, consultants cannot necessarily help consultees make a commitment to change; they can only prescribe some solutions that the organization is capable of carrying out and tailor them to the unique aspects of the organization. Generalized prescriptions are rarely successful because they fail to consider the uniqueness of each organization.

**Case Example of Doctor–Patient Consultation.**    A counselor in a community counseling center was asked to be an internal consultant to improve the center's effectiveness in delivering services to its clients. She was chosen because of her effective diagnostic skills, her solid working knowledge of organizations, and her trustworthiness. The consultant was given "free run" of the center and was charged with defining the center's problem areas and prescribing some ways to effectively manage them. She began by informing all staff members of the nature of consultation. Interviews and surveys were used to gather data from the center's administration, staff, and former clients. Complete confidentiality was guaranteed to all involved. Information was sought on such factors as interpersonal relationships, views of the center's organizational climate, and the center's role and mission. Based on the analysis of the data, the consultant concluded that there was little consensus concerning the center's overall role and mission, which led to a lack of understanding of how the center was run and what the staff and administration were supposed to do. This lack of understanding in turn led to inadequacies in the area of program development.

The consultant prescribed a review and subsequent modification of the center's role and mission statement. Furthermore, she recommended development of a five-year strategic plan based on the modified role and mission statement and suggested that all employees be involved in each of these activities.

**The Process Model.**  Schein (1990c) points out that failure to involve the consultee in the diagnosis may lead him or her to misdiagnose the problems inadvertently. This led Schein (1987, 1988, 1999) to formulate his model of process consultation. The basic difference between this model and the purchase of expertise and doctor–patient models is that the consultant's expertise includes skills to involve the consultee in defining the problem, to form a team with the consultee, and to ensure that the consultation process focuses on the consultee's needs. The consultant's expertise lies in making individual consultees as well as groups of consultees more effective problem-solvers in the future (McLean, 2006). Process consultation may be in order when a consultant is needed to supplement the consultee's problem-solving skills—the consultee knows something is wrong and wants to figure out what it is and what to do about it.

Process consultation can be defined as guidance provided to some group by an individual "trained in group dynamics and organization development" (Kormanski & Eschbach, 1997, p. 137). French and Bell (1999) note that most organization development consultation easily falls under the framework of process consultation.

Process consultation is what the consultant does to help the consultee identify, understand, and change the process events that occur within an organization (Schein, 1978, 1999). The focus of consultation is not on the content of the problem, but rather on the process by which problems are solved. The consultee "owns" the problem (and continues to own it throughout the consultation process) and "purchases" the consultant's expertise in handling process events. Process consultation is designed to help consultees examine and deal with human and social events as they relate to problems the consultee tries to solve (French & Bell, 1999).

Process consultation is based on the premise that often things in an organization can be changed only if the consultee is involved in diagnosing the problem and generating solutions. Because of the complexity of problems in organizations and the consultees' familiarity with them, consultees' input into the diagnosis is crucial. In addition, advice given by consultants can be counterproductive in that it can cause resistance, power struggles, and resentment.

The relationship between the consultant and the consultee is extremely important. The consultant must create an environment of trust and credibility and help the consultee feel safe enough to own the problem and work on it throughout the consultation process. Such tasks demand empathy, respect, and genuineness on the part of the consultant. Process consultation works best when the following assumptions are met (Schein, 1987):

- The consultee is distressed somehow but does not know the source of the distress or what to do about it.

- The consultee does not know either what kind of assistance might be available or which consultant could provide the help needed.

- The nature of the problem is such that the consultee not only needs help in figuring out what is wrong, but would also benefit from participation in the diagnostic process.

- The consultee has "constructive intent," is motivated by goals and values that the consultant can accept, and has some capacity to enter into a helping relationship.

- The consultee is ultimately the only one who knows what form of intervention will work best in the situation.

- The consultee is capable of learning how to diagnose and solve his or her own organizational problems. (pp. 32–33)

In a nutshell, process consultation assumes that consultees must acquire and maintain ownership of their problems, that they do not fully understand these problems, and that they can learn to design and manage change on their own (Ledford, 1990).

The process consultation model is most applicable when a consultee with some problem-solving ability is willing to learn how to work out solutions without seeking content assistance or giving the problem to the consultant for diagnosis. By focusing on the *how* rather than the *what* of problem solving, the consultant and consultee work together, enabling the consultee to solve current concerns and similar ones in the future. Schein (1990c) admits that the need for content experts will increase in the future, but that their services will not be well-utilized unless their efforts are combined with process consultation.

*Consultation Goals.*  The primary goal of process consultation is to help consultees gain insight into the everyday events occurring within the organization. It attempts to teach consultees to act on those events and become more adept at identifying and modifying them in ways that achieve their goals (Schein, 1987). If the consultant and consultee are successful, the ultimate goal of increasing the organization's overall effectiveness is also met.

*Consultant Functions and Roles.*  The primary roles played by the process consultant are facilitator and catalyst. The consultant collaborates with the consultees such that consultation becomes a joint effort. Rather than providing content expertise, the consultant facilitates consultees process of self-discovery and self-exploration so that they are able to use their skills in identifying and addressing the problems at hand.

The consultant must be an expert in processes that occur at the individual, interpersonal, and intergroup levels; content expertise in the consultee's institution's area of perceived difficulty is not required. The consultant helps the consultee obtain insight into the everyday human activities in an organization (for example, who talks to whom about what), which are viewed as critical to the appropriate diagnosis of an organizational problem (Schein, 1988, 1999). The process consultant provides less structure and direct input than would a consultant operating in either the purchase of expertise or doctor–patient models. This lack of structure can be threatening to the consultee because of unpredictability inherent to process consultation (Ledford, 1990).

In addition to creating a climate conducive to consultee exploration and input, the process consultant assists in gathering data about the relationships within the organization and members' perceptions of organizational processes. The consultant then assists the consultee in making a diagnosis using these data, and process-oriented interventions such as agenda setting and feedback are made by the consultant and consultee. Finally, the consultant helps the consultee evaluate the consultation by looking for changes in values and interpersonal behaviors within the organization (Golembiewski, 1993e). The consultant's success is measured by how effectively consultees define and achieve their goals and whether the changes produced remain effective in the long run (Schmuck, 1995). Once the evaluation has been concluded, the consultant reduces involvement and terminates the consultation.

*Consultee Experience in Consultation.*  The consultee—a person within the organization and perhaps a manager—senses that something is not quite right in the organization, that things could be better, and that he or she wants them to improve. The consultee uses the consultant to translate vague feelings and perceptions into concrete actions to enhance the overall effectiveness of the organization (Bennis et al., 1985).

The major role of the consultee in this model is that of an active collaborator and teammate (Murrell, 1993). The consultee is assumed to have some problem-solving skills and be knowledgeable about his or her organization. The consultee provides the content of the consultation and participates in the processes at issue as the consultee's process skills dictate. The consultee then discusses content issues and the nature of the perceived problems, sets goals, and attempts to make plans for action (Schmuck, 1995). The consultation process itself helps the consultee define diagnostic steps that lead to action plans or organizational change (Bennis et al., 1985). Process consultation can be more demanding and threatening to consultees than other types of consultation because its open-ended emphasis may lead to uncomfortable areas or issues (Ledford, 1990).

*Application: Consultant Techniques and Procedures.*
The premise of process consultation is that organizations are merely networks of people. If these networks are not functioning effectively, there will be extreme difficulty in accomplishing the tasks of the organization. Process consultation attempts to enhance the overall functioning of the organization by helping the consultee change values and develop skills. In effect, the consultee's development is accomplished when the consultant models the desired values and skills. During this process, the consultee begins to take more and more responsibility for the diagnosis and implementation of procedures. As the desired skills and values become more evident in the consultee's behavior, the consultant gradually disengages from consultation.

There are seven overlapping steps to process consultation (Schein, 1988):

1.  making initial contact with the consultee organization
2.  defining the relationship, formal contacting, and creating a psychological contract
3.  selecting a setting and method of work
4.  gathering data and making a diagnosis
5.  intervening
6.  reducing involvement
7.  terminating

The process consultant spends a significant amount of time building relationships with consultees and assumes that, without trust, the consultee will not deal with the basic issues that are concerning the organization, and therefore consultation will not likely be successful. In addition to developing trust, the consultant selects a work site close to "where the action is." By being able to observe the real work of the organization, he or she is able to ask the right kinds of questions to help consultees explore things such as organizational culture and values.

The process consultant favors the use of interventions that maximize opportunities for consultee–consultant interactions. Consequently, observation, informal interviews, and group discussions are used frequently by process consultants. The process consultant considers data gathering to be a crucial process that should be conducted in a manner consistent with the consultee's values. Further, the process consultant believes that plans for gathering data should be general in nature because the only way to determine how to proceed is to use experiences resulting from initial data-gathering strategies.

As process consultation proceeds, the consultant can intervene in a variety of ways. Schein has categorized these in terms of their tactical goals—exploration, diagnosis, action alternatives, and confrontation—because the process consultant usually moves through these interventions in that order as the consultation process unfolds. The consultant uses exploratory questions to stimulate the consultee's thinking and to determine his or her views. Diagnostic interventions are used to involve the consultee in the diagnostic process, action alternatives help convince the consultee that something can be done about the situation, and confrontational interventions are used to test the consultee's motivation and willingness to act.

Regarding evaluation, the process consultant determines what outcomes might occur as a result of consultation and how they are to be measured. As its ultimate goal, process consultation attempts to improve organizational performance by changing values and interpersonal skills in key personnel.

**Case Example of Process Consultation.** A group of teachers at a secondary school was unsatisfied with the general quality of communication between the staff and students and wanted to improve the communication efforts of the staff as a whole. They asked Gene, the school counselor, to sit in at their meetings and act as a "sounding board," which he agreed to do.

Time at the end of each meeting was allocated for Gene to give feedback to the group. He was also asked to help the group stay on task and get through the problem-solving process. During the consultation Gene provided feedback to the group on its problem-solving skills, challenged it to define its goals more precisely, and suggested that group members develop specific ways to evaluate their attempts to communicate better. All in all, he helped the group members become more effective problem solvers. Finally, Gene provided feedback on the group's ways of gathering information from students and the types of interventions it developed for improving communication. When everyone involved was satisfied with the way things were going, Gene reduced involvement with the group and attended only every third meeting.

## COLLABORATION FROM AN
## ORGANIZATIONAL PERSPECTIVE

The aim of organizational collaboration is the same as organizational consultation: the enhanced functioning of the organization. As organizations have become complex, collaboration across elements of the organization has almost become an essential component of organizations' everyday routine (Rawlings, 2000). Because of the tremendous increase in "in-house" human service professionals, such as human resource development specialists, or-

ganizations are uniquely poised to maximize the benefits of collaboration. Structures such as self-directed work teams, quality circles, and project management teams all lend themselves to having the human service professional function as a collaborator. In organizations where collaboration is relatively new, human service professionals can train members of the organization in problem-solving skills and team functioning. The human service professional can then participate as a collaborator and take responsibility for the outcome of some aspects of the project, as well as providing consultation to, and receiving it from, fellow collaborators.

Because of its collaborative nature, the process consultation model may be the easiest to adapt to collaboration. Human services professionals will need to adapt the purchase of expertise and doctor–patient models to include a method for empowering fellow collaborators who can use their own expertise to a greater degree and develop a shared vision.

The emergence of the internal consultant role also has implications for collaboration in organizations (Caplan et al., 1994). Managers, for example, may find it more suitable to have some responsibility for some part of a plan rather than be seen as a person trying to consult with a subordinate, thereby walking the thin line between supervision and consultation (Caplan et al., 1994). Finally, although leaders of organizations see the need for collaboration, they sometimes have difficulty building the capacity for it (Rawlings, 2000). One method of building such capacity involves developing a shared vision, a shared understanding, and shared goals (Rawlings, 2000). Organizational collaboration has received more attention in the literature and has been used more frequently by all types of organizations.

## MULTICULTURAL ASPECTS RELATED
## TO ORGANIZATIONAL
## CONSULTATION

Schein's typology sets the stage for the effective practice of multicultural consultation. Those cultural groups that prefer structured, expert-based

---

**C A S E   11.1     Organizational Consultation for School Consultants**

---

Doris is a middle school consultant who was asked by the administration of her school to work with one of its interdisciplinary teams. The team consisted of a social studies teacher, a math teacher, a science teacher, and a language arts teacher.

The team leader had been complaining to the administration that certain team members consistently go "around" her rather than "through" her when communicating with the principal. This was in spite of the fact that the principal had reminded the other team members of proper protocol.

As Doris was determining how to approach the team, she realized that part of the problem was the principal's high level of approachability. The principal met with Doris and the team and asked them to work together on resolving the apparent problem the team was having. The principal mentioned that the team may want to use Doris for building some procedures for communicating outside of the team.

Doris started out by meeting with the team during its planning session. As she heard the intensity of the feelings among the team members, she decided that process consultation was in order. It was obvious to Doris that *how* things were being said was just as important as *what* was being said.

Doris suggested: (1) that the team knew it had a problem in internal and external communication (the team members, including the leader, agreed), (2) that the members were in the best position to determine how to resolve these issues, and (3) that they engage in a collaborative effort that would help them solve not only their current concern but similar ones in the future. She and the team agreed to meet for three sessions during the next month.

In playing the roles of facilitator and catalyst, Doris raised questions for exploration and helped the team look closely at itself and its communication processes. She raised the issue of authority when it appeared that there were differences in whether the team leader was "in charge" or a "group spokesperson." The team felt awkward as it attempted to be humane yet honest. The teachers had worked together for over 10 years but only recently had been placed together as a team.

At the close of the third session when Doris asked the team to evaluate her, themselves, and the progress that had been made, the members generally acknowledged that, she had been of great assistance as an objective facilitator. Though they had initially been defensive and looked for blame rather than taking responsibility for the problems they were experiencing, the members had come to agreement about the role of team leader, resolved their authority issue, and improved their communication in terms of concreteness and authenticity. Doris followed up in one last meeting a month later.

**Commentary**

Doris demonstrated some excellent skills in determining which approach to organizational consultation she might take. She noted the significant amount of emotion surrounding the team's functioning and accurately determined that process consultation, with its more interpersonal focus, was an appropriate method with which to start. She also astutely determined that if the goal was to get the team to collaborate more effectively, then the approach to consultation should be one, like process consultation, that places people in a position of collaborating to solve their problems.

---

consultation should find the purchase of expertise model attractive. Its focus on problem- solving and content expertise allows consultees the security of having a knowledgeable and skilled person leading the consultation process. The purchase of expertise model demands little in terms of self disclosure or expression of feeling. For those cultural groups that desire an expert and prefer assistance with problem definition and determining interventions, the doctor–patient model will be attractive. For those who prefer a nonhierarchical relationship, the purchase

of expertise model may not be attractive. By its focus on diagnosis, the doctor–patient model can readily take cultural variables into consideration. Like the purchase of expertise model, the doctor–patient model demands limited self-disclosure. For those groups that value the nature of the relationship, process consultation is an attractive model. Its focus on understanding the interpersonal process as an aspect of problem definition creates the necessity for a strong relationship between the consultant and the consultee. For cultural groups with strong self-

**C A S E  11.2    Organizational Consultation for Community Consultants**

The general manager of the local branch of AME Telephone Company contacted the local mental health agency for the purpose of developing and implementing a professional outplacement counseling program. The company was undergoing a downsizing mandated by its parent company. The general manager informed the director of the mental health agency that the parent company had made funds available for the purpose of counseling displaced workers. The manager noted that almost half of the unit's 56 workers were going to be laid off.

Maria, a community mental health consultant, was assigned to explore the possibilities of the agency working with the telephone company. Using the principles of program consultation, she spent a great deal of time with the manager discussing the nature of the telephone company, which was a typical bureaucracy many other telephone and utility companies she had worked with over the past 20 years. Everyone had their assigned duties and did them well. The general manager was aware of the bureaucratic structure and attempted to ensure adequate morale by having an upbeat newsletter and recognition of birthdays. He also used a personal touch by getting out and about in the divisions of the company, and he knew each employee by name.

After she had a feel for the nature of the organization, Maria informed the manager about some general principles of outplacement counseling and the possible structures that such a program could address. She noted the importance of the morale program with those employees remaining with the company, as well as the goodwill the program could develop with the departing employees. Maria and the manager discussed the positive impact that an outplacement program could have not only on the local unit, but also on the parent company's national reputation. Any outplacement program has three phases: preparing the company to make terminations, helping those employees who are terminated find new jobs, and assisting remaining employees to feel secure.

As Maria and the general manager roughed out an outline that Maria could develop into a program proposal, they concluded that the general manager himself should undergo some training in effective termination, determined that severance packages should be discussed with the employees being terminated prior to the offering of outplacement services, and discussed the nature of outplacement counseling services needed by the employees. Since the company was in a moderately rural area, many of the employees' families had lived in the area for generations. Hence, part of the counseling process would encourage employees to discuss their feelings concerning termination, myths and realities about finances, career counseling, and placement.

Maria and the manager discussed outplacement concepts that seemed particularly applicable to the employees being terminated at the telephone company: job hunts within and outside the local community; "creating your own job" strategies; and testing and assessment of a candidate's aptitudes; and skills. Finally, they determined what the outplacement counseling program could do for the remaining company employees and addressed occupational wellness.

Based on their discussion, Maria developed a proposal for the program and submitted it to the mental health agency director and the telephone company general manager for approval. The program included a detailed blueprint for how the program was to be implemented and an extensive evaluation procedure that included input from all employees as well as placement success data.

**Commentary**

Maria did an excellent job of being thorough in her approach to program consultation. Instead of plugging in a canned program, she analyzed the organization and considered some of its unique aspects. Notice how she educated the general manger and made him part of the intervention. Maria also looked at the outplacement counseling program from the perspective of the entire company by including something for the remaining employees. Such systemic thinking enhances the probability of successful program implementation.

The idea for this case study came from an article by Siobhan McGowan (1993) entitled "Employees, Managers Work It Out after Layoffs" in *Guidepost, 35*(10), 1, 10.

determination needs, this model allows for them to bring and use their own personal resources in the consultation process. Process consultation can be viewed as empowering to disenfranchised groups.

Finally, with the rise of coaching as a subset of consultation, coaching across diversity lines will require more attention in the future (Thomas, 2006).

## SUMMARY

Organizational consultation encompasses many types of consultation performed by consultants, internal or external. Consultants function as technical experts, diagnosticians, or process experts to increase overall effectiveness. The organization itself, or one of its parts, is the client, and consultees are people in the organization with whom the consultant works.

Organizational consultation has its roots in the fields of industrial technology, manufacturing productivity, the applied behavioral sciences, and managerial science. Important work in organizational consultation includes that of Blake and Mouton (1983), Schein (1987, 1988, 1999), Lippitt and Lippitt (1986), and French and Bell (1999).

The basic assumptions of organizational consultation are that the process is as important as the content; the behavior of individuals, groups, and organizations is cyclical in nature; and satisfied personnel make for effective organizations.

Organizations suffer because their personnel lack the knowledge, skills, or values to function at optimal levels of effectiveness. Organizational consultants, armed with a broad repertoire of techniques grounded in organizational theory, attempt to help consultees deal with the complexities of organizational life and enhance effectiveness.

Consulting with organizations is a little like feeding a hungry animal: in living its life, the organization uses up energy and becomes hungry. If it doesn't get some food (consultation), it cannot function optimally and will eventually starve to death.

## RECENT TRENDS

The major trends in organizational consulting are linked to several societal factors: the impact of living and working in an information society; the ever-increasing pace of change in all aspects of life; the growing awareness that change requires systemic thinking; the realization that change can be successfully accomplished only through social influence (Schein, 2006; Truscott et al., 2000); and increasing internationalization and diversity within organizations (Plummer, 1998; Rawlings, 2000). These factors have created the following general trends in organizational consulting: a continued reliance on computer hardware and software, a primary consideration of the effects of organizational culture and diversity on consultation efforts when selecting interventions, and the willingness and ability of organizational consultants to "wear many hats" when

they provide services. For example, as diversity continues to increase in the work force, consultants will need to be increasingly sensitive to workplace diversity issues related to organizational infrastructure, job satisfaction, relationships among staff, and work productivity (Sears et al., 2006; Steward, 1996).

One trend in organizational consultation is the tendency to combine process consultation with the purchase of expertise and doctor–patient models (Schein, 1990c, 1999; French & Bell, 1999). Schein (1990c) suggests that such combinations involve consultees at more significant levels in the consultation process and enhance the probability of success in consultation. By combining process consultation with other forms, the consultant ensures that the consultee is appropriately invested in the process, the appropriate problems are being worked on, the diagnosis is relevant and clear to pertinent parties, and the solutions generated are appropriate for the organizational context and culture (Rockwood, 1993; Schein, 1990c, 1999). Further, since consultation is a helping relationship, focus on process events such as the dynamics of communication is essential (Schein, 1999).

There has been an increase in consultants acting as coaches to mangers and administrators (Davison & Gasiorowski, 2006). As you most likely know, the term "coaching" has been all over the organizational consultation literature, yet there is very little in the literature that speaks to agreement on the definition of the term and very little empirical evidence about its effectiveness. Recently, Schein (2006) has suggested that coaching is a subset of consultation. Regardless of the coaching situation, consultation skills such as the ability to move easily among the expert, doctor–patient, and process roles is essential (Schein, 2006, p. 24).

One trend in education/training consultation has been the emergence of performance consultation (Robinson & Robinson, 1995). Performance consultation assumes that solutions proposed by education/training approaches often miss the mark because what are really needed are solutions that are based on *performance*. Performance consultation assumes that the focus should not be on skill acquisition because much of the research on training suggests that trainees do not follow through after the training. While the education/training approach focuses on training activities and experiences, performance consultation teaches the skills and knowledge related to specific job performance. In short, performance consultation makes the shift from what consultees need to learn to what they must do.

There has been increased involvement of organizational consultants in schools (Merrell et al., 2006). Consultants have been asked to assist in addressing a variety of issues such as those posed by the No Child Left Behind Act, school violence, and the achievement gap between majority and minority students.

Another trend is the emergence of diversity consultation. Diversity consultation recognizes the increasing diversity in the workplace and the importance of managing diverse work environments. Diversity consultation is used to deal with issues related to awareness, sociopolitical implications, open dialogue, cultural competence, and cultural norms (Ingraham, 2000; Thomas, 2006).

There is an increasing emphasis placed on determining how and when to apply models of organizational consultation. For example, Carson and Lowman (2002) discuss the implications of individual-level variables on organizational consultation. Fuqua and Kurpius (1993) have developed seven principles for assisting consultants in determining how best to select from among consultation models:

1.  Consultants should select models congruent with the perceived needs of consultees and the organization.

2.  Consultants should clearly articulate to consultees which model is being used.

3.  The major goal in model selection should be expanding consultees' conceptual framework.

4.  The model should allow consultees to generalize from the enhanced conceptual framework after the consultant exits.

5.  The most powerful implementations will involve development of the consultees.

6.  There is more positive power in sharing the application of models with consultees.

7.  The application of multiple models will more likely lead to consultation success than will applying a single model.

There is a trend toward creating standards for organizational consultation assessment and evaluation. Cooper and O'Connor (1993) have developed a conceptual framework for organizational consultation measures based on the focus of the intervention (i.e., specific individual, group, or organizational processes) and the target of the assessment (i.e., individual, group, or organizational processes). In addition, there is increasing emphasis on the fact that a combination of quantitative and qualitative assessment measures can be of great benefit to organizational consultants. This trend has created some significant issues related to effective assessment in organizational consultation (Cooper & O'Connor 1993; Fuqua et al., 1999; Levinson, 2002; see also Chapter 8).

As noted in Chapter 7, consultants are increasing being called upon to provide service in crisis and disaster situations (Gottlieb, 2005; McCarroll & Ursano, 2006; Stock, 2007). Organizations use consultants to review or create crisis management plans and to train organizational personnel in how to react. The idea is for the consultant to help the organization "plan pre-event interventions to minimize post-event consequences" (McCarroll & Ursano, 2007, p. 193).

## CONCLUSIONS

Because organizational consultation encompasses a variety of approaches, it is difficult to assess its major contributions. It has, however, clearly contributed to improving workplace conditions (e.g., through process consultation) and helping organizations become more diverse and accountable (e.g., through program consultation).

Organizational consultation has emphasized the interconnectedness between meeting human needs and organizational structure. The specialized types of consultation available in organizational consultation have increased. Organizational consultation's concept of the organization-as-client has helped organizations understand the importance of organizational culture; indeed, most organizations now realize that organizational culture strongly influences much individual behavior (French & Bell, 1999). Organizational consultation has also demonstrated that working with groups of consultees can be a cost-effective way to meet workers' needs and increase organizational effectiveness.

The criticisms of organizational consultation are frequently those directed at organization development; for example, that it has not fulfilled its early promise to integrate or systematize its interventions. The following criticisms were adapted from a critique of organizational consultation by Gallessich (1982, pp. 221–222). Unfortunately, they are still true today:

- It is too preoccupied with interpersonal process to the detriment of problem-related factors such as budgeting and technology.
- Its interventions are often "Band-Aids on an open wound" and hence are not effective in solving many organizational problems in the long run. (For example, there is an overreliance on the use of workshops to solve identified concerns.)

- Its results are often "cosmetic" or only involve "fine-tuning."
- Its consultants sometimes perform "dirty work" or "spy" for managers and other administrators.
- Its consultants sometimes produce such grand designs that their interventions in effect are worse than the organization's problems were in the first place.
- Its consultants sometimes try to apply methods of business and industry when providing organizational consultation to human service agencies.

There are yet other criticisms of organizational consultation. Some organizational consultants rely on one or two pet interventions, particularly workshops, and some cannot always take into account administrators' deeply rooted assumptions about administration and personnel—assumptions that may differ from those held by the consultant. Hence, there is at the outset of consultation tremendous potential for resistance that may never be overcome.

Schein (1987, 1988) noted that the purchase of expertise and doctor–patient models are limited because they rely on basic assumptions that are rarely met in practice. Therefore, they are at best superficial and, at worst, counterproductive.

Organizational consultation frequently does not accurately take into account the external forces operating on the organization or internal issues such as those related to diversity (Ingraham, 2000). Consulting with an organization on Madison Avenue would therefore require dealing with external forces quite different from those operating on an organization in the rural South. Organizational consultation is also criticized for not realizing its potential because researchers and practitioners have not developed better theories (Adlerfer, 1990) or they have jumped on new but untested initiatives (Block, 2000).

These criticisms reflect more the imperfections of practicing organizational consultants than imperfections in the models and their principles. Accordingly, better training procedures for organizational consultants are as likely to produce improvements, as would refinements in organizational consultation models.

## SUGGESTIONS FOR EFFECTIVE PRACTICE

- Be able to determine if you should be using the purchase of expertise, doctor–patient, or process model of consultation.

- Remember that your ultimate goal in organizational consultation is to assist the entire organization in some way.

- Use the dictum that *how* you do what you do is as important as *what* you do.

## QUESTIONS FOR REFLECTION

1. What historical forces led to the development of organizational consultation?

2. How can an organization be a client?

3. Differentiate among the purchase of expertise, doctor–patient, and process models of consultation.

4. Why are the purchase of expertise and doctor–patient models particularly limited?

5. Explain how both education/training and program consultation are examples of purchase of expertise consultation.

6. Why is program evaluation the most common function of the program consultant?

7. Process consultation aims for changes in values and skills of the consultees involved. How are these values and skills related to organizational effectiveness?

8. Is it really possible for a consultant to produce an accurate diagnosis of an organization's problem? Why or why not?

9. Why do so few consultees follow through on the prescriptions made by organizational consultants?

10. How can multicultural issues be dealt with at the organizational level?

# SUGGESTED SUPPLEMENTARY READINGS

If you are interested in organizational consultation, you may want to read some of the following books:

Conyne, R. K., and O'Neil, J. M. (Eds.). (1992). *Organizational consultation: A casebook.* Newbury Park, CA: Russell Sage Foundation. This text presents five case studies of organizational consultation in a variety of settings. Each case study follows a specified format. Of particular interest is the last chapter, which analyzes and synthesizes the case studies. This book is an excellent resource for learning the practical, hands-on side of organizational consultation.

Schein, E. H. (1988). *Process consultation: Its role in organization development*, Volume 1 (2nd ed.). Reading, MA: Addison-Wesley. This classic text is a must for anyone interested in consulting with organizations. Schein discusses process consultation in detail and in relation to the purchase of expertise and doctor–patient models.

Schein, E. H. (1999). *Process consultation revisited: Building the helping relationship.* Reading, MA: Addison-Wesley. Of particular interest is Schein's discussion of consultation as a helping relationship. Its business and industry orientation should not diminish the wealth of applicable information in this book for human service consultants/collaborators.

Schein, E. H. (2004). *Organizational culture and leadership.* (3rd ed.). San Francisco: Jossey-Bass. This is Schein's latest contribution to the field of process consultation. It is a resource for understanding the interpersonal dynamics in organizations. The material on organizational culture provides excellent information on the impact of culture on the practices of consultants and collaborators.

# 12

✳

# School-Based Consultation
# and Collaboration

**B**oth consultation and collaboration are effective in providing psychological services in schools.

A great deal of consultation and collaboration occurs in schools resulting in a time-efficient and cost-effective way to affect the well-being of students (ASCA, 2003; Davis, 2005; Merrell et al., 2006; Myrick, 2003). Because schools represent a microcosm of community life, they are excellent settings for consultation and collaboration. Mental health professionals—internal and external to school settings—consult and collaborate regularly with teachers, administrators, and parents/guardians who are often the first ones to note issues students may be having (Keys et al., 1998; Kratochwill & Pittman, 2002; Studer, 2005). When mental health/human service professionals are involved with staff development, parent groups, intervention teams, and program development—or when they are used as resources on a variety of topics—they are engaging in consultation or collaboration (see Pellitteri, 2000; Safran & Safran, 2001).

As a means by which psychological services are delivered in a school, consultation is an indirect service to students and attempts to help others work more effectively with students. Collaboration combines indirect and direct services to students. Thus, students are the ultimate beneficiaries of the consultant's services, and both the direct and ultimate beneficiaries of collaboration. Consultation and collaboration can occur as primary prevention (e.g., enhancing the school climate), secondary prevention (e.g., working with school administrators in developing programs for students at risk for teenage pregnancy), and tertiary prevention (e.g., consulting with a teacher about a child who is having difficulty in the classroom). Increasing attention has been given to providing primary prevention services to

263

those who have basic responsibility for students (teachers, administrators, and parents) that can positively affect school and home climates.

To be effective, mental health/human service consultants—internal and external—should be aware of the educational, social, and emotional needs of children. They must understand how to communicate with teachers, administrators, and parents; and they must be aware of the forces operating in the local building, at the school system level, and in the community at large (Salmon, 1993). For example, consultation should be explained to adults in the school in such a way that they are not threatened by another adult helping them with the difficulties they experience (Conoley & Wright, 1993). By working effectively with other professionals at school and with parents/guardians, school-based human service professionals can positively impact the lives of large numbers of children (Gutkin & Curtis, 1999) and can help resolve concerns, prevent future problems, and provide developmental strategies (Gerler, 1992). In addition, by providing these services, counselors and psychologists can broaden the scope of their influence in the school (Dougherty, 1992b).

The actual ways in which consultation and collaboration occur varies according to the model being employed. Keys et al. (1998) make some important clarifications regarding the distinction between consultation and collaboration. The problem-solving processes in collaboration and consultation are essentially the same. What varies is that, in collaboration, there is an emphasis on shared expertise throughout the entire process (Keys et al., 1998). The "triadic-dependent relationship" style of consultation is known as the "expert" mode of consultation. In the "collaborative dependent" style, the consultant functions not only as an expert but also as a facilitator and educator. The consultee, however, still depends on the expertise of the consultant. The consultant educates the consultee about the problem-solving process, and together they collaborate to identify and solve a problem. In other words, even though the consultant is collaborative, she or he is still "in charge" of the process. This style of consultation is often what consultants refer to when they say they "collaborate" with their consultees. Some authors (e.g., Keys et al., 1998) believe traditional models are effective for dealing with normal, developmental problems, but true collaboration and independent approaches are called for when dealing with more complex issues.

Schools are different than other organizations such as mental health centers or business and industry settings. Because the context in which consultation and collaboration occur is important (Zins & Erchul, 2002), I dedicate an entire chapter to these services in a school context. Even though you may not work in a school, it is highly likely that sooner or later you will collaborate or consult with school personnel. Awareness of consultation and collaboration in the context of a school is essential for all human service professionals.

This chapter surveys the scope of school consultation and collaboration. We will briefly discuss their history and examine the nature of consulting with administrators, including how school consultants can use organization development consultation with their administrators. In addition, we will survey methods of consulting and collaborating with teachers. Adlerian and instructional consultation are included in this discussion. From there we will discuss consulting and collaborating with parents, including parent case consultation and parent education. After a discussion of interagency collaboration, we will examine some pragmatic issues including those surrounding multicultural school consultation. Finally, we will reflect upon school consultation and collaboration in the 21st century.

Here are some questions to consider as you read this chapter:

1. In what ways is consultation in the school different from consulting in the community?

2. What is unique about consulting and collaborating with teachers?

3. What special factors does a consultant have to take into consideration when consulting or collaborating with parents?

4. What special ethical issues does interagency collaboration in the schools raise?

5. How can collaboration be viewed as the service of choice over consultation for school-based human service professionals to provide?

## RATIONALE FOR SCHOOL-BASED CONSULTATION AND COLLABORATION

As the mental health and instructional needs of students have become of increasing concern, interest in consultation and collaboration has increased commensurately (Gutkin & Curtis, 1999; Kanel, 2007). The increasing number of societal problems that school-aged youth encounter is increasing the need for consultation and collaboration services (Meyers, Meyers, & Grogg, 2004). Upwards to twenty percent of our youth suffer form mental health issues with barely over one-fourth receiving appropriate care (Greenberg et al., 2003).

Revisions to the Individuals with Disabilities Act (IDEA; Pub. L. 108–446, 2004) (Wilczynski, Mandal, & Fusilier, 2000), school violence, the No Child Left Behind Act, emphases on school reform and restructuring (Adelman & Taylor, 2007; Senge et al., 2000), as well as increased school accountability and high-stakes testing (Braden, 2002), have all led to an increased importance for consultation and collaboration in school settings. In addition, because administrators, parents, and other school support personnel affect the learning climate of the school, they are appropriate persons for consultative assistance (Hall & Mei-Ju, 1994).

School-based and non-school-based mental health professionals are increasingly called upon to assist with the organizational change necessitated by school improvement initiatives. To this end, school-based psychologists, counselors, and community mental health providers are being asked to provide consultation and collaboration to improve their own individual schools in these specific areas (Riley, 1996, p. 478):

- teaching, learning, and related standards
- use of technology
- governance, management, and accountability
- parent and community support and involvement
- system-wide improvements
- promotion of grassroots efforts
- dropout prevention strategies
- coordination with school-to-work programs
- milestones and timelines

### Case Example of School-Based Consultation

Consider this example:

You are a school counselor who is asked by a teacher to help him "increase the motivation to learn" of an academically gifted junior who is failing the teacher's chemistry class. You and the teacher discuss his concern in detail. You develop a plan in which you will interview the student about his lack of achievement and report back to the teacher. The teacher agrees to observe the student's behavior in the classroom and search for any possible clues. You both agree to meet during the teacher's planning period to share your experiences and develop the next steps.

This example is just one of a variety of ways in which school-based human service professionals consult. It is important to remember that all you have read about in this text so far is applicable to school consultation. For example, the information about organizations discussed in Chapter 8 applies to schools.

The underlying premise for school consultation is that, by helping the significant others of students such as teachers and parents make appropriate changes, consultants can contribute to substantive, positive outcomes for students (Gutkin & Curtis, 1999). Consulting has the potential to positively affect more students than working with individual students (Meyers, Gaughan, & Pitt, 1990). Thus, consultants have the ability to significantly impact the mental health and development of children by improving the skills and knowledge of parents and those professionals who work with children at school.

There are some concerns related to the use of consultation in the schools. For example, effective consultation takes time, yet the time constraints in schools are myriad. Furthermore, school administrators do not always view consultation as an important function in the school, and even when they do, other services such as testing and counseling compete for the time of counselors and psychologists.

### Case Example of School-Based Collaboration

Now consider this example:

You are a school counselor who asks a teacher to collaborate in order to "increase the motivation to learn" of an academically gifted junior who is failing the teacher's chemistry class. You and the teacher discuss his concern in detail. Together, you develop a plan in which you will interview the student about his lack of achievement and report back to the teacher. The teacher agrees to observe the student's behavior in the classroom and search for any possible clues. You both agree to meet during the teacher's planning period to share your experiences and develop the next steps. After you both engage in these tasks, you develop a plan that allows both of you to take responsibility for some aspect of the case.

This example provides a description of the basic rudiments of school-based collaboration. Notice how it differs from the example of school-based consultation in which the teacher took all of the responsibility for the implementation of the plan. School-based collaboration allows for individual expertise to

be used in a team situation. It builds relationships for other problem-solving activities such as consultation, maximizes productivity, and requires shared accountability (Cramer, 1998; Friend & Cook, 1996, 1997; Safran & Safran, 1998). Collaboration activities are typified by a cooperative relationship. The activities are cooperative in that the relationship is one among equals, given possible differences in expertise and need, with each partner having different contributions to make. The activities are accomplished through a partnership in that the distribution of labor involved is specified and agreed upon. When collaborating with teachers and parents, it is important to consider training them in the skills of collaboration rather than to assume they have those skills (Ikeda et al., 1996).

Collaboration is particularly appropriate for multidisciplinary team conferences. At these meetings, professionals and sometimes parents attempt to develop an appropriate educational or behavioral plan for a student. As early as the mid-1980s, Zins and Curtis (1984) suggested the importance of having all parties at such meetings skilled in consultation to overcome the possible shortcomings of these types of meetings. Collaboration, like an effective team, works best when the leadership of the process is shared over time (Shaw & Swerdlik, 1995).

There are some schools that use collaboration extensively to "invent and reinvent" meaningful educational experiences for students (Thousand et al., 1996). For example some schools rely extensively on ad hoc problem-solving teams. When this occurs, there is less of the "shut-the-door-of-my-classroom" attitude and more of a "let's-look-at-the-bigger-picture" attitude. Collaboration emphasizes shared accountability for outcomes and a shared responsibility for participation and decision making. School-based counselors and psychologists may well want to consider using collaboration whenever possible (Caplan & Caplan, 1993).

## HISTORICAL BACKGROUND

The history of what we now call school-based consultation and collaboration dates back to the 1920s.

As early as 1925, the role of school psychologists' functions would still be recognized today as closely allied to consultation (Bramlett & Murphy, 1998; Merrell et al., 2006). These included contributing to the study of children with learning problems and developing a mental health program in the school (French, 1990).

But it was during the 1950s that the term "consultation" began to be used regularly as part of the consultant's functioning. The 1954 Thayer Conference all but made consultation a part of the school psychologist's role. In the early 1960s, some school psychology researchers (see Lambert, 2000) wrote about school psychology being a suitable profession for the practice of school-based mental health consultation. Cottingham (1956) was among the first to recognize the need for special assistance for teachers by school-based counselors, which provided the basis for the consultation role in the elementary school. The rationale was that by acting as consultants, school-based human service professionals could assist the school in developing a climate conducive to student growth and development, hence creating an avenue by which all students could be affected. When school-based human service workers delivered only direct services such as individual and group counseling, their impact on the school climate was limited since it was virtually impossible to reach all children in the school (Dinkmeyer & Carlson, 1973).

Impetus for consulting with parents came from the work of Faust (1968), who noted that students' relationships with their parents could affect their learning ability at school. Therefore, Faust (1968) strongly advocated consulting with parents but cautioned school personnel against using the "brush fire" (p. 86) approach in dealing with crises that teachers and administrators have with parents. He advocated the idea of parent training groups as well as consulting with parents about their individual children. Faust (1968), however, gave priority to consulting with school personnel such as teachers and administrators over consulting with parents. Because of efficiency, he suggested that the most important form of consulting was with groups of teachers, not only with regard to student behavior

but also concerning curriculum development and classroom activities. Faust was also one of the first to call for counselors to engage in in-service programs for school personnel. For the school counseling profession, there was some initial resistance to consultation as some writers thought that it would take away from the school counselor's time with students (Myrick, 2003).

In 1966, a report by the joint Committee on the Elementary School Counselor (ACES/ASCA, 1966) made consulting an official role for school counselors along with counseling and coordination. The literature on consultation for school counselors was very limited at this time. Kahnweiler (1979) reported locating 12 articles on consultation in counseling journals written between 1964 and 1968. By 1972, however, there had been articles published for counselors on topics such as Adlerian consultation, behavioral consultation, in-service programs for teachers, and parent consultation.

Fullmer and Bernard (1972) and Dinkmeyer and Caldwell (1970) also advocated the role of school consultant as one who could provide in-service education to teachers on open communication and the wise use of tests, as well as on assisting work groups. Fullmer and Bernard were among the first to note that when consultation is successful, the consultant is made obsolete while at the same time increasing the long-term possibilities of enhancing consultation. These authors strongly advocated the use of group consultation.

Dinkmeyer and Carlson's (1973) text *Consulting: Facilitating Human Potential and Change Processes* advocated that school consultants be active change agents for improving the organizational climate of the school, thus expanding the concept of school consultant to include organizational consultation.

In 1975, the passage of Public Law 94-142 supported the use of consultation by school-based consultants regarding students with special needs. Subsequent federal and state legislation supported the use of consultation and collaboration as a viable method of indirect service in the schools. Hence, consultation was to be an effective way to assist regular education teacher with children who had special needs (Martens & Ardion, 2002). The 1990s saw increased attention to collaboration as an important service. Today, consultation and collaboration are important services provided by school-based consultants. As our society becomes even more culturally diverse and social and economic problems continue to grow, the demand for these services in the school will increase even more.

## CONSULTING AND COLLABORATING WITH SCHOOL ADMINISTRATORS

The school's leadership is a powerful force in determining the extent to which consultation and collaboration are considered acceptable services (Bramlett & Murphy, 1998; Raforth, 2006). Therefore, it is important that school psychologists and counselors not only inform administrators about these services, but also that they actually engage administrators in these services (Bramlett & Murphy, 1998; Paisley & Milsom, 2007; Raforth, 2006). Administrator support and acceptance of programs is essential for change to occur (McDougal et al., 2000). Administrators have priorities and pressures for which they may actively seek consultation (Hughes, 2000).

School-based consultants can consult with school administrators in a variety of ways. They frequently meet with principals to discuss particular children that have come to principals' attention. For example, a consultant may use a client-centered case approach with a principal who is trying to decide whether or not to suspend a student from school. In addition, principals often request consultation regarding programs that operate in the school (Illback et al., 1999; Jacob & Hartshorne, 2003). In another example, school consultants may be asked to evaluate their own in-school consultation programs or programs that involve cultural diversity (Pena, 1996), school reform (Colbert, Vernon-Jones, & Pransky, 2006), classroom-based group interventions (Robinson & Elias, 1993), and systemic change (Adelman & Taylor, 2007).

Other topics for which administrators seek consultation include school violence, substance abuse, high-stakes testing, professional development, planning for crisis situations, and professional competence issues (Blader & Gallagher, 2001; Jacob & Hartshorne, 2003). Administrators are typically concerned about the potential for disruptive behavior. As a result they frequently seek consultation on ways to manage behavior at the school, classroom, and individual levels (Luiselli, 2002; Sugai et al., 2000). When consulting with administrators about programs, consultants will want to ensure that the following factors are addressed: how the program will be introduced, how stakeholders will be engaged, how previous research affects program implementation, and how program resources will be prioritized (Rotheram-Borus, Bickford, & Milburn, 2001). Furthermore, school-based professionals will want to work closely with administrators to incorporate primary prevention programs into the school setting; for example, establishing prereferral intervention teams and problem-solving teams (Bahr & Kovaleski, 2006; Raforth, 2006; Raforth & Foriska, 2006) or in working to prevent school violence (Larson, Smith, & Furlong, 2002).

Principals frequently request school consultants to co-consult with external consultants when human services are the focus of the external consultants' assistance. Such collaboration can enhance the effectiveness of the external consultants' services (Johnston & Gilliland, 1987). As in other contexts, when human service professionals collaborate with administrators, they take on responsibility for some of the outcome.

There is a move toward increased organization development consultation on the part of school-based consultants (Curtis & Stollar, 2002; Dougherty & Dougherty, 1991; Dustin & Ehly, 1992) because school administrators increasingly want assistance with goals that involve the entire school (Hansen et al., 1990; Ehly, 1993). For example, total quality management (TQM) strategies are beginning to be used by school-based consultants (Smaby, Harrison, & Nelson, 1995). The TQM approach is usually implemented through the total quality group (TQG). School counselors and school psychologists can use TQG as a way of helping site-based management teams be most effective by focusing on group roles, social influence, and group stages either in providing staff development training in TQG or consulting with an existing TQG. Since case consultation and program consultation are covered elsewhere in this text, so I will focus here on organization development consultation.

## School Consultation and Organization Development Change

Increasingly, internal and external forces are requiring schools to accomplish necessary and challenging changes, and schools are looking to consultation and collaboration services for help (Cowan, 2007; Flaspohler, 2007; Hazel, 2007; Zins & Illback, 1995). There is a sharpening focus on organizational consultation in schools including groups of consultees, entire schools, and even school districts (Merrell et al., 2006; Zins & Erchul, 2002). Organizational development consultation is a series of planned and sustained efforts to apply the principles of behavioral science to improve the functioning of the school (see process consultation in Chapter 11). School counselors and school psychologists are being called upon to assist in implementing system-wide programs related to school reform that are driven by their central offices (Colbert et al., 2006; Knoff, 2002; Paisley & Milsom, 2007), consultation regarding the development of crisis intervention teams for responses to issues like school violence (Bramlett et al., 2002), and the implementation of positive psychology into the mainstream of the school (Akin-Little et al., 2004). These initiatives can include developing a collaboration program in each school, building assistance teams, determining the necessary processes for systems monitoring, assisting with strategic plans (Adelman & Taylor, 2007), and providing ongoing staff development. The goal is ongoing school renewal through the creation of a culture of change, teacher professionalism, and high expectations (Raforth & Foriska, 2006).

The impetus for organizational consultation in the school has come from the school reform movement (Curtis & Stollar, 1996), a renewed emphasis on public health principles in mental health (Hazel, 2007), and the realization that what often appears to be a child-focused problem is merely a symptom of a building or systems problem (Knoff, 2002). Merrell et al. (2006) and Greenberg et al. (2003) note issues that necessitate organizational-level change: preparing for an increasingly diverse student population; advances in technology; and the increasing severity and complexity of student needs. This approach appreciates and uses the unique characteristics of the school in the change process (Curtis & Stollar, 2002). In spite of the recent attention organization development has been receiving, its application to schools is not new (see, as examples, Illback & Zins, 1993). Organization development is a systematic process, using the principles and methods of behavioral science to increase the effectiveness of organizations such as schools (French & Bell, 1999). The target is the human side of the school, and the goal is to structure activities that assist that human side to be better problem solvers on their own (French & Bell, 1999). The change that is targeted must reflect the complexity of the school that is being changed (Zins & Illback, 1995). Organization development consultation usually starts with the administrator of the school who involves the school-based consultant and other professionals in the change process (Curtis & Stollar, 1996). Such consultation is a way of making carefully planned, predictable changes in the school (Elliott & Busse, 1993). Its goal is to enhance the school's effectiveness by helping school personnel understand and effectively act on problems and move toward self-renewal. This type of consultation can be long-term, lasting for several years. As a result, it can be quite time consuming (Larney, 2003). One of the first steps in using organization development consultation is to train the stakeholders and gatekeepers in problem solving (Knoff, 1995, 2002). Examples include developing a team to enhance a school's climate, creating a task force to increase the number of parent volunteers in a school, assisting a faculty to move from a self-contained classroom to team teaching, helping a planning team conduct a survey (Schmuck

& Runkel, 1985), creating and promoting effective problem-solving teams (Raforth & Foriska, 2006), and sustaining innovations (Adelman & Taylor, 2003).

When school-based consultants use organization development consultation, they generally adopt the systems approach described in Chapter 8, which allows them to observe and intervene in the school's subsystems (Knoff, 2002; Schmuck, 1995). For example, there may be a rift between teachers (the technological subsystem) and counselors (the supportive subsystem) concerning "pulling out" students for counseling services during class time. Organization development consultation would attempt to help these subsystems function more smoothly together. This view keeps in mind the school's ability to manage change. For example, if the cultural diversity of a school's student body is increasing, the school-based consultant may be placed in charge of a school-wide program to accommodate this change. Finally, organization development consultation looks to the satisfaction of school personnel, since satisfied workers are productive workers. The school-based consultant operating from an organization consultation perspective might well monitor the school's morale as one indicator of whether change is necessary.

Organization development consultation follows the steps presented in the generic model in Chapter 3 through 6, and its primary interventions include process observation and feedback, training, and survey feedback. The typical targets of organization development consultation are the school's structure (e.g., policies), processes (e.g., ways of planning), behavior (e.g., roles of personnel; see Illback et al., 1999) and capacity building (Nastasi, 2004). In another example, school-based consultants can assist their organizations to deal with unintended outcomes of school reform and high stakes testing, such as focusing the curriculum exclusively on tested subjects and dealing with repeated poor performance on the part of many students (Braden, 2002). School-based consultants typically ensure that programs related to organizational change are acceptable to stakeholders so that they can be more effectively institutionalized

(McDougal et al., 2000). When human service/mental health professionals collaborate from an organizational development framework, they take on responsibility for some aspect of the outcome.

**A Brief Example of Organization Development Consultation.**  Wes is a school-based consultant with training in organization development. His school is rapidly undergoing changes in the cultural diversity of its student body, for which his principal has asked for assistance in developing a plan to help the school adjust. Wes begins by assessing the degree to which the school is adjusting to the change and compares his findings with the desired state of affairs. He surveys the staff and conducts structured interviews with randomly selected teachers and support personnel.

Wes draws two conclusions as a result: The entire school staff is not well trained in multicultural education and has unrealistic fears of increased violence and vandalism at the school. Wes creates and submits to the principal a plan involving an in-service program on multicultural education, visitations by staff to schools with cultural diversity, and the development of a special committee to develop ongoing plans for adjustment and monitoring progress.

# CONSULTING AND COLLABORATING WITH TEACHERS

Interest on the part of teachers in consultation depends on many factors. Traditionally, school counselors and psychologists have worked with teachers to establish interventions in the regular classroom as a way to reduce special education placements (Kratochwill, Elliott, & Callan-Stoiber, 2002). These efforts have led to increased consultation activities with personnel such as special education teachers, teachers of children with behavioral disorders, and teachers in charge of programs for preschool children. School-based consultants have assisted teachers with both academically and behavioral challenged children as well as those with less severe concerns. More recently, school psychologists and counselors have engaged in collaboration with teachers as a method of providing service to students and their families. Hughes points to the bottom line for teachers in need of consultation: "Teachers typically have a student in their classroom for a limited period of time and are interested in interventions that offer quick results. Teachers are also interested in decreasing behaviors that interfere with smooth functioning of the classroom and that they experience as personally stressful" (2000, p. 323).

School consultation and collaboration can be effective and efficient ways to help teachers enhance their professional skills and to generalize the effects of psychoeducational interventions (Caplan & Caplan, 1993). For example, consultants can use social dynamic information to support the direct interventions of teachers in determining how the peer group and the classroom support undesirable behavior (Farmer, 2000). Many articles document teachers being helped with a variety of topics, such as conducting effective parent conferences (Johns, 1992), enhancing the self-concept of students (Braucht & Weime, 1992), choosing instructional methodologies (Margolis, 1990; Rosenfield, 2002a), engaging in conflict resolution (McFarland, 1992), acting as resources for teachers in gifted education (Landrum, 2001), dealing with other common problems (Stenho, 1995), consulting regarding military children (Horton, 2005), and dealing with issues related to being a beginning teacher (Knotek, Babinski, & Rogers, 2002). There is some empirical support that teachers can be trained to generalize consultation-related skills to their classroom following consultation (Riley-Tillman & Eckert, 2001). The nature of the consultation relationship and its influence on the teacher determine whether or not the teacher is going to follow through with the consultant's recommendations and implement the interventions (O'Keefe & Medway, 1997; Sterling-Turner, Watson, & Moore, 2002). There is some evidence that the number of teachers who are willing to engage is increased by the consultant being based in the school, consultation services being offered rather

than waiting for requests, the teachers perceiving that the consultant has excellent problem-solving skills, and the teachers perceiving that they themselves have good problem-solving skills (Stenger, Tollefson, & Fine, 1992). Consultants may need to dedicate time to training teachers to effectively implement interventions (Sterling-Turner et al., 2002). Consulting with high school teachers may vary from that with elementary teachers (Gray, Gutkin, & Riley, 2001). Because high school students have more than one teacher a day, consultants are at this level are more likely to engage in group consultation. Due to the nature of high school students, rewards for them are hard to determine, and when they are determined, administrators and parents may find them unacceptable.

One way to conceptualize school-based interventions is through a matrix of change agents and intervention categories (Lentz et al., 1996). Change agents include students themselves, peers, the home, the teacher, and other school adults. The general category of intervention includes contingency-based (e.g., praise after task completion), antecedent-based (e.g., changing prompts), teaching academic skills, teaching learning strategies, teaching appropriate social behaviors, and teaching coping or problem-solving strategies (e.g., personal problem-solving strategies).

On the other hand, in collaboration, in which most parties are providing direct service and have responsibility for part of the outcome, the issue becomes getting everyone "on board" with what needs to happen and when (Iverson, 2002).

There are a variety of models from which school consultants and their consultees can choose. Popular models such as education/training consultation (Shapiro, Dupaul, Bradley, & Bailey, 1996), behavioral consultation, and mental health consultation have already been discussed elsewhere in this text. I have chosen two other models that are popular in school consultation to discuss in this chapter: Adlerian consultation (Dinkmeyer, 2006; Dinkmeyer & Carlson, 1973; Dinkmeyer, Pew, & Dinkmeyer, 1979) and instructional consultation (Rosenfield, 1987, 2002a).

## Adlerian Consultation

Adlerian consultation with teachers is based on the works of Alfred Adler's individual psychology. The major proponents of Adlerian consultation in schools have been Don Dinkmeyer, Jon Carlson, and their colleagues. This discussion is based on writings by Carlson, Watts, & Maniacci (2006), Dinkmeyer (2006), Dinkmeyer and Carlson (2000), and Kottman (1995). Adlerian school consultation is based on several assumptions:

- Teachers cannot take responsibility for student behavior.
- Teachers should be more involved with encouragement than with praise.
- Teachers cannot always prevent failure on the part of students.
- Teachers need to try to meet the affective as well as the cognitive needs of students.
- The consultant talks directly to the teacher about their problem with the child as opposed to talking about the child exclusively.
- The consultee is to learn new skills to facilitate change.

**Case Consultation.**   How consultation proceeds with an individual teacher depends on his or her perceived needs, but usually a collaborative mode is employed (Carlson et al., 2006). In case consultation, Adlerian consultants frequently use a detailed referral form, which the teacher fills out prior to the first consultation session and which provides the consultation a beginning point. In addition to using the referral form, the consultant asks the teacher to tell his or her story in such a way that the dynamics of the teacher–student relationship are evident (Dinkmeyer, 2006; Kottman, 1995). As the teacher relates his or her beliefs about the child's behavior, the consultant tunes into the teacher's feelings so as to further understand the possible goal of the student's behavior.

The consultant may also observe the child in the teacher's classroom. The consultant and teacher then make a tentative hypothesis about the goal of the child's behavior and discuss possible alternatives

from which the teacher may choose. The alternatives are based on the realization that to change the student's behavior, the teacher must change his or her own behavior first. A recent trend in Adlerian consultation involves the use of narratives and anecdotes to assist with the consultation process (Mortola & Carlson, 2003). Advice-giving is avoided and is replaced by a process that integrates new skills with the consultee's belief system.   Adlerian consultation follows the following steps (Carlson et al., 2006, pp. 253–254):

- establish the tone
- get a specific description of the problem
- get a second specific example and clarify the goal of misbehavior and the teacher's troubling belief
- review the guidelines for reaching the goal
- solicit tentative solutions
- attain closure

**A Brief Example of Adlerian Case Consultation.**   Alfred, a school-based consultant, is working with Howard, a middle school teacher who has voluntarily sought out consultation regarding a seventh-grader who seems to be rapidly becoming the class clown. Howard has completed and submitted the referral form. Alfred establishes rapport with Howard, and together they get specific examples of the student's behavior and then determine Howard's feelings and reactions to the behavior. Howard reports that he is mostly annoyed because constantly reprimanding the boy gets in the way of his teaching the class. The consultant observes the student in class and conducts a diagnostic interview with him. In the meantime, Howard is keeping a record of the boy's acting out behavior. Alfred and Howard then hold a planning session and determine that the boy's primary goal is attention. They develop a plan in which Howard changes how he responds to the student. Alfred agrees to follow up with Howard within a week.

**C-Group.**   The C-group is a group Adlerian consultation method so named because all of the forces operant in the group begin with the letter C. These forces include consultation, collaboration, clarification, confrontation, cohesion, commitment, changes, concern, caring, confidentiality, and communication (Dinkmeyer & Carlson, 2000). The C-group is an alternative to traditional staff development training in which ideas about behavior are disseminated. The group is both didactic and experiential.

The typical group consists of four to six teachers and the consultant. It meets once a week for about an hour and has a life of about six to eight sessions. It is based on the rationale that most problems are interpersonal in nature, classroom and otherwise, and that these problems are best solved in an open, safe group setting. Teachers present problems they are having with individual students and the group discusses them.

The purposes of the consultation group are to help teachers understand patterns of student behaviors and ways to improve those patterns, as well as to provide teachers with an arena in which they can openly communicate, understand the practical application of Adlerian ideas about human behavior, and experience the rewards of group learning.

Outcomes for teachers include the satisfaction of sharing similar concerns, acquiring more effective ways of dealing with student misbehavior, understanding their interpersonal relations better, and learning about how to lead classroom discussions concerning affective topics.

**A Brief Example of a C-Group.** Loretta is a school consultant leading a C-group for a group of six elementary school teachers. The first meeting has all of the teachers sharing something about themselves with Loretta pointing out similarities in their concerns and building rapport among the teachers. In subsequent meetings, Loretta shares Adler's ideas on the purposive nature of human behavior, which gives the group a common ground for approaching their concerns. She also encourages the members to share anecdotes and helps them identify and share their feelings as they relate to such anecdotes. The concept of discouragement is discussed as well as practical methods of working with misbehavior. Loretta

maintains control over the group's process by keeping it focused and encourages the teachers to help one another with their concerns about students. During the group meeting Loretta passes out a variety of handouts on Adler's ideas on children. The group then applies this information to the children they are seeking to help.

## Instructional Consultation

Instructional consultation (Rosenfield, 1987, 1992, 2002b; Rosenfield & Gravois, 1996; Stringer, Reynolds, & Simpson, 2003) is a relatively new model for helping teachers modify their instructional behavior and more effectively create a learning environment for students. Gravois and Rosenfield note: "The model is based on the premise that quality instructional and management programming, matched to a student's assessed entry skills, increases student success, reduces behavioral difficulties, and avoids the need for special education evaluation and placement" (2006, p. 45). Instructional consultation and behavioral consultation have some basic common elements (Rosenfield 2002a, 2002b). As a form of consultee-centered consultation, the success of instructional consultation is dependent on the quality of the consultant–consultee relationship and the degree to which suggested interventions are carried out and followed up.

Instructional consultation is a collaborative process in which a problem is identified and interventions are selected and made. Since the planned interventions typically require that the consultee change his or her instructional style, a strong consultant–consultee relationship based on trust and mutual sharing is essential. A strong focus is placed on defining the problem in specific, measurable terms, and decisions are data driven (Wizda, 2004).

The most common roles of the instructional consultant appear to be those of collaborator and educational trainer but may also include being an advocate for a particular instructional technique or service for a given student. The consultant often functions as a fact finder and observes and collects data to define the problem more clearly. The consultant may assess the student's learning, the teacher's instructional style, and the teaching–learning process. The consultant attempts to collaborate whenever possible but is obviously an expert as far as instructional improvement goes.

Prior to accepting consultees, the consultant suggests a referral process within the school. With the process in place, teachers will be informed of the nature of consultation, its collaborative intent, and non-supervisory nature. They will also understand that they are in control of how the problems presented will be solved and that the consultant will function as a resource person.

The consultant clearly informs the consultee about the consultation process and its potential benefits. The consultee needs to enter the consultation relationship with an expectation of success, a non-defensive attitude, the motivation to discuss the problem situation openly, and a willingness to make changes. It is helpful if the consultee is knowledgeable about or willing to be trained in problem-solving strategies.

The consultation procedure includes the following steps: establishing a collaborative relationship, identifying the problem, observing the classroom, assessing curriculum-based learning, planning instructional interventions, and terminating.

The problem is identified in terms of the student behaviors that concern the teacher and the learning environment in which the student resides. Clarifying the problem at this stage requires strong communication skills from consultant and consultee. This stage often ends with a reconceptualization of the problem as the result of the interaction of instruction, the learning task, and student skills rather than merely as a deficit in the student (Knotek, Rosenfield, Gravois, & Babinski, 2003). The problem is conceptualized as an instructional mismatch.

The consultant often learns the teacher's instructional goals and plans prior to making objective and systematic observations of the student and the learning environment as a step in problem identification. The consultant's findings are discussed soon after the observation. Data collection and interpretation often lead to a reconceptualization of the data.

As the assessment of the problem is curriculum based, the consultant must understand the scope and sequence of the material as well as the teacher's attitudes about the curriculum. For example, is the teacher being driven to complete the coverage of certain material at the expense of mastery by the student? This assessment provides a basis for planning intervention strategies.

The consultant and teacher refine the problem, discuss alternatives, and brainstorm possible interventions that will improve the management of the student (e.g., time on task) and the management of learning (e.g., instructional style). From the list of available strategies, the teacher selects ones that are feasible from the point of view of time, resources, and classroom structure.

As these strategies are put into place, the consultant monitors the process on a regular basis and helps make modifications as necessary. Based on the results, the consultant and consultee will then terminate the relationship. The consultant typically makes and submits a complete write-up of the consultation experience.

Knotek et al. summarize instructional consultation by noting that the "traits of reframing the etiology of the problem, the collection of data to confirm or disconfirm ideas, the iterative brainstorming, and the generation of alternative hypotheses, resulted in a process of orderly reflection that supported the construction of new understandings of and approaches to the workplace problem" (2002, p. 325).

Recent developments in this model include the concept of instructional consultation teams (Gravois & Rosenfield, 2006; Knotek, Gravois, & Rogers, 2002; Rosenfield, 2002a, 2002b). These teams can have the impact of changing the school culture to be more accepting of a collaborative, problem-solving focus and can create a shift to arranging systemic variables from a traditional view which looks for deficits in a given student. There is a trend in conducting instructional consultation with Limited English Proficient (LEP) students and their families by using school interpreters (Lopez, 2000). The limited research on the use of interpreters in this way suggest that the pace of consultation will be slowed, the accuracy of communication will need to be monitored, and the use of the interpreter may affect how rapport with the family and student will be developed (Lopez, 2000). Instructional consultation is also an effective service in targeting English Language Learners' (ELL) language instructional needs in non-bilingual settings as the consultant can provide background materials, modeling, and intervention scripts (Lopez, 2006).

Another trend in instructional consultation is the use of curriculum-based assessment (CBA) (Burns, 2004; Wizda, 2004). CBA is a method that, in a systematic way, analyzes the instructional needs of a student and then designs instruction for optimal achievement (Burns, 2004; Gravois & Gickling, 2002). The idea is that academic problems are viewed as a mismatch between student skill level and how and/or what the student is being taught. Assessment is used repeatedly to help determine what and/or how the student should be taught (Gravois & Gickling, 2002). The referring teacher's skills are developed so that they can be used effectively with similar students in the future (Wizda, 2004). One other recent development is that the language used in IC has moved to the forefront, and the actual words used in the consultation relationship are considered to be the subject of study in IC in order to maximize the effectiveness of consultation (Rosenfield, 2004). Consultants may need to instruct teachers in assessment techniques as well as behaviorally oriented instructional strategies (Begeny, 2006).

**A Brief Example of Instructional Consultation[1].** Wilma is a 4th-grade teacher who has recently had a new student, Maria, enter her room from another school district. School records indicated that her attendance over the past three years had been erratic. Wilma had placed Maria in the slower reading group. Maria is a quiet, unassuming child who appears to listen to directions in class but has not been able to complete classroom work assigned to her, especially in reading. She stays at her seat for about five minutes during independent work time and then begins to move around the room. Because Wilma has had such a small amount of written work from Maria, she has little information to help her discover Maria's reading level, and there are no test scores in her school records. Wilma feels this child would be better served by more individual attention and that she should be removed from her classroom for at least a part of the day for special services. Wilma has no assistant and states that she cannot slow the progress of the class for this one student.

Wilma came to the first meeting with the consultant convinced that moving the child from the classroom was the best option. After listening carefully to Wilma's explanation of the problem, the consultant presented the advantages of working together to identify specific areas of concern in Maria's academic performance. Although Wilma was still unsure she could comfortably commit the extra time needed to help Maria, she was willing to work with the consultant to define Maria's reading problem more fully. Wilma and the consultant agreed to two classroom visits for the consultant and a follow-up meeting. The observations were planned to systematically assess Maria's reading performance level as well as her interactive patterns with the teacher, other students, and the classroom environment as a whole. The consultant and teacher discussed the instruction that would be taking place on observation days and the objectives Wilma planned to achieve. The consultant planned to review the scope and sequence expectations of fourth-grade reading materials so that she could more adequately determine Maria's instructional level.

After the classroom observations, the consultant and Wilma discussed what the consultant had learned from observing Maria, the classroom environment, Wilma's relationship with Maria, and the performance of the other children with respect to Maria. From this information they refined the instructional problem to be addressed. The consultant agreed to formally assess Maria's current reading instructional level, and permission forms for this were sent to Maria's parents.

---

[1.] The author would like to thank Carole Williford for this case study.

Once these data were collected, Wilma and the consultant met once more to determine how best to meet Maria's reading needs. They brainstormed potential approaches—from peer teaching to classroom volunteer parents—and Wilma chose the best alternative. They planned step-by-step intervention strategies and agreed to talk by phone weekly to make any needed modifications in the interventions. Once Wilma was satisfied with Maria's progress, they agreed to terminate. The consultant documented the consultation through a written report.

*A Final Note on Consultation with Teachers.* There is, in my opinion, a bottom line for effectively consulting with teachers. When consultants work with teachers, it is very important that teachers do not view consultation as a process with the following underlying message: "How can I (the consultant) help you do your job better without my having to do anything myself?" For consultation with teachers to be effective, teachers need to perceive the consultation process as an enterprise with an equitable workload distribution that requires minimal time, all the while being optimally helpful. Further, it is critical that teachers perceive that their input into the problem-solving process is valued. As you might guess, collaboration may well often be the service of choice for work with teachers. For example, school-based counselors and psychologists might well recommend collaboration when dealing with teachers on students' homework completion issues (Margolis, McCabe, & Alber, 2004).

# CONSULTING AND COLLABORATING WITH PARENTS/GUARDIANS/ EXTENDED FAMILIES

Schools are consciously attempting to assist children and increase parental/guardian involvement in the school (Esler et al., 2002; Sheridan et al., 2006; Van Velsor & Cox, 2000). The diversity of the settings in which children are raised is considerable and varies by race (Carlson, 2006). Because families influence a student's academic, social, and behavioral competencies, consultation and collaboration with families are essential and has been on the rise (Christenson & Buerkle, 1999). The benefits of partnerships between parents and schools have been demonstrated time and again (Amatea, Daniels, Bringman, & Vandiver, 2004). Among other things, this initiative is due to the increasing social problems that our country is experiencing along with their impact on the schools. There is relatively strong evidence that parent consultation is effective for a variety of school-related behavioral and emotional concerns (Guli, 2005). Evidence with ethnic minorities is limited due to lack of adequate research (Guli, 2005). Additionally, family involvement in the school can positively impact academic achievement (Christenson & Buerkle, 1999; Freer & Watson, 1999) and can have positive effects for the family as well. In spite of the need, parents often have low levels of involvement in the schools (Esler et al., 2002). Further, we need to distinguish parent involvement (which is typically a one-way flow of information from the school to the parent/guardian) and parent collaboration (which is a two-way communication effort based on joint efforts to assist the child) (Cox, 2005). Please note that in this chapter when I use the term "parent," I include the terms "single parent," "guardian," and "extended families" to enhance readability. That said, much of the literature in consultation and collaboration ignores the importance that caregivers other than parents can play in the lives of children.

The need for parental involvement is well stated by Riley: "Thirty years of research make it clear: Parents and families are pivotal to children's learning" (1996, p. 480). Consulting and collaborating with parents has received increasing attention (Hughes et al., 2001; Kratochwill & Pittman 2002). School-based consultation and collaboration can be keys to parent involvement on a broader scale. There are great numbers of parents who are confused about their roles and relationships with their children (Kottman, 1995; Kottman & Wilborn, 1992). Changes in our society have increased the stress levels of parenting significantly. The family and school are both very powerful forces in influencing the learning and development of children. This implies that human service professionals in the schools are expected to have significant contact with parents, largely through consultation and collaboration. For example, school-based consultants often use parent consultation as an adjunct to counseling students (Athanasiou, 2001). Some authors (e.g., Weiss, 1996) suggest that it is best for mental health/human services professionals to assume that all parents are interested in their child's welfare and try to involve even those who consistently reject invitations for involvement.

Contrary to some of what you might find in the literature, there is no "one" eclectic model of parent consultation or collaboration. As a consultant or collaborator, you need to be aware of the models in the literature and then form your own personal model. Parent consultation usually takes the form of either direct case consultation about a given child, parent education, or technology training; hence the increasing popularity of the term "parent involvement" (Kratochwill & Pittman, 2002; Sheridan, Kratochwill, & Bergan, 1996). These approaches to working with parents are often used interchangeably. However, as Sheridan (1993b) points out, there are several differences. These approaches vary in terms of the breadth of information provided (with parent education being highest), the depth of skill development (with parent consultation being the highest), the specificity of skill/knowledge imparted (with parent consultation being the highest), and individuality of focus (with parent consultation being the highest). See Chapter 10 for coverage of conjoint behavioral consultation that includes service to parents as well as educational personnel.

In addition to consultation, there has been increased emphasis on home–school collaboration (Esler et al., 2002). Due to collaboration's emphasis on mutual accountability for outcomes, parents may more likely become involved when they are offered this service. In this manner, parents become instigators of change rather than the target of change. They have the type of relationship, one of equals, that builds trust. Even if human services professionals are gearing their efforts toward the psychological well-being of the child, it is best to link these efforts to the academic achievement of the child as the academic success of their children is a top priority of parents.

Through consultation and collaboration, human service/mental health professionals can help parents to assist their children in the successful accomplishment of developmental tasks and prevent early school problems from impacting normal childhood development (Conroy & Mayer, 1994).

Parent consultation and collaboration create the opportunity for the school and parents to work as a team for the benefit of the school and family (Downing & Harrison, 1991). Many times, consultants provide a variety of services to parents simultaneously. Knoff and Batsche (1993) report a program that combines parent training, tutoring, and support. These activities involve training parents in tutoring, in their children's academic curriculum, and in behavior management; supervision of parent's tutoring with their and others' children; consultation with parents as they initiate tutoring in their home; and the creation of parent drop-in centers designed to encourage parental participation in the schools.

Finally, school-based consultants will want to make sure that all parents are aware of consultation and collaboration services and feel welcome to use them. At the same time, school-based consultants may want to redefine their job roles to include more parent consultation. Research has shown that parent consultation can be effective in assisting with school-based behavioral and emotional problems of students (Guli, 2005).

## Parent Case Consultation

Parents may seek out consultation for a variety of reasons ranging from concern over their child's moving into or out of the school to worries about their child's academic, emotional, or social behavior (Kottman, 1995; Ritchie & Partin, 1994). There are many approaches to parent case consultation, among the more popular of which are the Adlerian, behavioral (Kratochwill, Elliott, & Callan-Stoiber, 2002), and mental health approaches. Behavioral consultation is the most popular, and the behaviorally based conjoint behavioral consultation (Sheridan, 2006) described in Chapter 10 is rapidly gaining popularity (Guli, 2005). There has been some application of family therapy and solutions-based models to parent consultation (Nicoll, 1992; Sommers-Flanagan, 2007). Regardless of the model used, a positive consultation experience can promote increased involvement by parents in the school life of their child and improve family relationships (Kottman, 1995; Sheridan, 1993b). A rule of thumb is to provide the parent with viable options for interventions and allow them to select the ones with the highest likelihood of success as they see it. You should note that there is very little empirical research that supports the efficacy of parent consultation (Sheridan, Kratochwill, & Bergan, 1996).

**A Brief Example of Parent Case Consultation Using a Generic Model.** Sunny is a school consultant who has been approached by a parent named Mardy. Recently tested for the academically gifted program at her school, Mardy's daughter had failed to meet the program's criteria and was concerned that she would lose her friends, many of whom were already in the program. Mardy was worried about how she had taken the news.

Sunny quickly established with Mardy that they would be collaborating. Sunny assessed the parent's feelings about her daughter not being included in the program. Mardy noted that she just didn't meet the program's criteria and that that was okay. Mardy was not disappointed in her child or the school but wanted advice on how to help her daughter deal with this "defeat." Sunny provided Mardy with some information on how children take such setbacks and discussed the family dynamics that had occurred since the child had not made the program.

Mardy confessed that so far her strategy for helping had amounted to reassurance. Sunny and Mardy agreed that Mardy would use active listening with her daughter about the situation. In addition, Mardy would increase the time spent with her daughter doing special things, like going horseback

riding, and would have her daughter invite some of her girlfriends to their house for a stay over. Sunny helped Mardy put all of these activities into a plan and followed up by phone two weeks later to assist her with any loose ends.

## Parent Education and Training

Although school-based consultants work with teachers more frequently than they do parents due to easier access (Merrell et al., 2006), parent consultation is also a major activity. Parent education and training are variations of the education/training consultation model discussed in Chapter 11. Parent education tends to be high on breadth of information provided, low on skill development, low on specificity of information, and low on focusing on the concerns of individual parents (Hoard & Shepard, 2005; Sheridan, Welch, & Orme, 1996). Parent education groups have a variety of different possible goals such as improving communication, developing effective parenting skills, and increasing knowledge of child development (Carlson et al., 2006; Gmeinder & Kratochwill, 1998). Parent education is one way of promoting parent involvement in the schools (Conroy & Mayer, 1994). Parent education is typically conducted as an intervention for an existing condition (Hoard & Shepard, 2005; Valdez, Carlson, & Zanger, 2005) and often subsumes parent training, with the basic difference being that parent training includes the acquisition of specific parenting skills (Sheridan et al., 1996) or skills related to help their children improve academic performance (Rhoades & Kratochwill, 1998). For example, school psychologists and counselors can provide workshops for parents on helping children cope with divorce due to the fact that many parents lack the skill to help children cope effectively with the changes brought on by divorce (Parker, 1994). More recently, school-based consultants have been involved in training nonmainstream parents on how to "navigate" the school system by learning its ins and outs and engage in their children's learning (Koonce & Harper, 2005).

Parent training groups are frequently based on the premise that parents can learn to help their children when they are taught by methods that go beyond didactic instruction, like modeling (Carlson et al., 2006; Watson & Robinson, 1996).

There are three popular types of parent education groups (Kramer, 1990): parent effectiveness training (PET) based on the work of Carl Rogers (Gordon, 1970), Adlerian approaches (Carlson et al., 2006; Dinkmeyer & Carlson, 2000; Dinkmeyer & McKay, 1996; Kottman, 1995), and behavioral approaches based on social learning theory (Becker, 1971). These approaches or individual aspects of them can be provided to parents through multiweek parent programs, monthly parent nights, or through faculties such as a parent resource library (Conroy & Mayer, 1994). Online approaches to parent education are becoming increasingly popular. The empirical evidence related to parent education programs is limited, of varying quality, and mixed (Hoard & Shepard, 2005). The empirical research on parent education and parent training is limited in scope and quality; practicing consultants should be cautious in estimating parent education's benefits (Hoard & Shepard, 2005; Kramer, 1990; Valdez et al., 2005). One of the biggest challenges faced by consultants is getting parents who need parent education to attend; those who resist may need special consideration (Downing & Downing, 1991). There is some evidence that consultants can train parents to conduct parent groups effectively, thus freeing up the consultant for other activities (Kottman & Wilborn, 1992). There is trend to develop brief, focused community-based individual consulting sessions for interested parents, but more research is needed (Sommers-Flanagan, 2007).

**A Brief Example of Parent Education from an Adlerian Perspective.**    Sylvia is a school consultant conducting a group of seven parents that meets once a week for eight weeks. To teach the Adlerian theory of human behavior as it relates to child-rearing and family life—one of her major goals—Sylvia provides each parent with the book *Raising a Responsible Child* (Dinkmeyer & McKay, 1996), the content of which forms the basis of the group's discussions.

During each session, the group discusses the activities and homework assignments from the previous session, as well as the current reading.

Sylvia then leads the group in an exercise related to the reading, which the group likewise discusses, and assigns a new reading and homework assignment. Sylvia attempts to get the group members to practice in their homes what they are learning in the group and provides motivational support to the parents as they implement what they have been learning.

Here are some bottom line suggestions for working with parents:

- Be multiculturally sensitive and competent.
- Remember that most children do not come from a traditional, intact family.
- Avoid judgmental comments about the child or the parent/custodian.
- Make the parents active partners in the attempts to change their behavior and their children's behavior.
- At all times give the honest impression of being competent, caring, and qualified.
- Use the existing strengths of the child and parents as the foundation for recommending strategies.
- Advocate for the child and the parents.
- Find an alternative to consultation if parents are unwilling to recognize a problem or are not willing or able to implement a problem-solving process.

## Home–School Collaboration

In home–school collaboration, the goal is to create effective partnerships between school-based professionals and parents to enhance student learning (Christenson & Buerkle, 1999; Minke, 2006). Home–school collaboration is "the relationship between families and schools where parents and educators work together to promote the academic and social development of children" (Cox, 2005, p. 473). Through collaboration, parents are not on their own, but have the assistance of a trained professional who is willing to partner with and provide assistance to their child. School personnel can learn detailed information about the child and the family and engage parents in jointly defined goals. According to Esler et al. (2002), basic considerations in home school collaboration include:

- a preventive, problem-solving approach
- both educators and families are critical in socializing learners
- broad opportunities for parent participation are essential
- building relationships with parents can take time and effort

In collaborating with parents, school-based professionals will want to ensure that parents are true partners, are viewed as experts on their children, and have responsibility for some of the outcomes related to the goals of collaboration. It is also important to keep a solutions-oriented perspective during collaboration to help the parent remain focused on behavior change.

**A Brief Example of Parent Collaboration.** Kyrie is a school psychologist who is collaborating with a parent, Shameika, regarding her child Al. Shameika has initiated the collaboration due to her concern that Al, a sixth grader, is falling in with an inappropriate peer group. Kyrie and Shameika create a collaboration based on shared responsibility with a solution-based focus. Kyrie agrees to invite Al to a group she is forming in which the students discuss interpersonal relationships with their peers. Shameika agrees to work with Al on broadening the number of extracurricular activities in which he engages, thus setting the stage for new and more appropriate peer relationships. Together they develop a plan along with a timeline. Shameika details for Kyrie some of Al's behaviors at home to assist her in working with Al in the group. Kyrie suggests some ways for Shameika to get Al involved in additional extracurricular activities in ways that Al would feel he had some say. Kyrie gets Al's permission to discuss in general what they talk about in the group. The two adults communicate regularly over the phone on the progress they are making. In time Al gets

involved in extracurricular activities that have more desirable peer groups. The skills he has learned in the group allows him to relate better to his peers. Kyrie and Shameika agree to follow up regularly with each other to monitor Al's progress.

## Cross-Cultural Considerations When Working with Parents

Children today are less likely to reside with both biological parents, and this fact varies significantly by race. There is little research that identifies evidence-based practices for such social situations (Carlson, 2006). That said, parent involvement is positively related to the academic and social success of students (Lott & Rogers, 2005). School counselors and psychologists will want to remember that, in our increasingly diverse society, they will encounter issues related to cultural and linguistic diversity when working with parents. In addition, as Jeltova and Fish note: "There is now acknowledgement that parents may be biological, adoptive, step, or foster, that they may be single or in a couple, and that they may be married, divorced, widowed, remarried, or in a partnership, gay, straight, or transgender" (2005, p. 18). Culture directly influences the family in a significant manner (Ortiz & Flanagan, 2002; Sheridan, 2000). Cultural issues can amplify the complexity of consultation (Brown, 1997; Nastasi, 2006; Ramirez & Smith, 2007; Soo-Hoo, 1998). For example, consultants will need to remember that some cultural groups view achievement in terms of the individual while others view it through group cooperation. This difference can impact the way a consultant works with parents about the school-related issues their child is facing (Diller, 2007). In addition, consultants can work to ensure that schools are responsive and attentive to removing any barriers non-mainstream parents encounter in their attempts to obtain a quality education for their children, welcoming their input and active participation. Nastasi suggests that the focus for consultants should be on "empowering parents to navigate the public education system, (b) effectively integrating cultural considerations into consultation and intervention efforts, and (c) educating both families and school personnel" (2005, pp. 114–115). For example, school-based consultants can assist parents in developing relationships with school personnel who typically come from the mainstream culture. In another example, they can focus on nonmainstream students' strengths, engage in culturally sensitive communication, and demonstrate a culturally sensitive understanding and valuing of parents' coping strategies in activities such as conducting parent support and empowerment groups (Lott, 2003; Lott & Rogers, 2005).

School consultants will be asked to help address the developmental needs of an increasing number of students from culturally diverse backgrounds (Simcox, Nuijens, & Lee, 2006; Tarver Behring & Ingraham, 1998). By the year 2020, it is estimated that the number of school-age children that will come from minority groups is over 50 percent. There are six dimensions of racial/ethnic variability that consultants should be knowledgeable about: notions of kinship, roles and status, sex-role socialization, language, religion/spirituality, and ethnic identity (Lee, 1995). Lee points out that in their consultative function, school-based professionals can bridge potential gaps between the school and parents through "incorporation of the inherent strengths of families and communities into the educational process" (p. 13) and by promoting the use of cultural diversity as a way to enhance the soundness of the education of students. Lott and Rogers (2005) echo these points. Consultants will want to exercise caution in making any kind of generalizations regarding any characteristics of a given culture. There is diversity within culturally diverse groups (i.e., individual differences), and these need to be taken into account (Nastasi, 2006; Nastasi et al., 2000; Ramirez & Smith, 2007). For example, variables such as socioeconomic status and geographic location influence and shape a family's values (Ortiz & Flanagan, 2002).

When consulting with parents in cross-cultural situations, consultants need to consider the impact of culture on children's academic achievement, children's behavior, modes of parental communication and expectations, and the family system itself (Brown, 1997; Maital, 2000; Minke, 2006). The impact of culture on variables such as these can be accounted for by doing the following things when consulting (Moseley-Howard, 1995, pp. 343–344):

- Remain aware of the systemic impact upon the child.
- Evaluate the cultural milieu of the child and the degree of acculturation.
- Evaluate strengths of the culture of origin and its adaptive characteristics.
- Focus on development/readiness and all aspects of cognitive style.
- Be aware of characteristics influenced by culture that may have an impact on assessment and intervention results.

The interested reader is referred to the following articles on the best practices for considering cultural factors in working with nonmainstream families: general considerations (Lott & Rogers, 2005); gay, lesbian, bisexual, and transgender families (Jeltova & Fish, 2005); families in poverty (Guishard, Fine, Doyle, Jackson, Staten, & Webb, 2005); African American parents (Koonce & Harper, 2005); bilingual families (Ochoa & Rhodes, 2005); Latinos (La Roche & Shriberg, 2004); and migrant families (Clare, Jimenez, & McClendon, 2005).

# INTERAGENCY COLLABORATION

Agencies such as the school, social services, the local mental health center, the child evaluation center, family services organization, and often the family itself collaborate together to help selected children and their families (Bemak, Murphy, & Kaffenberger, 2005; Staton et al., 2007). The rationale for interagency collaboration, in the case of students, is that the social and/or educational problems of a child affect all aspects of his or her life such as the home and school. The shared responsibility for the case shifts the focus from what the school can do to what the community should do to provide services (Hobbs & Collison, 1995). The shared responsibility necessitates solid agreement on the roles and responsibilities of individual collaborators. You can imagine the complexity of this collaboration effort with different agencies with different mission statements and procedures for providing services. Further, the collaborating professionals will want to recognize that their team will have a distinct "personality" that will impact how the team will function (Garrett, 1998).

The need for effective prevention programs serving at-risk youths and their families has increased. This has involved a shift from single-setting practice to school/community-based and -linked interagency service (Bemak et al., 2005; Hodges, Hernandez, & Nesman, 2003; Short & Talley, 1999; Swenson et al., 2000). Counselors in school and community settings can be instrumental in developing and maintaining mental health programs for today's youth. Because school counselors and school psychologists have a primary responsibility for addressing the social and personal needs of students, they are thereby involved in school-community collaboration (Geroski, Rodgers, & Breen, 1997; Hobbs & Collison, 1995). They will work on interagency teams to plan, coordinate, evaluate, and provide direct services to students and their families. In addition, school-based professionals work with human service agency personnel to provide primary and secondary prevention programs in the school or community such as those related to bully-proofing the school and developing programs for students at risk. As with other forms of collaboration, interagency collaboration requires cultural competence (Staton et al., 2007). For example, school and community consultants working on health and educational issues for migrant families will need to be knowledgeable about the cultural values of these families (Clare, Jimenez, McClendon, 2005). School-based personnel can function within collaborative teams in capacities such as making interventions at school, monitoring overall progress at school and home, and making suggestions to community-based mental health professionals.

Whereas more traditional expert modes of consultation were adequate in the past, the complexity of the problems faced by today's youths and their parents suggest that a more collaborative approach may be in order. "School-linked and school-based programs, with services located either at the school or in the community, offer a promising model for service delivery, and collaborative planning between schools and community has become critical to the success of such efforts" (Keys et al., 1995, p. 123). Collaboration has become increasingly popular, as school and community agencies have understood the fragmentation of at-risk youth services. Consultants must develop multifaceted programs for at-risk youth and their families because the problems faced by these groups are multi-causal and must be solved by addressing a larger context: there is no single answer to such problems (Cummings et al., 2004; Keys et al., 1998; Lerner, 1995).

Although school and community counselors provide case-related services on a regular basis, collaborative consultation efforts are relatively new. These efforts have come about as schools and agencies have realized that no one person or no one organization can solve the complex issues and problems that need to be dealt with; hence service integration has been introduced among schools and agencies. In collaboration there are multiple experts who come together to "jointly identify problems to be addressed . . . to determine strategies and the role each person plays in implementing these strategies to carry out their roles interdependently, and to monitor progress" (Keys et al., 1998, p. 124). Both school and community consultants, in order to use collaboration effectively, must see themselves as connected to a broader community (Nastasi, 2005).

By ensuring that collaboration services are delivered in a timely, efficient, and integrated manner, the consultant encourages collaboration efforts that focus on the healthy development of the child and his or her family. To deliver services of this level of quality, the collaborating team needs to ensure commitment from all parties, encourage effective communication, have strong leadership, have an understanding of the culture of the collaborating agencies, engage in serious preplanning, commit adequate resources, and minimize turf issues

(Johnson, Zorn, Yung Tam, LaMontagne, & Johnson, 2003).

In order to maximize the probability that an effective plan will be designed and implemented, the collaborating professionals will want to meet soon after the child and his or her family have been identified as needing services. By having several professionals as well as the family itself involved in planning and implementing the interventions that are part of the plan, a broad knowledge base is applied to the plan. On the other hand, it is essential that each collaborating professional recognizes the philosophical orientation, service limitations, and mission of the other agencies involved as part of the collaborating team (Swenson et al., 2000). By having an awareness of boundary issues, collaborating professionals can be prepared to implement their "piece of the pie" without doing anything counterproductive to the efforts of other collaborating professionals. These issues highlight the importance of developing interagency policies that provide for a broad-based and comprehensive delivery system (Breznay, 2001; Quinn & Cumblad, 1994).

The collaborating professionals will usually select a team facilitator, frequently a school counselor or school psychologist who will convene meetings, ensure documentation of meeting discussions, and make sure that progress on the individual collaborator's work with the family is discussed during meetings. The team facilitator will make sure that the plan is made and carried out with adjustments made as necessary. Further, the team facilitator has the responsibility to make sure an evaluation of the plan is made and shared. The facilitator has the collaborating professionals develop some kind of form that will enable the team to monitor the plan. For example, the plan will have the following sections: the problem identified along with the date of identification, a description of the goal developed to deal with the problem, a description of the intervention used to meet the goal, a notation of which collaborating professionals were to do what and by when, and a section describing the outcome of the intervention.

When working with families, it is important to empower the family so that there is not a hierarchical difference between the family and the school (Short & Talley, 1999). When collaborating with parents, every attempt should be made to provide them with maximum input into meaningful participation in the collaboration team's work with them and their child (Friend & Cook, 1996). This type of group consensus on how to proceed and follow up can increase the chances of success. Consistent use of language among various agencies, even to the point of developing a common brochure describing services, can minimize misunderstanding by parents as well as some school personnel (Ikeda et al., 1996).

Interagency collaboration can take time in terms of being out of the school building and the amount of necessary paperwork. Ways to minimize the constraints of time include rotating team meeting sites and using technology to store, retrieve, and communicate information (Hobbs & Collison, 1995). Collaboration involves trade-offs. School personnel have to give up some power in order to get the benefits of community responsibility.

Due to managed care, a trend in interagency collaboration includes increased involvement of health care service agencies with school and community integrated planning and service provision (Knoff, 1996). When professionals in these settings look across their settings and circumstances, they will be able to define concerns and generate solutions in a joint manner (Hellkamp, 1996), often using strategic planning (Knoff, 1996). Such strategic planning emphasis will determine who will provide services, how they will be provided, and whether health care reform will determine the provision of services (e.g., a certain limit on the number of sessions a family may have that insurance will pay for). Further interagency collaboration will need to consider results-based planning and budgeting systems to ensure for adequate services (Orland, 1999). School-based professionals will want to be aware of the following trends in interagency collaboration: a movement toward providing incentives for achieving results, a change in focus from service providers to service recipients, and a change from supporting projects to supporting changes in the system (Jehl, 1999). The limited research on interagency consultation suggests that shared physical space, mechanisms for both formal and informal communication, team coordination, organizational support, and collaborative decision making all contribute to success (Nicholson et al., 2000).

## PRAGMATIC ISSUES

There are a variety of pragmatic issues that face school-based psychologists and counselors in their consultation and collaboration activities due to the school setting.

### Ethical Issues

All of the ethical issues discussed in Chapter 7 apply to school-based situations, though two of them take on particular significance in a school setting: confidentiality and informed consent (Dougherty, 1992a). As every practicing human service professional knows, maintaining confidentiality in a school is difficult because there is a tendency in many schools for personnel to share information about students in inappropriate ways. It is easy to imagine how breaking teacher confidentiality unnecessarily could have disastrous effects. School-based counselors and psychologists must ensure that the limits to confidentiality are clearly defined and mutually agreed upon for each consultation and collaboration relationship (Jacob & Hartshorne, 2003).

Many school professionals are just becoming familiar with their own roles as consultants and collaborators, and the persons with whom they work such as teachers, administrators, and parents are often not familiar with exactly what constitutes consultation and collaboration and how they differ (Hughes et al., 1993). Therefore, counselors and psychologists need to explain their services whenever necessary. As an example, time constraints in schools often create conditions for very brief informal consultation. Consultants will want to be alert for ethical issues related to the welfare of the client system and the integrity of the consultation process (Harrison, 2004). Multicultural issues clearly affect school consultation and collaboration. The chang-

ing demographics of the student population in our society dictate that school-based professionals will encounter such issues in their daily practice. For example, the use of interpreters can raise issues of confidentiality in school settings (Lopez, 2000). In another example, school-based consultants will need to ensure that assessment and intervention practices are culturally appropriate (Castillo, Quintana, & Zamarripa, 2000).

School-based counselors and psychologists and external consultants may have to deal with the ethical issue of deciding whether to end a consultation or collaboration relationship and engage in advocacy roles to ensure that students receive the services to which they are entitled (McMahon & Pruett, 1998). Counselors and psychologists can be placed in the predicament of trying to help a system that truly does not want assistance and, as a result, the students in the system suffer.

### Working with Other School-Based Professionals

Because there may be several professionals in a school working to assist the same child, family, or program, there is the potential for both collaboration and conflict. I am of the opinion that collaboration is the most desirable way to proceed in such cases. Idol and Baran (1992) suggest some practical ways for collaboration to be enhanced and conflict minimized: Consultants should clearly define their roles and responsibilities with one another on an ongoing basis, adopt a model of consultation/collaboration that all are comfortable with as a common ground for working together, attempt to obtain minimum competency in the skills necessary for implementing the adopted model of consultation, and adopt a framework consisting of problem-solving stages (like those discussed in Chapters 3–6 in this text) to guide the implementation of their model.

There are many examples of school psychologists and counselors collaborating with school-based management teams, student assistance teams (SAT), student study teams (SST), teacher assistance teams, multidisciplinary teams, and department- and grade-level teams (McLoughlin, Kubick, & Lewis, 2002; Paisley & Milsom, 2007; Ross, Powell, & Elias, 2002). Teams are an increasingly popular outcome of school reform including reform aimed at cultural competency (Simcox, Nuijens, & Lee, 2006). Teams allow for many tasks that cannot be adequately performed by individuals; the effects of teams are more than the effects of individuals working alone (French & Bell, 1999). Their goal is to assist the school and home to meet the educational and behavioral needs of students. To assist teams to function effectively, school-based consultants can work to minimize the barriers that inhibit team effectiveness: unfamiliar tasks, extensive time demands, procedural complexity, limited intervention resources, and limited administrative support (Doll et al., 2005). Further, they will want to ensure that teacher input is valued, interventions are well defined, and the team has some accountability for outcomes (Slonski-Fowler & Truscott, 2004).

## Systems View of the School

A systems view of schools is a useful framework for understanding the organizational context of consultation (see Chapter 8). It also allows for a multi-level service delivery model that can include individuals, classrooms, and the entire school. System-level change demands that all aspects of education be examined in terms of multiple levels and be based on multiple partnerships among stakeholders (Manz, 2007). As a result all students receive services that match their needs (Hojnoski, 2007). School-based consultants will be increasingly called upon to provide system-level services (Conyne & Mazza, 2007; Hojnoski, 2007; Merrell et al., 2006; Paisley & Milsom, 2007) to assess readiness for change as well as to encourage and sustain changes (Adelman & Taylor, 2007). The idea is that consultants will use existing structures and processes within the school to initiate, maintain, and evaluate system-level changes (Hoffman et al., 2006; Jeltova & Fish, 2005; Adelman & Taylor, 2007; Taylor & Dymnicki, 2007). This view allows for issues related to student learning and behavior to be viewed beyond the student and more from the perspective

of environmental context. In a systems view of consultation, the student is examined in the context of school and family units. These units and their interaction (for example, teacher attitudes, parent child-rearing practices, communication patterns between parents and the school) then become eligible for attention and modification. Individual change can be facilitated when the wider system that directly interrelates with the student is considered (French & Bell, 1999).

Systems theory assumes the school to be the target for consultation intervention; to consult with a teacher represents a linear view of the child being responsible for negative behavior, and the teacher for correcting it. This may reinforce in the teacher's mind that the child, not the system, has the problem.

One concern is that not all teachers are comfortable with systems approaches; some want more concrete ways of approaching perceived problems. In addition, many school consultants have not been trained in systems methods. Finally, the systems view typically dictates that the consultant examine the child in interaction with a variety of levels of the ecosystem such as home, school, and community, thus complicating the nature of the consultation relationship (Hoffman et al., 2006; Sheridan, Welch, & Orme, 1996).

## Developing a Framework for Prevention and Intervention

Prevention programs are seeing resurgence in schools. The idea is to provide a more prevention-oriented model in addition to the common case models we have already learned about (Hojnoski, 2007). Social and emotional learning (SEL) can provide an integrated framework for programs dealing with students' social, academic, and behavioral needs (Zins, 1995; Zins, Bloodworth, Weissberg, & Walberg, 2004). SEL assists schools to see that social, emotional, and academic development need to be looked at together and are thus all part of the school's responsibility (Manz, 2007). Greenberg et al. (2003) note that "school-based prevention and youth development interventions are most beneficial when they simultaneously enhance students' personal and social assets, as well as improve the quality of the environments in which students are educated" (p. 467). School-based consultants are especially qualified to assist with such prevention efforts (Bramlett et al., 2002), particularly in ensuring that these programs are contextualized to the school in which they are being placed and that they contain elements that promote social and emotional learning (SEL) such as communication skills, conflict resolution, and study habits (Carlson, 2007). Other models include prevention efforts related to responding to traumatizing events such as acts of terrorism by working with schools and families on resiliency training and preparedness (Alpert & Duckworth Smith, 2003). SEL programs do not yet have a strong research base due to the complexity of their implementation and measurement (Tanyu, 2007). That said, successful implementation of SEL programs require understanding that schools are multilevel systems with complex policies that support implementation. The consultant must also be aware that human dynamics and empowerment are involved (Tanyu, 2007).

Among the many goals of school-based consultation are the ideas that problems can be prevented by creating and implementing primary prevention programs and consultants can effectively work with school personnel on preventative goals (Meyers, 2002). Some research suggests that consultees adapt prevention programs to their perceived needs when implementing them and that implementation of intervention programs is difficult (Larson & Samdal, 2007). Consultee-centered, program, education/ training, and organizational consultation and collaboration are methods to accomplish this (Meyers, 2002; Meyers et al., 2004). For example, a school-based consultant may help to develop a team of stakeholders to collaborate together in coordinating a program related to school attendance. In another example, consultants can provide education/training consultation regarding mental health promotion, and the public health model to school personnel and parents (Nastasi, 2004). In yet another example, a school and community consultants work together on a prevention program involving community members to restrict access to tobacco

among school-aged youth (Jason, Pokorny, Ji, & Kunz, 2005). There is a growing body of evidence that prevention programs can be effective (Metropolitan Area Child Study Research Group, 2007).

## Time Constraints

As you might recall from Chapter 8, time constraints are a large and real issue for conducting effective consultation. A limitation of school consultation and collaboration is that both take time to do well (Gottlieb, 2006; Welch, 2000; Wilczynski et al., 2000). With increasing accountability in our schools, there is very little free time at school for the people who work there, so it can be difficult for counselors and psychologists to engage teachers and administrators in these services, let alone parents who must often take time off from work to come to the school for any reason. The school environment encourages engagement in short consultations and collaborative efforts (Davis, 2005). More recently Caplan and Caplan have stressed the importance of "orderly and unhurried reflection during consultation discussions" (1993, p. 43). On the other hand, counselors and psychologists need to find strategies to effectively cope with the very real time constraints placed upon consultation and collaboration during the school day. Effective time management on the part of school professionals is one obvious help in creating time for consultation and collaboration. Recent research has supported that collaboration is valued by school personnel and that adequate time is found to conduct it (Welch & Tulbert, 2000). Consultants can likely have more positive impact on the consultation process by using their limited time to observe and assess the problem and then model and coach, rather than by just talking to the consultee (Watson & Robinson, 1996) and helping student assistance teams run efficiently (Doll et al., 2005).

Five other strategies include early release/late arrival of students, use of substitutes, teaching strategies that free up personnel (Friend & Cook, 1996), the limited use of the telephone and/or e-mail (Kruger et al., 2001), and videoconferencing or the telephone (Reese et al., 2006) for accomplishing some of the tasks related to consultation and collaboration, plus the use of group methods as appropriate. Another option is to adjust the school culture so that consultation and collaboration are seen as systematic, organized activities through which the school psychologist or school counselor provides assistance (Fall, 1995).

## MULTICULTURAL SCHOOL CONSULTATION

"Ethnic and linguistic minority children constitute the most rapidly growing segment of the youth population of the United States. In fact, ethnic minority youth now constitute 35 percent of the U.S. public school population and more than 50 percent of the student population in many urban school districts . . ." (Quintana et al., 2000, p. 435). These demographic changes that are reflected in the students in our schools impact the delivery of consultation and collaboration (Merrell et al., 2006). School-based consultants will increasingly be called upon to work with school personnel and parents to meet the needs of these students. *Multicultural school consultation* is an approach to consultation that takes into account how cultural issues affect the consultation process (Ingraham, 2000; Rogers, 2000). Multicultural consultation is more a way of looking at consultation than a distinct model. Ingraham (2000) points out several components of multicultural school consultation:

- domains for consultant learning and development (e.g., understanding the cultural context for consultation)

- domains of consultee learning and development (e.g., avoiding overemphasis on culture)

- cultural variations in the consultation constellation (e.g., taking into account cultural differences among the consultant, consultee, and client system)

- contextual and power influences (e.g., minimizing power differentials between the consultant and the consultee)

- hypothesized methods for supporting consultee and client success (e.g., using consultation methods matched with the consultee's style)

Taken together, these dimensions provide a framework for dealing with the multicultural issues that arise in consultation. Within this framework, consultants take into account both individual differences and cultural issues so as not to overemphasize cultural variables; culture goes beyond characteristics such as race and language. For example, this framework helps to avoid *intervention paralysis,* the inability to determine an intervention due to uncertainty in how to select culturally appropriate interventions (Ingraham, 2000). There is some evidence that modifications to traditional consultation approaches when consulting with teachers and parents of culturally diverse backgrounds are important; these modifications may vary by culture (Tarver Behring et al., 2000). As Merrell et al. note: We "must adopt practices and service delivery models that reduce bias, meet individual needs, and result in better outcomes for all children and their families" (2006, p. 59). As one example, more research is needed that validates the effectiveness of parent education and parent training with ethnic minorities (Hoard & Shepard, 2005).

## SCHOOL CONSULTATION IN THE 21ST CENTURY

What trends are occurring in school consultation in the first decade of the new millennium? What needs will school personnel and parents calling for assistance from school consultants have? I will next describe some of the ways consultants may be using their skills. Merrell et al. (2006) have pointed out trends in school psychology (and, in this author's opinion, there are similar trends in school counseling and school social work) that will impact the delivery of school-based consultation and collaboration. Consultation and collaboration will:

1. focus more on positively impacting all students in additional to those with major concerns;

2. develop culturally sensitive interventions that apply to increasing demographic changes in the school population;

3. engage in system-level initiatives (e.g., entire school) in addition to those that are individual-related; and

4. use date-driven decision making to select and evaluate interventions.

The limited use of the telephone and/or e-mail to accomplish some tasks (such as follow-up) is on the increase. These methods help to save time but may also have disadvantages when compared to face-to-face contact. Chapter 7 of this text reviews some related ethical issues.

Schools are dramatically expanding their services to prekindergarten children. Public education is being offered to children at risk from birth onward and to all three- and four-year-olds (Fine & Kontos, 1992; Hohenshil & Brown, 1991). Therefore, school-based consultants will increasingly be asked to offer services to the significant others of prekindergarten children (Bacon & Dougherty, 1992; Sheridan et al., 2006) including interventions related to response to intervention (RTI) (Barnett et al., 2007). Further, consultants will increase their work as liaisons between school systems and early childhood settings (Hojnoski & Missal, 2006).

School-based consultants will help their schools create a positive climate with regard to the school reform movement's continuing impact on public education (Colbert et al., 2006). As we have noted, school-based consultants have increasingly been called on to help schools deal with four major concerns related to school reform: children at risk, reintegration of special students, school-community integration of services, and restructuring of schools (Beck, 1994; Curtis & Stollar, 2002; Mayer et al., 1993). In addition to their typical consultation practice, school-based

consultants will be involved in projects designed to promote collegiality in the school, promote social and emotional learning through prevention programs (Zins et al., 2004), develop programs for students at risk as academic standards are increased, develop study skills programs, and ensure that the socio-affective domain is included in any curriculum planning. Other areas in which consultation and collaboration will be needed include quality assurance, parent involvement, supporting teacher competence, building student-focused community networks (Dwyer & Gorin, 1996), itinerant consultation in early childhood education (Harris & Klein, 2004), and developing peer teacher consultation groups (Blase, J., & Blase, J. C., 2006).

The controversy over traditional assessment and response to intervention (RTI) (Barnett et al., 2007; Willis & Dumont, 2006) continues and will influence consultant behavior. RTI developed from applied behavioral analysis and provides a history of interventions and their impact. RTI guides problem solving by using "data-based decision making as a basis for modifying, titrating, or changing the nature of interventions" (Gresham, 2006, p. 526). In other words, assessment is seen as needing to be related to the selection of interventions and their evaluation. RTI requires intervention at multiple levels to address both the organization's and individuals' needs (Cowan, 2007).

The infusion of positive psychology to increase the well-being of the individuals in the school through mental health and behavioral consultation is also receiving more attention (Akin-Little, Little & Delligatti, 2004; Foster & Lloyd, 2007; Larson & Samdal, 2007; Love, 2007). Consultants will increasingly translate the finding of positive psychology into interventions that focus on "what is going right" with the client system. In a related initiative, the positive behavior support (PBS) movement (Barnett et al., 2007; Carr, 2007; Hojnoski, 2007; Scott & Martinek, 2006; Sugai et al., 2000) will continue to provide an approach that allows consultants to help develop support and interventions (behavioral and/or academic) at the individual, classroom or school-levels (Cowan, 2007). PBS employs a preventative and positive influence approach. Maintaining effec-

---

**C A S E   12.1      Consultation for School Consultants[1]**

---

Dr. Purdy, a professor of counseling in a southeastern university, was asked by the principal of a local elementary school, Mrs. Abdujaparov, to provide consulting services. Principal Abdujaparov explained that they were just beginning the process of developing a school-wide positive behavioral support program (PBS) and knew that Dr. Purdy had assisted other schools in successfully implementing like programs. Within the next several weeks, Dr. Purdy and the principal met and discussed the consulting fee and the team's tentative implementation time line, then arranged suitable regular meeting times for the rest of the academic year.

Before the first meeting with the PBS leadership team, Dr. Purdy researched different aspects of the school, including its geographic location, academic status, the percentage of students on free or reduced lunch, the number of teachers with advanced degrees and/or national certification, and the last four years of disciplinary reports. He also spoke informally with two different parents he knew who had children attending that particular school.

In the first meeting, after introducing himself and explaining his experience with PBS, he spent the rest of the hour getting to know the team (asking about their hopes and hesitations regarding implementing PBS), and finished the day by taking a tour of the school. In subsequent meetings, Dr. Purdy found the team exceptionally spirited and talkative, and they would often veer off on tangents about different problem areas within the school (i.e., buses, cafeteria). At first, Dr. Purdy allowed the team some leeway when they strayed from the topic, but as the weeks progressed he began speaking up more quickly, often summarizing the teacher's complaint and finding ways to integrate the complaint into the PBS planning process. In time, other team members began modeling Dr. Purdy's style of redirecting, and the meetings became more productive. The majority of the detail work was delegated to different team members to be completed between

meetings, and Dr. Purdy regularly provided feedback to questions, mainly through email.

Shortly after the initial meetings began, Dr. Purdy asked if he could attend the next full faculty and staff meeting where the PBS process was going to be introduced. During this meeting he took special care to insure all faculty and staff that their feedback was welcome and needed, and that no final approval or implementation would take place without their knowledge.

As expected, it took a full academic year for all aspects PBS to be implemented. Throughout the process, Dr. Purdy assisted the team in many ways: he collaborated with team members to determine efficient ways to implement PBS procedures while keeping all staff abreast of developments, he wrote brief articles in the school's monthly newsletter highlighting favorable outcomes other schools had experienced after establishing their PBS plans, he attended several PTO meetings to discuss the benefits of PBS and highlight their progress, and he assisted the team in analyzing the data so problem areas could be addressed. With all procedures in place, Dr. Purdy ended his involvement in the project but assured the team that he was available for future consulting if needed.

**Commentary**

In this example, Dr. Purdy was wise to keep the stakeholders abreast of the PBS implementation process through faculty and PTO meetings and newsletter articles because nothing compromises consultation quicker than to impose one's expertise on a reluctant staff. This is not to say that every stakeholder will welcome changes with open arms; some resistance is to be expected, but people are much more willing to accept reorganization when they feel they have had opportunities for providing input into the process. Thus, it is vital to the success of consultation to make the process as transparent and collaborative as possible.

---

[1] The author would like to thank Russ Curtis for this case study.

---

tive practices is emphasized. Functional behavioral assessment is often used in PBS. Students receiving PBS learn about themselves, social skills and community-buildingskills.

In a related trend, consultants will increasingly be using a community vision that emphasizes fulfillment rather than a therapeutic vision when working in in-

teragency collaboration with regard to transitioning students with disabilities to community life (Michaels & Lopez, 2005). This will involve a person-centered, strength-based orientation rather than a deficit-based orientation (Smith & Nevin, 2005).

The multiple issues brought about by high-stakes testing, such as teacher burnout, will be fertile areas for consultation. With the significant rate of turnover in school personnel—as much as 50 percent of teachers leaving before completing five years of service—and the aging of school faculty members, school-based consultants will increasingly be called upon to facilitate teacher support groups through a variety of models including consultee-centered consultation (Babinsky & Rogers, 1998). These groups may range from mentoring groups and teacher support groups to burnout prevention and stress management groups (Jellinek, 1990).

In their work with prevention programs, school-based consultants will increasingly be involved in helping to determine research-based practices, determining program accountability, advocating for programs that view the school and its surrounding community as the unit of change, providing research-based training programs in preventive techniques for stakeholders, looking at prevention more from a public health perspective,

focusing on positive psychology (e.g., subjective well-being) (Seligman & Csikszentmihalyi, 2000), and functioning as part of the support system to keep programs going (Graden, 2004; Greenberg et al., 2003; Meyers et al., 2004; Nastasi, 2004). For example, by taking a public health perspective, consultants can engage in organizational consultation that builds an infrastructure for sustained and institutionalized problem solving (Nastasi, 2004).

School-based consultants are increasingly called upon to act as organizational consultants during a disaster, national emergency (Costello, Phelps, & Wilczenski, 1994; Halpern & Tramontin, 2007; Studer, 2005), or local crisis (such as violence in the school). School-based consultants help schools develop crisis plans. They train and work with teachers, parents, and other mental health colleagues concerning appropriate crisis intervention, coordination of the response to the crisis, and engage in postcrisis debriefing activities.

## SUGGESTIONS FOR EFFECTIVE PRACTICE

- As you plan the work in your practice, deliberately take into consideration the very real time constraints that school personnel face.

- Remember that many, if not most, of the students you will serve will not come from intact families.

- Bear in mind the importance of cultural diversity in your practice of school consultation and collaboration.

- Remember that schools are among the slowest of organizations to change.

## QUESTIONS FOR REFLECTION

1. What strikes you as most notable about the history of school-based consultation?

2. To what degree do you see organizational consultation as a viable option when consulting with school administrators?

3. Do you see any possible pitfalls in consulting with school administrators who may also be your immediate superiors?

4. To what degree can Adlerian case consultation be used effectively at the elementary, middle, and secondary school levels?

5. Why is the Adlerian C-group a good alternative to traditional in-service programs for teachers?

6. Do you think that most school-based consultants are adequately trained in the teaching-

learning process to employ instructional consultation effectively? Why?

7.  What are some special factors consultants need to take into account when consulting with parents?

8.  Which of the pragmatic issues covered in this chapter has the most relevance to your practice as a consultant?

9.  What changes are going to impact how school-based consultants deliver their services in the 21st century?

10. To what degree can the mental health and behavioral models discussed in earlier chapters be implemented in a school setting?

## SUGGESTED SUPPLEMENTARY READINGS

Ingraham, C. L. (2000). Consultation through a multicultural lens: Multicultural and cross-cultural consultation in schools. *School Psychology Review, 29,* 320–343. This article offers a model of consultation called multicultural school consultation. The article offers a conceptual framework for multicultural consultation and makes suggestions for future research.

Gutkin, T. B., and Curtis, M. J. (1999). School-based consultation theory and practice: The art and science of indirect service delivery. In C. R. Reynolds and T. B. Gutkin (Eds.), *The handbook of school psychology* (3rd ed., pp. 598–637). New York: Wiley. This chapter covers a variety of topics on school-based consultation, including its characteristics, rationale for services, major approaches, and contemporary and future issues. Broad in scope, consultants will find a wealth of information in this chapter.

Ortiz, S. O., & Flanagan, D. P. (2002). Best practices in working with culturally diverse children and families. In A. Thomas and J. Grimes (Eds.), *Best practices in school psychology* (3 rd ed., pp. 1049–1060). Washington, DC: National Association of School Psychologists. This is an excellent article that provides a wealth of information for consultants who work with culturally diverse populations. The authors apply their views on multicultural helping to families in a very practical way.

# 13

***

# Case Study Illustrations of Consultation and Collaboration

The purpose of this chapter is to help you apply theory to practice and obtain a more realistic picture of what transpires in consultation. It is important to remember that there are many different ways to carry out these services.

Recall that some approaches deal with the entire organization as the client (for example, process consultation), whereas some work with consultees who are delivering direct services to clients (e.g., client–centered case mental health consultation). Therefore, strict comparison among the various approaches to the three models of consultation and collaboration is not possible because the different approaches are used to accomplish different things.

The next section describes a human service organization, Acme Human Services Center, in terms of its environment, people, structure, and activities. To demonstrate the many approaches to consultation, we will assume this human service organization delivers direct services to clients. Assume that, for each approach, the consultant has all the data mentioned for Acme Human Services Center, gathered in various ways from various sources. Each approach to consultation is then applied within this human service organization. Assume also that the contact persons in the organization know what kind of consultation is needed. (In reality, this happens only occasionally; thus, the overall context in which each consultation model is illustrated is somewhat unrealistic. However, the given illustration of each consultation approach will be very realistic.)

Each approach to consultation is discussed in terms of its goals, the consultant's role and function, the consultee's experience in consultation, and the application of the approach. The final case study, a composite of various approaches, illustrates how the ideas, goals, concepts, and techniques from various approaches can be synthesized and applied by a consultant in a given setting.

After we finish the Acme case studies, we will compare school-based consultation and collaboration by using transcripts of two very similar cases. You will have to read these two transcripts very carefully to detect the more-or-less subtle differences in the processes involved in these services. I have deliberately chosen the situation for consultation and collaboration so that you can quickly develop an appreciation for similarities and differences through comparing and contrasting the same case.

As you read the chapter, I suggest you remember the following:

- There are several ways to go about expertly performing each approach to consultation and collaboration.

- Most of the approaches are highly flexible with regard to how consultation and collaboration might proceed.

Consider the following questions as you read through this chapter:

- Are the various approaches to consultation and collaboration more alike than they are different?

- Based on the case studies in this chapter, are there any skills that consultants need that are common to all the approaches discussed?

- How can you use this chapter to help you develop your own personal model of consultation and collaboration?

- Which of the different models seem most attractive to you personally?

- In what ways would you apply the approaches presented in this chapter differently than the author did?

Assume that you are equally talented in each of the approaches to mental health, behavioral, and organizational consultation. Imagine further that you are called into a human service organization and asked to perform, in turn, each approach to consultation. You would be asked to perform the client-centered case, consultee-centered case, program-centered administrative, and consultee-centered administrative approaches to mental health consultation. You would next be asked to provide the behavioral case, behavioral technology training, and behavioral system approaches to behavioral consultation. You would then be asked to perform the education/training, program, doctor–patient, and process approaches to organizational consultation.

Finally, you would need to ask yourself several questions before proceeding with each approach:

- What assumptions do I need to make according to the approach I am about to use?

- What are the goals of the approach I am about to use?

- What consultant roles and functions will be demanded of me?

- What will my consultees experience during the consultation process?

- In specific terms, how will I go about applying this particular approach?

Illustrations of each approach to consultation or collaboration in more or less the same context can provide you several learning experiences, including:

- a real-life feel for how the approaches work

- a deeper understanding of how the approaches converge and diverge in theory and practice

- an opportunity to begin developing personal preferences for some approaches over others

In addition, the studies are a basis for forming your own personal model of consultation and collaboration, a lifelong process of development based on your professional and personal experiences. The keys to a useful personal model of these services are fourfold:

1. Know your own values about life in general and these services in particular.

2. Know your personal and professional strengths and limitations.

3. Know and be able to practice as many approaches to consultation and collaboration as possible.

4. Know what the organizations you are serving really need from you before you start.

## THE CASE: ACME HUMAN SERVICES CENTER

### A Description of the Organization

Acme Human Services Center is a private institution that provides a variety of counseling and psychological services in a wide portion of a rural southeastern state. The Center is located in a city with a population of 90,000 and provides services to many of the small surrounding communities. The population base is 70 percent white, 20 percent African American, and 10 percent other minorities, including Latinos and Asian Americans. Textiles, furniture manufacturing, automobile assembly, and agriculture are the main industries of the area, which has been labeled economically depressed. There is a high unemployment rate and a moderate crime rate. Referendums for civic improvements such as schools and recreation centers are continually voted down by the populace. A four-year university in the area provides a variety of cultural, recreational, and social events. The casual observer would note the presence of modern churches, parks, music and drama organizations, and library facilities.

In competition with the Center, which has been in operation for 10 years under the same director, are two other small private practice corporations, a small number of individuals in private prac-

tice, and a local community mental health center that has been in existence for 20 years and has recently been told to divest itself of direct service programs. The Center has a professional staff of 15: one psychiatrist, one nurse, two doctoral-level psychologists, two doctoral-level counselors, two master's-level school psychologists, two master's-level counselors, two master's-level clinical psychologists, and three master's-level social workers. Two clerical staff members and one mental health technician also work there.

To provide community-based services, the Center offers a variety of outpatient programs. Its clients are referred by schools, physicians, juvenile and adult court systems, the social services department, and occasionally the local mental health center. The basic realm of services is divided into several categories, including adult mental health services, child and adolescent mental health services, substance-abuse services, community consultation services, and employee assistance program services. Plans for providing mental retardation services and positive behavioral support consultation are being considered.

The Center has no written mission statement. Its founder, a psychiatrist, feels that its mission is to help citizens develop and maintain an adequate level of social and personal well-being and dignity. Dramatic growth over the past four years due to the addition of the substance abuse and employee assistance programs has led to a doubling of the organization's income and the hiring of five additional staff during that time.

## THE ORGANIZATION'S PROBLEMS

When the director of the organization last reviewed its progress, he listed problems that had emerged so that steps could be taken to solve them. He thought that such a procedure would help the organization maintain and perhaps enhance its financial position. As he reflected on the past four years, he listed the following problems:

- an increase in referrals of cocaine-related substance abusers with no true "experts" on the staff to handle them

- a lack of knowledge about how to evaluate the effectiveness of the employee assistance programs

- increasing concern over the deteriorating relationship between the staffs of the child and adolescent program and the adult program

- too much of the decision-making responsibility in the hands of one leader for an increasingly complex organization

- insufficient time for program heads to consult on cases

- a lack of definite direction in the substance abuse program

- an increase in the number of "acting out" adolescents as clients

- an increase in requests from schools for assistance in classroom management techniques

- the need for each program to clarify its own specific goals and objectives

- a growing concern over staff morale in general

Although the agency director knew that he had a few staff people who could function as internal consultants, he felt that objectivity was at a premium and thus decided to seek outside consultation for each of the problem areas. The director, himself a well-known consultant, was easily able to identify an effective type of consultation that would be likely to solve each problem.

Because the staff had no true experts in cocaine-related substance abuse, an education/training organizational consultation was selected. The inability to evaluate the employee assistance programs could be resolved through program evaluation consultation. Because the deterioration of the relationships between the two staffs was a mystery as far as the director was concerned, a doctor–patient type of organizational consultation was in order. The centralization of

leadership in an increasingly complex organization called for a review of how decisions are made and what other possibilities existed, and thus a process form of organizational consultation seemed appropriate.

Because program heads were increasingly taxed with other duties, they had little time to consult with the psychologists, counselors, and social workers who provided direct services to clients; client-centered and possibly consultee-centered case mental health consultation seemed correct for this problem. The lack of definite direction in the substance-abuse program called for either program-centered administrative or consultee-centered program mental health consultation. The increasing number of requests from schools for assistance in classroom management techniques and school violence reduction required training the agency's staff, so behavioral technology training consultation was needed. Each program could formulate its own specific goals and objectives with the assistance of behavioral system consultation. Finally, the increasing number of "acting out" adolescents clearly required behavioral case consultation.

## Existing Data on the Organization

The organization's internal environment is frantically paced: everyone seems so busy that there is little time for social interaction at work. Office doors remain closed during the day, even when clients are not being seen. Paperwork appears to be backlogged in spite of computer-assisted office support and electronic databases. A trained observer would label the environment as unstable and heterogeneous.

The organization's personnel are cordial with one another, yet relationships tend to be superficial. Efficiency and productivity are high but come at a price, for little discussion occurs relative to the direction the Center should take. Although personnel feel secure about their jobs, it is evident that morale and a sense of teamwork are declining. The competition between the child and adolescent program and the adult program has caused some intense (but suppressed) negative feelings between some program members.

The organization is bureaucratic: The Center director makes all decisions and only infrequently consults with program directors. Lines of communication follow a vertical chain of command, and thus the ideas of many of the therapists are not solicited. Employees were hired for specific purposes and are to work only to achieve those purposes. The rules of the organization, although explicitly stated in a manual, are never discussed. The director keeps a complete but disorganized set of records.

Change occurs at the Center in a "top-down" fashion. Typically, members are informed of changes through memoranda, although the nature of changes is described without any rationale. Clearly there is the assumption that each change will be acceptable and willingly carried out without discussion.

The Center does not place adequate emphasis on the personal or professional growth of its staff. It assumes that talented people have been hired and that they will take care of their own professional and personal needs. No attempts are made to include employees in the emotional "ownership" of the Center. An environment that nurtures employee growth is lacking, and networking is not used as a supplement to the director's leadership.

As a whole, the organization is in trouble. Although the Center is growing rapidly in response to the demand for diversified services, it is run as if it were still a small operation with a simple mission. The organization is still doing what it does well, but the price it is paying has alerted the director to the need for consultation.

## THE APPROACHES TO CONSULTATION AND COLLABORATION

In each of the approaches illustrated in this section, you can assume that the consultant engages in all the appropriate behaviors expected of a highly professional, competent consultant. Most approaches to consultation adhere to some version of the generic model previously discussed. You can also assume that the consultant proceeds in the same sequence as the generic model. Thus, a good working relationship is established, a problem defined, a contract agreed upon, and entry accomplished. For the sake of brevity, I do not describe these basics of effective consultation behavior in each illustration. Rather, I attempt to provide the essence of each approach so that you can make appropriate comparisons and contrasts.

### Mental Health Consultation

**Client-Centered Case Approach.** Client-centered case consultation does not deal with issues residing within the consultee. Rather, the contract specifies that I, as a mental health consultant, examine the consultee's client concerning some professional matter and write a report that includes recommendations. I operate in a fashion analogous to the doctor–patient approach to organizational consultation, except that the diagnosis and prescription are based on data concerning a client, not some aspect of the organization.

My focus is on the client, and my aim is to advise the consultee on how to "fix" some problem concerning the client under consideration. I examine the client, make some form of assessment and diagnosis, and provide the consultee with a report containing suggestions and recommendations to help the client. I spend very little time with the consultee.

A counselor from the Center seeks my help in determining how to go about getting a mother and teenage daughter to communicate openly during their counseling sessions. I function as an expert in parent–child interactions and use my expertise in diagnosing the causes of toxic relationships and in prescribing remedies for improving them. The counselor is to provide me with as much pertinent information as possible regarding the difficulties the clients are having in communicating with each other in general and in the counseling sessions in particular. She gathers additional information on the client's family and relates it to me, and she is responsible for reading my report and determining whether to implement the recommendations I make.

I meet with the counselor for one session at the Center, during which I build a relationship with her and get a feel for her perceptions of the particulars of the work-related problem. I assess her general abilities as she discusses the case. As I consider the strengths and weaknesses of the Center, I come to the realization that my consultee is likely to get very little individual or group supervision on this case because of the very busy state of affairs at the Center. I realize that I need to devise a plan that is short term and well within the counselor's level of expertise. My assessment is that she is a talented professional but has had relatively little experience in helping parents and children work through communication difficulties during the counseling process.

Next I interview the mother and daughter, first together and then separately. My talk with the mother reveals that she had found out about and told her husband about a sexual experience of their daughter. I pursue this topic in terms of the current state of affairs in the mother–daughter relationship.

Based on all the information I have gathered, I write up a report for the counselor and discuss it with her at our final meeting. After telling her that she is under no obligation to follow through on my recommendations, I proceed to share them with her. I suggest that she see the mother and daughter on an individual basis for two or three sessions to get to know each of them better and to develop a more trusting relationship with each. This would create the conditions that enable the mother and daughter to communicate more effectively in subsequent sessions together. I also suggest that she utilize a nondirective counseling style for the purpose of enhancing the relationship between the mother and daughter. These recommendations are well within the professional competencies of the counselor and have a high probability of being successful. No special training is necessary, nor were there any increased demands for supervision. As a final step, I arrange for a follow-up session in about six weeks.

**Consultee-Centered Case Approach.**    In applying consultee-centered case consultation, my primary goal is to improve the ability of my consultee to work more effectively with the current client and with similar clients in the future. I am retained as a consultant because no one at the Center has sufficient time for routine consultation. I am available to all staff. The case at hand involves a psychologist with a female client who, in the words of the psychologist, "has a lot of anger inside of her that she needs to express." As I listen, I develop a strong hunch that some of the unresolved needs of the consultee are blocking his effectiveness in the case. I play the roles of detective, expert, and educator in this approach to mental health consultation. I determine what emotional and cognitive factors within the consultee are blocking progress in the case and give the consultee specific information he can use to help the client.

While discussing the case, the consultee mentions how much anger the client has and how important it is for the client to deal with that anger. He discusses the case with some emotion, even a sense of desperation. He knows that I am going to make some recommendation to him, but he seems driven to convince me that I should recommend that anger be the central focus of the therapy.

As a matter of procedure, I do not interview or examine the client, but proceed by listening to my consultee's subjective view of the case. I determine that he is suffering from a lack of professional objectivity and that there is little available supervisory assistance from members of the Center. In deciding to make some interventions designed to help the consultee regain more professional objectivity, I ask him specific, detailed questions about the client's anger and the therapy interventions that have been used thus far, since I'm more interested in his version of the case than I am in the actual facts. I'm hoping that by discussing the client's need to express anger, the consultee will develop a broader, more objective perspective on the case.

I determine that theme interference is causing the lack of objectivity. It is as if the consultee is saying, "Unless she deals with the repressed anger in our therapy sessions, we will never make progress in therapy." He cannot see that there are several ways to help the client besides helping her get in touch with and express her anger. I attempt to use theme interference reduction through a combination of techniques.

First, I keep the discussion on the client and remain calm in discussing the case. In addition, I remain very calm and objective about my relationship with the consultee. Finally, I tell him a parable about a former client of mine who was similar to his. The client in my story never dealt with her repressed anger but still benefited tremendously from therapy. As I discuss the story, I notice a sense of reduced tension in the consultee about the case. He seems more objective and hopeful, and I close the session by calmly scheduling a follow-up meeting. I express continued hopefulness and interest in the progress of the case.

## Program-Centered Administrative Approach

When applying program-centered administrative consultation, I work with the Center's director and the head of the substance-abuse program, both of whom want to develop a sense of direction for the program. My specific goal is to help them develop that sense of direction and therefore fix the program. My general goals are to enhance the overall functioning of the program and increase the program development skills of the director and the program head.

My role is that of an expert familiar with substance-abuse programs and how they operate. I collect information on the program and how it works, analyze that information, and recommend some solutions. I use my expertise in organizational theory to determine how to collect the information I need. My consultees discuss with me why they hired me in the first place and what they think they want from consultation. They point out some of the organization's idiosyncrasies and make suggestions about which staff I should contact in gathering information on the program.

The administrators help me develop a timetable for consultation and the methods by which they will sanction my work throughout the Center. They provide me with as much information about the organization as possible, respond openly to my questions, and then develop a list of their reasons why the substance abuse program has a lack of direction. Finally, they wish me good luck and let me know that they are available any time I have questions or need anything. They realize that they will have limited contact with me. The program concerns treatment, not prevention.

In concentrating on management and giving some attention to program accomplishments, I examine agency records on unemployment rates, arrests for drug use and possession, and substance-use driving offenses. I interview key staff and administrators and find out that no one uses the information. Further, there are no records on the types of substances clients are abusing. No outcomes are recorded as a part of the program's objectives. Counselors and therapists in the program see clients as part of their caseloads but have little input into the overall workings of the program.

I proceed through the stages of formulating a simplistic solution, first becoming very confused about the entire situation and then getting a firm grasp of the consultation problem. Based on this information, I develop a set of tentative recommendations, which I feed back to all parties involved irrespective of their ranks within the organization. Based on the reactions I get, I modify those recommendations. The final list of recommendations looks something like this:

- Use available data to determine community needs relative to substance abuse and, based on current staff, modify the program.

- Set objectives and develop a philosophy for the program.

- Point out that alcohol and cocaine abuse are on the rise in the community and that treatment of these illnesses could become the central focus of the program.

- Keep detailed databases that include the records of the contacts personnel have with substance-abuse cases.

These recommendations and the report that contains them are distributed to the appropriate people at the Center. It is up to the director to determine if and how my recommendations are to be implemented. I then set up a follow-up session to occur six months from the date of the report's distribution.

## Consultee-Centered Administrative Approach

As a consultant applying consultee-centered administrative consultation, I am involved in the most complex and demanding type of mental health consultation. I am asked to work with the director and the head of the substance-abuse program regarding the program's lack of direction. The difference between this consultation and the example just described under program-centered mental health consultation is that its main goal is to enhance the consultee's program development and maintenance skills, and its secondary goal is to improve specific programs.

My role is that of both expert and facilitator. I expect consultation to take a long time because I involve the consultees in every step along the way to help them improve their skills in developing plans and strategies related to the successful running of the substance-abuse program. I need the skills of knowing about organizations, how they are best managed, and how they change for the better. I also need the skill of "reading" an organization to pinpoint possible problem areas. I move about the Center as if I were a member and try to understand it from the employees' perspective. Because my role is complex, I need to make sure that the administrator lets everyone involved know precisely what my role is to be.

The director and program head are involved with me as much as possible in this collaborative effort. They lay the groundwork for my presence within the organization and provide the necessary sanctions. They arrange times for me to meet with everyone involved in the substance-abuse program so that I can present my findings.

As I begin to "float" through the Center, I make sure that no one regards me as a "spy" for the director. I want everyone in the program to see me as a

helper, not a threat to their security. I am careful to build trusting relationships not only with the director and program head, but also with all members of the program. The consultees know that their skills will be enhanced by gathering and discussing the data; I therefore get them to uncover what is needed to give the program a sense of direction. I help them use group meetings, interviews, and questionnaires as data collection devices and then help them discuss the data in meetings involving the entire program staff. As the consultees discuss the information, I notice that they incorrectly think they know what is happening in the program and where it is going. In helping them be more objective in analyzing the data, I point out some key factors: there is no philosophy surrounding the program, and there are no written objectives and goals. My observations increase their objectivity. In being very patient and in trying not to force my ideas on them, I take a relatively nondirective stance and ask them what they think various kinds of data mean.

Through my efforts the director and program head realize that if the substance-abuse program had a well-defined sense of direction complete with philosophy, goals, objectives, plus a strategic plan for the next five years, then a great deal of stress would be alleviated for all the parties involved. The director then appoints the head of the substance-abuse program to head a committee charged with developing such direction. It consists entirely of substance-abuse program employees, who are paid an honorarium beyond their normal salaries for their work. I agree to help the program head run this committee and to help him try out new leadership styles and techniques as the committee attempts to fulfill its charge.

**Ecological Perspective.**   In using the ecological perspective to mental health consultation, I employ a preventative approach. My "client" is Acme itself—a unique institution and not "just another human service center." Therefore, my first task is to become very familiar with the internal environment at Acme and with the community surrounding it. I examine the history of Acme's development in the community and review its orientation procedures for new staff and how people are acknowledged on an everyday basis.

My interventions are aimed at helping the organization develop long-term adaptive processes so it can continue to flourish as its external and internal environments change. I empower the staff to help one another and scan the entire organization for the resources (that is, people, events, and places) that are over- and underused. I believe that the power for change resides in the consultees, so, as I build strong collaborative relationships with all the staff, I try to develop strong relationships with the consultees and make special note of their strengths.

Though the staff feel well paid and professionally appreciated, the interviews with selected staff members reveal a conflict between two teams and a general concern over not having any voice in how the Center should be run. I help the members set up a network of effective communication in which they can support and act as resources for each other. I also suggest that the director establish work groups to enhance staff "ownership" of what goes on in the Center. I encourage the staff to develop special events at work that are not work related, such as "birthday breaks" and fun "bull sessions." Finally, I help develop a procedure for a community advisory group and an internal professional development group. My written report to the director (with a copy to each staff member) summarizes the elements and findings of the consultation and schedules two follow-up sessions three and six months later.

### Behavioral Consultation

**Case Approach.**    As in client-centered case mental health consultation, my main objective in behavioral case consultation is to assist the consultee with a work-related problem in a given case. The difference between the two approaches is that in behavioral case consultation my work is within a behavioral framework. I work as a consultant in the Center and am available one day a week. My consultee is a master's level social worker at the Center whose client is a schoolteacher who wants to overcome his fear of flying in airplanes. I am an expert in behavioral tech-

nology and its application to counseling/therapy. I keep that role of expert throughout the consultation process, although I collaborate whenever possible with the consultee. Although I control the process of consultation, the consultee determines the best course of action to take in regard to the case. I provide knowledge concerning the learning principles related to phobias about flying and make sure that all the stages of the consultation process are successfully accomplished.

As my link to the client, the consultee provides me with as much specific information as possible concerning the case. I lead her through the stages of problem identification, problem analysis, plan implementation, and problem evaluation. We verify that a phobia about flying in airplanes exists and determine that the client does not possess "free floating" anxiety, but only a few situation-specific anxieties. Our goal is to have the client actually ride in an airplane with minimal anxiety, and we determine that this can be easily measured by having the client use a checklist during the flight and by intermittently taking his pulse rate.

I illustrate how the process of classical conditioning has probably occurred and created the client's phobia. The consultee and I then examine how this conditioning maintains the client's phobia. Next, we plan how the consultee will use systematic desensitization with the client. Because the consultee does not know the procedure, I train her and monitor her handling of the case. I show her how to apply the general technique to the specific needs of the client by helping her develop a personalized strategy. I give her some books and videotapes so that she can do some independent studying. I role-play systematic desensitization procedures with her, taking the role of her client. We design an evaluation that includes not only the successful completion of the desensitization strategy, but also whether the client actually flies in an airplane with acceptable levels of anxiety. We then arrange for a follow-up session in three months. When she feels ready, the consultee prepares to follow through on what she has learned.

**Behavioral Technology Training Approach.**
When I consult from a behavioral technology

training approach, I focus on enhancing my consultees' general and/or specific skills in this area. The Center, particularly the child and adolescent program, was receiving more and more requests for classroom management strategies and school violence reduction strategies from the local school system. None of the staff had professional experience with schools, but most had good general behavioral technology skills. Because of my expertise in behavioral technology and my many years of working with school systems in such training, I was retained to train the entire staff of the child and adolescent program in behavioral classroom management skills and in school violence reduction procedures.

My goal is to increase the consultees' skills in classroom management techniques so that they in turn can use behavior technology with schoolteachers concerned with classroom management and school violence. I make sure that the consultees have enough accurate information concerning classroom management behavioral technology, have developed related competencies, and have a positive attitude toward the use of these skills. The consultees should learn as best they can, integrate their knowledge about behavioral technology approaches to classroom management into their consultation skills, and attempt to create a positive attitude toward the use of behavioral technology in the classroom.

Based on input from all the parties involved, including school personnel, I develop and implement a training plan using lectures, modeling, behavioral rehearsal, feedback, and reinforcement as my primary tools. Modeling followed by rehearsal and practice with feedback are stressed so that the consultee is able to perform the required skills well. I go to great lengths to demythologize behavior modification in the classroom and provide rules of thumb for proceeding with classroom management procedures, such as conducting observations and establishing token economies and "time-out" procedures. I have the Center's director announce specifically why this training is important to the consultees and the Center; he also comments on the types of rewards the consultees can expect from participation in the training.

I evaluate the training in several ways, first with a questionnaire that reveals attitudes toward the training itself and then with a test that has the consultees state specifically what they have learned and their attitudes toward their newly acquired knowledge and skills. A very important part of the evaluation comes six months later, when I observe the staff consult with teachers on classroom management procedures derived from behavioral technology. At that time, I assess the degree to which they have transferred their knowledge and skills to actual school settings and how effectively they use those skills.

**Behavioral System Approach.**  My goal in this approach is to enhance the efficiency and effectiveness of the Center in terms of its stated function. The director invites me to "take a look at the Center" and then make some recommendations. He notes that the Center is growing very rapidly and that its affairs are in a constant state of disarray.

As an expert in behavioral technology and systems theory, I accomplish my goals by collaboratively guiding the director and program heads through defining and assessing the system, making selected interventions, and evaluating the effects. I use behavioral technology to help the organization function more efficiently.

As joint collaborators, the consultees determine what is to be done in consultation and how the results of consultation will be used. To accomplish this, they provide me with as much accurate information as they can. As the change agents within the Center, they have both the power and perspective to accomplish the goals of consultation.

I proceed by helping the consultees define the Center in terms of its structure and activities. We observe what goes on in the everyday routine for a week, share our perceptions, and come to a consensus. Once we have characterized the Center adequately, we are ready to assess it. We design questionnaires and arrange to observe the various subsystems to evaluate the overall system. We try to answer the question, "What are the effects of the Center's structure and activities on the behavior of its members?" The major answer we obtain is that there is lack of direction among the members because there are no defined goals and objectives for the various programs the Center offers. The consultees and I determine that the highest priority must be given to having each program develop, spell out, and adhere to a set of behavioral goals and objectives. We next set behavioral outcome goals that include what is to be accomplished, when, by whom, and under what conditions.

Criteria are set up to assess the quality of these goals, which are then evaluated. I suggest that the various programs modify their activities and structure to coincide with their newly written behavioral goals and objectives. The consultees agree. We then develop an evaluation to determine how well each program behaves according to its specific goals and objectives. I arrange for a follow-up in six months to help the consultees discuss these evaluations and make appropriate adjustments.

## Organizational Consultation

**Education/Training Approach.** As I consult with Acme Human Services Center within the education/training framework, I attempt to enhance the overall effectiveness of the organization by improving the professional effectiveness of the members of the substance-abuse program with respect to cocaine-related substance-abuse counseling. I assume that a blend of didactic and experiential learning is the best approach. The members of the substance-abuse team would probably need information related to cocaine abuse and some skills in working with drug abusers.

As a consultant using this approach, I function as an expert technological advisor, teacher, and trainer. Because I realize that the staff of the substance-abuse program is small and consists of skilled professionals, I tailor my consultation to their specific needs and am quite specific in the education and training I provide them.

The role of the consultees is that of learners. They have all volunteered for the consultation and meet my expectations that they will be interested and cooperative learners and will invest themselves in the consultation process. They realize that

they need some assistance in working with cocaine abusers and are highly involved in the entire consultation process.

My first step is to conduct a needs assessment of the consultees to make sure that they perceive a need for education and training in cocaine abuse. Furthermore, I want to assess what they know and can already do in relation to working with cocaine abusers; I also want to determine what they must learn in order to work more effectively. I construct a questionnaire to acquire this information and hold a brief meeting with each consultee. I then hold one meeting with the entire group to determine whether the information I received from them accurately reflects their perceptions of their needs.

I plan the education/training based on the results of the needs assessment, which indicates that the staff requires information and training in diagnosing cocaine abuse, particularly in determining patterns of pathological use, impairments of social and occupational functioning related to its use, duration of the disturbance, and the probability of relapse into abuse. Utilizing the principles of adult learning, I assume that the participants are self-directing, can discuss many of their own experiences pertinent to the topic, and are ready to learn. For the primary tools of consultation, I plan a series of activities around the expressed needs of the consultees: lectures with audiovisual aids, several small group discussions, modeling and practice of diagnostic skills related to cocaine abuse, and feedback. I determine that four sessions of two hours each are needed to accomplish the goals of consultation.

As I implement the education/training consultation, I create a climate of mutual respect and am particularly careful not to "speak down" to the consultees or flaunt my knowledge of cocaine abuse. I am very open about what I know and don't know about the topic and about my experiences in working with cocaine abusers.

During the course of consultation, I include some of my own successes and failures with cocaine abusers. I remain flexible, keep a professional yet light atmosphere, and use humor when appropriate. I provide a great deal of time for practice of the skills required by the consultees, particularly during the last two sessions. In evaluating the education and training, I use pre- and post-intervention questionnaires on the consultees' knowledge of cocaine abuse and behavioral checklists to determine their levels of functioning in applying their newly acquired skills. I have them evaluate the consultation in terms of its effect, adequacy, and value. Finally, I arrange for a follow-up meeting in 60 days to assess the impact of the training and iron out any anticipated problems.

**Program Approach.**   As a consultant with a program orientation, I am very much interested in working with the Acme Human Services Center in evaluating the relative success of its employee assistance programs. The goal of a program evaluation consultation is to improve current decision making about how a program should function. I have been hired to answer the question, "To what degree are the goals of the employee assistance program being met?" In addition, I have been retained to assist the Center director and the program heads to be more effective program evaluators in their own right.

My role is that of technological expert in program evaluation. I attempt to provide accurate, timely, and useful information to the director and program heads. I use as much of a collaborative approach as the skills of the consultees permit. I meet with the consultees to review the goals of the employee assistance program, develop a possible program evaluation design, and present it to the consultees for their feedback. I then obtain their feedback and redesign the evaluation accordingly. Much of my time is spent in preparing and planning the evaluation design.

The consultees provide me with as much information as possible about the program, for such information will be needed when I design the evaluation. I spend a lot of time with the consultees to become very familiar with the program and ask the director to give the head of the employee assistance program a great deal of time so that she will feel free to cooperate. I also discuss with the director what he intends to do with the results of the program evaluation. His reply indicates that my

evaluation will be used for modifying the programs (if necessary) and for running the program on a day-to-day basis.

After preparing the program evaluation design, I collect some of the data and have consultees collect the rest. To evaluate the goals of the employee assistance program, data is collected on how many clients are served, the effects of the services for them, attitudes of clients and providers toward the program, and attitudes of members of the organizations in which employee assistance programs are provided (including those who did not partake of the services). We collected this data by using questionnaires and surveys, observing the programs (but not the direct delivery of services to clients), conducting interviews of a few randomly selected volunteer service providers and clients, and examining the program's records on the number of clients for the various services offered and the duration of those services.

After collecting the data, I analyze them, bearing in mind the four standards of proper evaluation: accuracy, utility, feasibility, and propriety. I keep all the appropriate parties involved and apprised of my findings as they emerge. My findings indicate that only 3 percent of the employees use the employee assistance program for an average of three contacts. Reasons for this scant participation are the stigma of being seen going to a counselor at work and fear that confidentiality will somehow be broken. Attitudes of clients and service providers are quite positive in terms of the perceived effectiveness of the services provided.

Nonusers of the program indicate that they would be more likely to participate if services were provided at the Center, not at the work site, and if the program did not have a reputation for serving only substance abusers. Intervention measures that counselors took with their clients resulted in positive gains by the clients.

My final task is to present this data to the director and program head. I suggest that all personnel involved in the program be present at a "feedback meeting," in which I outline the results of the evaluation and facilitate a planning session based on the evaluation. At that meeting, I use graphics to explain the evaluation and what the data mean. I avoid jargon but take care not to appear condescending.

I then facilitate a planning session in which plans are made to publicize the program more thoroughly and promote it as a positive growth experience for the participants. Plans are also made to permit the employees the option of coming to the Center for services. I then summarize the evaluation, describe the next steps in which the consultees engage, and make arrangements for a follow-up visit.

**Doctor–Patient Approach.**    The director had no idea why there was friction between the child and adolescent program and the adult program. When an organization knows that something is wrong but doesn't know the reason, the doctor–patient model of consultation can be very helpful. As a consultant using this approach, my job is to find out what is wrong and prescribe a solution. The organization has purchased my expertise in diagnosis and prescription concerning the conflict between the two programs. I realize that my very presence is an intervention that affects how the problem will be diagnosed. Because of this, I spend time building effective relationships with the parties involved in and affected by the consultation to increase the probability that the information obtained from the parties involved will be straightforward and honest.

My primary goal is to define the problem that is causing friction between the two programs and recommend a viable solution. I assume that the friction is merely a symptom of some broader problem. At this time, I am not concerned about helping the organization enhance its diagnostic and prescriptive abilities. In the doctor–patient approach, I function as an expert. I create relationships with the appropriate parties, collect and analyze information, make a diagnosis, and prescribe a solution.

I must be able to "read" the organization and determine what data to obtain and how to obtain it. The consultees are the "patients"; I need them to describe the symptoms of the problem as they see

them. I attempt to create conditions in which they can provide truthful, complete information, and so I ensure that they understand and are willing to implement my solution. I gather data about the organization's purpose, structure, internal relationships, leadership, and program for rewards. I gather this data by interviewing each member of each program about their program and their perceptions of the other program. Confidentiality is assured to all involved.

From these interviews the child and adolescent program emerges as one that perceives itself to be out of favor with the director; the members see themselves as "second-class citizens" in his eyes and they question how they fit into his future plans. Some members even think that the entire program might be scrapped so that the organization could become involved to a greater degree in the more profitable adult service area. In addition, the head of the adult program is seen as a favorite of the director who has undue influence in the day-to-day operation of the entire agency. These factors have caused the strain between the two programs.

Based on this analysis, I formulate some solutions that are tailored to the organization and its capability for solving its own problems. First, I recommend a series of group meetings between the members of the two programs using third-party conflict resolution. Second, I recommend that the director make a written statement concerning the short- and long-term future of each program. Third, I recommend that he should appoint all program heads to an advisory committee that he will chair. Finally, I encourage him to implement these changes.

**Process Approach.**    The Center's director knows that the leadership style of the organization must change. He used to believe that an effective leader needed to control all the factors related to running an organization: employees' work-related behavior, record keeping, and decision making. This procedure worked relatively effectively until the Center started to grow in size and complexity. The director then continually found himself in a reactive posture he described in this way: "I feel like I am running from one brush fire to another. I am putting in 16-hour days. All the stress is affecting how I relate to clients and my employees. I think I need my own personal employee assistance program!"

As a process consultant, I realize that leadership is a process variable in managing any organization. The director already knows that leadership style changes are imperative, so I am confident that some substantial progress can be made in changing how the organization is managed. He has asked me to observe him in action for one week to get a feel for how he manages, and he also asked me to observe each of the program heads for two days. These observations give me some ideas about their decision-making styles and underlying assumptions about the nature of human beings that inevitably influence leadership style. My goals as a process consultant are to help the director and the program heads become aware of their everyday leadership and decision-making behaviors and to help them identify and modify these behaviors in ways that are consistent with their goals. I accomplish these outcomes by being a facilitator of self-discovery for each consultee.

I assist in gathering data to shed light on leadership and decision-making procedures as they relate to the current state of affairs within the organization. In addition, I help the consultees diagnose what is being done and what yet needs to be done. The director's goal is to delegate more authority, decision-making responsibility, and administrative tasks to the program heads. The program heads' goal is to develop leadership and decision-making skills that are necessary for their new responsibilities. Their roles are those of active collaborators; they must translate their vague perceptions into specific insights and then act on those insights.

I provide minimum structure in carrying out my assignment and use clarifying questions and probes to stimulate the consultees' thoughts on their own current behavior. As human service professionals with administrative experience, the consultees have decision-making and problem-solving skills on which I can capitalize. They also suggest interventions they think would be helpful. In this case, they ask for feedback on their leadership and decision-making skills. I proceed by helping the consultees set goals and by observing them as they attempt to accomplish them. I help the consultees gather data concerning employees' perceptions of the leadership styles and decision-making procedures within the organization. Based on all this data, I help the consultees diagnose their problem —the need for practice in leadership and decision-making skills that involve input from all levels of the organization. I act as "director" and set up several role-playing situations in which the consultees practice the new skills. The director, for example, practices setting agendas for meetings, delegating authority, soliciting input from subordinates, and creating a strategic planning committee.

The heads practice confrontation meetings, assertive behavior, and conflict resolution skills. After each role-playing segment, I coach the consultees in how they can increase their leadership and decision-making skills in an interpersonally effective manner. In addition, I make a few structural recommendations concerning how lines of authority can be set up within a small organization like the Center. I then help them develop ways to monitor their own progress in these areas.

## SCHOOL-BASED CONSULTATION EXAMPLE

### Background

Ms. Gentry, a fifth-grade teacher, has requested the assistance of Ms. Hall, a school psychologist, in dealing with a student who has difficulty with self-control. Ms. Gentry and Ms. Hall have met before to discuss other students. They have a good rapport with one another and share a strong respect for each other's professional abilities.

C1 (CONSULTANT): Ms. Gentry, hi, it's good to see you. How's it going?

T1 (TEACHER): Oh, better I guess. You know I really appreciate your meeting with me. I'm so frustrated. This kid is really disrupting the whole class, and I don't know what to do about it.

C2: This is Tommy. He's the ten-year-old you mentioned the other day . . .

T2: Yes. You know he's a bright kid, but I just can't get him to stay focused. He's always out of his seat with a thousand excuses . . . the bathroom, the water fountain, the trash can. And, of course this interferes with the work of the other students. As you know, we tested him but he doesn't qualify for any special services. He's of normal intelligence, and there's no LD or ADHD indications.

C3: Hmm. Okay, let me see . . . no special needs, normal IQ, but he consistently gets out of his seat, and when he's up he's not only not working himself, but he also gets others off task. Anything else?

T3: No that's about it. You know, he's not a bad child. He doesn't mean to cause problems. He's just very social and very active.

C4: Okay, so there don't seem to be emotional problems either. He's just out of control and doesn't seem able to follow the class rules.

T4: Right. He just acts without thinking. He's not manipula-tive or mean. He needs to learn to control himself. I don't know what to do! I've got to do something. Tommy's not learning a thing, and he's keeping the rest of the class from learning too. My test scores this year are going to stink. Can you help?

C5: Yes, we can work together on this. We could use the problem-solving formula we've used in the past. We'll get some more details on what's going on with Tommy. Goals will probably help once I get a more precise picture of what's going on. We'll establish some realistic goals and then design a plan. If it's okay with you, we'll use this little form I've developed to help us save time. (See Figure 13.1.)

T5: Thanks. I appreciate your listening and your help. Maybe we could use a plan like the one we used for Jimmy. You know, it's nice to have a counselor like you. Your plans are sensible and easily implemented.

## Consultant and Teacher Reflections

CONSULTANT: *At times it may be easier to utilize a ready-made form. This form can either be completed independently or during an interview with the teacher. With some teachers, this may lower the initial resistance to the consultative process. Some teachers become quite protective of their planning time. They may get as little as 45 minutes a day for planning and grading. These behaviors seem to call for a behavioral management situation. Does Ms. Gentry have the time and skills*

**Global Goals**

1.  *Tommy learns to realize potential.*
2.  *More effective learning environment for the whole class.*

**Specific Goals**

*Tommy remains in seat during seatwork and discussion.*

Plan:
Noted Obstacles:
Baseline Data:
Monitoring Data:
Conclusions:

*Tommy develops insight as to how his behavior affects others.*

Plan:
Noted Obstacles:
Baseline Data:
Monitoring Data:
Conclusions:

*Tommy participates in discussion.*

Plan:
Noted Obstacles:
Baseline Data:
Monitoring Data:
Conclusions:

*Tommy follows directions.*

Plan:
Noted Obstacles:
Baseline Data:
Monitoring Data:
Conclusions:

**FIGURE 13.1**    Consultation summary sheet

to apply the consistency required to implement a behavior management program?

TEACHER: *I wonder what is going on with this child. There's something wrong because he is not doing the work. Could it be my teaching style or approach to him? How* am I going to explain his behavior if the principal walks in to observe the class? Worse yet, what if the entire class gets off task while the principal is there in my room? Well, at least this consultant is listening to me and seems to understand. I really need that. I wonder if the *consultant is going to get the impression that I can't motivate or control the class. I wonder if the consultant will think I complain too much.*

C6: Well, thanks. Let's hope we can make some changes for the better. Okay, you basically said, "Good kid, good intentions, average IQ, no emotional or learning problems, just out of control." Tell me more. How long has this been going on?

T6: Tommy's behavior has been a problem since the beginning of the year. I've tried different techniques in dealing with Tommy's behavior, but nothing seems to work. For example, after leaving his seat in the middle of a test, he knocked a little girl's paper off her desk. She became very upset and wasn't able to finish her test. This seemed to be the last straw so to speak. At this time I called for a parent–teacher conference with Tommy's mother and father. When I informed them of the problem, they seemed surprised and concerned. During this time I asked them about Tommy's behavior at home. His parents told me that they usually did not have problems with Tommy at home, except at bedtime. His parents don't sound very strict. I got the impression that their expectations of him are only that he eat with the family and be in bed on time. Tommy basically decides what he does with his time. His mother felt that Tommy's behavior could easily be controlled by explaining the rules to him. She didn't seem to understand that I had already made several attempts to control his behavior, including explaining the rules, but always failed.

C7: That's got to be frustrating to have tried different types of behavior control and gotten nowhere and then find that there are not many expectations at home. Maybe we can design something new that gets better results. Is that your primary concern?

T7: That is definitely my primary concern because his behavior is not only disrupting his academic achievement but disrupting the concentration of the class as a whole.

C8: I think we have a pretty good idea about the nature of the problem. Now let's talk a little bit about goals. What would you like to see happen regarding Tommy's behavior?

## Consultant and Teacher Reflections

CONSULTANT: *Tommy's parents sound loose. I wonder what kind of messages Tommy's parents send him about how to respond to Ms. Gentry's expectations? I also wonder if Tommy's acting out behavior is a result of lack of control, attention getting, rebelliousness, or something else. A behavior management program may be effective with the first two causes, but, if he is motivated by rebelliousness, I wonder if such a program would work.*

TEACHER: *Well maybe I am too strict. Who knows? You know I tried those things I mentioned to the consultant, but did I try hard enough and long enough and do them correctly? Why are these parents so lenient with this child?*

T8: Basically, I would like for Tommy to be able to perform up to his potential in the classroom. He needs to get some control over his behavior in order to concentrate. He needs to change his behaviors so he's not distracting to the other kids in the classroom.

C9: Those things really seem to go hand in hand. If he is able to gain some control over his behavior, he should be less likely to disturb the other children in the class. You would also like him to work more toward his academic potential. Those really seem like good global goals for Tommy. In order to help him most effectively we need to clarify two things: What do we mean by saying Tommy will be working to his academic potential? And regarding behavior—what would Tommy be doing if he did have more control over his actions? Do you agree that these are the two areas we should focus on?

T9: I believe that his behavior is affecting his academic performance and, if changed, will positively impact his performance in class. So, I believe his behavior should be the main focus of our intervention.

C10: Okay, do you mind if I jot this down as we go? Let's begin with Tommy's having more control over his behavior. Can you list five things that you would like to see Tommy doing that he's not doing now? Or five behaviors that you'd like to see him do less frequently? This will help us set some specific goals.

T10: First of all, I would like Tommy to be aware of other children and how his behavior affects them. I would like for him to remain in his seat more often. I would like for him to be able to listen and interact appropriately in class discussions. And I would like for him to be able to follow instructions better.

C11: Those four suggestions seem like very good ones for a start. Let me summarize our goals: We talked about the global goals of helping Tommy to learn and achieve up to his potential as well as to obtain some control over his behavior in order for you to have a more effective learning climate for the whole class. The more specific goals that you stated include giving him some insight into how his behavior affects others. You would also like him to remain in his seat more. You want him to participate in class discussions. And lastly, you would like him to follow instructions more consistently. Are those some of the ideas that you had in mind?

T11: Yes. That about sums it up.

C12: Okay, now let's take each of these goals and see how we might measure progress in each area. For example, how would we know that Tommy better understands how his behavior affects other children in the classroom?

T12: I don't know, maybe through observations or his journaling. I would imagine if other goals are progressing that he would have a better understanding about how his behavior is affecting others.

C13: Sure, progress in other areas may give us some insight. That sounds really good. I did have one thought. What would happen if you had a five- or ten-minute weekly meeting with Tommy to discuss some things that happened during that day or the week to create an awareness of other people's feelings? For example, you could say, "I wonder how Mary felt when you went by and knocked down her paper?"

T13: Five or ten minutes ... I could do that. I certainly spend more time on him than that now.

C14: We could use that then as one means of measuring progress toward our goal. Does that sound okay?

T14: Yes.

C15: Well, let's move on to the next goal of having Tommy stay in his seat more often. How do you think we might measure progress toward that goal?

T15: I suppose I could watch and observe over time. Perhaps take some data each day and note how the behavior decreases over time.

C16: Yes. One of the things we could do in this situation would be to take a baseline of Tommy's behavior as well as determining the standard amount of times other kids get out of their seats in a day. Then, as you said, we can observe and collect data to measure progress over time. What about measuring progress with listening and interacting during lessons? How would you measure progress regarding this goal?

T16: I'm not sure, can we talk about that?

C17: I see what you mean. That is a difficult goal to identify. How about eye contact? It's an indicator of attentiveness. Maybe you might note how well Tommy is maintaining eye contact. If you take note of how often he is able to maintain eye contact throughout the day, these behaviors may be a good measure of attentiveness. Perhaps we could come up with more specifics about that, but for now that seems like a

good general technique for obtaining information. Then interaction of course implies ...

T17: Right, that he's participating in class discussions and answering questions.

C18: Again, we could take a baseline of frequency of behavior then compare it over time. You know, you've got enough to do. Why don't I determine this baseline data for you unless you think my presence will make Tommy act differently? We haven't discussed a plan yet, but I would be willing to come into the class at some point in the day and get this data for you so you would still be able to concentrate on the rest of the class.

T18: Okay, thanks.

C19: Let's move on to our goal of following instructions. How would you measure progress toward that goal?

T19: I would observe his behaviors, establish a baseline, and note progress over time in the form of following instructions during the day or week.

C20: So we would actually measure progress by Tommy becoming more compliant. I do think that even though we are focusing primarily on changing Tommy's behavior, we may have to change some of your techniques and classroom management behaviors. For example, you may have to give Tommy more attention at the beginning of the implementation relative to other children in the class. Is this all right with you?

T20: I can do that.

## Consultant and Teacher Reflections

CONSULTANT: *If Tommy realizes that other students resent his behavior, it may worsen the situation. We need to emphasize how his popularity will grow with more participation and compliant behavior. How can I get Ms. Gentry to realize the importance of emphasizing his growth in popularity rather than the negative side of his current behavior? Journaling is such a subjective measure to use for feedback. The negative impact Tommy's behavior has had on others may well be too sensitive for him to directly express in a journal or interview with Ms. Gentry. Is this an appropriate measure of any of our goals? Test scores are probably more important than Ms. Gentry is letting on. Perhaps they themselves should be the target of change here. The focus on improving test scores could keep Ms. Gentry fully focused and invested in the process while providing some concrete feedback for Tommy.*

TEACHER: *Setting up goals and measuring progress. Is this going to work? What if I put all of this time and energy into Tommy and he doesn't change? Why does everything mean more work for me? At least the consultant seems to think that the things I will try will work and is willing to help out in the process. But give Tommy more attention? How can I possibly do that?*

C21: I believe we've come up with enough goals. Now I think we're ready to take a look at what techniques you've tried so far. This will probably give us some clues as to what directions we will take with any further plan and will also give us ideas about the best ways to work with Tommy. So, what have you tried so far, and what have you found to be helpful?

T21: When I first noticed Tommy's deviant behaviors, I would simply remind him to remain in his seat or to pay attention to the lesson, but he often would not comply. Then I moved his desk to the front of the class where I hoped he would be able to concentrate better, but this did not seem to help. I moved on to the removal of privileges such as time at recess as well as setting up a parent–teacher conference, which I mentioned previously. None of these things seemed to improve Tommy's behavior, though some worked better than others. The removal of privileges improved Tommy's behavior for a short period of time, but I don't enjoy using negative reinforcement with children. Especially since the effects seem to lessen after a few days. Tommy's mother suggested that I might reward him, but I have not implemented a plan using a reward system.

C22: You've really tried several good things. I'm a little concerned that none of them have been effective with Tommy. I understand your hesitance to use negative reinforcement, and since it has been only minimally effective, we won't include that in our plan. Do you feel that there is anything that you haven't tried that may be effective?

T22: No, I've tried all my usual tricks. I'm really frustrated with Tommy and his behavior. So I don't really know where to go from here. I can usually get through to kids, but nothing seems to work with Tommy.

C23: Since his parents suggest that he enjoys rewards, perhaps we could design a system of positive reinforcement. Kids his age really respond to rewards. Do you have any ideas in this area?

T23: Mrs. Jones uses some sort of system of sticker reinforcement that I could use for the whole class.

C24: That's a good idea. Tommy wouldn't feel singled out, and maybe he could benefit from some peer modeling. You can even take this system a step further by creating really cool stickers with clip art to get the kids really enthusiastic. Does that sound like something you would have time for? I know how busy you are.

T24: Sure that sounds like a good idea. I believe you're right in the effectiveness of the entire class. As much as Tommy doesn't realize how his behavior affects others, he does seem to be influenced by his peers and their behaviors.

C25: Right, that really builds in the peer modeling idea. When he sees other kids performing in a certain way for a certain reward, Tommy may get the idea. Okay, it seems like we have a lot of good ideas. How about if we take the goals and create some rules and a reward system? To keep this manageable in terms of time, we'll only keep records on Tommy's behavior.

T25: Maybe this will work. Tommy will know what's expected and will respond to the positive reinforcement he's used to at home.

C26: Of course, the structure of your class will be slightly different as a result of record keeping. We also want the reinforcement to be consistent. Do you anticipate any problems or difficulties in this area?

T26: Listen, the way I feel today, I will try anything.

C27: I know students like Tommy can be a real challenge. The next step, then, is that we need to outline a plan of action. We have our basic goals. We know what we want to accomplish. I see the plan as using a peer-modeling program based on sticker reinforcement to facilitate appropriate behavior for Tommy. Let's try to put the logistical aspects of the plan into operation. What do you think would be the first step in putting this program into place?

T27: Well, I feel like I need to touch base with Tommy's parents again to let them know what we're doing. Then perhaps present the idea to Tommy himself.

C28: You're right. Tommy is a vital part of this plan, but perhaps presenting the program to the class as a whole rather than isolating Tommy would create less self-consciousness in Tommy about his behavior. To assure the effectiveness of this program for Tommy you could give him a little more attention—more eye contact and one-on-one time—in addition to making sure he's meeting his goals.

T28: Right.

C29: I told you I'd do the baselines, so I'll take care of that.

T29: Okay.

C30: So, we'll start by talking to his parents. Then the second step would be for me to come in and baseline some of his behaviors. Then thirdly, you should develop a procedure for presenting the reward system to the class.

T30: Okay.

C31: Now that we know what we're going to do and how we're going to do it, when do you think you would be ready to start?

T31: Any time, as soon as possible. It should only take me a few days to set up a meeting with Tommy's parents. You can come in to the classroom whenever you have time within the next couple of weeks. Then we could proceed with the implementation of the reward system.

C32: Okay, I can come in about 9 AM on Wednesday. How does that sound?

T32: That would be fine.

C33: Look, I know you have very little free time, but I would like to give you a pamphlet on token economies that may act as a reference during the implementation of the plan. Then we need to figure out how our plan might be making progress.

T33: Well, we will be able to look at Tommy's baselines and then follow his progress. We could even plot the data we collect in class on a graph so that we have concrete evidence of change. Yeah, that works.

### Consultant and Teacher Reflections

CONSULTANT: *The negative reinforcement probably did not work because it is not used at home. I'm glad Ms. Gentry is not insisting on the use of negative reinforcement! I need to make sure that these techniques are clearly spelled out to Ms. Gentry and that they are implemented with integrity long enough to be effective. I'm not sure that what she has tried previously has been thoroughly implemented at a level consistent enough to be effective. I'm concerned about altering her class structure to assist record keeping. How can I minimize my intrusion into her regular classroom routine?*

TEACHER: *Okay, I am only investing five–ten minutes a day on Tommy. That doesn't sound like much, but I seldom get time to breathe as it is. Is it fair that Tommy gets all of this extra attention when other better-behaved students get less? Am I taking too much time away from Tommy? Maybe some of the other teachers are correct. Maybe there is no point in all of this extra effort for one child who doesn't "deserve it." Yet the consultant seems to think there is hope. I wonder. Okay, sticker program for the entire class . . . maybe Terry and Jackie's behavior can be addressed at the same time. What about the record keeping for all of this? That could be a lot. I wonder what system I could use that I'll feel comfortable with? All right, nine Wednesday morning. That's math time. What kind of process do I need to use for the consultant to get a baseline on Tommy? I can't forget to call Tommy's parents. I wish the consultant had offered to do that. She knows more about this than I do.*

C34: Good. Okay, what have we left out?

T34: I don't know. I feel good about this plan. It will definitely be a step in a positive direction for my class and Tommy.

C35: Can we schedule a time to get back together for about 20 minutes, perhaps during your planning period on Monday? Then we can make sure everything is ready and you can let me know some specific things I should look for regarding Tommy on Wednesday.

T35: Okay.

C36: I feel really good about our plan of action. We've put together a lot of good ideas, and I think it has a good chance of being successful. Now, let me be sure I've got this straight . . .

T36: Okay. We've gone through a problem-solving process in which we identified the problem as being certain aspects of Tommy's behavior. We then developed a plan involving peer modeling and a sticker reward system, which we used to develop a system of implementation.

C37: Great. So you feel good about this?

T37: Sure.

C38: Well listen, I really appreciate working with you, and I hope we can do this again. Tommy is fortunate to have a teacher like you. The kids respond to you, and I can see why. With all you've got going on you're still concerned about helping, not blaming, children like Tommy.

T38: Thanks. I try. And I guess if this doesn't work, we'll try something else.

## Consultant and Teacher Reflections

CONSULTANT: *Ms. Gentry seems to have bought into this process. I'm encouraged that she is approaching this from a broad-based perspective. I need to remember to reinforce her and to mention, in an appropriate way, her efforts to the principal. Hmm . . . I wonder if I should say anything to the principal. If I did, it could be misinterpreted by Ms. Gentry as well as others. Better not. This is the fourth case in which a token economy has been used this month. Maybe I should conduct some staff development training on the next workday. That would save a lot of us some time and perhaps plant some seeds for some future requests for consultation.*

TEACHER: *Baseline, sticker reward system, monitoring—these are going to take time. I'll try them, but I'm not sure about all of*

*this. Well, okay, I'll try it for a few weeks.*

# SCHOOL-BASED COLLABORATION EXAMPLE

## Background

Ms. Gentry, a fifth grade teacher, and Ms. Hall, a school counselor, decide to collaborate to assist a student who has difficulty with self-control. Ms. Gentry and Ms. Hall collaborated before to discuss other students. They have a good rapport with one another and share a strong respect for each other's professional abilities. As you read this case be sure to compare and contrast it with the preceding consultation case. In that way, you will notice both the similarities and differences between these two services. For example, in this case you note that the counselor takes much more responsibility for some of the outcome of the case than the psychologist in the preceding example did.

C1 (COLLABORATOR): Ms. Gentry, hi, it's good to see you. How's it going?

T1 (TEACHER): Oh, better I guess. You know I really appreciate your meeting with me. I'm so frustrated. This kid is really disrupting the whole class, and I don't know what to do about it.

C2: This is Tommy. He's the ten-year-old you mentioned the other day. I have noticed him in the hallway a lot recently.

T2: Yes. You know he's a bright kid, but I just can't get him to stay focused. He's always out of his seat with a thousand excuses . . . the bathroom, the water fountain, the trash can. And, of course this interferes with the work of the other students. As you know, we tested him but he doesn't qualify for any special services. He's of normal intelligence, and there's no LD or ADHD indications.

C3: Hmm. Okay, let me see . . . no special needs, normal IQ, but he consistently gets out of his seat, and when he's up he's not only not working himself, but he also gets others off task. I notice in the hall that he "gets in the faces" of other students a lot but in a playful manner. Anything else?

T3: No, that's about it. You know, he's not a bad child. He doesn't mean to cause problems. He's just very social and very active.

C4: Okay, so there don't seem to be emotional problems either. He's just out of control and doesn't seem able to follow the class rules. You know, that's exactly how he is in the hallway.

T4: Right. He just acts without thinking. He's not manipulative or mean. He needs to learn to control himself. I don't know what to do! I've got to do something. Tommy's not learning a thing, and he's keeping the rest of the class from learning, too. My test scores this year are going to stink. I sure would like for us to try to work together to help him.

C5: Me too. We could use the problem-solving formula we've used in the past. We'll get some more details on what's going on with Tommy. Goals will probably help once we get a more precise picture of what's going on. We'll establish some realistic goals and then design a plan. You can be in charge of the classroom part of it and I will counsel with him and be responsible for that. I think he will be willing to work with me, and I'll work on changing the same behaviors you're trying to change in class. If it's okay with you we'll use that little form we developed last year to help us save time. (See Figure 13.1; the teacher and the collaborator would use the same form that was used in the consultation example with the exception of adding a line for "Responsible Party" to indicate who is responsible for each goal.) You know, I really enjoy working with you. Together, we have a better chance of helping Tommy than either one of us would have alone.

T5: Maybe we could use a plan like the one we used for Jimmy. You know, it's nice to have a counselor like you. Your plans are sensible and easily implemented.

## Collaborator and Teacher Reflections

COLLABORATOR: *At times it may be easier to utilize a ready-made form. This form can either be completed independently or during an interview with the teacher. Some teachers may prefer to use a different form or none at all. It is more important to create the conditions in which the teacher is willing to add his or her expertise to assist me in putting together and implementing my part of the plan. For example, I know she can help me determine the things that Tommy and I can work on in counseling. Some teachers become quite protective of their planning time. They may get as little as 45 minutes a day for planning and grading. By collaborating, I might help Ms. Gentry to be even more willing to spend the time it takes to help Tommy. These behaviors seem to call for a behavioral management situation. Does Ms. Gentry have the time and skills to apply the consistency required to implement a behavior management program?*

TEACHER: *I wonder what is going on with this child. There's something wrong because he is not doing the work. Could it be my teaching style or approach to him? How am I going to explain his behavior if the principal walks in to observe the class? Worse yet, what if the entire class gets off task while the principal is there in my room? Well, at least Ms. Hall and I are going to work together. She listens to me and seems to understand. I really need that. I wonder if Ms. Hall is going to get the impression that I can't motivate or control the class. I wonder if she will think I complain too much. I'm glad she is going to work with Tommy in counseling. That way I*

*am not responsible for everything about getting him changed. Perhaps by working together we can make good progress in a short amount of time.*

C6: Well, thanks. Let's hope by working together and each having "a piece of the pie" in helping Tommy that we can make some changes for the better. Okay, you basically said, "Good kid, good intentions, average IQ, no emotional or learning problems, just out of control." That's my read on this too. Let's share some more about our perceptions of Tommy. For example, I am curious how long has this been going on.

T6: Tommy's behavior has been a problem since the beginning of the year. I've tried different techniques in dealing with Tommy's behavior, but nothing seems to work. For example, after leaving his seat in the middle of a test, he knocked a little girl's paper off her desk. She became very upset and wasn't able to finish her test. This seemed to be the last straw so to speak. At this time I called for a parent–teacher conference with Tommy's mother and father. When I informed them of the problem, they seemed surprised and concerned. At this time I asked them about Tommy's behavior at home. His parents told me that they usually did not have problems with Tommy at home, except at bedtime. His parents don't sound very strict. I got the impression that their expectations of him are only that he eat with the family and be in bed on time. Tommy basically decides what he does with his time. His mother felt that Tommy's behavior could easily be controlled by explaining the rules to him. She didn't seem to understand that I had already made several attempts to control his behavior, including explaining the rules, but always failed.

C7: That's got to be frustrating to have tried different types of behavior control and gotten nowhere and then find that there are not many expectations at home. Maybe we can design something new that gets better results. Is that your primary concern?

T7: That is definitely my primary concern because his behavior is not only disrupting his academic achievement but disrupting the concentration of the class as a whole.

C8: I think we have a pretty good idea about the nature of the problem. Now let's talk a little bit about goals. What would we like to see happen regarding Tommy's behavior?

## Collaborator and Teacher Reflections

COLLABORATOR: *Tommy's parents sound loose. I wonder what kind of messages Tommy's parents send him about how to respond to Ms. Gentry's expectations? Maybe we need to involve them in our attempts to help Tommy. I also wonder if Tommy's acting-out behavior is a result of lack of control, attention getting, rebelliousness or something else. A behavior management program may be effective with the first two causes, but if he is motivated by rebelliousness, I wonder if*

*such a program would work. All of this makes me think that I should work with him in counseling.*

TEACHER: *Well, maybe I am too strict. Who knows? I tried those things I mentioned to Ms. Hall, but did I try hard enough and long enough and do them correctly? Why are these parents so lenient with this child? Maybe Ms. Hall and I should make a home visit part of the plan.*

T8: Well, for my part, I would like for Tommy to be able to perform up to his potential in the classroom. He needs to get some control over his behavior in order to concentrate. He needs to change his behaviors so he's not distracting to the other kids in the classroom.

C9: I agree. That's what I want to do. Those things really seem to go hand in hand. If he is able to gain some control over his behavior, he should be less likely to disturb the other children in the class. We would also want him to work more toward his academic potential. Those really seem like good global goals for Tommy. In order to help him most effectively we need to clarify two things: What do we mean by saying Tommy will be working to his academic potential? And regarding behavior—what would Tommy be doing if he did have more control over his actions? I think that these are the two areas we should focus on. Do you agree?

T9: I believe that his behavior is affecting his academic performance and, if changed, will positively impact his performance in class.

So I believe his behavior should be the main focus of our intervention. Okay, I will jot this down as we go along.

C10: Great. Let's begin with Tommy's having more control over his behavior. Let's list some things that we would like to see Tommy doing that he's not doing now. Or some behaviors that we'd like to see him do less frequently. This will help us set some specific goals. For example, I want him to walk down the hallway without disturbing others. I also want him to learn better social skills through the counseling I'll be providing him.

T10: For me, well let's see. First of all, I would like Tommy to be aware of other children and how his behavior affects them. I would like for him to remain in his seat more often. I would like for him to be able to listen and interact appropriately in class discussions. And I would like for him to be able to follow instructions better.

C11: Those four suggestions seem like very good ones for a start. Let's summarize our goals: We talked about the global goals of helping Tommy to learn and achieve up to his potential as well as to obtain some control over his behavior in order for you to have a more effective learning climate for the whole class. The more specific goals that we stated include giving him some insight into how his behavior affects others. We would also like him to remain in his seat more. We want him to participate in class discussions. And lastly, we would like him to follow instructions more consistently.

T11: We also want him to learn better social skills and behave properly in the hallway. I know one thing, he's not gong to be in the hallway much any more. At any rate we are going to have to figure out how we know what kind of progress is being made.

C12: Good point. Let's take each of these goals and see how we might measure progress in each area. For example, how would we know that Tommy better understands how his behavior affects other children in the classroom?

T12: I don't know, maybe through observations or his journaling. I would imagine if other goals are progressing that he would have a better understanding about how his behavior is affecting others.

C13: Sure, progress in other areas may give us some insight. That sounds really good. I did have one thought. What would happen if you had a five- or ten-minute weekly meeting with Tommy to discuss some things that happened during that day or the week to create an awareness of other people's feelings? For example, you could say, "I wonder how Mary felt when you went by and knocked her paper off her desk?"

T13: Five or ten minutes . . . I could do that. I certainly spend more time on him than that now.

C14: We could use that then as one means of measuring progress toward our goal. Does that sound okay?

T14: Sounds okay to me. Well, let's move on to the next goal of having Tommy stay in his seat more often. How do you think we might measure progress toward that goal?

C15: What's your take on this?

T15: I suppose I could watch and observe over time. Perhaps take some data each day and note how the behavior decreases over time.

C16: Yes. One of the things we could do in this situation would be to take a baseline of Tommy's behavior as well as determining the standard amount of times other kids get out of their seats in a day. Then, as you said, we can observe and collect data to measure progress over time. What about measuring progress with listening and interacting during lessons? How would you measure progress regarding this goal?

T16: I'm not sure, can we talk about that?

C17: I see what you mean. That is a difficult goal to identify. How about eye contact? It's an indicator of attentiveness. Maybe you might note how well Tommy is maintaining eye contact. If you take note of how often he is able to maintain eye contact throughout the day, these behaviors may be a good measure of attentiveness. Perhaps we could come up with more specifics about that, but for now that seems like a good general technique for obtaining information. Then interaction of course implies . . .

T17: Right, that he's participating in class discussions and answering questions.

C18: Again, we could take a baseline of frequency of behavior then

compare it over time. You know, you've got enough to do. Why don't I determine this baseline data for you unless you think my presence will make Tommy act differently? We haven't discussed a plan yet, but I would be willing to come into the class at some point in the day and get this data for you so you would still be able to concentrate on the rest of the class. I'd like to share this information with you. Maybe you can give me some ideas for working with him in counseling after you look at it.

T18: Okay, thanks. Now let's talk about him following directions.

C19: Good idea. Our goal is for him to follow instructions better. How can we measure progress toward that goal?

T19: I would observe his behaviors, establish a baseline, and note progress over time in the form of following instructions during the day or week.

C20: So we would actually measure progress by Tommy becoming more compliant. I do think that even though we are focusing primarily on changing Tommy's behavior, we may have to change some of your techniques and classroom management behaviors. For example, you may have to give Tommy more attention at the beginning of the implementation relative to other children in the class. Is this all right with you?

T20: I can do that. In your counseling with him you can reinforce these behaviors. I wonder if he should be in a group rather than one-on-one with you. I guess I keep going back to the social skills and the fact that the group is a great place to practice them *in vivo*. We can talk about that later.

## Collaborator and Teacher Reflections

COLLABORATOR: *If Tommy realizes that other students resent his behavior, it may worsen the situation. We need to emphasize how his popularity will grow with more participation and compliant behavior. How can I get Ms. Gentry to realize the importance of emphasizing his growth in popularity rather than the negative side of his current behavior? Journaling is such a subjective measure to use for feedback. The negative impact Tommy's behavior has had on others may well be too sensitive for him to directly express in a journal or interview with Ms. Gentry. Is this an appropriate measure of any of our goals? Test scores are probably more important than Ms. Gentry is letting on. Perhaps they themselves should be the target of change here. The focus on improving test scores could keep Ms. Gentry fully focused and invested in the process while providing some concrete feedback for Tommy. I'm glad Ms. Gentry is willing to make some recommendations, like the group suggestion, to me. It shows that we are truly collaborating here. It's nice to have some external validation of my ideas, or even some new ones from an informed source.*

TEACHER: *Setting up goals and measuring progress. Is this going to work? What if I put all of this time and energy into Tommy and he doesn't change? Why does everything mean more work for me? At least Ms. Hall seems to think that the things I will try will work and*

*is willing to help out in the process. But give Tommy more attention? How can I possibly do that? I like how Ms. Hall was open to my idea about working with Tommy in a group. It is nice to see that I can help her some as she is helping me. Maybe we will get somewhere on all of this and I won't end up having to do all of the work.*

C21: I believe we've come up with enough goals. Now I think we're ready to take a look at what techniques we've tried so far. This will probably give us some clues as to what directions to take with Tommy. It will help us to develop a better plan and figure out some possible ways to work with Tommy. I don't have anything to report because I haven't had him in counseling before and haven't really done anything about his behavior in the classroom. What about you? What have you tried so far, and what have you found to be helpful with him in the classroom?

T21: When I first noticed Tommy's deviant behaviors, I would simply remind him to remain in his seat or to pay attention to the lesson, but he often would not comply. Then I moved his desk to the front of the class where I hoped he would be able to concentrate better, but this did not seem to help. I moved on to the removal of privileges such as time at recess as well as setting up a parent–teacher conference, which I mentioned previously. None of these things seemed to improve Tommy's behavior, though some worked better than others. The removal of privileges improved

Tommy's behavior for a short period of time, but I don't enjoy using negative reinforcement with children. Especially since the effects seem to lessen after a few days. Tommy's mother suggested that I might reward him, but I have not implemented a plan using a reward system. By the way, we need to involve the parents in this one. I think they are a piece of what's wrong.

C22: I agree with involving the parents. I think you've tried several good things. I'm a little concerned that none of them have been effective with Tommy. I understand your hesitance to use negative reinforcement, and since it has been only minimally effective, we won't include that in our plan. Do you feel that there is anything that you haven't tried that may be effective?

T22: No, I've tried all my usual tricks. I'm really frustrated with Tommy and his behavior. So I don't know where to go from here. I can usually get through to kids, but nothing seems to work with Tommy. Since his parents suggest that he enjoys rewards, perhaps we could design a system of positive reinforcement. Kids his age really respond to rewards. Do you have any ideas in this area?

C23: Well, sometimes sticker reinforcement works well with students like Tommy.

T23: Mrs. Jones uses some sort of system of sticker reinforcement that I could use for the whole class.

C24: That's a good idea. Tommy wouldn't feel singled out, and

maybe he could benefit from some peer modeling. Does that sound like something you would have time for? I know how busy you are.

T24: Sure, that sounds like a good idea; I was on the same track as you when you started talking. I can even take this system a step further by creating cool stickers with clip art to get the kids really enthusiastic. I believe we're right in the effectiveness of the entire class. As much as Tommy doesn't realize how his behavior affects others, he does seem to be influenced by his peers and their behaviors.

C25: Right, that really builds in the peer modeling idea. When he sees other kids performing in a certain way for a certain reward, Tommy may get the idea. Okay, it seems like we have a lot of good ideas. How about if we take the goals and create some rules and a reward system? We have to keep this thing manageable.

T25: To keep this manageable in terms of time, we'll only keep records on Tommy's behavior. Maybe this will work. Tommy will know what's expected and will respond to the positive reinforcement he's used to at home.

C26: Of course, the structure of your class will be slightly different as a result of record keeping. We also want the reinforcement to be consistent. Do you anticipate any problems or difficulties in this area?

T26: Listen, the way I feel today, I will try anything. I can do this.

C27: I know students like Tommy can be a real challenge. Part of me is wondering how I am going to convince him that counseling is in his best interest. Well, back to the reward system. The next step, then, is that we need to outline a plan of action. We have our basic goals. We know what we want to accomplish. I see the plan as using a peer-modeling program based on sticker reinforcement to facilitate appropriate behavior for Tommy. Let's try to put the logistical aspects of the plan into operation.

T27: Well, I think the first step in putting this program into place is to touch base with Tommy's parents again to let them know what we're doing. Then we could present the idea to Tommy himself.

C28: You're right. Maybe we should use your idea of a home visit to enlist their support and maybe their participation. Tommy is a vital part of this plan, but perhaps presenting the program to the class as a whole rather than isolating Tommy would create less self-consciousness in Tommy about his behavior. To assure the effectiveness of this program for Tommy, you could give him a little more attention—more eye contact and one-on-one time—in addition to making sure he's meeting his goals.

T28: Right.

C29: I told you I'd do the baselines, so I'll take care of that.

T29: Okay. So, we'll start by talking to his parents. Then the second step would be for you to come in and baseline some of his behaviors. Third, I should develop a procedure for presenting the reward system to the class.

C30: That will work for me. I'll think about the visit to the home and how we should go about approaching the parents. I'll think of some questions for you about how I might proceed with Tommy in counseling, like what he sees as rewarding and so forth.

T30: Okay.

C31: Now that we know what we're going to do and how we're going to do it, when do you think you would be ready to start?

T31: Any time, as soon as possible. It should only take you a few days to set up a meeting with Tommy's parents. You can come into the classroom whenever you have time within the next couple of weeks. Then we could proceed with the implementation of the reward system. I will create a list of information on Tommy you can use in counseling. I am assuming you are still thinking about working with him in a group?

C32: Yes, I might have a couple of sessions one-on-one to gain a relationship and get him used to the process so he can be more ready for a group. About the baselining, I can come in about 9 AM on Wednesday. How does that sound?

T32: That would be fine.

C33: Look, I know you have very little free time, but I would like to give you a pamphlet on token economies that may act as a reference during the implementation of the plan. Then we need to figure out how our plan might be making progress.

T33: Well, we will be able to look at Tommy's baselines and then follow his progress. We could even plot the data we collect in class on a graph so that we have concrete evidence of change. Yeah, that works. By the way, I have put together some of his work so you can get a feel for what he does academically.

## Collaborator and Teacher Reflections

COLLABORATOR: *The negative reinforcement probably did not work because it is not used at home. I'm glad Ms. Gentry is not insisting on the use of negative reinforcement! I need to make sure that these techniques are clearly spelled out to Ms. Gentry and that they are implemented with integrity long enough to be effective. I'm not sure that what she has tried previously has been thoroughly implemented at a level consistent enough to be effective. I'm concerned about altering her class structure to assist record keeping. How can I minimize my intrusion into her regular classroom routine? I am concerned that the parents will play "No problem" with us, defend Tommy as being okay, and imply that the problem is in the school. Ms. Gentry and I will need to make sure we are together on how we will approach the parents. I think Tommy can fit into a group. If his social skills are poor, the other kids may reject him pretty*

*quickly. I guess individual counseling at the beginning will prevent some of that.*

TEACHER: *Okay, I am only investing five–ten minutes a day on Tommy. That doesn't sound like much, but I seldom get time to breathe as it is. Is it fair that Tommy gets all of this extra attention when other better-behaved students get less? Am I taking too much time away from Tommy? Maybe some of the other teachers are correct. Maybe there is no point in all of this extra effort for one child who doesn't "deserve it." Yet Ms. Hall seems to think there is hope. I wonder. Okay, sticker program for the entire class . . . maybe Terry and Jackie's behavior can be addressed at the same time. What about the record keeping for all of this? That could be a lot. I wonder what system I could use that I'll feel comfortable with? All right, nine Wednesday morning. That's math time. What kind of process do I need to use for Ms. Hall to get a baseline on Tommy? We can't forget to call Tommy's parents. We have to make sure we are on the same wavelength before we approach them. I don't like home visits, but this one may be worth it. Something has to change with Tommy. Ms. Hall knows more about this than I do, but I know Tommy better. I'm glad Ms. Hall is going to do group work with Tommy. I don't think that individual counseling as the only treatment would work that well with Tommy. I am glad that she was open to my advice.*

C34: Good. Okay, what have we left out?

T34:   I don't know. I feel good about this plan. It will definitely be a step in a positive direction for my class and Tommy.

C35:   Can we schedule a time to get back together for about 20 minutes, perhaps during your planning period on Monday? Then we can make sure everything is ready and you can let me know some specific things I should look for with Tommy on Wednesday.

T35:   Okay.

C36:   I feel really good about our plan of action. We've put together a lot of good ideas, and I think it has a good chance of being successful. Now, let me be sure I've got this straight . . .

T36:   Okay. We've gone through a problem-solving process in which we identified the problem as being certain aspects of Tommy's behavior. We then developed a plan involving peer modeling and a sticker reward system, which we used to develop a system of implementation. Then we developed a plan whereby we would try to engage the parents in helping him by making a home visit. You are going to work with Tommy in counseling and I am going to get you some ideas on things I think might work for you when you counsel him.

C37:   Great. I feel good about this.

T37:   Me too. I think that by working together on this we can hopefully help Tommy.

C38:   Well listen, I really appreciate working with you, and I hope we can do this again. Tommy is fortunate to have a teacher like you. The kids respond to you, and I can see why. With all you've got going on you're still concerned about helping, not blaming, children like Tommy.

T38:   Thanks. I try. And I guess if this doesn't work, we'll try something else. By the way, a lot of counselors would just come in and work out something for *me* to do. Then they would go off and work with someone else. It makes me feel real good to know that I have a partner in this. I have support and someone who is working toward the same ends. It's a nice feeling to know that we are in this together.

## Collaborator and Teacher Reflections

COLLABORATOR:   *Ms. Gentry seems to have bought into this process. I'm encouraged that she is approaching this from a broad-based perspective. I need to remember to reinforce her and to mention, in an appropriate way, her efforts to the principal. Hmm . . . I wonder if I should say anything to the principal. If I did, Ms. Gentry as well as others could misinterpret it. Better not. Ms. Gentry's investment in this goes to show how sometimes collaboration is a better way to go than consultation. I think either service would work with her but I can think of many teachers who would want me to work with their students while they are working with the student also. This is the fourth case in which a token economy has been used this month. Maybe I should conduct some staff development training on the next workday. That would save a lot of us some time and perhaps plant some seeds for some future requests for collaboration. Better yet, I should ask for a few minutes at our next faculty meeting and discuss collaboration and consultation. It never hurts to keep these ideas in front of teachers and principals.*

TEACHER: *Baseline, sticker reward system, monitoring, and a home visit—these are going to take time. But so is Ms. Hall's counseling Tommy. I'll try my*

*end of this for a few weeks. After all, I won't be alone. It's not like we aren't going to help one another with each of our responsibilities in helping Tommy. All I can say is that I am relieved I'm not the only one responsible for helping Tommy change here.*

## SUMMARY

This chapter encourages you to begin assessing your own personal model of consultation and collaboration. It has applied the various approaches to mental health, behavioral, and organizational consultation to some work-related problem within a particular organization. Table 13.1 summarizes the major focus of each approach. In addition, we compared two transcripts of similar cases involving school-based consultation and collaboration to help you differentiate between these two services.

**T A B L E  13.1**    **The Major Focus of Several Consultation and Collaboration Approaches**

| APPROACH | MAJOR FOCUS |
|---|---|
| **Mental Health** | |
| Client-Centered Case | Helping a consultee with a client (with minimal contact with the consultee) |
| Consultee-Centered Case | Considers work-related problem to reside in the consultee; helping consultee by focusing on case |
| Program-Centered Administrative | Helping an administrator fix a program-related problem |
| Consultee-Centered Administrative | Helping an administrator and other consultees develop their skills to improve the mental health aspects of the organization and its programs |
| Ecological | Changing the human-environment interface |
| **Behavioral** | |
| Training | Training consultees to improve their general and/or specific skill areas of behavioral technology |
| System | Assisting an organization in being more effective by using behavioral technology |
| Case | Helping a consultee apply behavioral technology to a case |
| **Organizational** | |
| Educational/Training | Training or educating consultees to be more effective in some area |
| Program | Assisting an organization with some aspect of a program, frequently evaluation |
| Doctor–Patient | Entering an organization, diagnosing a problem, and prescribing a solution |
| Process | Assisting consultees in becoming better decision makers and problem solvers in the future |

# SUGGESTIONS FOR EFFECTIVE PRACTICE

- Remember to develop and follow your own personal model of consultation and collaboration.

- Read case studies and transcripts of consultation and collaboration cases often to maintain a sense of how others deal with the nuts and bolts of effective practice.

- Remember to do what you love, and love what you do!

# QUESTIONS FOR REFLECTION

1.  Which of the approaches just described in the Acme case most emphasize the quality of the consultation relationship?

2.  Of the Acme case problems just described, in which would consultation be the most difficult to evaluate adequately?

3.  In the Acme case, do you see similarities among behavioral system consultation, doctor–patient consultation, and process consultation? Explain your answer.

4.  Would you proceed in a manner different from mine if you were asked to perform process consultation with Acme? If so, how?

5.  What similarities did you notice in the school-based consultation and collaboration transcripts?

6.  What differences did you detect in the school-based consultation and collaboration transcripts?

7.  Based on your reading of this chapter, which approach appeals to you the most? Why?

8.  In which of the cases discussed would you most like to have been the consultant or a collaborating professional? Why?

9.  With which approach would you have the most difficulty in the role of consultant or collaborator? Why?

10. For which approaches would you actively seek out additional training?

# SUGGESTED SUPPLEMENTARY READINGS

Dougherty, A. M. (2009). *A casebook of psychological consultation and collaboration* (5th ed.). Belmont, CA: Wadsworth. This text provides several case studies of human services consultation and collaboration. The final chapter provides several practice cases. This case studies book is designed to accompany the present text. Its focus is to provide a nuts-and-bolts approach to understanding how to provide services in consultation and collaboration for counselors, psychologists, college student personnel, human resource specialists, and other human service professionals.

# Epilogue

I hope you have enjoyed and benefited from this book. Providing consultation and collaboration can be among the most challenging and enjoyable professional activities in which you engage. As you reflect on what you have read and practiced, let me leave you with some concluding thoughts.

There is no "one-minute–manager" type of consultation or collaboration. To be accomplished effectively, these services take time and planning—a difficult prospect in the "quick fix" society in which we live. The "Catch-22" is that effective consultation and collaboration take time, yet time is often hard to come by. The consultant and collaborator need to balance time and quality. That said, remember quick fixes are short lived and typically lead to diminishing returns.

Appreciate the challenge of the complexity of these services. Take care not to be overwhelmed by all the variables that affect their processes. If you give your best effort when you consult and collaborate and trust the process, then anxiety and doubt will not overburden you.

To enhance your effectiveness as a consultant and as a collaborator, continue your professional and personal development. You will need to become familiar with the literature on consultation and collaboration, have some supervised field experience in performing them, gain a sense of the organizational contexts in which they occur, and possess some degree of knowledge of who you are as a person. Taken together these will provide a cognitive map to guide your practice.

When in doubt, consider using collaboration. Collaboration minimizes the probability of a negative experience and at the same time maximizes the input into the problem-solving process. It is also empowering by nature. Consultation and collaboration involve relationships among people—they need to be performed with a personal touch. Each is more than a science, an art, or a craft: Each is all of these things along with commitment—to oneself as a helper, to the people with whom one is working, and to the ever-challenging task of trying to help others work more effectively.

Good luck and best wishes!

# Glossary

Because consultation and collaboration are neither well-defined nor have adequately developed their own identity, many of the terms used about them in the literature are vague and confusing.

Therefore, the glossary that follows contains some key terms used throughout this book. It is very important that you familiarize yourself with these terms to avoid confusion as you continue reading.

**Advocacy** a role consultants take on when they believe a certain course of action should be taken.

**Advocacy consultation** an expansion of the role of advocacy to a method of consultation entirely devoted to furthering some course of action.

**Behavioral consultation** one of the three major types of consultation; it attempts to assist consultees and their client systems through a systematic, problem-solving approach based on behavioral technology.

**Client** in some approaches to mental health and behavioral consultation, the person with whom the consultee is having a work-related or caretaking-related problem; in this instance the client constitutes the client system (see below). One of the goals of consultation is to improve the functioning of the client.

**Client system** the person, group, organization, or community with whom the consultee is having a work-related or caretaking-related problem. One of the goals of consultation is to improve the functioning of the client system.

**Collaboration** a service provided by a professional in which there is a shared responsibility for the outcome of the problem-solving process, including participation in interventions. Collaboration often occurs in teams of professionals and stakeholders working toward the same ends. Collaboration is characterized by mutual, reciprocal consultation among the parties involved.

**Collaborative consultation** the method of relating most consultants use when working with their consultees; it allows both parties to pool their strengths and resources in their efforts (however, the consultee typically carries out the plan developed in consultation). Any model of consultation can be implemented collaboratively.

**Consultant** a person, typically a human service professional, who delivers direct service to another person (consultee) who has a work-related or caretaking-related problem with a person, group, organization, or community (client system).

**Consultation** a type of helping relationship in which a human service professional (consultant) delivers assistance to another person (consultee) so as to solve a work-related or caretaking-related problem the consultee has with a client system.

**Consultee** the person, often a human service professional or a caretaker (e.g., a parent, teacher, or supervisor), to whom the consultant provides assistance with a work-related or caretaking-related problem. One of the goals of consultation is to improve the current and future functioning of the consultee.

**Cross-cultural consultation** consultation in which the relationship consists of parties who are culturally different from one another.

**Cultural competence** a set of knowledge, skills and attitudes in people and organizations that enable people and organizations to work effectively in cross-cultural contexts.

**Diagnosis** the second of the four stages of the consultation process. In this stage the problem to be solved in consultation is defined. Thus, in its simplest form, diagnosis is the equivalent of problem identification. In its more complex form, it is an ongoing process in which the target problem is continually redefined and worked on by gathering, analyzing, interpreting, and discussing data.

**Direct service** the assistance a consultant provides a consultee or that a consultee provides a client system. When consultants work with consultees, they are providing direct service to them. When consultees work with client systems, they provide direct service to them. This term is frequently contrasted with indirect service.

**Disengagement** the last of the four stages in the consultation process; it involves the winding down of consultation, including evaluation of the consultation, postconsultation planning, reduced contact, follow-up, and termination.

**Diversity** differences among groups based on characteristics such as race, gender, ethnicity, etc.

**Entry** the first of the four stages of the consultation process; it involves exploring the presenting problem, formulating a contract, and physically and psychologically entering the system in which consultation is to occur.

**External consultant** a consultant not permanently employed in the organization in which consultation is to occur.

**Generic model of consultation** a model of consultation that contains those characteristics common to the various types of consultation and the approaches to these types. It is what distinguishes consultation as a unique helping relationship.

**Human service organization** a broad term describing an organization that provides some form of contact with clients and aims to improve the well-being of those clients and, therefore, of society. Counseling centers, mental health centers, Head Start programs, homes for the mentally retarded, and social services departments are all examples of human service agencies.

**Implementation** the third of the four stages of the consultation process; it is the stage in which action is taken on the problem. It begins with formulating and choosing a problem-solving plan and includes implementing and evaluating that plan.

**Indirect service** the type of service provided to the client system by the consultant. The consultant affects the well-being of the client system by helping the consultee help the client system more effectively. It is one of the characteristics of consultation that differentiates it from other helping relationships. This term is frequently contrasted with indirect service.

**Internal consultant** a consultant who is employed in the organization in which consultation is to occur.

**Mental health consultation** one of the three major types of consultation; it attempts to focus on the psychological well-being of all the parties involved in consultation. Its ultimate goal is to create a more mentally healthy society.

**Multicultural consultation** an approach to consultation that takes into account how cultural issues affect the consultation process.

**Organization** a group of people put together for a common purpose. Almost all consultation, regardless of the type, occurs within some type of organization. It is one of the factors that influence the processes and outcomes of consultation.

**Organization contact person** the person in the organization in which consultation is being considered who initially contacts (or is contacted by) the consultant. This person is often a midlevel administrator who may or may not become a consultee. This person usually paves the way for the consultant's entry into the organization.

**Organizational consultation** one of the three major types of consultation; its primary goal is the enhancement of an organization's effectiveness. The organization itself is the client system, and the members of the organization involved in consultation are the consultees. Consultants frequently work together in teams when performing organizational consultation.

**Outreach** extending or making known available services to a target population.

**Parties-at-interest (stakeholders)** those people (who usually belong to the organization in which consultation occurs) who are not directly involved in consultation but are affected by the consultation process in some way. Parties-at-interest typically include contact persons and administrators. If the consultant belongs to an organization (for example, a mental health center), then those members of the consultant's organization indirectly affected by the consultation are also parties-at-interest.

**Tripartite** composed of three parts. With respect to consultation, it refers to the three parties involved: consultant, consultee, and client system.

**Work-related problem** the kind of problem considered to be suitable for the primary focus in consultation. In the case of consultation with people such as parents, the term *caretaking-related problem* is sometimes used instead. This term is often contrasted with *personal problems,* which are not directly dealt with in consultation.

# References

Adelman, H. S., & Taylor, L. (2003). On sustainability of project innovations as systemic change. *Journal of Educational and Psychological Consultation, 4*, 1–25.

Adelman, H. S., & Taylor, L. (2007). Systemic change for school improvement. *Journal of Educational and Psychological Consultation, 17*, 55–77.

Adelman, H. S., & Taylor, L. (1998). Toward a scale-up model for replicating new approaches to schooling. *Journal of Educational and Psychological Consultation, 8*, 197–230.

Adlerfer, C. P. (1990). Organizational consultation: The state of the field. *Journal of Applied Behavioral Science, 23*, 281–284.

Akin-Little, K. A., Little, S. G., & Delligatti, N. (2004). A preventative model of school consultation incorporating perspectives from positive psychology. *Psychology in the Schools, 41*, 155–162.

Allen, C. T., & Forman, S. G. (1984). Efficacy of methods of training teachers in behavior modification. *School Psychology Review, 13*(1), 26–32.

Allen, J. M. (1994). School counselors collaborating for success. *ERIC document #EDO-CG-94-27.* Greensboro, NC: ERIC/CASS.

Allen, S. J., & Graden, S. J. (1995). Best practices in collaborative problem solving for intervention design. In A. Thomas & J. Grimes (Eds.), *Best practices in school psychology* (3rd ed., pp. 667–678). Washington, DC: National Association of School Psychologists.

Allen, S. J., & Graden, S. J. (2002). Best practices in collaborative problem solving for intervention design. In A. Thomas & J. Grimes (Eds.), *Best practices in school psychology* (4th ed., pp. 565–582). Washington, DC: National Association of School Psychologists.

Alpert, J. L.(Ed.). (1982). *Psychological consultation in educational settings.* San Francisco: Jossey-Bass.

Alpert, J. L., & Duckworth Smith, H. (2003). Terrorism, terrorism threat, and the school consultant. *Journal of Educational and Psychological Consultation, 4*, 369–385.

Alpert, J., & Silverstein, J. (1985). Mental health consultation: Historical, present and future perspectives. In J. R. Bergan (Ed.), *School psychology in contemporary society* (pp. 121–138). Columbus, OH: Merrill.

Alpert, J. L., & Taufique, S. R. (2002a). Consultation training: A field in need of review, revision, and research. *Journal of Educational and Psychological Consultation, 13*(1&2), 7–11.

Alpert, J. L., & Taufique, S. R. (2002b). Consultation training: 26 years and three questions. *Journal of Educational and Psychological Consultation, 13*(1&2), 13–33.

Altrocchi, J. (1972). Mental health consultation. In S. E. Golarm & C. Eisdorfer (Eds.), *Handbook of community mental health* (pp. 477–508). New York: Appleton-Century-Crofts.

Amada, G. (1993). The role of the mental health consultant in dealing with disruptive college students. *Journal of College Student Psychotherapy, 8*, 121–127.

Amatea, E. S., Daniels, H., Bringman, N., & Vandiver, F. M. (2004). Strengthening counselor-teacher-family connections. *Professional School Counseling, 8*, 47–55.

American Association for Counseling and Development (1991). Multiculturalism as a fourth force in counseling. *Journal of Counseling and Development, 70*(1). Alexandria, VA: Author.

American Counseling Association (1995). *Ethical standards for Internet on-line counseling.* Alexandria, VA: Author.

American Counseling Association (2005). *Code of ethics and standards of practice* (Rev. ed.). Alexandria, VA: Author.

American Mental Health Counselors Association (2000). *Code of Ethics* (Rev. ed.). Alexandria, VA: Author.

American Psychological Association (1993). Guidelines for providers of psychological services to ethnic, linguistic, and culturally diverse populations. *American Psychologist, 48*(1), 45–48.

American Psychological Association (2002). *Ethical principles of psychologists and code of conduct* (Rev. ed.). Washington, DC: Author.

American Psychological Association (2003). Guidelines on multicultural education, training, research, practice, and organizational change for psychologists. *American Psychologist, 58*, 377–402.

American School Counselor Association (2003). *ASCA national model: A framework for comprehensive school counseling programs.* Alexandria, VA: Author.

American Society for Training and Development (2005). *Code of Ethics.* Alexandria, VA: Author.

Anderson, B. S. (1996). *The counselor and the law* (4th ed.). Alexandria, VA: American Counseling Association.

Anderson, D. (1992). A case for standards of counseling practice. *Journal of Counseling and Development, 71*, 22–26.

Anderson, T. K., Kratochwill, T. R., & Bergan, J. R. (1986). Training teachers in behavioral consultation and therapy: An analysis of verbal behaviors. *Journal of School Psychology, 24*, 229–241.

Anderson, W. R., Frieden, B. J., & Murphy, M. J. (Eds.). (1977). *Managing human services.* Washington, DC: International City Management Association.

Anton-Lahart, J., & Rosenfield, S. (2004). *Journal of Educational and Psychological Consultation, 5*, 41–62.

Aplin, J. C. (1978). Structural change vs. behavioral change. *Personnel and Guidance Journal, 56*(7), 407–411.

Armenakis, A. A., & Burdg, H. B. (1988). Consultation research: Contributions to practice and directions for improvement. *Journal of Management, 14*, 339–365.

Armstrong, I. R., & Wheatley, W. J. (1990). Diagnosing the needs of small business clients: A methodology for consultants. *Consultation, 8*, 25–40.

Arredondo, P. (1996). *Successful diversity management initiatives.* Thousand Oaks, CA: SAGE.

Arredondo, P., Shealy, C., Neale, M., & Winfrey, L. L. (2004). Consultation and interprofessional collaboration: Modeling for the future. *Journal of Clinical Psychology, 60*, 787–800.

Arredondo, P., Toporek, R., Brown, S. P., Jones, J., Locke, D. C., Sanchez, J., & Stadler, H. (1996). Operationalization of the multicultural counseling competencies. *Journal of Multicultural Counseling and Development, 24*(1), 42–78.

Ary, D., Jacobs, L. C., & Razavieh, A. (1985). *Introduction to research in education* (3rd ed.). New York: Holt, Rinehart & Winston.

Ashford, S. J., & Cummings, L. L. (1983). Feedback as an individual resource: Personal strategies of creating information. *Organizational Behavior and Human Performance, 32*, 370–398.

Association for Specialists in Group Work (1989). *Ethical guidelines for group counselors.* Alexandria, VA: Author.

Association for Specialists in Group Work (2000). *Professional standards for the training of group workers.* (Rev. ed.). Alexandria, VA: Author.

Athanasiou, M. S. (2001). Using consultation with a grandmother as an adjunct to play therapy. *Family Journal, 9*, 445–450.

Athanasiou, M. S., Geil, M., Hazel, C. E., & Copeland, E. P. (2002). A look inside school-based consultation: A qualitative study of the beliefs and practices of school psychologists and teachers. *School Psychology Quarterly, 17*, 258–298.

Atkinson, D. R. (2004). *Counseling American minorities* (6th ed.). Boston: McGraw-Hill.

Auster, E. R., Feeney-Kettler, K. A., & Kratochwill, T. R. (2006). Conjoint behavioral consultation: Application to the school-based treatment of anxiety disorders. *Education and Treatment of Children, 29,* 243–256.

Axelson, J. A. (1993). *Counseling and development in a multicultural society* (2nd ed.). Pacific Grove, CA: Thomson Brooks/Cole.

Axmith, M. (1997). The evolving workplace: Its implications for outplacement practice. In A. J. Pickman (Ed.), *Special Challenges in Career Management* (pp. 233–244). Mahwah, NJ: Lawrence Erlbaum Associates.

Baard, P. P. (1994). A motivational model for consulting with not-for-profit organizations: A study of church growth and participation. *Consulting Psychology Journal: Practice & Research, 46,* 19–31.

Babcock, N. L., & Pryzwansky, W. B. (1983). Models of consultation: Preferences of educational professionals at five stages of service. *Journal of School Psychology, 21,* 359–366.

Babinski, L. M., Jones, B. D., & DeWert, M. H. (2001). The role of facilitators and peers in an online support community for first year teachers. *Journal of Educational and Psychological Consultation, 12,* 151–169.

Babinski, L. M., & Rogers, D. L. (1998). Supporting new teachers through consultee-centered group consultation. *Journal of Educational and Psychological Consultation, 9,* 285–308.

Backer, T. E. (1985). The future of organizational consulting. *Consultation, 4*(1), 17–29.

Backer, T. E. (1988). Workplace drug abuse programs: Consultation issues and opportunities. *Consultation, 7,* 216–227.

Backer, T. E. (1993). Consulting on innovation and change with public mental health organizations: The Caplan approach. In W. P. Erchul (Ed.), *Consultation in community, school, and organizational practice* (pp. 149–162). Washington, DC: Taylor & Francis.

Backer, T. E., & Porterfield, J. (1998). Change at work: Why it hurts and what employers can do about it. In S. Klarreich (Ed.), *Handbook of Organizational Health Psychology* (pp. 203–215). Madison, CT: Psychological Press.

Bacon, E. H., & Dougherty, A. M. (1992). Consultation in preschool settings. *Elementary School Guidance and Counseling, 27,* 24–32.

Bahr, M. W., & Kovaleski, J. F. (2006). The need for problem-solving teams. *Remedial and Special Education, 27,* 2–5.

Baker, S. B., & Shaw, M. C. (1987). *Improving counseling through primary prevention.* Columbus, OH: Merrill.

Bandura, A. (1977). *Social learning theory.* Englewood Cliffs, NJ: Prentice-Hall.

Bangert, A. W., & Baumberger, J. P. (2005). Research and statistical techniques used in the *Journal of Counseling and Development*: 1990–2001. *Journal of Counseling and Development, 83,* 480–487.

Barak, A. (1994). A cognitive-behavioral educational workshop to combat sexual harassment in the workplace. *Journal of Counseling & Development, 8,* 595–602.

Bardon, J. (1986). Psychology and schooling: The interrelationships among persons, processes, and products. In S. N. Elliott & J. C. Witt (Eds.), *The delivery of psychological services in schools: Concepts, processes, and issues* (pp. 53–80). Hillsdale, NJ: Erlbaum.

Barlow, D. H., Hayes, S. C., & Nelson-Gray, R. O. (1999). *The scientist practitioner* (2nd ed.). New York: Pergamon Press.

Barlow, D. H., & Hersen, M. (1984). *Single case experimental designs* (2nd ed.). New York: Pergamon Press.

Barnett, D., & Lentz, F. E., Jr. (1993). Functional outcome analysis: A good heuristic that went a bridge too far. *School Psychology Quarterly, 8,* 231–237.

Barnett, D., VanDerHeyden, A. M., & Witt, J. C. (2007). Achieving science-based practice through response to intervention: What it might look like in preschools. *Journal of Educational and Psychological Consultation, 17,* 31–54.

Beaver, B. R., & Busse, R. T. (2000). Informant reports: Conceptual and research bases of interviews with parents and teachers. In E. S. Shapiro & T. R. Kratochwill (Eds.), *Behavioral assessment in schools* (2nd ed., pp. 257–287). New York: Guilford Press.

Beck, V. (1994). Opportunity plus: A school- and community-based tutorial program for elementary students. *Elementary School Guidance & Counseling, 29,* 156–160.

Becker, W. O. (1971). *Parents are teachers.* Champaign, IL: Research Press.

Beckhard, R. (1979). Organization changing through consulting and training. In D. P. Sinha (Ed.),

*Consultants and consultant styles* (pp. 17–44). New Delhi, India: Vision Books.

Beer, M. (1980). *Organization change and development: A systems view.* Glenview, IL: Scott, Foresman.

Beer, M., & Spector, B. (1993). Organizational diagnosis: Its role in organizational learning. *Journal of Counseling and Development, 71,* 642–650.

Beer, M., & Walton, R. E. (1990). Developing the competitive organization: Interventions and strategies. *American Psychologist, 45*(2), 154–161.

Begeny, J. C. (2006). Assessing pre-service teachers' training in empirically validated behavioral instruction practices. *School Psychology Quarterly, 21,* 262–285.

Beisser, A. R., & Green, R. (1972). *Mental health consultation and education.* Palo Alto, CA: National Press Books.

Bell, C. R., & Nadler, L. (Eds.) (1985). *Clients and consultants: Meeting and exceeding expectations* (2nd ed.). Houston: Gulf Publishing.

Bellack, A. S., & Hersen, M. (Eds.) (1985). *Dictionary of behavior therapy techniques.* New York: Pergamon Press.

Bellman, G. M. (1990). *The consultant's calling.* San Francisco: Jossey-Bass.

Bemak, F. Murphy, S. & Kaffenberger, C. (2005). Community-focused consultation: New directions and practice. In C. Sink (Ed.), *Contemporary school counseling* (pp. 327–357). Boston: Houghton Mifflin.

Benedek, D. M., Ursano, R. J., Fullerton, C. S., Vineburgh, N. T., & Gifford, R. K. (2006). Responding to workplace terrorism: Applying military models of behavioral health and public health response. *Journal of Workplace Behavioral Health, 1,* 21–33.

Bennis, W. G., Benne, K. D., Chin, R., & Corey, K. E. (Eds.) (1985). *The planning of change* (4th ed.). New York: Holt, Rinehart & Winston.

Benshoff, J. M., & Paisley, P. O. (1996). The structured peer consultation model for school counselors. *Journal for Counseling & Development, 74,* 314–318.

Bergan, J. R. (1977). *Behavioral consultation.* Columbus, OH: Merrill.

Bergan, J. R., & Kratochwill, T. R. (1990). *Behavioral consultation and therapy.* New York: Plenum.

Bergan, J. R., & Tombari, M. L. (1976). Consultant skill and efficiency and the implementation and outcomes of consultation. *Journal of School Psychology, 14*(1), 3–14.

Bernard, M. E., & DiGiuseppe, R. (2000). Advances in theory and practice of rational-emotive behavioral consultation. *Journal of Educational and Psychological Consultation, 11*(3&4), 333–355.

Berrios, R., & Lucca, N. (2006). Qualitative methodology in counseling research: Recent contributions and challenges for a new century. *Journal of Counseling and Development, 84,* 174–186.

Bersoff, D. N. (1996). The virtue of principle ethics. *The Counseling Psychologist, 24*(1), 86–91.

Bianco-Mathis, V., & Veazey, N. (1996). Consultant dilemmas: Lessons from the trenches. *Training and Development Journal (July),* 39–42.

Birnbrauer, H. (1987). Evaluation techniques that work. *Training and Development Journal, 41*(7), 53–55.

Bittel, L. R. (1972). *The nine master keys of management.* New York: McGraw-Hill.

Blader, J. C., & Gallagher, R. (2001). Consultation to administrators. *Child and Adolescent Psychiatric Clinics of North America, 10,* 185–197.

Blake, R. R., & Mouton, J. S. (1983). *Consultation: A handbook for individual and organization development* (2nd ed.). Reading, MA: Addison-Wesley.

Blase, J., & Blase, J. J. (2006). *Teachers bring out the best in teachers: A guide to peer consultation for administrators and teachers.* Thousand Oaks, CA: Corwin Press.

Block, P. (2000). *Flawless consulting: A guide to getting your expertise used* (2nd ed.). San Francisco: Jossey-Bass.

Blom-Hoffman, J., & Rose, G. S. (2007). Applying Motivational interviewing to school-based consultation: A commentary on "Has consultation achieved its primary prevention potential?," an article by Joseph E. Zins. *Journal of Educational and Psychological Consultation, 17,* 151–156.

Bloom, B. L. (1984). *Community mental health: A general introduction* (2nd ed.). Pacific Grove, CA: Thomson Brooks/Cole.

Boss, R. W. (1993). The psychological contract. In R. T. Golembiewski (Ed.), *Handbook of organizational consultation* (pp. 65–74). New York: Marcel Dekker, Inc.

Brack, G., Jones, E. S., Smith, R. M., White, J., & Brack, C. J. (1993). A primer on consultation theory: Building a flexible world view. *Journal of Counseling and Development, 71,* 619–628.

Braden, J. P. (2002). Best practices for school psychologists in educational accountability: High stakes testing and educational reform. In A. Thomas & J. Grimes (Eds.), *Best practices in school psychology* (4th ed., pp. 301–319). Bethesda, MD: National Association of School Psychologists.

Bradley, D. F. (1994). A framework for the acquisition of collaborative consultation skills. *Journal of Educational and Psychological Consultation, 5,* 51–68.

Bramlett, R. K., & Murphy, J. J. (1998). School psychology perspectives on consultation: Key contributions to the field. *Journal of Educational and Psychology Consultation, 9,* 29–55.

Bramlett, R. K., Murphy, J. J., Johnson, J., & Wallingsford, L. (2002). Contemporary practices in school psychology: A national survey of roles and referral problems. *Psychology in the Schools, 39,* 327–335.

Braucht, S., & Weime, B. (1992). The school counselor as consultant on self-esteem: An example. *Elementary School Guidance and Counseling, 26,* 229–236.

Brehm, J. W. (1966). *A theory of psychological reactance.* New York: Academic Press.

Brett, J. M., Goldberg, S. B., & Ury, W. L. (1990). Designing systems for resolving disputes in organizations. *American Psychologist, 45*(2), 162–170.

Breznay, S. (2001). Liaison teams: A strategy for building interagency collaboration in caring for children with serious emotional disturbances and their families. *Issues in Interdisciplinary Care, 3,* 101–106.

Brigman, G., Mullis, F., Webb, L., & White, J. (2005). *School counselor consultation.* Hoboken, NJ: Wiley.

Brown, D. (1988). Empowerment through advocacy. In D. J. Kurpius & D. Brown (Eds.), *Handbook of consultation: An intervention for advocacy and outreach* (pp. 5–17). Alexandria, VA: American Association for Counseling and Development.

Brown, D. (1993). Defining human services consultation. In J. E. Zins, T. R. Kratochwill, & S. N. Elliott (Eds.). *Handbook of consultation for children* (pp. 46–69). San Francisco: Jossey-Bass.

Brown, D. (1997). Implications of cultural values for crosscultural consultation with families. *Journal of Counseling and Development, 76,* 29–35.

Brown, D., Kurpius, D. J., & Morris, J. R. (1988). *Handbook of consultation with individuals and small groups.* Alexandria, VA: American Association for Counseling and Development.

Brown, D., Pryzwansky, W. B., & Schulte, A. C. (1995). *Psychological consultation: Introduction to theory and practice* (3rd ed.). Boston: Allyn & Bacon.

Brown, D., Pryzwansky, W. B., & Schulte, A. C. (2001). *Psychological consultation: Introduction to theory and practice* (4th ed.). Boston: Allyn & Bacon.

Brown, J. E. (1987). A systemic view of psychological consultation in the schools. *Canadian Journal of Counseling, 21,* 114–124.

Brubaker, J. C. (1978). Futures consultation: Designing desirable futures. *Personnel and Guidance Journal, 56,* 428–431.

Bundy, M. L., & Poppen, W. A. (1986). School counselors' effectiveness as consultants: A research review. *Elementary School Guidance and Counseling, 20,* 215–222.

Burges, B. (1976). *Facts and figures: A layman's guide to conducting surveys.* Boston: Institute for Responsive Education.

Burke, W. W. (1980). Organization development and bureaucracy in the 1980's. *Journal of Applied Behavioral Science, 16*(3), 423–437.

Burke, W. W. (1993). The changing world of organizational change. *Consulting Psychology Journal, 45,* 9–17.

Burns, M. K. (2004). Curriculum-based assessment in consultation: A review of three levels of research. *Journal of Educational and Psychological Consultation, 15,* 63–78.

Burrello, L. C., & Reitzug, U. C. (1993). Transforming context and developing culture in schools. *Journal of Counseling and Development, 71,* 669–677.

Busse, R. T., & Beaver, B. R. (2000). Informant report: Parent and teacher interviews. In E. S. Shapiro and T. R. Kratochwill (Eds.), *Conducting school-based assessments of child and adolescent behavior* (pp. 235–251). New York: Guilford Press.

Busse, R. T., Kratochwill, T. R., & Elliott, S. N. (1999). Influences of verbal interactions during behavioral consultations on treatment outcomes. *Journal of School Psychology, 37,* 117–143.

Butler, W. M., Leitenberg, H., & Fuselier, G. D. (1993). The use of mental health professional consultants to police hostage negotiation teams. *Behavioral Sciences and the Law, 11,* 213–221.

Buysse, V., Schulte, A. C., Pierce, P. P., & Terry, D. (1994). Models and styles of consultation: Preferences of professionals in early intervention. *Journal of Early Intervention, 18,* 302–310.

Calfee, B. E. (1997). Lawsuit prevention techniques. In *The Hatherleigh guide to ethics in therapy* (pp. 109–125). New York: Hatherleigh Press.

Campbell, C. A. (1992). The school counselor as consultant: Assessing your aptitude. *Elementary School Guidance and Counseling, 26,* 237–250.

Campbell, C. A. (1993). Strategies for reducing parent resistance to consultation in the schools. *Elementary School Guidance and Counseling, 28,* 83–91.

Caplan, G. (1970). *The theory and practice of mental health consultation.* New York: Basic Books.

Caplan, G. (1974). *Support systems and community health: Lectures in concept development.* New York: Behavioral Publications.

Caplan, G. (1977). Mental health consultation: Retrospect and prospect. In S. C. Plog & P. I. Ahmed (Eds.), *Principles and techniques of mental health consultation* (pp. 9–21). New York: Plenum.

Caplan, G. (1993a). Epilogue. In W. P. Erchul (Ed.), *Consultation in community, school, and organizational practice* (pp. 205–213). Washington, DC: Taylor & Francis.

Caplan, G. (1993b). Mental health consultation, community mental health, and population-oriented psychiatry. In W. P. Erchul (Ed.), *Consultation in community, school, and organizational practice* (pp. 41–55). Washington, DC: Taylor & Francis.

Caplan, G., & Caplan, R. B. (1993). *Mental health consultation and collaboration.* San Francisco: Jossey-Bass.

Caplan, G., & Caplan, R. B. (1999). *Mental health consultation and collaboration.* Prospect Heights, IL: Waveland. (Original work published in 1993).

Caplan, G., Caplan, R. B., & Erchul, W. P. (1994). Caplanian mental health consultation: Historical background and current status. *Consulting Psychology Journal: Practice & Research, 46,* 2–12.

Caplan, G., & Caplan-Moskovich, R. B. (2004). Recent advances in mental health consultation and mental health consultation. In N. M. Lambert, I. Hylander & J. H. Sandoval (Eds.), *Consultee-centered consultation: improving the quality of professional services in* schools and community organizations (pp. 21–35). Mahwah, NJ: Erlbaum.

Caplan-Moskovich, R. B., & Caplan, G. (2004). Consultee-centered consultation in low feasibility settings. In N. M. Lambert, I. Hylander & J. H. Sandoval (Eds.), *Consultee-centered consultation: Improving the quality of professional service in schools and community organizations* (pp. 187–201). Mahwah, NJ: Erlbaum.

Carlisle, H. (1982). *Management: Concepts, methods, and applications* (2nd ed.). Chicago: Science Research Associates.

Carlson, C. (2006). Single parenting and step-parenting. In G. G. Bear and K. M. Minke (Eds.). *Children's needs III: Development, prevention, and intervention* (pp. 783–797). Bethesda, MD: National Association of School Psychologists.

Carlson, D. L. (2007). From Dodge City to Emerald City: The importance of Joseph E. Zins' work in teacher education programs: A commentary on "The scientific base linking social and emotional learning to school success," a chapter by Joseph E. Zins, Michelle R. Bloodworth, Roger P. Weissberg, and Herbert J. Walberg. *Journal of Educational and Psychological Consultation, 17,* 219–223.

Carlson, J., Watts, R. E., & Maniacci, M. (2006). *Adlerian therapy: Theory and practice.* Washington, DC: American Psychological Association.

Carner, L. A. (1982). Developing a consultative contract. In J. L. Alpert (Ed.), *Psychological consultation in educational settings* (pp. 8–32). San Francisco: Jossey-Bass.

Carr, E. G. (2007). The expanding vision of positive behavior support: Research perspectives on happiness, helpfulness, hopefulness. *Journal of Positive Behavior Support, 9,* 3–14.

Carson, A. D., & Lowman, R. L. (2002). Individual-level variables in organizational consultation. In R. L. Lowman (Ed.), *Handbook of organizational consulting psychology: A comprehensive guide to theory, skills, and techniques* (pp. 5–26). San Francisco: Jossey-Bass.

Case, T. L., Vandenberg, R. J., & Meredith, P. H. (1990). Internal and external change agents. *Leadership & Organization Development Journal, 11*(1), 4–15.

Castillo, E. M., Quintana, S. M., & Zamarripa, M. X. (2000). Cultural and linguistic issues. In E. S. Shapiro and T. R. Kratochwill (Eds.),

*Conducting school based assessments of child and adolescent behavior* (pp. 274–306). New York: Guilford Press.

Chalofsky, N., & Lincoln, C. I. (1983). *Up the HRD ladder: A guide for professional growth.* Reading, MA: Addison-Wesley.

Champion, D. P., Kiel, D. H., & McLendon, J. A. (1990). Choosing a consulting role. *Training and Development Journal (February)*, 66–69.

Chapiro, J. (1981). What kind of a system is an organization and with what metaphors do we describe it? In R. Lippitt & G. Lippitt (Eds.), *Systems thinking—a resource for organization diagnosis and intervention* (Vol. 3, pp. 35–42). Washington, DC: International Consultants Foundation Series.

Cherniss, C. (1993). Preentry issues revisited. In R. T. Golembiewski (Ed.), *Handbook of organizational consultation* (pp. 113–118). New York: Marcel Dekker, Inc.

Cherniss, C. (1998). Teacher empowerment, consultation, and the creation of new programs in schools. *Journal of Educational and Psychological Consultation, 8*, 135–152.

Chin, R., & Benne, K. D. (Eds.) (1985). *The planning of change* (4th ed.). New York: Holt, Rinehart & Winston.

Chowanec, G. D. (1993). TQM: Evaluating service quality. *Consulting Psychology Journal, 45*, 31–32.

Christenson, S. L. (1995). Families and schools: What is the role of the school psychologist? *School Psychology Quarterly, 10*, 118–132.

Christenson, S. L., & Buerkle, K. (1999). Families as educational partners for children's school success: Suggestions for school psychologists. In C. R. Reynolds and T. B. Gutkin (Eds.), *The handbook of school psychology* (3rd ed., pp. 709–744). New York: Wiley.

Clare, M. M., Jimenez, A., & McClendon, J. (2005). Toma el tiempo: The wisdom of migrant families in consultation. *Journal of Educational and Psychological Consultation, 16*, 95–111.

Clayton, S., & Bongar, B. (1994). The use of consultation in psychological practice: Ethical, legal and clinical considerations. *Ethics & Behavior, 4*, 43–57.

Cleven, C. A., & Gutkin, T. B. (1988). Cognitive modeling of consultation processes: A means for improving consultees' problem definition skills. *Journal of School Psychology, 26*(4), 379–389.

Cohen, E., & Osterweil, Z. (1986). An "Issue-focused" model of mental health consultation with groups of teachers. *Journal of School Psychology, 24*(3), 243–256.

Colbert, R. D., Vernon-Jones, R., & Pransky, K. (2006). The social change feedback process: Creating a new role for counselors in education reform. *Journal of Counseling and Development, 84*, 72–82.

Cole, E., & Siegal, J. A. (Eds.) (2003). *Effective consultation in school psychology* (2nd ed.). Cambridge, MA: Hogrefe & Huber.

Cole, S. M., Thomas, A. R., & Lee, C. C. (1988). School counselor and school psychologist: Partners in minority family outreach. *Journal of Multicultural Counseling and Development, 16*, 110–116.

Colton, D. L., & Sheridan, S. M. (1998). Conjoint behavioral consultation and social skills training: Enhancing the play behaviors of boys with attention deficit hyperactivity disorder. *Journal of Educational and Psychological Consultation, 9*, 3–28.

Conoley, J. C., & Conoley, C. W. (1982). The effects of two conditions of client-centered consultation on student-teacher problem descriptions and remedial plans. *Journal of School Psychology, 20*, 323–328.

Conoley, J. C., & Conoley, C. W. (1985). The school consultant as advocate: A perspective for trainers. *School Psychology International, 6*(4), 219–224.

Conoley, J. C., & Conoley, C. W. (1990). Staff consultative work in schools. In N. Jones & N. Frederickson (Eds.), *Refocusing educational psychology* (pp. 84–103). London: Falmer.

Conoley, J. C., & Conoley, C. W. (1992). *School consultation: Practice and training* (2nd ed.). Boston: Allyn & Bacon.

Conoley, C. W., Conoley, J. C., & Gumm, W. B., II. (1992). Effects of consultee problem presentation and consultant training on consultant problem definition. *Journal of Counseling and Development, 71*, 60–62.

Conoley, C. W., Conoley, J. C., Ivey, D. C., & Scheel, M. J. (1991). Enhancing consultation by matching the consultees' perspectives. *Journal of Counseling and Development, 69*, 546–549.

Conoley, J. C., & Gutkin, T. B. (1986). School psychology: A re-conceptualization of service delivery realities. In S. N. Elliott & J. C. Witt (Eds.), *The delivery of psychological services in schools* (pp. 393–424). Hillsdale, NJ: Erlbaum.

Conoley, J. C., & Haynes (1992). Ecological perspectives. In R. D'Amato and B. Rothlisberg (Eds.), *Psychological perspectives on interaction* (pp. 177–189). White Plains, NY: Longman Publishing.

Conoley, J. C., & Wright, C. (1993). Caplan's ideas and the future of psychology in the schools. In W. P. Erchul (Ed.), *Consultation in community, school, and organizational practice* (pp. 177–192). Washington, DC: Taylor & Francis.

Conroy, E., & Mayer, S. (1994). Strategies for consulting with parents. *Elementary School Guidance & Counseling, 29,* 60–66.

Consultation I: Conceptual, structural, and operational dimensions (special issue). (1993a). *Journal of Counseling and Development, 71,* 596–708.

Consultation II: Prevention, preparation, and key issues (special issue). (1993b). *Journal of Counseling and Development, 71,* 115–223.

Conyne, R. K., & Mazza, J. (2007). Ecological group work applied to schools. *Journal for Specialists in Group Work, 32,* 19–29.

Conyne, R. K., & O'Neil, J. M. (Eds.). (1992). *Organizational consultation: A casebook.* Newbury Park, CA: Sage.

Conyne, R. K., Rapin, L. S., & Rand, J. M. (1997). A model for leading task groups. In H. Forester-Miller and J. A. Kottler (Eds.), *Issues and challenges for group practitioners* (pp. 117–130). Denver: Love Publishing Company.

Cook, D. W. (1989). Systematic need assessment: A primer. *Journal of Counseling and Development, 67,* 462–464.

Cooke, R. A. (1979). Managing change in organizations. In G. Zaltman (Ed.), *Management principles for non-profit agencies and organizations* (pp. 154–209). New York: AMACOM.

Cooper, S., & Hodges, W. F. (Eds.) (1983). *The mental health consultation field.* New York: Human Sciences Press.

Cooper, S. E., Monarch, N., Serviss, S. T., Gordick, D., & Leonard, L. H. (2007). Professional preparation and continuing education for beginning, entry, midlevel, and senior consulting psychologists. *Consulting Psychology Journal: Practice and Research, 59,* 1–16.

Cooper, S. E., & Newbold, R. C. (1994). Combining external and internal behavioral system consultation to enhance plant safety. *Consulting Psychology Journal, 46,* 32–41.

Cooper, S. E., & O'Connor, R. M., Jr. (1993). Standards for organizational consultation assessment and evaluation instruments. *Journal of Counseling and Development, 71,* 651–660.

Corey, G. (2005). *Theory and practice of counseling and psychotherapy* (7th ed.). Pacific Grove, CA: Thomson Brooks/Cole.

Corey, G., Corey, M. S., & Callanan, P. (2007). *Issues and ethics in the helping professions* (7th ed.). Pacific Grove, CA: Thomson Brooks/Cole.

Correa, V. I., & Tulbert, B. (1993). Collaboration between school personnel in special education and Hispanic families. *Journal of Educational and Psychological Consultation, 4,* 253–265.

Cosier, R. A., & Dalton, D. R. (1993). Management consulting: Planning, entry, performance. *Journal of Counseling and Development, 72*(2), 191–198.

Costello, M., Phelps, L., & Wilczenski, F. (1994). Children and military conflict: Current issues and treatment implications. *School Counselor, 41,* 220–225.

Cottingham, H. E. (1956). *Guidance in the elementary schools: Principles and practice.* Bloomington, IL: McKnight & McKnight.

Cottone, R. R. (2001). A social constructivism model of ethical decision making in counseling. *Journal of Counseling and Development, 79*(1), 39–45.

Counselman, E. F., & Weber, R. L. (1994). Leadership of mental health consultation groups: A model for group therapists. *International Journal of Group Psychotherapy, 44,* 349–360.

Covey, S. R. (1991). *Principle-centered leadership.* New York: Simon and Schuster.

Cowan, R. J. (2007). The use and perceived utility of peer mediated systems for school psychologists: A commentary on "Introduction to developing peer-mediated support systems for helping professionals: Are we ready to practice what we preach?," an article by Joseph E. Zins, and on "Consultation with Professional peers: A national survey of the practices of school psychologists," an article by Joseph E. Zins and John J. Murphy. *Journal of Educational and Psychological Consultation, 17,* 185–189.

Cowan, R. J., & Sheridan, S. M. (2003). Investigating the acceptability of behavioral interventions in applied conjoint behavioral consultation: Moving from analog conditions to naturalistic settings. *School Psychology Quarterly, 18,* 1–21.

Cowles, C. A., & Washburn, J. J. (2005). Psychological consultation on program design of intensive management units in juvenile correctional facilities. *Professional Psychology: Research and Practice, 36,* 44–50.

Cox, D. D. (2005). Evidence-based interventions using home-school collaboration. *School Psychology Quarterly, 20,* 473–497.

Cox, T. (2001). *Creating the multicultural organization.* San Francisco: Jossey-Bass.

Cramer, S. F. (1998). *Collaboration.* Boston: Allyn & Bacon.

Crego, C. A. (1985). Ethics: The need for improved consultation training. *Counseling Psychologist, 13*(3), 473–476.

Criddle, W. D. (2007). Adapting REBT to the world of business. *Journal of Rational-Emotive & Cognitive-Behavior Therapy, 25,* 87–106.

Crone, D. A., Hawken, L. S., & Bergstrom, M. K. (2007). A demonstration of training, implementing, and using functional behavioral assessment in 10 elementary and middle school settings. *Journal of Positive Behavioral Interventions, 9,* 15–29.

Crose, R., & Kixmiller, J. S. (1994). Counseling psychologists as nursing home consultants: What do administrators want? *Counseling Psychologist, 22,* 104–114.

Cross, P. (1984). *Adults as learners.* San Francisco: Jossey-Bass.

Cummings. J. A., Harrison, P. L., Dawson, M. M., Short, R. J., Gorin, S., & Palomares, R. S. (2004a). The 2002 conference on the future of school psychology: Implications for consultation, intervention, and prevention services. *Journal of Educational and Psychological Consultation, 5,* 239–256.

Cummings. J. A., Harrison, P. L., Dawson, M. M., Short, R. J., Gorin, S., & Palomares, R. S. (2004b). Follow-up to the 2002 futures conference: Collaborating to serve all children, families, and schools. *Journal of Educational and Psychological Consultation, 5,* 335–344.

Curtis, M. J., & Metz, L. W. (1986). System level intervention in a school for handicapped children. *School Psychology Review, 15,* 510–518.

Curtis, M. J., & Stollar, S. A. (1996). Applying principles and practices of organizational change to school reform. *School Psychology Review, 25,* 409–417.

Curtis, M. J., & Stollar, S. A. (2002). Best practices in system-level change. In A. Thomas and J. Grimes (Eds.), *Best Practices in School Psychology* (4th ed., pp. 223–243). Washington, DC: National Association of School Psychologists.

Daly III, E. J., & Murdoch, A. (2000). Direct observation in the assessment of academic skills problems. In E. S. Shapiro and T. R. Kratochwill (Eds.), *Behavioral assessment in schools: Theory, research, and clinical foundations* (2nd ed., pp. 46–73). New York: Guilford Press.

Daniels, T. D., & Dewine, S. (1990). Communication process as target and tool for consultancy intervention: Rethinking a hackneyed theme. *Journal of Educational and Psychological Consultation, 2,* 303–322.

Darnell, A. J., & Kupermine, G. P. (2006). Organizational culture competence in mental health service delivery: A multilevel analysis. *Journal of Multicultural Counseling and Development, 34,* 194–207.

Das, A. K. (1995). Rethinking multicultural counseling: Implications for counselor education. *Journal of Counseling and Development, 74*(1), 45–52.

David, R. J., & Strang, D. (2006). When fashion is fleeting: Transitory collective beliefs and the dynamics of TQM consulting. *Academy of Management Journal, 49,* 215–233.

Davis, J. M., & Hartsough, C. S. (1992). Assessing psychosocial environment in mental health consultation groups. *Psychology in the Schools, 29,* 224–228.

Davis, K. M. School-based consultation. In C. Sink (Ed.), *Contemporary school counseling* (pp. 297–326). Boston: Houghton Mifflin.

Davison, M., & Gasiorowski, F. (2006). The trend of coaching: Adler, the literature, and marketplace would agree. *The Journal of Individual Psychology, 62,* 188–201.

Deck, M. D. (1992). Training school counselors to be consultants. *Elementary School Guidance and Counseling, 26,* 221–228.

Deitz, P. E., & Reese, J. T. (1986). The perils of police psychology: 10 strategies for minimizing role conflicts when providing mental health services and consultation to law enforcement agencies. *Behavioral Sciences and the Law, 4*, 385–400.

Delbecq, A. L., Van De Ven, A. H., & Gustafson, D. H. (1975). *Group techniques for program planning: A guide to nominal group and delphi processes.* Glenview, IL: Scott, Foresman.

Denton, C. A., Hasbrouck, J. E., & Sekaquaptewa, S. (2003). The consulting teacher: A descriptive case study in responsive systems consultation. *Journal of Educational and Psychological Consultation, 4*, 41–73.

Dewar, A. L. (1980). *The quality circle guide to participation management.* Englewood Cliffs, NJ: Prentice-Hall.

Dickinson, D. J., & Adcox, S. (1984). Program evaluation of a school consultation program. *Psychology in the Schools, 21*, 336–342.

Dickinson, D. J., & Bradshaw, S. P. (1992). Multiplying effectiveness: Combining consultation with counseling. *School Counselor, 40*, 118–124.

Diller, J. V. (2007). *Cultural diversity: A primer for human services.* Belmont, CA: Thomson Brooks/Cole.

Dinkmeyer, D., Jr. (2006). School consultation using individual psychology. *Journal of Individual Psychology, 62*, 180–187.

Dinkmeyer, D., & Caldwell, E. (1970). *Developmental counseling and guidance: A comprehensive school approach.* New York: McGraw-Hill.

Dinkmeyer, D., Jr., & Carlson, J. (2001). *Consultation: Creating school-based interventions* (2nd ed.). Philadelphia: Taylor & Francis.

Dinkmeyer, D., & McKay, G. (1996). *Raising a responsible child.* New York: Simon & Schuster.

Dinkmeyer, D. C., McKay, G., & Dinkmeyer, D., Jr. (1997). *Systematic training for effective parenting (STEP).* Circle Pines, MN: American Guidance Service.

Dinkmeyer, D. C., Pew, W. L., & Dinkmeyer, D. C., Jr. (1979). *Adlerian counseling and psychotherapy.* Monterey, CA: Thomson Brooks/Cole.

Dixon, D. N., & Dixon, D. E. (1993). Research in consultation: Toward better analogues and outcome measures. *Journal of Counseling and Development, 71*, 700–702.

Dodson-Chaneske, D. (1988). Mental health consultation to a police department. *Journal of Human Behavior and Learning, 5*, 35–38.

Dodson, W. W., & Vaccaro, B. (1988). Mental health consultation in campus discipline: A program of primary prevention. *Journal of American College Health, 37*(2), 85–88.

Doll, B., Haack, K., Kosse, S., Osterloh, M., Siemers, E., & Pray, B. (2005). The dilemma of pragmatics: Why schools don't use quality team consultation practices. *Journal of Educational and Psychological Consultation, 16*, 127–155.

Domitrovich, C. E., & Greenberg, M. T. (2000). The study of implementation: Current findings from effective programs that prevent mental disorders in school-aged children. *Journal of Educational and Psychological Consultation, 11*, 193–221.

Dorn, F. J. (1986). The road to workshop consultation: Some directions for the new traveler. *American Mental Health Counselors Journal, 8*(2), 53–59.

Douce, L. A. (1993). AIDS and HIV: Hopes and challenges for the 1990's. *Journal for Counseling and Development, 71*, 259–260.

Dougherty, A. M. (1992a). Ethical issues in consultation. *Elementary School Guidance and Counseling, 26*, 214–220.

Dougherty, A. M. (1992b). School consultation in the 1990s. *Elementary School Guidance and Counseling, 26*, 163–164.

Dougherty, A. M. (1996-97, Fall/Winter). The importance of effective communication in consultation. *The Consulting Edge, 4*, 1–2, 4–7.

Dougherty, A. M. (2009). *A casebook of psychological consultation and collaboration: A casebook* (5th ed.). Pacific Grove, CA: Thomson Brooks/Cole.

Dougherty, A. M. (2006a). Managing role conflicts in school counseling. In B. Herlihy and G. Corey (Eds.), *Boundary issues in counseling* (2nd ed., pp. 179–182). Alexandria, VA: American Counseling Association.

Dougherty, A. M. (2006b). Dual role conflicts in consultation. In B. Herlihy and G. Corey, *Boundary issues in counseling* (2nd ed., pp. 91–93). Alexandria, VA: American Counseling Association.

Dougherty, A. M., & Dougherty, L. P. (1991). Using your school counselor as an organizational consultant. *American Middle School Education, 12*(2), 37–44.

Dougherty, A. M., Dougherty, L. P., & Purcell, D. (1991). The sources and management of resistance to consultation. *School Counselor, 38*, 178–186.

Dougherty, A. M., Henderson, B. B., & Lindsey, B. (1997). The effectiveness of direct versus indirect confrontation as a function of stage of consultation: Results of an exploratory investigation. *Journal of Educational and Psychological Consultation, 8,* 361–372.

Dougherty, A. M., Henderson, B. B., Tack, F. E., Deck, M. D, Worley, V., & Page, J. R. (1997). The relation of facilitative conditions, consultant experience, and stage of consultation to consultees' perceptions of the use of direct confrontation. *Journal of Educational and Psychological Consultation, 8,* 21–40.

Dougherty, A. M., Tack, F. E., Fullam, C. B., & Hammer, L. A. (1996). Disengagement: A neglected aspect of the consultation process. *Journal of Educational and Psychological Consultation, 7,* 259–274.

Dougherty, A. M., & Taylor, B. L. B. (1983). Evaluation of peer helper programs. *Elementary School Guidance and Counseling, 18*(2), 130–136.

Downing, J., & Downing, S. (1991). Consultation with resistant parents. *Elementary School Guidance and Counseling, 25,* 296–301.

Downing, J., & Harrison, T. (1991). Parents' tough beat. *The School Counselor, 39,* 91–97.

Drotar, D. (1987). Psychological consultation in medical settings: Challenges and constraints. In J. R. McNamara and M. A. Appel (Eds.), *Critical issues, development, and trends in professional psychology* (Vol. 3, pp. 80–111). New York: Praeger.

Drum, D. J., & Valdese, L. E. (1988). Advocacy and outreach: Applications to college/university settings. In D. J. Kurpius & D. Brown (Eds.), *Handbook of consultation: An intervention for advocacy and outreach* (pp. 38–60). Alexandria, VA: American Association for Counseling and Development.

Duncan, C. F. (1995). Cross-cultural school consultation. In C. C. Lee (Ed.), *Counseling for diversity: A guide for school counselors and related professionals* (pp. 128–141). Boston: Allyn & Bacon.

Duncan, C. F., & Pryzwansky, W. B. (1988). Consultation research: Trends in doctoral dissertations 1978–1985. *Journal of School Psychology, 26,* 107–119.

Duncan, C., & Pryzwansky, W. B. (1993). Effects of race, racial identity development, and orientation style on perceived consultant effectiveness. *Journal of Multicultural Counseling and Development, 21,* 88–96.

Dunson III, R. M., Hughes, J. N., & Jackson, T. W. (1994). Effect of behavioral consultation on student and teacher behavior. *Journal of School Psychology, 32,* 247–266.

Dustin, D. (1993). School consultation in the nineties. *Paper presented at the annual convention of the American Counseling Association,* Atlanta, GA.

Dustin, D., & Ehly, S. (1984). Skills for effective consultation. *School Counselor, 32,* 23–29.

Dustin, D., & Ehly, S. (1992). School consultation in the 1990s. *Elementary School Guidance and Counseling, 26,* 165–175.

Dworkin, A. L., & Dworkin, E. P. (1975). A conceptual overview of selected consultation models. *American Journal of Community Psychology, 3*(2), 151–159.

Dwyer, K. P., & Gorin, S. (1996). A national perspective of school psychology in the context of school reform. *School Psychology Review, 25,* 507–511.

Edens, J. F. (1997). Home visitation programs with ethnic minority families: Cultural issues in parent consultation. *Journal of Educational and Psychological Consultation, 8,* 373–383.

Egan, G. (1985). *Change agent skills in helping and human service settings.* Pacific Grove, CA: Thomson Brooks/Cole.

Egan, G. (2006). *Essentials of skilled helping.* Belmont, CA: Wadsworth Thomson.

Egan, G. (2007). *The skilled helper* (8th ed.). Belmont, CA: Thomson Brooks/Cole.

Egan, G., & Cowan, M. A. (1979). *People in systems: A model for development in the human-service professions and education.* Pacific Grove, CA: Thomson Brooks/Cole.

Ehly, S. (1993). Overview of group interventions for special service providers. *Special Services in the Schools, 18,* 9–38.

Elliott, S. N., & Busse, R. T. (1993). Effective treatments with behavioral consultation. In J. E. Zins, T. R. Kratochwill, & S. N. Elliott (Eds.), *Handbook of consultation services for children* (pp. 179–203). San Francisco: Jossey-Bass.

Elliott, S. N., Busse, R. T., & Shapiro, E. S. (1999). Intervention techniques for academic performance problems. In C. R. Reynolds and T. B. Gutkin (Eds.), *The handbook of school psychology* (3rd ed., pp. 664–685). New York: Wiley.

Erchul, W. P. (1987). A relational communication analysis of control in school consultation. *Professional School Psychology, 2*(2), 113–124.

Erchul, W. P. (1993a). Reflections on mental health consultation: An interview with Gerald Caplan. In W. P. Erchul (Ed.), *Consultation in community, school, and organizational practice* (pp. 57–72). Washington, DC: Taylor & Francis.

Erchul, W. P. (1993b). Selected interpersonal perspectives in consultation research. *School Psychology Quarterly, 8*, 38–49.

Erchul, W. P. (1999). Two steps forward, one step back: Collaboration in school-based consultation. *Journal of School Psychology, 37*, 191–203.

Erchul, W. P., & Chewning, T. G. (1990). Behavioral consultation from a request-centered relational communication perspective. *Professional School Psychology, 5*, 1–20.

Erchul, W. P., & Conoley, C. W. (1991). Helpful theories to guide counselors' practice of school-based consultation. *Elementary School Guidance and Counseling, 25*, 204–211.

Erchul, W. P., DuPaul, G. J., Grissom, P. F., Vile Junod, R. E., Jitendra, A. K., Mannella, M. C. et al. (2007). Relationships among relational communication processes and consultation outcomes for students with attention deficit hyperactivity disorder. *School Psychology Review, 36*, 111–129.

Erchul, W. P., & Martens, B. K. (2002). *School consultation: Conceptual and empirical bases of practice.* New York: Kluwer/Plenum.

Erchul, W. P., & Raven, B. H. (1997). Social power in school consultation: A contemporary view of French and Raven's bases of power model. *Journal of School Psychology, 35*, 137–171.

Erchul, W. P., Raven, B. H., & Ray, A. G. (2001). School psychologists' perceptions of social power bases in teacher consultation. *Journal of Educational and Psychological Consultation, 12*, 1–23.

Erchul, W. P., Raven, B. H., & Whichard, S. M. (2001). School psychologist and teacher perceptions of social power in consultation. *Journal of School Psychology, 39*, 483–497.

Erchul, W. P., & Schulte, A. C. (1993). Gerald Caplan's contributions to professional psychology: Conceptual underpinnings. In W. P. Erchul (Ed.), *Consultation in community, school, and organizational practice* (pp. 3–39). Washington, DC: Taylor & Francis.

Erchul, W. P., & Schulte, A. C. (1996). Behavioral consultation as a work in progress. *Journal of Educational and Psychological Consultation, 7*, 345–354.

Erchul, W. P., & Sheridan, S. M. (Eds.) (2008). *Handbook of research in school consultation: Empirical foundations for the field.* New York: Lawrence Erlbaum Associates/Taylor & Francis Group.

Erchul, W. P., Sheridan, S. M., Ryan, D. A., Grissom, P. F., Killough, C. E., Mettler, D. W. (1999). Patterns of relational communication in conjoint behavioral consultation. *School Psychology Quarterly, 14*, 121–147.

Erhardt, K. E., Barnett, D. W., Lentz, F. E., Jr., Stollar, S. A., & Reifin, L. H. (1996). Innovative methodology in ecological consultation: Use of scripts to promote treatment acceptability and integrity. *School Psychology Quarterly, 11*, 149–168.

Ervin, R. A., & Erhardt, K. E. (2000). Behavior analysis and school psychology. In J. Austin and J. E. Carr (Eds.), *Handbook of Applied Behavioral Analysis* (pp. 113–131). Reno, NV: Context Press.

Esler, A. N., Godber, Y., & Christenson, S. L. (2002). Best practices in supporting home-school collaboration. In A. Thomas and J. Grimes (Eds.), *Best practices in school psychology* (4th ed., pp. 389–411). Bethesda, MD: National Association of School Psychologists.

Fagan, T. K. (1995). Trends in the history of school psychology in the United States. In A. Thomas and J. Grimes (Eds.), *Best practices in school psychology* (3rd ed., pp. 59–67). Washington, DC: National Association of School Psychologists.

Fall, M. (1995). Planning for consultation: An aid for the elementary school counselor. *The School Counselor, 43*, 151–156.

Fanibanda, D. K. (1976). Ethical issues of mental health consultation. *Professional Psychology, 7*, 547–552.

Farmer, T. W. (2000). The social dynamics of aggressive and disruptive behavior in school: Implications for behavior consultation. *Journal of Educational and Psychological Consultation, 11*(3&4), 299–321.

Faust, V. (1968). *The counselor-consultant in the elementary school.* Boston: Houghton Mifflin.

Feld, J. K., Bergan, J. R., & Stone, C. A. (1987). Behavioral consultation. In C. A. Maher &

S. G. Forman (Eds.), *A behavioral approach to education of children and youth* (pp. 183–219). Hillsdale, NJ: Erlbaum.

Ferguson, E. D. (2006). Work relations that enhance the well-being of organizations and individuals. *Journal of Individual Psychology, 62,* 80–84.

Fine, N., & Kontos, S. (1992). Indirect service delivery through consultation: Review and implications for early intervention. *Journal of Early Intervention, 16,* 221–233.

Finn, C. A., & Sladeczek, I. E. (2001). Assessing the social validity of behavioral interventions: A review of treatment acceptability measures. *School Psychology Quarterly, 16,* 176–206.

Fisher, R., & Brown, S. (1988). *Getting together.* New York: Penguin.

Fisher, R., Ury, W., & Patton, B. (1991). *Getting to yes: Negotiating without giving in* (2nd ed.). New York: Penguin.

Flanagan, D. P., & Miranda, A. H. (1995). Best practices in working with culturally different families. In A. Thomas and J. Grimes (Eds.), *Best practices in school psychology* (3rd ed., pp. 1049–1060). Washington, DC: National Association of School Psychologists.

Flanagan, D. P., & Ortiz, S. O. (2002). Best practices in intellectual assessment: Future directions. In A. Thomas and J. Grimes (Eds.), *Best practices in school psychology* (4th ed., pp. 1351–1372). Washington, DC: National Association of School Psychologists.

Flanagan, S. G., Cray, M. E., & Meter, D. V. (1983). A facility-wide consultation and training team as a catalyst in promoting institutional change. *Analysis and Intervention in Developmental Disabilities, 3,* 151–169.

Flaspohler, P. D. (2007). Making a difference in research and practice: A commentary on "Consulting to facilitate planned organizational change in schools," an article by Joseph E. Zins and Robert J. Illback. *Journal of Educational and Psychological Consultation, 17,* 125–132.

Ford, C. H. (1979). Developing a successful client-consultant relationship. In C. R. Bell & L. Nadler (Eds.), *The client-consultant handbook* (pp. 8–21). Houston: Gulf Publishing.

Fordyce, J. K., & Weil, R. (1971). *Managing with people.* Reading, MA: Addison-Wesley.

Fordyce, J. K., & Weil, R. (1978). Methods for finding out what is going on. In W. L. French, C. H. Bell, Jr., & R. A. Zawacki (Eds.), *Organization development: Theory, practice, and research* (pp. 121–129). Dallas, TX: Business Publications.

Forman, S. G. (1984). Behavioral and cognitive-behavioral approaches to staff development. In C. A. Maher, R. J. Illback, and J. E. Zins (Eds.), *Organizational psychology in the schools: A handbook for professionals* (pp. 302–322). Springfield, IL: Charles C. Thomas.

Forman, S. G. (1995). Organizational factors and consultation outcome. *Journal of Educational and Psychological Consultation, 6,* 191–195.

Foster, S. L., & Lloyd, P. J. (2007). Positive psychology principles applied to consulting psychology at the individual and group level. *Consulting Psychology Journal, 59,* 30–40.

Freer, P., & Watson, T. S. (1999). A comparison of parent and teacher acceptability ratings of behavioral and conjoint behavioral consultation. *School Psychology Review, 28,* 672–684.

French, J. L. (1990). History of school psychology. In T. B. Gutkin and C. R. Reynolds (Eds.), *The handbook of school psychology* (2nd ed., pp. 3–20). New York: Wiley.

French, J. R. P., Jr., & Raven, B. H. (1959). The bases of social power. In D. Cartwright (Ed.), *Studies in social power* (pp. 150–167). Ann Arbor, MI: Institute for Social Research.

French, W. L. (1972). Organizational development: Objectives, assumptions and strategies. In N. Margulies & A. P. Raia (Eds.), *Organizational development values, process, and technology* (pp. 31–49). New York: McGraw-Hill.

French, W. L., & Bell, C. H., Jr. (1999). *Organization development: Behavioral science interventions for organization improvement* (6th ed.). Englewood Cliffs, NJ: Prentice-Hall.

French, W. L., Bell, C. H., Jr., & Zawacki, R. A. (Eds.) (1978). *Organization development: Theory, practice, and research.* Dallas: Business Publications.

Friedlander, E., & Brown, L. D. (1974). Organization development. In M. R. Rosenzweig & L. W. Porter (Eds.), *Annual Review of Psychology, 25* (pp. 219–340). Palo Alto, CA: Annual Reviews.

Friend, M., & Cook, L. (1996). *Interactions: Collaboration skills for school professionals* (2nd ed.). New York: Longman.

Friend, M., & Cook, L. (1997). Student-centered teams in schools: Still in search of an identity. *Journal of Educational and Psychological Consultation, 8,* 3–20.

Frisby, C. L. (2006). Ethnic and racial diversity. In G. G. Bear and K. M. Minke (Eds.). *Children's needs III: Development, prevention, and intervention* (pp. 567–578). Bethesda, MD: National Association of School Psychologists.

Froehle, T. C., & Rominger, R. L., III. (1993). Directions in consultation research: Bridging the gap between science and practice. *Journal of Counseling and Development, 71,* 693–699.

Fuchs, D., & Fuchs, L. S. (1989). Exploring effective and efficient prereferral interventions: A component analysis of behavioral consultation. *School Psychology Review, 8*(2), 260–283.

Fuchs, D., Fuchs, L. S., Dulan, J., Roberts, H., & Fernstrom, P. (1992). Where is the research on consultation effectiveness? *Journal of Educational and Psychological Consultation, 3,* 151–174.

Fullmer, D. W., & Bernard, H. W. (1972). *The school counselor consultant.* Boston: Houghton Mifflin.

Fuqua, D. R., & Kurpius, D. J. (1993). Conceptual models in organizational consultation. *Journal of Counseling and Development, 71,* 607–618.

Fuqua, D. R., & Newman, J. L. (1983). Models, principles, and methods of data utilization in organizational consultation. *Paper presented at the American Personnel and Guidance Association Annual Convention,* Washington, DC.

Fuqua, D. R., & Newman, J. L. (1985). Individual consultation. *Counseling Psychologist, 13*(3), 390–395.

Fuqua, D. R., & Newman, J. L. (2006). Moral and ethical issues in human systems. *Consulting Psychology Journal: Practice and Research, 58,* 206–215.

Fuqua, D. R., Newman, J. L., & Dickman, M. M. (1999). Barriers to effective assessment in organizational consultation. *Consulting Psychology Journal, Practice and Research, 51,* 14–23.

Gabbard, C., & Halischak, K. (1993). Consulting opportunities: Working with student-athletes at a university. *Counseling Psychologist, 21,* 386–398.

Gallessich, J. (1982). *The profession and practice of consultation.* San Francisco: Jossey-Bass.

Gallessich, J. (1985). Toward a meta-theory of consultation. *Counseling Psychologist, 13*(3), 336–354.

Gallessich, J., Long, K. M., & Jennings, S. (1986). Training of mental health consultants. In F. V. Mannino, E. J. Trickett, M. E. Shore, M. G. Kidder, & G. Levin (Eds.), *Handbook of mental health consultation* (pp. 279–317). Rockville, MD: National Institute of Mental Health.

Gallup, J. (1998). How to gain access to a company as a consultant. In S. Klarreich (Ed.), *Handbook of Organizational Health Psychology* (pp. 43–54). Madison, CT: Psychological Press.

Garland, F. N. (1993). Combat stress control in the postwar theater: Mental health consultation during redeployment phase of Operation Desert Storm. *Military Medicine, 158,* 334–337.

Garmston, R. J., & Wellman, B. M. (1992). *How to make presentations that teach and transform.* Alexandria, VA: Association for Supervision and Curriculum Development.

Garrett, J. N. (1998). Local interagency coordinating council personality: A factor in consultation. *Journal of Educational and Psychological Consultation, 9,* 261–266.

Gemmill, G., & Costello, M. (1990). Group mirroring as a means for exploring the group shadow: A perspective for organizational consultation. *Consultation, 9,* 277–291.

Gemmill, G., & Wynkoop, C. (1990). The psychodynamics of the client–consultant nexus in organizational process consulting. *Consultation, 9,* 129–140.

Gerler, E. R., Jr. (1992). Consultation and school counseling. *Elementary School Guidance and Counseling, 26,* 162.

Gerler, E. R., Jr., & Myrick, R. D. (1991). The elementary school counselor's work with prekindergarten children: Implications for counselor education programs. *Elementary School Guidance and Counseling, 26,* 67–75.

Geroski, A. M., Rodgers, K. A., & Breen, D. T. (1997). Using the *DSM-IV* to enhance collaboration among school counselors, clinical counselors, and primary care physicians. *Journal of Counseling & Development, 75,* 231–239.

Gerstein, L. H. (2007). Counseling psychology's commitment to strengths: Rhetoric or reality? *The Counseling Psychologist, 34,* 276–292.

Gibbons, K. A., & Shinn, M. M. (2002). Best practices in evaluating psychoeducational services based on student outcome data. In A. Thomas and J. Grimes (Eds.), *Best practices in school psychology* (4th ed., pp. 159–172). Bethesda, MD: National Association of School Psychologists.

Gibbs, J. T. (1980). The interpersonal orientation in mental health consultation: Toward a model of ethnic variations in consultation. *Journal of Community Psychology, 8*, 195–207.

Gibbs, L. E. (2003). *Evidence-based practice for the helping professions: A practical guide with integrated multimedia.* Pacific Grove, CA: Thomson Learning.

Gibson, G. (1988). Consultation as advocacy and outreach in community mental health settings: Theory to practice. In D. J. Kurpius & D. Brown (Eds.), *Handbook of consultation: An intervention for advocacy and outreach* (pp. 27–37). Alexandria, VA: American Association for Counseling and Development.

Gibson, G., & Chard, K. M. (1994). Quantifying the effects of community mental health consultation interventions. *Consulting Psychology Journal, 46*, 13–25.

Gilmore, T. N. (1993). Issues in ending consultancies. In R. T. Golembiewski (Ed.), *Handbook of organizational consultation* (pp. 253–261). New York: Marcel.

Ginter, E. J., Scalise, J. J., & Presse, N. (1990). The elementary school counselor's role: Perceptions of teachers. *School Counselor, 38*, 19–23.

Glaser, E. M. (1981). Ethical issues in consultation practice with organizations. *Consultation, 1*(1), 12–16.

Glidewell, J. C. (1959). The entry problem in consultation. *Journal of Social Issues, 15*(2), 51–59.

Gmeinder, K. L., & Kratochwill, T. R. (1998). Short-term, home-based intervention for child noncompliance using behavioral consultation and a self-help manual. *Journal of Educational and Psychological Consultation, 9*, 91–117.

Goldstein, B. S. C. (1998). Creating a context for collaborative consultation: Working across bicultural communities. *Journal of Educational and Psychological Consultation, 9*, 367–374.

Goldstein, B. S. C., & Harris, K. C. (2000). Consultant practices in two heterogeneous Latino schools. *School Psychology Review, 29*, 368–377.

Goldstein, L., & Gilliam, P. (1990). Training system issues in the year 2000. *American Psychologist, 45*(2), 134–143.

Golembiewski, R. T. (1969). Organization development in public agencies: Perspectives in theory and practice. *Public Administration Review, 29*, 367–377.

Golembiewski, R. T. (1993a). Features of energizing data. In R. T. Golembiewski (Ed.), *Handbook of organizational consultation* (pp. 323–325). New York: Marcel Dekker, Inc.

Golembiewski, R. T. (1993b). Role analysis technique. In R. T. Golembiewski (Ed.), *Handbook of organizational consultation* (pp. 357–358). New York: Marcel Dekker, Inc.

Golembiewski, R. T. (1993c). Stakeholders in consultation. In R. T. Golembiewski (Ed.), *Handbook of organizational consultation* (pp. 367–371). New York: Marcel Dekker, Inc.

Golembiewski, R. T. (1993d). Third-party consultation. In R. T. Golembiewski (Ed.), *Handbook of organizational consultation* (pp. 393–398). New York: Marcel Dekker, Inc.

Golembiewski, R. T. (1993e). Toward a process orientation. In R. T. Golembiewski (Ed.), *Handbook of organizational consultation* (pp. 383–386). New York: Marcel Dekker, Inc.

Golembiewski, R. T., & Rauschenberg, F. (1993). Third-party consultation: Basic features and one misapplication. In R. T. Golembiewski (Ed.), *Handbook of organizational consultation* (pp. 393–398). New York: Marcel Dekker, Inc.

Golembiewski, R. T., & Sun, B. (1989). Consulting is definitely worth the cost: Success rates in OD and QWL Consultation. *Consultation, 8*, 203–208.

Gongora, J. N. (2004). Using consultee-centered consultation in a network intervention with health providers. In N. M. Lambert, I. Hylander & J. H. Sandoval (Eds.), *Consultee-centered consultation: Improving the quality of professional services in schools and community organizations* (pp. 171–185). Mahwah, NJ: Erlbaum.

Good, T. L., Wiley, A. R., Thomas, R. E., Stewart, E., McCoy, J., Kloos, B., Hunt, G. D., Moore, T., & Rappaport, J. (1997). Bridging the gap between schools and community: Organizing for family involvement in a low-income neighborhood. *Journal of Educational and Psychological Consultation, 8*, 277–296.

Goode, W. J., & Hatt, P. K. (1972). The collection of data by questionnaire. In N. Margulies & A. P. Raia (Eds.), *Organizational development: Values, process, and technology* (pp. 163–185). New York: McGraw-Hill.

Goodstein, L. D. (1978). *Consulting with human service systems*. Reading, MA: Addison Wesley.

Goodstein, L. D. (1985). Through a glass darkly: A commentary on Backer's "The future of organizational consulting." *Consultation, 4*(1), 30–33.

Gordon, T. (1970). *Parent effectiveness training*. New York: Wyden.

Gottlieb, B. H. (1974). Re-examining the preventive potential of mental health consultation. *Canada's Mental Health, 22*, 4–6.

Gottlieb, B. H. (1983). Opportunities for collaboration with informal support systems. In S. Cooper and W. F. Hodges (Eds.), *The mental health consultation field* (pp. 181–203). New York: Human Sciences Press.

Gottlieb, M. C. (2006). A template for peer ethics consultation. *Ethics & Behavior, 16*, 151–162.

Graden, J. L. (1989). Reactions to school consultation: Some considerations from a problem-solving perspective. *Professional School Psychology, 4*, 29–35.

Graden, J. L. (2004). Arguments for change to consultation, prevention, and intervention: Will school psychology ever achieve this promise? *Journal of Educational and Psychological Consultation, 5*, 345–359.

Granda, K. (1992). Consultant personal and working framework and its impact on member-authority relations in small groups. Unpublished doctoral dissertation, Northwestern University. *Dissertation Abstracts International, 53*(11), May 1993.

Gravois, T. A., & Gickling, E. E. (2002). Best practices in curriculum-based assessment. In A. Thomas & J. Grimes (Eds.), *Best practices in school psychology* (4th ed., pp. 885–898). Bethesda, MD: National Association of School Psychologists.

Gravois, T. A., Knotek, S., & Babinski, L. M. (2002). Educating practitioners as consultants: Development and implementation of the instructional consultation team consortium. *Journal of Educational and Psychological Consultation, 13*(1&2), 113–132.

Gravois, T. A., & Rosenfield, S. A. (2006). Impact of instructional consultation teams on the disproportionate referral and placement of minority students in special education. *Remedial and Special Education, 27*, 42–52.

Gray, C. L., Gutkin, T. B., & Riley, T. R. (2001). Acceptability of rewards among high school

teachers, parents, students, and administrators: Ecological implications for consultation at the high school level. *Journal of Educational and Psychological Consultation, 12*, 25–43.

Greenberg, M. T., Weissberg, R. P., O'Brien, M. U., Zins, J. E., Fredericks, L., Resnik, H., & Elias, M. J. (2003). Enhancing school-based prevention and youth development through coordinated social, emotional, and academic learning. *American Psychologist, 58*, 466–474.

Gregory, B. T., Armenakis, A. A., Moates, K. N., Albritton, M. D., & Harris, S. G. (2007). Achieving scientific rigor in organizational diagnosis: An application of the diagnostic funnel. *Consulting Psychology Journal: Practice and Research, 59*, 79–90.

Greiger, R. (2007a). Introduction to special issue. *Journal of Rational-Emotive & Cognitive-Behavior Therapy, 25*, 77–85.

Greiger, R. (2007b). One REBTERS model for business consulting. *Journal of Rational-Emotive & Cognitive-Behavior Therapy, 25*, 107–120.

Greiner, L. E. (1967). Patterns of organizational change. *Harvard Business Review*, (May/June), 119–130.

Greiner, L. E., & Metzger, R. O. (1983). *Consulting to management: Insights to building and managing a successful practice*. Englewood Cliffs, NJ: Prentice-Hall.

Gresham, F. M. (2006). Response to intervention. In G. G. Bear and K. M. Minke (Eds.). *Children's needs III: Development, prevention, and intervention* (pp. 525–540). Bethesda, MD: National Association of School Psychologists.

Gresham, F. M., & Kendall, G. K. (1987). School consultation research: Methodological critique and future research directions. *School Psychology Review, 16*, 303–316.

Gresham, F. M., & Lemanek, K. L. (1987). Parent education. In C. A. Maher and S. G. Forman (Eds.), *A behavioral approach to education of children and youth* (pp. 153–181). Hillsdale, NJ: Erlbaum.

Gresham, F. M., & Lopez, M. F. (1996). Social validation: A unifying concept for school-based consultation research and practice. *School Psychology Quarterly, 11*, 204–227.

Gresham, F. M., & Noell, G. H. (1993). Documenting the effectiveness of consultation outcomes. In J. E. Zins, T. R. Kratochwill, & S. N. Elliott (Eds.),

*Handbook of consultation services for children* (pp. 249–273). San Francisco: Jossey-Bass.

Gresham, F. M., Watson, T. S., Skinner, C. H. (2001). Functional behavioral assessment: Principles, procedures, and future directions. *School Psychology Review, 30,* 156–172.

Grigsby, R. K. (1992). Mental health consultation at a youth shelter: An ethnographic approach. *Child and Youth Care Forum, 21,* 247–261.

Grissom, P. F., Erchul, W. P., & Sheridan, S. M. (2003). Relationships among relational communication processes and perceptions of outcomes in conjoint behavioral consultation. *Journal of Educational and Psychological Consultation, 4,* 157–180.

Guishard, M., Fine, M., Doyle, C., Jackson, J., Staten, T., & Webb, A. (2005). The Bronx on the move: Participatory consultation with mothers and youth. *Journal of Psychological and Educational Consultation, 16,* 35–54.

Guli, L. A. (2005). Evidence-based parent consultation with school-related outcomes. *School Psychology Quarterly, 20,* 455–472.

Gutkin, T. (1993). Conducting consultation research. In J. E. Zins, T. R. Kratochwill, & S. N. Elliott (Eds.), *Handbook of consultation services for children* (pp. 227–248). San Francisco: Jossey-Bass.

Gutkin, T. B. (1996). Patterns of consultant and consultee verbalizations: Examining communication leadership during initial consultation interviews. *Journal of School Psychology, 34*(3), 199–219.

Gutkin, T. B. (1997). An introduction to the mini-series: The social psychology of interpersonal influence with adults. *Journal of School Psychology, 35,* 105–106.

Gutkin, T. B. (1999a). Collaborative versus directive/prescriptive/expert school-based consultation: Reviewing and resolving a false dichotomy. *Journal of School Psychology, 37,* 161–190.

Gutkin, T. B. (1999b). The collaboration debate: Finding our way through the maze: Moving forward into the future: A response to Erchul (1999). *Journal of School Psychology, 37,* 229–241.

Gutkin, T. B. (2002). Training school-based consultants: Some thoughts on grains of sands and building anthills. *Journal of Educational and Psychological Consultation, 13*(1&2), 133–146.

Gutkin, T. B., & Curtis, M. J. (1999). School-based consultation theory and practice: The art and

science of indirect service delivery. In C. R. Reynolds & T. B. Gutkin (Eds.). *The handbook of school psychology* (3rd ed., pp. 598–637). New York: Wiley.

Hagedorn, H. J., Beck, K. J., Nuebert, S. F., & Werlin, S. H. (1976). *Working manual of simple program evaluation techniques for community mental health centers.* Rockville, MD: Arthur D. Little, for the National Institute of Mental Health.

Hall, A. S., & Mei-Ju, L. (1994). An integrative consultation framework: A practical tool for elementary school counselors. *Elementary School Guidance & Counseling, 29,* 16–27.

Hall, L. E. (2005). *Dictionary of multicultural psychology: Issues, terms, and concepts.* Thousand Oaks, CA: Sage.

Halpern, J., & Tramontin, M. (2007). *Disaster mental health: Theory and practice.* Pacific Grove, CA: Thomson Brooks/Cole.

Hanko, G. (1987). Group consultation with mainstream teachers. *Educational and Child Psychology, 4*(3–4), 123–130.

Hansen, J. C., Himes, B. S., & Meier, S. (1990). *Consultation: Concepts and practices.* Englewood Cliffs, NJ: Prentice-Hall.

Hanson, W. E., Creswell, J. W., Plano Clark, V. L., Petska, K. S., Creswell, J. D. (2005). Mixed methods research designs in counseling psychology. *Journal of Counseling Psychology, 52,* 224–235.

Hardesty, P. H., & Dillard, J. M. (1994). The role of elementary school counselors compared with their middle and secondary school counterparts. *Elementary School Guidance & Counseling, 29,* 83–91.

Harris, K. C. (1991). An expanded view on consultation competencies for educators serving culturally and linguistically diverse exceptional students. *Teacher Education and Special Education, 14*(1), 25–29.

Harris, K. C., & Klein, M. D. (2004). An emergent discussion of itinerant consultation in early childhood special education. *Journal of Educational and Psychological Consultation, 15,* 123–126.

Harrison, M. I., & Shirom, A. (1999). *Frames and models in organizational diagnosis.* Thousand Oaks, CA: Sage.

Harrison, T. C. (2004). *Consultation for the Helping Professions.* Boston: Pearson.

Haverkamp, B. E, Morrow, S. L., & Ponterotto, J. G. (2005). A time and place for qualitative and mixed methods in counseling psychology research. *Journal of Counseling Psychology, 52,* 123–125.

Hawryluk, M. K., & Smallwood, D. L. (1986). Assessing and addressing consultee variables in school-based behavioral consultation. *School Psychology Review, 15*(4), 519–528.

Hayes, J., & Prakasam, R. (1989). Culture: The efficacy of different modes of consultation. *Leadership and Organization Development Journal, 10*(1), 24–32.

Haynes, R., Corey, G., & Moulton, P. (2003). *Clinical supervision in the helping professions.* Pacific Grove, CA: Thomson Brooks/Cole.

Hays, P. A. (1996). Addressing the complexities of culture and gender in counseling. *Journal of Counseling and Development, 74,* 332–338.

Hays, P. A. (2001). *Addressing cultural complexities in practice.* Washington, DC: American Psychological Association.

Hazel, C. E. (2007). Timeless and timely advice: A commentary on "Consultation to facilitate planned organizational change in schools," an article by Joseph E. Zins and Robert J. Illback. *Journal of Educational and Psychological Consultation, 17,*125–132.

Heller, K., & Monahan, J. (1983). Individual-process consultation. In S. Cooper and W. F. Hodges(Eds.), *The mental health consultation field* (pp. 19–25). New York: Human Sciences Press.

Hellkamp, D. T. (1996). A multidisciplinary collaborative management and consulting model: The inner workings and future challenges. *Journal of Educational and Psychological Consultation, 7,* 79–85.

Henning-Stout, M. (1993). Theoretical and empirical bases of consultation. In J. E. Zins, T. R. Kratochwill, and S. N. Elliott (Eds.), *Handbook of consultation services for children* (pp. 15–45). San Francisco: Jossey-Bass.

Henning-Stout, M. (1994). Consultation and connected knowing: What we know is determined by the questions we ask. *Journal of Educational and Psychological Consultation, 5,* 5–21.

Henning-Stout, M., & Brown-Cheatham, M. B. (1999). School psychology in a diverse world: Considerations for practice, research, and training. In C. R. Reynolds and T. B. Gutkin (Eds.), *The handbook of school psychology.* (3rd ed., pp. 1041–1055). New York: Wiley.

Henning-Stout, M., & Conoley, J. C. (1987). Consultation and counseling as procedurally diver-gent: Analysis of verbal behavior. *Professional Psychology: Research and Practice, 18,* 124–127.

Heppner, P. P., Kivlighan, D. M., Jr., & Wampold, B. E. (1999). *Research design in counseling* (2nd ed.). Pacific Grove, CA: Thomson Brooks/Cole.

Herlihy, B., & Corey, G. (2006). *Boundary issues in counseling* (2nd ed.). Alexandria, VA: American Counseling Association.

Herr, P. (2000). Downsizing and the accidental consultant. In E. B. Klein, F. Gabelnicky, & P. Iterr. *Dynamic consultation in a changing workplace* (pp. 211–231). Madison, CN: Psychological Press.

Hershenson, D. B., & Power, P. W. (1987). *Mental health counseling: Theory and practice.* New York: Pergamon Press.

Heyel, C. (Ed.) (1973). *Encyclopedia of management* (2nd ed.). New York: Van Nostrand Reinhold.

Hintze, J. M., Volpe, R. J., Shapiro, E. S. (2002). Best practices in the systematic direct observation of student behavior. In A. Thomas and J. Grimes (Eds.), *Best practices in school psychology* (4th ed., pp. 993–1006). Bethesda, MD: National Association of School Psychologists.

Hoard, D., Shepard, K. N. (2005). Parent education as parent-centered prevention: A review of school-related outcomes. *School Psychology Quarterly, 20,* 434–454.

Hobbs, B. B., & Collison, B. B. (1995). School-community agency collaboration: Implications for the school counselor. *The School Counselor, 43,* 58–65.

Hodges, S., Hernandez, M., & Nesman, T. (2003). A developmental framework for collaboration in child-serving agencies. *Journal of Child and Family Studies, 12,* 291–305.

Hodges, W. F., & Cooper, S. (1983). General introduction. In S. Cooper & W. E. Hodges (Eds.), *The mental health consultation field* (pp. 19–25). New York: Human Sciences Press.

Hogan, M. (2007). *Four skills of cultural diversity competence* (3rd ed.). Belmont, CA: Wadsworth.

Hohenshil, T. H. (1996). Editorial: Role of assessment and diagnosis in counseling. *Journal of Counseling and Development, 75,* 64–67.

Hohenshil, T. H., & Brown, M. B. (1991). Public school counseling services for prekindergarten children. *Elementary School Guidance and Counseling, 26,* 4–11.

Hoffman, M. A., Phillips, E. L., Noumair, D. A., Shullman, S., Gray, J., Homer, J. et al. (2006). Toward a feminist and multicultural model of consultation and advocacy. *Journal of Multicultural Counseling and Development, 34*, 116–128.

Hogan, M. (2007). *Four skills of cultural diversity competence: A process for understanding practice* (3rd ed.). Belmont, CA: Wadsworth–Thomson.

Hojnoski, R. L. (2007). Promising directions in school-based systems level consultation: A commentary on "Has consultation achieved its potential?," an article by Joseph E. Zins. *Journal of Educational and Psychological Consultation, 17*, 157–163.

Hojnoski, R. L., & Missal, K. N. (2006). Addressing school readiness: Expanding school psychology in early education. *School Psychology Review, 35*, 602–614.

Holcomb-McCoy, C. Assessing the multicultural competence of school counselors: A checklist. *Professional School Counseling, 7*, 178–186.

Holtz, H., & Zahn, D. (2004). *How to succeed as an independent consultant* (4th ed.). Hoboken, NJ: Wiley.

Hopko, D. R., & Hopko, S. D. (2003). Employee assistance programs: Opportunities for behavior therapists. *Behavior Therapist, 26*, 310–304.

Horton, D. (2005). Consultation with military children and schools: A proposed model. *Consulting Psychology Journal, 57*, 259–265.

Hosie, T. W. (1994). Program evaluation: A potential area of expertise for counselors. *Counselor Education and Supervision, 33*, 349–362.

Houk, J. L., & Lewandowski, L. J. (1996). Consultant verbal control and consultee perceptions. *Journal of Educational and Psychological Consultation, 7*, 107–118.

House, R. M., & Walker, C. M. (1993). Preventing AIDS through education. *Journal of Counseling and Development, 71*, 282–289.

Huckabay, M. A. (2002). The issue of dependency in organizational consultation: A response to Arvum Weiss's article. *Gestalt Review, 1*, 18–25.

Hughes, J. (1980). Organizational issues consultants need to bear in mind. *School Psychology Review, 9*, 103–107.

Hughes, J. (1983). The application of cognitive dissonance theory to consultation. *Journal of School Psychology, 21*, 349–357

Hughes, J. N. (1986). Ethical issues in school consultation. *School Psychology Review, 15*(4), 489–499.

Hughes, J. N. (2000). The essential role of theory in the science of treating children: Beyond empirically supported treatments. *Journal of School Psychology, 38*, 301–330.

Hughes, J. N., Barker, D., Kemenoff, S., & Hart, M. (1993). Problem ownership, casual attributions, and self-efficacy as predictors of teachers' referral decisions. *Journal of Educational and Psychological Consultation, 4*(4), 369–384.

Hughes, J. N., & DeForest, P. A. (1993). Consultant directiveness and support as predictors of consultation outcomes. *Journal of School Psychology, 31*, 355–373.

Hughes, J. N., & Falk, R. S. (1981). Resistance, reactance, and consultation. *Journal of School Psychology, 19*, 134–141.

Hughes, J. N., Grossman, P., & Barker, D. (1990). Teachers' expectancies, participation in consultation, and perceptions of consultant helpfulness. *School Psychology Quarterly, 5*, 167–179.

Hughes, J. N, Hasbrouck, J. E., Serdahl, E., Heidgerken, A., & McHaney, L. (2001). Responsive systems consultation: A preliminary evaluation of implementation and outcomes. *Journal of Educational and Psychological Consultation, 12*(3), 179–201.

Huse, E. E. (1978). Organization development. *Personnel and Guidance Journal, 56*(7), 403–406.

Huse, E. R. (1975). *Organization development and change.* St. Paul, MN: West.

Hyatt, S. P., & Tingstrom, D. H. (1993). Consultant's use of jargon during intervention presentation: An evaluation of presentation modality and type of intervention. *School Psychology Quarterly, 8*, 99–109.

Hylander, I. (2003). Toward a grounded theory of the conceptual change process in consultee-centered consultation. *Journal of Educational and Psychological Consultation, 4*, 263–280.

Hyman, A. (1993). A model for psychological consultation with retarded adults living in community residences. *Journal of Developmental and Physical Disabilities, 5*, 369–376.

Idol, L. (1998). Collaboration in the schools: A master plan for staff development. *Journal of Educational and Psychological Consultation, 9*, 155–163.

Idol, L., & Baran, S. (1992). Elementary school counselors and special educators consulting together: Perilous pitfalls or opportunities to collaborate? *Elementary School Guidance and Counseling, 26,* 202–213.

Ikeda, M. J., Tilly, W. D., Stumme, J., Volmer, L., & Allison, R. (1996). Agency-wide implementation of problem solving consultation: Foundations, current implementation, and future directions. *School Psychology Quarterly, 11,* 228–243.

Illback, R. J., & Zins, J. E. (1993). Organizational perspectives in child consultation. In J. E. Zins, T. R. Kratochwill, & S. N. Elliott (Eds.). *Handbook for consultation services for children* (pp. 87–109). San Francisco: Jossey-Bass.

Illback, R. J., Zins, J. E., Maher, C. A. (1999). Program planning and evaluation: Principles, procedures, and planned change. In C. R. Reynolds and T. B. Gutkin (Eds.), *The handbook of school psychology* (3rd ed., pp. 907–932). New York: Wiley.

*Individuals with Disabilities Education Act (IDEA) Public Law* 105–17, (1997). Washington, DC: U.S. Government Printing Office.

*Individuals with Disabilities Education Improvement Act of 2004. Public Law* 108–446. (2004). Washington, DC: U.S. Government Printing Office.

Ingraham, C. L. (2000). Consultation through a multicultural lens: Multicultural and cross-cultural consultation in schools. *School Psychology Review, 29,* 320–343.

Ingraham, C. L. (2003). Multicultural consultee-centered consultation: When novice consultants explore cultural hypotheses with experienced teacher consultants. *Journal of Educational and Psychological Consultation, 4,* 329–362.

Ingraham, C. L. (2004). Multicultural consultee-centered consultation: Supporting consultees in the development of cultural competence. In N. M. Lambert, I. Hylander & J. H. Sandoval (Eds.), *Consultee-centered consultation: Improving the quality of professional services in schools and community organizations* (pp. 133–170). Mahwah, NJ: Erlbaum.

Ingraham, C. L., & Meyers, J. (2000a). Annotated bibliography for the mini-series on multicultural and crosscultural consultation in schools. *School Psychology Review, 29,* 426–428.

Ingraham, C. L., & Meyers, J. (2000b). Introduction to multicultural and cross-cultural consultation in schools: Cultural diversity issues in school consultation. *School Psychology Review, 29,* 315–319.

International Society for Mental Health Online (2000). Suggested principles for the online provision of mental health principles. Retrieved February 3, 2007, from http://www.ismho.org/suggestions.html.

Iscoe, I. (1993). Gerald Caplan's conceptual and qualitative contributions to community psychology: Views from an old timer. In W. P. Erchul (Ed.), *Consultation in community, school, and organizational practice* (pp. 87–98). Washington, DC: Taylor & Francis.

Isgar, T., & Isgar, S. (1993). High-performing teams. In R. T. Golembiewski (Ed.), *Handbook of organizational consultation* (pp. 417–418). New York: Marcel Dekker.

Ivancevich, A. L., Szilagyi, D., Jr., & Wallace, M. C., Jr. (1977). *Organizational behavior and performance.* Santa Monica, CA: Scott, Foresman.

Ivancevich, J. M., Matteson, M. T., Freedman, S. M., & Phillips, J. S. (1990). Worksite stress management interventions. *American Psychologist, 45*(2), 252–261.

Iverson, A. M. (2002). Best practices in problem-solving team structure and process. In A. Thomas and J. Grimes (Eds.), *Best practices in school psychology* (4th ed., pp 657–669). Bethesda, MD: National Association of School Psychologists.

Ivey, A. E., Ivey, M. B., & Simek-Morgan, L. (1993). *Counseling and psychotherapy: A multicultural perspective* (3rd ed.). Boston: Allyn & Bacon.

Jackson, D. N., & Hayes, D. H. (1993). Multicultural issues in consultation. *Journal of Counseling and Development, 72*(2), 144–147.

Jacob, S. (2002). Best practices in utilizing professional ethics. In A. Thomas and J. Grimes (Eds.), *Best practices in school psychology* (4th ed., pp. 77–87). Bethesda, MD: National Association of School Psychologists.

Jacob, S., & Hartshorne, T. S. (2003). *Ethics and law for school psychologists* (4th ed.). Hoboken, NJ: John Wiley & Sons.

James, R. K., & Dougherty, A. M. (1985). Doing your own dog and pony show: A guide for the perplexed school counselor. *School Counselor, 20,* 11–18.

Janis, I. L., & Mann, L. (1977). *Decision making: A psychological analysis of conflict, choice, and commitment.* New York: Free Press.

Jason, L. A., Pokorny, S. B., Ji, P., & Kunz, C. (2005). Developing community-school-university partnerships to control youth access to tobacco. *Journal of Educational and Psychological Consultation, 16*, 201–222.

Jeger, A. M., & McClure, G. (1982). An experiential evaluation and process analysis of a behavioral consultation program. In A. M. Jeger and R. S. Slotnick (Eds.), *Community mental health and behavioral-ecology: A handbook of theory, research, and practice* (pp. 389–401). New York: Plenum.

Jeger, A. M., & Slotnick, R. S. (Eds.) (1982). *Community mental health and behavioral ecology: A handbook of theory, research, and practice.* New York: Plenum.

Jehl, J. D. (1999). Comprehensive services for children and families: The federal role. *Journal of Educational and Psychological Consultation, 10*, 281–296.

Jellinek, M. S. (1990). School consultation: Evolving issues. *Journal of American Academy of Child and Adolescent Psychiatry, 29*, 311–314.

Jeltova, I., & Fish, M. C. (2005). Creating school environments responsive to gay, lesbian, bisexual, and transgender families: Traditional and systemic approaches for consultation. *Journal of Educational and Psychological Consultation, 6*, 17–33.

Jennings, K. R. (1988). Testing a model of quality circle processes: Implications for practice and consultation, *Consultation, 7*(1), 19–28.

Jenster, P. V., & Bigler, W. R. (1989). Analyzing the strategy-culture linkage: A procedural guide for consultants. *Consultation, 8*, 25–40.

Jerrell, J. M., & Jerrell, S. L. (1981). Organizational consultation in school systems. In J. C. Conoley (Ed.), *Consultation in schools* (pp. 133–156). New York: Academic Press.

Jitendra, A. K., DuPaul, G. J., Volpe, R.J.,Tresco, K. E., Junod, R. E. V., Lutz, L. G. et al. (2007). Consultation-based academic intervention for children with attention deficit hyperactivity disorder. *School Psychology Review, 36*, 217–236.

Johns, K. M. (1992). Lowering beginning teacher anxiety about parent-teacher conferences through role playing. *School Counselor, 40*, 146–152.

Johnson, C. D., & Johnson, S. K. (1988). Advocacy and outreach through consultation: Applications to educational settings. In D. J. Kurpius & D. Brown (Eds.), *Handbook of consultation: An intervention for advocacy and outreach* (pp. 61–76). Alexandria, VA: American Association for Counseling and Development.

Johnson, J. J., & Pugach, M. C. (1996). The emerging third wave of collaboration: Beyond problem solving. In W. Stainbach and S. Stainback (Eds.), *Controversial issues confronting special education* (2nd ed., pp. 196–204). Boston: Allyn & Bacon.

Johnson, L. J., Zorn, D., Yung Tam, B. K., LaMontagne, M., & Johnson, S. A. (2003). Stakeholders views of factors that impact successful interagency collaboration. *Exceptional Children, 69*, 195–210.

Johnston, R., & Gilliland, B. E. (1987). A program for effective interaction between school systems and consultants. *School Counselor, 35*, 110–119.

Jones, K. M., & Lungaro, C. J. (2000). Teacher acceptability of functional assessment-derived treatments. *Journal of Educational and Psychological Education, 11*(3&4), 323–332.

Jones, S. (1986). Addressing internal politics: A role for modeling in consultant-client interaction. *Small Group Behavior, 17*, 67–81.

Jordan, A. E., & Meara, N. M. (1990). Ethics and the professional practice of psychologists: The role of virtue and principles. *Professional Psychology: Research and Practice, 21*, 107–114.

Juras, J. L., Mackin, J. R., Curtis, S. E., & Foster-Fishman, P. G. (1998). Key concepts of community psychology: Implications for consulting in educational and human service settings. *Journal of Educational and Psychological Consultation, 8*, 111–133.

Kahnweiler, W. M. (1979). The school counselor as consultant: A historical review. *Personnel and Guidance Journal, 57*, 374–379.

Kamphaus, R. W., Reynolds, C. R., & Imperato-McCammon, C. (1999). Roles of diagnosis and classification in school psychology. In C. R. Reynolds and T. B. Gutkin (Eds.), *The handbook of school psychology* (3rd ed., pp. 292–306). New York: Wiley.

Kampwirth, T. J. (2006). *Collaborative consultation in the schools* (3rd ed.). Upper Saddle River, NJ: Merrill-Prentice Hall.

Kanel, K. (2007). *A guide to crisis intervention* (3rd ed.). Pacific Grove, CA: Thomson Brooks/Cole.

Kanfer, F. H., & Goldstein, A. P. (Eds.) (1991). *Helping people change* (4th ed.). New York: Pergamon Press.

Kaplan, L. S., Geoffroy, K. E., & Burgess, D. G. (1993). Counselors as consultants during a national crisis. *School Counselor, 41,* 60–64.

Karg, R. S., & Wiens, A. N. (2005). Improving diagnostic and clinical interviewing. In G. P. Koocher, J. C. Norcross, & S. S. Hill III (Eds.), *Psychologists' desk reference* (2nd ed., pp. 13–16). NY: Oxford University Press.

Karoly, P., & Harris, A. (1986). Operant methods. In F. H. Kanfer & A. P. Goldstein (Eds.), *Helping people change* (pp. 111–144). New York: Pergamon Press.

Katz, D., & Kahn, R. L. (1978). *The social psychology of organizations* (2nd ed.). New York: Wiley.

Katz, D., & Kahn, R. L. (1990). *The social psychology of organizations* (4th ed.). New York: Wiley.

Katzell, R., & Thompson, D. (1990). Work motivation: Theory and practice. *American Psychologist, 45*(2), 144–153.

Kazdin, A. E. (2001). *Behavior modification in applied settings* (6th ed.). Pacific Grove, CA: Thomson Brooks/Cole.

Keller, H. R. (1981). Behavioral consultation. In J. C. Conoley (Ed.), *Consultation in schools: Theory, research, and procedures* (pp. 59–99). New York: Academic Press.

Kelley, R. E. (1981). *Consulting: The complete guide to a profitable career.* New York: Scribner's.

Kelly, J. G. (1983). Consultation as a process of creating power: An ecological view. In S. Cooper & W. F. Hodges (Eds.), *The mental health consultation field* (pp. 153–171). New York: Human Sciences Press.

Kelly, J. G. (1987). An ecological paradigm: Defining mental health consultation as a preventative service. *Prevention in Human Services, 4*(3–4), 1–36.

Kelly, J. G. (1993). Gerald Caplan's paradigm: Bridging psychotherapy and public health practice. In W. P. Erchul (Ed.), *Consultation in community, school, and organizational practice* (pp. 75–85). Washington, DC: Taylor & Francis.

Kets De Vries, M. F. R., & Associates (Eds.) (1991). *Organizations on the couch.* San Francisco: Jossey-Bass.

Keys, S. G., Bemak, F., Carpenter, S. L., & King-Sear, M. E. (1998). Collaborative consultant: A new role for counselors serving at-risk youths. *Journal of Counseling & Development, 7,* 123–133.

Khandwalla, P. N. (1977). *The design of organizations.* New York: Harcourt Brace Jovanovich.

Kirkpatrick, D. L. (1998). *Evaluating training programs: The four levels* (2nd ed.). San Francisco: Berrett-Koehler. Madison, WI: American Society for Training and Development.

Kitchener, K. S., & Harding, S. S. (1990). Dual role relationships. In B. Herlihy and L. B. Golden (Eds.), *American Association for Counseling and Development ethical standards casebook* (4th ed., pp. 146–154). Alexandria, VA: American Association for Counseling and Development.

Klein, D. (1969). Some notes on the dynamics of resistance to change: The defender role. In W. G. Bennis, K. D. Benne, & R. Chin (Eds.), *The planning of change* (2nd ed., pp. 498–507). New York: Holt, Rinehart & Winston.

Klein, D. C. (1983). Future directions for consultation by mental health systems. In S. Cooper & W. F. Hodges (Eds.), *The mental health consultation field* (pp. 221–229). New York: Human Sciences Press.

Kloos, B., McCoy, J., Stewart, E., Thomas, R. E., Wiley, A., Good, T. L., Hunt, G. D., Moore, T., & Rappaport, J. (1998). Bridging the gap: A community-based, open systems approach to school and neighborhood consultation. *Journal of Educational and Psychological Consultation, 8,* 175–196.

Knoff, H. M. (1988). Clinical supervision, consultation, and counseling: A comparative analysis for supervisors and other educational leaders. *Journal of Curriculum and Supervision, 3,* 240–252.

Knoff, H. M. (1996). The interface of school, community, and health care reform: Organizational directions toward effective services for children and youth. *School Psychology Review, 25,* 446–464.

Knoff, H. M. (2002). Best practices in facilitating school reform, organizational change and strategic planning. In A. Thomas and J. Grimes (Eds.), *Best practices in school psychology* (4th ed., pp. 235–253). Bethesda, MD: National Association of School Psychologists.

Knoff, H. M., & Batsche, G. M. (1993). A school reform process for at-risk students: Applying Caplan's organizational consultation principles to guide prevention, intervention, and home-school cooperation. In W. P. Erchul (Ed.), *Consultation in community, school, and organizational practice* (pp. 123–147). Washington, DC: Taylor & Francis.

Knoff, H. M., & Curtis, M. J. (1996). Organizational change and school reform: School psychology at a professional crossroad: Introduction to the miniseries. *School Psychology Review, 25,* 406–408.

Knoff, H. M., Kottman, T., & Wilborn, B. L. (1992). Parents helping parents: Multiplying the counselor's effectiveness. *School Counselor, 40,* 10–14.

Knoff, H. M., McKenna, A. E, & Riser, K. (1991). Toward a consultant effectiveness scale: Investigating the characteristics of effective consultants. *School Psychology Review, 20,* 81–96.

Knoff, H. M., Sullivan, P., & Liu, D. (1995). Teachers' ratings of effective school psychology consultants: An exploratory factor analysis study. *Journal of School Psychology, 33,* 39–57.

Knotek, S. E. (2003). Making sense of jargon during consultation: Understanding consultees' social language to effect change in student study teams. *Journal of Educational and Psychological Consultation, 14,* 181–207.

Knotek, S. E. (2004). Evaluation issues and strategies in consultee-centered consultation. In N. M. Lambert, I. Hylander & J. H. Sandoval (Eds.), *Consultee-centered consultation: Improving the quality of professional services in schools and community organizations* (pp. 391–400). Mahwah, NJ: Erlbaum.

Knotek, S. (2006). Administrative crisis consultation after 9/11: A university's system response. *Consulting Psychology Journal: Practice and Research, 58,* 162–173.

Knotek, S. E., Babinski, L. M., Rogers, D. L. (2002). Consultation in new teacher groups: School psychologists facilitating collaboration among new teachers. *California School Psychologist, 7,* 39–50.

Knotek, S. E., Rosenfield, S. A., Gravois, T. A., & Babinski, L. M. (2003). The process of fostering consultee development during instructional consultation. *Journal of Educational and Psychological Consultation, 4,* 303–328.

Knotek, S. E., & Sandoval, J. (2003). Current research in consultee-centered consultation. *Journal of Educational and Psychological Consultation, 4,* 243–250.

Knowles, M. S., Holton, E. F., & Swanson, R. A. (2000). *The adult learner: The definitive classic on education and training* (5th ed.). Woburn, MA: Butterworth-Heinemann.

Knox, A. B. (1977). *Adult development and learning: A handbook on individual growth and competence in the adult years.* San Francisco: Jossey-Bass.

Knox, A. B. (1986). *Helping adults learn.* San Francisco: Jossey-Bass.

Koonce, D. A., & Harper, W., Jr. (2005). Engaging African American parents in the schools: A community-based consultation model. *Journal of Educational and Psychological Consultation, 6,* 55–74.

Kormanski, C., & Eschbach, L. (1997). From group leader to process consultant. In H. Forester-Miller and J. A. Kottler (Eds.), *Issues and challenges for group practitioners* (pp. 133–164). Denver: Love Publishing Company.

Kottman, T. (1995). *Partners in play.* Alexandria, VA: American Counseling Association.

Kottman, T., & Wilborn, B. L. (1992). Parents helping parents: Multiplying the counselor's effectiveness. *School Counselor, 40,* 10–14.

Kovach, B. E. (1998). Pyramids, circles, and teams: Confronting leadership issues. *Consulting Psychology Journal, 50,* 164–172.

Kramer, J. J. (1990). Training parents as behavior change agents: Successes, failures, and suggestions for school psychologists. In T. B. Gutkin and C. R. Reynolds (Eds.), *The handbook of school psychology* (2nd ed., pp. 683–702). New York: Wiley.

Kratochwill, T. R., & Bergan, J. R. (1990). *Behavioral consultation in applied settings: An individual guide.* New York: Plenum.

Kratochwill, T. R., Elliott, S. N., & Busse, R. T. (1995). Behavioral consultation: A five-year evaluation of consultant and client outcomes. *School Psychology Quarterly, 10,* 87–110.

Kratochwill, T. R., Elliott, S. N., & Callan-Stoiber, K. (2002). Best practices in school-based problem-solving consultation. In A. Thomas and J. Grimes (Eds.), *Best practices in school psychology* (4th ed., pp. 583–608). Washington, DC: National Association of School Psychologists.

Kratochwill, T. R., Elliott, S. N., & Carrington Rotto, P. (1995). Best practices in school-based behavioral consultation. In A. Thomas and J. Grimes (Eds.), *Best practices in school psychology* (3rd ed., pp. 519–537). Washington, DC: National Association of School Psychologists.

Kratochwill, T. R., Mace, F. C., & Bissel, M. S. (1987). Program evaluation and research. In C. A. Maher & S. G. Foreman (Eds.), *A behavioral approach to education of children and youth* (pp. 253–288). Hillsdale, NJ: Erlbaum.

Kratochwill, T. R., & Pittman, P. H. (2002). Expanding Problem-solving consultation training: Prospects and frameworks. *Journal of Educational and Psychological Consultation, 13*(1&2), 69–95.

Kratochwill, T. R., Sheridan, S. M., Carlson, J., Lasecki, K. L. (1999). Advances in behavioral assessment. In C. R. Reynolds and T. B. Gutkin (Eds.), *The handbook of school psychology* (3rd ed. pp. 350–382). New York: Wiley.

Kratochwill, T. R., & Shernoff, E. S. (2004). Evidence-based practice: Promoting evidenced-based practice interventions in school psychology. *School Psychology Review, 33*, 34–48.

Kratochwill, T. R., & Stoiber, K. C. (2000a). Empirically supported interventions and school psychology: Conceptual and practice issues–Part II. *School Psychology Quarterly, 15*, 233–253.

Kratochwill, T. R., & Stoiber, K. C. (2000b). Uncovering critical research agendas for school psychology: Conceptual dimensions and future directions. *School Psychology Review, 29*, 591–603.

Kratochwill, T. R., & Van Someren, K. R. (1985). Barriers to treatment success in behavioral consultation: Current limitations and future directions. *Journal of School Psychology, 23*, 225–239.

Kratochwill, T. R., & Van Someren, K. R. (1995). Barriers to treatment success in behavioral consultation: Current limitations and future directions. *Journal of Educational and Psychological Consultation, 6*, 125–143.

Kress, J. S., Cimring, B. R., & Elias, M. J. (1998). Community psychology consultation and the transition to institutional ownership and operation of intervention. *Journal of Educational and Psychological Consultation, 8*, 231–253.

Kressel, K., Bailey, J. R., & Forman, S. F. (1999). Psychological consultation in higher education: Lessons from a university faculty development center. *Journal of Educational and Psychological Consultation, 10*, 51–82.

Kruger, L. J., & Struzziero, J. (1998). Computer-mediated peer support of consultation: Case description and evaluation. *Journal of Educational and Psychological Consultation, 8*, 75–90.

Kruger, L. J., & Struzziero, J., Kaplan, S. K., Macklem, G., Watts, R., & Weksel, T. (2001). The use of e-mail in consultation: An exploratory study of consultee outcomes. *Journal of Educational and Psychological Consultation, 12*, 133–149.

Kuehnel, T. G., & Kuehnel, J. M. (1983a). Consultation training from a behavioral perspective. In J. L. Alpert and J. Meyers (Eds.), *Training in consultation* (pp. 85–103). Springfield, IL: Charles C. Thomas.

Kuehnel, T. G., & Kuehnel, J. M. (1983b). Mental health consultation. In S. Cooper & W. E. Hodges (Eds.). *The mental health consultation field* (pp. 39–56). New York: Human Sciences Press.

Kuh, G. D. (1993). Appraising the character of a college. *Journal of Counseling and Development, 71*, 661–668.

Kurpius, D. J. (1978). Consultation theory and process: An integrated model. *Personnel and Guidance Journal, 56*(6), 335–338.

Kurpius, D. J. (1985). Consultation interventions: Successes, failures, and proposals. *Journal of Counseling Psychology, 13*(3), 368–389.

Kurpius, D. J. (1986). Consultation: An important human and organizational intervention. *Journal of Counseling and Human Service Professions, 1*(1), 58–66.

Kurpius, D. J. (1987). Response to "Consultation in special education." *Journal of Learning Disabilities, 20*(8), 495.

Kurpius, D. J., Brack, G., Brack, C. J., & Dunn, L. B. (1993). Maturation of systems consultation: Subtle issues inherent in the model. *Journal of Mental Health Consultation, 15*, 414–429.

Kurpius, D. J., & Fuqua, D. R. (1993a). Introduction to the special issues. *Journal of Counseling and Development, 71*, 596–597.

Kurpius, D. J., & Fuqua, D. R. (1993b). Fundamental issues in defining consultation. *Journal of Counseling and Development, 71*, 598–600.

Kurpius, D. J., Fuqua, D. R., & Rozecki, T. (1993). The consulting process: A multidimensional approach. *Journal of Counseling and Development, 71*, 601–606.

Kurpius, D. J., & Lewis, J. E. (1988). Introduction to consultation: An intervention for advocacy and outreach. In D. J. Kurpius & D. Brown (Eds.), *Handbook of consultation: An intervention for advocacy and outreach* (pp. 1–4). Alexandria, VA: American Association for Counseling and Development.

Kurpius, D. J., & Robinson, S. E. (1978). An overview of consultation. *Personnel and Guidance Journal, 56*(6), 321–323.

Kurpius, D. J., & Rozecki, T. (1992). Outreach, advocacy, and consultation: A framework for prevention and intervention. *Elementary School Guidance and Counseling, 26*, 176–189.

Kurpius, D. J., & Rozecki, T. G. (1993). Strategies for improving interpersonal communication. In J. E. Zins, Kratochwill, T. R., and S. N. Elliott (Eds.), *Handbook of consultation services for children* (pp. 137–158). San Francisco: Jossey-Bass.

Lamb, C. S. (1992). Managing disruptive students: The mental health practitioner as a consultant for faculty and staff. *Journal of College Student Psychotherapy, 7*, 23–39.

Lambert, N. M. (2000). School psychology—more than the sum of its parts: Legends on journeys through time. *School Psychology Review, 29*, 120–137.

Landrum, M. S. (2001). Resource consultation and collaboration in gifted education. *Psychology in the Schools, 38*, 457–466.

Lange, A., & Grieger, R. (1993). Integrating RET into management consulting and training. *Journal of Rational-Emotive & Cognitive-Behavior Therapy, 11*, 51–57.

Larney, R. (2003). School-based consultation in the United Kingdom: Principles, practice and effectiveness. *School Psychology International, 24*, 5–19.

LaRoche, M., & Maxie, A. (2003). The considerations in addressing cultural differences in psychotherapy. *Professional Psychology: Research and Practice, 35*, 194–200.

LaRoche, M., & Shriberg, D. (2004). High stakes exams and Latino students: Toward a culturally sensitive education for Latino children in the United States. *Journal of Educational and Psychological Consultation, 5*, 205–223.

Larson, J., Smith, D. C., & Furlong, M. J. (2002). Best practices in school violence prevention. In A. Thomas and J. Grimes (Eds.), *Best practices in school psychology* (4th ed., pp. 1081–1097). Bethesda, MD: National Association of School Psychologists.

Larson, T., & Samdal, O. (2007). Implementing second step: Balancing fidelity and program adaptation.

*Journal of Educational and Psychological Consultation, 17*, 1–29.

Latham, G. P., & Lee, T. W. (1986). Goal setting. In E. A. Locke (Ed.), *Generalizing from laboratory to field settings* (pp. 101–117). Lexington, MA: Lexington Books.

Lawson, H. A. (1998). Academically based community scholarship, consultation as collaborative problem-solving, and a collective-responsibility model for the helping fields. *Journal of Psychological and Educational Consultation, 9*, 195–232.

Ledford, G. E., Jr. (1990). Smart clients, foolish questions: On dumb questions and the clients who love them. *Consultation, 9*, 323–328.

Lee, C. C. (1995). School counseling and cultural diversity: A framework for effective practice. In C. C. Lee (Ed.), *Counseling for diversity: A guide for school counselors and related professionals* (pp. 3–17). Boston, MA: Allyn & Bacon.

Lee, C. C., & Richardson, B. L. (1991). *Multicultural issues in counseling: New approaches to diversity.* Alexandria, VA: American Counseling Association.

Lee, R. J. (1993). Getting things done in changing organizations. In R. T. Golembiewski (Ed.), *Handbook of organizational consultation* (pp. 495–499). New York: Marcel Dekker.

Lee, S. W., & Jamison, T. R. (2003). Including the FBA process in student assistance teams: An exploratory study of team communications and intervention selection. *Journal of Educational and Psychological Consultation, 4*, 209–239.

Lentz, F. E., Allen, S., J., & Erhardt, K. E. (1996). The conceptual elements of strong interventions in school settings. *School Psychology Quarterly, 11*(2), 118–136.

Leonard, P. Y., & Gottsdanker-Willekens, A. E. (1987). The elementary school counselor as consultant for selfconcept enhancement. *School Counselor, 34*, 245–255.

Lerner, R. M. (1995). *America's youth in crisis: Challenges and opportunities for programs and policies.* Thousand Oaks, CA: Sage.

Levine, H. Z. (1985). Consensus on employee assistance programs. *Personnel, 62*(4), 14–19.

Levinson, H. (1993). Looking ahead: Caplan's ideas and the future of organizational consultation. In W. P. Erchul (Ed.), *Consultation in community, school, and organizational practice* (pp. 193–204). Washington, DC: Taylor & Francis.

Levinson, H. (2002). Psychological consultation to organizations: Linking assessment and intervention. In R. L. Lowman (Ed.), *Handbook of organizational consulting psychology: A comprehensive guide to theory, skills, and techniques* (pp. 415–449). San Francisco: Jossey-Bass.

Lewin, K. (1945). Research center for group dynamics. *Sociometry, 8*(2), 9.

Lewin, K. (1951). *Field theory in social sciences.* New York: Harper & Row.

Lewis, J. A., & Lewis, M. D. (1986). *Counseling programs for employees in the workplace.* Pacific Grove, CA: Thomson Brooks/Cole.

Lewis, J. A., Lewis, M. D., Daniels, J. A., & D'Andrea, M. J. (2003). *Community counseling: Empowerment strategies for a diverse society* (3rd ed.). Pacific Grove, CA: Thomson Brooks/Cole.

Lewis, J. A., Lewis, M. D., & Souflee, S., Jr. (1991). *Management of human service programs* (2nd ed.). Pacific Grove, CA: Thomson Brooks/Cole.

Lewis, T. J., & Newcomer, L. L. (2002). Examining the efficacy of school-based consultation: Recommendations for improving outcomes. *Child & Family Behavior Therapy, 24,* 165–181.

Liberman, R. P., Kuehnel, T. G., Kuehnel, J. M., Eckman, T., & Rosenstein, J. (1982). The behavioral analysis and modification project for community mental health. In A. M. Jeger and R. S. Slotnick (Eds.), *Community mental health and behavioral ecology: A handbook of theory, research, and practice* (pp. 95–112). New York: Plenum.

Lincoln, Y. S., & Guba, E. G. (1985). *Naturalistic inquiry.* Newbury Park, CA: Sage.

Lindberg, S. P. (1996) The mental health counselor and hospice. In W. J. Weikel and A. J. Palmo (Eds.), *Foundations of mental health counseling* (2nd ed., pp. 229–231). Springfield, IL: Thomas Books.

Lippitt, G. (1969). *Organizational renewal: Achieving viability in a changing world.* New York: Dutton.

Lippitt, G. L. (1982a). *Organizational renewal: A holistic approach to organization development* (2nd ed.). Englewood Cliffs, NJ: Prentice-Hall.

Lippitt, G. L. (1982b). Managing conflict in today's organizations. *Training and Development Journal* (July), 1–5.

Lippitt, G. L. (1993). Models of organizational change. In R. T. Golembiewski (Ed.), *Handbook of organizational consultation* (pp. 501–508). New York: Marcel Dekker.

Lippitt, G. L., Langseth, P., & Mossop, J. (1985). *Implementing organizational change.* San Francisco: Jossey-Bass.

Lippitt, G., & Lippitt, R. (1986). *The consulting process in action* (2nd ed.). La Jolla, CA: University Associates.

Lippitt, G. L., & Nadler, L. (1979). Emerging roles of the training director. In C. R. Bell & L. Nadler (Eds.), *The client-consultant handbook* (pp. 44–49). Houston: Gulf Publishing.

Lippitt, R. (1983). Ethical issues and criteria in intervention decisions. In S. Cooper and W. F. Hodges (Eds.), *The mental health consultation field* (pp. 139–151). New York: Human Sciences Press.

Lochman, J. E., Dunn, S. E., & Klimes-Dougan, B. K. (1993). An intervention and consultation model from a social cognitive perspective: A description of the anger coping program. *School Psychology Review, 22,* 458–471.

Lochman, J. E., Lampron, L. B., Gemmer, T. C., Harris, S. R., & Wyckoff, G. M. (1989). Teacher consultation and cognitive-behavioral interventions with aggressive boys. *Psychology in the Schools, 26,* 179–188.

Locke, E. A., & Latham, G. P. (1984). *Goal setting: A motivational technique that works.* Englewood Cliffs, NJ: Prentice-Hall.

Locke, E. A., & Latham, G. P. (2002). Building a practically useful theory of goal setting and task motivation: A 35-year odyssey. *American Psychologist, 57,* 705–717.

Locker, B. Z. (1997). Job loss and organizational change: Psychological perspectives. In A. J. Pickman (Ed.), *Special challenges in career management* (pp. 13–24). Mahwah, NJ: Lawrence Erlbaum.

Logan, W. L. (1997). Peer consultation group: Doing what works for counselors. *Professional School Counseling, 1,* 4–6.

Lopez, E. C. (2000). Conducting instructional consultation through interpreters. *School Psychology Review, 29,* 378–388.

Lopez, E. C. (2006). Targeting English language learners, tasks, targets, and treatments in instructional consultation. *Journal of Applied School Psychology, 22,* 59–79.

Lorsch, J. W., & Lawrence, P. (1972). The diagnosis of organizational problems. In N. Margulies & A. P. Raia (Eds.), *Organizational development: Values, process, and technology* (pp. 218–228). New York: McGraw-Hill.

Lott, B. (2003). Recognizing and welcoming the standpoint of low-income parents in the public schools. *Journal of Educational and Psychological Consultation, 4,* 91–104.

Lott, B., & Rogers, M. R. (2005). School consultants working for equity with families, teachers, and administrators. *Journal of Educational and Psychological Consultation, 16,* 1–16.

Love, K. B. (2007). Close but no cigar (yet): A commentary on "Has consultation achieved its primary prevention potential?", an article by Joseph E. Zins. *Journal of Educational and Psychological Consultation, 17,* 165–169.

Lowman, R. L. (1985). Ethical practice of psychological consultation: Not an impossible dream. *Counseling Psychologist, 13*(3), 466–472.

Lowman, R. L. (Ed.) (2006). *The ethical practice of psychology in organizations* (2nd ed.).

Luiselli, J. K. (2002). Focus, scope, and practice of behavioral consultation to public schools. *Child & Family Behavior Therapy, 24,* 5–21.

Luke, R. A., Jr. (1993). Workplace issues in the '90s. In R. T. Golembiewski (Ed.), *Handbook of organizational consultation* (pp. 525–534). New York: Marcel Dekker.

Lum, D. (2007). *Culturally competent practice: A framework for understanding diversity & justice issues* (3rd ed.). Belmont, CA: Thomson Brooks/Cole.

Lundberg, C. C. (1985). Consultant feedback: A metaphor technique. *Consultation, 4*(2), 145–151.

Lundberg, C. C. (1993). Knowing and surfacing organizational culture. In R. T. Golembiewski (Ed.), *Handbook of organizational consultation* (pp. 535–547). New York: Marcel Dekker.

Lusky, M. B., & Hayes, R. L. (2001). Collaborative consultation and program evaluation. *Journal of Counseling and Development 79*(1), 26–38.

Lutzker, J. R., & Martin, J. A. (1981). *Behavior change.* Pacific Grove, CA: Thomson Brooks/Cole.

Maas, K., & Mann-Feder, V. (1994). Successful consultation in youth care: The role of initial contracting. *Journal of Child & Youth Care, 9*(3), 59–65.

MacLennan, B. W. (1986). The organization and delivery of mental health consultation in changing times. In F. V. Mannino, E. J. Trickett, M. F. Shore, M. G. Kidder, & G. Levine (Eds.), *Handbook of mental health consultation* (pp. 319–345). Rockville, MD: National Institute of Mental Health.

MacLennan, B. W., Quinn, R. D., & Schroeder, D. (1975). The scope of community mental health consultation. In E. V. Mannino, B. W. MacLennan, & M. E. Shore (Eds.), *The practice of mental health consultation* (pp. 3–24). Rockville, MD: National Institute of Mental Health.

MacLeod, I. R., Jones, K. M., Somers, C. L., & Havey, J. M. (2001). An evaluation of the effectiveness of school-based behavioral consultation. *Journal of Educational and Psychological Consultation, 12*(3), 203–216.

MacMann, G. M., Barnett, D. W., Allen, S. J., Bramlett, R. K., Hall, J. D., & Ehrhardt, K. E. (1996). Problem solving and intervention design: Guidelines for the evaluation of technical adequacy. *School Psychology Quarterly, 11,* 137–148.

MacNealy, M. S. (1999). *Strategies for empirical research in writing.* Boston: Allyn & Bacon.

Maher, C. A. (1981). Interventions with school social systems: A behavioral-systems approach. *School Psychology Review, 10*(4), 499–510.

Maher, C. A. (1993). Providing consultation services in business settings. In J. E. Zins, T. R. Kratochwill, & S. N. Elliott (Eds.), *Handbook of consultation services for children* (pp. 317–328). San Francisco: Jossey-Bass.

Maher, C. A., Cook, S. A., & Kruger, L. J. (1987). Human resource development. In C. A. Maher & S. G. Forman (Eds.), *A behavioral approach to education of children and youth* (pp. 221–252). Hillsdale, NJ: Erlbaum.

Maher, C. A., & Illback, R. J. (1983). Planning for organizational change in schools: Alternative approaches and procedures. *School Psychology Review, 12,* 460–466.

Maital, S. L. (1996). Integration of behavioral and mental health consultation as a means of overcoming resistance. *Journal of Educational and Psychological Consultation, 7,* 291–303.

Maital, S. L. (2000). Reciprocal distancing: A systems model of interpersonal processes in cross-cultural consultation. *School Psychology Review, 29*, 389–400.

Maloney, H. N. (1991). Congregational consultation. *Prevention in Human Services, 1*(3), 289–315.

Mang, M. (2004). Use of metaphors, parables, and anecdotes in consultee-centered consultation: School-based applications. In N. M. Lambert, I. Hylander, & J. H. Sandoval (Eds.), *Consultee-centered consultation: Improving the quality of professional services in schools and community organizations* (pp. 301–312). Mahwah, NJ: Erlbaum.

Mann, P. A. (1978). Mental health consultation in school settings. *Personnel and Guidance Journal, 56*(6), 369–373.

Mann, P. A. (1983). Transition points in consultation entry, transfer, and termination. In S. Cooper & W. E. Hodges (Eds.), *The mental health consultation field* (pp. 99–105). New York: Human Sciences Press.

Mannino, F. V., MacLennan, B. W., & Shore, M. E. (Eds.) (1975). *The practice of mental health consultation.* New York: Gardner.

Mannino, F. V., & Shore, M. E. (1986). Understanding consultation: Some orienting dimensions. *Counseling Psychologist, 13*(3), 363–367

Margolis, H. (1990). Helping implement co-operative learning. *School Psychology International, 11*, 309–318.

Manz, P. H. (2007). Cultivating fertile grounds: Enhancing and extending the scientific base of social and emotional learning: A commentary on "The scientific base linking social and emotional learning on school success," a chapter by Joseph E. Zins, Michelle R. Bloodworth, Roger P. Weissberg, and Herbert J. Walberg. *Journal of Educational and Psychological Consultation, 17*, 211–218.

Margolis, H., McCabe, P. P., & Alber, S. R. (2004). Resolving struggling readers' homework difficulties: How elementary school counselors can help. *Journal of Educational and Psychological Consultation, 15*, 79–110.

Margulies, N., & Raia, A. P. (1972). Emerging issues in organization development. In N. Margulies and A. P. Raia (Eds.), *Organizational development: Values, process, and technology* (pp. 475–478). New York: McGraw-Hill.

Marks, E. S. (1995). *Entry strategies for school consultation.* New York: Guilford.

Maris, T. L. (1985). Characteristics of successful management consultants. *Consultation, 4*(3), 258–263.

Marshall, C., & Rossman, G. B. (1995). *Designing qualitative research* (2nd ed.). Thousand Oaks, CA: Sage Publications.

Martens, B. K. (1993). A behavioral approach to consultation. In J. E. Zins, T. R. Kratochwill, and S. N. Elliott (Eds.), *Handbook of consultation services for children* (pp. 65–86). San Francisco: Jossey-Bass.

Martens, B. K., & Ardoin, S. P. (2002). Training school psychologists in behavior support consultation. *Child and Family Behavior Therapy, 24*, 147–163.

Martens, B. K., Kelly, S. Q., & Diskin, M. T. (1996). The effects of two sequential-request strategies on teachers' acceptability and use of a classroom intervention. *Journal of Educational and Psychological Consultation, 7*, 211–221.

Martens, B. K., Lewandowski, L. J., & Houk, J. L. (1989). The effects of entry information on the consultation process. *School Psychology Review, 18*, 225–234.

Martens, B. K., & Witt, J. C. (1988). Expanding the scope of behavioral consultation: A systems approach to classroom behavior change. *Professional School Psychology, 3*(4), 271–281.

Martin, R. P. (1983). Consultant, consultee, and client explanations of each others' behavior in consultation. *School Psychology Review, 12*, 35–41.

Mason, E. J., Demers, S. T., & Middleton, E. J. (1984). Integrating consultation and program evaluation in school psychology. *Journal of School Psychology, 22*, 273–283.

Mathias, C. E. (1992). Touching the lives of children: Consultative interventions that work. *Elementary School Guidance and Counseling, 26*, 190–201.

Matson, J. (1985). Modeling. In A. S. Bellack & M. Hersen (Eds.), *Dictionary of behavior therapy techniques* (pp. 150–151). New York: Pergamon Press.

Matuszek, P. A. (1981). Program evaluation as consultation. In J. C. Conoley (Ed.), *Consultation in schools* (pp. 179–200). New York: Academic Press.

Mayer, G. R., Mitchell, L. K., Clementi, T., Clemet-Robinson, E., Myatt, R., & Bullara, D. T. (1993). A dropout prevention program for at-risk high school students: Emphasizing consulting to promote positive classroom climates. *Education and Treatment of Children, 16*, 135–146.

Mazade, N. A. (1983). In conclusion the past, present, and future in consultation. In S. Cooper & W. E. Hodges (Eds.), *The mental health consultation field* (pp. 233–242). New York: Human Sciences Press.

Mazade, N. A. (1985). Issues in consultation. *Consultation, 4*(1), 7–16.

McAuliffe, G. (1993). Career as an imaginative quest. *American Counselor, 2*(1), 13–16, 36.

McCarroll, J. E., & Ursano, R. J. (2006). Consultation to groups, organizations, and communities. In E. C. Ritchie, P. J. Watson & M. J. Friedman (Eds.), *Interventions following mass violence and disasters: Strategies for mental health practice* (pp. 193–205). New York: Guilford.

McCarthy, M. M., & Sorenson, G. P. (1993). School counselors: Legal duties and liabilities. *Journal of Counseling and Development, 72*(2), 159–167.

McCollum, M. G. (1981). Recasting a role for mental health educators. *American Mental Health Counselors Journal, 3*(1), 37–47.

McDougal, J. L., Clonan, S. M., & Martens, B. K. (2000). Using organizational change procedures to promote the acceptability of prereferral intervention services: The school-based intervention team project. *School Psychology Quarterly, 15*, 149–171.

McDougall, L. M., Reschly, D. J., & Corkery, J. M. (1988). Changes in referral interviews with teachers after behavioral consultation training. *Journal of School Psychology, 26*, 225–232.

McFarland, W. P. (1992). Counselors teaching peaceful conflict resolution. *Journal of Counseling and Development, 71*, 18–21.

McGowan, S. (1993). Employees, managers work it out after layoffs. *Guidepost, 35*(10), 1–10.

McKeachie, W. J., & Hofer, B. K. (2001). *McKeachie's teaching tips: Strategies, research, and theory for college and university teachers.* (11th ed.). Boston: Heath.

McLean, G. N. (2006). *Organization development.* San Francisco: Berrett-Koehler Publishers.

McLoughlin, C. S., Kubrick, Jr.,R. J., & Lewis, M. (2002). Best practices in promoting safe schools. In A. Thomas and J. Grimes (Eds.), *Best practices in school psychology* (4th ed., pp 1181–1194). Bethesda, MD: National Association of School Psychologists.

McMahon, T. J., & Pruett, M. K. (1998). On the proverbial horns of an ethical dilemma: School consultation, child advocacy, and adversarial intervention. *Journal of Educational and Psychological Consultation, 9*, 75–85.

Meade, C. J., Hamilton, M. K., & Yuen, R. K-W. (1982). Consultation research: The time has come the walrus said. *Counseling Psychologist, 4*, 39–51.

Medway, E. J. (1989). Further considerations on a cognitive problem-solving perspective on school consultation. *Professional School Psychology, 4*, 21–27.

Meeks, S. (1996). Psychological consultation to nursing homes: Description of a six-year practice. *Psychotherapy, 33*, 19–29.

Meichenbaum, D. (1977). *Cognitive-behavior modification: An integrative approach.* New York: Plenum.

Meichenbaum, D. (1985). *Stress inoculation training.* New York: Pergamon Press.

Melnick, J. (2003). Making the learning last. *Gestalt Review, 7*, 1–4.

Mendoza, D. W. (1993). A review of Gerald Caplan's *Theory and practice of mental health consultation. Journal of Counseling and Development, 71*, 629–635.

Merrell, K. W., Ervin, R. A., Gimpel, G. A. (2006). *School psychology for the 21st century.* New York: Guilford Press.

Merron, K. (1993). Let's bury the term "resistance." *Organization Development Journal, 11*(4), 77–86.

Metropolitan Area Child Study Research Group (2007). Changing the way children "think" about aggression: Social cognitive effects of a preventative intervention. *Journal of Consulting and Clinical Psychology, 75*, 160–167.

Meyers, B., Meyers, J., and Gelzheiser, L. (2001). Observing leadership roles in shared decision making: A preliminary analysis of three teams. *Journal of Educational and Psychological Consultation, 12*(4), 277–312.

Meyers, J. (1981). Mental health consultation. In J. C. Conoley (Ed.), *Consultation in schools: Theory, research, and procedures* (pp. 35–58). New York: Academic Press.

Meyers, J. (1985). Consultation as a basis for delivery of school psychological services. *Programs in School Psychology, 40*(1), 3–4.

Meyers, J. (2002). A 30 year perspective on best practices for consultation training. *Journal of Educational and Psychological Consultation, 13*(1&2), 35–54.

Meyers, J., Brent, D., Faherty, E., & Modafferi, C. (1993). Caplan's contributions to the practice of psychology in schools. In W. P. Erchul (Ed.), *Consultation in community, school, and organizational practice* (pp. 99–122). Washington, DC: Taylor & Francis.

Meyers, J., Gaughan, E., & Pitt, N. (1990). Contributions of community psychology to school psychology. In T. B. Gutkin & C. R. Reynolds (Eds.), *The handbook of school psychology* (2nd ed., pp. 198–217). New York: Wiley.

Meyers, J., Meyers, A B., & Grogg, K. (2004). Prevention through consultation: A model to guide future developments in the filed of school psychology. *Journal of Educational and Psychological Consultation, 5*, 257–276.

Meyers, J., & Nastasi, B. K. (1999). Primary prevention in school settings. In C. R. Reynolds and T. B. Gutkin (Eds.), *The handbook of school psychology* (3rd ed. pp. 764–799). New York: Wiley.

Meyers, J., Parsons, R. D., & Martin, R. (1979). *Mental health consultation in the schools*. San Francisco: Jossey-Bass.

Meyers, B., Valentino, C. T., Meyers, J., Boretti, M., & Brent, D. (1996). Implementing prereferral intervention teams as an approach to school-based consultation in an urban school setting. *Journal of Educational and Psychological Consultation, 7*, 119–149.

Meyers, J., & Yelich, G. (1989). Cognitive-behavioral approaches in psychoeducational consultation. In J. N. Hughes and R. J. Hall (Eds.), *Cognitive-behavioral psychology in the schools* (pp. 501–535). New York: Guilford.

Michaels, C. A., & Lopez, E. C. (2005). Collaboration and consultation in transition planning: Introduction to the mini-theme. *Journal of Educational and Psychological Consultation, 16*, 255–261.

Miller, T. W. (2006). Telehealth issues in consulting psychology practice. *Consulting Psychology Journal: Practice and Research, 58*, 82–90.

Minke, K. M. (2006). Parent-teacher relationships. In G. G. Bear and K. M. Minke (Eds.). *Children's needs III: Development, prevention, and intervention* (pp. 73–85). Bethesda, MD: National Association of School Psychologists.

Miranda, A. H. (1993). Consultation with culturally diverse families. *Journal of Educational and Psychological Consultation, 4*, 89–93.

Miranda, A. H. (2002). Best practices in increasing crosscultural competence. In A. Thomas and J. Grimes (Eds.), *Best practices in school psychology* (4th ed., pp 353–362). Bethesda, MD: National Association of School Psychologists.

Mitchell, T. R. (1978). *People in organizations: Understanding their behavior*. New York: McGraw-Hill.

Moleski, S. M., & Kiselica, M. S. (2005). Dual relationships: A continuum ranging from the destructive to the therapeutic. *Journal of Counseling and Development, 83*, 3–11.

Morasky, R. L. (1982). *Behavioral systems*. New York: Praeger.

Mortola, P., & Carlson, J. (2003). "Collecting an anecdote": The role of narrative in school consultation. *The Family Journal: Counseling and Therapy for Couples and Families, 11*, 7–12.

Moseley-Howard, G. S. (1995). Best practices in considering the role of culture. In A. Thomas and J. Grimes (Eds.), *Best practices in school psychology* (3rd ed., pp. 337–345). Washington, DC: National Association of School Psychologists.

Mowder, B. A., Willis, W. G., & Widerstrom, A. H. (1986). Consultation and handicapped preschoolers: Priorities, goals, and models. *Psychology in the Schools, 23*, 373–379.

Murphy, J. J. (1999). Common factors of school-based change. In B. L. Duncan and S. D. Miller (Eds.), *The heart and soul of change: What works in therapy* (pp. 361–386). Washington, DC: APA.

Murrell, K. L. (1993). Process consulting. In R. T. Golembiewski (Ed.), *Handbook of organizational consultation* (pp. 579–582). New York: Marcel Dekker, Inc.

Myers, B., & Arena, M. P. (2001). Trail consultation: A new direction in applied psychology. *Professional psychology: Research and practice, 32*, 386–391.

Myers, D. W. (1988). Preparation for EAP consulting work. *Consultation, 7*, 204–215.

Myrick, R. D. (2003). *Development guidance and counseling: A practical approach* (4th ed.). Minneapolis, MN: Educational Media.

Nabors, L. A., Ramos, V., & Weist, M. D. (2001). Use of focus groups as a tool for evaluating programs for children and families. *Journal of Educational and Psychological Consultation, 12*(3), 243–256.

Nadler, D. A. (1977). *Feedback and organization development: Using data-based methods.* Reading, MA: Addison-Wesley.

Nadler, L. (1980). *Corporate human resources development: A managerial tool.* New York: Van Nostrand Reinhold.

Nastasi, B. (2004). Meeting the challenges of the future: Integrating public health and public education for mental health promotion. *Journal of Educational and Psychological Consultation, 15*, 295–312.

Nastasi, B. (2005). School consultants as change agents in achieving equity for families in public schools. *Journal of Educational and Psychological Consultation, 6*, 113–125.

Nastasi, B. K. (2006). Multicultural issues in school psychology practice: Introduction. *Journal of Applied School Psychology, 22*, 1–11.

Nastasi, B., Varjas, K., Bernstein, R., Jaysena, A. (2000). Conducting participatory culture-specific consultation: A global perspective on multicultural consultation. *School Psychology Review, 29*(3), 401–413.

National Association of School Psychologists (2000). *Professional conduct manual,* Bethesda, MD: Author.

National Association of Social Workers. (1999). *Code of ethics* (Rev. ed.). Silver Springs, MD: Author.

National Board for Certified Counselors. (1998). *Standards for the ethical practice of webcounseling.* Alexandria, VA: Author.

National Board for Certified Counselors. (2002). *National board for certified counselors code of ethics.* Alexandria, VA: Author.

National Organization for Human Service Education. (1995). *Ethical standards of the national organization for human service organizations.* Author.

Naumann, W. C., Gutkin, T. B., & Sandoval, S. R. (1996). The impact of consultant race and student race on perceptions of consultant effectiveness and intervention acceptability. *Journal of Educational and Psychological Consultation, 7*, 151–160.

Neilsen, E. H. (1984). *Becoming an OD practitioner.* Englewood Cliffs, NJ: Prentice-Hall.

Nevis, E. (1987). *Organizational consulting.* Cleveland, OH: Gestalt Institute of Cleveland Press.

Newman, J. L. (1993). Ethical issues in consultation. *Journal of Counseling and Development, 72*(2), 148–156.

Newman, J. L., & Fuqua, D. R. (1984). Data-based consultation in student affairs. *Journal of College Student Personnel, 25*, 206–212.

Newman, J. L., Gray, E. A., & Fuqua, D. R. (1996). Beyond ethical decision making. *Consulting Psychology Journal, 48*, 230–236.

Newman, J. L., Robinson-Kurpius, S. E., & Fuqua, D. R. (2002). Issues in the ethical practice of consulting psychology. In R. L. Lowman (Ed.), *Handbook of organizational consulting psychology: A comprehensive guide to theory, skills, and techniques* (pp. 733–758). San Francisco: Jossey-Bass.

Nicholson, D., Artz, S., Armitage, A., & Fagan, J. (2000). Working relationships and outcomes in multidisciplinary collaborative practice settings. *Child & Youth Care Forum, 29*, 39–69.

Nicoll, W. G. (1992). A family counseling and consultation model for school counselors. *School Counselor, 39*, 351–361.

Noble, B., & Dickinson, D. J. (1988). Utility of school psychologists' recommendations: Perception of elementary teachers. *Psychology in the Schools, 25*, 412–418.

Noell, G. H. (1996). New directions in behavioral consultation. *School Psychology Quarterly, 11*, 187–188.

Noell, G. H. (2002). Direct assessment of clients' instructional needs: Improving academic, social, and emotional outcomes. In M. L. Kelley, D. Reitman, & G. H. Noell (Eds.), *Practitioners guide to empirically based measures of school behavior* (pp. 63–68). New York: Kluwer Academic/Plenum Publishers.

Noell, G. H., & Gresham, F. M. (1993). Functional outcome analysis: Do the benefits of consultation and prereferral intervention justify the costs? *School Psychology Quarterly, 8*, 200–226.

Noell, G. H., Roane, H. S., VanDerHeyden, A. M., Whitmarsh, E. L., & Gatti, S. L. (2000). Programming for the generalization of communication to the classroom following assessment and training outside of the classroom. *School Psychology Review, 29*, 429–442.

Noell, G. H., & Witt, J. C. (1996). A critical re-evaluation of five fundamental assumptions underlying behavioral consultation. *School Psychology Quarterly, 11,* 189–203.

Noell, G. H., & Witt, J. C. (1998). Toward a behavior analytic approach to consultation. In T. S. Watson and F. M. Gresham (Eds.). *Handbook of Child Behavior Therapy* (pp. 41–57). New York: Plenum Press.

Noell, J. C., Witt, J. C., Slider, N. J., Connell, J. E., Gatti, S. L., Williams, K. L. et al. (2005). Treatment implementation following behavioral consultation in schools: A comparison of three follow-up strategies. *School Psychology Review, 34,* 87–106.

Norris, D. A., Burke, J. P., & Speer, A. L. (1990). Tri-level delivery: An alternative consultation model. *School Psychology Quarterly, 5,* 89–110.

Nuttall, E. V., De Leon, B., & Valle, M. (1990). Best practices in considering cultural factors. In A. Thomas and J. Grimes (Eds.). *Best practices in school psychology* (2nd ed., pp. 219–233). Washington, DC: NASP.

O'Callaghan, J. B. (1993). *School-based collaboration with families.* San Francisco: Jossey-Bass.

Ochoa, S. H., & Rhodes, R. L. (2005). Assisting parents of bilingual students to achieve equity in public schools. *Journal of Educational and Psychological Consultation, 6,* 75–94.

O'Connell, J. J. (1990). Process consulting in a content field: Socrates in strategy. *Consultation, 9,* 199–208.

O'Conner, W. A., & Lubin, B. (1984). *Ecological approaches to clinical and community psychology.* New York: Wiley.

O'Driscoll, M. P., & Eubanks, J. L. (1992). Consultant and client perceptions of consultant competencies: Implications for OD consulting. *Organization Development Journal, 10*(4), 53–59.

Offermann, L. R., & Gowing, M. K. (1990). Organizations of the future. *American Psychologist, 45*(2), 95–108.

Oher, J. M. (1993). Survey research to measure EAP customer satisfaction: A quality improvement tool. *Employee Assistance Quarterly, 8*(4), 41–75.

O'Keefe, D. J., & Medway, F. J. (1997). The application of persuasion research to consultation in school psychology. *Journal of School Psychology, 35,* 173–193.

Oktay, J. S. (2004). Grounded theory. In D. K. Padgett (Ed.). *The qualitative research experience* (pp. 23–47). Belmont, CA: Thomson Brooks/Cole.

O'Neill, P., & Trickett, E. J. (1982). *Community consultation.* San Francisco: Jossey-Bass.

Orland, M. E. (1999). Financing more integrated children and family services: Current practice and opportunities for reform. *Journal of Educational and Psychological Consultation, 10,* 251–267.

Ortiz, S. O. (2006). Multicultural practices in school psychology practice: A critical analysis. *Journal of Applied School Psychology, 22,* 151–167.

Ortiz, S. O., & Flanagan, D. P. (2002). Best practices in working with culturally diverse children and families. In A. Thomas and J. Grimes (Eds.), *Best practices in school psychology* (4th ed., pp. 337–351). Bethesda, MD: National Association of School Psychologists.

Osterweil, Z. O. (1987). A structured process of problem definition in school consultation. *School Counselor, 34*(5), 345–352.

Osterweil, Z. O. (1988). A structured integrative model of mental health consultation in schools. *International Journal for the Advancement of Counselling, 11,* 37–49.

Osterweil, Z., & Plotnik, R. (1989). Mental health consultation: An evaluation of the issue-focused model. *School Psychology International, 10,* 293–299.

Otani, A. (1989). Client resistance in counseling: Its theoretical rationale and taxonomic classification. *Journal of Counseling and Development, 67,* 458–461.

Pace, L. A., & Argona, D. Z. (1994). Participatory action research. In French, W. L., Bell, Jr., C. H., & Zawacki, R. A. (Eds.). *Organizational development and transformation: Managing effective change* (4th ed., pp. 509–717). Homewood, IL: Richard D. Irwin.

Pace, T. M., Mullins, L. L., Chaney, J. M., & Olson, R. A. (1995). Psychological consultation with primary care physicians: Obstacles and opportunities in the medical setting. *Professional Psychology: Research and Practice, 26,* 123–131.

Padgett, D. K. (Ed.) (2004). *The qualitative research experience.* Pacific Grove, CA: Thomson Learning.

Paisley, P. O., & Milsom, A. (2007). Group work as an essential contribution to transforming school counseling. *Journal for Specialists in Group Work, 32,* 9–17.

Parker, R. J. (1994). Helping children cope with divorce: A workshop for parents. *Elementary School Guidance & Counseling, 29*, 137–148.

Parr, G. (1993). Educational reforms in Texas and their implications for school counselors. *School Counselor, 41*, 44–47.

Parsons, R. D. (1996). *The skilled consultant.* Boston: Allyn & Bacon.

Parsons, R. D., & Meyers, J. (1984). *Developing consultation skills.* San Francisco: Jossey-Bass.

Partin, R. L. (1993). School counselors' time: Where does it go? *School Counselor, 40*, 274–281.

Patterson, C. H. (1986). *Theories of counseling and psychotherapy* (4th ed.). New York: Harper & Row.

Patton, M. Q. (1986). *Utilization-focused evaluation.* Beverly Hills, CA: Sage.

Pearson, B., & Piazza, N. (1997). Classification of dual relationships in the helping professions. *Counselor Education and Supervision, 37*, 89–99.

Pedersen, P. B. (1997). The cultural context of the American Counseling Association code of ethics. *Journal of Counseling and Development, 76*, 23–28.

Pellitteri, J. (2000). Music therapy in the special education setting. *Journal of Educational and Psychological Consultation, 11*(3&4), 379–391.

Pena, R. A. (1996). Multiculturalism and educational leadership: Keys to effective consultation. *Journal of Educational and Psychological Consultation, 7*, 315–325.

Perry, M. A., & Furukawa, M. J. (1986). Modeling methods. In E. H. Kanfer & A. P. Goldstein (Eds.), *Helping people change* (pp. 66–110). New York: Pergamon Press.

Peters, T. (1988). *Thriving on chaos.* New York: HarperCollins.

Petti, T. A., Cornely, P. J., & McIntyre, A. (1993). A consultative study as a catalyst for improving mental health services for rural children and adolescents. *Hospital and Community Psychiatry, 44*, 262–265.

Petty, R. E., Heesacker M., & Hughes, J. N. (1997). The elaboration likelihood model: Implications for the practice of school psychology. *Journal of School Psychology, 35*, 107–136.

Pfeiffer, J. W., & Jones, J. E. (Eds.) (1974). *A handbook of structured experiences for human relations training* (Vol. 3). La Jolla, CA: University Associates.

Pfeiffer, J. W., & Jones, J. E. (Eds.). (1977). Ethical considerations in consulting. In J. E. Jones and J. W. Pfeiffer (Eds.), *The 1977 annual handbook for group facilitators* (pp. 217–224). La Jolla, CA: University Associates.

Pickman, A. J. (1994). *The complete guide to outplacement counseling.* Hillsdale, NJ: Lawrence Erlbaum.

Piersel, W. C., & Gutkin, T. B. (1983). Resistance to school-based consultation: A behavioral analysis of the problem. *Psychology in the Schools, 20*, 311–320.

Pinkerton, R., & Temple, R. D. (2000). Mental health consultation and psychology internship training. *Professional Psychology: Research and Practice, 31*, 315–320.

Pipes, R. B. (1981). Consulting in organizations: The entry problem. In J. C. Conoley (Ed.), *Consultation in schools—theory, research, procedures* (pp. 11–33). New York: Academic Press.

Plummer, D. L. (1998). Approaching diversity training in the year 2000. *Consulting Psychology Journal, 50*, 181–189.

Pohlman, C., Hoffman, L. B., Dodds, A. H., & Pryzwansky, W. B. (1998). Utilization of school-based professional services: An exploratory analysis of perceptions of mentor teachers and student teachers. *Journal of Educational and Psychological Consultation, 9*, 347–365.

Polkinghorne, D. E., & Gribbons, B. C. (1999). Applications of qualitative research strategies to school psychology research problems. In C. R. Reynolds and T. B. Gutkin (Eds.), *The handbook of school psychology* (3rd ed., pp. 108–136). New York: Wiley.

Ponterotto, J. G. (2005). Qualitative research in counseling psychology: A primer on research paradigms and philosophy of science. *Journal of Counseling Psychology, 52*, 126–136.

Ponti, C. R., & Flower, J. C. (1993). Consulting in elementary and secondary schools. In J. E. Zins, T. R. Kratochwill, & S. N. Elliott (Eds.), *Handbook of consultation services for children* (pp. 277–290). San Francisco: Jossey-Bass.

Prein, H. (1987). Strategies for third-party interventions. *Human Relations, 40*, 699–720.

Prilleltensky, I., Peirson, L., & Nelson, G. (1998). The application of community psychology values and guiding concepts to school consultation. *Journal of Educational and Psychological Consultation, 8*, 153–173.

Pruett, M. K. (1998). Statement of purpose for legal and ethical issues in consultation. *Journal of Educational and Psychological Consultation, 9*, 73–74.

Pryzwansky, W. B. (1989). Some further thoughts about the problem-finding challenge of consultation. *Professional School Psychology, 4*, 37–40.

Pryzwansky, W. B. (1993). Ethical consultation practice. In J. E. Zins, T. R. Kratochwill, & S. N. Elliott (Eds.), *Handbook of consultation services for children* (pp. 329–348). San Francisco: Jossey-Bass.

Pryzwansky, W. B. (1996). Professionals' peer-mediated learning experiences: Another idea whose time has come. *Journal of Educational and Psychological Consultation, 7*, 71–78.

Pryzwansky, W. B. (2003). Finally, a contemporary treatment of consultee-centered consultation. *Journal of Educational and Psychological Consultation, 4*, 363–368.

Pryzwansky, W. B., & Noblit. G. W. (1990). Understanding and improving consultation practice: The qualitative case study approach. *Journal of Educational and Psychological Consultation, 1*, 293–307.

Pugh, D. S. (1966). Modern organizational theory: A psychological and sociological study. *Psychological Bulletin, 66*(4), 235–251.

Putnam, R. F., Luiselli, J. K., & Jefferson, G. L. (2002). Expanding technical assistance consultation to public schools: District-wide evaluation of instructional and behavioral support practices for students with developmental disabilities. *Child & Family Behavior Therapy, 24*, 113–128.

Quinn, K., & Cumblad, C. (1994). Service providers' perceptions of interagency collaboration in their communities. *Journal of Emotional and Behavioral Disorders, 2*, 109–116.

Quintana, S. M., Castillo, E. M., Zamarripa, M. X. (2000). Assessment of ethnic and linguistic minority children. In E. S. Shapiro and T. R. Kratochwill (Eds.), *Behavioral assessment in schools: Theory, research and clinical foundations* (2nd ed., pp. 435–463). New York: Guilford Press.

Quirk, M. P., Strosahl, K., Kreilkamp, T., & Erdberg, P. (1995). Personality feedback consultation to families in a managed mental health care practice.

*Professional Psychology Research and Practice, 26*, 27–32.

Raforth, M. A., & Foriska, T. (2006). Administrator participation in promoting effective problem-solving teams. *Remedial and Special Education, 27*, 130–135.

Ramirez, S. Z., Lepage, K. M., Kratochwill, T. R., & Duffy, J. L. (1998). Multicultural issues in school-based consultation: Conceptual and research considerations. *Journal of School Psychology, 36*, 479–509.

Ramirez, S. Z., & Smith, K. A. (2007). Case vignettes of school psychologists' consultations involving Hispanic youth. *Journal of Educational and Psychological Consultation, 17*, 79–93.

Randolph, D. L., & D'Ilio, V. R. (1990). Factors influencing perceptions of consultant effectiveness. *Psychology: A Journal of Human Behavior, 27*(13), 12–19.

Randolph, D. L., & Graun, K. (1988). Resistance to consultation: A synthesis for counselor-consultants. *Journal of Counseling and Development, 67*, 182–184.

Rawlings, D. (2000). Collaborative leadership teams: Oxymoron or new paradigm? *Consulting Psychology Journal, 52*, 36–48.

Redmon, W. K., Cullari, S., & Farris, H. E. (1985). An analysis of some important tasks and phases in consultation. *Journal of Community Psychology, 13*, 375–386.

Reed, C., Greer, A., McKay, C., & Knight, C. (1990). Process issues in consultancy. *Journal of Adolescence, 13*(4), 387–400.

Reese, R. J., Conoley, C. W., & Brossart, D. F. (2006). The attractiveness of telephone counseling: An empirical investigation of client perceptions. *Journal of Counseling and Development, 84*, 54–60.

Register, D. (2002). Collaboration and consultation: A survey of board certified music therapists. *Journal of Music Therapy, 39*, 305–321.

Remley, T. P., Jr. (1988). Consultative advocacy differentiated from legal advocacy. In D. J. Kurpius & D. Brown (Eds.), *Handbook of consultation: An intervention for advocacy and outreach* (pp. 18–26). Alexandria, VA: American Association for Counseling and Development.

Remley, T. P., Jr. (1993). Consultation contracts. *Journal of Counseling and Development, 72*, 157–158.

Remley, T. P. (2007). The relationship between law and ethics. In B. Herlihy and G. Corey (Eds.), *American Counseling Association ethical standards casebook* (6th ed., pp. 285–292). Alexandria, VA: American Counseling Association.

Remley, T. P. & Herlihy, B. (2007). *Ethical, legal, and professional issues in counseling* (2nd ed. updated). Upper Saddle River, NJ: Merrill/Prentice-Hall.

Reppucci, N. D. (1977). Implementation issues for the behavior modifier as institutional change agent. *Behavior Therapy, 8,* 594–605.

Reppucci, N. D., & Saunders, J. (1983). Focal issues for institutional change. *Professional Psychology: Research and Practice, 14,* 514–528.

Reschly, D. J., & Wilson, M. (1995). School psychology practitioners and faculty: 1986 to 1991—trends in demographics, roles, satisfaction, and system reform. *School Psychology Review, 24,* 62–80.

Resnick, H., & King, J. (1985). Shadow consultation: Intervention in industry. *Social Work, 30,* 447–450.

Rhoades, M. M., & Kratochwill, T. R. (1992). Teacher reactions to behavioral consultation: An analysis of language and involvement. *School Psychology Quarterly, 7,* 47–59.

Rhoades, M. M., & Kratochwill, T. R. (1998). Parent training and consultation: An analysis of a homework intervention program. *School Psychology Quarterly, 13,* 241–264.

Rice, A. K. (1969). Individual, group, and intergroup process. *Human Relations, 22,* 565–584.

Ridley, C. R., & Mendoza, D. W. (1993). Operationalizing organizational effectiveness: The preeminent consultation task. *Journal of Counseling and Development, 72*(2), 168–177.

Riley, R. W. (1996). Improving America's schools. *School Psychology Review, 25,* 477–484.

Riley-Tillman, T. C., & Chafouleas, S. M. (2003). Using interventions that exist in the natural environment to increase treatment integrity and social influence in consultation. *Journal of Educational and Psychological Consultation, 14,* 139–156.

Riley-Tillman, T. C., & Eckert, T. L. (2001). Generalization programming and school-based consultation: An examination of consultees' generalization of consultation-related skills. *Journal of Educational and Psychological Consultation, 12*(3), 217–241.

Rimm, D. C., & Cunningham, H. M. (1985). Behavior therapies. In S. J. Lynn & J. P. Garske (Eds.), *Contemporary psychotherapies models and methods* (pp. 221–259). Columbus, OH: Merrill.

Ritchie, M. H. (1982). Parental consultation: Practical considerations. *School Counselor, 29,* 402–410.

Ritchie, M. H., & Partin, R. L. (1994). Parent education and consultation activities of school counselors. *School Counselor, 41,* 165–170.

Rivard, J. C., Johnsen, M. C., Morrissey, J. P., & Starrett, B. E. (1999). The dynamics of interagency collaboration: How linkages develop for child welfare and juvenile justice sectors in a system of care demonstration. *Journal of Social Service Research, 25*(3), 57–77.

Roberts, A. H., & Rust, J. O. (1994). Role and function of school psychologists, 1992–93: A comparative study. *Psychology in the Schools, 31,* 113–119.

Robinson, B. A., & Elias, M. J. (1993). Stabilizing classroom-based group interventions: Guidelines for special services providers and consultants. *Special Services in the Schools, 8,* 159–177.

Robinson, D., & Robinson, J. C. (1995). *Performance consulting.* San Francisco: Berrett-Kohler.

Robinson, S. E., & Gross, D. R. (1985). Ethics of consultation: The Canterville ghost. *Counseling Psychologist, 13*(3), 444–465.

Rockwood, G. R. (1993). Edgar Schein's process versus content consultation models. *Journal of Counseling and Development, 71,* 636–638.

Rogawski, A. S. (1978). The Caplanian model. *Personnel and Guidance Journal, 56,* 324–327.

Rogers, C. R. (1961). *On becoming a person.* Boston: Houghton Mifflin.

Rogers, M. R. (2000). Examining the cultural context of consultation. *School Psychology Review, 29,* 414–418.

Rosen, C. S., Young, H. E., & Norris, F. H. (2006). On a paved road with good intentions, you still need a compass. In E. C. Ritchie, P. J. Watson, & M. J. Friedman (Eds.), *Interventions following mass violence and disasters: Strategies for mental health practice* (pp. 206–223). New York: Guilford.

Rosenfield, S. A. (1985). Teacher acceptance of behavioral principles. *Teacher Education and Special Education, 8*(3), 153–158.

Rosenfield, S. A. (1987). *Instructional consultation.* Hillsdale, NJ: Erlbaum.

Rosenfield, S. A. (1991). The relationship variable in behavioral consultation, *Journal of Behavioral Consultation, 1*, 329–336.

Rosenfield, S. A. (1992). Developing school-based consultation teams: A design for organizational change. *School Psychology Quarterly, 7*, 27–46.

Rosenfield, S. A. (2002a). Best practices in instructional consultation. In A. Thomas and J. Grimes (Eds.), *Best practices in school psychology* (4th ed., pp. 609–623). Bethesda, MD: National Association of School Psychologists.

Rosenfield, S. A. (2002b). Developing instructional consultants: From novice to competent to expert. *Journal of Educational and Psychological Consultation, 13*(1&2), 97–111.

Rosenfield, S. A. (2004). Consultation as dialogue: The right words at the right time. In N. M. Lambert, I. Hylander & J. H. Sandoval (Eds.), *Consultee-centered consultation: Improving the quality of professional services in schools and community organizations* (pp. 337–347). Mahwah, NJ: Erlbaum.

Rosenfield, S. A., & Gravois, T. A. (1996). *Instructional consultation teams: Collaborating for change.* New York: Guilford.

Rosenfield, S. A., & Gravois, T. A. (1999). Working with teams in the school. In C. R. Reynolds and T. B. Gutkin (Eds.), *The handbook of school psychology.* (3rd ed., pp. 1025–1040). New York: Wiley.

Rosenthal, S. L. (1993). Educational consultation in the context of a medical setting. *Journal of Educational and Psychological Consultation, 4*(4), 391–394.

Ross, G. J. (1993). Peter Block's flawless consulting and the homunculus theory: Within each person is a perfect consultant. *Journal of Counseling and Development, 71*, 639–641.

Ross, J. A., & Regan, E. M. (1990). Strategies of experienced and inexperienced consultants. *Alberta Journal of Educational Research, 36*(2), 157–180.

Ross, M. R., Powell, S. R., & Elias, M. (2002). New roles for school psychologists: Addressing the social and emotional learning needs of students. *School Psychology Review, 31*, 43–52.

Rotheram-Borus, M. J., Bickford, B., Milburn, N. G. (2001). Implementing a classroom-based social skills training program in middle childhood. *Journal of Educational and Psychological Consultation, 12*(2), 91–111.

Rowley, W. J., & MacDonald, D. (2001). Counseling and the law: A cross-cultural perspective. *Journal of Counseling and Development, 79*, 422–429.

Rubin, H. (2002). *Collaborative leadership.* Thousand Oaks, CA: Sage.

Rudestam, K. E. (1982). *Experiential groups in theory and practice.* Pacific Grove, CA: Thomson Brooks/Cole.

Rusnack, B. L. (1989). The consultant's role. In M. L. Henk (Ed.), *Social work in primary care* (pp. 98–112). Newbury Park, CA: Sage.

Russell, M. L. (1978). Behavioral consultation: Theory and process. *Personnel and Guidance Journal, 56*(6), 346–350.

Russell-Chapin, L. A., & Stoner, C. R. (1995). Mental health counselors as consultants for diversity training. *Journal of Mental Health Counseling, 17*, 146–156.

Safran, S. P. (1991). The communication process and school-based consultation: What does the research say? *Journal of Educational and Psychological Consultation, 2*, 343–370.

Safran, S. P., & Safran, J. S. (1998). Prereferral consultation and intervention assistance teams revisited: Some new food for thought. *Journal of Educational and Psychological Consultation, 8*, 93–100.

Safran, J. S., & Safran, S. P. (2001). School-based consultation for asperger syndrome. *Journal of Educational and Psychological Consultation, 12*(4), 385–395.

Sales, B. D., Miller, M. O., & Hall, S. R. (2005). *Laws affecting clinical practice.* Washington, DC: American Psychological Association.

Salmon, D. (1993). Anticipating the school consultant role: Changes in personal constructs following training. *School Psychology Quarterly, 8*, 301–317.

Salmon, D., & Lehrer, R. (1989). School consultant's implicit theories of action. *Professional School Psychology, 4*, 173–187.

Salzman, M. B. (2002). A culturally congruent consultation at a Bureau of Indian Affairs boarding school. *Journal of Individual Psychology, 58*, 132–147.

Salzman, M. B. (2005). Contextualizing the symptom in multicultural consultation: Anger in a cultural-historical context. *Journal of Educational and Psychological Consultation, 6*, 223–237.

Sampson, J. P., Jr., Kolodinsky, R. W., & Greeno, B. P. (1997). Counseling on the information highway: Future possibilities and potential problems. *Journal of Counseling and Development, 75*, 203–212.

Sandland, K., & Dougherty, A. M. (1985). Using the nominal group technique with incarcerates. *Journal of Offender Counseling, 6,* 25–30.

Sandoval, J. (1996). Constructivism, consultee-centered consultation, and conceptual change. *Journal of Educational and Psychological Consultation, 7,* 89–97.

Sandoval, J. (2003). Constructing conceptual change in consultee-centered consultation. *Journal of Educational and Psychological Consultation, 4,* 251–261.

Sandoval, J. (2004). Conceptual change in consultee-centered consultation. In N. M. Lambert, I. Hylander & J. H. Sandoval (Eds.), *Consultee-centered consultation: Improving the quality of professional services in schools and community organizations* (pp. 37–44). Mahwah, NJ: Erlbaum.

Saver, K., & Downes, B. (1991). PIT crew: A model for teacher collaboration in an elementary school. *Intervention in School and Clinic, 27*(2), 116–120.

Schein, E. H. (1969). *Process consultation: Its role in organization development* (1st ed.). Reading, MA: Addison-Wesley.

Schein, E. H. (1978). The role of the consultant: Content expert or process facilitator? *Personnel and Guidance Journal, 56*(6), 339–343.

Schein, E. H. (1985). *Organizational Culture and Leadership: A Dynamic View.* San Francisco: Jossey-Bass, Inc.

Schein, E. H. (1987). *Process consultation: Lessons for managers and consultants* (Vol. 2). Reading, MA: Addison-Wesley.

Schein, E. H. (1988). *Process consultation: Its role in organization development* (Vol. 1, 2nd ed.). Reading, MA: Addison-Wesley.

Schein, E. H. (1990a). Back to the future: Recapturing the OD vision. In E. Massarick (Ed.), *Advances in Organization Development* (Vol. 1, pp. 13–26). Norwood, NJ: Ablex.

Schein, E. H. (1990b). Organizational culture. *American Psychologist, 45*(2), 109–119.

Schein, E. H. (1990c). Models of consultation: What do organizations of the 1990s need? *Consultation, 9,* 261–275.

Schein, E. H. (1993). Legitimating clinical research in the study of organizational culture. *Journal of Counseling and Development, 71,* 703–708.

Schein, E. H. (1999). *Process consultation revisited: Building the helping relationship.* Reading, MA: Addison-Wesley.

Schein, E. H. (2004). *Organizational culture and leadership.* (3rd ed.). San Francisco: Jossey-Bass.

Schein, E. H. (2006). Consultation and coaching revisited. In M. Goldsmith and L. S. Lyons (Eds.). *Coaching for leadership* (2nd ed., pp. 17–25). San Francisco, CA: Wiley.

Schein, E. H., & Greiner, L. E. (1977). Can organization development be fine tuned to bureaucracies? *Organization Dynamics, 5*(3), 48–61.

Schindler-Rainman, E. (1985). Invited commentary: The modern consultant's renaissance person. *Consultation, 4*(3), 264–267.

Schmidt, J. J. (1993). *Counseling in schools.* Needham Heights, MA: Allyn & Bacon.

Schmidt, J. J., & Osborne, W. L. (1981). Counseling and consulting: Separate processes or the same? *Personnel and Guidance Journal, 59,* 168–171.

Schmuck, R. A. (1976). Process consultation and organization development. *Professional Psychology, 7,* 626–635.

Schmuck, R. A. (1983). System-process mental health models. In S. Cooper & W. R. Hodges (Eds.), *Mental health consultation field* (pp. 71–90). New York: Human Sciences Press.

Schmuck, R. A. (1990). Organization development in schools: Contemporary concepts and practices. In T. B. Gutkin & C. R. Reynolds (Eds.), *The handbook of school psychology* (2nd ed., pp. 899–919). New York: Wiley.

Schmuck, R. A. (1995). Process consultation and organization development. *Journal of Educational and Psychological Consultation, 6,* 199–206.

Schmuck, R. A., & Runkel, P. J. (1985). Organization development in schools. *Consultation, 4,* 236–259.

Schottle, D. A., & Peltier, G. L. (1996). Should schools employ behavior management consultants? *Journal of Instructional Psychology, 23*(2), 128–130.

Schulte, A. C., & Osborne, S. S. (2003). When assumptive worlds collide: A review of definitions of collaboration in consultation. *Journal of Educational and Psychological Consultation, 14,* 109–138.

Schwiebert, V., & Myers, J. E. (1994). Midlife care givers: Effectiveness of a psychoeducational intervention for midlife adults with parent-care responsibilities. *Journal of Counseling and Development, 72,* 627–632.

Schwiebert, V., & Myers, J. E. (1997). Short term group treatment for adult children caring for aging parents: A psychoeducational approach. *Therapeutic Strategies with the Older Adult, 3*(6), 4–11.

Scott, T. M., & Martinek, G. (2006). Coaching positive behavior support in school settings: Tactics and data-based decision making. *Journal of Positive Behavior Interventions, 8,* 165–173.

Scriven, M. (1967). The methodology of evaluation. In R. Tyler, R. Gagne, & M. Scriven (Eds.), *Perspectives on curriculum evaluation (AERA Monograph Series on Curriculum Evaluation).* Chicago: Rand McNally.

Sears, R., Rudisill, J., Mason-Sears, C. (2006). *Consultation skills for mental health professionals.* Hoboken, NJ: Wiley.

Seligman, M. P., & Csikszentmihalyi, M. (2000). Positive psychology: An introduction. *American Psychologist, 60,* 410–421.

Senge, P., Cambron-McCabe, N., Lucas, T., Smith, B., Dutton, J., & Kleiner, A. (2000). *Schools that learn.* New York: Doubleday.

Shadish, W. R., Cook, T. D., & Campbell, D. T. (2002). *Experimental and quasi-experimental designs for generalized causal influence.* Boston: Houghton Mifflin.

Shapiro, E. S., DuPaul, G. J., Bradley, K. L., & Bailey, L. T. (1996). A school-based consultation program for service delivery to middle school students with attentiondeficit/hyperactivity disorder. *Journal of Emotional & Behavioral Disorders, 4,* 73–81.

Shaw, H. E., & Shaw, S. F. (2006). Critical ethical issues in online counseling: Assessing current practices with an ethical intent checklist. *Journal of Counseling and Development, 84,* 41–53.

Shaw, S. R., & Swerdlik, M. E. (1995). Best practices in facilitating team functioning. In A. Thomas and J. Grimes (Eds.), *Best practices in school psychology* (3rd ed., pp. 153–159). Washington, DC: National Association of School Psychologists.

Sheeley, V. L., & Herlihy, B. (1986). The ethics of confidentiality and privileged communication. *Journal of Counseling and Human Service Professions, 1*(1), 141–148.

Sheridan, S. M. (1992). Consultant and client outcomes of competency-based behavioral consultation training. *School Psychology Quarterly, 7,* 245–270.

Sheridan, S. M. (1993a). Functional outcome analysis: Do the costs outweigh the benefits? *School Psychology Quarterly, 8,* 227–230.

Sheridan, S. M. (1993b). Models for working with parents. In J. E. Zins, T. R. Kratochwill, & S. N. Elliott (Eds.), *Handbook of consultation services for children* (pp. 110–133). San Francisco: Jossey-Bass.

Sheridan, S. M. (1997). Conceptual and empirical bases of conjoint behavioral consultation. *School Psychology Quarterly, 12,* 119–133.

Sheridan, S. M. (2000). Considerations of multiculturalism and diversity in behavioral consultation with parents and teachers. *School Psychology Review, 29,* 344–353.

Sheridan, S. M., Clarke, B. L., Knoche, L. L., & Edwards, C. P. (2006). The effects of conjoint behavioral consultation in early childhood settings. *Early Education and Development, 7,* 593–617.

Sheridan, S. M., Eagle, J. W., Cowan, R. J., Mickelson, W. (2001). The effects of conjoint behavioral consultation: Results of a 4-year study. *Journal of School Psychology, 39,* 361–385.

Sheridan, S. M., Eagle, J. W., & Doll, B. (2006). An examination of the efficacy of conjoint behavioral consultation with diverse clients. *School Psychology Quarterly, 21,* 396–417.

Sheridan, S. M., & Kratochwill, T. R. (1992). Behavioral parent-teacher consultation: Conceptual and research considerations. *Journal of School Psychology, 30,* 117–139.

Sheridan, S. M., Kratochwill, T. R., & Bergan, J. R. (1996). *Conjoint behavioral consultation.* New York: Plenum Press.

Sheridan, S. M., Kratochwill, T. R., & Elliott, S. N. (1990). Behavioral consultation with parents and teachers: Delivering treatment for socially withdrawn children at home and at school. *School Psychology Review, 19,* 33–52.

Sheridan, S. M., Welch, M., & Orme, S. F. (1996). Is consultation effective? A review of outcome research. *Remedial and Special Education, 17,* 341–354.

Sherwood, J. J. (1993). Essential differences between traditional approaches to consulting and a collaborative approach. In R. T. Golembiewski (Ed.),

*Handbook of organizational consultation* (pp. 687–691). New York: Marcel Dekker.

Shertzer, B., & Linden, J. D. (1979). *Fundamentals of individual appraisal.* Boston: Houghton Mifflin.

Short, R. J., Moore, S., & Williams, C. (1991). Social influence in consultation: Effect of degree and experience on consultees' perceptions. *Psychological Reports, 68,* 131–137.

Short, R. J., & Talley, R. C. (1999). Services integration: An introduction. *Journal of Educational and Psychological Consultation, 10*(3), 193–200.

Shosh, M. (1996). Counseling in business and industry. In W. J. Weikel and A. J. Palmo (Eds.), *Foundations of mental health counseling* (2nd ed., pp. 232–241). Springfield, IL: Thomas Books.

Shultz, J. (1984). Historical overview of OD counseling. In R. J. Lee & A. M. Freedman (Eds.), *Consultation skills reading* (pp. 1–3). Arlington, VA: National Training Labor Institute.

Silverman, M. M. (1993). Commentary: Consultation in a campus context: Collaboration, cooperation, and coordination. *Journal of College Student Psychotherapy, 7*(3), 49–55.

Simcox, A. G., Nuijens, K. & Lee, C. C. (2006). School counselors and school psychologists: Collaborative partners in promoting cultural competent schools. *Professional School Counselor, 9,* 272–277.

Simola, S. K. (2005). Organizational crisis management: Overview and opportunities. *Consulting Psychology Journal: Practice and Research, 57,* 180–192.

Sinha, D. P.(Ed.). (1979). *Consultants and consultant styles.* New Delhi, India: Vision Books.

Skinner, B. F. (1953). *Science and human behavior.* New York: Macmillan.

Skinner, C. H., Dittmer, K. I., & Howell, L. A. (2000). Direct observation in school settings: Theoretical issues. In E. S. Shapiro and T. R. Kratochwill (Eds.), *Behavioral assessment in schools* (2nd ed., pp. 19–77). New York: Guilford Press.

Sladeczek, I. E., Elliott, S. N., Kratochwill, T. R., Robertson-Mjaanes, S., & Stoiber, K. C. (2001). Application of goal attainment scaling to a conjoint behavioral consultation case. *Journal of Educational and Psychological Consultation, 12,* 45–58.

Slonski-Fowler, K. E., Truscott, S. D. (2003). General education teachers' perceptions of the prereferral

intervention team process. *Journal of Educational and Psychological Consultation, 5,* 1–39.

Smaby, M. H., Harrison, T. C., & Nelson, M. (1995). Elementary school counselors as total quality management consultants. *Elementary School Guidance & Counseling, 29,* 310–319.

Smart, D. W., & Smart, J. F. (1997). DSM-IV and culturally sensitive diagnosis: Some observations for counselors. *Journal of Counseling and Development, 75,* 392–398.

Smith, E. P., Connell, C. M., Wright, G., Sizer, M., Norman, J. M., Hurley, A., & Walker, S. N. (1997). An ecological model of home, school, and community partnerships: Implications for research and practice. *Journal of Educational and Psychological Consultation, 8,* 339–360.

Smith, R. M., & Nevin, A. (2005). Conceptualizing liberatory roles for educational and psychological consultants: Implications for transition planning. *Journal of Educational and Psychological Consultation, 16,* 263–286.

Snow, D. L., & Gersick, K. E. (1986). Ethical and professional issues in mental health consultation. In R. V. Mannino, E. J. Trickett, M. Shore, M. G. Kidder, & G. Levin (Eds.), *Handbook of mental health consultation* (pp. 393–431). Rockville, MD: National Institute of Mental Health.

Sommers-Flanagan, J. (2007). Single session consultations for parents: A preliminary investigation. *The Family Journal, 15,* 24–29.

Soo-Hoo, T. (1998). Applying frame of reference and reframing techniques to improve school consultation in multicultural settings. *Journal of Educational and Psychological Consultation, 9,* 325–345.

Sperry, L. (1996). *Corporate therapy and consulting.* New York: Brunner/Mazel, Inc.

Sperry, L. (2005). Establishing a consultation agreement. In G. P. Koocher, J. C. Norcross, & S. S. Hill III (Eds.), *Psychologists' desk reference* (2nd ed., pp. 666–669). NY: Oxford University Press.

Staton, A. R., Benson, A. J., Briggs, M. K., Cowan, E., Echterling, L. G., Evans, W. F. et al. (2007). *Becoming a community counselor.* Boston: Houghton Mifflin.

Stayer, E. M., & Dillard, J. W. (1986). A factor analysis approach to selecting a consultation style. *Psychology: A Quarterly Journal of Human Behavior, 23*(4), 1–8.

Steege, M., Brown-Chidsey, R., & Mace, F. C. (2002). Best practices in evaluating interventions. In A. Thomas and J. Grimes (Eds.), *Best practices in school psychology* (4th ed., pp. 517–533). Bethesda, MD: National Association of School Psychologists.

Steele, E. (1975). *Consulting for organizational change.* Amherst: University of Massachusetts Press.

Stein, R. H. (1990). *Ethical issues in counseling.* Buffalo, NY: Prometheus Books.

Steinberg, D., & Hughes, L. (1987). Work-centered issues in consultative work. *Journal of Adolescence, 10*(3), 309–316.

Stenger, M. K., Tollefson, N., & Fine, M. J. (1992). Variables that distinguish elementary teachers who participate in school-based consultation from those who do not. *School Psychology Quarterly, 7,* 271–284.

Stenho, J. J. (1995). Classroom consulting with reality therapy. *Journal of Reality Therapy, 15,* 81–86.

Sterling-Turner, H. E., Watson, T. S., & Moore, J. W. (2002). The effects of direct training and treatment integrity on treatment outcomes in school consultation. *School Psychology Quarterly, 17,* 47–77.

Sterling-Turner, H. E., Watson, T. S., Wildmon, M., Watkins, C, & Little, E. (2001). Investigating the relationship between training type and treatment integrity. *School Psychology Quarterly, 16,* 56–67.

Steward. R. J. (1996). Training consulting psychologists to be sensitive to multicultural issues in organizational consultation. *Consulting Psychology Journal, 8,* 180–189.

Stock, H. V. (2007). Workplace violence: Advances in consultation and assessment. In A. M. Goldstein (Ed.), *Forensic psychology: Emerging topics and expanding roles* (pp. 511–549). Hoboken, NJ: Wiley.

Stoiber, K. C., & Kratochwill, T. R. (2000). Empirically supported interventions and school psychology: Rationale and methodological issues–Part I. *School Psychology Quarterly, 15,* 75–105.

Strauss, A., & Corbin, J. (1990). *Basics of qualitative research: Grounded theory procedures and techniques.* Newbury Park, CA: Sage.

Stringer, S. J., Reynolds, G. P., & Simpson, F. M. (2003). *Journal of Instructional Psychology, 30,* 69–76.

Stroh, L. K., & Johnson, H. H. (2006). *The basic principles of effective consulting.* Mahwah, NJ: Erlbaum.

Strong, S. R. (1968). Counseling: An interpersonal influence process. *Journal of Counseling Psychology, 15,* 215–224.

Strother, J., & Jacobs, E. (1986). Parent consultation: A practical approach. *School Counselor, 33,* 292–296.

Studer, J. R. (2005). *The professional school counselor.* Belmont, CA: Thomson Brooks/Cole.

Stum, D. L. (1982). DIRECT: A consultation skills training model. *Personnel and Guidance Journal, 60,* 296–301.

Sue, S. (1998). In search of cultural competence in psychotherapy and counseling. *American Psychologist, 53,* 440–448.

Sugai, G., & Horner, R. (1999). Discipline and behavioral support: Practices, pitfalls, and promises. *Effective School Practices, 17,* 10–17.

Sugai, G., Horner, R. H., Dunlap, G., Hieneman, M., Lewis, T. J., Nelson, C. M., Scott, T., Liaupsin, C., Sailor, W., Turnbull, A., Turnbull III, H. R., Wickham, D., Wilcox, B., & Ruef, M. (2000). Applying positive behavior support and functional behavioral assessment in schools. *Journal of Positive Behavior Interventions, 2*(3), 131–143.

Sugai, G., Sprague, J. R., Horner, R. H., & Walker, H. M. (2000). Preventing school violence: The use of office discipline referrals to assess and monitor school-wide discipline interventions. *Journal of Emotional and Behavioral Disorders, 8,* 94–101.

Sullivan, W. P. (1991). Community mental health: A model for social work consultants. *Research on Social Work Practice, 1,* 289–315.

Sullivan, W. P., & Rapp, C. A. (1991). Improving client outcomes: The Kansas technical assistance project. *Community Mental Health Journal, 27,* 327–336.

Summers, I., & White, D. E. (1980). Creativity techniques: Toward improvement of the decision process. In S. Ferguson and S. Ferguson (Eds.), *Intercommunication: Readings in organizational communication* (pp. 338–348). Rochelle Park, NJ: Hayden.

Sundstrom, E., DeMeuse, K. P., & Futrell, D. (1990). Work teams. *American Psychologist, 45*(2), 120–133.

Swartz, D., & Lippitt, G. (1975). Evaluating the consulting process. *Journal of European Training, 4,* 309–326.

Swenson, C. C., Randall, J., Henggeier, S. W., & Ward, D. (2000). The outcomes and costs of an interagency partnership to serve maltreated children in state custody. *Children's Services: Social Policy, Research, and Practice, 3,* 191–209.

Swenson, L. C. (1997). *Psychology and law* (2nd ed.). Pacific Grove, CA: Thomson Brooks/Cole.

Talbott, J. A. (1988). The elements of community consultation. *New Directions for Mental Health Services, 37,* 69–84.

Tannenbaum, S., Greene, V., & Glickman, A. (1989). The ethical reasoning process in an organizational consulting situation. *Professional Psychology: Research and Practice, 2,* 229–235.

Tanyu, M. (2007). Implementation of prevention programs: Lessons for future research and practice: A commentary on "Social and emotional learning: Promoting the development of all students," a chapter by Joseph E. Zins and Maurice J. Elias. *Journal of Educational and Psychological Consultation, 17,* 257–262.

Tarver Behring, R. K., & Ingraham, C. L. (1998). Culture as a central component of consultation: A call to the field. *Journal of Educational and Psychological Consultation, 9,* 57–72.

Tarver Behring, S., Cabello, B., Kushida, D., Murguia, A. (2000). Cultural modifications to current school-based consultation approaches reported by culturally diverse beginning consultants. *School Psychology Review, 29,* 354–376.

Tashakkori, A., & Teddlie, C. (Eds.) (2003). *Handbook of the mixed methods in the behavioral and social sciences.* Thousand Oaks, CA: Sage.

Taylor, L., & Adelman, H. S. (1998). Confidentiality: Competing principles, inevitable dilemmas. *Journal of Educational and Psychological Consultation, 9,* 267–275.

Taylor, R. D., & Dymnicki, A. B. (2007). Empirical evidence of social and emotional learning's influence on school success: A commentary on "Building academic success on social and emotional learning: What does the research say?," a book edited by Joseph E. Zins, Roger P. Weissberg, Margaret C. Wang, and Herbert J. Walberg. *Journal of Educational and Psychological Consultation, 17,* 225–231.

Telzrow, C. F., & Beebe, J. J. (2002). Best practices in facilitating intervention adherence and integrity. In A. Thomas and J. Grimes (Eds.), *Best practices in school psychology* (4th ed., pp. 503–515). Bethesda, MD: National Association of School Psychologists.

Thomas, C. C., Correa, V. L., & Morsink, C. V. (1995). *Interactive teaming.* Englewood Cliffs, NJ: Prentice-Hall.

Thomas, K. G. F., Gatz, M., & Luczak, S. E. (1997). A tale of two school districts: Lessons to be learned about the impact of relationship building and ecology on consultation. *Journal of Educational and Psychological Consultation, 8,* 297–320.

Thomas, R. T., Jr. (2006). Coaching in the midst of diversity. In M. Goldsmith and L. S. Lyons (Eds.). *Coaching for leadership* (2nd ed., pp. 229–236). San Francisco, CA: Wiley.

Thousand, J. S., Villa, R. A., Paolucci-Whitcomb, P., & Nevin, A. (1996). A rationale and vision for collaborative consultation. In W. Stainback and S. Stainback (Eds.), *Controversial issues confronting special education* (2nd ed., pp. 205–218). Boston: Allyn & Bacon.

Tichy, N. M. (1983). *Managing strategic change: Technical, political, and cultural dynamics.* New York: Wiley.

Tilly III, W. D. (2002). Best practices in school psychology as a problem-solving enterprise. In A. Thomas and J. Grimes (Eds.), *Best practices in school psychology* (4th ed., pp. 21–36). Bethesda, MD: National Association of School Psychologists.

Tindal, G., Shinn, M. R., & Rodden-Nord, K. (1990). Contextually based school consultation: Influential variables. *Exceptional Children, 56,* 324–336.

Tingstrom, D. H., Little, S. G., & Stewart, K. J. (1990). School consultation from a social psychological perspective: A review. *School Consultation and Social Psychology, 27,* 41–50.

Tobias, L. L. (1990). *Psychological consulting to management.* New York: Brunner/Mazel.

Tobias, R. (1993). Underlying cultural issues that effect sound consultant/school collaboratives in developing multicultural programs. *Journal of Educational and Psychological Consultation, 4,* 237–251.

Tombari, M., & Davis, R. A. (1979). Behavioral consultation. In G. D. Phye & D. J. Reschly (Eds.), *School psychology perspectives and issues* (pp. 281–307). New York: Academic Press.

Topping, K. J., & Ehly, S. W. (2001). Peer assisted learning: A framework for consultation. *Journal of Educational and Psychological Consultation, 12,* 113–132.

Trickett, E. J. (1986). Consultation as a preventative intervention: Comments on ecologically based case studies. *Prevention in Human Services, 4,* 187–204.

Trickett, E. J. (1992). Prevention ethics: Explicating the context of prevention activities. *Ethics & Behavior, 2,* 91–100.

Trickett, E. J. (1993). Gerald Caplan and the unfinished business of community psychology: A comment. In W. P. Erchul (Ed.), *Consultation in community, school, and organizational practice* (pp. 163–176). Washington, DC: Taylor & Francis.

Trickett, E. J., Kelly, J. G., & Vincent, T. A. (1984). The spirit of ecological inquiry in community research. In E. Susskind & D. C. Klein (Eds.), *Community research.* New York: Praeger.

Truscott, S. D., Cosgrove, G., Meyers, J., & Eidle-Barkman, K. A. (2000). The acceptability of organizational consultation with prereferral intervention teams. *School Psychology Quarterly, 15,* 172–206.

Tunnecliffe, M. R., Leach, D. J., & Tunnecliffe, L. P. (1986). Relative efficacy of using behavioral consultation as an approach to teacher stress management. *Journal of School Psychology, 24,* 123–131.

Turco, T. L., & Skinner, C. H. (1991). An analysis of consultee verbal responses to structured consultant questions. *TACD Journal, 19*(1), 23–32.

Turnage, J. J. (1990). The challenge of new work place technology for psychology. *American Psychologist, 45* (2), 171–178.

Uhlemann, M. R., Lee, D. Y., & Martin, J. (1994). Client cognitive responses as a function of quality of counselor verbal responses. *Journal of Counseling and Development, 73,* 198–203.

Unger, D. G., Park, E. A., Antal, P., Tessell, P. A., Rigney, K., DeRasmo, K., & Kassess, J. (2000). *Journal of Educational and Psychological Consultation, 11,* 273–296.

Upah, K. R. F., & Tilly III, W. D. (2002). Best practices in designing, implementing, and evaluating quality interventions. In A. Thomas and J. Grimes (Eds.), *Best practices in school psychology* (4th ed., pp. 483–501). Bethesda, MD: National Association of School Psychologists.

United States Bureau of the Census. (2000). *2000 U.S. Census.* Washington, DC: U.S. Government Printing Office.

Valdez, C. R., Carlson, C., & Zanger, D. (2005). Evidence-based parent training and family interventions for school behavior change. *School Psychology Quarterly, 20,* 403–433.

Van Velsor, P. R., & Cox, D. L. (2000). Use of the collaborative drawing technique in school counseling practicum: An illustration of family systems. *Counselor Education and Supervision, 40,* 141–153.

Vernberg, E. M., & Reppucci, N. D. (1986). Behavioral consultation. In E. V. Mannino, E. J. Trickett, M. F. Shore, M. G. Kidder, and G. Levin (Eds.), *Handbook of mental health consultation* (pp. 49–80). Rockville, MD: National Institute of Mental Health.

Vogt, J. F. (1989). A temporary team framework for enhancing client-consultant relationships. *Organization Development, 7*(4), 58–66.

Wallace, W. A., & Hall, D. L. (1996). *Psychological consultation.* Pacific Grove, CA: Thomson Brooks/Cole.

Waltman, G. H. (1989). Social work consultation services in rural areas. *Human Services in the Rural Environment, 12*(3), 17–21.

Walton, R. E. (1987). *Managing conflict: Interpersonal dialogue and third party roles* (2nd ed.). Reading, MA: Addison-Wesley.

Washburn, J. J., Manley, Jr., T., & Holiwski, F. (2003). Teaching on racism: Tools for consultant training. *Journal of Educational and Psychological Consultation, 4,* 387–399.

Waszak, C., & Sines, M. C. (2003). Mixed methods in psychological research. In A. Tashakkori & C. Teddlie (Eds.), *Handbook of mixed methods in social and behavioral research* (pp. 557–576). Thousand Oaks, CA: Sage.

Watson, T., & Steege, M. (2003). *Conducting school-based functional behavioral assessments.* New York: Guilford Press.

Watson, T. S., & Robinson, S. L. (1996). Direct behavioral consultation: An alternative to traditional behavioral consultation. *School Psychology Quarterly, 11,* 267–278.

Watson, T. S., & Steege, M. W. (2003). *Conducting school-based functional behavioral assessments.* New York: Guildford.

Watson, T. S., Sterling, E., McDade, A. (1997). Demythifying behavioral consultation. *School Psychology Review, 26,* 467–474.

Webster, L., Knotek, S. E., Babinski, L. M., Rogers, D. L., & Barnett, M. M. (2003). Mediation of consultee's conceptual development in new teacher groups: Using questions to improve coherency. *Journal of Educational and Psychological Consultation, 4*, 281–301.

Weinrach, S. G., & Thomas, K. R. (1998). Diversity-sensitive counseling today: A postmodern clash of values. *Journal of Counseling and Development, 76,* 115–122.

Weisbord, M. R. (1976). Organizational diagnosis: Six places to look for trouble with or without a theory. *Group and Organizational Studies, 1,* 430–447.

Weisbord, M. R. (1984). Client contact: Entry and contract. In R. J. Lee & A. M. Freedman (Eds.), *Consultation skills readings* (pp. 63–66). Bethel, ME: National Training Laboratories Institute.

Weisbord, M. R. (1985). The organization development contract revisited. *Consultation, 4*(4), 305–315.

Weiss, H. (1996). Family-school collaboration: Consultation to achieve organizational and community change. *Human Systems, 7,* 211–235.

Weissenburger, J. W., Fine, M. J., & Poggio, J. P. (1982). The relationship of selected consultant/teacher characteristics to consultation outcomes. *Journal of School Psychology, 20,* 263–270.

Welch, M. (1998). The IDEA of collaboration in special education: An introspective examination of paradigms and promise. *Journal of Educational and Psychological Consultation, 9,* 119–142.

Welch, M. (2000). Collaboration as a tool for inclusion. In S. E. Wade (Ed.), *Inclusive education: A casebook and readings for prospective and practicing teachers* (pp. 71–96). Mahwah, NJ: Lawrence Erlbaum.

Welch, M., & Tulbert, B. (2000). Practitioners' perspectives of collaboration: A social validation and factor analysis. *Journal of Educational and Psychological Consultation, 11*(3&4), 357–378.

Welfel, E. R. (2002). *Ethics in counseling and psychotherapy: Standards, research, and emerging issues* (2nd ed.). Pacific Grove, CA: Thomson Brooks/Cole.

Werner, J. L., & Tyler, J. M. (1993). Community-based interventions: A return to community mental health center's origins. *Journal of Counseling and Development, 71,* 689–692.

West, J. F., & Idol, L. (1987). School consultation (Part 1): An interdisciplinary perspective on theory, models, and research. *Journal of Learning Disabilities, 20*(7), 388–408.

West, J. F., & Idol, L. (1993). The counselor as consultant in the collaborative school. *Journal of Counseling and Development, 71,* 678–683.

Wheeler, D. D., & Janis, I. J. (1980). *A practical guide for making decisions.* New York: Free Press.

White Kress, V. E., Eriksen, K. P., Rayle, A. D., & Ford, S. J. W. (2005). The *DSM-IV-TR* and culture: Considerations for counselors. *Journal of Counseling and Development, 83,* 97–104.

White, L. J., & Loos, V. E. (1996). The hidden client in school consultation. *Journal of Educational and Psychological Consultation, 7,* 161–177.

Wickstrom, K. F., & Witt, J. C. (1993). Resistance within school-based consultation. In J. E. Zins, T. R. Kratochwill, and S. N. Elliott (Eds.), *Handbook of consultation services for children* (pp. 159–178). San Francisco: Jossey-Bass.

Wigtil, J. V., & Kelsey, R. C. (1978). Team building as a consulting intervention for influencing learning environments. *Personnel and Guidance Journal, 56*(7), 412–416.

Wilcoxon, S. A. (1990). Developing consultation contracts: Applying foundational principles to critical issues. *Journal of Independent Social Work, 4*(3), 17–28.

Wilczynski, S. M., Mandal, R. L., & Fusilier, I. (2000). Bridges and barriers in behavioral consultation. *Psychology in the Schools, 37,* 495–504.

Wilkinson, L. A. (2005). Bridging the research-to-practice gap in school-based consultation: An example using case studies. *Journal of Educational and Psychological Consultation, 6,* 175–200.

Wilkinson, L. A. (2006). Monitoring treatment integrity. *School Psychology International, 27,* 426–438.

Willems, E. P. (1974). Behavioral technology and behavioral ecology. *Journal of Applied Behavioral Analysis, 7,* 151–156.

Williams, R. T. (1982). An overview of consultation and education in the rural community. In P. A. Keler & J. D. Murray (Eds.), *Handbook of rural community mental health* (pp. 122–134). New York: Human Sciences Press.

Williams, W. L. (2000). Behavioral consultation. In J. Austin and J. E. Carr (Eds.), *Handbook of Applied Behavioral Analysis* (pp. 375–397). Reno, NV: Context Press.

Willis, J. O., & Dumont, R. (2006). And never the twain shall meet: Can response to intervention and cognitive assessment be reconciled? *Psychology in the Schools, 43*, 901–908.

Wintersteen, R. T., & Young, L. (1988). Effective professional collaboration with family support groups. *Psychosocial Rehabilitation Journal, 12*, 19–31.

Witt, J. C. (1990a). Face-to-face verbal interaction in school-based consultation: A review of the literature. *School Psychology Quarterly, 5*, 199–210.

Witt, J. C. (1990b). Complaining, precopernian thought and the univariate linear mind: Questions for school based behavioral consultation research. *School Psychology Review, 19*, 367–377.

Witt, J. C., & Elliott, S. N. (1983). Assessment in behavioral consultation: The initial interview. *School Psychology Review, 12*, 42–49.

Witt, J. C., Gresham, F. M., & Noel, G. H. (1996a). What's behavioral about behavioral consultation? *Journal of Educational and Psychological Consultation, 7*, 327–344.

Witt, J. C., Gresham, F. M., & Noel, G. H. (1996b). The effectiveness and efficiency of behavioral consultation: Differing perspectives about epistemology and what we know. *Journal of Educational and Psychological Consultation, 7*, 355–360.

Witt, J. C., & Martens, B. K. (1988). Problems with problem-solving consultation: A re-analysis of assumptions, methods, and goals. *School Psychology Review, 17*, 211–226.

Wizda, L. (2004). An instructional consultant looks to the future. *Journal of Educational and Psychological Consultation, 5*, 277–294.

Wolf, R. S., & Pillemer, K. (1994). What's new in elder abuse programming? *The Gerontologist, 34*, 126–129.

Woody, R. H. (1989). Public policy, ethics government, and the law. *Professional School Psychology, 4*, 75–83.

Woody, R. H., & Associates. (1984). *The law and the practice of human services.* San Francisco: Jossey-Bass.

Wubbolding, R. (1990). Professional issues: Consultation and ethics, Part I. *Journal of Reality Therapy, 9*(2), 71–74.

Wubbolding, R. (1991a). Professional issues: Consultation and ethics, Part II. *Journal of Reality Therapy, 10*(2), 55–59.

Wubbolding, R. E. (1991b). Professional issues: Consultation: III. *Journal of Reality Therapy, 11*(1), 76–80.

Yolles, S. F. (1970). Foreword. In G. Caplan, *The theory and practice of mental health consultation.* New York: Basic Books.

Zand, D. E. (1978). Collateral organization: A new change strategy. In W. L. French, C. H. Bell, Jr., & R. A. Zawacki (Eds.), *Organization development: Theory, practice, and research* (pp. 293–307). Dallas: Business Publications.

Zifferblatt, S. M., & Hendricks, C. G. (1974). Applied behavioral analysis of societal problems: Population change, a case in point. *American Psychologist, 29*, 750–761.

Zins, J. E. (1993). Enhancing consultee problem-solving skills in consultation. *Journal of Counseling and Development, 72*(2), 185–190.

Zins, J. E. (1995). Has primary prevention achieved its potential? *The Journal of Primary Prevention, 15*, 285–301.

Zins, J. E. (1998). Expanding the conceptual foundations of consultation: Contributions of community psychology. *Journal of Educational and Psychological Consultation, 8*, 107–110.

Zins, J. E. (2002). Building a strong future for educational and psychological consultation. *Journal of Educational and Psychological Consultation, 13*(1&2), 5–6.

Zins, J. E., Bloodworth, M. R., Weissberg, R. P., & Walberg, H. J. (2004). The scientific base for linking social and emotional learning to school success. In J. E. Zins, R. P. Weissberg, M. C. Wang, & H. J. Walberg (Eds.), *Building academic success on social and emotional learning: What does the research say?* (pp. 2–22). New York: Teachers College Press.

Zins, J. E., & Curtis, M. J. (1984). Building consultation into the educational service delivery system. In C. A. Maher, R. J. Illback, & J. E. Zins (Eds.), *Organizational psychology in the schools: A handbook for professionals* (pp. 213–242). Springfield, IL: Thomas.

Zins, J. E., Elias, M. J., Greenberg, M. T., & Pruett, M. K. (2000). Promoting quality implementation in prevention programs. *Journal of Educational and Psychological Consultation, 11*, 173–174.

Zins, J. E., & Erchul, W. P. (2002). Best practices in school consultation. In A. Thomas and J. Grimes (Eds.),

*Best practices in school psychology* (4th ed., pp. 625–643). Bethesda, MD: National Association of School Psychologists.

Zins, J. E., & Illback, R. J. (1995). Consulting to facilitate planned organizational change in schools. *Journal of Educational and Psychological Consultation, 6,* 237–245.

Zins, J. E., Kratochwill, T. R., & Elliott, S. N. (1993). Current status of the field. In J. E. Zins, T. R. Kratochwill, and S. N. Elliott (Eds.), *Handbook*

*of consultation services for children* (pp. 1–12). San Francisco: Jossey-Bass.

Zins, J. E., Weissberg, R. P., Wang, M. C., & Walberg, H. J. (Eds.). (2004). *Building school success through social and emotional learning.* New York: Teachers College Press.

Zusman, J. (1972). Mental health consultation: Some theory and practice. In J. Zusman & D. L. Davidson (Eds.), *Practical aspects of mental health consultation.* Springfield, IL: Charles C. Thomas.

# Name Index

# Subject Index